T0419671

GLOBAL CHALLENGES OF DIGITAL TRANSFORMATION OF MARKETS

ECONOMIC ISSUES, PROBLEMS AND PERSPECTIVES

Additional books and e-books in this series can be found on Nova's website under the Series tab.

GLOBAL CHALLENGES OF DIGITAL TRANSFORMATION OF MARKETS

ELENA DE LA POZA

AND

SERGEY E. BARYKIN

EDITORS

nova
science publishers
New York

NOTICE TO THE READER

Library of Congress Cataloging-in-Publication Data

Names: de la Poza, Elena, editor. | Barykin, Sergey E., editor.
Title: Global challenges of digital transformation of markets / Elena de la Poza (editor) Professor, Finance, Universitat Politècnica de València, Valencia, Spain, Sergey E. Barykin (editor) Professor, Economics, Peter the Great St. Petersburg Polytechnic University, St Petersburg, Russia.
Description: New York : Nova Science Publishers, 2021. | Series: Economic issues, problems and perspectives | Includes bibliographical references and index. |
Identifiers: LCCN 2021031340 (print) | LCCN 2021031341 (ebook) | ISBN 9781536197549 (hardcover) | ISBN 9781536198645 (adobe pdf)
Subjects: LCSH: Business logistics--Technological innovations. | Marketing--Management. | Personnel management.
Classification: LCC HD38.5 .G565 2021 (print) | LCC HD38.5 (ebook) | DDC 658.8--dc23
LC record available at https://lccn.loc.gov/2021031340
LC ebook record available at https://lccn.loc.gov/2021031341

Published by Nova Science Publishers, Inc. † New York

CONTENTS

PREFACE

As rapid changes are brought on by the advent of breakthrough technologies and by the challenges facing humanity, existing business models are to be consistently updated and reinvented. In fact, innovative business models need to be adopted, focused on generating novel state-of-the-art products and technologies that have not yet gained wide circulation, and on searching for new markets or marketing opportunities, which would allow to sell the goods and services produced in the increasingly digitized economy.

This book is devoted to the challenges of digital transformation in logistics and supply chain management, digitization of trade networks and global markets, with a primary focus on business processes and marketing transformation. Thus, the book is structured into four parts due to the nature of the research contained in it.

The first ten chapters of the book are related to digital technologies in logistics and supply chain management, considering the current trends in optimization and digital transformation of business processes. The experience of developing logistics solutions for the tasks of the digital agenda in different countries is analyzed. A further focus is on the national and regional models of cooperation for organizing logistics networks based on digital technologies.

The second component of the book includes seven chapters (chapter 11-17) and focuses on various issues of digitization of trade networks and global markets. Digital transformation of society and. The trends that have changed the world's commodity markets, such as Big Data, artificial intelligence, augmented reality are addressed in this section.

The third part of the book (chapter 18-38) deals with research related to digital finance and banking (chapter 22, 27, 28, 30, 33); consumer behavior and smart management (chapter 20, 25, 31, 32, 35, 38); strategic planning in the context of digitization of the economy (chapter 23, 24, 26, 34); business processes transformation in the digital economy (chapter 18, 19) and transformation of marketing competences and communications in the age of digitization (chapter 21, 29, 37).

Finally, the fourth fragment of the book (chapters 39, 40 and 41) argue different aspects of HR-management in the age of digital transformation. Modern trends and technologies of HR-management are analyzed. Such subjects as human capital investment, change management, and new requirements on the quality of human resources in the context of digitization are considered.

Dr. Elena de la Poza
Universitat Politècnica de València

Dr. Sergey E. Barykin
Peter the Great St. Petersburg Polytechnic University

In: Global Challenges of Digital Transformation of Markets ISBN: 978-1-53619-754-9
Editors: E. de la Poza and S. E. Barykin © 2021 Nova Science Publishers, Inc.

Chapter 1

ASSESSMENT OF STABILITY OF NETWORK LOGISTICS BUSINESS

S. E. Barykin[1], S. M. Sergeev[1,], I. V. Kapustina[1] and Elena de la Poza[2]*

[1]Peter the Great St.Petersburg Polytechnic University, Russia
[2]Center for Economic Engineering (INECO).
Universitat Politècnica de València, Spain

ABSTRACT

Digital logistics platforms are based on technologies for inter-machine exchange of information flows online and decision-making algorithms for processing the incoming data of an economic nature. While there is a full range of hardware available for equipping all links of logistics management, including servers, peripheral sensors, adapters for high-speed mobile networks, and cloud platforms, algorithmic (intelligent) software, or Brainware, still remains the subject of discussion. This study considers the stability of the behavior of mathematical models characterizing the transfer processes in networks with complex structure. This problem is highly important for logistics of both a wide range of discrete cargo, and for quasi-continuous cargo, for example, liquid hydrocarbons. An integral functional is taken as the criterion of the logistics operator. The solution is obtained based on a system in the class of integrable functions that adequately describe the transfer of masses with a complex internal rheology. A generalized solution of the system is a function that defines the variational statement of the initial boundary-value problem. The consideration is extended beyond the framework of classical continuously differentiable solutions because the physical nature of transfer of goods and cargo flows through logistics networks has to be described more accurately.

Keywords: logistics, digitalization, mathematical model, sustainability, optimization

---

* Corresponding Author's Email: sergeev2@inbox.ru.

1. INTRODUCTION

Building a sustainable supply chain means balancing reliability and flexibility. Both of these properties of the supply chain can act as a safety cushion against uncertainties and should be taken into consideration when planning. Legacy logistics solutions, have not justified themselves in the digital age. Decentralized communication is giving way to more precise and modern solutions. The combination of optimization modeling and data analysis is a basic technology that allows you to create a fairly detailed model of the real supply chain of its digital counterpart Idea -. The goal of creating a digital twin is to manage the risks in the supply chains, thereby making them more reliable and resilient in the event of any failures. Modern technologies allow you to collect large amounts of data on supply chains online. The management technologies used in supply chains enable the identification of critical hot spots and timely warning of incidents that may have a critical impact on the supply chain(S. Y. Barykin, Bochkarev, Kalinina, and Yadykin 2020). It can successfully act as a replacement for expensive field monitoring methods, without causing any damage to the physical object. A digital twin refers to an evolving digital profile of the historical and current behavior of a physical object or process that helps optimize business performance(Kapustina et al., 2020).

Rapid changes in the field of high technology leads to changes in all spheres of life. Enterprises need to transform their workforce to achieve a sustainable competitive advantage. The introduction of high-tech solutions leads to a change in the format and content of almost any work, as well as a rethinking of approaches to personnel planning(Bril, Kalinina, et al., 2020). When developing a business plan for a new enterprise, the main issues are market assessment and-sales forecast opportunities to attract investment. When drawing up a business plan for an existing enterprise, another important issue arises - the use of internal resources of the enterprise, assets and personnel. Therefore, when developing an enterprise plan, there is a need for a special financial and economic analysis of the object and the preparation of key financial indicators of business planning standards(Bril, Evseeva, et al., 2020).

It is necessary to consider the issue of training personnel for the digital industry in the context of creating teams at enterprises in scientific organizations and universities that have the necessary digital competencies and digital literacy, that is, the ability to use modern methods, experimentation and research technologies to develop globally competitive products. This competence becomes an integrator of the technological, ethical, and cognitive aspects of education. In this paradigm, the basis of the methodological approach to solving the problem of personnel training is a problem-oriented scientific approach, and the model of creating mirror engineering centers is a possible model for scaling competencies, spreading knowledge and developing network interaction(S. Barykin, Borovkov, Rozhdestvenskiy, Tarshin, et al., 2020).

A digital ecosystem is a self-organizing, sustainable system with digital platforms at the base, which form a single information environment where the members of the ecosystem can interact when no hard functional ties between them exist. The base of a digital ecosystem is the diverse platform technologies which form a single information environment for all members: society, business and government. The development of platform technologies contributes to the scaling up of digital ecosystems, which are beyond the business environment and B2B and B2C relationships. The digital environment is used to connect members, exchange information and resources, organize processes and coordinate objectives. One of the most important features of a DES is its ability to self-organize and the lack of a managing or supervising member of the ecosystem. The main difference between digital ecosystems and traditional ecosystems is that the organization of business in the latter is based on management decision making by a human. Meanwhile, management decision making in digital ecosystems is for the most part automated and carried out without human participation, thanks to the diverse tools which exist such as artificial intelligence, computer vision and so on(S. Y. Barykin, Kapustina, Kirillova, Yadykin, et al., 2020).

The process of managing the organization's personnel within the digital ecosystem, while maintaining the basic goal setting, is transformed from an instrumental point of view. The transition from a traditional HR system to a digital one involves a difference between how staff interact with each other and with management. The key factor in the digital interaction system is the ability of each employee to freely contact the information and analytical center. The digital interaction system also differs from the traditional one by expanding the channels for exchanging information and analytics. Considering the tasks of personnel management in the digital era, it can be shown that the problem of digital personnel management is the scientific search for the features of employee interaction in the new technological structure of Industry 4.0 under the influence of the flow of innovations, there is a change. It includes improvements in performance, reliability, quality, and safety (Sergey Barykin, Kalinina, Aleksandrov, Konnikov, et al., 2020).

Over the past decade, technologies and equipment that can radically change the approach to managing the processes of cargo movement and cargo transportation have become widespread. This includes the possibility of machine-readable exchange of information about goods and cargo among themselves. The structure of relations between participants in this segment of the economy has become more complex. This is due to the processes of consolidation in commercial structures, which leads to an increase in the complexity of managing such business objects, as well as a multiple increase in the time and money spent on ensuring the material flows of goods and cargo necessary to maintain a competitive business. To solve such large-scale problems, the use of scientifically based mathematical models is required. This approach will allow us to use the digital footprint of processes in the logistics network and develop an algorithmic basis for a whole range of software tools for more efficient management of the logistics industry (S. Y. Barykin, Kapustina, Sergeev, and Yadykin 2020).

It is necessary to find an economically optimal management of the flows of goods and cargo based on digital information about their movement, taking into account the stochastic nature of the volumes and directions of flows. At the same time, it is necessary to choose and justify the methodology for calculating the node DC terminals included in the network structure of logistics activities. The obtained set of mathematical relations allows us to simulate the operation of a network distribution center as a node element of a logistics system that functions on the principles of 3PL operator in conditions of stochastic nature of incoming and shipped goods flows (Shmatko et al., 2021).

Mathematical modeling of evolutionary processes of transfer of different goods and cargoes, both discrete and quasi-continuous, is considered in a number of fundamental studies(A. P. Zhabko, Shindyapin, and Provotorov 2019). One of the main requirements imposed in real logistics business is that the stability of the behavior of mathematical models is to be assessed for finding the potential applications of the obtained results(Borisoglebskaya et al., 2019). There are multiple reasons for this, related to both the real situation and the instability of external conditions. In particular, the input data initiating the process are given with a certain error; in addition, indicators that are important in logistics, such as traffic, the throughput of supply chain segments, waiting times for loading and unloading, customs procedures for cross-border transportation, and other factors, can also be estimated only by random distribution functions (Aleksei P. Zhabko, Nurtazina, and Provotorov 2019).

The standard approaches relied on classical methods for studying the solution stability in systems of differential equations, introduced by Lyapunov. The solution was assumed to be stable if it changed little for small perturbations of the initial condition and for any moment of time.

Several studies, for example, (Provotorov 2008) proposed mathematical models of logistic processes in networks using methods combining graph theory and equations of mathematical physics, including the well-developed tools of the theory of optimal decision-making (Podvalny, Podvalny, and Provotorov 2017). In this paper, we provide the stability conditions for the solution of an evolutionary parabolic system with distributed parameters on a graph which is the prototype of the logistic transport network (Provotorov, V. V. and Provotorova E.N 2017). At the same time, the mathematical model reflects the evolutionary process of the transfer of goods and cargo along a spatial network(Artemov et al., 2019). The parabolic system is considered in the class of integrable functions that adequately describe the transfer of masses with a complex internal rheology. A generalized solution or weak solution of the system in this case is an integrable function that determines the variational statement of the initial boundary-value problem.

Accordingly, the answer to the question about the influence of changes in the initial data on the behavior, and analysis of the mathematical model (primarily the solutions of the initial boundary-value problems governing the model) takes on an additional importance from the economic standpoint. Thus, in general, the issue at hand is risk assessment of investing funds and the stability of the business model.

2. PROBLEM STATEMENT

The main results in the mathematical theory of stability are well developed in the class of ordinary differential equations. However, because there is a requirement to adequately describe economic processes where the efficiency criterion contains at least two variables, one of which is time, these differential systems have to be abandoned in numerous applications in favor of considering evolutionary partial differential equations, due to the complexity of mathematical models. This practically important case is analyzed in our study. We consider the stability of an evolutionary system with distributed parameters, generating a mathematical model, on a graph (network) with unlimited increase in the time variable.

3. MAIN FORMALISMS

We use the definitions and notations adopted in (Provotorov, Sergeev, and Part 2019). The logistics network is illustrated with a graph of arbitrary rheology Γ, which is a bounded directed geometric graph with the edges γ, parameterized by the segment $[0,1]$. Here $\partial\Gamma$ and $J(\Gamma)$ denote the sets of boundary ζ and internal ξ nodes of the graph; Γ_0 is the union of all edges of γ_0 that do not contain endpoints; $\Gamma_t = \Gamma_0 \times (0,t)$ ($\gamma_t = \gamma_0 \times (0,t)$), $\partial\Gamma_t = \partial\Gamma \times (0,t)$ ($t \in (0,T]$, $T < \infty$ is an arbitrary fixed constant).

The Lebesgue integral over Γ or Γ_t is used throghout the study:

$$\int_{\Gamma} f(x)dx = \sum_{\gamma} f(x)_{\gamma} dx \ \text{ or } \ \int_{\Gamma_t} f(x,t)dxdt = \sum_{\gamma_t} f(x,t)_{\gamma} dxdt,$$

$f(\cdot)_{\gamma}$ corresponds to the restriction of the function $f(\cdot)$ to the edge γ.

Let us introduce the definition of the required spaces and sets: $C(\Gamma)$ is the space of continuous functions on Γ; $L_p(\Gamma)$ $(p = 1,2)$ is the Banach space of functions measurable on Γ_0, summable with pth degree; spaces $L_p(\Gamma_T)$ are defined similarly; $L_{2,1}(\Gamma_T)$ is the space of functions from $L_1(\Gamma_T)$ with the norm defined by the ratio

$$\|u\|_{L_{2,1}(\Gamma_T)} = \int_0^T (\int_{\Gamma} u^2(x,t)dx)^{1/2} dt.$$

We use the equivalents of the Sobolev spaces(Volkova, Gnilitskaya, and Provotorov 2014): $W_2^1(\Gamma)$ is the space of functions from $L_2(\Gamma_T)$ with a generalized first-order derivative also belonging to $L_2(\Gamma_T)$ (Provotorov, Ryazhskikh, and Gnilitskaya 2017); $W_2^{1,0}(\Gamma_T)$ is the space of functions from $L_2(\Gamma_T)$ with a generalized first-order derivative with respect to x belonging to $L_2(\Gamma_T)$ (the space $W_2^1(\Gamma_T)$ is introduced similarly); $V_2(\Gamma_T)$ is the set of all functions $u(x,t) \in W_2^{1,0}(\Gamma_T)$ with a finite norm:

$$\| u \|_{2,\Gamma_T} \equiv \max_{0 \le t \le T} \| u(\cdot,t) \|_{L_2(\Gamma)} + \| u_x \|_{L_2(\Gamma_T)} \tag{1}$$

and continuous with respect to t in the norm $L_2(\Gamma)$, i.e., such that given $\Delta t \to 0$, $\| u(x,t + \Delta t) - u(x,t) \|_{L_2(\Gamma)} \to 0$ is uniform on $[0,T]$.

Let us introduce the space of states of a parabolic system, and auxiliary spaces. For this purpose, let us consider a bilinear form:

$$\ell(\mu,v) = \int_{\Gamma} \left(a(x) \frac{d\mu(x)}{dx} \frac{dv(x)}{dx} + b(x)\mu(x)v(x) \right) dx \tag{2}$$

with fixed measureable functions $a(x)$, $b(x)$, which are bounded on Γ_0, summable with a square:

$$0 < a_* \le a(x) \le a^*, |b(x)| \le \beta, x \in \Gamma_0$$

4. GENERAL MATHEMATICAL MODEL

Using the terms introduced for modeling the movement of goods along the logistics network structure, we can adopt a rigorous mathematical formulation to translate the processes to a form accessible for algorithmic description. We apply the following statement(Provotorov and Provotorova 2017). Let the function $u(x) \in W_2^1(\Gamma)$ be such that $\ell(u,v) - \int_{\Gamma} f(x)\eta(x)dx = 0$ for any $\eta(x) \in W_2^1(\Gamma)$ ($f(x) \in L_2(\Gamma)$ is a fixed function).

Then, for any edge $\gamma \subset \Gamma$, the restriction $a(x)_\gamma \dfrac{du(x)_\gamma}{dx}$ is continuous at the endpoints of the edge γ. Let us denote by $\Omega_a(\Gamma)$ the set of functions $u(x)$ satisfying these conditions and relations:

$$\sum_{\gamma \in R(\xi)} a(1)_\gamma \frac{du(1)_\gamma}{dx} = \sum_{\gamma \in r(\xi)} a(0)_\gamma \frac{du(0)_\gamma}{dx}$$

at all nodes of the graph, which is the image of the logistics network $\xi \in J(\Gamma)$ (here $R(\xi)$ and $r(\xi)$ are the sets of edges γ, oriented, respectively, << towards the node ξ

\>> and <<away from the node ξ >>). The closure of the set $\Omega_a(\Gamma)$ in the norm $W_2^1(\Gamma)$ is denoted by $W^1(a,\Gamma)$. If we assume that the functions $u(x)$ from $\Omega_a(\Gamma)$ also satisfy the boundary condition $u(x)|_{\partial\Gamma} = 0$, then we obtain the space $W_0^1(a,\Gamma)$. Next, let $\Omega_a(\Gamma_T)$ be the set of functions $u(x,t) \in V_2(\Gamma_T)$, whose traces are defined on the sections of the region Γ_T by the plane $t = t_0$ $(t_0 \in [0,T])$ as functions of the class $W_0^1(a,\Gamma)$ and satisfy the relations:

$$\sum_{\gamma \in R(\xi)} a(1)_\gamma \frac{\partial u(1,t)_\gamma}{\partial x} = \sum_{\gamma \in r(\xi)} a(0)_\gamma \frac{\partial u(0,t)_\gamma}{\partial x} \tag{3}$$

for all nodes of the logistics network $\xi \in J(\Gamma)$. The closure of the set $\Omega_a(\Gamma_T)$ in the norm (1) is denoted by $V^{1,0}(a,\Gamma_T)$; from here it obviously follows that the condition $V^{1,0}(a,\Gamma_T) \subset W_2^{1,0}(\Gamma_T)$ is satisfied.

Another subspace of the space $W_2^{1,0}(\Gamma_T)$ is $W^{1,0}(a,\Gamma_T)$, closing the set of smooth functions satisfying the relations (3) for all nodes $\xi \in J(\Gamma)$ and for any $t \in [0,T]$ in the norm $W_2^{1,0}(\Gamma_T)$ (the space $W^1(a,\Gamma)$ is introduced similarly); the absorption condition $W^{1,0}(a,\Gamma_T) \subset W_2^{1,0}(\Gamma_T)$ is satisfied.

Thus, the space $V^{1,0}(a,\Gamma_T)$ describes the set of states of a parabolic system, and $W^{1,0}(a,\Gamma)$ and $W^1(a,\Gamma)$ describe auxiliary spaces within the framework of this approach. The difference between the elements of the space $V^{1,0}(a,\Gamma_T)$ and the elements of $W^{1,0}(a,\Gamma)$ is that the latter have no continuity with respect to the time variable *t*. This is fundamentally important for generating economic indicators characterizing the transfer of goods. Indeed, an integrated criterion reflecting the costs of transferring goods depends both on the distance traveled and on time. Such dependences exhibit jumps due to changes in tariffs for multimodal transportation, approaching the expiry date of a wide range of fast-moving consumer goods (FMCG), transport lease conditions, port infrastructure, demurrage, detention, or contractual penalties for short delivery or late shipment, and other factors accompanying logistics operations.

Let us consider the following parabolic equation in the spaces $W^{1,0}(a,\Gamma)$ and $V^{1,0}(a,\Gamma_T)$:

$$\frac{\partial y(x,t)}{\partial t} - \frac{\partial}{\partial x}\left(a(x)\frac{\partial y(x,t)}{\partial x}\right) + b(x)y(x,t) = f(x,t) \tag{4}$$

representing a system of differential equations with distributed parameters of the economic criterion on each edge γ of the graph Γ as an image of a logistics network; $f(x,t) \in L_{2,1}(\Gamma_T)$. The state $y(x,t)$ $(x,t \in \overline{\Gamma}_T)$ of system (4) in the region $\overline{\Gamma}_T$ is determined by a generalized solution $y(x,t)$ of Eq. (4), satisfying the initial and boundary conditions:

$$y|_{t=0} = \varphi(x), \quad x \in \Gamma, \quad y|_{x \in \partial\Gamma_T} = 0 \tag{5}$$

$\varphi(x) \in L_2(\Gamma)$. Above, we have already established that the functions $a(x)$ and $b(x)$ are summable with a square. It follows from the condition $y(x,t) \in V^{1,0}(a,\Gamma_T)$ that the mapping of the economic criterion to the graph $y:[0,T] \to W_0^1(a,\Gamma) \subset L_2(\Gamma)$ is a continuous function, so that the first equality in (5) holds true and is definable almost always. In this case, we consider the first initial boundary-value problem (4), (5) or the Dirichlet boundary condition in relations (5).

Let us present the main statements and steps for the proof of the validity of the results obtained, necessary for the study of solution stability. The main practical applications are analysis of management strategies adopted by managers of logistics services and risk management of logistics business processes. Let us first consider the solution in the auxiliary space $W^{1,0}(a,\Gamma_T)$, then in the space $V^{1,0}(a,\Gamma)$. Complete proofs are given in(Volkova and Provotorov 2014).

Let us define that a generalized solution of the initial boundary-value problem (4), (5) of class $W_2^{1,0}(\Gamma_T)$ is a function $y(x,t) \in W^{1,0}(a,\Gamma_T)$ that satisfies the integral identity:

$$-\int_{\Gamma_T} y(x,t)\frac{\partial\eta(x,t)}{\partial t}dxdt + \ell_T(y,\eta) =$$

$$= \int_{\Gamma} \varphi(x)\eta(x,0)dx + \tag{6}$$

$$+ \int_{\Gamma_T} f(x,t)\eta(x,t)dxdt$$

for any $\eta(x,t) \in W^1(a,\Gamma_T)$ equal to zero at $t = T$; $\ell_t(y,\eta)$ is the bilinear form defined by the relation:

$$\ell_t(y,\eta) = \int_{\Gamma_t}\left(a(x)\frac{\partial y(x,t)}{\partial x}\frac{\partial\eta(x,t)}{\partial x} + b(x)y(x,t)\eta(x,t)\right)dxdt;$$

$$t \in (0,T].$$

Determining the solvability of problems and (4), (5) in the space $W^{1,0}(a,\Gamma_T)$ (and $V^{1,0}(a,\Gamma_T)$), a special basis of the space $W_0^1(a,\Gamma)$ is used, which is a system of generalized eigenfunctions of the boundary-value problem for eigenvalues (spectral problem):

$$-\frac{d}{dx}\left(a(x)\frac{du(x)}{dx}\right)+b(x)u(x)=$$
$$= \lambda u(x), u(x)|_{\partial\Gamma}=0 \tag{7}$$

in the functional class $W^1(a,\Gamma)$ (Golosnoy et al., 2019).

It follows then that, assuming (2), the spectral problem (7) has a countable set of real eigenvalues $\{\lambda_i\}_{i\geq1}$ (numbered in ascending order with respect to their multiplicities) with a limit point at infinity (the eigenvalues λ_i are positive, except possibly a finite number of the first ones). The system of generalized eigenfunctions $\{u_i(x)\}_{i\geq1}$ forms a basis in $W_0^1(a,\Gamma)$ and $L_2(\Gamma)$, orthonormal in $L_2(\Gamma)$ and orthogonal in the sense of the scalar product(Provotorov et al., 2020).

Since we take into account the economic meaning of variables in practical applications, it follows from the condition that $b(x) \geq 0$ should be non-negative that all eigenvalues of spectral problem (7) are positive. The positivity of the eigenvalues is the determining factor for establishing the stability property of parabolic evolutionary systems with distributed parameters on the graph.

5. Study of Solution Stability

Let us carry out a mathematically substantiated study for the stability parameters of the solution found for system (4), which describes the dynamics of the logistic process, formalized as the transfer of goods and cargo over the network. The transport network, in turn, is presented in the form of a mathematical graph. Suppose that $0 \leq b(x) \leq \beta$ for $x \in \Gamma$, which guarantees that the eigenvalues $\lambda_i, i \geq 1$ are positive. Let us consider the resulting system (4) on the set $\Gamma_\infty = \Gamma_0 \times (0,\infty)$. Let us introduce the notations $\Gamma_{t_0,t} = \Gamma_0 \times (t_0,t)$, $\partial\Gamma_{t_0,t} = \partial\Gamma \times (t_0,t)$ $(0<t_0<t<\infty)$, $\Gamma_{t_0,\infty} = \Gamma_0 \times (t_0,\infty)$, $\partial\Gamma_{t_0,\infty} = \partial\Gamma \times (t_0,\infty)$; evidently, $\Gamma_{t_0,t} \subset \Gamma_t$. As above, $f(x,t) \in CL_{2,1}(\Gamma_T)$, with $\int_t^{t+1} \| f(\cdot,\varsigma)\|_{L_2(\Gamma)}^2 \, d\varsigma \leq A$ for any $t \geq 0$.

Let the state of system (4) be described by the function $\bar{y}(x,t) \in V^{1,0}(a, \Gamma_{t_0,\infty})$, which is a generalized solution of Eq. (4) in the region $\Gamma_{t_0,\infty}$ with the initial and boundary conditions:

$$y\big|_{t=t_0} = \bar{\varphi}(x), \quad x \in \Gamma, \quad y\big|_{x \in \partial\Gamma_{t_0,\infty}} = 0.$$

the function $y(x,t) \in V^{1,0}(a, \Gamma_{t_0,\infty})$ is a weak solution of Eq. (4) in the region $\Gamma_{t_0,\infty}$ with the initial and boundary conditions:

$$y\big|_{t=t_0} = \varphi(x), \quad x \in \Gamma, \quad y\big|_{x \in \partial\Gamma_{t_0,\infty}} = 0$$

The state $\bar{y}(x,t)$ of system (4) is assumed to be unperturbed, and that of $y(x,t)$ is assumed to be perturbed. It follows from previous analysis of the generalized solution of problem (4), (5)) that the states $\bar{y}(x,t)$, $y(x,t)$ are defined in the region $\Gamma_{t_0,\infty}$, satisfy the corresponding initial and boundary conditions, and belong to the space $V^{1,0}(a, \Gamma_{t_0,\infty})$ at $f(x,t) \in CL_{2,1}(\Gamma_\infty)$.

Below, we propose the definition for the stability of a solution to the initial boundary-value problem (4), (5) (stability of the unperturbed state of system (4)) as an equivalent of Lyapunov stability.

Let us assume that the unperturbed state $\bar{y}(x,t)$ of system (4) is called stable if for any $t_0 > 0$ and $\varepsilon > 0$, there is $\delta(t_0, \varepsilon) > 0$, such that at $\|\varphi - \bar{\varphi}\|_{L_2(\Gamma)} < \delta(t_0, \varepsilon)$ $\|y(\cdot,t) - \bar{y}(\cdot,t)\|_{W^1(a,\Gamma)} < \varepsilon$ is fulfilled at $t \geq t_0$, where $y(x,t)$ is the perturbed state of system (4).

Similarly to the definition for the stability of the unperturbed state of system (4), we can introduce the definition for the uniform stability of the unperturbed state of system (4) in the region $\Gamma_{t_0,\infty}$. For system (4), we can introduce definitions of the asymptotic and exponential stability of the unperturbed state of system (3) in the region $\Gamma_{t_0,\infty}$. Because system (4) is linear, all definitions can be reformulated for the zero (trivial) state of the system (4).

Let us prove that given the above condition $0 \leq b(x) \leq \beta$, $x \in \Gamma$, the unperturbed state of the system (4) is stable in the region Γ_T. This follows from the fact that, due to the linearity of equation (4), the function $\theta(x,t) = y(x,t) - \bar{y}(x,t)$ is an element of the space $V^{1,0}(a, \Gamma_{t_0,\infty})$ and is a generalized solution of the initial boundary-value problem for the homogeneous equation (4), satisfying the initial and boundary conditions:

$$\theta\mid_{t=t_0} = \phi(x), \quad x \in \Gamma, \quad \theta\mid_{x\in\partial\Gamma_{t_0,\infty}} = 0$$

where $\phi(x) = \varphi(x) - \overline{\varphi}(x)$. Therefore, the initial boundary-value problem (4) is uniquely generalized solvable, its solution has the representation $\theta(x,t) = \sum\limits_{i=1}^{\infty} \phi_i e^{-\lambda_i t} u_i(x)$, $\phi_i = (\phi, u_i)$ and is the limit of the weakly converging sequence of $\{\theta^N\}_{N\geq 1}$ approximations:

$$\theta^N(x,t) = \sum_{i=1}^{N} \phi_i e^{-\lambda_i t} u_i(x)$$

and the following inequality holds simultaneously:

$$\|\theta^N\|_{2,\Gamma_t} \leq \sum_{i=1}^{N} \phi_i^2 e^{-2\lambda_i t}, N = 1, 2, \dots.$$

Considering the limit in the last inequality at $N \to \infty$, we obtain the estimate:

$$(e^{-2\lambda_i t} < 1, \ i = 1, 2, \dots) \ \|\theta\|_{2,\Gamma_t} \leq C^* \|\phi\|_{L_2(\Gamma)}$$

for any $t \in [t_0, \infty]$; C^* is a constant independent of t. The latter means that

$$\|\theta(\cdot,t)\|_{W^1(a,\Gamma)} \leq C^* \|\phi\|_{L_2(\Gamma)}$$

Let us fix $\varepsilon > 0$, taking $\delta = \dfrac{\varepsilon}{C^*}$, then, since

$$\|\phi\|_{L_2(\Gamma)} = \|\varphi - \overline{\varphi}\|_{L_2(\Gamma)} < \delta$$

the inequality $\|\theta(\cdot,t)\|_{W^1(a,\Gamma)} = \|y(\cdot,t) - \overline{y}(\cdot,t)\|_{W^1(a,\Gamma)} < \varepsilon$ follows for any $t > t_0$, which was required to obtain the stability conditions.

CONCLUSION

Data flow processing algorithms reflecting the current state of cargo movements are the core of digital logistics platforms. The efficiency of a logistics operator directly depends on the quality of management decisions made. Since the operation of all links of a logistics chain is influenced by random perturbations, it is necessary to study the stability of the obtained solutions to confirm the practical possibility of switching to leading planning indicators. The technique proposed in the paper is a continuation of the standard approaches using classical methods for studying the solution stability in systems of differential equations. However, the dynamics of network processes of goods transfer plotted on graphs with different topologies requires mathematical models associated with solving initial boundary-value problems in the class of differential equations with respect to the distributed parameters. This reflects the conditions imposed on the solution of equations describing systems with parameters distributed on the graph. In this paper, we provide the stability conditions for the solution of an evolutionary parabolic system with distributed parameters on a graph which is the prototype of the logistic transport network. We used a quality functional integrating the economic indicators of the process depending on time and on the parameter of goods transfer. Solving the problem posed and applying a generalized solution is a complicated task because the quality functional is not continuous with respect to its arguments. This is due to the real conditions of logistics operations. The most typical ones are inevitable time delays and stevedoring costs for loading and unloading operations, customs procedures, changes in mileage rates for multimodal transportation, the influence of the time factor on the costs of renting transportation services and port/station infrastructure, demurrage, detention, or contractual penalties for short delivery or late shipment, stringent restrictions on the delivery schedule for most FMCG goods and other types of goods with short expiry dates. Furthermore, other perturbations can have a considerable effect on economic indicators, such as congestion of transport routes and variable density of average traffic, sensitivity to adverse weather conditions, especially in the air and sea transportation segment, as well as possible complications of a political nature, for example, sanctions and force majeures, gaining a particularly prominent role during the COVID-19 pandemic. All these are components of problems in supply chain management, increasing in complexity in the context of business consolidation into network structures. The results obtained allow to estimate the influence of changes in the initial data on the behavior and analysis of the mathematical model, primarily the solutions of the initial boundary-value problems that determine the model. This theoretical solution gains a much more important economic meaning. It can be concluded that, in general, the issues to be considered are risk assessment of investing funds and the sustainability of the business model used by the logistics operator.

REFERENCES

Artemov, M. A., E. S. Baranovskii, A. P. Zhabko, and V. V. Provotorov. 2019. "On a 3D Model of Non-Isothermal Flows in a Pipeline Network." *Journal of Physics: Conference Series* 1203 (1): 0–9. https://doi.org/10.1088/1742-6596/1203/1/012094.

Barykin, S., A. Borovkov, O. Rozhdestvenskiy, A. Tarshin, and V. Yadykin. 2020. "Staff Competence and Training for Digital Industry." *IOP Conference Series: Materials Science and Engineering* 940 (1). https://doi.org/10.1088/1757-899X/940/1/012106.

Barykin, Sergey Yevgenievich, Andrey Aleksandrovich Bochkarev, Olga Vladimirovna Kalinina, and Vladimir Konstantinovich Yadykin. 2020. "Concept for a Supply Chain Digital Twin." *International Journal of Mathematical, Engineering and Management Sciences* 5 (6): 1498–1515. https://doi.org/10.33889/IJMEMS.2020.5.6.111.

Barykin, Sergey Yevgenievich, Irina Vasilievna Kapustina, Sergey Mikhailovich Sergeev, and Vladimir Konstantinovich Yadykin. 2020. "Algorithmic Foundations of Economic and Mathematical Modeling of Network Logistics Processes." *Journal of Open Innovation: Technology, Market, and Complexity* 6 (4): 1–16. https://doi.org/10.3390/joitmc6040189.

Barykin, Sergey Yevgenievich, Irina Vasilievna Kapustina, Tatiana Viktorovna Kirillova, Vladimir Konstantinovich Yadykin, and Yevgenii Aleksandrovich Konnikov. 2020. "Economics of Digital Ecosystems." *Journal of Open Innovation: Technology, Market, and Complexity* 6 (4): 1–16. https://doi.org/10.3390/joitmc6040124.

Barykin, Sergey, Olga Kalinina, Igor Aleksandrov, Evgenii Konnikov, Vladimir Yadikin, and Mikhail Draganov. 2020. "Personnel Management Digital Model Based on the Social Profiles' Analysis." *Journal of Open Innovation: Technology, Market, and Complexity* 6 (4): 1–20. https://doi.org/10.3390/joitmc6040152.

Borisoglebskaya, L. N., V. V. Provotorov, S. M. Sergeev, and E. S. Kosinov. 2019. "Mathematical Aspects of Optimal Control of Transference Processes in Spatial Networks." *IOP Conference Series: Materials Science and Engineering* 537 (4). https://doi.org/10.1088/1757-899X/537/4/042025.

Bril, Alexander, Olga Kalinina, Sergey Barykin, and Anna Burova. 2020. "The Methodological Features of the Economic Evaluation of Personnel Management Operational Projects." In *Innovations in Digital Economy*, edited by Dmitrii Rodionov, Tatiana Kudryavtseva, Mohammed Ali Berawi, and Angi Skhvediani, 143–54. Cham: Springer International Publishing.

Bril, Alexander, Svetlana Evseeva, Olga Kalinina, Sergey Barykin, and Elena Vinogradova. 2020. "Personnel Changes and Labor Productivity in Regulatory Budget Monitoring." *IOP Conference Series: Materials Science and Engineering* 940 (1). https://doi.org/10.1088/1757-899X/940/1/012105.

Golosnoy, A. S., V. V. Provotorov, S. M. Sergeev, L. B. Raikhelgauz, and O. Ja Kravets. 2019. "Software Engineering Math for Network Applications." *Journal of Physics: Conference Series* 1399 (4). https://doi.org/10.1088/1742-6596/1399/4/044047.

Kapustina, Irina, Olga Kalinina, Alina Ovchinnikova, and Sergei Barykin. 2020. "The Logistics Network Digital Twin in View of Concept of the Non-Destructive Quality Control Methods." *E3S Web of Conferences* 157. https://doi.org/10.1051/e3sconf/202015705001.

Podvalny, S. L., E. S. Podvalny, and V. V. Provotorov. 2017. "The Controllability of Parabolic Systems with Delay and Distributed Parameters on the Graph." *Procedia Computer Science* 103 (October 2016): 324–30. https://doi.org/10.1016/j.procs.2017.01.115.

Provotorov, V V. 2008. "Eigenfunctions of the Sturm-Liouville Problem on a Star Graph." *Sbornik: Mathematics* 199 (10): 1523–45. https://doi.org/10.1070/sm2008v199n10abeh003971.

Provotorov, V. V., and E. N. Provotorova. 2017. "Synthesis of Optimal Boundary Control of Parabolic Systems with Delay and Distributed Parameters on the Graph." *Vestnik Sankt-Peterburgskogo Universiteta, Prikladnaya Matematika, Informatika, Protsessy Upravleniya* 13 (2): 209–24. https://doi.org/10.21638/11701/spbu10.2017.207.

Provotorov, V. V., and Provotorova E.N. 2017. *"Optimal Control of the Linearized Naver-Stokes System in a Netlike Domain,"* 431–43.

Provotorov, V. V., D. V. Danilevich, A. A. Fedotov, S. M. Sergeev, and O. Ja Kravets. 2020. "Digital Management by Supply Networks in Engineering." *IOP Conference Series: Materials Science and Engineering* 862 (3). https://doi.org/10.1088/1757-899X/862/3/032024.

Provotorov, V. V., S. M. Sergeev, and A. A. Part. 2019. "Solvability of Hyperbolic Systems with Distributed Parameters on the Graph in the Weak Formulation." *Vestnik Sankt-Peterburgskogo Universiteta, Prikladnaya Matematika, Informatika, Protsessy Upravleniya* 15 (1): 107–17. https://doi.org/10.21638/11702/spbu10.2019.108.

Provotorov, V. V., V. I. Ryazhskikh, and Yu A. Gnilitskaya. 2017. "Unique Weak Solvability of a Nonlinear Initial Boundary Value Problem with Distributed Parameters in a Netlike Domain." *Vestnik Sankt-Peterburgskogo Universiteta, Prikladnaya Matematika, Informatika, Protsessy Upravleniya* 13 (3): 264–77. https://doi.org/10.21638/11701/spbu10.2017.304.

Shmatko, Alexey, Sergey Barykin, Sergey Sergeev, and Anuphat Thirakulwanich. 2021. *"Modeling a Logistics Hub Using the Digital Footprint Method — The Implication for Open Innovation Engineering."*

Volkova, A S, and V V Provotorov. 2014. "Generalized Solutions and Generalized Eigenfunctions of Boundary-Value Problems on a Geometric Graph." *Russian Mathematics* 58 (3): 1–13. https://doi.org/10.3103/S1066369X14030013.

Volkova, A S, Yu. A Gnilitskaya, and V V Provotorov. 2014. "On the Solvability of Boundary-Value Problems for Parabolic and Hyperbolic Equations on Geometrical Graphs." *Automation and Remote Control* 75 (2): 405–12. https://doi.org/10.1134/S0005117914020192.

Zhabko, A. P., A. I. Shindyapin, and V. V. Provotorov. 2019. "Stability of Weak Solutions of Parabolic Systems with Distributed Parameters on the Graph." *Vestnik Sankt-Peterburgskogo Universiteta, Prikladnaya Matematika, Informatika, Protsessy Upravleniya* 15 (4): 457–71. https://doi.org/10.21638/11702/spbu10.2019.404.

Zhabko, Aleksei P., Karlygash B. Nurtazina, and Vyacheslav V. Provotorov. 2019. "About One Approach to Solving the Inverse Problem for Parabolic Equation." *Vestnik Sankt-Peterburgskogo Universiteta, Prikladnaya Matematika, Informatika, Protsessy Upravleniya* 15 (3): 323–36. https://doi.org/10.21638/11702/spbu10.2019.303.

In: Global Challenges of Digital Transformation of Markets ISBN: 978-1-53619-754-9
Editors: E. de la Poza and S. E. Barykin   © 2021 Nova Science Publishers, Inc.

Chapter 2

ALGORITHM FOR SUPPORTING MULTIMODAL LOGISTICS IN CONDITIONS OF MARKET UNCERTAINTY

V. V. Provotorov[1,*], V. V. Bakharev[2], N. V. Dedyukhina[3], N. V. Ostrovskaya[4], M. S. Loskutova[4] and N. S. Mayer[4]

[1]Voronezh State University, Voronezh, Russia
[2]Peter the Great St. Petersburg Polytechnic University, Russia
[3]Department of Accounting and Audit,
Emperor Alexander I St. Petersburg State Transport University,
St. Petersburg, Russia
[4]Financial University under the Government of
the Russian Federation (Moscow), St. Petersburg branch, Russia

ABSTRACT

There are two key directions related to solving the problem of end-to-end digitalization in the multimodal transportation segment. The first is technical support of Machine-to-Machine (M2M) interaction using a number of technologies, such as the availability and standardization of machine-readable codes with corrective properties, consistency of GPS/GLONASS/BEIDOU geolocation protocols, and others. The second task consists in developing logistics support algorithms, generally within the framework of the 3PL concept (Third-Party Logistics). While there is a diverse range of technical equipment available for M2M, the second problem has to be solved by applying mathematical modeling using optimization methods based on economically substantiated criteria. The article proposes a methodology for constructing control algorithms that connect both modern cross-docking and pick-by-line technologies, and methods of

* Corresponding Author's Email: sergeev2@inbox.ru.

mathematical programming under uncertainty of the environment. This approach is based on analysis of the world experience in digital tracking, confirming that the main effect during implementation is achieved precisely due to the capabilities of formalized algorithms using the mathematical theory of optimal processes and is many times greater than the simple reduction of freight forwarding costs.

Keywords: control algorithm, multimodal transportation, machine-to-machine communication, digital tracking, stochastic models

1. INTRODUCTION

The properties of flexibility and reliability of the supply chain allow you to navigate in conditions of uncertainty and should be taken into account when planning. The combination of optimization modeling and data analysis is a basic technology that allows you to create a fairly detailed model of the real supply chain of its digital counterpart Idea. The goal of creating a digital twin is to manage the risks in the supply chains, thereby making them more reliable and resilient in the event of any failures. Modern technologies allow you to collect large amounts of data on supply chains online. The management technologies used in supply chains enable the identification of critical hot spots and timely warning of incidents that may have a critical impact on the supply chain (S. Y. Barykin, Bochkarev, Kalinina, and Yadykin 2020). It can successfully act as a replacement for expensive field monitoring methods, without causing any damage to the physical object.

Intensive development in the field of high technologies is reflected in all spheres of life. More and more elements are involved in the process of digitalization Enterprises need to transform their workforce to achieve a sustainable competitive advantage (Bril, Kalinina, et al. 2020). The introduction of high-tech solutions leads to a change in the format and content of almost any work, as well as a rethinking of approaches to personnel planning. When developing a business plan for a new enterprise, the main issues are market assessment and-sales forecast opportunities to attract investment. When drawing up a business plan for an existing enterprise, another important issue arises - the use of internal resources of the enterprise, assets and personnel. Therefore, when developing an enterprise plan, there is a need for a special financial and economic analysis of the object and the preparation of key financial indicators of business planning standards (Bril, Evseeva, et al. 2020).

A digital ecosystem is a self-organizing, sustainable system with digital platforms at the base, which form a single information environment where the members of the ecosystem can interact when no hard functional ties between them exist. The base of a digital ecosystem is the diverse platform technologies which form a single information environment for all members: society, business and government. The development of platform technologies contributes to the scaling up of digital ecosystems, which are beyond the business environment and B2B and B2C relationships. The digital environment is used to connect members, exchange information and resources, organize processes and coordinate objectives. One of the most important features of a DES is its ability to self-organize and the lack of a managing or supervising member of the ecosystem. The main difference between digital ecosystems and traditional ecosystems is that the organization of business in the latter is based on management decision making by a human. Meanwhile, management decision making in digital ecosystems is for the most part automated and carried out without human participation, thanks to the diverse tools which exist such as artificial intelligence, computer vision and so on (S. Y. Barykin, Kapustina, Kirillova, Yadykin, et al. 2020). A digital twin refers to an evolving digital profile of the historical and current behavior of a physical object or process that helps optimize business performance (Kapustina et al. 2020)

The process of managing the organization's personnel within the digital ecosystem, while maintaining the basic goal setting, is transformed from an instrumental point of view. The transition from a traditional HR system to a digital one involves a difference between how staff interact with each other and with management. The key factor in the digital interaction system is the ability of each employee to freely contact the information and analytical center. The digital interaction system also differs from the traditional one by expanding the channels for exchanging information and analytics. Considering the tasks of personnel management in the digital era, it can be shown that the problem of digital personnel management is the scientific search for the features of employee interaction in the new technological structure of Industry 4.0 under the influence of the flow of innovations, there is a change. It includes improvements in performance, reliability, quality, and safety (Sergey Barykin, Kalinina, Aleksandrov, Konnikov, et al. 2020).

Over the past decade, technologies and equipment that can radically change the approach to managing the processes of cargo movement and cargo transportation have become widespread. This includes the possibility of machine-readable exchange of information about goods and cargo among themselves. The structure of relations between participants in this segment of the economy has become more complex. This is due to the processes of consolidation in commercial structures, which leads to an increase in the complexity of managing such business objects, as well as a multiple increase in the time and money spent on ensuring the material flows of goods and cargo necessary to maintain a competitive business. To solve such large-scale problems, the use of scientifically based mathematical models is required. This approach will allow us to use the digital footprint of processes in the logistics network and develop an algorithmic basis for a whole range of software tools for more efficient management of the logistics industry (S. Y. Barykin, Kapustina, Sergeev, and Yadykin 2020).

It is necessary to find an economically optimal management of the flows of goods and cargo based on digital information about their movement, taking into account the stochastic nature of the volumes and directions of flows. At the same time, it is necessary to choose and justify the methodology for calculating the node DC terminals included in the network structure of logistics activities. The obtained set of mathematical relations allows us to simulate the operation of a network distribution center as a node element of a logistics system that functions on the principles of 3PL operator in conditions of stochastic nature of incoming and shipped goods flows (Shmatko et al. 2021).

It is necessary to consider the issue of training personnel for the digital industry in the context of creating teams at enterprises in scientific organizations and universities that have the necessary digital competencies and digital literacy, that is, the ability to use modern methods, experimentation and research technologies to develop globally competitive products. This competence becomes an integrator of the technological, ethical, and cognitive aspects of education. In this paradigm, the basis of the methodological approach to solving the problem of personnel training is a problem-oriented scientific approach, and the model of creating mirror engineering centers is a possible model for scaling competencies, spreading knowledge and developing network interaction (S. Barykin, Borovkov, Rozhdestvenskiy, Tarshin, et al. 2020).

Globalization provides a wide field for business opportunities. The coverage of potential consumers is virtually unlimited geographically. Managers of the logistics department are tasked with choosing the economically optimal option from the available variety of solutions. Since enterprises from any segment of the economy operate under uncertainty of demand, mathematical tools should be used (Pilipenko et al. 2019), with the functional resulting from the condition of profit maximization typically serving as the criterion.

A number of problems arise with the transition to the concept of Machine-to-Machine interaction(S. Krasnov et al. 2019), related to identifying the objects (goods in any container) and tracking their movements. Intelligent automation tools such as laser and radio frequency scanners, robotic warehouse complexes, in-process autonomous transport based on machine-readable codes have become widespread (Sergey Krasnov, Sergeev, Zotova, et al. 2019). So, a wide array of tools can be used to solve the identification problem, ranging from linear barcodes and two-dimensional Quick Response Codes (QR) to recognition tools based on RFID (Radio Frequency Identification) tags.

The decision to use a specific tool depends on the conditions of the object's location throughout the entire track, as well as restrictions on the equipment used during transportation. According to EAN/UCC (European Article Number / Uniform Code Council) and ITF (Interleaved Two of Five) standards (Borisoglebskaya, Provotorova, and Sergeev 2019b), the maximum allowed encoding is from 10208 to 23648 characters. The size of the information array depends on the possibility for error correction, starting from the lower L level (allows to recover up to 7% of the information lost) with intermediate M and Q levels, ending with the upper H level (recovering up to 30% of the information lost due to the influence of the external environment and other adverse factors).

Modern machine-to-machine interaction relies on cloud-based Internet solutions, therefore, logistic algorithms (Borisoglebskaya, Provotorova, et al. 2019) include both individual units and large quantities of cargo, organized into packages, as a control objects. In this case, combined schemes are used, based on RFID tags containing the addresses of individual units and requiring to access the forwarding server. This identification makes it possible to switch to M2M algorithms for cross-docking procedures and pick-by-line selection (Borisoglebskaya, Provotorov, et al. 2019), which are present in the vast majority of logistic schemes.

The difference in these technologies is that cross-docking does not imply a change in machine labeling during 3PL (Third Party Logistics) processing by the operator. Its advantages are the high speed of processing the SKU (Stock Keeping Unit) for an item. The time spent within the DC (distribution center) is minimized. The pick-by-line technology includes SKU processing, reorganization of cargo units, in particular, fragmentation. Thus, the goods arrive to the unloading area rather than the stock. Accordingly, each of the smaller items should have its own machine-readable labeling with complete information.

This type of interaction covers exceptionally large data arrays, containing millions of records, each with a dimension of 10,000–15,000 characters, since the global trend is to consolidate commercial structures in a network under a single brand, carrying out a unified distribution and marketing policy. In addition, distribution centers formed as component nodes and the concept of third-party logistics emerged based on SCM (supply chain management) technologies (Sergey Krasnov, Sergeev, Titov, et al. 2019) within the paradigm of commercial networks. Today, 3PL providers are active in the commercial segment, primarily in retail chains.

Due to the flexibility of M2M technologies and alternative modes of transportation, as well as expanding range of functions, higher levels of services such as 4PL and 5PL have appeared. Such forms are more common in other segments of the economy, for example, in P2P (Peer-to-Peer or Partner-to-Partner) networks, online auctions, etc. In this study, we consider their potential for applying the obtained results.

2. PROBLEM STATEMENT

This study analyzes digital technologies within the framework of the interaction between Machine-to-Machine and standard machine-readable codes with corrective properties, with the aim to make a transition to end-to-end automation of the most common segment of multimodal transportation within 3PL logistics.

Analyzing the world experience in digital tracking, we concluded that the main effect during implementation, far greater than a simple reduction in freight forwarding costs, can be achieved only by using the capabilities offered by formalized algorithms based on the mathematical theory of optimal processes(Provotorov, Sergeev, and Part 2019). The practical focus of the study is that the results are oriented towards multimodal logistics and constructing a scalable model. This will allow to develop the results for higher levels of third-party logistics.

3. MAIN MATHEMATICAL FORMALISMS

Let us introduce the formalisms necessary for constructing the mathematical model. We assume that a multimodal transport operator (MTO) plans its operations under market uncertainty, which is reflected in a set of random variables ci, where $i = 1,2,\ldots,m$. This includes the quantitative values of delivery requests represented by the set of acceptable values of x, the volumes of raw materials, components, traffic, consolidated supply, and their known distribution functions based on the results of statistical analysis of market data. The corresponding indicators of the expected value $m_i = E(c_i)$ and variance D_i are influenced by such market factors as demand, prices, personnel maintenance, risks. The only restriction is Lindeberg's condition: for any $\tau >$ 0,

$$\lim_{x \to 0} \frac{1}{B_n^2} \sum_{k=1}^{n} \int_{|x-m_k|>\tau \cdot B_n} (x-m_k)^2 c_k(t)dt = 0 \ ,$$

must be satisfied, where $B_n = \sqrt{\sum_{k=1}^{n} D_k}, c_k(t)$ is the distribution density, t is the time.

Moreover, the dependences of the values of c_i typically exhibit seasonal variations (Borisoglebskaya et al. 2020). For this we use the following expression obtained in (Fedotov et al. 2020): $m_i = A_{0j} + \sum_k A_{ki} Cos(2\pi \frac{1}{12}(k + \theta_i))$, where k is the number of the planning period, A_{0i}, A_{1i}, θ_i are the coefficients of the Fourier series.

Next, we introduce the controlled variables $x_j : x_j \geq 0; j = 1,2,\ldots,n$, reflecting both the volume of traffic by specific modes of transport and the routes chosen, also including the impact of throughput and the data for the indicators of distribution centers used as route nodes.

The goal is to find the variables $x_j, j = 1,2,\ldots,n$ given the stochastic nature of information about the actual values taken for $c_j, j = 1,2,\ldots,n$.

Next, we introduce the deterministic quantities $a_{ij}, j = 1,2,\ldots,m, j = 1,2,\ldots,n$ as well as parameters b_i, which define the model constraints. These include such values as the characteristics of transport in terms of carrying capacity, schedule of the railway or port, the volume of warehouses, stevedoring performance, the costs for maintaining warehouses, rent, energy.

Let us formulate the problem in terms of separable functions. The functional $\sum_{j=1}^{n} c_j x_j$ has to be optimized given the constraints $\sum_{j=1}^{n} a_{ij} x_j = b_i, i = 1,2,\ldots,m$.

The simplest interpretation of a set of constraints is, for example, the deadweight of a consolidated transport pool.

Analyzing the potential steps that can be taken to optimize the quality functional, we should note that if only the variables x_j, $j = 1,2,...,n$ are determined in the absence of complete information on the values of c_j, the desired solution of the optimal expected value of $E\left[\sum_{j=1}^{n} c_j x_j\right]$ with these constraints is reduced to solving the equivalent of the usual deterministic problem of linear programming. For this, based on the properties of random functions, the functional of the condition is rewritten as $\sum_{j=1}^{n} E\left[c_j\right]x_j$. In this case, the expected values of the corresponding coefficients of the initial problem were chosen as the coefficients in the expression for the objective function.

However, the problem of stochastic linear programming cannot be solved by a simple method in cases when even some of the values of x_j require information to be determined more accurately.

One of the solution methods (Provotorov et al. 2020) is based on the mathematical theory of games, considered in detail in (Borisoglebskaya, Provotorova, and Sergeev 2019a); however, additional factors have to be taken into account for a multidimensional model. Notably, an extended planning horizon is always considered and the problem is solved in several stages; furthermore, if the optimization vector has a large dimension, iterative procedures that are convenient for programming should be formed. If these conditions are provided, another method can be proposed for obtaining the desired result, described below.

4. ALGORITHM

Let a unit of a commercial trading network compose a plan for multimodal transportation and the workload of distribution centers for a known extended time horizon.

The total volume of the set of cargoes required for business operations during the planning period is limited to T (the dimension is arbitrary, for example, in tons or cargo packages).

At the start of each of the periods comprising the planned horizon, the enterprise must calculate the following controllable variables:

- x_1 is the amount of goods and cargo transported by one mode (for example, railway cars);
- x_2 is the number of goods and cargo transported by the second mode (typically by motor vehicles);
- x_3 are the goods and cargo processed at distribution centers.

To complete the delivery of x_1, a_1x_1 units of the first type of transport are required for the planning period, respectively, a_2x_2 units of the second type are required for the delivery of x_2 for the planning period. Let us introduce the notations D_1 and D_2 to quantitatively characterize the maximum fleet for each type of transport.

Next, let us introduce the prices for the cargo unit of the first type of transport, equal to r_1, and for the second, equal to r_2. At the same time, the costs for each transportation are equal to $r_j(a_j x_j)$ for each track j ($j = 1,2$). The model should take into account the associated costs for maintaining a unit of transport, stevedoring, insurance, etc. Their volume directly depends, for example, on the choice of delivery terms. It is known that these costs can differ considerably for the CIF (Cost, Insurance and Freight) or FOB (Free On Board) (Golosnoy et al. 2019) terms commonly used (according to Incoterms), Let us set them equal to e_j for servicing a unit of each mode of transport j ($j = 1,2$). Thus, $e_j x_j$ are the total associated costs for type j. To form an optimization criterion, we calculate the amount of costs Q:

$$Q = (a_1 x_1 r_1 + e_1) x_1 + (a_2 x_2 r_2 + e_2) x_2 + c_3 x_3 \tag{1}$$

where c_3 is the cost of handling a cargo unit from x_3. Then, introducing the notations c_j = $r_j a_j + e_j$ ($j = 1,2$), we can rewrite the criterion in the form $Q = \sum_{j=1}^{3} c_j x_j$.

Notice that provided that a_j ($j = 1,2$), c_j ($j = 1,2,3$) and D_j are deterministic, the problem can become trivial and be reduced to solution by the linear programming method. In commercial applications, Q should be minimized to account for the constraints.

$$\sum_{j=1}^{3} x_j = T, a_1 x_1 + s_1 = D_1, a_2 x_2 + s_2 = D_2, x_j \geq 0, s_j \geq 0, \tag{2}$$

where s_i is the shortage of the corresponding transport units.

Due to the market uncertainty described above, enterprise managers can have real data available on the costs for r_1, r_2 (and, accordingly, the values of c_1, c_2) in practice, with only a certain time lag after a decision is made for the values of x_1, x_2, x_3.

Besides, the values of a_1, a_2 as well as potential levels of D_1, D_2 available in the transport pool occupy a certain range of random variables. Therefore, the indicators s_1, s_2 only become known in practice after the exact data on the values of a_j and D_j arrive. It follows that the coefficients a_j and D_j are random under market uncertainty (S. M. Sergeev et al. 2020), and the structure of the model's constraints is not fully defined.

To complete the optimization problem, it is necessary to take into account that the multimodal transport operator delivers an additional amount of cargo that was not specified in the contract at a higher price. This formally corresponds to the excess of $a_j x_j$ over D_j.

To take this factor into account, (t_1, t_2) is added to the left-hand side of balance ratios (2), and $(f_1 t_1 + f_2 t_2)$ to the objective function formula (1). This is interpreted by the values of $t_i \geq 0$ as the excess over contractual volumes for transport j, and $(f_i t_i)$ introduces the coefficient f_j for the price increase of the delivery of t_i cargo units.

Let us finally formulate the optimization problem as searching for the minimum costs of the extended criterion Q^*. We introduce the following formalisms:

$$Q^* = \sum_{j=1}^{3} c_j x_j + f_1 t_1 + f_2 t_2 \text{, with the constraints}$$

$$a_1 x_1 + s_1 - t_1 = D_1 \text{; } a_2 x_2 + s_2 - t_2 = D_2 \text{; } \sum_{j=1}^{3} x_j = T \text{.}$$

The cost increase factors for directions f_i have a random nature, their values at the start of the planning period and at the moment when the indicators for x_j are determined are known only at the level of the probability distribution function. Additionally, the real data for t_i, and, accordingly, s_i, are calculated after the values of the random variables that govern this mathematical model are found.

5. RESULTS

The solution to this problem can be reduced to an iterative algorithm for machine-to-machine communication. At the same time, the data for cargo indicators, such as dimensions, weight, destination, maximum storage times and restrictions on the type of transport, are embedded in the QR code and read by a computer automatically. This serves as the initial data for the calculation. Let us now give the main steps comprising the flowchart of the algorithm.

1. The values of x_1, x_2, x_3 are calculated by the simplex method using a personal computer, based on the data determined only with respect to the values of e_1, e_2 and c_3.
2. The analytics on random variables c_1, c_2, f_1, f_2, a_1, a_2, D_1, D_2 and the degree of their correlation with the values of x_1, x_2, x_3 are obtained from market monitoring and Internet surveys.
3. The values of c_1, c_2, t_1, t_2, are calculated on a PC.
4. We calculate x_1, x_2, x_3 from the condition of minimizing the functional Q^*.

Because risk management is mandatory in real commercial operations, it is possible to find the final number W of the states characterized by a set of indicators $(f_1, f_2, a_1, a_2, D_1, D_2)$ and the vector $\overline{P}$ of their probabilities of the same dimension. To program the algorithm, let us bring these states into a matrix Ω of size $W \times 6$. If $W = 3$, then the matrix and the vector have the form

$$\Omega = \begin{Vmatrix} f_{11}, f_{12} & a_{11}, a_{12} & D_{11}, D_{12} \\ f_{21}, f_{22} & a_{21}, a_{22} & D_{21}, D_{22} \\ f_{31}, f_{32} & a_{31}, a_{32} & D_{31}, D_{32} \end{Vmatrix}, \quad \overline{P} = (p_1, p_2, p_3), \quad \sum_i p_i = 1.$$

In this case, the calculation is carried out using the expected values.

We obtain $E[a_j] = \sum_{q=1}^{3} p_q a_{qj}$, and, knowing $E[r_j]$ and e_j, we define

$E[c_j] = E[r_j] \cdot E[a_j] + e_j, j = 1,2$. The final formulation of the model is as follows:

Minimize the expression

$$E[c_1]x_1 + E[c_2]x_2 + c_3 x_3 + p_1 [f_{11}t_{11} + f_{12}t_{12}] +$$
$$+ p_2 [f_{21}t_{21} + f_{22}t_{22}] + p_3 [f_{31}t_{31} + f_{32}t_{32}]$$

under the following constraints:

$$\sum_{j=1}^{3} x_i = T;$$

$$a_{11}x_1 + s_{11} - t_{11} = D_{11}; \; a_{12}x_2 + s_{12} - t_{12} = D_{12}; \; a_{21}x_1 + s_{21} - t_{21} = D_{21};$$
$$a_{22}x_2 + s_{22} - t_{22} = D_{22}; \; a_{31}x_1 + s_{31} - t_{31} = D_{31}; \; a_{32}x_2 + s_{32} - t_{32} = D_{32}.$$

6. CALCULATION

The described technique allows to program the iterative algorithm on a computer. As an example, four datasets were taken that differ in terms of the number of transport units and the location of the distribution center. It was assumed within the model that decisions are made for the entire track without the participation of managers, which is equivalent to machine-to-machine communication. However, this implies that all information necessary for the solution is contained in machine-readable code.

Figures 1-4 show the results of computer simulation of the planning undertaken by a multimodal transport operator in case of machine-to-machine interaction. Different types of constraints on the transport pool and on the position of the distribution center in the supply chain are considered. Notice that the ordinate axis represents the initial values corresponding to the deterministic problem. Analysis of the data obtained allows us to conclude that the decisions made are strongly dependent not only on the degree of market uncertainty σ, but also on the role of configuration and technologies used in the delivery process.

For example, if the distribution center is located between the transitions from one type of transport to another (Figures 1, 2), its load decreases, but if its location is in the region of the final recipient (Figures 2, 3), it plays the role of an emergency stock compensating for the uneven demand.

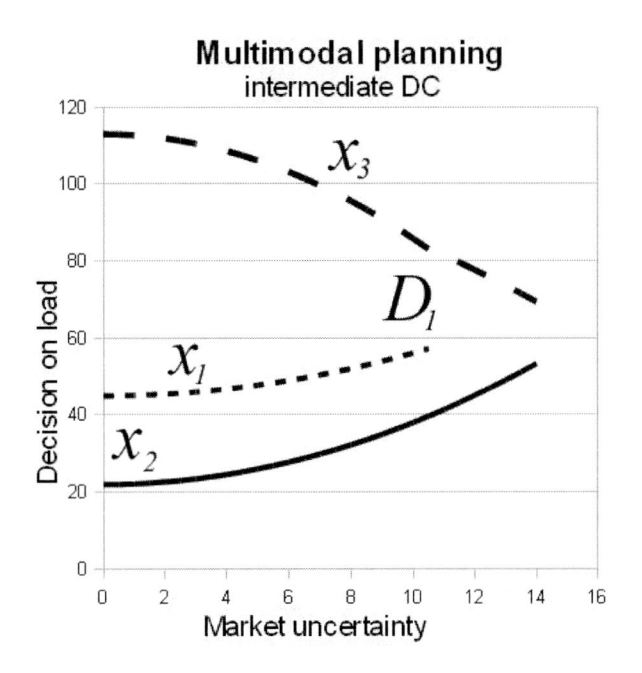

Figure 1. Plan for constraint with respect to D_1.

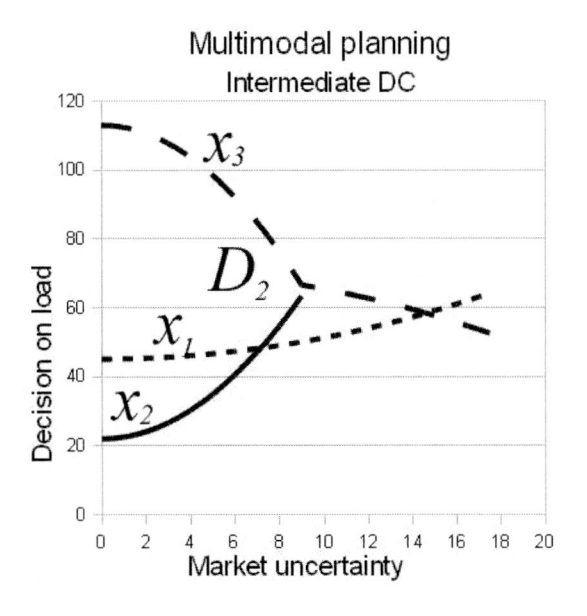

Figure 2. Plan for constraint with respect to D_2.

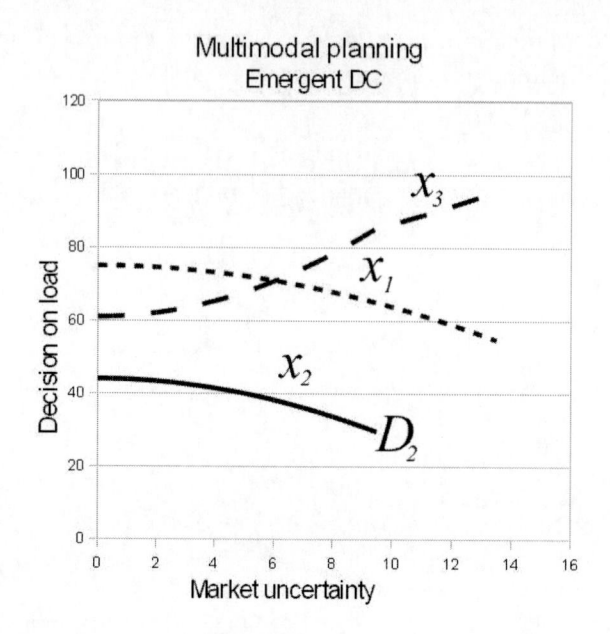

Figure 3. Plan for constraint with respect to D_2.

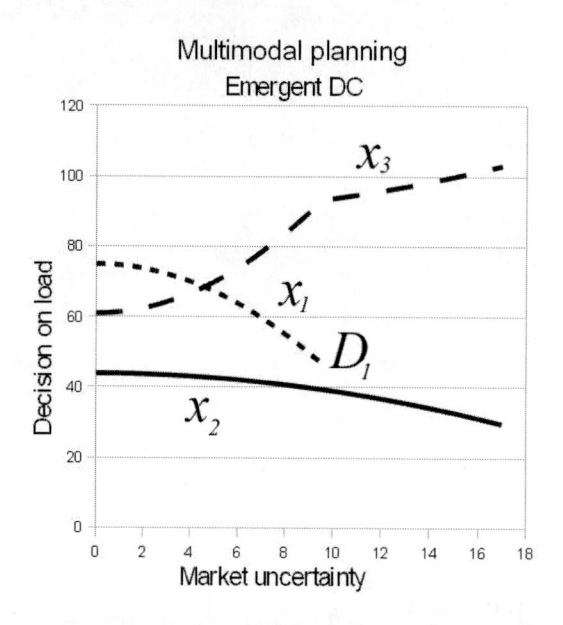

Figure 4. Plan for constraint with respect to D_1.

The formulas obtained for a particular example for three gradations of the set of indicators are in fact scalable and allow to write the algorithm in matrix form. The dimension of the model is not limited, as not only parameters associated with multimodal transportation but also related processes, such as cross-docking or pick-by-line, included in the general chain of machine-to-machine interaction, can act as control variables. A separate process is simultaneous optimization taking into account the Private Label segment (S. Sergeev and Kirillova 2019), accounting for up to 25% of the turnover of retail chains. A distinctive characteristic of some of the variables is that they are deterministic with respect to this position but zero variance should be taken for their distribution parameters, and the same expressions are applied.

The parameters can also include such indicators as customs clearance, border control, including traffic delays when crossing state borders, and changes of carrier, which are important for cross-border commerce. At the same time, the dimension of machine-readable codes on transported cargo should be controlled so that it contains the information necessary for the algorithm.

CONCLUSION

The results obtained make it possible to create a set of algorithms for monitoring software for a wide range of equipment. It is primarily a tool for automating decision-making in planning the processes of a multimodal transport operator. In addition, cloud-based technologies of machine-to-machine interaction can be used to implement some of the procedures via the controllers of automated warehouses, robotic stackers, and in-process automated transport. Intelligent forwarding systems will allow not only to exclude human forwarders from the technological process but also to dramatically improve the economic performance by reducing costs, choosing the optimal inter-transport interaction, meeting the storage conditions accounting for the risks associated with the limited storage and transportation periods.

This can serve as a basis for full-fledged CFS (cargo forwarding services) and automatic systems meeting the requirements. M2M interaction algorithms can make it possible to monitor the location and the conditions of the goods online along the entire logistic leg, notify the receiving services about the arrival of goods, unloading and warehouse operations. In addition, payments can be made simultaneously and automatically in real time for both freight forwarding services and customs duties, excise taxes and other payments associated with the movement of goods.

The practical focus of the study is that the results are oriented towards multimodal logistics, which makes the model scalable towards higher levels of third-party logistics. Since up to 90% of the global volume of flows of raw materials and finished products is distributed multimodally, implementing the proposed models will bring not only economic benefits, reducing the load on global traffic, but also improve the environment and provide a significant social effect. Calculations with a computer model based on the algorithms developed in the paper serve as a convenient tool that managers of commercial networks with a convenient tool can use for planning current activities, taking into account market uncertainty at all stages, both with consumers and with suppliers throughout the business chain, including distribution centers as independent nodes of machine-to-machine interaction.

Equipping the computers of managers of networked commercial enterprises with such subsystems in the shell of expert systems will provide a powerful tool for planning, generating competitive advantages and, accordingly, an economic effect.

REFERENCES

Barykin, S., A. Borovkov, O. Rozhdestvenskiy, A. Tarshin, and V. Yadykin. 2020. "STAFF COMPETENCE and TRAINING for DIGITAL INDUSTRY." *IOP Conference Series: Materials Science and Engineering* 940 (1). https://doi.org/10.1088/1757-899X/940/1/012106.

Barykin, Sergey, Olga Kalinina, Igor Aleksandrov, Evgenii Konnikov, Vladimir Yadikin, and Mikhail Draganov. 2020. "Personnel Management Digital Model Based on the Social Profiles' Analysis." *Journal of Open Innovation: Technology, Market, and Complexity* 6 (4): 1–20. https://doi.org/10.3390/joitmc6040152.

Barykin, Sergey Yevgenievich, Andrey Aleksandrovich Bochkarev, Olga Vladimirovna Kalinina, and Vladimir Konstantinovich Yadykin. 2020. "Concept for a Supply Chain Digital Twin." *International Journal of Mathematical, Engineering and Management Sciences* 5 (6): 1498–1515. https://doi.org/10.33889/IJMEMS.2020.5.6.111.

Barykin, Sergey Yevgenievich, Irina Vasilievna Kapustina, Tatiana Viktorovna Kirillova, Vladimir Konstantinovich Yadykin, and Yevgenii Aleksandrovich Konnikov. 2020. "Economics of Digital Ecosystems." *Journal of Open Innovation: Technology, Market, and Complexity* 6 (4): 1–16. https://doi.org/10.3390/joitmc6040124.

Barykin, Sergey Yevgenievich, Irina Vasilievna Kapustina, Sergey Mikhailovich Sergeev, and Vladimir Konstantinovich Yadykin. 2020. "Algorithmic Foundations of Economic and Mathematical Modeling of Network Logistics Processes." *Journal of Open Innovation: Technology, Market, and Complexity* 6 (4): 1–16. https://doi.org/10.3390/joitmc6040189.

Borisoglebskaya, L. N., V. V. Provotorov, S. M. Sergeev, and E. S. Kosinov. 2019. "Mathematical Aspects of Optimal Control of Transference Processes in Spatial Networks." *IOP Conference Series: Materials Science and Engineering* 537 (4). https://doi.org/10.1088/1757-899X/537/4/042025.

Borisoglebskaya, L. N., E. N. Provotorova, and S. M. Sergeev. 2019a. "Commercial Software Engineering under the Digital Economy Concept." *Journal of Physics: Conference Series* 1399 (3). https://doi.org/10.1088/1742-6596/1399/3/033029.

———. 2019b. "Promotion Based on Digital Interaction Algorithm." *IOP Conference Series: Materials Science and Engineering* 537 (4). https://doi.org/10.1088/1757-899X/537/4/042032.

Borisoglebskaya, L. N., E. N. Provotorova, S. M. Sergeev, and A. P. Khudyakov. 2019. "Automated Storage and Retrieval System for Industry 4.0 Concept." *IOP Conference Series: Materials Science and Engineering* 537 (3): 0–6. https://doi.org/10.1088/1757-899X/537/3/032036.

Borisoglebskaya, L. N., S. M. Sergeev, E. N. Provotorova, and A. A. Zaslavskiy. 2020. "Digital Algorithms for Supply Chain Automation of Mechanical Engineering Production." *IOP Conference Series: Materials Science and Engineering* 862 (4). https://doi.org/10.1088/1757-899X/862/4/042025.

Bril, Alexander, Svetlana Evseeva, Olga Kalinina, Sergey Barykin, and Elena Vinogradova. 2020. "Personnel Changes and Labor Productivity in Regulatory Budget Monitoring." *IOP Conference Series: Materials Science and Engineering* 940 (1). https://doi.org/10.1088/1757-899X/940/1/012105.

Bril, Alexander, Olga Kalinina, Sergey Barykin, and Anna Burova. 2020. "The Methodological Features of the Economic Evaluation of Personnel Management Operational Projects." In *Innovations in Digital Economy*, edited by Dmitrii Rodionov, Tatiana Kudryavtseva, Mohammed Ali Berawi, and Angi Skhvediani, 143–54. Cham: Springer International Publishing.

Fedotov, A. A., S. M. Sergeev, E. N. Provotorova, T. V. Prozhogina, and O. Yu Zaslavskaya. 2020. "The Digital Twin of a Warehouse Robot for Industry 4.0." *IOP Conference Series: Materials Science and Engineering* 862 (3): 0–6. https://doi.org/10.1088/1757-899X/862/3/032061.

Golosnoy, A. S., V. V. Provotorov, S. M. Sergeev, L. B. Raikhelgauz, and O. Ja Kravets. 2019. "Software Engineering Math for Network Applications." *Journal of Physics: Conference Series* 1399 (4). https://doi.org/10.1088/1742-6596/1399/4/044047.

Kapustina, Irina, Olga Kalinina, Alina Ovchinnikova, and Sergei Barykin. 2020. "The Logistics Network Digital Twin in View of Concept of the Non-Destructive Quality Control Methods." *E3S Web of Conferences* 157. https://doi.org/10.1051/e3sconf/202015705001.

Krasnov, S., E. Zotova, S. Sergeev, A. Krasnov, and M. Draganov. 2019. "Stochastic Algorithms in Multimodal 3PL Segment for the Digital Environment." *IOP Conference Series: Materials Science and Engineering* 618 (1). https://doi.org/10.1088/1757-899X/618/1/012069.

Krasnov, Sergey, Sergey Sergeev, Aleksandr Titov, and Yelizaveta Zotova. 2019. "Modelling of Digital Communication Surfaces for Products and Services Promotion." *IOP Conference Series: Materials Science and Engineering* 497 (1). https://doi.org/10.1088/1757-899X/497/1/012032.

Krasnov, Sergey, Sergey Sergeev, Elizaveta Zotova, and Nadezhda Grashchenko. 2019. "Algorithm of Optimal Management for the Efficient Use of Energy Resources." *E3S Web of Conferences* 110. https://doi.org/10.1051/e3sconf/201911002052.

Pilipenko, O. V., E. N. Provotorova, S. M. Sergeev, and O. V. Rodionov. 2019. "Automation Engineering of Adaptive Industrial Warehouse." *Journal of Physics: Conference Series* 1399 (4). https://doi.org/10.1088/1742-6596/1399/4/044045.

Provotorov, V. V., D. V. Danilevich, A. A. Fedotov, S. M. Sergeev, and O. Ja Kravets. 2020. "Digital Management by Supply Networks in Engineering." *IOP Conference Series: Materials Science and Engineering* 862 (3). https://doi.org/10.1088/1757-899X/862/3/032024.

Provotorov, V. V., S. M. Sergeev, and A. A. Part. 2019. "Solvability of Hyperbolic Systems with Distributed Parameters on the Graph in the Weak Formulation." *Vestnik Sankt-Peterburgskogo Universiteta, Prikladnaya Matematika, Informatika,*

Protsessy Upravleniya 15 (1): 107–17. https://doi.org/10.21638/11702/spbu10. 2019.108.

Sergeev, S., and T. Kirillova. 2019. "Information Support for Trade with the Use of a Conversion Funnel." *IOP Conference Series: Materials Science and Engineering* 666 (1). https://doi.org/10.1088/1757-899X/666/1/012064.

Sergeev, Sergey M., Anna A. Kurochkina, Olga V. Lukina, and Vilena E. Zasenko. 2020. "Interactive Algorithm for Estimating Consumer Demand for Tourism Services for Sustainable Operation of the Transport Industry." *IOP Conference Series: Materials Science and Engineering* 918 (1). https://doi.org/10.1088/1757-899X/918/1/012219.

Shmatko, Alexey, Sergey Barykin, Sergey Sergeev, and Anuphat Thirakulwanich. 2021. *"Modeling a Logistics Hub Using the Digital Footprint Method — The Implication for Open Innovation Engineering."*

In: Global Challenges of Digital Transformation of Markets ISBN: 978-1-53619-754-9
Editors: E. de la Poza and S. E. Barykin   © 2021 Nova Science Publishers, Inc.

Chapter 3

Stochastic Algorithms for Managing the Flows of Material Resources of a Logistics Hub

V. V. Provotorov[1,], S. E. Barykin[2], N. V. Ostrovskaya[3], E. S. Volkova[3] and Bilal Khalid[4]*

[1]Voronezh State University, Voronezh, Russia
[2]Peter the Great St. Petersburg Polytechnic University, Russia
[3]Financial University under the Government of the Russian Federation (Moscow)
St. Petersburg branch, Russia
[4]Business School, King Mongkut's Institute of Technology Ladkrabang,
Bangkok, Thailand

Abstract

Digital logistics platforms have already become a major trend in the recent years, making dramatic advances during the COVID-19 pandemic. The architecture of modern logistics industry exhibits a tendency towards consolidation of commerce into networks. Making decisions in such a business environment is difficult due to imperfect algorithms, which is the main obstacle to increasing the economic feasibility of logisitcs. This study considers the development of an algorithmic basis for the software shell of the control server processing the flow of data on the movement of goods and cargo through a network. Because it is more profitable to use two-stage rather than single-stage nodes for intermediate storage and processing in modern commercial networks, the mathematical model should reflect the complex structure of such a logistics hub. The algorithms were developed acccounting for the stochastic nature of the flows of goods and cargo due to the market uncertainty of the operating conditions of the logistics hub.

Keywords: logistics, network, commerce, mathematical model

---

* Corresponding Author's Email: sergeev2@inbox.ru.

1. INTRODUCTION

With the ongoing globalization of trade and production, as commercial structures for trading goods and services merge into transnational networks, the concept of hubs and distribution systems that include large terminals and warehouses acting as providers of 3PL (Third Party Logistics) services is steadily gaining popularity. They have extensive functions, adapting flexibly to specific segments of commerce. Searching for algorithms in the Demand-driven Techniques/Logistics (DDT) paradigm is an important problem, allowing logistics networks to swiftly respond to market fluctuations and potentially optimizing distribution flows passing through network hubs. While successful projects on optimal algorithms of warehouse logistics services have been implemented in retail(Pilipenko et al. 2019)(S. Krasnov et al. 2019), the problem of organizing flows in large hubs and terminals of logistics networks cannot be solved within the framework of the deterministic approach. The results that are applicable in practice can be found by developing mathematical models(Sergey Krasnov, Sergeev, Zotova, et al. 2019) based on methods for describing the stochastic dynamics characterizing the movement of goods. In this case, not only financial and economic indicators are taken as criteria: time constraints imposed by the shelf life of products, current movement, customs or other procedures for handling goods and related information are also taken into account.

Over the past decade, technologies and equipment that can radically change the approach to managing the processes of cargo movement and cargo transportation have become widespread. To solve such large-scale problems, the use of scientifically based mathematical models is required. This approach will allow us to use the digital footprint of processes in the logistics network and develop an algorithmic basis for a whole set of software tools for more effective management of the logistics industry (S. Y. Barykin, Kapustina, Sergeev, and Yadykin 2020).

It is necessary to find an economically optimal management of the flows of goods and cargo based on digital information about their movement, taking into account the stochastic nature of the volumes and directions of flows. At the same time, it is necessary to choose and justify the methodology for calculating the DC node terminals that are part of the network structure of logistics activities. The resulting set of mathematical relations allows us to model the operation of a network distribution center as a nodal element of a logistics system operating on the principles of a 3PL operator in the conditions of the stochastic nature of incoming and shipped commodity flows (Shmatko et al. 2021).

Changes in the high-tech sector also oblige enterprises to transform their workforce in order to achieve a sustainable competitive advantage. The introduction of high-tech solutions leads to a change in the format and content of almost any work, as well as to a rethinking of approaches to personnel planning (Bril, Evseeva, et al. 2020).

It is necessary to consider the issue of training personnel for the digital industry in the context of creating teams in enterprises (Bril, Kalinina, et al. 2020), scientific organizations and universities that have the necessary digital competencies and digital literacy. In this paradigm, the methodological approach to solving the problem of personnel training is based on a problem-oriented scientific approach, and the model of creating mirror engineering centers is a possible model for scaling competencies, spreading knowledge and developing network interaction (S. Barykin, Borovkov, Rozhdestvenskiy, Tarshin, et al. 2020).

The combination of optimization modeling and data analysis is the basic technology that allows you to create a sufficiently detailed model of the real supply chain of its digital counterpart Idea -. The goal of creating a digital twin is to manage risks in supply chains, thereby making them more reliable and resilient in the event of any failures. Modern technologies allow us to collect large amounts of data on supply chains online (S. Y. Barykin, Bochkarev, Kalinina, and Yadykin 2020). A digital twin is an evolving digital profile of the historical and current behavior of a physical object or process that helps optimize business performance (Kapustina et al. 2020).

A digital ecosystem is a self-organizing, sustainable system based on digital platforms that form a single information environment in which ecosystem members can interact in the absence of rigid functional links between them. The basis of the digital ecosystem is a variety of platform technologies that form a single information environment for all its participants: society, business and the state (S. Y. Barykin, Kapustina, Kirillova, Yadykin, et al. 2020).

The process of managing the organization's personnel within the digital ecosystem, while maintaining the basic goal setting, is transformed from an instrumental point of view. The transition from a traditional HR system to a digital one involves a difference between how employees interact with each other and with management. The key factor in the system of digital interaction is the ability of each employee to freely contact the information and analytical center. The digital interaction system also differs from the traditional one by expanding the channels for exchanging information and analytics. Considering the tasks of personnel management in the digital age, it can be shown that the problem of digital personnel management is the scientific search for the features of employee interaction in the new technological structure of Industry 4.0 under the influence of the flow of innovations and changes occurring in it. It includes improvements in performance, reliability, quality, and security (Sergey Barykin, Kalinina, Aleksandrov, Konnikov, et al. 2020).

2. OBJECTIVES

This paper analyzes the activities of a two-stage warehouse subsystem of large transport logistics hubs as nodes of logistics networks. The distribution center (DC) serves as the upper level; it is typically a large object combining warehouse complexes of Class A (the Knight Frank classification). Since the type, container, and characteristics of cargoes are of no particular importance for mathematical description (Borisoglebskaya, Provotorova, and Sergeev 2019b), all types of storage facilities are included in the concept of DC. At the same time, such parameters as the temperature regime, differences between packaged, liquid and loose cargo, expiry date are reflected in their formalized economic indicators. The second level is the local SW (Store Warehouse) situated as close as possible to the consumer. As a rule, one DC contains several SW objects combined in a spoke-hub distribution system.

3. Developing a Mathematical Description

Let us introduce a number of formalisms(Borisoglebskaya, Provotorova, et al. 2019) necessary for composing the mathematical model.

Here w is the stock level of the DC/SW; $w \geq 0$; $v$is theshipment quantity expressed in standard SKU (stockkeepingunit) units; $r = w + v$ reflects the total stock volume; z is the stochastic variable of the demand expressed in standard units, $z \geq 0$; $p(z)$ is the distribution function z; $D$is the volume of the request in commodity units per unit of time; L is the duration of the time interval that it takes to fulfill the order; D_L is the volume of demand in units or the rate of demand for the planned period of time L.

Because the process is separable, $D_L = D \cdot L$is fulfilled; $TC(v)$ is the function of dependence of total costs; FC (fixed cost) with the condition $FC > 0$ reflects the overhead costs; $\Phi(r)$ is the expected cost function; β satisfying the condition $\beta > 0$ are the maintenance costs; γ are the losses.

The value of Ω^* defined as $\Omega^* = \dfrac{\gamma - c}{\gamma + \beta}$ is the critical relationship $0 < \Omega^* < 1$; the non-negative quantity$S$equals the smallest integer from a natural series of values for which the following inequality holds true:

$$\Omega(S) = \sum_{z=0}^{S} p(z) \geq \Omega^* ;\ \varphi(r \mid w)$$ are the average costs, equal to the costs for when

the stock volume is equal to r with the initial volume w.

Let us analyze the EOQ (Economic Order Quantity) of the model in terms of its stability against market uncertainty. The stability of economic operations of a distribution (Borisoglebskaya, Provotorov, et al. 2019) enterprise is determined by the choice of calculated parameters of the EOQ, the indicator Δ^*. Such analysis should allow to assess competitiveness in the conditions of market uncertainty. It follows from expression (Sergey Krasnov, Sergeev, Titov, et al. 2019) for the optimal value of

$$\Delta^* = \sqrt{\dfrac{2FC \cdot D}{\beta}}$$ that the growth realtive to the amount of overhead costs FC is below a

linear dependence. This is due to the dependence of Δ^* on the root of the rate of the demand D and the inverse of the costs β for maintenance of warehouse stocks. With a twofold fluctuation in the demand rate, EOQ increases only within 40%. Accordingly, when β doubles in price, the required EOQ decreases only by 30%. Analysis of the formula for calculating T^* that is the time between the dates when stocks are replenished $T^* = \dfrac{EOQ}{D} = \dfrac{\Delta^*}{D} = \sqrt{\dfrac{2FC}{\beta D}}$, it follows that given an increase in the rate of demand D, Δ^* grows, but the interval determined by the optimal value of T shortens. In real-life conditions, this manifests as more frequent requests made by the DC to suppliers to maintain damping reserve stocks. The fundamental choice of EOQ with restrictions on multiplicity is of fundamental importance for assessing the dynamics of the distribution warehouse (Provotorov, Sergeev, and Part 2019). This type of procedure is typically due to packaging standards or logistics, and appears both in the form of minimum supply volumes and in packaging units. In practice, the calculation of Δ^* is reduced to selecting $\tilde{\Delta}$ that is maximally close to optimal. Then the real multiple order is calculated by the formula:

$$\tilde{\Delta} = \tau\Delta^* = \tau\sqrt{2KM/h}\,,$$ where $\tau > 0$. Then, following the formula for calculating the average costs $AC = \dfrac{FC \cdot D}{\Delta} + cD + \dfrac{\beta\Delta}{2}$, the variable component can be represented as

$$VC(\tau) = \frac{FC \cdot D}{\Delta^*} + \frac{\beta \cdot \Delta^*}{2} = \frac{FC \cdot D\sqrt{\beta}}{\tau\sqrt{2FC \cdot D}} + \frac{\beta r\sqrt{2FC \cdot D}}{2\sqrt{\beta}}$$

The actual multiple value is substituted here instead of Δ^*, and the fixed cost component equal to cD is excluded. Analyzing the expression

$$\xi = VC(\tau)/VC(1) = \frac{\left(\tau^{-1} + \tau\right)}{2}$$

and the computations of the variable component of costs depending on the value of τ, we can conclude that $\tilde{\Delta}$ has low sensitivity, which is reflected in Figure 1.

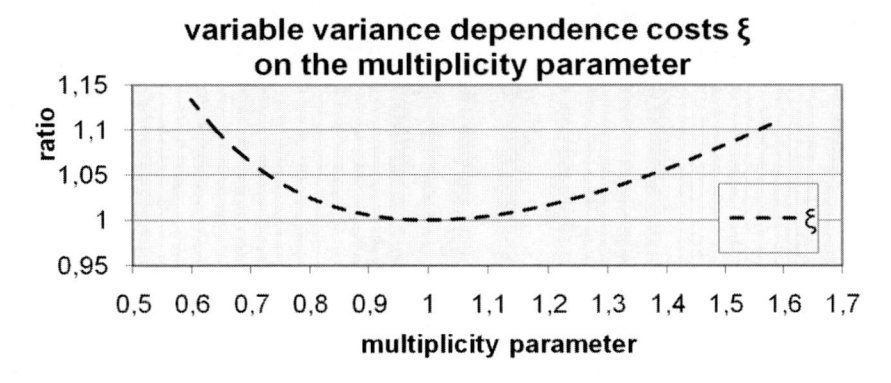

Figure 1. Sensitivity calculation.

At the same time, the deviation of variable costs does not exceed 10% or $VC(\tau) \leq 1.1 \cdot VC(1)$ in the interval $0.55 \leq \tau \leq 1.6$, that is, the factor of multiplicity, expressed in the deviation of $\tilde{\Delta}$ from the optimum Δ^*, has very little effect. For the purposes of our analysis, let us preserve the half range by introducing $\tau' = \tau^{-1}$, taking into account that the ratio $\dfrac{VC(\tau)}{VC(1)}$ is invariant to the substitution of τ with τ'.

The real operation of distribution centers and emergency (Borisoglebskaya et al. 2020) warehouses of any structures is characterized by a discrete nature, both of the volumes of the goods placed, and of the planning periods for replenishment of stocks.

To obtain simulation results given a discrete number of goods and time periods, as well as multiple commodity units, let us regard the parameter D in the model to be the number of goods due to demand in a unit period.

Deliveries DT of units of goods are accompanied by expenses C_T, where $T = 1,2,...$ is a natural number. This is equivalent to C_T as an indicator reflecting the expenses over a period of T planning time units. We calculate it by the formula:

$$C_T = FC + cDT + \frac{1}{2}\beta D(T-1)T .$$

The optimal operating mode is determined from the minimum of C_T/T. Accounting for $T = 1, 2,...$, its implementation is equivalent to searching for

$$\min_T \left[\frac{FC}{T} + cD + \frac{1}{2}\beta D(T-1) \right] .$$

Differentiating and equating to zero, we solve the equation with respect to T. We obtain the result T as: $T^* = \sqrt{2FC/\beta D}$. It follows that EOQ or Δ^* is calculated as: $\Delta^* = D \cdot T^* = \sqrt{2FC \cdot D/\beta}$. As a final step, we round T^* both up and down. This allows to complement the procedure with an economic calculation to find the most profitable option.

The economic indicators for assessing the performance of a distribution center are generated with a certain period. The mathematical model from (Fedotov et al. 2020) can be used to link the calculations with the costs of maintaining warehouse stocks.

The online communication mode proves that the DC is partially in a state of contractually deferred compliance. The share of such time is calculated using the formula $-s/\Delta$, where it is taken that $s \leq 0$, i.e., a negative critical level is allowed. The volume of goods for the period of negative stocks at the distribution center is equal to $(-s/2)$ units of goods. This implies an economically determined loss of demand, reduced to a unit planning period and calculated as $-s^2/2\Delta$. This produces integral losses in fines, loss of reputation and lost profits. The coefficient γ (> 0) reflects the losses for unsatisfied demand in a single period for a unit of goods. We obtain AC

that is the size of the average costs for the period: $AC =$
$$\frac{FC \cdot D}{\Delta} + cD + \frac{(\beta + \gamma)S^2}{2\Delta} - \gamma S + \frac{\gamma}{2}\Delta.$$

At the same time, γ is an integral indicator; to find the optimal operating mode of the distribution center, let us find its minimum. Differentiating AC with respect to S that is the emergency stock after the DC is replenished, we obtain the optimal stock volume:

$$S^* = \left(\frac{\gamma}{\beta + \gamma}\right)\Delta.$$

Calculating the optimal EOQ taking into account S^*, as a result, we have Δ^*, S, s:

$$\Delta^* = \sqrt{2FC \cdot D\left(\frac{1}{\beta} + \frac{1}{\gamma}\right)}, S = \sqrt{2FC \cdot D\left(\frac{\gamma}{\beta(\beta + \gamma)}\right)}, s = -\sqrt{2FC \cdot D\left(\frac{\beta}{\gamma(\beta + \gamma)}\right)}.$$

4. FORMING A GENERAL MODEL

The results obtained from simulation of a single item can now be extended to the entire assortment matrix.

It was assumed above for the dynamic model formed on the intervals of the planning horizon that the operation costs *FC*, as well as the costs for maintaining current stocks were deterministic. $L > 0$ almost always in real-life operation of the DC, so let us introduce z_L, actual consumer demand in the interval from receiving a request for a product and making a delivery. The parameter z_L is a random variable following its own distribution law. The inequality $z_L > s$ implies a delay in receiving the goods.

Such a scheme is implemented in the DC oriented towards the cross-docking technology. The presence of an SW allows to optimize (Provotorov et al. 2020) the level of emergency stocks in limited local storage facilities. The spoke-hub paradigm of distribution is in demand precisely because a 3PL player solves many problems, in particular, rental costs, distance from the consumer, limitations on the shelf life of goods.

The control algorithms are selected based on the criterion for the performance of the distribution center. This criterion is in turn chosen based on a number of parameters with multidirectional action. The most relevant part of programming the procedure for finding the extremum of the functional is reflecting the cost reduction provided that the tasks set by the business are completed.

Let us introduce the distribution function $p_L(z_L)$ as the dependence of the actual consumption in a forecast period *L*. Since the postulates of stationarity, ordinariness and absence of aftereffect are taken into account by the very formulation of the problem on the choice of constraints for developing the functional, we can assume that the distribution function $p_L(z_L)$ obeys Poisson's law on the interval $T: p_L(T) = (M_rT)^{z_L} \cdot e^{-M_rT} / Z_L!$. On the one hand, such a representation greatly facilitates analysis and obtaining theoretical results. However, the condition that the expected value and the standard deviation confirming such a hypothesis be equal is not always satisfied in practice. The implementation of the mathematical model (Borisoglebskaya, Provotorova, and Sergeev 2019a) always includes developing a software package allowing to adopt an arbitrary form of the distribution function $p_L(z_L)$ in the calculations, expanding the capabilities of the model.

Let us introduce a characteristic of expenses θ_s for satisfying the requirements for the delivery into the target functional. According to the expressions obtained for finding EOQ, the following can be written for them: $\theta_s = FC \cdot D/\Delta + cD$.

In addition, let us define the costs of maintaining stocks by adding an estimate of the probable losses (Golosnoy et al. 2019). Let us consider various situations in the planning interval between successive requirements to replenish the warehouse. Let us take into account the case of demand (S. M. Sergeev et al. 2020) corresponding to the inequality $z_L < S$ and the alternative. For this purpose, we introduce the expressions for the distribution function $p_L(z_L)$ into the previously obtained equations for calculation in the given planning interval, obtaining the following:

$$\sum_{z_L=0}^{s} \frac{1}{2}[s+(s-z_L)]p_L(z_L) + \sum_{z_L>s} \frac{1}{2}[s+0]p_L(z_L) =$$
$$\frac{1}{2}\left[s + \sum_{z_L=0}^{s}(s-z_L)p_L(z_L)\right].$$

Based on M_L that is the expected value of $p_L(z_L)$, we obtain the average level of stocks in the planning period from the moment of loading to the next order:

$$\frac{1}{2}\left[(s-M_L+\Delta)+s\right] = \frac{1}{2}(2s-M_L+\Delta) \tag{1}$$

We introduce the results obtained taking into account the weight coefficients into the functional of economic indicators of the DC. We define the weight coefficient $\mu = M_L/\Delta$ equal to the proportion of the planning interval corresponding to the standby mode for the expected level of warehouse resources. The average level is taken with the weight coefficient $(1 - M_L/\Delta)$, as an addition to μ.

After transformation, we obtain the expression for $\tilde{r}$, the average resource level reduced to a unit period:

$$\tilde{r} = \frac{M_L}{2\Delta}\left[-2s + M_L - \Delta + s + \sum_{z_L=0}^{s}(s-z_L)p_L(z_L)\right] +$$

$$+\frac{1}{2}(2s - M_L + \Delta).$$

Since the ratio $\sum_{z_L=0}^{s}(s-z_L)p_L(z_L) = s - M_L - \sum_{z_L>s}(s-z_L)p_L(z_L)$ is satisfied for any

arbitrary $p_L(z_L)$, the possible shortage of goods as $\sum_{z_L>s}(s-z_L)p_L(z_L)$ expressing in

terms of $p_L(z_L)$, we calculate the expected shortage per unit time of the planning period in terms of the weight coefficient D/Δ. Formalizing the obtained expressions (S. Sergeev and Kirillova 2019) gives the costs $\tilde{\Phi}$ for maintenance of the DC in a single planning period.

$$\tilde{\Phi} = \frac{FC \cdot D}{\Delta} + cD + \beta\left(\frac{\Delta}{2} - M_L + s\right) +$$

$$+\left(\frac{\beta M_L}{2\Delta} + \frac{D\gamma}{\Delta}\right)\sum_{z_L>s}(z_L-s)p_L(z_L). \tag{2}$$

Now the problem on determining the optimal control of the flow of goods in the distribution center can be solved. For this purpose, we need to find the extremum of the expression $\tilde{\Phi}$ by calculating the partial derivative and solving the equation $\frac{\partial E[AC]}{\partial \Delta} = 0$ with respect to the variable Δ entering it. After simple transformations, we obtain the desired optimal value in the form of the expression:

$$\Delta^* = \sqrt{\frac{2FC \cdot D}{\beta} + \left(M_L + \frac{2D\gamma}{\beta}\right)\sum_{z_L>s}(z_L-s)p_L(z_L)}. \tag{3}$$

Since the solution to the problem can be considered complete provided that the integer parameters are found, then, making a transition to the discrete form of the statistical distribution $\Omega_L(r) = \sum_{z_L=0}^{r}p_L(z_L)$, we obtain as a result the optimal control value of s^* given $(s^* > 0)$ as the smallest integer corresponding to the inequality $\Omega_L(s^*) > \Omega^*$, where

$$\Omega^* = 1 - \frac{\beta\Delta}{\beta M_L/2 + D\gamma} \tag{4}$$

This will give the required critical operation level of the distribution center.

It can be concluded from the obtained results of modeling the operation of a DC under market uncertainty that the planned purchases and the level of stocks are the most economically profitable only if conditions (3) and (4) are simultaneously fulfilled.

Only this approach to managing emergency stocks can allow to reach minimum costs corresponding to an optimal business strategy. In this case, the desired value is calculated using the formula following the above logic for the calculation of s^*:

$$
\min \tilde{\Phi} = cD + \sqrt{2\beta \left[FC + \left(\frac{\beta M_L}{2D} + \gamma \right) D \sum_{z_L > s} (z_L - s^*) p_L(z_L) \right]} +
$$
$$
+ \beta(s^* - M_L)
$$

(5)

Calculations using this expression allow to forecast the feasibility of generating stocks for a specific demand item. Since the assortment of DC warehouses is so extensive that it is physically impossible to keep stocks for the entire range of goods, preliminary analysis of demand levels, the probability of an order for a specific item and losses incurred if the item is not in stock will allow to optimize both maintenance costs and the space required. A separate issue is the stochastic nature of the value L. This situation happens not only in trade, for example, when delivering goods from various warehouses, during cross-border deliveries, when there may be occasional delays due to customs procedures and queues at the border, but also in the service sector, where the range of probable reasons for the variation in L is much wider. The resulting model is completely adequate in this case as well, with the difference that the structure of the distribution function $p_L(z_L)$ changes; however, since, as indicated above, no restrictions were imposed on its form, the simulation results are fully achieved with an increase in the dimension of the functions.

5. EXAMPLE OF DC CALCULATION

The calculation based on specific values of cargo flows, assortment and parameters of warehouses was carried out using the reports of the Barcelona Port Authority and in cooperation with the Faculty of Economics and Business of Universitat de Barcelona.

The port of Barcelona annually serves about 10,000 large ships with the total cargo up to 50 million tons. Various types of cargo are handled, including general, loose and liquid. The developed mathematical model does not consider sea transport as an element of logistics schemes or carriers. In this calculation, we used data on the segment of warehousing serving ships as customers who consume goods and services. The port infrastructure provides the following services for this purpose:

- ships are provided with rations, including products under the port's own brand. The assortment of these goods is extremely high, includes 18,400 items, has a limited shelf life, and requires special storage conditions. Since about 1,500 cruise ps, liners, and ferries are loaded annually, these operations make up a significant share in the movement of commodity stocks;

- both technical and drinking water is supplied;
- refueling services are provided;
- ships are supplied with all kinds of chemicals, lubricants, refrigeration and climatic equipment;
- energy and steam are provided both in the dock and by supplying batteries (including removable) or other power sources and types of energy;
- consumables are supplied;
- products are supplied for current maintenance of the ship's machines, including repair parts;
- other types of supplies are provided, such as personal hygiene products, clothing, medicines, etc.

First, we carried out computer simulation for the movement of a single-product load (Figure 2) depending on the distribution law of $p_L(z_L)$ according to Eqs. (1, 2), and for a 4-product load (Figure 3).

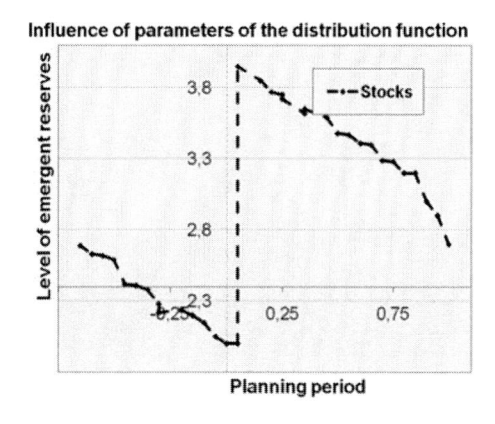

Figure 2. Analysis ofdistribution function.

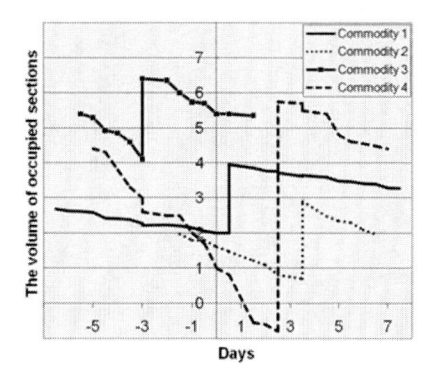

Figure 3. Movement of DC stocks.

Analyzing the results, we can observe that a calculated negative load level is generated in some cases (see the dashed curve in Figure 2). The reason for this is that a deferred demand forms in the DC reserve, due to the presence of a time lag between the request for a certain item and its execution. This behavior is quite common for online interaction and allows to both plan the business operations of the distribution center, optimizing its volumes, and minimize the costs for allocation in the SW and the spaces required.

Next, the movement of the total load of the distribution center was simulated for a large assortment in the standard mode and using Eqs. (3–5). The results obtained can be used to assess the available resources for optimizing the storage space, which allows either to do handle the operations with smaller areas, or the potential additional resources for increasing the number of vessels served by this DC.

Analysis of the results gives reason to assume that the total flow can be modeled using a distribution function that differs from the Poisson type. The basis for this assumption is that, firstly, hundreds of flows are summed in real operation of a DC, which satisfies the conditions of the central limit theorem, and in addition, Lindeberg's condition on their comparable intensities is fulfilled. To summarize the results, let us consider the most common model of Gaussian probability distribution. Its advantage is that it does not impose the condition that the expected value and the standard deviation be equal, which is characteristic of Poisson processes and is inconvenient in practice.

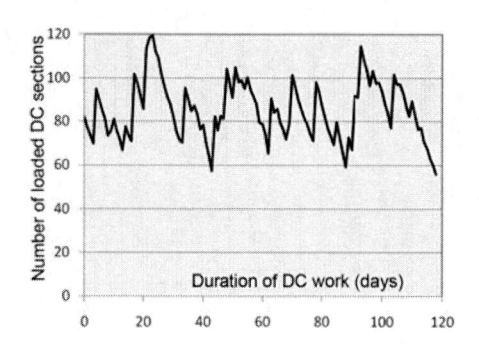

Figure 4. Standard operation.

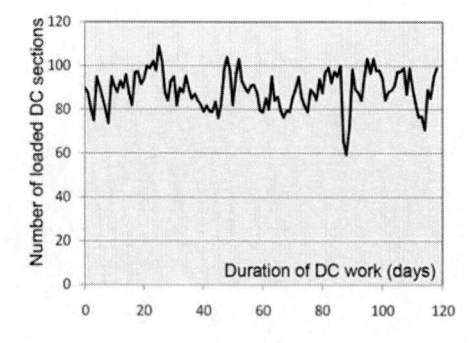

Figure 5. Optimal operation.

To apply the methods for modeling the planned operations of a distribution center under market uncertainty, we introduce a reduced random value. For this purpose, (z_L) has to be redefined as a centered and normalized value of u_χ. Let us calculate the characteristics of the expected value M_L and variance $V_L = \sum_{z_L > 0} (z_L - M_L)^2 p_L(z_L)$. Then,

$u_\chi = \dfrac{\chi - M_L}{\sqrt{V_L}}$ and, respectively, $\chi = M_L + u_\chi \sqrt{V_L}$ can be found. Based on the expression

previously obtained for $\Omega^* = 1 - \dfrac{\beta \Delta}{\beta M_L / 2 + D\gamma}$, we write the standard expression of the

Gaussian function as $G(u) = \int_{-\infty}^{u} \dfrac{1}{\sqrt{2\pi}} e^{-t^2/2} dt$, as well as the integral function

corresponding to it, normalized as: $G^*(u) = \int_{u}^{\infty} (t-u) \dfrac{1}{\sqrt{2\pi}} e^{-t^2/2} dt$. It follows, then for the

estimated calculations that the following equation can be used provided that the distribution function $p_L(z_L)$ is assumed to be normal:

$\sum_{z_L > \chi} (z_L - \chi) p_L(z_L) \approx \sqrt{V_L} \cdot G^*(u_\chi)$. To calculate u_χ, the condition $G(u_\chi) = \Omega^*$ is used

instead of the previous one $\Omega_L(s^*) > \Omega^*$, and the optimal value of Δ^* is found from the equation:

$$\Delta^* = \sqrt{\dfrac{2FC \cdot D}{\beta} + \left(M_L + \dfrac{2D\gamma}{\beta} \right) \sqrt{V_L} \cdot G^*(u_\chi)}.$$

CONCLUSION

A modern logistics hub or distribution warehouse complex of a large port is a sophisticated commercial structure. Optimizing the operation of such a structure should involve scientific methods based on mathematical models using methods from the theory of stochastic processes and the theory of optimal solutions. Calculations indicate the increasing such indicators as the intensity of using the warehouse spaces, uniform loading, reduction of losses due to exceeded shelf life require substantial resources.

As a result, the economic efficiency of the entire hub or complex of distribution warehouses can be improved; taking into account the capital investments and significant turnover of such a business, this will generate a significant increase in profits, providing a competitive advantage in the rapidly developing market for providing services of port and land hubs and distribution centers.

REFERENCES

Barykin, S., Borovkov, A., Rozhdestvenskiy, O., Tarshin, A. & Yadykin, V. (2020). "STAFF COMPETENCE and TRAINING for DIGITAL INDUSTRY." *IOP Conference Series: Materials Science and Engineering*, 940 (1). https://doi.org/10.1088/1757-899X/940/1/012106.

Barykin, Sergey, Olga Kalinina, Igor Aleksandrov, Evgenii Konnikov, Vladimir Yadikin. & Mikhail Draganov. (2020). "Personnel Management Digital Model Based on the Social Profiles' Analysis." *Journal of Open Innovation: Technology, Market, and Complexity*, 6 (4), 1–20. https://doi.org/10.3390/joitmc6040152.

Barykin, Sergey Yevgenievich, Andrey Aleksandrovich Bochkarev, Olga Vladimirovna Kalinina. & Vladimir Konstantinovich Yadykin. (2020). "Concept for a Supply Chain Digital Twin." *International Journal of Mathematical, Engineering and Management Sciences*, 5 (6), 1498–1515. https://doi.org/10.33889/IJMEMS.2020.5.6.111.

Barykin, Sergey Yevgenievich, Irina Vasilievna Kapustina, Tatiana Viktorovna Kirillova, Vladimir Konstantinovich Yadykin. & Yevgenii Aleksandrovich Konnikov. (2020). "Economics of Digital Ecosystems." *Journal of Open Innovation: Technology, Market, and Complexity*, 6 (4), 1–16. https://doi.org/10.3390/joitmc6040124.

Barykin, Sergey Yevgenievich, Irina Vasilievna Kapustina, Sergey Mikhailovich Sergeev. & Vladimir Konstantinovich Yadykin. (2020). "Algorithmic Foundations of Economic and Mathematical Modeling of Network Logistics Processes." *Journal of Open Innovation: Technology, Market, and Complexity*, 6 (4), 1–16. https://doi.org/10.3390/joitmc6040189.

Borisoglebskaya, L. N., Provotorov, V. V., Sergeev, S. M. & Kosinov, E. S. (2019). "Mathematical Aspects of Optimal Control of Transference Processes in Spatial Networks." *IOP Conference Series: Materials Science and Engineering*, 537 (4). https://doi.org/10.1088/1757-899X/537/4/042025.

Borisoglebskaya, L. N., Provotorova, E. N. & Sergeev, S. M. (2019a). "Commercial Software Engineering under the Digital Economy Concept." *Journal of Physics: Conference Series*, 1399 (3). https://doi.org/10.1088/1742-6596/1399/3/033029.

———. (2019b). "Promotion Based on Digital Interaction Algorithm." *IOP Conference Series: Materials Science and Engineering*, 537 (4). https://doi.org/10.1088/1757-899X/537/4/042032.

Borisoglebskaya, L. N., Provotorova, E. N., Sergeev, S. M. & Khudyakov, A. P. (2019). "Automated Storage and Retrieval System for Industry 4.0 Concept." *IOP Conference Series: Materials Science and Engineering*, 537 (3), 0–6. https://doi.org/10.1088/1757-899X/537/3/032036.

Borisoglebskaya, L. N., Sergeev, S. M., Provotorova, E. N. & Zaslavskiy, A. A. (2020). "Digital Algorithms for Supply Chain Automation of Mechanical Engineering Production." *IOP Conference Series: Materials Science and Engineering* 862 (4). https://doi.org/10.1088/1757-899X/862/4/042025.

Bril, Alexander, Svetlana Evseeva, Olga Kalinina, Sergey Barykin. & Elena Vinogradova. (2020). "Personnel Changes and Labor Productivity in Regulatory Budget Monitoring." *IOP Conference Series: Materials Science and Engineering*, 940 (1). https://doi.org/10.1088/1757-899X/940/1/012105.

Bril, Alexander, Olga Kalinina, Sergey Barykin. & Anna Burova. (2020). "The Methodological Features of the Economic Evaluation of Personnel Management Operational Projects." In *Innovations in Digital Economy*, edited by Dmitrii Rodionov, Tatiana Kudryavtseva, Mohammed Ali Berawi, and Angi Skhvediani, 143–54. Cham: Springer International Publishing.

Fedotov, A. A., Sergeev, S. M., Provotorova, E. N., Prozhogina, T. V. & Yu Zaslavskaya, O. (2020). "The Digital Twin of a Warehouse Robot for Industry 4.0." *IOP Conference Series: Materials Science and Engineering*, 862 (3), 0–6. https://doi.org/10.1088/1757-899X/862/3/032061.

Golosnoy, A. S., Provotorov, V. V., Sergeev, S. M., Raikhelgauz, L. B. & Ja Kravets, O. (2019). "Software Engineering Math for Network Applications." *Journal of Physics: Conference Series*, 1399 (4). https://doi.org/10.1088/1742-6596/1399/4/044047.

Kapustina, Irina, Olga Kalinina, Alina Ovchinnikova. & Sergei Barykin. (2020). "The Logistics Network Digital Twin in View of Concept of the Non-Destructive Quality Control Methods." *E3S Web of Conferences*, *157*. https://doi.org/10.1051/e3sconf/202015705001.

Krasnov, S., Zotova, E., Sergeev, S., Krasnov, A. & Draganov, M. (2019). "Stochastic Algorithms in Multimodal 3PL Segment for the Digital Environment." *IOP Conference Series: Materials Science and Engineering*, 618 (1). https://doi.org/10.1088/1757-899X/618/1/012069.

Krasnov, Sergey, Sergey Sergeev, Aleksandr Titov. & Yelizaveta Zotova. (2019). "Modelling of Digital Communication Surfaces for Products and Services Promotion." *IOP Conference Series: Materials Science and Engineering*, 497 (1). https://doi.org/10.1088/1757-899X/497/1/012032.

Krasnov, Sergey, Sergey Sergeev, Elizaveta Zotova. & Nadezhda Grashchenko. (2019). "Algorithm of Optimal Management for the Efficient Use of Energy Resources." *E3S Web of Conferences*, 110. https://doi.org/10.1051/e3sconf/201911002052.

Pilipenko, O. V., Provotorova, E. N., Sergeev, S. M. & Rodionov, O. V. (2019). "Automation Engineering of Adaptive Industrial Warehouse." *Journal of Physics: Conference Series*, 1399 (4). https://doi.org/10.1088/1742-6596/1399/4/044045.

Provotorov, V. V., Danilevich, D. V., Fedotov, A. A., Sergeev, S. M. & Ja Kravets, O. (2020). "Digital Management by Supply Networks in Engineering." *IOP Conference Series: Materials Science and Engineering*, 862 (3). https://doi.org/10.1088/1757-899X/862/3/032024.

Provotorov, V. V., Sergeev, S. M. & Part, A. A. (2019). "Solvability of Hyperbolic Systems with Distributed Parameters on the Graph in the Weak Formulation." *Vestnik Sankt-Peterburgskogo Universiteta, Prikladnaya Matematika, Informatika,*

Protsessy Upravleniya, 15 (1), 107–17. https://doi.org/10.21638/11702/spbu10. 2019.108.

Sergeev, S. & Kirillova, T. (2019). "Information Support for Trade with the Use of a Conversion Funnel." *IOP Conference Series: Materials Science and Engineering*, 666 (1). https://doi.org/10.1088/1757-899X/666/1/012064.

Sergeev, Sergey M., Anna A. Kurochkina, Olga V. Lukina. & Vilena E. Zasenko. (2020). "Interactive Algorithm for Estimating Consumer Demand for Tourism Services for Sustainable Operation of the Transport Industry." *IOP Conference Series: Materials Science and Engineering*, 918 (1). https://doi.org/10.1088/1757-899X/918/1/012219.

Shmatko, Alexey, Sergey Barykin, Sergey Sergeev. & Anuphat Thirakulwanich. (2021). "*Modeling a Logistics Hub Using the Digital Footprint Method — The Implication for Open Innovation Engineering.*"

In: Global Challenges of Digital Transformation of Markets ISBN: 978-1-53619-754-9
Editors: E. de la Poza and S. E. Barykin   © 2021 Nova Science Publishers, Inc.

Chapter 4

DIGITAL TRANSFORMATION SCM IN VIEW OF COVID-19 FROM THAILAND SMES PERSPECTIVE

Bilal Khalid[1] and Elena Naumova[2,]*

[1]KMITL Business School, King Mongkut's Institute of technology Ladkrabang, Bangkok, Thailand
[2]Saint Petersburg State Maritime Technical University, Saint-Petersburg, Russia

ABSTRACT

Digital transformation involves the use of digital technologies to reorganize the operational processes and make them more effective and efficient. The article covers the problem of digital transformation of supply chain management (SCM) due to the changing business environment, and the desire to meet the customers' demand. The authors prove that the supply chain management processes are altered, such as reduction of product design and a manufacturing period, faster delivery of products to customers, easily meeting the preferences and demands of customers and faster and effective decision-making supported by big data and analytical decision techniques. In Thailand, digital transformation has been considered critical, particularly with the SMEs, which account for a significant proportion of the country's GDP. Some of the techniques that should be involved in the digitalization process include adoption of a learning culture, roadmap to development, creation of awareness, collaboration and support. In the wake of COVID-19, digital transformation has proved more essential through e-commerce and online transactions. Within this COVID-19 pandemic period and in future, the software and applications that could be used by SMEs in their process of digitalization include 3D-printers, Computer Aided Manufacturing (CAM), Computer Aided Design (CAD), Product Lifecycle Management (PLC), Customer Relationship Management programs, Virtual Assistance, Artificial Intelligence, Total Quality Management (TQM), Just in Time (JIT), Just in Time (JIT), Lean Manufacturing (LM) among others. Some of the initiatives that could be

* Corresponding Author's Email: elenanaumova@mail.ru.

implemented by the government include developing legal and regulatory framework of SMEs, supporting digitalization of SCM.

Keywords: digital transformation, supply chain management, digitalization process, small and medium enterprises

1. INTRODUCTION

With the rapid growth of the internet in the recent past and the increase in internet users, how people conduct their daily activities, including business and financial transactions, has changed. The rapid development in technology has led to the emergence of e-commerce and the development of new forms of conducting banking and financial transactions (Alalwan et al. 2016). Overall, these changes could be termed as 'digital transformation,' which implies the changes occurring in strategies used to create jobs and income. Digital transformation involves using flexible management models geared towards gaining competitive advantage in the competitive business environment, meeting the customers' everchanging demands and preferences, and adopting the complex process of digitalizing and automating the business operations in the overall supply chain process. The automation is enabled by advancements in technology and the internet, in all aspects of supply chain management, including designing, manufacturing, marketing, sales, and the management models (Shareef et al. 2018). A significant component of digital transformation is the digital payments. Digital payment is a form of e-commerce that has been introduced as a more convenient and efficient and faster way of conducting financial transactions. Digital payment refers to various means of making payments using digital instruments (Baabdullah et al. 2017). Digital transformation goes beyond the mere software and hardware updates to incorporate the evolution of both the institutional and operational ecosystems of the business entities, to be in-line with the growth of technology, new ways of thinking as well as benefiting from the digitization process (Avirutha 2018). Digitalization refers to applying flexible business models such as digital payment methods like mobile money, electronic cars, working robots, and big data analytics.

Technically, digital transformation involves the rearrangement of technology, business processes, and models, intending to deliver additional value to customers, employees, and stakeholders, within the changing digital environment (Vatanasakdakul 2008; Vatanasakdakul, Aoun, and Chen 2017). The major factor influences the speed of digital transformation is customer demands. The supply chain management processes are altered, such as reduction of product design and a manufacturing period, faster delivery of products to customers, easily meeting the preferences and demands of customers and faster and effective decision-making supported by big data and analytical decision techniques. Additionally, digital transformation has played a critical role in increasing business operations efficiency and reducing the cost. The traditional business model has become outdated and replaced by more enhanced, knowledge-based, and flexible models to give a real-time response to customers' inquiries. The Industry 4.0 has brought significant changes in the business world, which include practicality of the manufacturing processes, simplified supply chain processes, reduced costs of infrastructure and energy, more qualified human power, and increased levels of profit and performance, (Brock and von Wangenheim 2019). However, those who take full advantage of the digital transformation manage to adapt and change with the technology levels.

The main pillar of digital transformation has been the innovation accelerator factors, including the Internet of Things (IoT), the 3D printing technology, big data analytics, artificial intelligence arguments, and virtual reality, software integration, blockchain, cybersecurity, and cloud computing (Ariyapruchya et al. 2017).

2. MATERIALS AND METHODS

Within this COVID-19 pandemic period and in future, the software and applications that could be used by SMEs (small and medium enterprises) in their process of SCM (supply chain management) digitalization include 3Dprinters, Computer Aided Manufacturing (CAM), Computer Aided Design (CAD), Product Lifecycle Management (PLC), Customer Relationship Management programs, Virtual Assistance, Artificial Intelligence, Total Quality Management (TQM), Just in Time (JIT), Just in Time (JIT), Lean Manufacturing (LM) among others. As the SMEs are making their effort in digital transformation, the Thailand government has a role to play in ensuring that the process of digital transformation is stimulated. Some of the initiatives that could be implemented by the government include developing legal and regulatory framework, supporting digitalization of SMEs. The government could also provide incentives, to the SMEs that are investing in the process of digital transformation.

2.1. Driving Factors Expediting Digital Transformation

Technological advancement and innovation, sensor technology (ST): Innovation is a critical ingredient to economic growth since it makes technology cheaper. Counties with more advanced technological levels experience rapid economic growth. More entrepreneurs should start working on digital platforms. Digital technologies enable SMEs to access global knowledge networks and markets at lower costs.

Social media, electronic commerce, and internet economy in business practices: Technological advancements have significantly traditional ways of conducting business transactions. In this era, technological advancements have provided avenues through which online business transactions and communication occur. Electronic commerce (e-commerce) is an excellent example of products of technological advancement. The World Trade Organization (WTO) defines e-commerce as the manufacture, distribution, and delivery of products and services using telecommunication. The digital transformation helps small businesses to compete competitively in the local and global markets by offering innovative products and services.

Globalization

Apart from increasing the mobility of products, services, and capital globally, digital transformation has also increased interactions and communications between societies and governments of different countries. This has enhanced cross-border economic integration that enables people from different parts of the world to conduct business transactions through digital platforms (Jones and Pimdee 2017).

Fourth Industrial Revolution

Through informational technologies, it is predicted that the fourth industrial revolution will be characterized by automated machines that would digitalize the production process. These machines would achieve personalized manufacturing; hence products produced would increasingly meet the personal demands of individuals. This would also help to avoid excessive use of energy, water, and other natural resources in the production process.

Artificial intelligence involves introducing smart software that investigates how the human brain thinks and learns how people interpret and solve problems. These softwares use such case studies to study human behavior and imitate their thinking. Through this, such softwares do not use the programmers' minds; instead, they interpret problems on their own and make their independent judgments (de Kervenoael et al. 2020). Some robots are being used in the manufacturing process. These robots have artificial intelligence; hence they do not require human intervention. Intelligent software's leave room for more improvements.

Internet of Things (IoT)

This involves a technology that connects devices over the internet. It allows connected devices to share data. This makes it easier for data collection, analysis, and processes. The automated system allows sending and receiving data and communication between the connected devices and other network devices and systems through the IP addresses of interconnected devices. IoT is more operative in relating time, work, and money-saving.

Effects of Generation Z on the Market

Generation Z includes people born between 1996 and 2001. Such a group of people comprises 25 percent of the world population. They were born into a digital world with digital devices such as mobile phones. Unlike the previous generation that used verbal communication, generation Z prefers online communication such as creating videos, following trends from the vlog, creating, and subscribing to channels.

They desire to play active roles in the product designing stage (Schallmo, Williams, and Boardman 2017).

Blockchain

This involves a decentralized ciphering record book that supports Bitcoin. Bitcoin is a digital currency that is accepted everywhere and is not controlled by anyone. Since 2012, Bitcoin has been distributed through an encrypted database technology that provides follow-up.

Cloud Computing

This is an internet-based information service that enables people to access and share computer sources on requests from computers and other devices. It enables people to store their files in their user computers rather than in data centers. This enables them to access their store files from anywhere without necessarily using their original computers. Applications such as Microsoft Office and Itune have ensured that software is distributed from the web browser rather than downloading them in computers.

Increase Use of Smartphones

Over the last few years, there have been increased smartphones. Currently, more than 1 billion phones are sold every year. This is because smartphones are offering computer skills. In 2018, more than 73 percent of its adult citizens in Turkey were using phones. Seventy-seven percent of them are using smartphones.

3D Printers

These are devices that rapidly print out models designed in 3D without using any fixtures or mold. Even though they produce high-quality models, they have a lower cost of product design and manufacturing. It has also increased the pace of designing houses. For instance, using 3D printers, more than ten houses can be established in China in a single day. 3D can also be used in medical applications, lowering mold cost, model making, and robot design, plastic plasters, prosthesis, among other applications.

Chatbots

These are software applications designed to back up verbal human speaking and imitate written messages in the service sector. Examples of chatbots include Google assistant, Alexa, and Siri.

Big Data

This involves data that computers are unable to process. Big data involves large amounts of structured, semi-structured, or unstructured data that has the potential of being mined to produce meaningful information. For instance, it enables designers to derive meaningful information about the demand for their potential customers to produce products that will meet the demand of their customers (Fountas et al. 2015; Klerkx, Jakku, and Labarthe 2019). Data analytics and big data provide SMEs with opportunities to develop a better understanding of their industries and improve their general business environment.

Augmented Reality (AR)

This involves physical reality extensions that are added by information generated by computers to the real environment. It includes text, sound, videos, graphics, GPs, and even smell. This increases productivity and reduces the cost that would be used to achieve given environments for production. Augmented reality technology can be used in the medical field in studying organisms and offering virtual training of surgeries. In real estate markets, it can be used in conducting visits to fully digital properties.

Developing a Circular Economy

Through digital technologies, this economy seeks to match demand to supply skills or under-utilized assets through intermediaries. The digital technology achieves this with speed and effectiveness. Through this economy, consumers become producers. It also minimizes wastage since something is only produced when there is a need for it.

Nanotechnology (N)

Nano is a measuring unit that is one-billionth of a given parameter (Nazir 2019). Nanotechnology involves technological materials that are at measure between 1 to 100 nanometers. Such materials are at least one dimensional. Nanotechnology Is a scientific knowledge that use of structure and size-dependent properties different from those associated with atoms by manipulating and controlling matter predominantly in the nanoscale (Pelletier and Cloutier 2019).

Digital Supply Chain (DSC)

This comprises hardware, software, and communication networks that support the interaction between orchestrates and globally distributed organizations. This enhances partnership activities in supply chains. Some of the activities facilitated by DSC include purchases, storage, moving, and sell of products. DSC seeks to increase global connectivity, transparency, scalability, proactive, innovation, flexibility, and intelligence (Barann et al. 2019).

Robotics

Using robots in routine recurring production activities help in reducing production cost. Robots are more flexible and perform such activities faster and more efficiently. Robots with ergonomic designs and better materials are being designed to drive vehicles with little or no human intervention. Through this, robotics will help in shifting capital and labor-intense production while managing societal expectations.

Advanced Manufacturing Technologies

These involve sophisticated technologies that are used in manufacturing industries. They include the technologies used in manufacturing Computer Numerical Control (CNC), manufacturing systems, smart sensors, non-smart and non-flexible automation systems, automatic robotics, and cyber-physical systems.

2.2. Digital Transformation in Thailand

The effort has received significant backing from the government as well as the private sector. It was focused that the IT spending in Thailand by the end of year 2020 would be US$11 billion. At the same it, it projected that by the end of year 2021, digital transformation is expected to contribute approximately US$9 billion to the GDP of Thailand, and at the same time increase the GDP growth rate by an approximated rate of 0.4% per annum. These findings are according to the research titles 'Unlocking the Economic Impact of Digital Transformation in Asia-Pacific'. The study indicates that there will be a dramatic acceleration of the digital transformation pace in Thailand, considering that by the end of year 2017; approximately 4% of the GDP in Thailand was derived from the digital products and services. these are the products and services which are created through the application of digital technologies such as mobility, internet of things (IoT), artificial intelligence as well as cloud computing. A large proportion of this spending is channeled to managed cloud services, which implies that digital transformation is playing a critical role, as well as being considered as a significant aspect. The research has suggested that more than 55% of the Thailand CEOs suggest that there is need for digital transformation. The critical aspect that needs to be addressed, according to (von Leipzig et al. 2017), is whether there is fear or resistance to spend.

2.3. Tactical Stage of Transformation

Inferring from (Buasuwan 2018), the benefit emanating from business transformation is clear. However, most of the companies in Thailand are stuck in their tactical stage of their journey to implementing digital transformation. By the year 2021, digital transformation is expected to contribute approximately 48% to the regions GDP, specifically from digital transformation products and services. However, studies have shown that Thailand has been lagging in the region, and eventually trailing behind other countries such as Singapore, Japan and South Korea. The major identified impediments to the full adoption and implementation of the digital transformation is the lack of technical knowledge and organizational silos. However, the collaborating of Thailand government and other technology partners have enabled the companies operating in the country to experience a steady growth and it is expected that this trend will continue. According to the recent study, 44% companies operating in Thailand considered digital transformation as their number one priority, while the second in priority was the infrastructure modernization, while the third was the cybersecurity.

Inferring from (Kircova 2012), the reason for digital transformation being considered as the most preferred results from the fact that many companies and businesses are facing great pressure of remaining competitive in the face of digital disruption across industries. The most affected countries include the financial services, logistics and telecommunications. Though the level of adoption and implementation of digital transformation is not equal in all the industries, some of the industries that have made great effort in digital transformation include banking sector, insurance sector, and financial sector. (Ndayizigamiye and Khoase 2018) observes that the commercialization of 5G networks could significantly boost the process of digital transformation in the manufacturing sector. It is observed that the Thailand's national framework of 4.0 has adopted and included significant strategic initiatives, which are geared towards driving adoption and implementation of smart manufacturing techniques in various sectors, and its associated driving technologies such as internet of things (IoT), artificial intelligence or machine learning (AI/ML), robotics, 3-D printing as well as mobile connectivity.

2.4. Digital Transformation of SMEs in Thailand

In Thailand, small and medium enterprises (SMEs) as a sector has been considered as a stable and significant one of the country's economy. By the year 2019, the sector was contributing more than 45% of the country's gross domestic products (GDP). It also constitutes to approximately 99% of the total establishment in the country, with an employment of approximately 69% of the total workforce in the country. Other contributions of Thai SMEs is the processing of the export raw materials. The digitalization of SMEs in Thailand has been considered a critical aspect over a long period of time. In the year 2018, three agencies, the Digital Promotion Agency (DEPA), United Overseas Bank (UOB), and Finlab came in to same terms and signed a Memorandum of Understanding (MOU), whose objective was to establish the smart business transformation program that was geared towards helping the SMEs in the process of digital development and transformation. Over the period of hits operation, the Smart Business Transformation program has been considered vital in Thailand as it is aimed to deepen and enhance the digital capabilities of the SMEs. Through the program, the SMEs were to benefit, and have been benefitting from the network of experts, technology leaders and mentors, which are provided to them by the DEPA, UOB (Thai) and The Finlabs. This program and the support given by the inherent organization are as are result of the recognition of the need and desire by Thai SMEs to grab the opportunities which are opening up in the Thailand and the overall region, though the adoption of the digital transformation. The program was also developed to be concurrent with the Thailand Digital government Plan 2017-2021, which was initiated by the government to develop and implement digital capabilities within all sectors involved. the major sectors that the program focused on included agriculture, tourism, education, medical professional's disaster prevention as well as public administration. These are crucial in the process of driving social and economic progress (Leung and Cossu 2019). Having a sustainable digital transformation among strategy for SMEs is critical, as it have the capabilities of creating a sustainable global digital market. Digital transformation, if adopted and implemented appropriately, it has the capacity of resulting into the increased business growth, regardless of the unpredictable business opportunities and economic challenges through reduction of the business cost, investments stimulation and increasing the levels of employment as well as revenue (Hinings, Gegenhuber, and Greenwood 2018). This will make the process of SMEs stronger as well as ready to forge to the future. For the SMEs to fully implement the process of digital transformation, there are various stages and process that they should adopt. These are discussed in the following section.

Data-Based Transformation

This is an aspect where the process of digital transformation is guided by findings grounded on statistical findings. It is the process of innovation, where each person is responsible for the implementation of a particular section. The owner or manager of the concerned SME should be responsible for implementing the transformation. The analysis process would include evaluation of the local challenges, risks and customer expectations. The needs and requirements of SMEs needs to be considered, as a mechanism of ensuring that there are measurable goals (Li et al. 2018). It is the responsibility of the management of SMEs to evaluate and analyze various digital topics, and the technologies, which could contribute positively towards the exploration of new business models. This would act as a benchmark and training which would support the SMEs.

Adoption of a Learning Culture

According to (Sebastian et al. 2017) adopting a 'learning culture' is vital as long as digital transformation of SMEs in Thailand is concerned. A leaning culture, according to (Sousa and Rocha 2019) implies the organizational conventions, practices, values and processes, which are geared towards encouraging employees to develop new knowledge and competence. With the unprecedented changes in the global society, and the increased evolution in technology, there is a great need for the SMEs to have technologically skilled employees, push the current employees to be technologically minded as well as develop the skills and abilities to detect the inherent gaps. The SMEs should focus on competing for the new markets and opportunities with market giants such as Facebook, Apple, Google and Amazon. The digital skilled employees should be given a priority, as they have the expertise to steer the start-ups forwards in the digital transformation journey.

Roadmap Development

Inferring from (Sagarik et al. 2018) SMEs in Thailand needs to define and develop simple steps, which are geared towards the achieving the set goals and objectives of digital transformation. The first step in this process is the definition of digital transformation objectives. These objectives should be defined with respect to four aspects; time, finances, space and quality. The overall roadmap would be composed of the following steps:

- Designing the SMEs new digital strategy;
- Analysis of the existing business model of the concerned SME;
- Analysis of the customers' requirements, needs, tastes and preferences;
- Performance of the digital evaluation and expectations;
- Setting the overall digital transformation objectives;
- Development of the competence in terms of digital transformation process;
- Setting effective best practices that would be used as benchmark for digital transformation;
- Developing the digital transformation business models options and information technology use;
- Developing the evaluation framework, value network as well as feedback from customers.

Creation of Awareness

The next step is the creation of awareness through campaign, aimed at informing people on the importance of supporting the environment 'To use IT to develop my business'. The SMEs owners should be eliminated on the importance of evaluating how effective IT tools are, in terms of return on investment (ROI, sales, and performance). There is also the need to link the expectations with the reality, which is IT user friendly. The SMEs owners and managers should be informed regarding the available trainings of the IT, and how effective and transparent communications could be established between their IT specialists regarding what is expected of them.

Collaboration

In the globalized business word, creation of business connection is vital, especially for the SMEs with the innovative labs and research institutions (Reis et al. 2018). It is necessary for the SMEs establish connections with the companies and stakeholders that that expertise in their field of operation, and as well obtain the consultancy services. Collaboration is considered vital in guiding the SMEs through the current trends, as well as demonstrating their importance, on the basis of practical examples and real-life examples which could be copied.

Support

As long as the SMEs are making their effort towards implementation of the digital transformation, there is also the need to have them supported, in terms of need analysis and implementation of feasible objectives (Ustundag and Cevikcan 2018). It is recommended that government of Thailand should take the initiative of supporting the SMEs, which are making efforts towards digital transformation. Some of the stakeholder that could help SMEs in their digital transformation include Trade Association and Chambers, as well as external supporters such as research institutes could significantly help the implementation of the digital transformation process.

3. RESULTS

COCID-19 has created the urgency of digital transformation. While COVID-19 has caused unprecedented challenges and issues to the businesses, societies and economies of the world, it has also given a clear glimpse into the future. The future is expected to have an environment where digital transactions are expected to be central in every transaction both social and commercial. It is expected that the world where digital is the preferred method of having customers' interaction, financial transaction as well as running the automated systems, which promote the productivity, is expected to continue even after post COVID-19 (Wongwuttiwat and Lawanna 2018). This digital transformation has affected both large enterprises as well as SMEs. There is an accelerated enterprise digital transformation, associated with the paradigm shift bringing about the operation of the 'new normal', which, as well, creates a standard over which the enterprises could be evaluated. In the future, SMEs will be ready to adapt to the increasingly volatile conditions faster, and make efforts to operate in the environments, which are sensitive and accommodative to all stakeholders. Therefore, the COVID-19 has fastened the SMEs to stay ready for accommodating the needs of the stakeholders such as the employees' customers and suppliers. The Figure 1 below illustrates the four steps necessary for the SMEs to move from digital transformation to enterprise transformation.

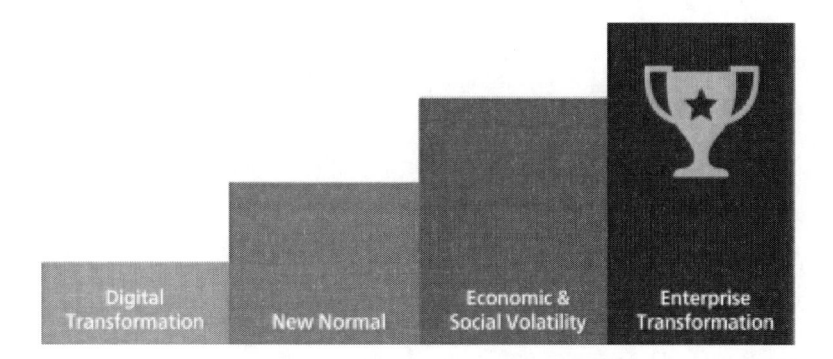

Figure 1. From Digital Transformation to Enterprise Transformation.

As the concept, 'COVID-19 has forced us online' Thailand and SMEs in particular is not an exceptional. The enterprises have been forced to adapt to the new way of conducting businesses, the new 'normal' way of operations. The status quo has been significantly disrupted, and business are forced to quickly adjust to a new way of conducting their business operations. The SMEs has no option apart from considering to enhancing their operations in terms of digitalized transactions and operations.

According to the Abeam's Digital Transformation matrix, there are four areas that the SMEs could adopt, that could lead to them towards having a complete digital transformation process, particularly in the wake of a pandemic, like the one of COVID-19. This matrix could help the digitized SMEs to operate effectively even in a lower revenue environment (Figure 2).

Based on the Abeam's Digital Transformation matrix, the first step towards digital transformation is the identification of new business opportunities. With the disruption of old ways of doing business, due to COVID-19, the SMEs has, to explore new digital methods and technologies of conducting their operations and meeting the customers' needs (Calipinar and Ulas 2013). These include virtual replacement of the previous physical offerings, and make them the easy ways of accessing their customers. The next step is the enhancement of products and services, which involves SMEs capitalizing on business opportunities, which are beyond their traditional bounds. The SMEs should focus on the areas, which are overlapping of complementary to their major business activities, as they would long-term as well as have a competitive edge. The third aspect is the business process improvement, which involves adoption of processes such as e-commerce, which uses automated and online transactions processes (Moreira, Ferreira, and Seruca 2018). It is a process of Business Process Reengineering (BPR), which is critical in the identification of the existing business process inefficiencies, and restructuring them towards delivering effective processes.

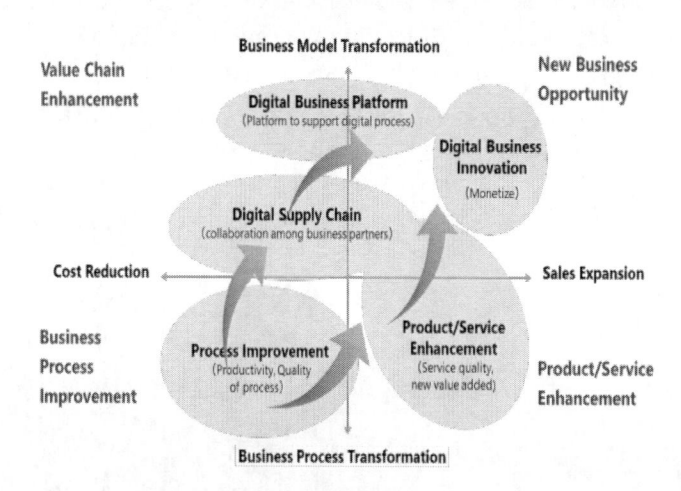

Figure 2. Abeam's Digital Transformation matrix.

There are various studies that have been aspect of digital transformation. These studies have identified various factors that influence the adoption and use of information and communication technology (ICTs) in an organization as a means of achieving digital transformation. These factors are include: 1) firms characteristics, such as size and type of the business, past experiences, privacy and security aspects such as limited knowledge on the technology application, internet security issues, hardware and software management; 2) lack of a well-defined roadmap of digital transformation; 3) lack of a good information sharing programs and meeting the legislations required for digital transformation; 4) and poor implementation environment. However, it is vital to consider that SMEs have access various information technology applications, which could be utilized to support their business activities. These including using Google Analytics to perform their online marketing and competition analysis, Pay-pal for conducting online transactions, Facebook for creating online business presence, marketing and advertisements, and other communication and collaboration channels such as skype, TeamViewer, WhatsApp and Massager. In this process, there are various software and program that could be used by SMEs in the process of digital transformation as described in the table below (Table 1).

Table 1. Software and program used by SMEs in the process of digital transformation

Function or Department	Program or Software to use
Human resource management (HRM)	Customer Relationship Management programs, Virtual Assistance, Artificial Intelligence, Mobile working and networking, Audio and Video Online platforms, Augmented Reality,
Customer management, sales and marketing	Virtual guidance and remote maintenance, Customers touch point, real-time purchase activities, demand forecasting, customer feedback management, customers digital training
New Product Development and design	3Dprinters, Computer Aided Manufacturing (CAM), Computer Aided Design (CAD), Product Lifecycle Management (PLC),
Demand Forecasting	Big data analytics, personalized products orders, fair support software
Manufacturing	Total Quality Management (TQM), Just in Time (JIT), Just in Time (JIT), Lean Manufacturing (LM)

4. DISCUSSION

In the context of SMEs digital transformation process, there may various variations, based on the type of SME concerned. Different types of sectors have different needs of digitalization. Therefore, there is a significant need for to categorize the SMEs based on their size and sector. The digital transformation process involves revolution of the

SMEs operational strategies, as well as the culture of the concerned organization. There are eight dimensions of digital transformation, which include strategy, leadership, products, operations, culture, people, governance and technology (Vial 2019) with some special features of project being realized in digital economy (Barykin, Kalinina, et al. 2021; Barykin, Kapustina, Sergeev, et al. 2021; Barykin, Bochkarev, et al. 2021; Barykin, Kapustina, Valebnikova, et al. 2021). There are three levels of digital transformations that could be adopted by SMEs. The first level is 'unaware' which describes the companies that do not offer any form of digital transformation and there are no traces of digital transformation available. This implies that the SMEs found in this level do not offer any digital products or services. The second level of digital transformation is referred to as the 'conceptual' level. The SMEs in this level are in the little levels of digital transformation. They offer little products of digital products and services, but they have not set a well-structured digital strategy. The third level is referred to as the 'defined' level of digital transformation, which are SMEs which are in advanced levels of digital transformation. At this level, the past experiences of digitalization are consolidated to form a comprehensive digitalization expertise, and an effective digital strategy. A SME could only be considered to be 'transformed' after the implementation of the full and clear digital strategy across all business and operations models of the SME. The defined digital strategy has a a good capacity of transforming the business and operations strategies of the company.

CONCLUSION

Digital transformation involves the rearrangement of technology, business processes, and models, intending to deliver additional value to customers, employees, and stakeholders, within the changing digital environment. Driven by the changing business environment, and the desire to meet the customers demand, the supply chain management processes are altered, such as reduction of product design and a manufacturing period, faster delivery of products to customers, easily meeting the preferences and demands of customers and faster and effective decision-making supported by big data and analytical decision techniques. In Thailand, digital transformation has been considered critical, particularly with the SMEs, which account for a significant proportion of the country's GDP. By the year 2021, digital transformation is expected to contribute approximately 48% to the regions GDP, specifically from digital transformation products and services. With this advancement in technology, and digital transformation, SMEs stand a significant opportunity to enhance their digital presence, in line with the Thailand Digital government Plan 2017-2021. For SMEs to have a successful SCM digitalization there are several aspects that should be considered. These include adoption of a learning culture, roadmap to development, creation of awareness, collaboration and support in supply chains.

In the period of COVID-19, digital transformation has proved more essential, as it provides digitalized ways of conducting businesses, without direct contact. It has created an environment where digital transactions are expected to be central in every transaction both social and commercial. There are various tools that could be use by SMEs in their process of digitalization, which include 3Dprinters, Computer Aided Manufacturing (CAM), Computer Aided Design (CAD), Product Lifecycle Management (PLC), Customer Relationship Management programs, Virtual Assistance, Artificial Intelligence, Total Quality Management (TQM), Just in Time (JIT), Just in Time (JIT), Lean Manufacturing (LM). The digital transformation process is enabled by advancement in global technology, and the use f internet, available even to the SMEs. It is advisable that SMEs should focus on the areas, which are overlapping of complementary to their major business activities, as they would long-term as well as have a competitive edge. As the SMEs are making their effort in digital transformation, the Thailand government has a role to play in ensuring that the process of digital transformation is stimulated. Some of the initiatives that could be implemented by the government include developing legal and regulatory framework, supporting digitalization of SMEs. The government could also provide incentives, to the SMEs that are investing in the process of digital transformation. This way, the overall process would be beneficial to all the stakeholders.

REFERENCES

Alalwan, Ali Abdallah, Yogesh K. Dwivedi, Nripendra P. P. Rana. & Michael D. Williams. (2016). "Consumer Adoption of Mobile Banking in Jordan." *Journal of Enterprise Information Management.* https://doi.org/10.1108/jeim-04-2015-0035.

Ariyapruchya, Kiatipong, Thanapat Reungsri, Ricardo Alfredo Habalian, Julian Latimer Clarke. & Smita Kuriakose. (2017). *Thailand Economic Monitor,* August 2017. *Thailand Economic Monitor,* August 2017. https://doi.org/10.1596/30248.

Avirutha, A. (2018). "The Impact of Digital Transformation to Business Performance in Thailand 4.0 Era." *Veridian E-Journal, Silpakorn University (Humanities ....*

Baabdullah, Abdullah, Ali Abdallah Alalwan, Nripendra P. Rana, Yogesh K. Dwivedi. & Vishanth Weerakkody. (2017). "Assessing Consumers' Intention to Adopt Mobile Internet Services in the Kingdom of Saudi Arabia." In *AMCIS 2017 - America's Conference on Information Systems: A Tradition of Innovation.*

Barann, Benjamin, Andreas Hermann, Ann-Kristin Cordes, Friedrich Chasin. & Jörg Becker. (2019). "Supporting Digital Transformation in Small and Medium-Sized Enterprises: A Procedure Model Involving Publicly Funded Support Units." In *Proceedings of the 52nd Hawaii International Conference on System Sciences.* https://doi.org/10.24251/hicss.2019.598.

Barykin, Sergey Yevgenievich, Andrey Aleksandrovich Bochkarev, Sergey Mikhailovich Sergeev, Tatiana Anatolievna Baranova, Dmitriy Anatolievich Mokhorov, and Aleksandra Maksimovna Kobicheva. 2021. "A Methodology of Bringing Perspective Innovation Products to Market." *Academy of Strategic*

Management Journal 20 (2): 19. https://www.abacademies.org/articles/a-methodology-of-bringing-perspective-innovation-products-to-market.pdf.

Barykin, Sergey Yevgenievich, Olga Vladimirovna Kalinina, Irina Vasilievna Kapustina, Victor Andreevich Dubolazov, Cesar Armando Nunez Esquivel, Elmira Alyarovna Nazarova, and Petr Anatolievich Sharapaev. 2021. "The Sharing Economy and Digital Logistics in Retail Chains: Opportunities and Threats." *Academy of Strategic Management Journal* 20 (2): 1–14. https://www.abacademies.org/articles/the-sharing-economy-and-digital-logistics-in-retail-chains-opportunities-and-threats.pdf.

Barykin, Sergey Yevgenievich, Irina Vasilievna Kapustina, Sergey Mikhailovich Sergeev, Olga Vladimirovna Kalinina, Viktoriia Valerievna Vilken, Yuri Yevgenievich Putikhin, and Lydia Vitalievna Volkova. 2021. "Developing the Physical Distribution Digital Twin Model within the Trade Network." *Academy of Strategic Management Journal* 20 (1): 1–24. https://www.abacademies.org/articles/developing-the-physical-distribution-digital-twin-model-within-the-trade-network.pdf.

Barykin, Sergey Yevgenievich, Irina Vasilievna Kapustina, Olga Aleksandrovna Valebnikova, Natalia Viktorovna Valebnikova, Olga Vladimirovna Kalinina, Sergey Mikhailovich Sergeev, Marisa Camastral, Yuri Yevgenievich Putikhin, and Lydia Vitalievna Volkova. 2021. "Digital Technologies for Personnel Management: Implications for Open Innovations." *Academy of Strategic Management Journal* 20 (2): 1–14. https://www.abacademies.org/articles/digital-technologies-for-personnel-management-implications-for-open-innovations.pdf.

Brock, Jürgen Kai Uwe. & Florian von Wangenheim. (2019). "Demystifying Ai: What Digital Transformation Leaders Can Teach You about Realistic Artificial Intelligence." *California Management Review.* https://doi.org/10.1177/1536504219865226.

Buasuwan, Prompilai. (2018). "Rethinking Thai Higher Education for Thailand 4.0." *Asian Education and Development Studies.* https://doi.org/10.1108/AEDS-07-2017-0072.

Calipinar, Hatice. & Dilber Ulas. (2013). "Model Suggestion for SMEs Economic and Environmental Sustainable Development." In *Small and Medium Enterprises: Concepts, Methodologies, Tools, and Applications.* https://doi.org/10.4018/978-1-4666-3886-0.ch023.

Fountas, S., Carli, G., Sørensen, C. G., Tsiropoulos, Z., Cavalaris, C., Vatsanidou, A., Liakos, B., Canavari, M., Wiebensohn, J. & Tisserye, B. (2015). "Farm Management Information Systems: Current Situation and Future Perspectives." *Computers and Electronics in Agriculture.* https://doi.org/10.1016/j.compag.2015.05.011.

Hinings, Bob, Thomas Gegenhuber. & Royston Greenwood. (2018). "Digital Innovation and Transformation: An Institutional Perspective." *Information and Organization.* https://doi.org/10.1016/j.infoandorg.2018.02.004.

Jones, Charlie. & Paitoon Pimdee. (2017). "Innovative Ideas: Thailand 4.0 and the Fourth Industrial Revolution." *Asian International Journal of Social Sciences.* https://doi.org/10.29139/aijss.20170101.

Kervenoael, Ronan de, Alexandre Schwob, Inci Toral Manson. & Chatlada Ratana. (2020). "Business-to-Business and Self-Governance Practice in the Digital Knowledge Economy: Learning from Pharmaceutical e-Detailing in Thailand." *Asian Business and Management.* https://doi.org/10.1057/s41291-020-00141-z.

Kircova, İbrahim. (2012). "İnternette Pazarlama - Ücretsiz Indirin [Internet Marketing - Free Download]." *Beta Basım Yayım Dağıtım.* 2012. https://docplayer.biz.tr/7328389-Internette-pazarlama-prof-dr-ibrahim-kircova.html.

Klerkx, Laurens, Emma Jakku. & Pierre Labarthe. (2019). "A Review of Social Science on Digital Agriculture, Smart Farming and Agriculture 4.0: New Contributions and a Future Research Agenda." *NJAS - Wageningen Journal of Life Sciences.* https://doi.org/10.1016/j.njas.2019.100315.

Leipzig, T. von, Gamp, M., Manz, D., Schöttle, K., Ohlhausen, P., Oosthuizen, G., Palm, D. & von Leipzig, K. (2017). "Initialising Customer-Orientated Digital Transformation in Enterprises." *Procedia Manufacturing.* https://doi.org/10.1016/j.promfg.2017.02.066.

Leung, Wing Fai. & Alberto Cossu. (2019). "Digital Entrepreneurship in Taiwan and Thailand: Embracing Precarity as a Personal Response to Political and Economic Change." *International Journal of Cultural Studies.* https://doi.org/10.1177/1367877918821234.

Li, Liang, Fang Su, Wei Zhang. & Ji Ye Mao. (2018). "Digital Transformation by SME Entrepreneurs: A Capability Perspective." In *Information Systems Journal.* https://doi.org/10.1111/isj.12153.

Moreira, Fernando, Maria João Ferreira. & Isabel Seruca. (2018). "Enterprise 4.0 - The Emerging Digital Transformed Enterprise?" In *Procedia Computer Science.* https://doi.org/10.1016/j.procs.2018.10.072.

Nazir, Salman. (2019). "CIO Interview with Ali Aurangzeb, Head of Global Marketing and Deputy Head of Digital Transformation, NETSOL Technologies, Inc." *Journal of Global Information Technology Management.* https://doi.org/10.1080/1097198X.2019.1603738.

Ndayizigamiye, Patrick. & Refiloe Gladys Khoase. (2018). "Inhibitors of the Adoption of E-Commerce by SMMES in Two South African Cities." *International Journal of EBusiness and EGovernment Studies.*

Pelletier, Claudia. & Martin Cloutier, L. (2019). "Challenges of Digital Transformation in SMEs: Exploration of IT-Related Perceptions in a Service Ecosystem." In *Proceedings of the 52nd Hawaii International Conference on System Sciences.* https://doi.org/10.24251/hicss.2019.597.

Reis, João, Marlene Amorim, Nuno Melão. & Patrícia Matos. (2018). "Digital Transformation: A Literature Review and Guidelines for Future Research." In *Advances in Intelligent Systems and Computing.* https://doi.org/10.1007/978-3-319-77703-0_41.

Sagarik, Danuvas, Pananda Chansukree, Wonhyuk Cho. & Evan Berman. (2018). "E-Government 4.0 in Thailand: The Role of Central Agencies." *Information Polity.* https://doi.org/10.3233/IP-180006.

Schallmo, Daniel, Christopher A. Williams. & Luke Boardman. (2017). "Digital Transformation of Business Models-Best Practice, Enablers, and Roadmap." *International Journal of Innovation Management.* https://doi.org/10.1142/S136391961740014X.

Sebastian, Ina, Jeanne Ross, Cynthia Beath, Martin Mocker, Kate Moloney. & Nils Fonstad. (2017). "How Big Old Companies Navigate Digital Transformation." *MIS Quarterly Executive.*

Shareef, Mahmud Akhter, Abdullah Baabdullah, Shantanu Dutta, Vinod Kumar. & Yogesh K. Dwivedi. (2018). "Consumer Adoption of Mobile Banking Services: An Empirical Examination of Factors According to Adoption Stages." *Journal of Retailing and Consumer Services.* https://doi.org/10.1016/j.jretconser.2018.03.003.

Sousa, Maria José. & Álvaro Rocha. (2019). "Digital Learning: Developing Skills for Digital Transformation of Organizations." *Future Generation Computer Systems.* https://doi.org/10.1016/j.future.2018.08.048.

Ustundag, Alp. & Emre Cevikcan. (2018). *Industry 4.0: Managing The Digital Transformation. Industry 4.0: Managing The Digital Transformation.*

Vatanasakdakul, Savanid. (2008). "Introducing Cultural Fit Factors to Investigate the Appropriateness of B2B Technology Adoption to Thailand." In *21st Bled EConference "ECollaboration: Overcoming Boundaries Through Multi-Channel Interaction" - Proceedings.*

Vatanasakdakul, Savanid, Chadi Aoun. & Yang (Nicole) Chen. (2017). "Chasing Success: An Empirical Model for IT Governance Frameworks Adoption in Australia." *Science, Technology and Society.* https://doi.org/10.1177/0971721817702278.

Vial, Gregory. (2019). "Understanding Digital Transformation: A Review and a Research Agenda." *Journal of Strategic Information Systems.* https://doi.org/10.1016/j.jsis.2019.01.003.

Wongwuttiwat, Jittima. & Adtha Lawanna. (2018). "The Digital Thailand Strategy and the ASEAN Community." *Electronic Journal of Information Systems in Developing Countries.* https://doi.org/10.1002/isd2.12024.

In: Global Challenges of Digital Transformation of Markets ISBN: 978-1-53619-754-9
Editors: E. de la Poza and S. E. Barykin   © 2021 Nova Science Publishers, Inc.

Chapter 5

DIGITAL CONVERSION OF LIFE CYCLE PROCESSES TRANSPORTATION AND LOGISTICS SYSTEMS

Alexey Nekrasov[1,] and Anna Sinitsyna[2]*
[1]Moscow Automobile and Road Construction State Technical University,
Moscow, Russia
[2]Russian University of Transport, Moscow, Russia

ABSTRACT

The article discusses an innovative approach to managing the life cycle of a transport and logistics system, based on the concept of proactive management. New processes are recommended to ensure the survivability and adaptation of complex organizational and technical objects in the context of digital transformation and the transition to the concept of Industry 4.0. As the basis of a highly efficient integrated TLS, there is a coordinated interaction of enterprises within the stages of the "design - operation - operational control - check and corrective actions - check of the control system" life cycle. The main idea in transforming the life cycle management system is the effective use of a consistent representation of the system and the environment in initially incompatible organizational and technical systems of the digital supply chain. New principles for the formation of COTO should be aimed at ensuring integrated safety and sustainable transport based on the integration of logistics engineering processes.

Keywords: digital transformation; supply chain; transport and logistics systems

---

* Corresponding Author's Email: tehnologistic@mail.ru.

1. Introduction

One of the significant trends in the development of digital transformation is the digital transformation of processes that support the entire life cycle of the transport and logistics system, as an essential element of the supply chain. The digitalization of the transport and logistics sector makes extensive use of the innovative tools of Industry 4.0, including changes in management methodology, technology for determining strategic directions for the development of regional transport and logistics systems, the transformation of life cycle processes and infrastructure (Yakovlev et al., 2019; Bulatova et al., 2019; Colombo et al., 2017; Nekrasov and Sinitsyna 2020).

Assessment of efficiency can be based on different methods, from the transition of the transport and logistics system (TLS) to an IT platform to the automation of logistics processes. Digital transformation based on a life cycle model can bring significant benefits, as it ensures the integration of all processes and the achievement of high productivity and sustainability of the transport system and the entire supply chain. This applies to digital twins and the improvement of quality control methods, built based on the digitalization of supply chains, reflecting all processes of the product life cycle (Barykin, Kapustina, Sergeev, et al. 2021).

Mainly complex organizational and technical objects (COTO) are used as such models in the context of digital transformations. They enable the integration of digital information and communication technology (ICT) processes and lifecycle processes that span the entire TLS and digital supply chain. In the current environment, the most important is an integrated approach that combines the use of ICT processes and logistics based on the infrastructure of the system life cycle. This translates into lower costs and lower response times to customer requests. As a result, we get the management of TLS as a single digital ecosystem.

Traditional (functional) logistics, dealing with the placement of production, warehouses, customers, and modeling supply chains to optimize costs and order time, in modern conditions implies refocusing on adaptive-digital methods. A new approach is required, the one based on the system mechanism of integrated management not only in supply chains but also that of processes in an enterprise based on the interaction of intelligent and Internet technologies (the Internet-of-things type).

2. Materials and Methods

The systems, means and complexes used are usually characterized by multi-dimensionality, multi-structuralism, indefinite functioning, hierarchy, excessive elements and connections, variety of implementing functions and processes, and mobility of components. The higher complexity of the existing COTOs requires more controlled parameters characterizing functioning processes. Research and practical experience show that managerial delays and mistakes as well as incorrect process monitoring can lead to serious negative consequences. All of this largely depends on the level of sustainability of logistical processes, which provide for the efficiency of the main elements of the system (production) for the whole life-cycle of both the production and infrastructure (Scholz-Reiter, Kolditz, and Hildebrandt 2009; Grant 2016).

In modern conditions, the infrastructure of the life-cycle of the transportation-logistics system can provide for conditions of innovative development, forming the demand for robot-oriented loading and transportation equipment and modern technological solutions, including logistic engineering and transport construction.

For example, it is impossible to imagine system approach implementation at railway transport without logistic engineering in warehousing, commercial operation Effective functioning of any system requires integration, which will define the interaction of different companies, logistic operators in the common system passenger and freight services, and the possible changes of each element (network configuration, rolling-stock type, transport mode) should be considered in connection with other transport modes ("About Priority Directions of Development of Transport and Logistics Business of the Holding "RZD." Transformation of the Business Model of the Holding "RZD" n.d.) (see Figure 1).

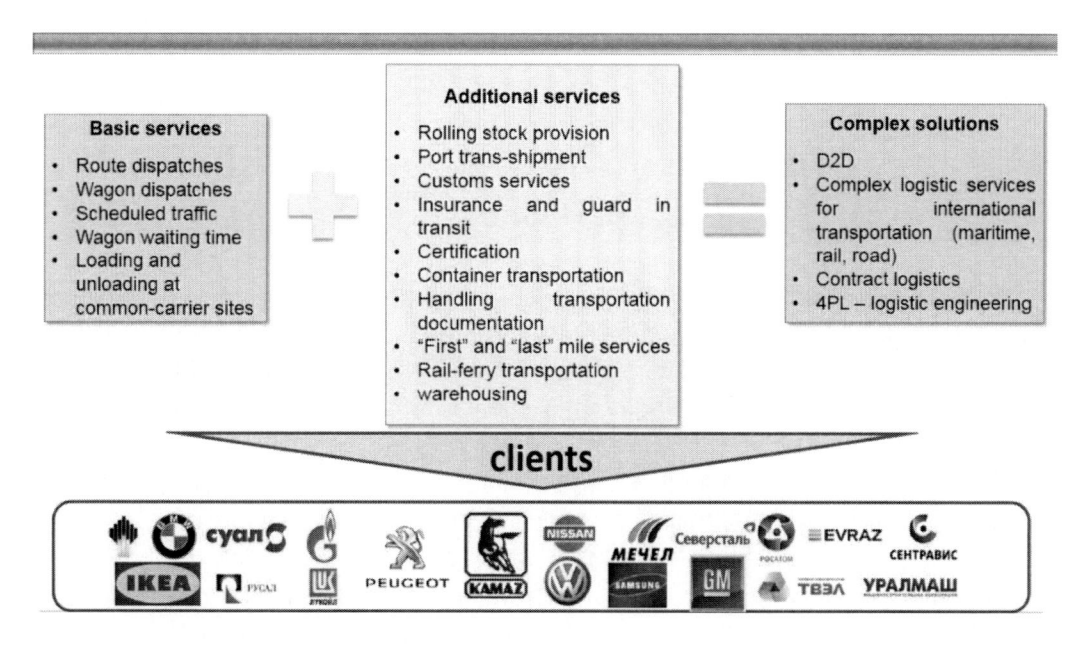

Figure 1. Freight services of JSC Russian Railways.

Digital transformation based on a life cycle model can bring significant benefits since it ensures the integration of all processes and the achievement of high productivity and sustainability of the transport system and the entire supply chain.

It is important to bear in mind that lack of resources (caused by a number of objective and subjective reasons) makes it impossible to keep up the required operational level of modern COTOs, which are to be usable in cases of faults, accidents, or disasters, and thus are to be sustainable. For this purpose it is possible to recommend new methods of proactive management, which are accompanied by intentional reconfiguration of COTOs and provide a complex system forecast and higher efficiency, basing on a large array of electronic data. Proactive management connects a physical object (infrastructure) with COTO's life-cycle processes using digital information-communication technologies.

Proactive COTO infrastructure management unlike traditionally used reactive management (aimed at the rapid reaction and further avoidance of incidents) implies prevention of incidents basing on creating in a monitoring and managerial system principally new forecasting and preventing opportunities in the formation and implementation of managerial activities basing on the system (complex) modeling (Guzzella and Sciarretta 2007; Novikov 2016; Sokolov et al., 2014).

Now there are various types of organizing proactive monitoring and COTO management, including proactive technologies of managing structural dynamics of managing the objects concerned. These technologies include: changing ways and aims of COTO functioning, their content, the operational sequence in various conditions, relocating elements and subsystems of COTOs, redistribution and decentralization of functions, tasks, management algorithms, information flows between COTO levels, using flexible (shortcut) technologies of COTO management, structural reconfiguration of COTOs in case of degradation (Demoly et al., 2013; Hicks and McGovern 2009).

3. RESULTS

Proactive (preventive) monitoring and management technologies in a COTO can be considered as prospective technologies in managing the complexity of compound systems (transportation-logistic objects), thanks to which the objects remain sustainably operational at carrying out tasks in the forecast conditions to the required degree.

The modern development of international transportation and progressive transportation-logistics technologies implies using several transport modes with its interaction with different life-cycle stages, which characterizes a transport system as capable of effective cooperation due to geographical and functional diversification and autonomy of separate supply chain stages. Introducing modern technologies, including new through digital technologies in the near future will be aimed not only at cutting costs, increasing reliability and safety of all stages, but also at mobile compatibility of transportation life-cycle processes.

High efficiency of transport is directly linked to both structure (processes) of enterprises, and the equipment and production assets used, which are employed at different life-cycle stages of systems. All this increases the complexity of COTOs, which include transportation and transportation-logistics services (Prinz, Kreggenfeld, and Kuhlenkötter 2018).

Each transportation-logistics system is based not only on using new transportation technologies at a single enterprise of a network, dealing with receiving, handling and delivery to the final customer, but also on the creation of numerous models of sustainable interaction life-cycle. Integration of transportation-logistics processes and production assets included into infrastructure (terminals, warehouses, lifting and transportation equipment, rolling-stock, etc) provides for higher growth of the productivity of the whole system, and not single employees and workstations.

Thus methodology, technological solutions and tools of organizational interaction based on proactive management should be based on integrated new generation transportation-logistic systems (ITLS) combining subsystems of transportation-logistics services, supply stages and provide sustainability and client orientation at a more efficient level. That is one of the priorities of cyber-physical systems, provided for in the strategy of the Industry 4.0 (Tantik and Anderl 2017; Mohd Ali et al., 2019; Meyer and Davis 2004; Issa et al., 2018).

The formation and introduction of high-quality and complex systems of freight handling based on the integration of transport network members is to be based on adaptivity, safety and sustainability. A highly-effective ITLS is based on coordination and interaction of enterprises at the life-cycle stages "design – operation- operational control – check-up and correction – management system monitoring". This framework forms the life-cycle processes of proactive management. This direction is aimed at providing not only the sustainability of transport but also the competitive infrastructure of the Russian national economy. Possibly types of COTO stages based on structural dynamics methodology are presented in Figure 2.

Thus, a task is set and solved not only to cut expenses at each stage of a supply chain but also to carry out a complex assessment of transportation-logistics infrastructure. Due to this, a balance should be found between stability (equilibrium) and reconfiguration of processes between different life-cycle models shown in Table 1 (Zezulka et al., 2018).

A new technological framework known as Industry 4.0 provides for further integration of a network of machines that will be able to autonomously change production patterns, keeping up high efficiency. The increased integration of "intelligent" works into industrial and transport infrastructure will mean much lower energy consumption and higher labor productivity.

The creation of digital technologies M2M (Machine-to-Machine) and IoT (Internet of Things) will enable logistic companies to develop supply chain management systems and enterprise management systems via machine interaction technologies (Pipia et al., 2019). M2M-technology enables a remote device to transmit to the data processing center the data about a monitored object – COTO.

Table 1. Structure types in structural dynamics

Types of multi-structure conditions / Structure types	jth level of ITLS and FMIS				
	$S_0^{(j)}$	$S_1^{(j)}$	...	$S_K^{(j)}$	
Topological structure			...		The diagram of structural changes in ITLS and FMIS
Technological structure			...		
Technical structure			...		
Software and mathematical provision structure			...		
Information provision structure			...		
Organizational structure			...		

4. DISCUSSION

However, the main challenge is not to increase information volume and automation via cyber-physical (robot-oriented) systems, but to form the management of self-governance, which is the most effective way to resist uncertainty (risks) of the environment), to support COTO's structures and functions in new models of life-cycle management. That is why the priority directions in the digital transformation of the IT sphere are the strategy of adaptive and proactive systems, adaptive management, and adaptive enterprise (Elphick and Beer 1981).

Central to the toolkit of such systems is the restructuring of the digital process control of pilot projects focused on engineering approaches (Bolsunovskaya et al., 2019).

The priority of the range of tools in such systems and enterprises is improving the life-cycle management processes. Under these conditions, the efficiency will first of all depend on its success in developing innovative technologies and adaptive enterprises (see Figure 2).

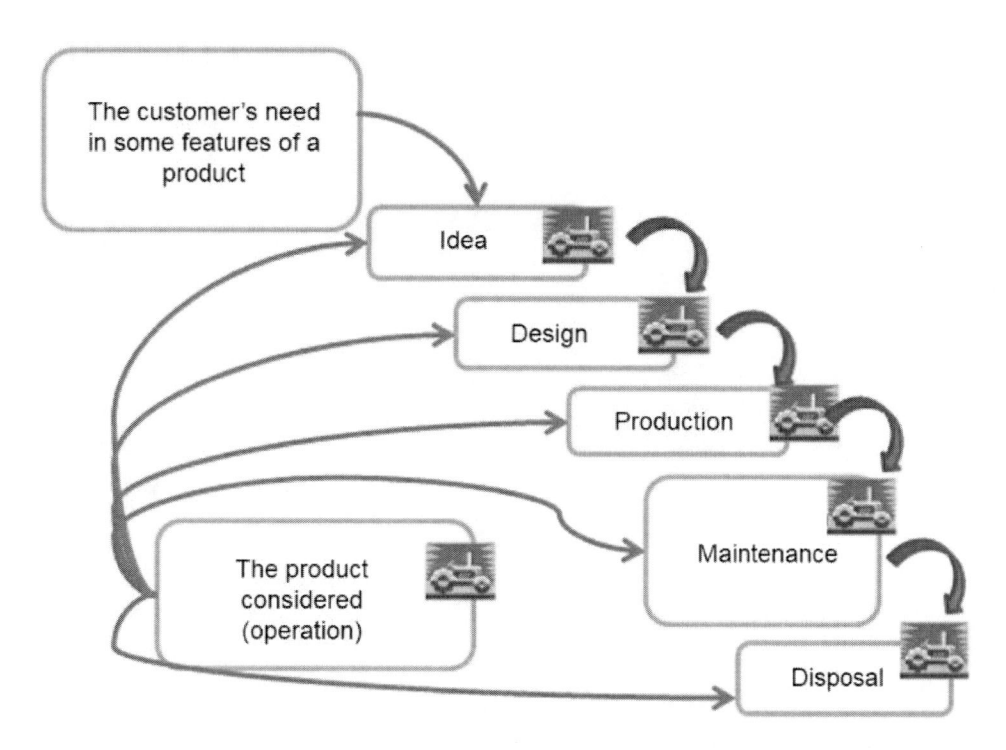

Figure 2. Life-cycle transformation of infrastructure equipment.

CONCLUSION

Thus, considering the problem of transformation of integrated transport and logistics systems into a "digital" environment, it is necessary to create a new look and characteristics of ITLS, which should correspond to global changes taking place in the modern world, based on the strategy of Industry 4.0 and digital transformation of processes as an IT sphere, and the transport and logistics sector. This will create conditions for the adaptation of the transport and logistics infrastructure to the modern service-oriented sector of the Russian economy.

New COTO-forming principles should be aimed at national security and sustainable transport development. The priority among business models of "knowledge economy" and logistical technologies should go to ITLS life-cycle management models with a long time-line. One of the main ideas of the life cycle management system is the effective use of a consistent representation of the system and its environment in initially incompatible organizational and technical systems (objects) of the digital supply chain.

This approach is global in nature and creates new opportunities for the digital transformation of transport and logistics infrastructure while implementing the concept of Industry 4.0. The main driving force in global transport systems is the need for highly efficient ICT and transportation processes based on the use of logistics engineering integration methods, which ensures the complexity of management and growth of TLS productivity, which determines the most optimal level of integration of ICT technologies and business in the digital supply chain.

REFERENCES

"About Priority Directions of Development of Transport and Logistics Business of the Holding "RZD." Transformation of the Business Model of the Holding "RZD." n.d. Accessed February 4, 2021. https://cargo.rzd.ru/.

Barykin, Sergey Yevgenievich, Irina Vasilievna Kapustina, Sergey Mikhailovich Sergeev, Olga Vladimirovna Kalinina, Viktoriia Valerievna Vilken, Yuri Yevgenievich Putikhin, and Lydia Vitalievna Volkova. 2021. "Developing the Physical Distribution Digital Twin Model within the Trade Network." *Academy of Strategic Management Journal* 20 (1): 1–24. https://www.abacademies.org/articles/developing-the-physical-distribution-digital-twin-model-within-the-trade-network.pdf

Bolsunovskaya, Marina, Svetlana Shirokova, Aleksandra Loginova, and Michail Uspenskij. 2019. "The Development and Application of Non-Standard Approach to the Management of a Pilot Project." *IOP Conference Series: Materials Science and Engineering* 497 (1). https://doi.org/10.1088/1757-899X/497/1/012024.

Bulatova, Nadezhda, Evdokia Dugina, Elena Dorzhieva, and Maria Siniavina. 2019. "Technology for Determining Strategic Directions for the Development of a Regional Transport and Logistics System under Digitalization." In *ACM International Conference Proceeding Series*. https://doi.org/10.1145/3372177.3373353.

Colombo, Armando W., Stamatis Karnouskos, Okyay Kaynak, Yang Shi, and Shen Yin. 2017. "Industrial Cyberphysical Systems: A Backbone of the Fourth Industrial Revolution." *IEEE Industrial Electronics Magazine*. https://doi.org/10.1109/MIE.2017.2648857.

Demoly, Frédéric, Olivier Dutartre, Xiu Tian Yan, Benoît Eynard, Dimitris Kiritsis, and Samuel Gomes. 2013. "Product Relationships Management Enabler for Concurrent Engineering and Product Lifecycle Management." *Computers in Industry*. https://doi.org/10.1016/j.compind.2013.05.004.

Elphick, Clive H., and Stafford Beer. 1981. "Brain of the Firm." *The Journal of the Operational Research Society*. https://doi.org/10.2307/2581406.

Grant, Delvin. 2016. "Business Analysis Techniques in Business Reengineering." *Business Process Management Journal*. https://doi.org/10.1108/BPMJ-03-2015-0026.

Guzzella, Lino, and Antonio Sciarretta. 2007. *Vehicle Propulsion Systems: Introduction to Modeling and Optimization. Vehicle Propulsion Systems (Second Edition): Introduction to Modeling and Optimization.* https://doi.org/10.1007/978-3-540-74692-8.

Hicks, Christian, and Tom McGovern. 2009. "Product Life Cycle Management in Engineer-to-Order Industries." *International Journal of Technology Management*. https://doi.org/10.1504/IJTM.2009.024913.

Issa, Ahmad, Bumin Hatiboglu, Andreas Bildstein, and Thomas Bauernhansl. 2018. "Industrie 4.0 Roadmap: Framework for Digital Transformation Based on the Concepts of Capability Maturity and Alignment." In *Procedia CIRP*. https://doi. org/10.1016/j.procir.2018.03.151.

Meyer, Christopher, and Stan Davis. 2004. "It's Alive: The Coming Convergence of Information, Biology, and Business." *Choice Reviews Online*. https://doi.org/10. 5860/choice.41-6633.

Mohd Ali, Munira, Rahul Rai, J. Neil Otte, and Barry Smith. 2019. "A Product Life Cycle Ontology for Additive Manufacturing." *Computers in Industry* 105: 191–203. https://doi.org/10.1016/j.compind.2018.12.007.

Nekrasov, A. G., and A. S. Sinitsyna. 2020. "Digital Transformation Infrastructure and Transportation Logistics Systems." In *IOP Conference Series: Materials Science and Engineering*. https://doi.org/10.1088/1757-899X/832/1/012052.

Novikov, Dmitry A. 2016. *Cybernetics: From Past to Future CYBERNETICS: From Past to Future*.

Pipia, Luca, Jordi Muñoz-Marí, Eatidal Amin, Santiago Belda, Gustau Camps-Valls, and Jochem Verrelst. 2019. "Fusing Optical and SAR Time Series for LAI Gap Fillingwith Multioutput Gaussian Processes." *Remote Sensing of Environment*. https://doi.org/10.1016/j.rse.2019.111452.

Prinz, Christopher, Niklas Kreggenfeld, and Bernd Kuhlenkötter. 2018. "Lean Meets Industrie 4.0 - A Practical Approach to Interlink the Method World and Cyber-Physical World." In *Procedia Manufacturing*. https://doi.org/10.1016/j.promfg. 2018.03.155.

Scholz-Reiter, B., J. Kolditz, and T. Hildebrandt. 2009. "Engineering Autonomously Controlled Logistic Systems." *International Journal of Production Research*. https://doi.org/10.1080/00207540701581791.

Sokolov, Boris V., Vyacheslav A. Zelentsov, Olga Brovkina, Victor F. Mochalov, and Semyon A. Potryasaev. 2014. "Complex Objects Remote Sensing Forest Monitoring and Modeling." In *Advances in Intelligent Systems and Computing*. https://doi.org/10.1007/978-3-319-06740-7_37.

Tantik, Erdal, and Reiner Anderl. 2017. "Potentials of the Asset Administration Shell of Industrie 4.0 for Service-Oriented Business Models." *Procedia CIRP* 64: 363–68. https://doi.org/10.1016/j.procir.2017.03.009.

Yakovlev, Andrei, Tatyana Lebedeva, Svetlana Malyutenkova, and Natalya Kepp. 2019. "Methodological Fundamentals of Quality Management Theory in Condition of Digital Economy." In *IOP Conference Series: Materials Science and Engineering*. https://doi.org/10.1088/1757-899X/497/1/012136.

Zezulka, F., P. Marcon, Z. Bradac, J. Arm, T. Benesl, and I. Vesely. 2018. "Communication Systems for Industry 4.0 and the IIoT." *IFAC-PapersOnLine*. https://doi.org/10.1016/ j.ifacol.2018.07.145.

In: Global Challenges of Digital Transformation of Markets ISBN: 978-1-53619-754-9
Editors: E. de la Poza and S. E. Barykin © 2021 Nova Science Publishers, Inc.

Chapter 6

BUSINESS PROCESS TRANSFORMATION IN AIR CARGO LOGISTICS

Benjamin Bierwirth[*], Robert Brylka and Ulrich Schwanecke

Hochschule RheinMain, Wiesbaden, Germany

ABSTRACT

Recently, urgent shipments of medical equipment around the world to curb the Covid-19 pandemic have emphasized once more the relevance of air cargo logistics. Unlike the passenger section of aviation where almost all consumer directed processes have been digitized during the last decade processes in air cargo are still very manual. In this paper, we want to demonstrate, therefore, for air cargo how an integrated approach using different digitized technologies may help in transforming ground handling processes. In the project, a comprehensive camera-based barcode scanning AI-algorithm was developed to identify multiple shipments on a pallet while being loaded and in motion. The barcode scanning has proven to be very robust, thus a high reliability could be achieved. Additionally, a cloud platform was set up to enhance transparency for the logistics planner as well as the receiving logistics partner. The cloud platform also serves to trigger and manage an automated truck which transports the goods between the supply chain partners. In addition, the cloud platform is meant to relieve the logistics planner from time-consuming manual re-planning tasks and gives the supply chain partners an ex-ante information enabling short-term down-side supply chain optimization. While the overall operation of the concept could be proven further developments in autonomous driving are needed before a complete process-automatization can be achieved.

Keywords: business process transformation, camera-based barcode reading, artificial intelligence, air cargo

---

* Corresponding Author's Email: benjamin.bierwirth@hs-rm.de.

1. INTRODUCTION

1.1. Air Cargo Business Processes

Air cargo is the fastest mode of transport and very reliable, but also the most expensive. Usually, the relevance of air cargo can be highlighted by the fact that it is used for roughly a third of the value in global cross-border logistics while at the same time covering less than five percent in terms of weight or volume. In these days, the relevance of air cargo has become even clearer when the Covid-19 pandemic has required many urgent transports of medical equipment. Beside urgent shipments, air cargo is used for products with high values or of volatile market demand.

As a rule, an air cargo transport chain consists of several companies: a forwarder, several trucking companies, and at least an airline (a detailed description of processes and partners can be found in (Brylka, Schwanecke, and Bierwirth 2020) and (Bierwirth et al. 2019)). Usually, air cargo networks are designed as hub-and-spoke-networks meaning that all air cargo shipments from a certain region are consolidated at one hub airport from where they are flown to another airport in the destination region. From there, the shipments are then transported to their ultimate destination. Unlike the networks of global express companies such as UPS, FEDEX or DHL which usually have their own hubs and own aircrafts, air cargo is flown in dedicated freighters and in the belly holds of passenger planes. Most passenger airlines make use of the extended business model transporting air cargo with their passenger planes.

As shipments are usually transported on crates or pallets special loading equipment is needed for the safe and efficient transport in aircrafts. On behalf of the airline, a cargo handling agent takes care of the consolidation and safe packaging of various air cargo shipments for one flight. Prior to that, bigger forwarders operating their own warehouses at hub airports consolidate all air cargo shipments for one region (e.g., all shipments from Europe with a destination in South Korea are consolidated). With bigger shipments the rate per kg decreases.

Air cargo handling requires a lot of flexibility being a volatile network with m:n-connections between forwarders and carriers with changing Origin-to-Destination-demands. Within Europe, the forwarder networks rely on trucking to the hub airport. Due to traffic situations (traffic jams, accidents) some trucks may not arriveon time at the hub. As a result, some shipments cannot be consolidated in the forwarder hub and the ground handling agent has to face deviations between the booking (number of pieces, weight, dimensions) and the actual delivered cargo.

Shipments have to be delivered to the cargo handling agent before the so-called Latest Acceptance Time, LAT. This is inevitable for the handling agent to process shipments and to avoid delays. It is, however, prone to create unwelcome peaks at the hand-ling agents facilities.

What is more, information quality and information exchange within the supply chain partners has been found to be quite weak, so each partner focuses on the optimization of processes within his own domain. Thus, the overall business process with its low level of digitization turns out to be quite inefficient.

Our SmartAirCargoTrailer project aims to improve this business process with the combination a several digitized technologies because neither existing solutions such as the automated handling and sorting systems of the courier, express and parcel (CEP) service providers cannot cope with the variation of air cargo shipment sizes and weights.

In this paper we describe our approach and the results of a first real-life test with a smart trailer to optimize transparency, costs and quality in this ground handling process.

We first briefly describe the related work, and then present our method which includes an in-depth description of the process and an overview of the technologies and solutions we used. In the Evaluation chapter we describe the tested scenarios and the results. Finally, we give a short conclusion and discuss possible future work.

1.2. Related Work

While there is a large number of publications in the field of aviation, the majority of papers focus on passenger transport. In the field of air cargo many papers address network optimization problems or present approaches to improve the load planning or consolidation problem. The advantages of information sharing in supply chain management has been document in several publications as well. In the following we give a brief overview on relevant literature which specifically address the ground handling processes in air cargo.

Feng et al. give an overview on air cargo operations (Feng, Li, and Shen 2015). The air cargo supply chain with a focus on the processes between forwarders and cargo handling agents can be found (Bierwirth and Schocke 2017). An airport classification defined in (Mayer 2016) can be used to identify cargo hubs. Lange analyses the reasons for departure delays caused by air cargo operations (Lange 2019). Liu et al. develop a model to calculate costs of flight delays caused by late package deliveries (Liu, Yin, and Hansen 2019). Selinka et al. provide an analytical solution for truck handling at air cargo terminals (Selinka, Franz, and Stolletz 2016) while Azadian et al. formulate an algorithm to optimize air cargo pick-up and deliveries (Azadian, Murat, and Chinnam 2017). Brandt and Nickel focus on the planning problem of air cargo (Brandt and Nickel 2019). Detailed analyses or approaches for certain processes in the air cargo supply chain can be found in (Monse 2002; Chan et al. 2006; Yan, Shih, and Shiao 2008; Lau et al. 2009; Bierwirth 2009). A more specific description of the processes and the concept of the SmartAirCargoTrailer project can be found in (Bierwirth et al. 2019).

While AGVs (Automatic Guided Vehicle) are common in production since decades, applications in transport are rare. The AGVs of Container Terminal Altenwerder (CTA) in Hamburg are centrally managed in a closed environment without other vehicles or human beings around and they navigate with the help of transponders in the ground (Ranau 2011). (DHL Trend Research 2014) gives an overview of AGVs already applied. While platooning is tested to increase efficiency on highways (Ellwanger and Wohlfarth 2017), autonomous trucks are deployed in on-site applications delivering goods from one building to another or in moving swap bodies ("DB Schenker Tests Automated 'Wiesel' Swap-Body Transporter I Deutsche Bahn AG" n.d.).

(Sörös and Flörkemeier 2013) and (Namane and Arezki 2017) describe state of the art method to localize barcodes. A deep learning based localization pipeline is developed in (Hansen et al. 2017). Concepts to deblur and sharpen barcode images are described in (Yahyanejad and Ström 2010) and (Kupyn et al. 2018). A detailed description of the developed algorithm can be found in (Brylka, Schwanecke, and Bierwirth 2020).

2. MATERIALS AND METHODS

Our project was focused on ground handling processes in air cargo logistics, especially short distance transports between a forwarder hub warehouse and an airline cargo handling agent facility.

Typically, the total process duration for these transports is several hours although driving is less than 30 minutes. The remaining time consists of waiting, documents processing, and checking unloaded cargo (completeness, damages). Many times, differences between documents and the actual (unloaded) pieces occur. As transports take place shortly before the Latest Acceptance Time (LAT) missing pieces have to be searched at the forwarder facility under high time pressure. Otherwise the complete shipment will miss its flight. This increases the time pressure both on the forwarder and the cargo handling agent (as the latter tries to process the late delivered missing pieces). Damages, wrong loadings or other mistakes lead to an increase of quality issues and a decrease of efficiency. Ongoing processes have to be stopped to search for the missing pieces and extra transports have to take place to deliver the missing pieces.

As already mentioned, the planning and operation of down-stream supply chain processes suffer from the lack of information. For example, in exports heavy shipments are placed on the bottom of an air cargo pallet and lighter shipments are put on top. As many shipments arrive only shortly before LAT, work on the air cargo pallets could only start when enough shipments and esp. the heavy ones are delivered. The cargo handling agent receives booking information from the airline, but quite often the no-show-rate or differences between the shipment and the bookings occur. As a result, planning based on booking figures is not feasible.

Import-wise, the challenges are comparable: As only few import shipments are time-critical the forwarder focuses on status updates for these shipments and organizes an extra transport (which is inefficient as other import shipments will not be picked up as the forwarder has not monitored their status).

Our project SmartAirCargoTrailer is meant above all to optimize the short distance transport process. In detail, any quality problems should be detected at the origin warehouse. Additionally, costs should be minimized. To achieve these objectives our approach basically consists of minor changes in the process and the combination of three technologies: Camera-based barcode scanning, cloud platform for transparency and steering and autonomous trucks. The principle is shown in Figure 1.

2.1. Changes in the Process

We decided to use a swap-body to allow for a direct loading of all shipments that are ready to be transported (see Figure 2). In today's process the shipments are buffered close to the truck dock. Shortly before LAT, a truck is ordered which will be then loaded with all shipments that have been buffered. As the employees rush to achieve delivery prior to LAT erroneous loadings occur. To directly load the swap-body allows for more time to identify and to correct mistakes. This concept implies, however, that one truck dock would be constantly blocked for these short-distance transports. From an efficiency point of view, its advantage is the increased utilization of the truck as it only has to load or unload the swap-body instead being idle during the complete loading process which can easily take up to 30 minutes.

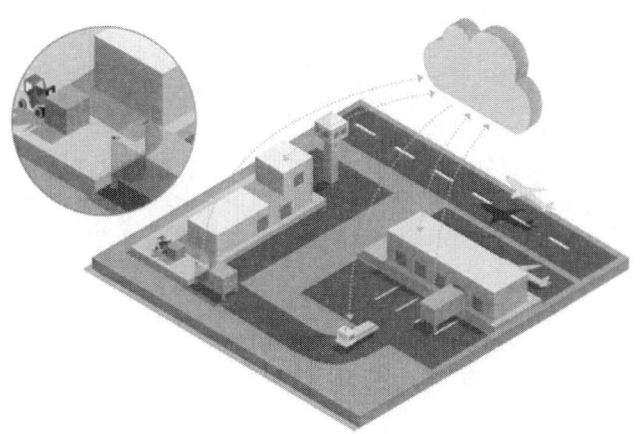

(Source: Fraunhofer IML).

Figure 1. Overview of the SmartAirCargoTrailer concept.

Figure 2. SmartAirCargoTrailer swap body in front of the forwarder warehouse.

Preferably, the labels of all shipments should be clearly readable on the outside as they cannot be read from the camera-based barcode scanning system. Typically, this would not require any change as most warehouse management system operate with barcode scanners and require the scanning of each shipment, after being taken out of an rack.

Beside these changes no changes to the material handling equipment (e.g., forklifts) and their operation were required.

2.2. Camera-Based Barcode Scanning

AWB labels consist of a barcode. To avoid process interruption ensuring the identification of all processed shipments scanning while being loaded into the truck is necessary. As multiple shipments are loaded at a time (on a crate with a forklift) typical barcode scanning solutions are not suitable. Additionally, the width and heights of a truck loading ramp has to be covered (2.5 x 2.5 m). Forklifts operate with up to 20 km/h, so the shipments and the barcodes show a lot of movement.

A setup with five12 megapixel cameras was needed to cover all sides (Figure 3). But even with high resolution cameras and high frame rates the images of the barcodes are blurred. To optimize image quality and to increase data processing, an AI-based solution was developed. In (Brylka, Schwanecke, and Bierwirth 2020) our AI-based image processing pipeline is described in detail.

We decided to install the camera system into a swap-body trailer to ensure flexibility and to make sure no changes to the warehouse were necessary. As the swap-body has no power supply a battery system was installed which allowed for a shift long operation of the system.

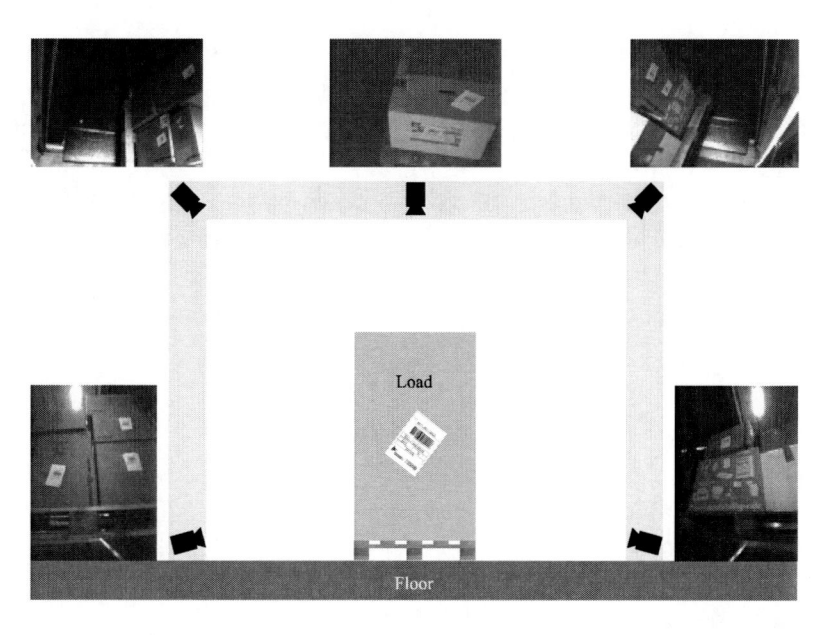

Figure 3. Schematic setup of the camera system. The cargo is monitored by five cameras.

Once a movement is detected by one of the cameras the recording and barcode identification algorithm starts. Identified barcodes will then be sent to the cloud platform for further processing. As we focused on the AWB numbers only other detected barcodes on shipments (e.g., the product EAN barcode or barcodes on forwarder labels) were discarded.

2.3. Cloud Platform

The cloud platform is the central data processing hub with a web-based frontend. Prior to the loading a load plan is uploaded. All planned shipments are indicated in grey. The camera-system transmits the detected barcodes to the cloud which indicates which shipments have been loaded. Complete shipments (all pieces loaded) are shown in green. Shipments only parts of which have been loaded, with still some pieces missing, are indicated in orange. Wrong shipments are indicated in red.

The information and loading status is available for the forklift driver, the operations manager and the down-stream supply chain partner. So quality issues at the outbound facility (in exports the forwarder) can be identified immediately and solved before the truck leaves the warehouse. At the same time, the down-stream partner receives reliable data to prepare the following consolidation and packing processes.

The cloud platform manages the truck operation: Based on multiple criteria, a truck will be ordered to pick up the swap-body. In the simplest case, the truck will be ordered when loading is complete (all shipments on the uploaded list are loaded). The platform would also trigger a warning to the operations manager if the LAT of a loaded shipment has been reached. If the operations manager does not react, the transport will be triggered anyway although the loading is not complete. This is to avoid that time-critical shipments miss their flight. A transport could be also triggered if the swap-body is full. For the import process a transport could be triggered if one or a list of urgent shipments are loaded.

However, the cloud platform offers the down-stream supply chain partner, the cargo handling agent, also the possibility to manually trigger a transport. This could be warranted if the cargo handling agent wants to reduce the peaks before LAT and wants to start pre-building air cargo pallets which would require heavy shipments first.

2.4. Autonomous Truck

To further increase efficiency a conventional truck will be replaced by an autonomous truck. Besides being cost-intensive, there is an increasing truck driver shortage in Germany which is a challenge for trucking companies. As the transports are very short, the job is even less attractive.

Tests of highly automated driving on closed, non-public areas have been reported already in the past ((Stahn, Stark, and Stopp 2007) and (Meinel 2018)). The CargoCity South of Frankfurt Airport which we have chosen as testbed may be considered a follow-up on this line of development. On the one hand this area is private area with controlled entry, on the other hand all kinds of vehicles can be operated there. Thus, transports between one forwarder hub and two cargo handling agents could be tested under real-time conditions.

3. RESULTS

3.1. Test Scenarios

After being tested under laboratory conditions and with a small-scale demonstrator with just one camera (see Figure 4), testing in a real-world scenario and full scale was being planned.

To verify our setup prior to the tests the dimensions and location of the barcode labels on 117 shipments were measured. The maximum of each dimension was less than 250 cm, while the mean was 110 cm in length, 78 cm in width and 94 cm in height. 18 pieces had their label placed on the top side. While the maximum height was 95 cm, the minimum was only 30 cm. The average height was 56 cm. For the other 99 pieces, the label position was at least 25 cm above the ground and a maximum height of 187 cm. The average was 81 cm.

Figure 4. Installation in the laboratory at the House of Logistics and Mobility (HOLM) (Left) and small-scale demonstrator with one camera at Transport Logistic trade fair in Munich (Right).

Figure 5. Pallet with test shipments while being loaded onto the smart trailer.

Although copies of real labels and comparable boxes and pallets were used, the testing had to take place with dummy freight due to insurance issues. The dummy shipments were set up in their dimensions and the location of the labels to resemble real air cargo pieces.

We have created a total of five scenarios which always included one export transport and one import transport. Each test required the loading and unloading of five pallets with mostly six boxes each (an example is shown in Figure 5). For all scenarios, a loading list with the expected AWBs was uploaded in the cloud platform.

In the first two scenarios, one AWB consists of two pieces (boxes) which are loaded on the same pallet. Ideally, after moving a pallet through the camera gate three AWBs would be detected, each with a piece count of two. The second scenario differed from the first as the LAT of shipment would trigger the transport whereas in the first scenario the completion of the list only would trigger the transport.

Scenario 3 and 4 had one AWB where the two pieces are loaded on two different pallets. After loading the first of the pallets this AWB remains orange with a piece count of 1 and will only be completed with the loading of the second pallet with the missing piece. The difference of scenario 4 consists in the triggering by the downside supply chain partner instead of the algorithm.

Scenario 5 presents some challenges for the automatic detection as one pallet with two small pieces had the labels placed on top. One pallet contained a piece with an AWB that is not on the list (to verify the misloading identification function). And the remaining three pallets had the labels positioned in a challenging form (only partly visible, labeled around a corner).

On the last testing day, various real shipments are tested with the camera system. This is foreseen as a standalone test without the cloud platform. While the detection and identification results were generated immediately the verification was done afterwards.

Beside the detection rate qualitative data are gathered through a short survey conducted among the logistics employees, mainly the forklift drivers.

Figure 6. Example of a real shipment with six pieces being tested on the last day.

The transports were planned between the forwarder facility and two cargo handling agents. Due to the unavailability of the planned autonomous truck a conventional swap body mover was used. We installed a tablet computer on the forklifts which did the loading or unloading so that the web-frontend was visible for the driver. A mobile hotspot made the internet connection for the tablet and the camera system. The tests took place from Sep, 2nd till Sep, 11th 2019.

Table 1. Test results per scenario

Scenario	Total number of barcodes	Number of barcode readings	Detection rate
1 (Sep, 2nd)			
Loading Export	30	30	100%
Unloading Export	*Technical problem*		
Loading Import	30	29	97%
Unloading Import	30	28	93%
2 (Sep, 3rd)			
Loading Export	30	30	100%
Unloading Export	30	29	97%
Loading Import	30	29	97%
Unloading Import	30	29	97%
3 (Sep, 4th)			
Loading Export	28	26	93%
Loading Export (2nd run)	28	26	93%
Unloading Export	28	26	93%
Loading Import	28	27	96%
Unloading Import	*Technical problem*		
4 (Sep, 9th)			
Loading Export	*Technical problem*		
Unloading Export	23	20	87%
Loading Import	24	23	96%
Unloading Import	24	21	88%
5 (Sep, 10th)			
Loading Export	23	21	91%
Unloading Export	23	21	91%
Loading Export (2nd run)	23	20	87%
Unloading Export (2nd run)	23	20	87%
Loading Import	23	19	83%
Unloading Import	23	22	96%
Real cargo shipments (Sep, 11th)			
Loading/Unloading	21	14	67%
Total numbers	**552**	**510**	**92%**

3.2. Results of the Camera-Based Barcode Scanning

During the tests a total of 552 pieces were loaded or unloaded. Of these 510 labels were identified correctly which equals a detection rate of 92 per cent. Table 1 shows the detection rate of each test event. Three tests had to be canceled due to problems with the mobile network (no connection).

The analysis of the missed barcode labels revealed a number of reasons – some of them could be solved with an improved algorithm.

- Two pieces where the labels were placed exactly at the same height were sometimes identified as only one piece (the label with less recognition being discarded by the algorithm as a misreading). A better position tracking of the labels will help to reduce these errors.
- Labels on the front were not detected reliably which was due to the motion detection, which triggered the image processing algorithm. The system identified the moving pallet too late and took only very few pictures (which are then also very blurred and distorted due to their position) which made the analysis quite challenging. The algorithm and the camera position were updated after the cause was identified.
- Damaged labels, labels which were bend around a corner and labels which were mostly concealed could not be read. These errors would have also occurred with a traditional barcode scanner.

4. Discussion

The results of test showed that the camera system is reliable. Nevertheless human interaction would still be needed for extraordinary shipments or if barcodes are not readable. The first step therefore is the elimination of the manual barcode scanning of outgoing shipments, which would increase efficiency in the warehouse where it is applied. The automated triggering of truck transports based on completeness or LAT relieves the transport manager from a time consuming task, which is prone to errors. Therefore efficiency and quality can be increased. The two effects mentioned above represent an approach to automation based on digitization, but do not qualify as a full business process transformation.

The tests with the autonomous truck were successful, but showed room for improvement. A short to midterm implementation of autonomous trucks – even in this simplified environment – seems not realistic. The truck was able to automatically dock at the warehouse and do all the required maneuverings, but in congested traffic situations where other trucks would park or stop outside designated parking spaces the limits of todays technology and algorithms become visible. Outside the yard switching lanes or intersections represent challenges. The test with the conventional truck showed that the concept already improves truck efficiency.

To transform the whole business process a more pull oriented supply chain thinking has to develop. Especially the down-stream supply chain partners have to leverage the value of the information flow. By pulling heavy shipments once they are ready, peak situations at the facility of the handling agent can be avoided. Import-wise the number of transports could be reduced significantly if the forwarder pulls all shipments that passed the customs process and not the specially monitored urgent ones.

CONCLUSION

The approach has the potential to significantly improve the short-distance transportation although autonomous driving requires still a lot of further research. The tests have shown that even with a conventional truck transportation could be improved. The cloud platform shows a lot of potential for better collaboration and an improved supply chain, but more time and more research will be necessary for this advanced process to become the standard procedure.

Most promising in our project appears the camera system we have developed to deliver high detection rates without interfering with the process. A follow-up project has already being started to detect and take into account more shipment attributes (such as Dangerous Goods labels and dimensions). The information gained through the cameras could be furthermore used for claims management as the automatically taken pictures prove the condition of the shipments on arrival and departure of a facility.

To leverage the full potential of the business transformation described here legal regulation regarding air cargo security has to be changed in order to complement today´s existing requirements of in-person presentation of shipment documentation. In view of the acceleration of digitization and contact-free processes triggered by the present Covid-19 pandemia hopes as to the further development in business process transformation such as presented here for the field of air cargo may not be unwarranted.

ACKNOWLEDGMENTS

This work is part of the research project Smart AirCargo Trailer funded by Landes-offensive zur Entwicklung Wissenschaftlich-ökonomischer Exzellenz (LOEWE 3). We gratefully acknowledge the cooperation partners Cargo Steps GmbH & Co. KG, Fraport AG, Fraunhofer Institute for Material Flow and Logistics, LUG Aircargo Handling GmbH, and Sovereign Speed FRA GmbH.

REFERENCES

Azadian, Farshid, Alper Murat. & Ratna Babu Chinnam. (2017). "An Unpaired Pickup and Delivery Problem with Time Dependent Assignment Costs: Application in Air Cargo Transportation." *European Journal of Operational Research*. https://doi.org/ 10.1016/j.ejor.2017.04.033.

Bierwirth, Benjamin. (2009). "Optimierung Der Sicherheits- Kontrolle i Dn Er u L Ftfracht- Transportkette [Optimization of security controls in the freight transport chain]." *Vortrag Gehalten Auf Dem Kolloquium "Luftfracht Und Luftsicherheit,"* no. November.

Bierwirth, Benjamin. & Kai-Oliver Schocke. (2017). "Lead-Time Optimization Potential of Digitization in Air Cargo." *Digitalization in Supply Chain Management and Logistics*.

Bierwirth, Benjamin, Ulrich Schwanecke, Thomas Gietzen, Daniel Andrés López. & Robert Brylka. (2019). "SmartAirCargoTrailer: Autonomous Short Distance Transports in Air Cargo." In *Hamburg International Conference of Logistics (HICL) 2019*.

Brandt, Felix. & Stefan Nickel. (2019). "The Air Cargo Load Planning Problem - a Consolidated Problem Definition and Literature Review on Related Problems." *European Journal of Operational Research*. https://doi.org/10.1016/j.ejor.2018. 07.013.

Brylka, R., Schwanecke, U. & Bierwirth, B. (2020). "Camera Based Barcode Localization and Decoding in Real-World Applications." *2020 International Conference on Omni-Layer Intelligent Systems (COINS)*, 1–8.

Chan, Felix T. S., Rajat Bhagwat, Kumar, N., Tiwari, M. K. & Philip Lam. (2006). "Development of a Decision Support System for Air-Cargo Pallets Loading Problem: A Case Study." *Expert Systems with Applications*. https://doi.org/10. 1016/j.eswa.2005.09.057.

"DB Schenker Tests Automated 'Wiesel' Swap-Body Transporter I Deutsche Bahn AG [DB Schenker Tests Automated 'Wiesel' Swap-Body Transporter I Deutsche Bahn AG]." n.d. Accessed February 5, 2021. https://www.deutschebahn.com/en/presse/ press_releases/DB-Schenker-tests-automated-Wiesel-swap-body-transporter- 3183398.

DHL Trend Research. (2014). *Self-Driving Vehicles in Logistics. DHL Customer Solutions & Innovation*. http://www.dhl.com/content/dam/downloads/g0/about_us/ logistics_insights/dhl_self_driving_vehicles.pdf.

Ellwanger, S. & Wohlfarth, E. (2017). "Truck Platooning Application." In *IEEE Intelligent Vehicles Symposium, Proceedings*. https://doi.org/10.1109/ IVS.2017.7995840.

Feng, Bo, Yanzhi Li. & Zuo Jun Max Shen. (2015). "Air Cargo Operations: Literature Review and Comparison with Practices." *Transportation Research Part C: Emerging Technologies*. https://doi.org/10.1016/j.trc.2015.03.028.

Hansen, Daniel Kold, Kamal Nasrollahi, Christoffer B. Rasmusen. & Thomas B. Moeslund. (2017). "Real-Time Barcode Detection and Classification Using Deep

Learning." In *IJCCI 2017 - Proceedings of the 9th International Joint Conference on Computational Intelligence*. https://doi.org/10.5220/0006508203210327.

Kupyn, Orest, Volodymyr Budzan, Mykola Mykhailych, Dmytro Mishkin. & Jiři Matas. (2018). "DeblurGAN: Blind Motion Deblurring Using Conditional Adversarial Networks." In *Proceedings of the IEEE Computer Society Conference on Computer Vision and Pattern Recognition*. https://doi.org/10.1109/CVPR.2018.00854.

Lange, Anne. (2019). "Does Cargo Matter? The Impact of Air Cargo Operations on Departure on-Time Performance for Combination Carriers." *Transportation Research Part A: Policy and Practice*. https://doi.org/10.1016/j.tra.2018.10.005.

Lau, H. C. W., Chan, T. M., Tsui, W. T., Ho, G. T. S. & Choy, K. L. (2009). "An AI Approach for Optimizing Multi-Pallet Loading Operations." *Expert Systems with Applications*. https://doi.org/10.1016/j.eswa.2008.03.024.

Liu, Yulin, Mogeng Yin. & Mark Hansen. (2019). "Economic Costs of Air Cargo Flight Delays Related to Late Package Deliveries." *Transportation Research Part E: Logistics and Transportation Review*. https://doi.org/10.1016/j.tre.2019.03.017.

Mayer, Robert. (2016). "Airport Classification Based on Cargo Characteristics." *Journal of Transport Geography*. https://doi.org/10.1016/j.jtrangeo.2016.05.011.

Meinel, Holger H. (2018). "Radarsensors and Autonomous Driving—Yesterday, Today and Tomorrow!" *Elektrotechnik Und Informationstechnik*. https://doi.org/10.1007/s00502-018-0627-2.

Monse, Michael. (2002). "Regionalisierung Bodenschutzbezogener Daten in Brandenburg [Regionalization of soil protection-related data in Brandenburg]." *International Journal of Phytoremediation*. https://doi.org/10.1080/03650340212668.

Namane, Abderrahmane. & Madjid Arezki. (2017). "Fast Real Time 1D Barcode Detection from Webcam Images Using the Bars Detection Method." In *Lecture Notes in Engineering and Computer Science*.

Ranau, Michael. (2011). "Planning Approach for Dimensioning of Automated Traffic Areas at Seaport Container Terminals." *Operations Research/ Computer Science Interfaces Series*. https://doi.org/10.1007/978-1-4419-8408-1_10.

Selinka, Gregor, Axel Franz. & Raik Stolletz. (2016). "Time-Dependent Performance Approximation of Truck Handling Operations at an Air Cargo Terminal." *Computers and Operations Research*. https://doi.org/10.1016/j.cor.2014.06.005.

Sörös, Gábor. & Christian Flörkemeier. (2013). "Blur-Resistant Joint 1D and 2D Barcode Localization for Smartphones." In *Proceedings of the 12th International Conference on Mobile and Ubiquitous Multimedia, MUM 2013*. https://doi.org/10.1145/2541831.2541844.

Stahn, Roland, Tobias Stark. & Andreas Stopp. (2007). "Laser Scanner-Based Navigation and Motion Planning for Truck-Trailer Combinations." In *IEEE/ASME International Conference on Advanced Intelligent Mechatronics, AIM*. https://doi.org/10.1109/AIM.2007.4412422.

Yahyanejad, Saeed. & Jacob Ström. (2010). "Removing Motion Blur from Barcode Images." In *2010 IEEE Computer Society Conference on Computer Vision and Pattern Recognition - Workshops, CVPRW 2010.* https://doi.org/10.1109/CVPRW.2010.5543258.

Yan, Shangyao, Yu Lin Shih. & Fei Yen Shiao. (2008). "Optimal Cargo Container Loading Plans under Stochastic Demands for Air Express Carriers." *Transportation Research Part E: Logistics and Transportation Review.* https://doi.org/10.1016/j.tre.2007.01.006.

In: Global Challenges of Digital Transformation of Markets ISBN: 978-1-53619-754-9
Editors: E. de la Poza and S. E. Barykin   © 2021 Nova Science Publishers, Inc.

Chapter 7

STRUCTURING INDICATORS IN ASSESSING THE EFFECTIVENESS OF DIGITAL TRANSFORMATION OF LOGISTICS

Irina V. Sukhorukova[*], Gennady P. Fomin and Denis A. Maksimov

Plekhanov Russian University of Economics, Moscow, Russia

ABSTRACT

The relevance of the study is due to the practical need for an optimal set of criteria for assessing digital transformation in logistics that satisfies many contradictory constraints and criteria. The subject of the research is the mechanisms of communication between indicators for assessing digital transformation in management systems and optimization of material flows and services and related information and cash flows. This will allow solving the problem as an integral management tool. The optimal solution contributes to the achievement of strategic, tactical or operational goals of the business due to the efficient from the standpoint of minimizing costs and meeting the requirements of end users for the quality of goods and services in managing material and service flows, as well as related flows of information and financial resources. To solve the problem, there are various optimization methods, each of which has both advantages and disadvantages. In this regard, a research task arises to use the advantages and eliminate the disadvantages in the form of a composition of methods in multi-criteria optimization. Therefore, the purpose of this study is to combine the methods of system analysis and various mathematical methods in combination with the methods of multi-criteria optimization for the formation of criteria for assessing digital transformation in logistics. In this regard, it became necessary to develop a methodology that allows finding a variety of solutions in

[*] Corresponding Author's Email: suhorukovaira@yandex.ru.

service nodes. As a result, an algorithm for structuring indicators for assessing the effectiveness of digital transformation in logistics was built.

Keywords: digital transformation in logistics, structuring indicators, multi-criteria, target function

1. INTRODUCTION

The digital revolution is rapidly coming to every country. The fourth industrial revolution and the digital economy will be difficult for emerging economies, so the risks may be more opportunities to realize competitive advantages (Junge and Straube 2020; Kayikci 2018; Evtodieva et al., 2019; Cozmiuc and Petrisor 2018). It is very important to choose for the digital development of Russia only what can be predictably and profitably implemented (Aleksandrov, Fedorova, and Parshukov 2020; Irina V. Sukhorukova and Chistiakova 2018; Zeltser et al., 2019; Irina Sukhorukova and Chistyakova 2019; Ordanini and Pol 2001; Chaudhuri, Monteleoni, and Sarwate 2011). This circumstance is due to the fact, that we are at the very beginning of the industrial transformation, and the impact cannot be predicted (Ma et al., 2018; Chako 2000; De Bernardi et al., 2020; Galstyan et al., 2019). Of course, highly developed and modern transport and logistics resources are key factors in the country's economic competitiveness. Roads, railways, the inland waterway system, seaports and airports facilitate the unification of production, agricultural and resource areas, centers of population and employment, and international exchanges. Maintaining and improving efficient transport and logistics infrastructures for the movement of people and goods continues to be important in national and global markets, given the projected population growth and the inevitable dramatic changes in industry, energy, especially in the oil, gas and agricultural sectors (Rudenko, Rodionova, and Stepanova 2019; Lyapina, Tarasova, and Fedotova 2020; I Sukhorukova and Chistiakova 2018). The movement of goods and production components between manufacturers, the growth of urban logistics, international supply chains and logistics are already at the intersection of phenomena such as the digital economy (Treiblmaier 2018; Zekos 2003; Gorlov et al., 2020; Parshukov, Aleksandrov, and Fedorova 2020; Kharin, Kuzin, and Mnatsakanyan 2019; Balashova and Maiorova 2020; Makarenko et al., 2018). It should be noted that in each final product, logistics accounts for 10%, and in the Russian economy about 20%. Logistics costs vary greatly and can be negligible for purely digital products sent over the Internet up to 60%, such as oil.

2. MATERIALS AND METHODS

The subject of the research is the mechanisms of communication between indicators for assessing digital transformation in management systems and optimization of material flows and services and related information and cash flows. Methodology: a set of logically linked methods for movement and goal achievement: evaluating the effectiveness. This will allow solving the problem as an integral management tool. The optimal solution contributes to the achievement of strategic, tactical or operational goals of the business due to the efficient from the standpoint of minimizing costs and meeting the requirements of end users for the quality of goods and services in managing material and service flows, as well as related flows of information and financial resources. To solve the problem, there are various optimization methods, each of which has both advantages and disadvantages. In this regard, a research task arises on the use of advantages and elimination of disadvantages in the form of a composition of methods in multicriteria optimization. Therefore, the purpose of this study is to combine the methods of system analysis and various mathematical methods in combination with the methods of multi-criteria optimization for the formation of criteria for assessing digital transformation in logistics. In this regard, it became necessary to develop a methodology that allows finding a variety of solutions in service nodes. From an economic point of view, we consider several objective functions, each of which has an optimal solution for its eigenvalues of independent variables. As a conceptual model for managing the digital transformation of logistics, it is advisable to propose the following scheme: People – Information – Product - Profit.

In this regard, it is necessary to form and combine into a single whole in the logistics management system: competitive employees, competitive information and competitive products. The economy is always based on human capital, which is the main driving force behind the socio - economic development of modern society. It is necessary to integrate it into a single whole as a system, which is possible by creating its structure according to strict rules of structuring and quantification. The success of the participants in logistics operations is assessed according to different indicators. The desire to see everything and immediately indicates the need to build relationship trees according to groups of structure levels, to determine their intermediate criteria, which are ultimately combined into a criterion for assessing the effectiveness of digital transformation of logistics. It is important to note that the proposed method makes it possible to use both qualitative and quantitative indicators and, through their weight convolution, arrive at the unification of indicators of any group.

3. RESULTS

The scale of research in logistics is truly enormous. To imagine and cover the movement of continuous flows of different physical nature directly only in Russia with its network of railways, river and sea routes, automobile, informational not only on the internet, but especially money, is not very easy, but necessary. You can cover this volume by concentrating tracking of benchmarks that allow you to assess the effectiveness of digital transformation in logistics. The proliferation of digital technologies encourages companies in the transport industry to analyze their market opportunities and study the competitive environment to determine potential growth opportunities. Companies must continually create conditions to serve their customers. The fact that order fulfillment and return is still part of the business process, even if e-commerce is used, explains why successful e-commerce implementations are associated with logistics companies. Physical objects are constantly being moved, processed, stored, sold, delivered and used around the world.However, trucks and containers often leave half-loaded and often return empty, and road freight services have an overall efficiency of less than 10%. This inefficiency has a huge impact on the environment and on the profitability of both the manufacturer and the carrier. Products are mostly stored in networks of warehouses and distribution centers and are not available quickly, nor with low transport costs, nor are they where they are needed. The modern economy is highly dependent on transport and logistics. This leads to a sharp increase in freight traffic. So in France for the period up to 2025, an increase in freight traffic is expected by 37%.

In the process of merging the virtual and real worlds, a hybrid world will be formed in which the Internet of things and augmented reality will dominate. The main result of the digital transformation of the economy is that organizations of all types need to learn how to use a new combination of computers, information and communication technologies and human knowledge in order to remain competitive in the global market. Companies must continually scan their environment to create new ways to serve their customers, and this requires tracking criteria.

The success of the participants in logistics operations is assessed by criteria. The main criterion for assessing the efficiency of the logistics system is the amount of logistics costs in the supply chain management by the formation of profit when the material flow passes through the supply chain. The analysis of the effectiveness of logistics activities can be carried out by correlating the profits and losses incurred arising in the supply chain. The criteria for evaluating efficiency include the following: General logistics costs. The level of quality of the logistics service. The aggregate performance of the organization. The cumulative duration of logistic operations. The quality of the logistics activities carried out and the level of logistics service. The total costs can be divided according to their area of origin: Internal and external operating costs. Administration costs of the logistics system. Costs associated with logistic risks. Logistics costs can be classified by functional area: Transport costs. Warehouse costs. Handling costs. Inventory management costs. Order management costs. Operating costs of automated systems. Costs for the formation and maintenance of stocks of raw materials and materials. Costs for the maintenance and sale of finished products. However, the main costs are inventory management and shipping costs. The criterion for assessing the effectiveness of the logistics system is the quality indicator of the logistics service provided and is determined by assessing the satisfaction of consumer expectations. Compliance with the terms of service provision with the terms declared by the client. Warranties for the services provided. Complete fulfillment of contractual obligations. Ease of establishing contact with the service provider. Correctness of personnel in the provision of services. The next indicator of the efficiency of the functioning of the logistics system is the indicator - return on investment in the logistics infrastructure. Reflects the efficiency of investments in logistics divisions, such as: storage facilities (warehouses of various types and purposes, cargo terminal and terminal complexes); transport units of various types of transport; transport communications (roads and railways, railway access roads, etc.); repair and auxiliary units serving transport and storage facilities; telecommunication system, information and computer system. In general, to assess the effectiveness of a logistics system, it is necessary to evaluate it as an integral organism, with functioning connections both within the system and outside it. Consequently, the efficiency of the logistics system is reflected in the availability of stocks, productivity, the quality of the logistics service provided, as well as the efficiency of investments in the infrastructure of the system. At the same time, technology and model innovations related to digitalization are transforming the transport industry in terms of increasing its efficiency and increasing the possibilities for shaping the architecture of the transport logistics of the future. Therefore, the problem arises of assessing the effectiveness of digital transformation of logistics, taking into account the above criteria and indicators.

To solve this problem, there are various methods of multicriteria optimization, each of which has both advantages and disadvantages. In this regard, a research task arises to use the advantages of existing methods and eliminate the disadvantages in the form of a composition of methods in carrying out multi-criteria optimization. There are mathematical methods that make it possible to justify the choice of a solution in multi-criteria conditions. However, the researcher is interested in such a method that would take into account the opinion of the participants in logistics operations, therefore, the solution to the problem begins with an extensive survey of all participants in the performance of logistics operations from start to finish. Thus, a list of indicators-characteristics of logistics is typed. Then, using the principles of systems analysis - structuring and quantification, we build the structure of the system of indicators, distributing them into groups with an indication of the links between them. Based on the data presented, we determine the weight of the indicators of the digital transformation of logistics, we use, for example, the method of paired comparisons, according to which the element of paired comparison is determined as follows:

$$b_{ij} \begin{cases} 1, \text{ if the compared characteristics are equivalent in importance;} \\ 2, \text{ if the } i^{th} \text{ characteristic is more important than the } j^{th} \text{ characteristic;} \\ 0, \text{ if the } i^{th} \text{ characteristic is less important than the } j^{th} \text{ characteristic.} \end{cases} \qquad (1)$$

then we calculate the sum of points for each indicator:

$$S_i = \sum_{j=1}^{n} b_{ij} \qquad (2)$$

and we determine the weight of each individual indicator:

$$M_i = \frac{S_i}{n^2} = \frac{S_i}{49} \qquad (3)$$

In this case, it is necessary to take into account the fulfillment of an additional condition:

$$\sum_{i=1}^{n} M_i = 1,0 \qquad (4)$$

In different groupings of indicators and options for application, this method ultimately allows you to build a hierarchical structure of a system of indicators for digital transformation of logistics. In this system, it is obvious that the indicators of the upper level are emerging and highlighted, which means the particular integral criteria. These particular criteria are suitable for assessing the effectiveness of the digital transformation of logistics. There are mathematical methods that allow, under these conditions, multi-criteria, nevertheless, to justify the choice of a solution. Of course, a solution that would simultaneously satisfy all conflicting requirements, as a rule, does not exist, which means that the decision is made in conditions of risk. For the first time this problem of multicriteria optimization arose in the work of the Italian economist V. Pareto during a mathematical study of commodity exchange in the trade process. To solve it, methods have been developed based on the folding of criteria, indicators or characteristics, where instead of a set of particular criteria, one scalar criterion is considered, obtained by combining particular criteria. Distinguish between multiplicative and additive methods of criteria folding. We assume that the criteria are commensurable, for example, the vector of the weighting coefficients of the criteria characterizing the importance of each criterion is normalized and determined, then a new objective function is constructed and the scalar criterion optimization problem is solved. In this case, the method of moving from multiple indicators P1,P2,...Pn to one given by a new function of the form called convolution or generalized criterion method, where Mj are weight coefficients, and their sum.

$$Q = \sum_{i-1}^{n} MiPi \qquad (5)$$

$$\sum_{i=1}^{n} M_i = 1,0 \qquad (6)$$

The more Mj the more the j-th criterion makes a contribution to the generalized criterion Q. It should be noted, that the greater the value of the Pj criterion, then this is not always good, for example, costs versus profits, therefore it is necessary to enter a point assessment of these criteria Bi (pi). On the scale "worse – better," where indeed the higher the value of the score Bi (pi), the better the indicator. Therefore, in order to avoid errors, it is necessary for objectivity purposes to introduce a 5 or 10 point scale for assessing qualitative and quantitative indicators with a gradation of intervals from bad (0) to the best (10). Then the scalar criterion optimization problem is solved. It can be proved that solving a problem with a scalar criterion is efficient for the problem. Then we reasonably find an integral assessment of the effectiveness of digital transformation of logistics according to the model:

$$Q(a_i) = \sum_{i=1}^{n} M\,i \times Б_i(p_i) \tag{7}$$

4. DISCUSSION

To get to this model, a huge amount of work must be done beforehand. First of all, it is necessary to depict a geographical map of the movement of flows: products, financial and information, then the service nodes in which service indicators appear: service waiting time, queue length, service time, service intensity, time spent in the system. This necessitates the use of methods of queuing theory in cooperation with methods of graph theory, which will provide the solution of stream problems of minimum cost and the horizon of objectivity in the formation of solutions. As a result of the study, a mechanism for a comprehensive analysis of the effective functioning of the logistics system is proposed. The developed algorithm makes it possible to evaluate it as an integral organism, with functioning connections both within the system and outside it. The efficiency of the logistics system is reflected in the availability of stocks, productivity, the quality of the logistics service provided, as well as the efficiency of investments in the system infrastructure. At the same time, innovations, technologies and models associated with digitalization are transforming the transport industry in terms of increasing its efficiency and increasing the possibilities for shaping the architecture of transport logistics of the future.

CONCLUSION

The practical significance lies in the fact that an algorithm for structuring indicators is proposed to form an integral assessment of the effectiveness of digital transformation of logistics, taking into account multi-criteria, attracting mathematical methods and models for large-scale control at all levels of management and ensuring equal awareness, objectivity and openness of mutual understanding on the state of logistics by all participants in the process, both top and bottom with the ability to change the scope of the problem.

REFERENCES

Aleksandrov, Igor, Marina Fedorova, and Alexey Parshukov. 2020. "E-Commerce in Russian Rural Areas as a Tool for Regional Development." In *E3S Web of Conferences.* https://doi.org/10.1051/e3sconf/202017513046.

Balashova, E. S., and K. S. Maiorova. 2020. "Analysis of Directions of Digital Technologies Introduction into Industrial Complex." *St. Petersburg State Polytechnical University Journal. Economics* 13 (2): 18–29.

Bernardi, Paola De, Danny Azucar, Canio Forliano, and Mattia Franco. 2020. "Innovative and Sustainable Food Business Models." In *Contributions to Management Science.* https://doi.org/10.1007/978-3-030-33502-1_7.

Chako, George K. 2000. "Synergizing Invention and Innovation for Missions and Markets." *Asia Pacific Journal of Marketing and Logistics.* https://doi.org/10.1108/13555850010764686.

Chaudhuri, Kamalika, Claire Monteleoni, and Anand D. Sarwate. 2011. "Differentially Private Empirical Risk Minimization." *Journal of Machine Learning Research.*

Cozmiuc, Diana, and Ioan Petrisor. 2018. "Industrie 4.0 by Siemens: Steps Made Next." *Journal of Cases on Information Technology.* https://doi.org/10.4018/JCIT.2018010103.

Evtodieva, T. E., D. V. Chernova, N. V. Ivanova, and N. S. Kisteneva. 2019. "Logistics 4.0." In *Contributions to Economics.* https://doi.org/10.1007/978-3-030-11754-2_16.

Galstyan, A. G., L. M. Aksyonova, A. B. Lisitsyn, L. A. Oganesyants, and A. N. Petrov. 2019. "Modern Approaches to Storage and Effective Processing of Agricultural Products for Obtaining High Quality Food Products." *Herald of the Russian Academy of Sciences.* https://doi.org/10.1134/S1019331619020059.

Gorlov, Ivan F., Gilyan V. Fedotova, Alexandra V. Glushchenko, Marina I. Slozhenkina, and Natalia I. Mosolova. 2020. "Digital Technologies in the Development of the Agro-Industrial Complex." In *Lecture Notes in Networks and Systems.* https://doi.org/10.1007/978-3-030-29586-8_26.

Junge, Anna Lisa, and Frank Straube. 2020. "Sustainable Supply Chains - Digital Transformation Technologies' Impact on the Social and Environmental Dimension." In *Procedia Manufacturing.* https://doi.org/10.1016/j.promfg.2020.02.110.

Kayikci, Yasanur. 2018. "Sustainability Impact of Digitization in Logistics." In *Procedia Manufacturing.* https://doi.org/10.1016/j.promfg.2018.02.184.

Kharin, Alexander, Vladimir Kuzin, and Albert Mnatsakanyan. 2019. "Innovations and Digital Transformation of the Russian Fishery Complex." In *ACM International Conference Proceeding Series.* https://doi.org/10.1145/3372177.3373354.

Lyapina, Svetlana, Valentina Tarasova, and Marina Fedotova. 2020. "Problems of Analyst Competency Formation for Modern Transport Systems." *Transport Problems.* https://doi.org/10.21307/TP-2020-021.

Ma, Yixuan, Zhenji Zhang, Alexander Ihler, and Baoxiang Pan. 2018. "Estimating Warehouse Rental Price Using Machine Learning Techniques." *International Journal of Computers, Communications and Control.* https://doi.org/10.15837/ijccc.2018.2.3034.

Makarenko, S. A., N. Sukhina, S. M. Krymov, S. V. Martynenko, and A. Adamenko. 2018. "*Testing Economic Systems of Capitalist Countries by the World Economic Crisis.*" In.

Ordanini, Andrea, and Annalisa Pol. 2001. "Infomediation and Competitive Advantage in B2b Digital Marketplaces." *European Management Journal.* https://doi.org/10.1016/S0263-2373(01)00024-X.

Parshukov, Aleksey, Igor Aleksandrov, and Marina Fedorova. 2020. "Developing the Sector of Remote Services in Rural Areas to Raise the Employment and Care of the Environment." In *E3S Web of Conferences.* https://doi.org/10.1051/e3sconf/202021707027.

Rudenko, Andrey, Valentina Rodionova, and Valeriya Stepanova. 2019. "*Social Fears in the Context of Security Concern: Social and Philosophical Analysis.*" In, 1144–55. https://doi.org/10.1007/978-3-319-90835-9_129.

Sukhorukova, I., and Natalia A. Chistiakova. 2018. "Economic Regulation And Mathematical Modeling Of Insurance Product Cost Method." *Regional Science Inquiry*, 195–203.

Sukhorukova, Irina, and Natal'ya Chistyakova. 2019. "Insurance of the Termination Risk of Projects with Joint Companion Activity." *Journal of Reviews on Global Economics* 8 (499): 269–74. https://doi.org/10.6000/1929-7092.2019.08.23.

Sukhorukova, Irina V., and Natalia A. Chistiakova. 2018. "Optimization of the Formation of the Capital Structure of the Insurance Company, Taking into Account the National Specifics of Insurance." *Journal of Reviews on Global Economics.* https://doi.org/10.6000/1929-7092.2018.07.12.

Treiblmaier, Horst. 2018. "The Impact of the Blockchain on the Supply Chain: A Theory-Based Research Framework and a Call for Action." *Supply Chain Management.* https://doi.org/10.1108/SCM-01-2018-0029.

Zekos, Georgios I. 2003. "MNEs, Globalisation and Digital Economy: Legal and Economic Aspects." *Managerial Law.* https://doi.org/10.1108/03090550310770875.

Zeltser, R. Ya., O. Bielienkova, Ye. V. Novak, and D. Dubinin. 2019. "Digital Transformation of Resource Logistics and Organizational and Structural Support of Construction." *Science and Innovation* 15: 34–46.

In: Global Challenges of Digital Transformation of Markets ISBN: 978-1-53619-754-9
Editors: E. de la Poza and S. E. Barykin   © 2021 Nova Science Publishers, Inc.

Chapter 8

DIGITAL TRANSFORMATION CHALLENGES IN SUPPLY CHAIN MANAGEMENT: A CASE STUDY OF ALPINE BIOMEDICAL

Poonam Chauhan[1,], Atishay Choudhary[1,**] and Anisha Padiyar[1,***]*

[1]K. J. Somaiya Institute of Management, Mumbai, India

ABSTRACT

The performance of business is improved upon by digital transformation as world today is increasingly interconnected. The increasingly competitive marketplace requires firms to adopt digital technologies to expand and manage their present position. The healthcare diagnostic devise sector is no exception and has embraced digitization across different verticals to remain agile and adaptive. The cost optimization strategy for healthcare services at global level have been targeting the diagnostic device and testing industry.

Alpine Biomedicals Industries is engaged in developing manufacturing and marketing of broad range of rapid tests in India.. It has expertise in biotechnology and IVD (In vitro diagnostics) and has taken initiatives towards the digital transformation of its supply chain to meet the industry demands. The case illustrates their efforts to move to digital processes and the challenges in execution. At the same time, it showcases their customary and traditional Diagnostic devices production is being challenged by developing prerequisites, such as more participative health care services empowered by the adoption of digital supply chain which guarantee to accomplish small impressions and more accurate results.

Keywords: Point of Care Diagnostics, Digital Supply Chain, Customer Centricity

---

[*] Corresponding Author's E-mail: poonam@somaiya.edu.
[**] Corresponding Author's E-mail: atishay.c@somaiya.edu.
[***] Corresponding Author's E-mail: anisha.padiyar@somaiya.edu.

1. INTRODUCTION

Alpine Biomedicals Pvt Ltd is an ISO 9001:2015 & WHO GMP certified company engaged in developing, manufacturing and marketing of broad range of rapid tests in India. The tests are used for In-vitro diagnosis of hormones and human diseases. Their product range includes rapid test for detection of Malaria Antigen, Malaria Antibody, HCG/Pregnancy, Syphilis, Salmonella typhi, Dengue and Chikungunya (Appendix 1, Appendix 2). These test products are CE certified for professional use and have been widely accepted in Indian Markets. Alpine biomedicals also have a self-contained R&D and QC lab. (Appendix 3).

Alpine Biomedicals are Customer centric for which they focus on improving the products and processes to enhance the quality of finished product and being cost competitive. They also provide OEM (Original Equipment Manufacturing) services which helps their customers to focus on marketing and revenue generation for their brand. The OEM services include products like uncut sheets, semi-finished goods, branded OEM specific design.

Customers who got benefits form Alpine OEM Specific design:

- HLL Life care;
- Kerala medical services corporation ltd.;
- Gujarat Pradesh corporation ltd.;
- Medisure pvt. Ltd;
- Surya laboratories;
- Magnum 350 laboratories;
- Vikath life care.

1.1. Biomedical Diagnostic Industry

Diagnostic devices are devices used to identify the nature or cause of a certain phenomenon, usually related to a medical condition ("UST Global and Gravity Supply Chain Solutions Join Hands to Deliver an Integrated Single Platform for End-to-End Supply Chain Visibility" n.d.).

Examples of diagnostic devices are magnetic resonance imaging apparatuses, temperature sensors or pacemakers. The Biomedical Diagnostic Industry consists of medical devices for Point of Care diagnostics under In-vitro Diagnostic markets and In vivo Diagnostics. Point of care diagnostics includes Glucometer, blood pressure monitors, oxymeters, pregnancy tests, etc. In vivo diagnostic devices include endoscopy or pacemakers. The Key players in the Point of care diagnostics and testing are AccuBio Tech, Roche, Danaher, Abbott, Siemens, Nova Biomedical and Johnson & Johnson. Bill and Melinda Gates foundation launched Cepheid's platform for Tuberculosis in India ("Fortune Business Insights™|Global Market Research Report &

Consulting" n.d.). The challenges with POC delivery is that the diagnostics have to be miniaturized modified and adapted which becomes expensive and difficult which can slow down commercialization.

1.2. Innovation at Alpine Biomedicals

As stated earlier the working at Alpine Biomedicals is engaged to add value to the customers experience at affordable pricing and innovations (Appendix 4). With the advent of Technology and accessibility to internet connection and smart phones, data tracking and storage in simplified and classified manner has become very convenient (Roussel, Kuenn and Schoepke 2002). Alpine Biomedicals has also jumped on the movement of Digitalization and has swapped their old supply chain practices of procurement and distribution with new online and web-based systems.

Post the transformation to the digital supply chain process, they garnered quite a few achievements, some of the recent accolades ("Covid-19 IgG/IgM Antibody Test - Alpine" n.d.) are as follows:

- They worked as sub-contractor and manufactured more than 20 million HCG test kits for HLL Lifecare Ltd. (A Govt. Of India Enterprise) Product Name – Nishchay
- They manufactured more than 4 million Malaria Pf/Pv Test kits in Single Quarter for a Govt. Tender
- They also developed COVID-19 IgG/IgM Antibody test which is approved from ICMR-NIV Pune

2. MATERIALS AND METHODS

The traditional supply chain had limited visibility, lacked real time data updates, couldn't adapt to changing times and less responsive to changing market conditions.

2.1. Business Process: Supply Chain Management

Designing effective supply chain structures provides competitive advantages for the companies. It can improve the bottom line by significantly reducing the costs of carrying inventory. It is expected to be sustainable and resilient (Büyüközkan and Berkol 2011). The supply chain is no longer linear but an integrated network of nodes that are well matched and paired (Lewis and Voehl 2020; Samal 2019; Supply and Survey 2013). These improvements lead to better production and sales forecast, just in time inventory and operational efficiency (Heinbuch 1995).

Further, the digital transformation of supply chain can enhance the capability to reach the market in short span of time, fulfilling customer expectation while reducing cost and improve visibility of supply chain (Korpela, Hallikas and Dahlberg 2017; Nasiri et al. 2020; Garay-Rondero et al. 2019). The digital SCM consists of the Intelligent Control Tower which manages monitors, makes decisions and manages execution across functions and companies to optimize the entire network. The digitization allows for balancing the inventory with fluctuating demand, factors in the risk and facilitates certainty in decision making. The digitization of SCM could range from digitize all transaction, connecting digitally with vendors and partners, replacing manual task with computers, improved visibility and tracking (Sanders and Swink 2019).

2.2. Digital Transformation of Supply Chain Management

The current supply chain management practices at Alpine Biomedicals were developed by a third-party vendor, creating value and optimally utilizing the time, manpower and finances. The other production related documents were made available. The company also follows mail order system for procurement of materials. The new system design encompasses effective upstream operation for inventory management which simplifies the raw material tracking along with superior downstream management of finished goods dispatched, new orders, sales and deliveries (Moon 2009; Sridharan, Caines and Patterson 2005). Alpine Biomedicals end user i.e., customers are Hospitals, Diagnostic Labs, Government organizations and pharmacies.This digital system ensures product safety and traceability.

Supply chains in healthcare diagnostic devices/testing kits are becoming increasingly complex especially with the significant disruption due to COVID-19 and global economic issues. The traditional supply chains have struggled to address the evolving production and customer demand. The purchase orders processing, the SKU management and delivery schedules have been pressured due to crises The digitization allows for balancing the inventory with fluctuating demand, factors in the risk and facilitates certainty in decision making (Jafarnejad et al. 2019). The digitization of SCM could range from digitize all transaction, connecting digitally with vendors and partners, replacing manual task with computers, improved visibility and tracking (McKone-Sweet, Hamilton and Willis 2005).

2.3. Goals of Digital Transformation of SCM

The goal of Digital supply chain model at Alpine Biomedicals enabled by new technology, is to differentiate their value proposition (Berman 2012) from the competitorson the following parameters:

1. End-to-end transparency- enabling visibility across the entire supply network

2. High levels of agility- driving flexible and proactive response of supply network levers
3. Connected environment- enhancing cross-functional collaboration across all partners and functions
4. Resource optimization -promoting a cohesive environment for humans and machines
5. Holistic decision making- promoting optimal network efficiency, reduced cost, and increase in revenue

The entire supply chain model then transforms into a more legitimate, dynamic, integrated supply network (Grau, Zeng and Xiao 2012; Maffia et al. 2012; Guido 2015). Ultimately, the DSCN digital core uses input from its multiple nodes to self-strengthen, thereby accelerating production, distribution, and delivery to customers by providing real-time information to make informed decisions, anticipate risks, and provide better end-to-end visibility (Skjoett-Larsen 1999). The authors also take into account the features of both trade networks' digitalization and bringing new products to market (Barykin, Bochkarev, et al. 2021; Barykin, Kapustina, Sergeev, et al. 2021).

2.4. The Procedural framework

To adopt Digital Supply Chain Network Alpine Biomedicals has worked on six fundamental procedural (Pisano 1991; Ross and Jayaraman 2009; Sarkis 2003; Christopher and Towill 2000) are described as follows:

1. Digital Development: This capability leverages technology to conceptualize, design, and launch products, ensuring cross-functional collaboration through the product lifecycle and improving design efficiency to develop high-quality products. It reduces R&D expenses and product maintenance costs and increases manufacturing flexibility. Reduction in manual intervention results in fewer errors, delays, and inefficiencies, which help the company respond quickly to changing customer requirements.
2. Synchronized Planning: This capability aligns strategic business objectives with financial goals and operational plans across various functions within the business. This helps to effectively anticipate customer demand and optimize inventory in the overall network.
3. Intelligent Supply: This capability helped in more effectively collaborate with strategic partners and improve the customer and supplier experiences by adopting advanced electronic platforms for requisitions and invoices. It also helps anticipate supply risks to proactively optimize end-to-end operations.
4. Smart Factory: This capability uses a calculated balance of human intelligence and machine intelligence to drive improvements in business

performance and worker safety based on production and demand data. Itprovides safe and ergonomic work environments for employees. Smart factories also take a proactive approach to maintenance to optimize planned downtime and predict potential outages.

5. Dynamic Fulfillment: This is an interconnected and cross-enterprise capability that enables alpine to deliver the right product to the right customer at the right time, enhancing customer experience.

Risk of product recalls due to counterfeit products is reduced as well, protecting brand reputation. It also helps enable intelligent customer order management, improving customer experience and reducing obsolescence costs.

3. RESULTS

More customized software enables Alpine Biomedical to design and execute own supply chain methodologies accurately and quickly and give much more prominent visibility into supply chain (Lambert, García-Dastugue and Croxton 2005). Ultimately which gave power to advance usage of assets and work, improve stock and delivery precision, convey the ideal request unfailingly, and react quicker to client openings and market variances (Habib 2011).

3.1. Impact of Digitized SCM at Alpine Biomedicals

The main advantages that were seen post the adoption of customized supply chain software was as follows:

1. Greater productivity without increasing manpower
2. Lower operational costs.
3. Improved pricing negotiations
4. Reduced chargeback errors.
5. Elimination of rebate overpayments.
6. Minimized regulatory violations and risk.
7. Enhance customer satisfaction.
8. Enlargement of brand image and reputation.
9. Reduced business process complexity.

Even after the many benefits come from a Digital supply chain process there were many hurdles in the way while implementing them that arose from the customer side, employee side and monetary investment and technological infrastructure up gradation which was required.

4. DISCUSSION

Following were some of the internal challenges that Alpine Biomedicals faced in adoption of digital SCM:

1. Staff Resistance- Resistance from staff can be in many forms and the reason for most often times is a fear that the business is moving away from the existing employee's core skills (Patterson, Grimm and Corsi 2003). Obsessed about being replaced by young 'digital natives' or replaced by machines and automation are enough reason for staff to resist, and in extreme cases, sabotage digital transformation efforts.

2. Non-digital customer segments- potential loss of revenue from the customers who currently rely or use traditional channels of SC to access services and engage with your organization. This is when the digital transformation has to take the risk of taking resource away from these traditional channels and favour the experimentation of new Digital channels (Ghobakhloo and Fathi 2020).

3. Decrease in usual productivity- loss of time and resource a business will incur, in diverting those assets to the digital transformation. During this period the companies has to hire more staff or generate additional investment for the transformation efforts.

4. Weak IT infrastructure to adopt digital practices.

Following were the external challenges at distributer's and customer's hospital, pharmacies, laboratories end:

1. Margin of Profit: Medical Devices have a high value per unit, however the margins are low for intermediaries this is majorly because there is supplier power at the retailers, wholesalers and manufacturers.

2. Life cycle of Product: Post the approval of process, it takes many years for the patent to develop into a product that is market ready, post the patent expiry, other alternatives enter the market, sometimes the companies reduce the price.
   Emerging technologies again shorten life cycle and creates pressure on distribution channels.

3. Inadequate Supply chain education: Lack of awareness on the concepts of Supply chain management, improper integration between all entities, makes the managers and other last mile customers ill-equipped.

Even at this moment Alpine Biomedical hasn't gone cent percent digital and still comprises of some amount of physical documentation due to habit and scared behavior of technology and fear that important bills and data may get deleted or lost.

To address this problem and to bridge the gap in varying degree of employee understanding, the company organizes Staff Trainings thrice a year to make the employees accustomed to the digital developments and make them proficient.

CONCLUSION

The digital transformation market is expected to grow at a CAGR of 22.7% from 2019 to reach $3,294 billionby 2025 ("Digital Transformation Market Is Expected to Grow at a CAGR of 22.7% to Reach $3,294 Billion by 2025 - Exclusive Report by Meticulous Research®" n.d.). It is admirable on the part of Alpine Biomedicals to have adopted the digital route in spite of the various roadblocks initially given the limitation of resources and infrastructure.

The determination to address the gaps will support in creating a sustainable roadmap that would help them achieve higher targets and volume in the coming years. The Biomedical Diagnostics Industry especially the In-vitro is Point of Care diagnostics are gaining huge popularity among the customers due to the ease of tests, small size, accurate results, rapid result, diagnosis for a variety of conditions, repeatability of certain devices and been perceived as one time investment and health tracking devices.

With the advent of the millennial era there is an immense demand of rapid efficiency and Point of Care Diagnostics to do exactly that. They currently hold a market share of USD 28.5 Billion with CAGR of 10.4%. The future would unveil if the expectations of consumer match their current perceptions.

ACKNOWLEDGMENT

We would like to thank our Corporate Guide Mr. Gaurav Garg, Head of Quality control and Quality Assurance at Alpine Biomedicals, for his guidance and facilitation along each and every step of the research. This endeavor would not have been fruitful without his constant encouragement and inputs. We have been fortunate to learn many aspects of Digital Transformation of Supply Chain Management from Alpine Biomedicals.

We would also like to express our gratitude to Mr. Sahil kalra (CEO, Alpine biomedicals Pvt Ltd) for his vital inputs and support which shaped the direction of this study. We thank the entire Alpine Biomedicals Team for giving us this opportunity to study their business processes.

We express our sincere thanks to our institute, K J Somaiya Institute of Management for consistent support and encouragement.

APPENDIX

Appendix 1. Products Manufactured at Alpine Biomedicals

- Rapid Immunochromatography test for Malaria Ag (All Forms);
- Rapid Immunochromatography test for Pregnancy;
- Rapid Immunochromatography test for Dengue IgM/IgM;
- Rapid Immunochromatography test for Dengue NS1;
- Rapid Immunochromatography test for Syphilis;
- Rapid Immunochromatography test for IgM antibodies to S.typhi;
- Rapid Immunochromatography test for COVID-19 IgM/IgM Antibody.

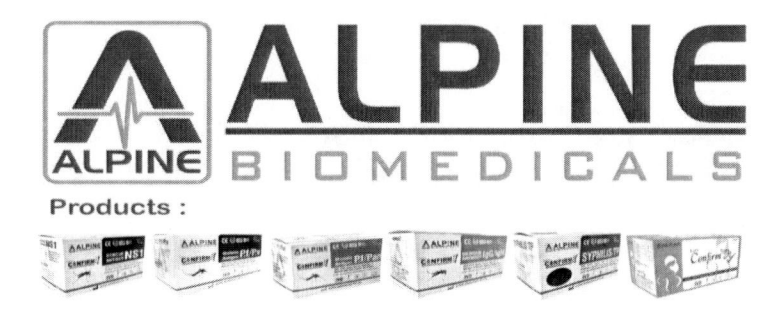

Appendix 2. Certificate of Compliance

Appendix 3. Facility Overview

Alpine Biomedicals Premises — Production Area -1 — Production Area-2 — QC Lab

Appendix 4. Approval form NIV & CDSCO

16.04.2020

Guidance on Rapid antibody kits for COVID-19

Not recommended for diagnosis of COVID-19 infection
- Can be done on blood/serum/plasma samples
- Test result is available within 30 minutes
- Test comes positive after 7-10 days of infection
- The test remains positive for several weeks after infection
- Positive test indicates exposure to SARS-CoV-2
- Negative test does not rule out COVID-19 infection

These tests are not recommended for diagnosis of COVID-19 infection

Till date, 23 antibody based rapid tests have been validated at NIV Pune, and the following were found to be satisfactory. 9 of these kits are manufactured in India.

S.No.	Kit Detail	*Lot no./Batch no.
1.	SARS-CoV-2 Antibody test (Lateral flow method): Guangzhou Wondfo Biotech, Mylan Laboratories Limited (CE-IVD) M R Roofs Private Ltd Abbott Laboratories Cadila Healthcare Limited (Zydus Cadila)	W19500309 W19500302 W19500351 W19500338
2.	COVID-19 IgM IgG Rapid Test: BioMedomics (CE-IVD)	20200226
3.	COVID-19 IgM/IgG Antibody Rapid Test: ZHUHAI LIVZON DIAGNOSTICS (CE-IVD)	CK2003010410
4.	New Coronavirus (COVID-19) IgG/IgM Rapid Test: Voxtur Bio Ltd, India	PCCV200301S
5.	COVID-19 IgM/IgG Antibody Detection Card Test: VANGUARD Diagnostics, India	RCOVID200301T
6.	Makesure COVID-19 Rapid test: HLL Lifecare Limited, India	CVCT030420 CVCT0204203 CVCT0104202
7.	YHLO iFlash-SARS-CoV-2 IgM and IgG detection kit (additional equipment required): CPC Diagnostics	20200206
8.	ACCUCARE IgM/IgG Lateral Flow Assay kit: LAB-CARE Diagnostics (India Pvt. Ltd)	CVC 200401
9.	Abchek COVID-19 IgM/IgG Antibody Rapid Test: NuLifecare	NUL/COV-19/R&D/001
10.	One Step Corona Virus (COVID-19) IgM/IgG Antibody Test: ALPINE BIOMEDICALS	A10420 A20420
11.	COVID 19 IgM/IgG Rapid Test Kit: Medsource Ozone Biomedicals (ver 2.0)	COV-002
12.	Immuno Quick Rapid Test for Detection of Novel Coronavirus (COVID-19) IgM/IgG Antibodies: Immuno Science India Pvt. Ltd	E142001
13.	Standard Q Covid -19 IgM/IgG Duo test – One Step Rapid Antibody test: SD Biosensors	E054002 E054004
14.	COVID-19 IgG/IgM Rapid Test Kit Rafael Diagnostic: BMT Diagnostics	COV20030059 COV20030059-1

*Above listed kits are validated with the mentioned batch number only. Responsibility for batch to batch consistency lies with the manufacturer.

REFERENCES

Barykin, Sergey Yevgenievich, Andrey Aleksandrovich Bochkarev, Sergey Mikhailovich Sergeev, Tatiana Anatolievna Baranova, Dmitriy Anatolievich Mokhorov, and Aleksandra Maksimovna Kobicheva. 2021. "A Methodology of Bringing Perspective Innovation Products to Market." *Academy of Strategic Management Journal* 20 (2): 19. https://www.abacademies.org/articles/a-methodology-of-bringing-perspective-innovation-products-to-market.pdf.

Barykin, Sergey Yevgenievich, Irina Vasilievna Kapustina, Sergey Mikhailovich Sergeev, Olga Vladimirovna Kalinina, Viktoriia Valerievna Vilken, Yuri Yevgenievich Putikhin, and Lydia Vitalievna Volkova. 2021. "Developing the Physical Distribution Digital Twin Model within the Trade Network." *Academy of Strategic Management Journal* 20 (1): 1–24. https://www.abacademies.org/articles/developing-the-physical-distribution-digital-twin-model-within-the-trade-network.pdf

Berman, Saul J. 2012. "Digital Transformation: Opportunities to Create New Business Models". *Strategy and Leadership*. https://doi.org/10.1108/10878571211209314.

Büyüközkan, Güçlin and Çidem Berkol. 2011. "Designing a Sustainable Supply Chain Using an Integrated Analytic Network Process and Goal Programming Approach in Quality Function Deployment". *Expert Systems with Applications*. https://doi.org/10.1016/j.eswa.2011.04.171.

"*Covid-19 IgG/IgM Antibody Test - Alpine.*" n.d. Accessed February 8, 2021. http://www.alpinebiomedicals.com/product/covid-19-igg-igm-antibody-test/.

"*Digital Transformation Market Is Expected to Grow at a CAGR of 22.7% to Reach $3,294 Billion by 2025 - Exclusive Report by Meticulous Research®.*" n.d. Accessed February 8, 2021. https://www.globenewswire.com/news-release/2020/02/05/1980062/0/en/Digital-Transformation-Market-is-Expected-to-Grow-at-a-CAGR-of-22-7-to-Reach-3-294-Billion-by-2025-Exclusive-Report-by-Meticulous-Research.html.

"*Fortune Business Insights™/Global Market Research Report & Consulting*". n.d. Accessed February 8, 2021. https://www.fortunebusinessinsights.com/.

Garay-Rondero, Claudia Lizette, Martinez-Flores, Jose Luis, Smith, Neale R., Caballero Morales, Santiago Omar and Aldrette-Malacara, Alejandra. 2019. "Digital Supply Chain Model in Industry 4.0". *Journal of Manufacturing Technology Management*. https://doi.org/10.1108/JMTM-08-2018-0280.

Ghobakhloo, Morteza and Fathi, Masood. 2020. "Corporate Survival in Industry 4.0 Era: The Enabling Role of Lean-Digitized Manufacturing". *Journal of Manufacturing Technology Management*. https://doi.org/10.1108/JMTM-11-2018-0417.

Grau, David, Lei Zeng and Yang Xiao. 2012. "Automatically Tracking Engineered Components through Shipping and Receiving Processes with Passive Identification Technologies". *Automation in Construction*. https://doi.org/10.1016/j.autcon.2012.05.016.

Guido, Ron. 2015. "Creating a Supply Chain in the New Age of Commerce". *EBN Online.*

Habib, Mamun. 2011. "Supply Chain Management (SCM): Theory and Evolution". In *Supply Chain Management - Applications and Simulations.* https://doi.org/10.5772/24573.

Heinbuch, S. E. 1995. "A Case of Successful Technology Transfer to Health Care. Total Quality Materials Management and Just-in-Time". *Journal of Management in Medicine.* https://doi.org/10.1108/02689239510086524.

Jafarnejad, Ahmad, Momeni, Mansoor, Razavi Hajiagha, Seyed Hossein and Faridi Khorshidi, Maryam. 2019. "A Dynamic Supply Chain Resilience Model for Medical Equipment's Industry". *Journal of Modelling in Management.* https://doi.org/10.1108/JM2-11-2018-0195.

Korpela, Kari, Hallikas, Jukka and Dahlberg, Tomi. 2017. "Digital Supply Chain Transformation toward Blockchain Integration". In *Proceedings of the 50th Hawaii International Conference on System Sciences (2017).* https://doi.org/10.24251/hicss.2017.506.

Lambert, Douglas M., García-Dastugue, Sebastián J. and Croxton, Keely L. 2005. "An Evaluation of Process-Oriented Supply Chain Management Frameworks". *Journal of Business Logistics.* https://doi.org/10.1002/j.2158-1592.2005.tb00193.x.

Lewis, Ralph, and Voehl, Frank. 2020. "Supply Chain Management*". In *Macrologistics Management: A Catalyst for Organizational Change.* https://doi.org/10.4324/9781003077121-6.

Maffia, Michele, Mainetti, Luca, Patrono, Luigi and Urso, Emanuela. 2012. "Evaluation of Potential Effects of RFID-Based Item-Level Tracing Systems on the Integrity of Biological Pharmaceutical Products". *International Journal of RF Technologies: Research and Applications.* https://doi.org/10.3233/RFT-2012-022.

Martin, Christopher and Towill, Denis R. 2000. "Supply Chain Migration from Lean and Functional to Agile and Customised". *Supply Chain Management.* https://doi.org/10.1108/13598540010347334.

McKone-Sweet, Kathleen E., Hamilton, Paul and Willis, Susan B. 2005. "The Ailing Healthcare Supply Chain: A Prescription for Change". *Journal of Supply Chain Management.* https://doi.org/10.1111/j.1745-493X.2005.tb00180.x.

Moon, Michael. 2009. "Centers of Excellence in Digital Supply Chains". *Journal of Digital Asset Management.* https://doi.org/10.1057/dam.2009.8.

Nasiri, Mina, Juhani Ukko, Minna Saunila and Tero Rantala. 2020. "Managing the Digital Supply Chain: The Role of Smart Technologies". *Technovation.* https://doi.org/10.1016/j.technovation.2020.102121.

Patterson, Kirk A., Grimm, Curtis M. and Corsi, Thomas M. 2003. "Adopting New Technologies for Supply Chain Management". *Transportation Research Part E: Logistics and Transportation Review.* https://doi.org/10.1016/S1366-5545(02)00041-8.

Pisano, Gary P. 1991. "The Governance of Innovation: Vertical Integration and Collaborative Arrangements in the Biotechnology Industry". *Research Policy*. https://doi.org/10.1016/0048-7333(91)90054-T.

Ross, Anthony D. and Vaidyanathan Jayaraman. 2009. "Strategic Purchases of Bundled Products in a Health Care Supply Chain Environment". *Decision Sciences*. https://doi.org/10.1111/j.1540-5915.2009.00228.x.

Roussel, Joseph, Kuenn, Hans and Schoepke Phil. 2002. "Unlocking the Value from Supply Chain Planning Solutions". *Supply Chain Forum: An International Journal*. https://doi.org/10.1080/16258312.2002.11517095.

Samal, Sarat K. 2019. "Logistics and Supply Chain Management". *International Journal of Psychosocial Rehabilitation*. https://doi.org/10.37200/IJPR/V23I6/PR190779.

Sanders, Nada R. and Swink, Morgan. 2019. "Digital Supply Chain Transformation: Visualizing the Possibilities". *Supply Chain Management Review*.

Sarkis, Joseph. 2003. "A Strategic Decision Framework for Green Supply Chain Management". *Journal of Cleaner Production*. https://doi.org/10.1016/S0959-6526(02)00062-8.

Skjoett-Larsen, Tage. 1999. "Supply Chain Management: A New Challenge for Researchers and Managers in Logistics". *The International Journal of Logistics Management*. https://doi.org/10.1108/09574099910805987.

Sridharan, Uma V., Caines, W. Royce and Patterson, Cheryl C. 2005. "Implementation of Supply Chain Management and Its Impact on the Value of Firms". *Supply Chain Management*. https://doi.org/10.1108/13598540510612785.

Supply, Global, and Chain Survey. 2013. "Next-Generation Supply Chains Efficient, Fast and Tailored". *Pwc-Report*.

"*UST Global and Gravity Supply Chain Solutions Join Hands to Deliver an Integrated Single Platform for End-to-End Supply Chain Visibility*". n.d. Accessed February 8, 2021. https://www.prnewswire.com/news-releases/ust-global-and-gravity-supply-chain-solutions-join-hands-to-deliver-an-integrated-single-platform-for-end-to-end-supply-chain-visibility-301065060.html.

In: Global Challenges of Digital Transformation of Markets ISBN: 978-1-53619-754-9
Editors: E. de la Poza and S. E. Barykin   © 2021 Nova Science Publishers, Inc.

Chapter 9

LOGISTICS CONCEPT OF KNOWLEDGE TRANSFER

A. A. Mikheev[1], S. E. Barykin[2], S. M. Sergeev[2,] and I. V. Kapustina[2]*

[1]Moscow State Institute of International Relations (University) of the Ministry of Foreign Affairs of the Russian Federation, Moscow, Russia
[2]Peter the Great St. Petersburg Polytechnic University, St. Petersburg, Russia

ABSTRACT

Currently, Russian scientific schools are developing innovative approaches to the development of the economy based on the concept of knowledge. The article offers a logistics approach to the study of the ways of forming the intellectual market of Russia. The combinatorics of transactions in logistics supply chains confirms the validity of involving a logistics provider in the monitoring of knowledge transfer.transfer of masses with a complex internal rheology. A generalized solution of the system is a function that defines the variational statement of the initial boundary-value problem. The consideration is extended beyond the framework of classical continuously differentiable solutions because the physical nature of transfer of goods and cargo flows through logistics networks has to be described more accurately.

Keywords: Logistics, Blockchain in supply, Knowledge Economy, International Knowledge Transfer

1. INTRODUCTION

Clusters of the new non-resource intellectual economy of Russia are formed due to innovative development, which is most clearly manifested through the high

---

* Corresponding Author's E-mail: sergeev2@inbox.ru.

dynamics of mobile communication coverage, which allows the formation of integrated markets.

The logistics concept for managing knowledge flows leads to the introduction of a new conceptual category of "socio-economic learning system", the organization of the space of which is represented as a development framework formed by specified territorial networks of settlement, infrastructure and production, providing specific economic mechanisms for the dissemination and adaptation of innovations.

The negative economic impact of the coronavirus crisis (CVC) could be studied at both the national and international levels (Genkin and Mikheev 2020) on the basis of the research methodology of the knowledge flows.

So, the fundamental theory for studing the flows of different resources could be chosen the logistics methodology implementing in various fields of knowledge (Ilin, Kalinina and Barykin 2018).

The authors attempt to consider the knowledge flows in current crisis from the point of view of the logistics approach which could be used for exploring both the financial flows (Kalinina, Kapustina et al. 2019) and knowledge transfer.

2. LITERATURE REVIEW

The development of the knowledge economy can be based on the interaction of the academic and business environment with the involvement of intellectual property (Kalinina, Alekseeva et al. 2019) and moral values, ideals, and corporate culture of specialists in various fields (Kalinina et al. 2018) on the basis of the approach of innovation activity to professional education considered as a system of interrelated types of work (Shahroom and Hussin 2018; Chen 2010).

Considering the approach in the context of rethinking the interweaving of financial and material resources flows (Kalinina, Balchik and Barykin 2018), one can put forward arguments in support of the theoretical position that the optimization of the financial management system at the level of groups of companies and individual organizations, together with the strengthening of the role of financial planning, is a factor of development at the micro - and meso-level (Vilken et al. 2019).

The features of the formation of the triple resource flow (materials, finance and information) could be considered on the basis of the wholistic view. Personnel flows could be studied in close connection with the development of socio-economic systems on an integrative theoretical basis (Barykin, Kalinina, et al. 2021; Barykin, Kapustina, Sergeev, et al. 2021).

On the basis of logistic approach to the management of different resources in an organization, which provides a theoretical basis for extending logistics management concept (Kalinina et al. 2020) being developed by the representatives of the St. Petersburg scientific school of logistics (Barykin, Bochkarev, et al. 2021; Barykin, Kapustina, Valebnikova, et al. 2021; Barykin, Smirnova, Sharapaev, et al. 2021).

3. PROBLEM STATEMENT

It can be shown that business continuity management is a flow process aimed at regulating the orderly movement of information, structured, directed and receiving different vectors in space and time (Figure 1).

The categorical minimum of development based on the concept of flow management involves the formation of a knowledge transfer system based on the following factors:

- system management,
- innovative development;
- organizational innovation.

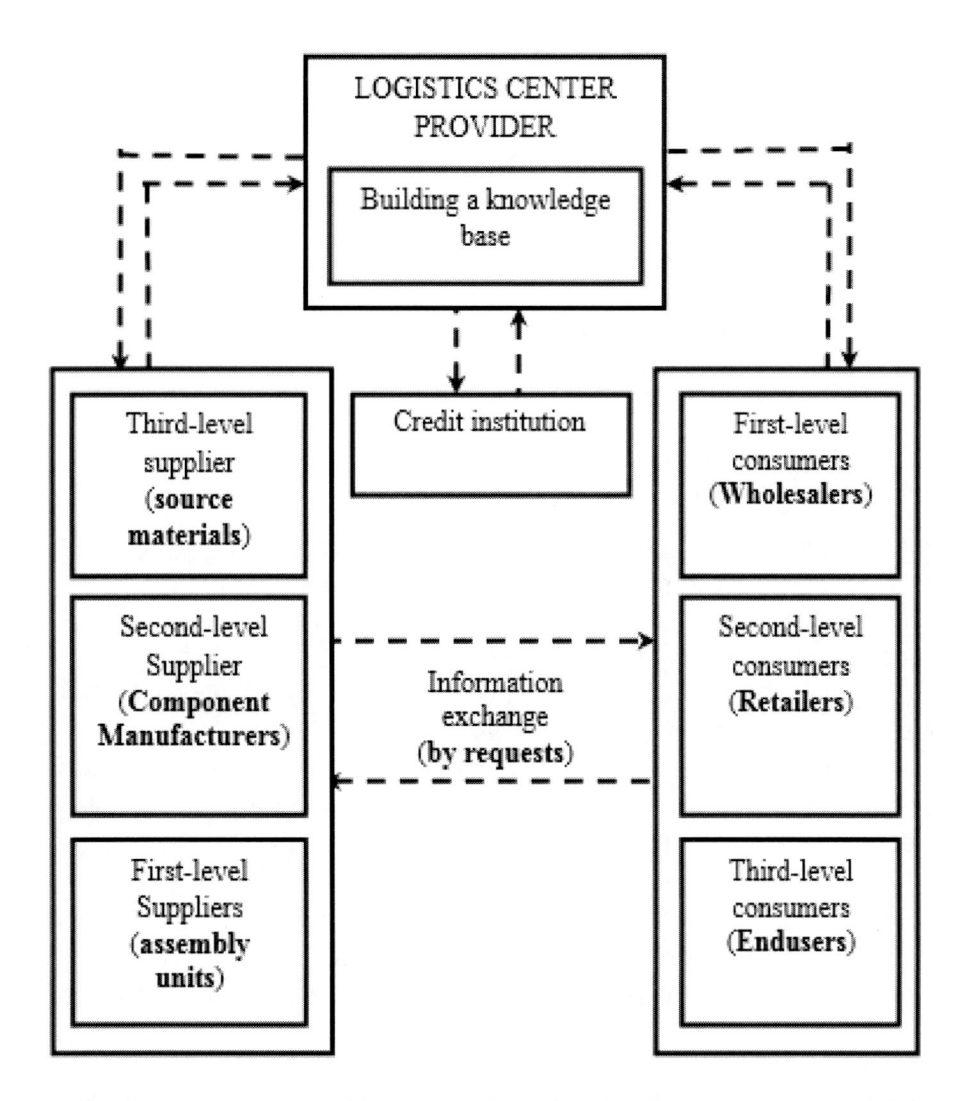

Figure 1. Continuous monitoring of information flows by a logistics provider − − − information resource flow.

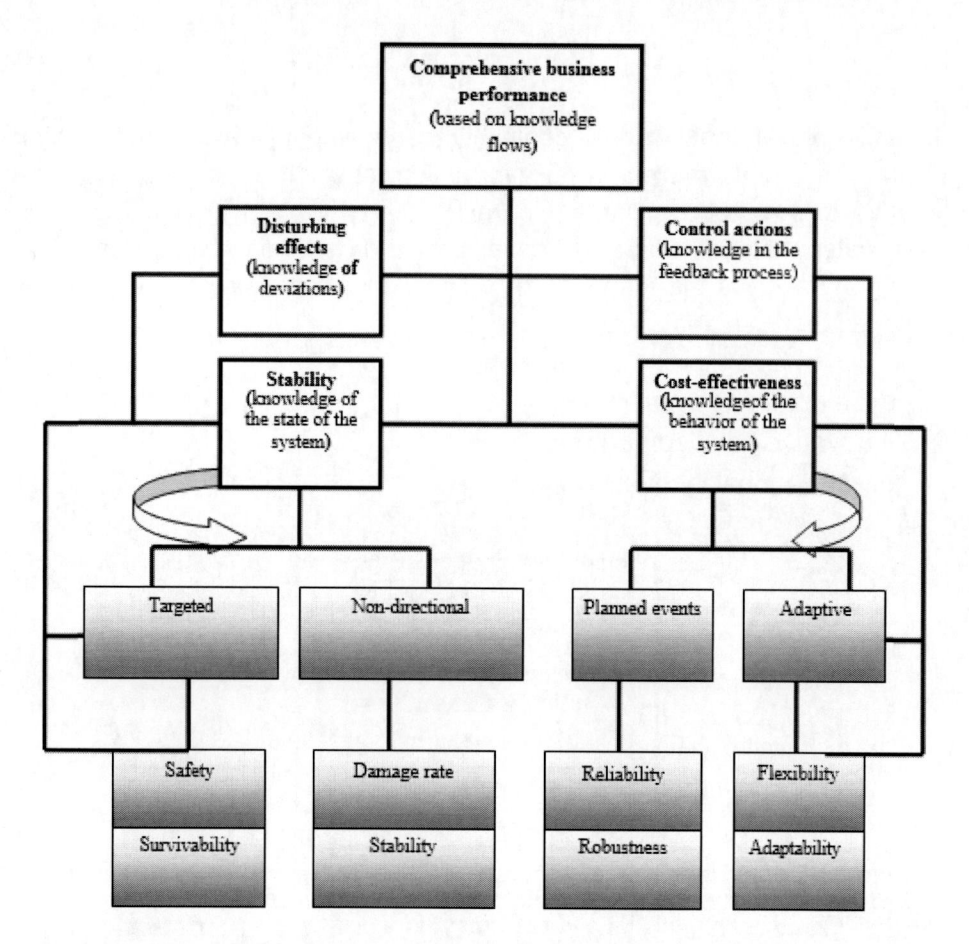

Figure 2. The relationship between the properties of supply chains and the main categories in the assessment of uncertainty.

Generally recognized properties of the supply chain are the categories that characterize the object of research in the temporal aspect from the point of view of purposeful provision of the organization's resource flows, managed with the help of knowledge flows, under conditions of uncertainty (Figure 2).

The analysis of the practices and principles laid down in the national business continuity management standards allows us to formulate a general conceptual approach that is based on the management of information flows (knowledge) and should mediate the concept of business continuity management and the logistics of flow management for a particular firm. Consider the activities of a logistics provider in the knowledge transfer system (Figure 3).

Transaction 1: The logistics provider generates knowledge about the need for a certain amount of materials or the provision of services.

Transaction 2. The logistics provider informs the suppliers about the parameters of the material flow.

Transaction 3: Selection of suppliers by the logistics provider.

Transaction 4: The logistics provider informs customers about the order options.

Transaction 5: Financial flow from customers to the logistics provider.

Transaction 6: Customers inform the logistics provider about the inventory of material and financial resources.

Transaction 7: Customers inform the logistics provider and the financial needs to pay for material resources.

Transaction 8: Customers ' financial needs are matched against investment opportunities.

Transaction 9: Customers send financial resources to a logistics intermediary for subsequent transfer to suppliers-Transaction 10.

Transaction 11: Flow of material resources from the supplier to the customers.

Transaction 12: The logistics intermediary distributes resources to customers based on knowledge of inventory and material needs.

4. METHODOLOGY

The authors could prove that dividing the planning period T into n time intervals for studying financial, material and information flows in the time interval $\Delta t_k = t_k - t_{k-1}$ ($k = 1, 2,..., n$). Let us assume that at some interval, a transaction, for example, related to the information flow (i) takes place, and transactions related to the flows of financial (f) and material (m) resources are zero. In the next interval, there is a financial flow instead of the flow of information and material resources. In the subsequent intervals of Δt_k, Δt_{k+1}, and Δt_n, all transactions are possible.

It can be shown that in the interval Δt_k, only one of the two transaction states is characteristic, which explains the occurrence of 2^{3n} states at n time intervals in relation to transactions.

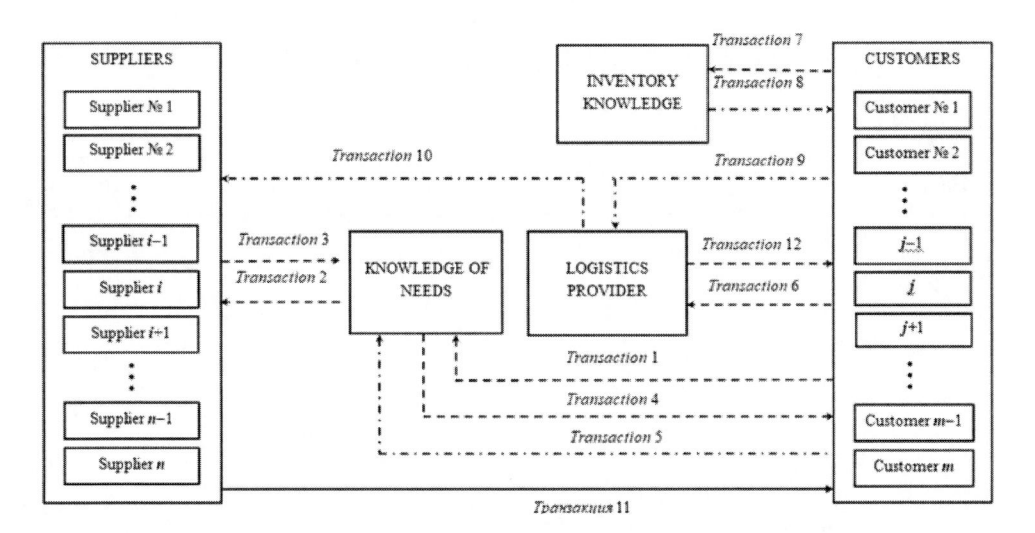

Figure 3. Monitoring by a logistics provider of knowledge transfer: ‒ ‒ ‒ information resource flow; ‒ · ‒ · financial resource flow; ▬▬▬ flow of material resources.

The interaction of the totality of information, material and financial flows can be studied within the framework of the conceptual apparatus of knowledge transfer, considering the concept of entropy of a single flow (studied as a whole). The concept of entropy of a single (considered as a whole) flow allows us to study the interaction of a set of information, material and financial flows from the perspective of knowledge transfer. Let's compare the combinations of transactions that occur with the same probability (Table 1).

**Table 1. Probabilities of combinations of transactions
with equal probability**

Item No.	Combination of elements	Probability
1	$\{0, f, m\}$	0.125
2	$\{i, 0, m\}$	0.125
3	$\{i, f, 0\}$	0.125
4	$\{0, 0, m\}$	0.125
5	$\{i, 0, 0\}$	0.125
6	$\{0, f, 0\}$	0.125
7	$\{0, 0, 0\}$	0.125
8	$\{i, f, m\}$	0.125

**Table 2. Probabilities of combinations of transactions
with different probabilities**

Item No.	Combination of elements	Probability
1	$\{0, f, m\}$	0.01
2	$\{i, 0, m\}$	0.9
3	$\{i, f, 0\}$	0.03
4	$\{0, 0, m\}$	0.013
5	$\{i, 0, 0\}$	0.011
6	$\{0, f, 0\}$	0.014
7	$\{0, 0, 0\}$	0.007
8	$\{i, f, m\}$	0.015

Combinations are equally probable, which leads to the greatest uncertainty, explained by the lack of confidence in the occurrence of any outcome of the eight, since the probabilities of any combination of transactions are equal (maximum entropy). Consider combinations with different probability of occurrence (Table 2).

If we assume that one of the threads must arise so that a single flow took a value of either material flow, financial, and, in the absence of both, the information flow – and then, always be a single stream has the form of one of the combinations from 1 to 3 in tables 1 – 2. So, likely 3^n transaction status at n intervals of time, is practically implemented through mechanisms to manage logistics provider resource flows for 12 transactions.

CONCLUSION

Thus, the formation of the development economy involves the transfer of knowledge (Urbancová, Vnoučková and Laboutková 2016; Amesse and Cohendet 2001; Clarke 2001; Silin 2012), managed using the methods of logistics theory with the involvement of the entire set of intellectual potential, the expansion of modern methodologies, conceptual developments designed primarily to ensure sustainable economic development, as well as to develop new archetypes of management of ecological and socio-economic systems:

- socially oriented;
- economically reliable;
- environmentally friendly.

The concept of knowledge transfer is related to the concept of business continuity, which considers a number of approaches, including the analysis of business impacts on the basis of information collection, which involves the management of knowledge flows (knowledge transfer) (Evans 2007; Dalkir 2011; Urbancová and Fejfarová 2015).

It refers to the continuity of critical activities and processes that produce or ensure the delivery of products or services to consumers. Theoretical approaches to the development and implementation of a business continuity management system could be considered in the event of crisis.

REFERENCES

Amesse, Fernand and Cohendet, P. 2001. "Technology Transfer Revisited from the Perspective of the Knowledge-Based Economy". *Research Policy.* https://doi.org/ 10.1016/S0048-7333(01)00162-7.

Barykin, Sergey Yevgenievich, Andrey Aleksandrovich Bochkarev, Sergey Mikhailovich Sergeev, Tatiana Anatolievna Baranova, Dmitriy Anatolievich

Mokhorov, and Aleksandra Maksimovna Kobicheva. 2021. "A Methodology of Bringing Perspective Innovation Products to Market." *Academy of Strategic Management Journal* 20 (2): 19. https://www.abacademies.org/articles/a-methodology-of-bringing-perspective-innovation-products-to-market.pdf.

Barykin, Sergey Yevgenievich, Olga Vladimirovna Kalinina, Irina Vasilievna Kapustina, Victor Andreevich Dubolazov, Cesar Armando Nunez Esquivel, Elmira Alyarovna Nazarova, and Petr Anatolievich Sharapaev. 2021. "The Sharing Economy and Digital Logistics in Retail Chains: Opportunities and Threats." *Academy of Strategic Management Journal* 20 (2): 1–14. https://www.abacademies.org/articles/the-sharing-economy-and-digital-logistics-in-retail-chains-opportunities-and-threats.pdf.

Barykin, Sergey Yevgenievich, Irina Vasilievna Kapustina, Sergey Mikhailovich Sergeev, Olga Vladimirovna Kalinina, Viktoriia Valerievna Vilken, Yuri Yevgenievich Putikhin, and Lydia Vitalievna Volkova. 2021. "Developing the Physical Distribution Digital Twin Model within the Trade Network." *Academy of Strategic Management Journal* 20 (1): 1–24. https://www.abacademies.org/articles/developing-the-physical-distribution-digital-twin-model-within-the-trade-network.pdf.

Barykin, Sergey Yevgenievich, Irina Vasilievna Kapustina, Olga Aleksandrovna Valebnikova, Natalia Viktorovna Valebnikova, Olga Vladimirovna Kalinina, Sergey Mikhailovich Sergeev, Marisa Camastral, Yuri Yevgenievich Putikhin, and Lydia Vitalievna Volkova. 2021. "Digital Technologies for Personnel Management: Implications for Open Innovations." *Academy of Strategic Management Journal* 20 (2): 1–14. https://www.abacademies.org/articles/digital-technologies-for-personnel-management-implications-for-open-innovations.pdf.

Barykin, Sergey Yevgenievich, Elena Aleksandrovna Smirnova, Petr Anatolievich Sharapaev, and Angela Bohuovna Mottaeva. 2021. "Development of the Kazakhstan Digital Retail Chains within the EAEU E-Commerce." *Academy of Strategic Management Journal* 20 (2): 1–18. https://www.abacademies.org/articles/development-of-the-kazakhstan-digital-retail-chains-within-the-eaeu-ecommerce-market.pdf

Chen, Xiaoguang. 2010. "Education, Innovation and Economic Growth". In *Investing in Human Capital for Economic Development in China*. https://doi.org/ 10.1142/9789812814425_0003.

Clarke, Thomas. 2001. "The Knowledge Economy". *Education + Training*. https://doi.org/10.1108/00400910110399184.

Dalkir, Kimiz. 2011. "Knowledge Management". In *Understanding Information Retrieval Systems: Management, Types, and Standards*. https://doi.org/10.4018/jksr.2012070105.

Evans, James R. 2007. "Impacts of Information Management on Business Performance". *Benchmarking*. https://doi.org/10.1108/14635770710761906.

Genkin, Artem S. and Mikheev, Alexey A. 2020. "Influence of Coronavirus Crisis on Food Industry Economy". *Foods and Raw Materials,* 8 (2): 204 - 15. https://doi.org/10.21603/2308-4057-2020-2-204-215.

Ilin, I., Kalinina, O. and Barykin, S. 2018. "Financial Logistics Innovations in IT Project Management". In *MATEC Web of Conferences,* Vol. 193. https://doi.org/10.1051/matecconf/201819305062.

Kalinina, O., Alekseeva, L., Varlamova, D., Barykin, S. and Kapustina, I. 2019. "Logistic Approach to Intellectual Property". In *E3S Web of Conferences,* Vol. 110. https://doi.org/10.1051/e3sconf/201911002103.

Kalinina, O., Balchik, E. and Barykin, S. 2018. "Innovative Management Neural Network Modelling Based on Logistic Theory". In *MATEC Web of Conferences,* Vol. 239. https://doi.org/10.1051/matecconf/201823904021.

Kalinina, O., Firova, S., Barykin, S. and Kapustina, I. 2020. Development of the Logistical Model for Energy Projects' Investment Sources in the Transport Sector. Edited by M. Pasetti and V. Murgul. *Advances in Intelligent Systems and Computing,* Vol. 982. Springer Verlag. https://doi.org/10.1007/978-3-030-19756-8_29.

Kalinina, O., Kapustina, I., Burova, A., Firsova, S., Barykin, S. and Sedyakina A. 2019. "Financial Logistics Theory as Innovative Approach to Management". In *Proceedings of the 33rd International Business Information Management Association Conference, IBIMA 2019: Education Excellence and Innovation Management through Vision 2020.*

Kalinina, O., Suschenko, V., Shchegolev, V. and Barykin, S. 2018. "Logistic Development and Use of Personnel Motivation System Based on the Chosen Strategy of Sports Organization". In *MATEC Web of Conferences,* Vol. 193. https://doi.org/10.1051/matecconf/201819305063.

Shahroom, Aida Aryani and Hussin, Norhayati. 2018. "Industrial Revolution 4.0 and Education". *International Journal of Academic Research in Business and Social Sciences.* https://doi.org/10.6007/ijarbss/v8-i9/4593.

Silin, Fouad. 2012. "Knowledge Transfer". In *Society of Petroleum Engineers - Abu Dhabi International Petroleum Exhibition and Conference 2012, ADIPEC 2012 - Sustainable Energy Growth: People, Responsibility, and Innovation.* https://doi.org/10.2118/161658-ms.

Urbancová, Hana and Fejfarová, Martina. 2015. "Vertical Knowledge Transfer in Czech Organizations". *Business: Theory and Practice.* https://doi.org/10.3846/btp.2015.477.

Urbancová, Hana, Vnoučková, Lucie and Laboutková, Šárka. 2016. "Knowledge Transfer in a Knowledge-Based Economy". *E a M: Ekonomie a Management.* https://doi.org/10.15240/tul/001/2016-2-005.

Vilken, V., Kalinina, O., Barykin, S. and Zotova, E. 2019. "Logistic Methodology of Development of the Regional Digital Economy". In *IOP Conference Series: Materials Science and Engineering,* Vol. 497. https://doi.org/10.1088/1757-899X/497/1/012037.

In: Global Challenges of Digital Transformation of Markets ISBN: 978-1-53619-754-9
Editors: E. de la Poza and S. E. Barykin   © 2021 Nova Science Publishers, Inc.

Chapter 10

SMART SUPPLY CHAINS' DEVELOPMENT WITHIN THE ECOSYSTEMS OF DIGITAL TRANSPORT CORRIDORS

S. E. Barykin[1], A. A. Mikheev[2], S. M. Sergeev[1,] and I. V. Kapustina[1]*

[1]Peter the Great St. Petersburg Polytechnic University, Russia
[2]Moscow State Institute of International Relations (University) of the Ministry of Foreign Affairs of the Russian Federation, Moscow, Russia

ABSTRACT

The coronavirus pandemic in 2020 has significantly changed supply chain management processes. At the moment, supply chain management practices are being adapted to the conditions of the pandemic and post-pandemic, and trends are being laid for the further development of logistics activities in the context of the digitalization of the economy. In the context of the transition to smart supply chains in the post-tandem environment, the project to create an ecosystem of digital transport corridors (ECTS) on the territory of the EAEU should be noted. The purpose of the study is to study the priority tools for digital transformation of the supply chain in the transition from supply chain 3.0 to smart supply chain. The authors propose an algorithm for step-by-step evaluation of possible tools. As a tool, you can use blockchain technologies.

Keywords: logistics, blockchain in supply, digitalization, mathematical model, sustainability, optimization

---

* Corresponding Author's Email: sergeev2@inbox.ru.

1. INTRODUCTION

In the context of the pandemic, business is suddenly faced with a new reality. In particular, there was a violation of previously stable logistics links between various counterparties. At the same time, the pandemic has led to a change in a number of patterns of consumer behavior and the explosive growth of local online commerce (Remko 2020; Kilpatrick and Barter 2020; Mollenkopf, Ozanne, and Stolze 2020). Accordingly, supply chain management practices have become more complex in the context of the pandemic. The companies that have previously invested in the digitalization of their logistics activities and the introduction of smart supply chains have shown the greatest efficiency in the new conditions. Accordingly, at present, the problem of building and managing smart supply chains is of the greatest relevance both in the theoretical aspect and in the empirical plan. Domestic and foreign researchers consider various aspects of smart supply chain management.

The process of Supply Chain Management (SCM) provides the movement of batches of raw materials, necessary components and finished products produced by the enterprise for the communication of such components of the logistics system of the enterprise as the purchasing subsystem, the production subsystem and the sales subsystem (Croxton et al. 2001).

The supply chain management system of the enterprise provides a link between the production activities and the sales activities of the enterprise. Accordingly, the SCM system should adapt as flexibly as possible to the company's current strategy and quickly adapt to the current economic model. There are many examples of such an adaptation of the SCM system to the development of the world economy. In particular, the industrialization that took place at the end of the XIX century led to a tendency to dramatically increase the overall size of merchant ships, especially those used for international transportation, as well as to the emergence and rapid development of the railway cargo transportation industry. The development of globalization processes in the second half of the XX century led to the widespread use of container transport ("Container Supply Chain Management: Facts, Problems, Solution" 2011). Vertically integrated companies, which spread in various sectors of the economy at the end of the XX century, were engaged in creating complex multi-element supply chain management systems that function on the basis of a complex of information flows, forecasts and plans for the movement of material flows within huge trade and production holdings.

Since the 1980s, the world has been experiencing a third industrial revolution, also called the digital revolution "Industry 3.0". As part of this revolution, manufacturers of goods and services are making a widespread transition from analog technologies to the use of digital technologies. The main driving forces of the digital revolution are the widespread use of information and communication technologies, the spread of computer technology-personal computers and mobile devices, the comprehensive penetration of the Internet, and the reduction in the cost of computer technology and communication services on the Internet.

At the same time, experts predict that in the future the world is waiting for the fourth industrial revolution (that is, the spread of "Industry 4.0") (Tjahjono et al. 2017; Garay-Rondero et al. 2019). Within the framework of the fourth industrial revolution, the mass introduction of various cyber-physical systems in the production of goods and services is expected. Cyberphysical systems are characterized by simultaneous existence in the virtual space and in the physical world. The difference between the concept of "Industry 3.0" and the concept of "Industry 4.0 "is as follows:" Industry 3.0 "is aimed at automating individual production processes and introducing single machines, while the concept of" Industry 4.0 " provides for the complete transformation of the totality of all physical assets available to the enterprise, followed by their integration into a separate digital ecosystem, which also includes partners who participate in the value chain. The implementation of the concept of "Industry 4.0" within a separate enterprise and the achievement of the economic effect of its implementation require the functioning of well-established processes for obtaining information and analyzing data, as well as the implementation of data exchange.

2. LITERATURE REVIEW

Aslam H., Qadeer A., Rashid K., Rehman S. consider the possibilities of improving the efficiency of supply chain management in the context of digitalization (Frederico and Garza-reyes 2020).

Chiang C., Kocabasoglu Hillmer C., Suresh N. The directions of changes in logistics activities under the conditions of pandemic and post-pandemic restrictions are investigated (Chiang, Kocabasoglu-Hillmer, and Suresh 2012).

Giordano G. A. considers hybrid supply chains in terms of transforming them into smart supply chains (Giordano 2020).

So, the issues of smart supply chain management have been studied by domestic and foreign researchers.

The process of digital transformation implies the transition of the enterprise to functioning within the framework of the "Industry 4.0" concept. In the process of digital transformation of the company's activities, digitalization and integration of a set of business processes within the functioning of the entire company is provided. Thus, digitalization extends to many processes, starting from the development of products produced by the enterprise and ending with sales activities and warranty service to consumers (Verny et al. 2020). It should be noted that it is preferable to form a special approach to the practice of performing specific tasks in the company, when each new project is not worked on by any separate structural division of the company, but for each new project, each time a new team is formed from employees of various divisions of the company, that is, the development of a matrix management structure in the company. The authors take into account the negative economic impact of the coronavirus crisis (CVC) at both the national and international levels (Genkin and Mikheev 2020).

Thus, we can say that the digital transformation of an enterprise is a process that involves not only the transformation of production technology, but also a change in the corporate culture and way of thinking in the company. As part of the digital transformation of the activities of any enterprise, its supply chain management system is changing.

The success of the SCM system operating in the enterprise is evaluated according to the following three criteria: the level of efficiency, reduction of logistics costs and reduction of the required time for the turnover of each unit of production.

A significant increase in the efficiency of the SCM system operating in the enterprise is achieved by restructuring the existing logistics network of a particular enterprise. As part of the restructuring and optimization of the logistics network, it is necessary to conduct a deep analysis to determine the main directions of the transformation of the logistics network: production sites, the number of necessary production capacities, as well as platforms and warehouses that determine the direction and capacity of physical flows – raw materials, materials, finished products – between different participants in a particular supply chain, and also affect the optimal distribution of finished products produced by the enterprise in the necessary logistics nodes for further delivery of products to the consumer (Bag et al. 2020).

In the new post-pandemic environment, it is important to ensure the availability and flexibility of logistics. It is important for business to have a stable connection with various logistics service providers, as well as the ability to quickly scale transportation, and transparency of business processes (Barykin, Kapustina, Sergeev, et al. 2020). A promising trend in logistics is the use of various digital platforms that unite many customers and a number of transport and logistics companies (Barykin, Bochkarev, et al. 2020; Barykin, Kapustina, Kirillova, et al. 2020). With the help of digital platforms, the parties can quickly conclude a wide range of digital contracts, exchange transport booking requests and electronic documents as quickly as possible, as well as control the delivery of a variety of goods in real time.

At present, in the era of widespread digital transformation of enterprises ' activities and changes in consumer behavior in the context of the spread of information and communication technologies, there is an increase in competition between enterprises. In order to maintain their competitiveness, companies will have to transform their business model. One of the directions of such transformation is the The Bill of Materials (BoM) being the list of the parts or components that are required to build a product. The BoM provides the manufacturer's part number and the quantity needed for each component (APM and CPC 2020).

Another area of transformation of the business model of the enterprise in the framework of Industry 4.0 is the concept of servitization, which involves the replacement of various goods with complex services that are based on these goods. In particular, this concept has now spread to software, various types of content (books, music) (Frederico and Garza-reyes 2020).

3. MATERIALS AND METHODS

It is necessary to analyze the main elements of the supply chain before planning and executing logistics operations, and then periodically update the results of the analysis. The algorithm for redesigning the SCM system is shown in Figure 1.

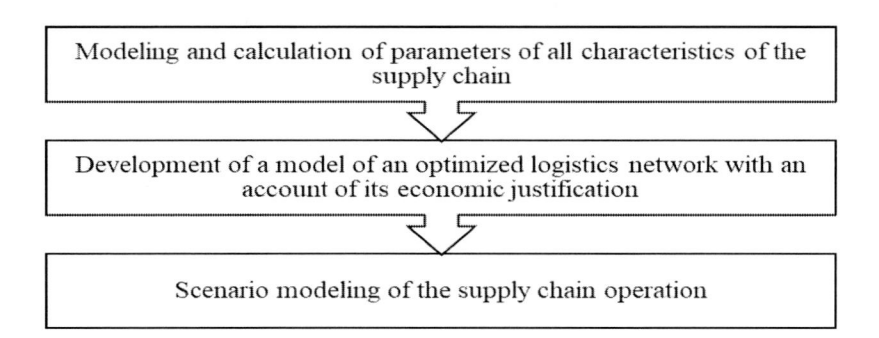

Figure 1. SCM system redesign algorithm.

The redesign of the SCM system makes it possible to reduce the logistics budget of the enterprise by an average of 5-10%, in addition, it increases the efficiency of the process of planning logistics operations within the supply chain.

As a basic principle of interaction with the client in the framework of Industry 4.0, omnichannel is used. The omnichannel principle assumes that any customer has the opportunity to order a specific product or service at any time, in any place, using any communication channel with the company, offline or online.

Traditional supply chains will respond to the constant changes in the economic environment. Accordingly, in the future, the transformation of supply chains and the formation of digital supply networks of the matrix type is expected, in which each link of the supply network at any given time affects the entire supply network as a whole and the efficiency of its functioning.

DHL experts addressed the analysis of the problems faced by various industries in the context of the Covid-19 pandemic. They formulated the following trends in the transformation of logistics activities and supply chain management practices in the future (Figure 2).

The Covid-19 pandemic has shown the inefficiency of traditional linear supply chains. After companies massively analyze the consequences of the Covid-19 pandemic for themselves and identify a set of bottlenecks in their supply chains, there will be a need to form a new model of supply chain management, which will be based on the construction of digital ecosystems (Barykin, Bochkarev, et al. 2021; Barykin, Kapustina, Valebnikova, et al. 2021; Barykin, Smirnova, Sharapaev, et al. 2021). Instead of a set of linear supply chains, companies can in the future implement services that allow automating the set of stages of logistics activities. Thus, within the digital ecosystem, all logistics business processes are transferred to an electronic format: procurement, work with counterparties, exchange of data and documents, sales activities, delivery financial transactions.

<table>
<tr><td>Logistics specialists will be guided by the sustainability of supplies, not the cost. Keeping the chains intact will be critical</td><td>Changes in consumer behavior will require the adaptation of transport flows and warehouse networks to the new realities. Digitalization will affect those processes in cargo transportation that were not previously reached</td></tr>
<tr><td>The need for effective management of the lifecycle of contracts with suppliers will create the need for digitalization and automation of this area</td><td>Information systems will have to support the option of remote work of employees with documents and data</td></tr>
</table>

Figure 2. Trends in the transformation of logistics activities and supply chain management practices (Jamal et al. 2019).

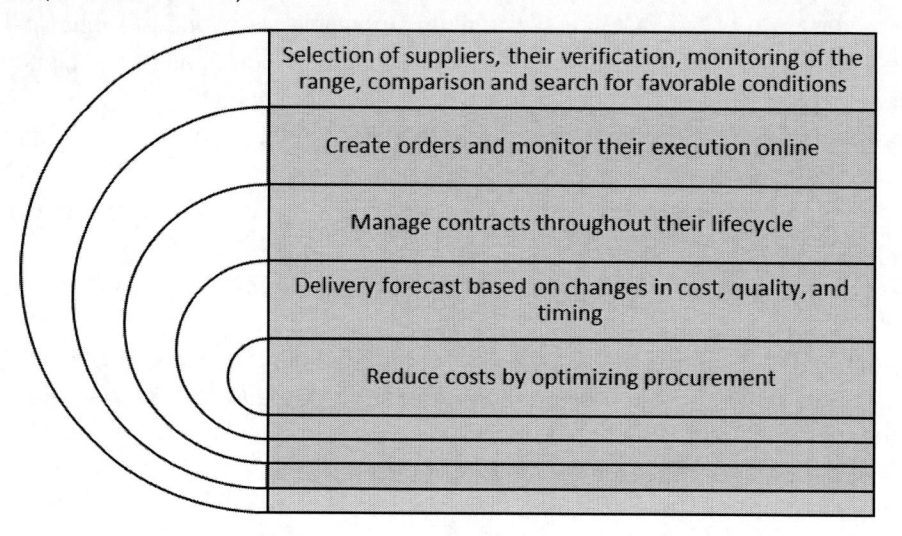

Selection of suppliers, their verification, monitoring of the range, comparison and search for favorable conditions

Create orders and monitor their execution online

Manage contracts throughout their lifecycle

Delivery forecast based on changes in cost, quality, and timing

Reduce costs by optimizing procurement

Figure 3. Functions of marketplaces and platforms for the rapid exchange of orders.

In order to establish an optimal process of interaction with a variety of suppliers, companies can use various platforms and marketplaces to quickly exchange a variety of orders with counterparties. This will allow you to automate the procurement processes, which as a result become transparent both for the company and for the business partners involved in them. The key functions of such platforms are shown in Figure 3.

Quarantine restrictions led to the termination of supplies of raw materials and components for many industries, which were forced to stop their activities. In order to ensure a sufficient level of stability in the supply of raw materials and components in the future, it is important to diversify logistics channels and work with suppliers. In the future, companies should not limit themselves to working only with direct suppliers of raw materials and components, choosing the capabilities of other suppliers belonging to the second and third level.

The coronavirus pandemic, which began in 2020, revealed several key logistics challenges faced by many companies: the process of forecasting demand, the lack of significant diversification of suppliers, a significant increase in the load on the logistics system, outdated formats for interacting with counterparties, and a low level of efficiency of manual data processing. Let's take a closer look at each of these problems.

The problem of demand forecasting. Plans for the production and marketing of goods and the supply chain were formed without taking into account the coronavirus pandemic. The need for mass prevention of morbidity and large-scale lockdowns have led to a sharp change in many consumer patterns of behavior. Accordingly, manufacturers of goods, distributors and retailers in the context of the pandemic were not prepared for the resulting sharp increase in the level of demand for certain categories of goods (medical masks, disposable gloves, toilet paper), and a drop in the level of demand for other categories of goods. This led simultaneously to such effects as interruptions in the supply of certain categories of goods, unclaimed stocks of other categories of goods, and the need for companies to restructure their logistics processes.

The problem of the lack of significant diversification of suppliers. In the context of the pandemic, the supply chains of various enterprises did not have time to adapt to sudden changes. Companies whose supply strategy largely depended on a limited number of direct suppliers were forced to hastily transform production plans and reallocate production capacity in the face of the pandemic.

The problem of increasing the load on the logistics system. The growth in the level of demand for certain product groups led to an increase in the load on the logistics systems of manufacturers of these products (Barykin, Kalinina, et al. 2021; Barykin, Kapustina, Sergeev, et al. 2021). Companies that produce the most popular products in the context of the pandemic are faced with the need to redistribute finished products in a new way within the distribution networks and look for many additional cargo carriers.

4. RESULTS OF THE STUDY

The author could show that trend towards online shopping has increased as a result of the pandemic, and consumers have become more likely to experiment with remote access to goods and services (Figure 4).

Prior to the coronavirus pandemic, approximately 70% of all orders from online stores were delivered to customers through various order pick-up points. However, during the period of quarantine restrictions in Russia, since March 30, shopping and entertainment centers have been suspended, and, accordingly, points for issuing orders from online stores have been closed. As a result, the share of deliveries through pick-up points decreased by 40%. Due to the fact that many points of delivery of orders were closed, and the population observed the self-isolation regime, there was an increase in the volume of delivery of orders from online stores "to the door" by 2.5 times. The growth in demand for delivery after March 30 significantly exceeded the pre-New Year peaks, which the Russian online retail was not ready for: there was an increase in the order collection time by 1.5-2 times, as a result, most market players had an increase in the delivery time of orders by an average of 50%. The increased demand for the delivery service from online stores has shown that there are problems with optimizing routes and meeting delivery deadlines.

The increase in the delivery time of online orders did not affect the cost of delivery at all: the cost of courier delivery "to the door" is still on average 5 times higher than pickup. In June, due to the gradual removal of the regime of increased sanitary and epidemiological readiness in a number of regions, the demand for courier delivery "to the door" decreased by an average of 10% compared to April-May 2020. However, in the online retail market, the request to reduce the cost of courier delivery "to the door" is still relevant.

According to the forecast of Price Water Coopers, as a result of the pandemic, the growth of e-commerce in Russia may accelerate (Figure 5):

Digitalization of retail contributes to the personalization of interaction with customers and the adaptation of sellers ' offers to the constantly and rapidly changing needs of many consumers (Strønen 2020). Using the express delivery service allows consumers to save time and at the same time brings online service and offline service to consumers, leveling the usual time difference that previously existed between them. Currently half of Russian consumers are not yet ready to completely abandon offline purchases and switch to online purchases. Accordingly, in order to ensure further growth of e-commerce turnover, many domestic retailers will have to undergo a digital transformation in the future.

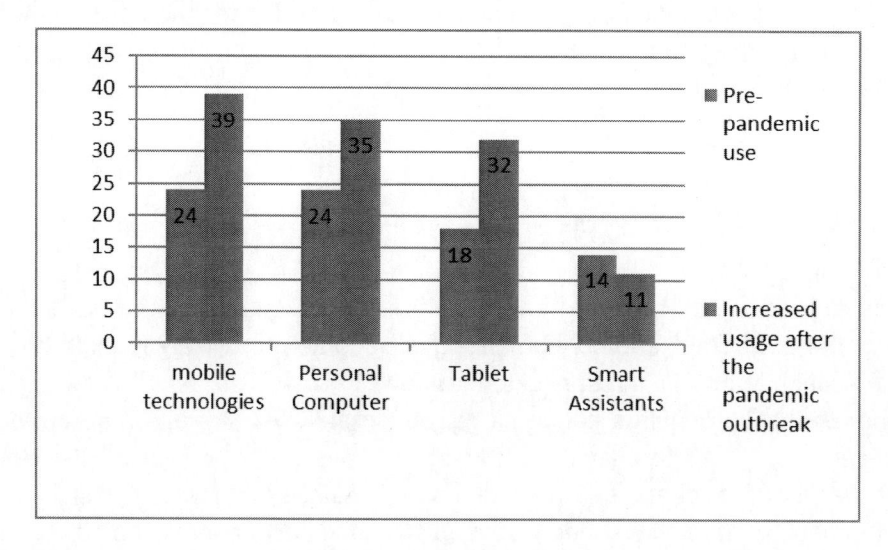

Figure 4. Consumers ' use of digital channels to make purchases.

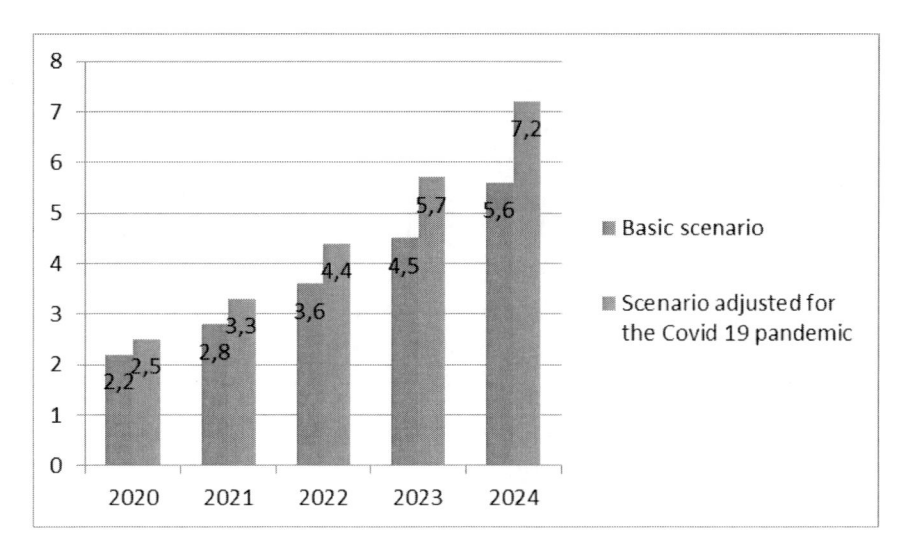

Figure 5. Forecast of Internet sales in Russia, trillion Rubles.

Most companies in the context of the pandemic have begun to reduce costs, including reducing their own costs for implementing digital transformation programs. However, the companies that increased revenue and profits during the pandemic did not stop the process of digital transformation. The leaders of the supply chain rating, according to Gartner ("Top 25 Supply Chain Companies for 2020" n.d.), are among the first to introduce digital technologies. These investments help logistics service market players to thrive even in such difficult economic conditions.

RBC, conducting a study of the impact of the Covid-19 pandemic on Russian business, invited enterprises in various industries to assess the positive effects of the pandemic on business (Figure 6).

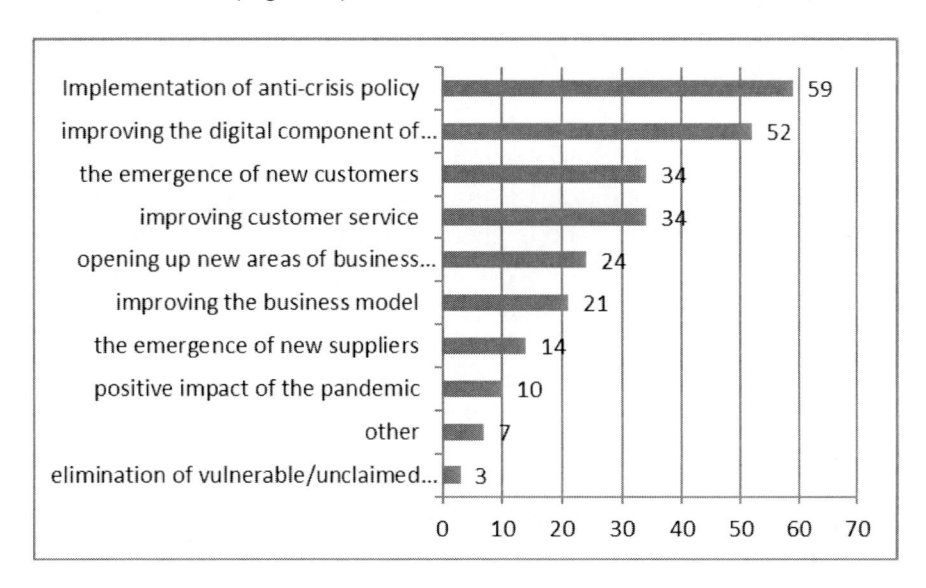

Figure 6. Positive business impacts of the Covid-19 pandemic, highlighted by companies in the logistics industry.

As positive consequences of the pandemic, more than half of the surveyed representatives of the logistics industry noted the implementation of anti-crisis policy (named by 59% of respondents) and the improvement of the digital component of the business (named by 52% of respondents).

It should be noted that today 54% of companies in the world continue to carry out paper document management instead of electronic, which leads to an increase in the processing time of orders by such companies, a lack of sufficient transparency in supply chains and suboptimal management decision-making ("Unicorn Tradeshift On Why Digital Will Become Default Post-COVID" 2020).

The introduction of electronic document management allows you to reduce the amount of routine work of employees, as well as to achieve transparency in relations with many counterparties. Thus, the introduction of electronic document management allows you to:

- reduce staff labor costs and labor costs;
- to achieve the provision of shipments of goods without the participation of a person;
- reduce possible errors caused by the impact of the human factor;
- provide effective management of the total number of warehouse operations.

The Covid-19 pandemic has forced all business entities to focus on ensuring fairly stable cash flows, as well as minimizing liquidity risk. Fintech has already transformed traditional business models, but until recently, researchers and practitioners paid relatively little attention to the process of digitalizing the back office functions of the enterprise and the work of the enterprise with accounts payable.

Electronic factoring should be noted as a promising tool that allows you to automate the work with accounts payable. It allows debtors to gain greater control over their suppliers and reduce the size of a possible cash gap. In turn, electronic factoring allows suppliers to reduce the period of possible deferred payment on the part of debtors. As a result of the use of electronic factoring, debtors can conduct a set of transactions in real time, as well as manage the duration of deferred payment, establishing mutually beneficial and trusting relationships with suppliers.

In the context of the transition to smart supply chains in the post-tandem environment, the project to create an ecosystem of digital transport corridors (EDTC) on the territory of the EAEU should be noted. This project is expected to be implemented by the efforts of all the EAEU countries by 2025. At the first stage of the project to create an EDTC, all the countries that are members of the EAEU will have to determine the set of priority areas, key elements and services of the ecosystem being formed. According to a preliminary expert assessment, the total cost of forming the EDTC system until 2025 is estimated at 10 billion rubles. At the same time, the total economic effect of the formation of the EDTC system is estimated tentatively at 154 billion rubles.

The implementation of the EDTC project will help in the future to simplify the processes of cargo delivery and declaration of transported goods, to level some of the barriers in mutual trade between the EAEU countries. The formed EDTC system will allow in the future to identify the most convenient routes and optimal conditions for cargo transportation, using a set of legally significant electronic documents, as well as optimizing the functions of state control in the process of cargo transportation. To implement the project of creating the EDTC, it is necessary to form a unified information and digital environment on the territory of the EAEU, which will function both on the territory of the EAEU member States and at the supranational level.

In the near future, the instability of previously formed supply chains is expected, however, in the future, there will be a radical change in most existing business processes and the emergence of new initiatives in the field of digitalization and automation of supply chain management.

5. DISCUSSION

In modern conditions, logistics ceases to be a related activity of the enterprise, acting as part of its value proposition. Since in modern conditions there is a regular transformation and modernization of the value propositions of economic entities, this makes it necessary to frequently change the design of existing logistics networks. At the same time, it is noted that the classical approaches to the implementation of logistics activities, which are aimed exclusively at such aspects as planning and execution of standard operations, in modern conditions simply do not keep up with the emerging changes and begin to slow down the development of the enterprise as a result.

It is important to note that in modern conditions, there is an effective automation of many functions related to logistics activities. For this purpose, digital integrations "client — contractor" are used, the introduction of digital document management, which allows you to maintain a digital archive of various events and documents. We can say that over the past 30 years, a person can no longer successfully compete with a machine in such areas of activity as data analysis and performing predictive risk calculation. Accordingly, it can be expected that in the foreseeable future, most of the routine tasks of logistics activities will move to the digitized back office of the logistics department.

On the contrary, such a field of activity as logistics network engineering, which actually turns out to be their periodic reengineering, currently cannot function without the use of human intuition, as well as strategic thinking, which are complemented by the latest tools for implementing big data analysis and artificial intelligence systems. As part of the logistics network engineering process, digitalization is necessary at such a stage as the development and implementation of a specific logistics strategy: with the help of digital tools, data collection, analysis of the collected data, analysis of the needs of a specific customer, development of various logistics models, modeling of possible changes in the external environment, testing of various logistics models for their sensitivity to changes in the external environment, formation of a flexible library of strategic scenarios. When performing these operations, a person acts not as a performer, but as a designer and engineer.

Currently, we can talk about the beginning of the era of hybrid management of logistics supply chains. As in many other industries, the logistics services market is expected to differentiate players into two large groups (Figure 7).

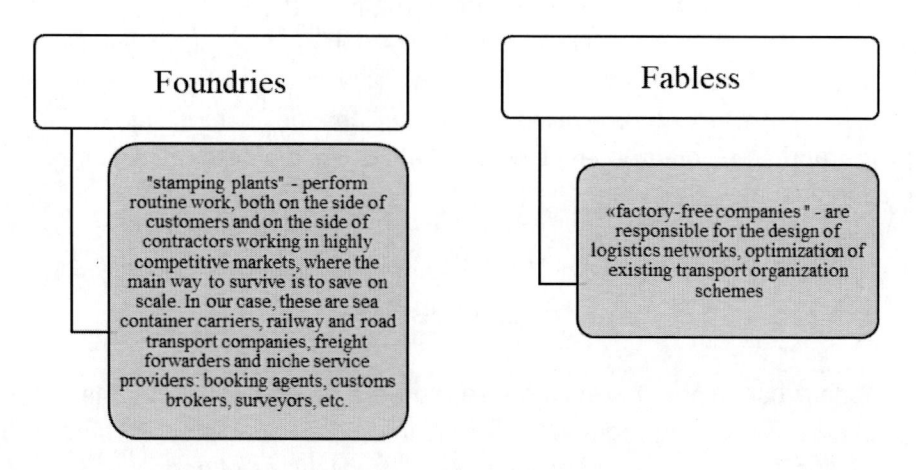

Figure 7. Groups of players in the logistics services market.

One of the key issues for companies that have decided to make the transition from supply chain 3.0 to smart supply chain is the problem of setting key priorities in the field of supply chain transformation (Tjahjono et al. 2017; Nasiri et al. 2020). Within each of the supply chain management processes, several alternative digital tools can be identified to transform the corporate supply chain.

In order to effectively address the challenge of moving from a supply chain 3.0 to a smart supply chain, the company needs to prioritize the tools of digital transformation of the supply chain. As an approach to the selection of priorities, an algorithm for step-by-step evaluation of possible tools is proposed, which includes the following operations.

First, it is necessary to identify the functions that are undergoing digital transformation in each corporate supply chain management process. Secondly, it is necessary to create a list of digital transformation tools for each of the selected supply chain management functions. The third stage of the proposed algorithm is the selection of criteria for evaluating digital transformation tools. Such criteria may include the technical feasibility of implementing the tool, the time required for implementing the tool, the cost of implementing the digital transformation tool in the supply chain, and so on. At the next stage, significance coefficients should be determined for each of the selected criteria, illustrating the importance of each of the criteria in forming the final assessment. The fifth stage is to evaluate each instrument of digital transformation of the supply chain and weigh them in accordance with the coefficients established in the previous stage. Finally, the final stage of evaluating the tools for digital transformation of the supply chain is the calculation of the final weighted average estimates and the selection of the optimal tools for implementing the transition from the supply chain 3.0 to the smart supply chain.

At the same time, it should be noted that there is a contradiction between the needs of business and the practices of implementing digital transformation of companies. In the process of implementing digital transformation, each company forms its own transformation strategy, setting its own priorities within this strategy. When developing a digital transformation strategy, the specialists who manage this process select projects whose implementation is of primary importance for the company. At the same time, supply chain management often does not fall into the primary focus of digital transformation directors. This is due to the gap in competencies: specialists managing the process of digital transformation are not sufficiently oriented in logistics activities, while specialists in the field of logistics may not be sufficiently oriented in the implementation of digital transformation of the enterprise's activities. The contradiction lies in the fact that without changing the company's supply chain management system, it is impossible to optimally manage the company's transforming value propositions. At the same time, companies often lack the human resources and technological resources to effectively automate the supply chain management process.

Thus, outsourcing of such a function as logistics engineering will be a natural solution for an economic entity engaged in digital transformation. At the same time, it should be taken into account that there is a stable reduction in the period between operations of restructuring logistics chains. In such conditions, logistics engineering involves managing a huge number of different participants who are engaged in the logistics process. This model of logistics activity is called "Supergrid Logistics" (Supergrid Logistics).

CONCLUSION

The transformation of logistics or, in other words, the sphere of supply chain management is an integral part of the process of digital transformation of the entire global economy. The COVID-19 pandemic and the response measures have accelerated the digitalization process. As a number of new virtual consumer habits strengthen, the transition to the digital world will become even faster for those market participants who have the desire and ability to invest in the relevant technologies

Structural changes in the logistics industry are associated in modern conditions not so much with the technical methods of order execution, but with the transformation of the decision-making process and the speed of adaptation of the system to various changes in the overall strategy of the company and the external environment.

REFERENCES

APM, Elaine Stattler, and Joyce Anne Grabel CPC. 2020. "THE SUPPLY CHAIN." In *The Master Guide to Controllers' Best Practices*, 337–45. Wiley Online Books. https://doi.org/https://doi.org/10.1002/9781119723349.ch9.

Bag, Surajit, Lincoln C. Wood, Sachin K. Mangla, and Sunil Luthra. 2020. "Procurement 4.0 and Its Implications on Business Process Performance in a Circular Economy." *Resources, Conservation and Recycling* 152 (September 2019): 104502. https://doi.org/10.1016/j.resconrec.2019.104502.

Barykin, Sergey Yevgenievich, Andrey Aleksandrovich Bochkarev, Sergey Mikhailovich Sergeev, Tatiana Anatolievna Baranova, Dmitriy Anatolievich Mokhorov, and Aleksandra Maksimovna Kobicheva. 2021. "A Methodology of Bringing Perspective Innovation Products to Market." *Academy of Strategic Management Journal* 20 (2): 1–19. https://www.abacademies.org/articles/a-methodology-of-bringing-perspective-innovation-products-to-market.pdf.

Barykin, Sergey Yevgenievich, Andrey Aleksandrovich Bochkarev, Olga Vladimirovna Kalinina, and Vladimir Konstantinovich Yadykin. 2020. "Concept for a Supply Chain Digital Twin." *International Journal of Mathematical, Engineering and Management Sciences* 5 (6): 1498–1515. https://doi.org/https://doi.org/10.33889/IJMEMS.2020.5.6.111.

Barykin, Sergey Yevgenievich, Irina Vasilievna Kapustina, Tatiana Viktorovna Kirillova, Vladimir Konstantinovich Yadykin, and Yevgenii Aleksandrovich Konnikov. 2020. "Economics of Digital Ecosystems." *Journal of Open Innovation: Technology, Market, and Complexity* 6 (124): 16. https://doi.org/10.3390/joitmc6040124.

Barykin, Sergey Yevgenievich, Irina Vasilievna Kapustina, Sergey Mikhailovich Sergeev, and Vladimir Konstantinovich Yadykin. 2020. "Algorithmic Foundations of Economic and Mathematical Modeling of Network Logistics Processes." *Journal of Open Innovation: Technology, Market, and Complexity* 6 (4): 16. https://doi.org/10.3390/joitmc6040189.

Barykin, Sergey Yevgenievich, Olga Vladimirovna Kalinina, Irina Vasilievna Kapustina, Victor Andreevich Dubolazov, Cesar Armando Nunez Esquivel, Elmira Alyarovna Nazarova, and Petr Anatolievich Sharapaev. 2021. "The Sharing Economy and Digital Logistics in Retail Chains: Opportunities and Threats." *Academy of Strategic Management Journal* 20 (2): 1–14. https://www.abacademies.org/articles/the-sharing-economy-and-digital-logistics-in-retail-chains-opportunities-and-threats.pdf.

Barykin, Sergey Yevgenievich, Irina Vasilievna Kapustina, Sergey Mikhailovich Sergeev, Olga Vladimirovna Kalinina, Viktoriia Valerievna Vilken, Yuri Yevgenievich Putikhin, and Lydia Vitalievna Volkova. 2021. "Developing the Physical Distribution Digital Twin Model within the Trade Network." *Academy of Strategic Management Journal* 20 (1): 1–24. https://www.abacademies.org/

articles/developing-the-physical-distribution-digital-twin-model-within-the-trade-network.pdf.

Barykin, Sergey Yevgenievich, Irina Vasilievna Kapustina, Olga Aleksandrovna Valebnikova, Natalia Viktorovna Valebnikova, Olga Vladimirovna Kalinina, Sergey Mikhailovich Sergeev, Marisa Camastral, Yuri Yevgenievich Putikhin, and Lydia Vitalievna Volkova. 2021. "Digital Technologies for Personnel Management: Implications for Open Innovations." *Academy of Strategic Management Journal* 20 (2): 1–14. https://www.abacademies.org/articles/digital-technologies-for-personnel-management-implications-for-open-innovations.pdf.

Barykin, Sergey Yevgenievich, Elena Aleksandrovna Smirnova, Petr Anatolievich Sharapaev, and Angela Bohuovna Mottaeva. 2021. "Development of the Kazakhstan Digital Retail Chains within the EAEU E-Commerce." *Academy of Strategic Management Journal* 20 (2): 1–18. https://www.abacademies.org/articles/development-of-the-kazakhstan-digital-retail-chains-within-the-eaeu-ecommerce-market.pdf.

Chiang, Chung Yean, Canan Kocabasoglu-Hillmer, and Nallan Suresh. 2012. "An Empirical Investigation of the Impact of Strategic Sourcing and Flexibility on Firm's Supply Chain Agility." *International Journal of Operations and Production Management* 32 (1): 49–78. https://doi.org/10.1108/01443571211195736.

"Container Supply Chain Management: Facts, Problems, Solution." 2011. *Lecture Notes in Engineering and Computer Science*.

Croxton, Keely L., Sebastián J. García-Dastugue, Douglas M. Lambert, and Dale S. Rogers. 2001. "The Supply Chain Management Processes." *The International Journal of Logistics Management*. https://doi.org/10.1108/09574090110806271.

Frederico, Guilherme, and Jose Arturo Garza-reyes. 2020. "*Supply Chain Strategy Reboot - Supply Chain Management Review*," no. July.

Garay-Rondero, Claudia Lizette, Jose Luis Martinez-Flores, Neale R. Smith, Santiago Omar Caballero Morales, and Alejandra Aldrette-Malacara. 2019. "Digital Supply Chain Model in Industry 4.0." *Journal of Manufacturing Technology Management*. https://doi.org/10.1108/JMTM-08-2018-0280.

Genkin, Artem S. and Mikheev, Alexey A. 2020. "Influence of Coronavirus Crisis on Food Industry Economy". *Foods and Raw Materials,* 8 (2): 204 - 15. https://doi.org/10.21603/2308-4057-2020-2-204-215.

Giordano, Geoff. 2020. "A Hybrid Supply Chain." *Plastics Engineering* 76 (5): 9–11. https://doi.org/10.1002/peng.20304.

Jamal, Noriza Mohd, Wee Sin Yi, Thoo Ai Chin, and Norhalimah Idris. 2019. "Effects of Supply Chain Flexibility towards Supply Chain Collaboration and Supply Chain Agility." *International Journal of Supply Chain Management* 8 (1): 170–73.

Kilpatrick, Jim, and Lee Barter. 2020. "COVID-19: Managing Supply Chain Risk and Disruption." *Deloitte*.

Mollenkopf, Diane A., Lucie K. Ozanne, and Hannah J. Stolze. 2020. "A Transformative Supply Chain Response to COVID-19." *Journal of Service Management*. https://doi.org/10.1108/JOSM-05-2020-0143.

Nasiri, Mina, Juhani Ukko, Minna Saunila, and Tero Rantala. 2020. "Managing the Digital Supply Chain: The Role of Smart Technologies." *Technovation.* https://doi.org/10.1016/j.technovation.2020.102121.

Remko, van Hoek. 2020. "Research Opportunities for a More Resilient Post-COVID-19 Supply Chain – Closing the Gap between Research Findings and Industry Practice." *International Journal of Operations and Production Management.* https://doi.org/10.1108/IJOPM-03-2020-0165.

Strønen, Fred. 2020. "Drivers for Digitalization in Retail and Service Industries." In *Proceedings of the 16th European Conference on Management Leadership and Governance, ECMLG 2020.* https://doi.org/10.34190/ELG.20.071.

Tjahjono, B., C. Esplugues, E. Ares, and G. Pelaez. 2017. "What Does Industry 4.0 Mean to Supply Chain?" *Procedia Manufacturing.* https://doi.org/10.1016/j.promfg.2017.09.191.

"Top 25 Supply Chain Companies for 2020." n.d. Accessed March 14, 2021. https://www.gartner.com/en/supply-chain/trends/the-gartner-supply-chain-top-25-for-2020.

"Unicorn Tradeshift On Why Digital Will Become Default Post-COVID." 2020. August 31, 2020. https://techblogwriter.co.uk/tradeshift/?fbclid=IwAR0Qvs0J26-o0713ln CinrB7fcJ1MQXWlvH9FHXNX8ekD4WhhFYbmljJbgA.

Verny, Jérôme, Ouail Oulmakki, Xavier Cabo, and Damien Roussel. 2020. "Blockchain & Supply Chain: Towards an Innovative Supply Chain Design." *Projectics/Proyéctica/Projectique* n°26 (2): 115. https://doi.org/10.3917/proj.026.0115.

In: Global Challenges of Digital Transformation of Markets ISBN: 978-1-53619-754-9
Editors: E. de la Poza and S. E. Barykin © 2021 Nova Science Publishers, Inc.

Chapter 11

ONLINE FOOD TRADE IN NON-CAPITAL REGIONS

Olga Chkalova[*], Inna Bolshakova[†], Natalia Kopasovskaya[‡], Maksim Tcvetkov[§] and Irina Tcvetkova[‖]

Lobachevsky State University of Nizhni Novgorod, Nizhni Novgorod, Russia

ABSTRACT

The authors investigated the development of online food trade in the regions of the Volga Federal District. The result was conclusions about the development of this sphere of trade outside megacities. To conduct the study, the regions were classified into four groups (quadrants) according to indicators reflecting economic development and the demographic situation. Existing enterprises selling food products online are grouped in accordance with the extension of their functions. The combination of two classifications made it possible to identify groups of regions with the best, average, and worst prospects for the development of online food trade and to determine the criteria for region assessment. At the same time, new practices in conducting online food trade were analyzed, as well as the specifics of changing these forms during a pandemic. The proposed approach to the classification of regions and enterprises can be used to analyze the competitive situation in the market for online food trade while considering regional features. Using the results of the analysis, market players can plan their initial entry into the market or the expansion of their activities.

Keywords: online food trade, non-capital regions, classification, percentage of urban population, level of income, trading enterprises

---

[*] Corresponding Author's Email: ochkalova@iee.unn.ru.
[†] Corresponding Author's Email: bolshakova.iep@yandex.ru.
[‡] Corresponding Author's Email: kopasovskay@iee.unn.ru.
[§] Corresponding Author's Email: macvetkov@yandex.ru.
[‖] Corresponding Author's Email: cvetkova@iee.unn.ru.

1. INTRODUCTION

Lorem ipsum dolor sit amet, consectetuer adipiscing elit. Maecenas porttitor congue massa. Fusce posuere, magna sed pulvinar ultricies, purus lectus malesuada libero, sit amet commodo magna eros quis urna.

Online trade has long been widespread and familiar to consumers, who have been widely using both domestic and foreign online stores to purchase non-food goods. Buying groceries online has become the next stage in the development of Internet commerce. In academic literature, global theoretical studies on the Internet food trade market are contained in the works by M. D. De-Juan-Vigaray and A. I. E. Seguí (De-Juan-Vigaray and Seguí 2019), O. Wang, S. Somogyi et al. (O. Wang, Somogyi, and Charlebois 2020).

In mid-2019, Moody's agency forecasted an active growth in the development of online food trade (about 20% per year). At the same time, the study noted that the percentage of this form of trade in food products will not exceed 1% of the market and will not compete significantly with traditional sales methods.

The question of what factors affect the development of online grocery retail most has been studied for a long time. The studies by H. T. Keh and E. Shieh (Keh and Shieh 2001), S. Prasad and M. Sharma (Prasad and Sharma 2016), P. K. Chintagunta, J. Chu et al. (Chintagunta, Chu, and Cebollada 2012) are devoted to this. The studies by T. Hansen (Hansen 2005), C. Hand et al. (Hand et al. 2009), H. H. Wang, N. Hao et al. (H. H. Wang et al. 2019) are focused on consumer behavior in online grocery retail.

A study conducted in late 2018 by the authors of this paper showed that online grocery stores promptly attracted low-mobility groups (mothers with young children, people who do not leave their homes for health reasons), suburban residents, as well as office workers seeking food delivery to their workplace. However, many consumers were wary of the delivery of expired goods, poorly sorted fruits and vegetables, or did not want to change the usual daily shopping routines in nearby convenience stores, etc.

However, the general trend for a steady increase in the use of online grocery stores was obvious, and various online platforms began to actively expand their operation in Russia. Participants in this market segment were both traditional companies (X5 RetailGroup, Spar, METRO) and numerous intermediaries at the federal and regional levels.

In 2019, the Click & Collect system was widely introduced, as well as stores without buyers (Dark Store) serving online trading. Naturally, their main activity was concentrated in Moscow and St. Petersburg. It was in these cities that the Perekrestok chain stores began to develop their delivery. In early March 2020, the online branch of Perekrestok, according to the X5 Retail Group, reached the level of 10 thousand orders daily.

The problem of regional development of online grocery retail for countries with a population of less than 100 million people (Germany, France, Belgium) has been studied by C. Seitz et al. (Seitz et al. 2017), S. F. Fedoseeva (Fedoseeva, Herrmann, and Nickolaus 2017), G. Goethals et al. (Goethals, Carugati, and Leclercq 2009). The study by K. R. Tanskanen (Tanskanen, Yrjölä, and Holmström 2002) are devoted to the same problem in Finland (with a population a little over 5 million). In contrast, Hanus, G. (Hanus 2016), and M. Lingyu et al. (Lingyu, Lauren, and Zhijie 2019) investigated this problem for such populous countries as the USA, India and China.

In general, throughout 2019 and in early 2020, the segment of online food trade functioned in an experimental mode: new formats were tested, the territorial presence of players was expanded, new consumer groups were attracted. The rapid development of the segment leads to the fact that new product launches are featured only in brief news reports and operational statistical reports. A deeper systematic study has not been conducted, which is why the present study is relevant. The development of individual business models in food retail was considered by K. K. Boyer and G. T. M. Hult (Boyer and Hult 2005), Aaiden and Ellen ("Global Strategic Business Management: Focusing On the Strategic Business Unit of Amazon Whole Foods" 2019), as well as Q. Hu, Q. Xu and B. Xu (Hu, Xu, and Xu 2019). It is noteworthy that in modern research attention is increasingly paid to the problem of successful promotion of online grocery supermarkets. The factors in the successful promotion of online food retailers have been studied by R. Ladhari, M. C. Rioux et al. (Ladhari et al. 2019), A. Zhang, C. Liang and J. Yin (Zhang, Liang, and Yin 2018), K. Anshu and L. Gaur (Anshu and Gaur 2019), I. This problem has been studied not only by foreign scientists but also by Russian ones (e.g., Krasyuk (I. A. Krasyuk and Medvedeva 2019; I. Krasyuk and Medvedeva 2019), Parshukov (Parshukov, Aleksandrov, and Fedorova 2020)).

In the second half of March, due to the pandemic, all food market participants noted a significant increase in online food orders (iGooods.ru, Utkonos, SberMarket, etc.) and faced a lack of resources for organizing work. Again, the main increase in online sales was recorded in Moscow and St. Petersburg. One of the results of the crisis will probably be that many consumers, having not considered online food services previously for various reasons, will have to familiarize themselves with these services. This will provide an additional impetus to the development of the industry in the long term, especially in the capital regions. Therefore, the study of the experience gained in online food trade should be of even greater interest.

The purpose of this article was to study the development of the forms and scale of activity of online food stores in non-capital regions. At the first stage of the study (2018-2019), the authors focused on studying Nizhny Novgorod, which is not a metropolitan region, but is located near Moscow and has a population of over a million. At the second stage (2019-2020), the research object was scaled to the Volga Federal District. This, in the authors' opinion, should make it possible to identify the differences and similarities in the development of online food trade in regions with different social and economic characteristics.

Thus, the objectives of the study are:

- group the studied regions according to pre-selected criteria;
- highlight the main development features of online food trade in the studied regions, with the main emphasis on the forms and scope of online trade coverage
- compare the characteristics of the regions and the features of Internet commerce development, identifying the existing relationships.

Information about the availability, territory of operation, product range, terms of delivery was obtained from open sources (websites of trading enterprises in the regions). The estimation of per capita income and the percentage of urban population is based on the data by the Federal State Statistic Service for 2018.

2. MATERIALS AND METHODS

2.1. Criteria Selection and Region Grouping

As the object of study, 14 regions, republics, and territories of the Volga Federal District were selected. To structure the study, the regions were divided into four groups according to two criteria: demographic and economic.

The online food trade assumes that the commercial enterprise is close to the consumer. In this case, the delivery time of the order will not exceed several hours. With a large number of deliveries in a limited area, the company organizes optimal routes and reduces costs, while ensuring a high level of service. Therefore, online grocery stores are extremely interested in capital regions, where a huge number of potential customers are concentrated.

However, the use of the population indicator to characterize the region in the context of this study is hardly valid, since this indicator also takes into account the residents of small settlements remote from large centers, who are mostly not targeted by online food trade at the present stage.

Therefore, for the grouping of regions according to the demographic criterion, the percentage of permanent urban population was chosen as the indicator. Its average value in the Volga Federal District is 72.1%. This choice enabled a different way of ranking the regions. While the population of Bashkortostan is greater than that of the Nizhny Novgorod region, and the Orenburg region and Udmurtia are ahead of the Kirov region, the situation is the opposite in terms of the percentage of permanent urban population. This impacts the attractiveness of these regions from the perspective of online trade development.

The economic criterion must reflect the material security of the inhabitants of the region. Having a certain income level, the consumer will not mind placing an order totaling over 1500 or 2000 rubles to get free delivery. The monetary income per capita on average per month (rubles) was used as an indicator for this criterion, according to Federal State Statistic Service data for 2018.

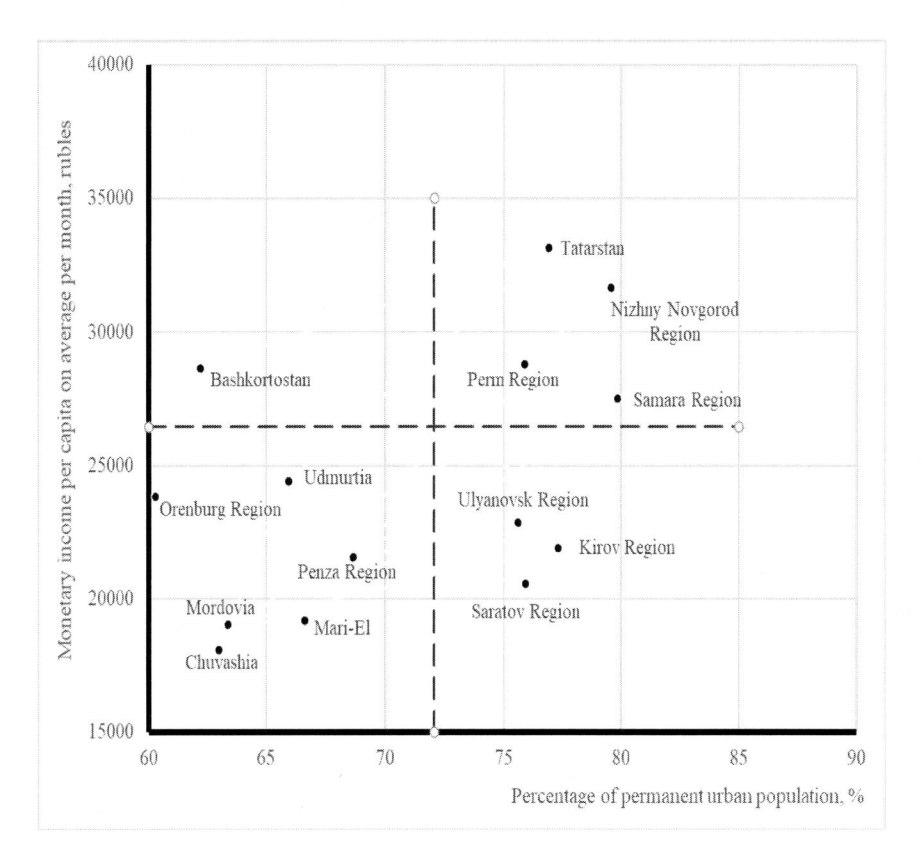

Figure 1. Subjects of the Volga Federal District grouped by the percentage of urban population and the level of income.

In this case, all regions were divided relative to the average indicator value for the Volga Federal District (26,436 rubles), as shown in Figure 1. Citizens' income exceeds the average value in five regions only, primarily in Tatarstan and the Nizhny Novgorod region. These regions are also characterized by a high proportion of the urban population. Among the regions with a low urban population, the majority turned out to be in the group with low cash incomes (six regions).

Thus, 14 subjects of the Volga Federal District were divided into 4 groups:

- high incomes, high urban population - four regions (1st quadrant of the matrix);
- high incomes, low urban population - one region (2nd quadrant);
- low incomes, low urban population - six regions (3rd quadrant);
- low incomes, high urban population - three regions (4th quadrant of the matrix).

2.2. Grouping of Online Trading Enterprises by the Volume of Functions Performed

Table 1 presents the Internet commerce modes that were identified. These are listed in order of broadening their range of services. In total, five groups of enterprises involved in the sale of food products online have been singled out. The presented grouping can be expanded and supplemented depending on the application.

Table 1. Classification of online food trading enterprises by the range of functions performed

Group name	Functions Performed
1.Commodity aggregators (intermediaries, not online stores)	Bringing together sellers and buyers in the local market; Providing help in finding the right product on the websites of different sellers.
2.Online food delivery services from retail chains (intermediaries, not online stores)	Delivery of goods from retail chains, promotion of own brand and the brands of partner networks
3.Online stores of manufacturing or wholesale and retail companies (online direction of offline business)	Online wholesale and retail of the food assortment of a manufacturing enterprise or a wholesale warehouse, possibly through an intermediary; Do not participate in pricing.
4. Online store of a stationary retail outlet (or without a stationary outlet).	A full range of retail operations online selling a range (often narrow) of foods within a single outlet
5. Federal or local retail chains that carry out offline and online trading	A full range of retail services with a wide range of food products within a trading network, coordination of the network.

2.2.1. Intermediary Companies (First and Second Groups)

The first group is commodity aggregators, intermediaries, whose main task is to bring together sellers and buyers in the local market. They perform a minimum of functions. These aggregators include RegMarkets.ru, Yandex Market, and iGooods.ru.

For the buyer, search using the aggregator does not begin with the choice of the store that sells the goods, but with selecting the necessary products. The service allows one to find a product, then select a seller, go to its online store and place an order there.

An aggregator is not an online store. It does not sell or deliver goods but offers the entire product line in its online catalog. A commodity aggregator can facilitate the organization of Internet commerce in any locality where there are real sellers who are ready to use the Internet to promote their product range.

The services of such intermediaries are used by:

- large retail chains that do not want to develop their own online service (Lenta, METRO, Carousel that all use iGooods.ru);
- small shops that do not have the financial capabilities and experience to develop their own online platforms;
- wholesale companies offering large shipments with delivery to any customers based on an online order.

Aggregators earn credibility with customers by providing them with complete information about the seller's reputation and quality of the product, and by posting various reviews and ratings. The commodity aggregators RegMarkets.ru and Yandex Market operate in all cities of the Volga Federal District.

The second group is online food delivery services from retail chains. Their main functions are the delivery of goods from retail chains, the promotion of their own brand, and the brands of partner networks.

Such services are much more involved in the process of product sales than aggregators. They independently recruit and train personnel for order fulfillment, select orders directly in the trading floors of stores, monitor the quality of ordered goods, determine the time and cost of delivery, allow customers to compare prices for goods, and choose the best offers. The costs of online trading for such services are significantly higher.

One such large-scale project is Sbermarket (formerly known as Instamart). It offers its services in 29 Russian cities and cooperates with five federal retail chains (Lenta, METRO, Auchan, Azbuka Vkusa, and VkusVill). Economies of scale allow large players to offer better shipping terms.

Medium and small projects are trying to occupy their own niche, trying to differ from a powerful competitor. They extend their activities to multiple regions (Produktoff, vGastronom) or even only to one city (Hyper v Dom, Gamma Online, Dostavushka, etc.).

A special kind of delivery service is one that appeared as a result of the general tendency to 'uberize' some areas of activity. Platforms like YouDo, Dostavista, MetnisKabanchikom, and others do not specialize in food delivery. They allow customers to find among the many registered participants one who is ready to fulfill their specific order for the selection and delivery of products.

Numerous taxi services operate on the same principle. And it is not surprising that during the coronavirus pandemic, it was the taxi drivers, having long worked in such an 'uberized' field, who began to perform mass delivery functions, including that of food products.

The services of the second group are a classic logistic intermediary that performs some of the functions of a seller. Accordingly, their features do not differ much from those of logistics intermediaries in general.

2.2.2. Other Companies (Third, Fourth, and Fifth Groups)

The third group is online stores specializing in particular groups of food products and often representing a manufacturing or wholesale company. They can offer, for example, a wide variety of meat or fish products.

Their main function is online wholesale and retail of the food assortment of a manufacturing enterprise or a wholesale warehouse on its own or through an intermediary. They work on the formation of the assortment, inventory management, promotion of the manufacturer's trademark, delivery of goods to consumers, etc. As a rule, such stores are not involved in pricing and offline retail.

In almost every region of the Volga Federal District, there is a food operator of a large wholesale or manufacturing company trying to develop online retail in food products, as one of their areas of business (Gourmand Fresh, Produktov Den, the Nurly Internet supermarket, etc.). The company has its own warehouse complex, where often there are opportunities for independent production refinement of goods (such as packaging and freezing).

The fourth group is online stores of stationary retail outlets (or possibly without stationary outlets). They carry out the whole range of online and offline retail services but within one outlet. They independently create an offline and online assortment, bear the costs of inventory management, organizing and managing the website, determine the prices of goods in stores and on the website, as well as the cost and conditions of delivery, lay out the goods in an offline store, and select orders for online buyers.

As a rule, these enterprises have a special assortment: farm products, confectionery or snacks (possibly handmade), delicacies, national food products, culinary products made in-house, etc. A relatively wide product line, including the fresh category, or a narrow line of products (for example, dairy products, honey, vegetables, meat delicacies) can be offered for sale.

A special subgroup is premium segment enterprises offering an assortment of eco-products online. They offer exclusive (environmentally friendly, not containing preservatives, dyes, or thickeners) food products at prices above the average level in the city (region). Delivery is carried out mainly in one city and its environs only.

Several large local producers or small private farms are combined to create such a store. Examples are Fereko Farmer Ecological Products, ZnatnyiFermer, Luhari Village, among others. Such online stores sell food products on their own behalf or on behalf of the manufacturer, have free delivery in the city, and have no restrictions on the amount of the order.

The fifth group is federal or local retail chains that carry out both offline and online retail trade in a universal or wide range of food products under one or different own brands. Such enterprises perform the most complex set of tasks. In addition to all retail operations and processes, they coordinate the work of a whole network of offline stores and determine from which outlets products will be selected and delivered to customers.

Some examples are the online stores of the federal retail chains SPAR, U Palycha, and Myasnov, as well as local retail chains Yarmarka, Semya, etc. For instance, SPAR's online store offers a universal range of food products including the fresh category. In fact, this is the only online store operating under the same own brand online and offline with extremely fast delivery, within 2-4 hours.

3. RESULTS

Let us compare the region and enterprise groups in online food trading. The enterprises of the first group are essentially virtual logistics intermediaries. They do not carry out any offline functions (selection, delivery, etc.). Therefore, their expansion to a particular region is not too difficult. It is not surprising, therefore, that commodity aggregators are present in all regions of the Volga Federal District. Thus, below we will discuss group 2-5 enterprises.

3.1. First Quadrant

The first quadrant (Figure 1) is occupied by the most urbanized regions with above-average population incomes. There are online delivery services from various distribution networks (group 2) in almost all cities of the quadrant under consideration:

- federal services (Sbermarket, iGooods.ru);
- local services (Dostavushka, FresheF, Dostavista in Kazan; Gamma Online, Billibong in Samara; Food up in Nizhny Novgorod);
- services of searching for freelancers (MetnisKabanchikom and YouDo);
- federal services that do not specialize in food products (Ozon, Wildberries).

In the second half of 2019, despite the growing appeal of online food purchases, many of the stores of this type could not remain competitive: the vGastronom project (delivery from METRO) was closed in Nizhny Novgorod, the same happened to Produktoff in Samara, etc. However, with the outbreak of the coronavirus pandemic, new projects began to emerge and old projects were revived, in particular in Nizhny Novgorod and Kazan. One example is FrescheF (Kazan), which at the time was nearly closed down. The pandemic also forced federal services such as Ozon and Wildberries to actively engage in product delivery.

Online stores of manufacturing, wholesale, and retail companies (group 3) are not present in all cities and do not conduct such large-scale activities as group 2 enterprises. Many of them are in an unstable position and are experiencing serious financial problems. In 2019, one such project, Easy_if_you_Busy (Nizhny Novgorod) was closed. Some continue to operate, e.g., GURMAN FRESH (Kazan and Samara), meat-samara.ru (Samara), and Mango-product (Perm).

In the region, shops of farm products are actively developing: Fereko Farmer Ecological Products (Kazan), Ferma (Kazan), ZnatnyiFermer (Nizhny Novgorod), Lukhari Village (Samara), and IzAtlashevo (Perm).

One innovation in this group is the delivery of foods for cooking at home: korzinanadom.ru (Kazan), OsnovaZhizni, VkusnoGotovimDoma, Kilo Vkusa, Proviantmaster (Samara). The National Trademark project, functioning under the auspices of the presidential program to support manufacturers of the region, can be classified as an online store of a stationary retail outlet.

Trading networks that work offline and develop their own online sales system (group 5) are represented by a small number of players. The ones offering the fastest delivery are SPAR and Myasnov (Nizhny Novgorod). In Samara, there are delivery services from the Nearby and Nearby Farmer retail chains, as well as from U Palycha (a limited range). In Perm, the off-line trading network called Family is developing its own delivery under the DomoiDostavim brand name. In March-April, with increased demand for food delivery, an online sales system for the VkusVill retail chain began to operate in Kazan.

3.2. Second Quadrant

The second quadrant (Figure 1) includes only one region that has slightly higher than average per capita income with a small percentage of the urban population, Bashkiria. The capital of Bashkortostan, Ufa, has a population of over one million and is comparable in this respect with Nizhny Novgorod and other cities of the first quadrant.

Online delivery services (group 2) in the region are approximately the same as in the cities of the first quadrant. Local services are represented, in particular, by delivery and courier services Ufa Market 24 and dostavkana123.ru. In the second half of 2019, the online delivery market was not able to accommodate all the players. The project vGastronom (delivery from METRO) and Ufa Market 24 stopped their operations. While this process was slowed down somewhat during the pandemic, neither old projects were revived nor new projects launched, unlike the cities of the first quadrant.

Online shops of manufacturing, wholesale and retail companies (group 3) are represented by the following projects: Nurly (launched by a soft drinks factory), GURMAN-FRESH (by a Kazan wholesale and retail company trading in meat, fish, and seafood), and Pyshka (by a culinary shop). The Nurly project expands the range of delivered products through cooperation with METRO, but does not work with fresh-category goods.

Trading networks that work offline and develop their own online sales system (group 5) in Bashkiria's capital are Magazin-Yarmarka.RF of the local Yarmarka retail network and Ecofood-dostavka of the Ecofood hypermarket chain.

3.3. Third Quadrant

The third quadrant covers the most regions. The percentage of the urban population here does not exceed 70%. Unlike the regions of the first and second quadrants, there are no million-plus cities. The largest city, Izhevsk, has a population of less than 700 thousand people.

Among the local projects focused on the delivery of food products ordered online, there are the Marathon 2.0 courier service and the tornado.shop project by the local Caravan chain (Penza), the Gourmania online store with a limited product range and teoriyaedi.ru, a food delivery service for cooking at home (Izhevsk), Produktov Den, also with a limited range (Cheboksary), as well as the From Atlashevo farm products store (Cheboksary).

3.4. Fourth Quadrant

The fourth quadrant does not include a single million-plus city either. The largest city, Saratov, has a population of just over 800 thousand people. However, unlike the regions of the third quadrant, the percentage of urban residents is higher, ranging from 75% to 80%. In addition, there are no cities with a population of less than 400 thousand people among the central cities of the regions.

Online delivery services from retail chains (group 2) in the regions include standard federal services and local services, such as DostavkaProduktov and Internet Supermarket MEGA 64 (Saratov), Dostavim73 and Prodkarta (Ulyanovsk), Instashop (Kirov).

It is noteworthy that Saratov services work only with federal retail chains, while Ulyanovsk and Kirov services also cooperate with local retail chains Gulliver and Gurman (Ulyanovsk), FermerskiyeProdukty and PoleznyeProdukty (Kirov). However, in the near future (April or May), the Sbermarket service is to start working in Saratov, which will be able to push local services away from working with large federal networks.

Online stores of manufacturing, wholesale and retail companies (group 3) are available in Ulyanovsk. This is the EdaTUT online store by the production and wholesale Prodsoyuz Group of Companies and the water and product delivery service ZakazVody by Undorovsky Mineral Water Plant Volzhanka.

Online stores of stationary retail outlets (group 4) in Saratov, namely Eda Domoy, VezuEdu, SvoyoKhozyaistvo, and SvoyaFerma all have a limited product range (without the fresh category).

In Saratov, an attempt is being made to open a food delivery service for cooking at home.

Offline trading networks that develop their own online sales systems (group 5) operate in Kirov and Saratov. In Kirov, the Sistema Globus trading network sells a wide range of goods online, including its own brands and goods produced by the network.

4. Discussion

In general, the regions of the first quadrant under consideration are characterized by a variety of forms of online food trade, fairly strong competition in the markets, and the presence of market growth potential, which resulted in a noticeable increase in demand and increased activity of enterprises during the pandemic. To survive, the projects in these regions should actively seek their unique selling points, as done by Pyshka in Ufa (see below). Online stores of stationary retail outlets (group 4) in the region are more focused on customers with above-average incomes who value product quality and comfort. It is in the cities of the most prosperous first quadrant that a sufficient number of such buyers can be found.

In the near future, the networks of the first quadrant, which mainly offer a standard product range, are likely to face competition from federal delivery services and own delivery services by projects like Perekrestok, which have so far been developed only in Moscow and St. Petersburg, but the chain itself includes numerous stores across the country.

The main forms of online food sales have been tested in the regions of the second quadrant. However, only the businesses that were able to offer a unique product range continue to operate. For example, the product range offered by Pyshka is an interesting combination of part-cooked and cooked products, as well as pastries. Thus, the company bridges the gap between the markets for grocery delivery and ready meals delivered from caterers. This unique combination is likely to allow the company to develop successfully in the future.

A feature of these enterprises is the availability of a large range of goods from local Bashkir manufacturers. In Ecofood-dostavka's catalog, there are sections for gluten-free, lactose-free, dietary, diabetic, and vegan products. This makes the service unique, but does not eliminate the potential competition from federal retail chains, should they expand to this region with their own delivery services. The current demand does not yet encourage a variety of experiments or strong competition.

Online stores of stationary retail outlets (group 4) are underrepresented in the region. The online store of organic farm products called Bashfermer, which used to offer dairy and meat products by local producers, does not work today. The incomes of the urban population are not high enough to support the demand for expensive farm products, and the large rural population cannot be considered as target consumers.

In the regions of the third quadrant, one can observe enterprises of online food trade in all five groups. However, only a subset of the groups are present in each individual city. In addition, each group is represented by a single project in most cases. This quadrant is characterized by low competition and a decrease in the number of delivery services and online food stores throughout the second half of 2019. This trend has not changed even during the pandemic when the demand for online ordering and food delivery was expected to increase.

Online food trade in the fourth quadrant regions is quite active, but so far it lags behind the regions of the first quadrant in terms of variety and level of competition. In Ulyanovsk, only one store of this type can be considered fully online-functioning, Ferma73.ru. Some other stores are promoting their products via social networks and accept orders by phone, which is why they cannot be considered fully online. In Saratov, classic online sales of groceries are carried out by the Auchan sales network. However, the fresh category is not included in its online assortment. The PyatyiUrozhai chain of stores positions itself as a farm products store, but offers a wider range for delivery and, apparently, generates most of its revenue by selling other types of products.

CONCLUSION

The following conclusions can be drawn from the study conducted:

1. The classification of regions according to two selected criteria (income per capita and the percentage of urban population) makes it possible to identify

groups of regions with different characteristics. The regions of the first quadrant, with the highest rates, enjoy a variety of forms of online trading, intense competition, and the potential for growth in demand. In the regions of the second and fourth quadrants, many forms of online grocery selling are being tested; however, their diversity and intensity of competition are lower than in the first quadrant. In the regions of the third quadrant, online food trade is carried out by a small number of enterprises with a limited variety of forms.

2. During the pandemic of the first half of 2020, interest in selling food products online has increased, but only in the cities of the first quadrant did this entail the revival of some projects and the inclusion of food delivery in the activities of enterprises that had not previously offered such services.

3. With all the variety of forms of online food trade, the enterprises considered in the study are quite clearly divided into five proposed groups according to the function scope of these enterprises.

4. There are variations within the proposed groups of enterprises, such as successful (or unsuccessful) practices, the scale of activity, breadth, specialization, or combinations of assortments. However, these variations do not contradict the proposed classification of enterprises.

5. The proposed approach to the classification of regions and enterprises can be used to analyze the competitive situation in the market for online sales of food products in relation to different territories. The analysis involves the division of the regions under consideration into four quadrants, in each of which one can expect to find a distribution of the groups of online enterprises as shown in this study. Using the results of the analysis, market players can plan initial entry into the market or an expansion of their activities.

REFERENCES

[1] Anshu, Kumari, and Loveleen Gaur. 2019. "E-Satisfaction Estimation: A Comparative Analysis Using AHP and Intuitionistic Fuzzy TOPSIS." *Journal of Cases on Information Technology.* https://doi.org/10.4018/JCIT.2019040105.

[2] Boyer, Kenneth K., and G. Tomas M. Hult. 2005. "Extending the Supply Chain: Integrating Operations and Marketing in the Online Grocery Industry." *Journal of Operations Management.* https://doi.org/10.1016/j.jom.2005.01.003.

[3] Chintagunta, Pradeep K., Junhong Chu, and Javier Cebollada. 2012. "Quantifying Transaction Costs in Online/off-Line Grocery Channel Choice." *Marketing Science.* https://doi.org/10.1287/mksc.1110.0678.

[4] De-Juan-Vigaray, María D., and Ana I.Espinosa Seguí. 2019. "Retailing, Consumers, and Territory: Trends of an Incipient Circular Model." *Social Sciences.* https://doi.org/10.3390/socsci8110300.

[5] Fedoseeva, Svetlana, Roland Herrmann, and Katharina Nickolaus. 2017. "Was the Economics of Information Approach Wrong All the Way? Evidence from

German Grocery r(E)Tailing." *Journal of Business Research.* https://doi.org/10. 1016/j.jbusres.2017.07.006.

[6] "Global Strategic Business Management: Focusing On the Strategic Business Unit of Amazon Whole Foods." 2019. *Journal of Research on the Lepidoptera.* https://doi.org/10.36872/lepi/v51i1/301001.

[7] Goethals, Frank G., Andrea Carugati, and Aurélie Leclercq. 2009. "Differences in E-Commerce Behavior between Neighboring Countries - The Case of France and Belgium." *Data Base for Advances in Information Systems.* https://doi.org/ 10.1145/1644953.1644960.

[8] Hand, C., Francesca Dall Olmo Riley, Patricia Harris, Jaywant Singh, and Ruth Rettie. 2009. "Online Grocery Shopping: The Influence of Situational Factors." *European Journal of Marketing.* https://doi.org/10.1108/03090560910976447.

[9] Hansen, Torben. 2005. "Consumer Adoption of Online Grocery Buying: A Discriminant Analysis." *International Journal of Retail & Distribution Management.* https://doi.org/10.1108/09590550510581449.

[10] Hanus, Gabriela. 2016. "Consumer Behaviour during Online Grocery Shopping." *CBU International Conference Proceedings.* https://doi.org/10.12955/cbup. v4.737.

[11] Hu, Qifan, Qianyun Xu, and Bing Xu. 2019. "Introducing of Online Channel and Management Strategy for Green Agri-Food Supply Chain Based on Pick-Your-Own Operations." *International Journal of Environmental Research and Public Health.* https://doi.org/10.3390/ijerph16111990.

[12] Keh, Hean Tat, and Elain Shieh. 2001. "Online Grocery Retailing: Success Factors and Potential Pitfalls." *Business Horizons.* https://doi.org/10.1016/ S0007-6813(01)80050-1.

[13] Krasyuk, I., and Y. Medvedeva. 2019. "Resource Support in Business Analytics of Innovative Development of Trade and Technological Systems." In *Proceedings of the 33rd International Business Information Management Association Conference, IBIMA 2019: Education Excellence and Innovation Management through Vision 2020.*

[14] Krasyuk, Irina A., and Yuliya Y. Medvedeva. 2019. "Drives and Obstacle for the Development of Marketing in Russian Retailing." In *Proceedings of the 33rd International Business Information Management Association Conference, IBIMA 2019: Education Excellence and Innovation Management through Vision 2020.*

[15] Ladhari, Riadh, Magalie Christelle Rioux, Nizar Souiden, and Nour Eddine Chiadmi. 2019. "Consumers' Motives for Visiting a Food Retailer's Facebook Page." *Journal of Retailing and Consumer Services.* https://doi.org/10.1016/ j.jretconser.2018.07.013.

[16] Lingyu, Meng, Christenson Lauren, and Dong Zhijie. 2019. "Strategic Development of Fresh E-Commerce with Respect to New Retail." In *Proceedings of the 2019 IEEE 16th International Conference on Networking, Sensing and Control, ICNSC 2019.* https://doi.org/10.1109/ICNSC.2019.8743243.

[17] Parshukov, Aleksey E., Igor Aleksandrov, and Marina Fedorova. 2020. "Universal Classification of Goods and Services for Marketing and Logistics." In *E3S Web of Conferences*. https://doi.org/10.1051/e3sconf/202021707001.

[18] Prasad, Sarita, and Mukund Sharma. 2016. "Demographic and Socioeconomic Influences Shaping Usage of Online Channel for Purchase of Food & Grocery." *Indian Journal of Marketing*. https://doi.org/10.17010/ijom/2016/v46/i10/102851.

[19] Seitz, Christian, Ján Pokrivčák, Marián Tóth, and Miroslav Plevný. 2017. "Online Grocery Retailing in Germany: An Explorative Analysis." *Journal of Business Economics and Management*. https://doi.org/10.3846/16111699.2017.1410218.

[20] Tanskanen, Kari, Hannu Yrjölä, and Jan Holmström. 2002. "The Way to Profitable Internet Grocery Retailing – Six Lessons Learned." *International Journal of Retail & Distribution Management*. https://doi.org/10.1108/09590550 210423645.

[21] Wang, H. Holly, Na Hao, Qingjie Zhou, Michael E. Wetzstein, and Yong Wang. 2019. "Is Fresh Food Shopping Sticky to Retail Channels and Online Platforms? Evidence and Implications in the Digital Era." *Agribusiness*. https://doi.org/ 10.1002/agr.21589.

[22] Wang, Ou, Simon Somogyi, and Sylvain Charlebois. 2020. "Food Choice in the E-Commerce Era: A Comparison between Business-to-Consumer (B2C), Online-to-Offline (O2O) and New Retail." *British Food Journal*. https://doi.org/ 10.1108/BFJ-09-2019-0682.

[23] Zhang, Aihua, Chen Liang, and Junwan Yin. 2018. "How Can Dmall Do Better? Discussion on New Retail Marketing Mode Based on 4Cs Theory." In *ACM International Conference Proceeding Series*. https://doi.org/10.1145/3194188. 3194190.

In: Global Challenges of Digital Transformation of Markets ISBN: 978-1-53619-754-9
Editors: E. de la Poza and S. E. Barykin

Chapter 12

IDENTIFICATION OF SECTOR LEADERS: ANALYSIS OF AGRICULTURAL COMPANIES USING KOHONEN NETWORKS

Jakub Horak and Petr Suler*

School of Expertness and Valuation, Institute of Technology and Business,
Ceske Budejovice, Czech Republic

ABSTRACT

Agriculture is a sector of the national economy using natural resources to produce commodities essential for life. An agricultural business is dependent on natural conditions and processes that are hardly influenceable by humans. The risks of agricultural businesses are significantly higher than in industrial businesses. In today's age of digitization, the companies have the opportunity to use the tools of AI to analyze the market situation. This information can be important for the identification of competitors and potential competitors in a particular sector. The goal of the paper is to provide an analysis of the agricultural sector in the Czech Republic using Kohonen networks. Within the analysis, the leaders in the sector will be identified. Data of 4,201 businesses active in the agricultural sector in 2016 are used. The data set is subjected to cluster analysis using Kohonen networks. In order to identify the field leaders, variables such as the amount of assets, fixed assets, operational revenues, or earnings before tax are taken into consideration. In the analysis, the absolute and average values of individual clusters are further examined. As a result, the most successful clusters and companies in the sector of agriculture could be identified. Following the results obtained, it can be concluded that the future agriculture sector development can be predicted based on the results of 37 companies.

Keywords: agricultural companies, neural networks, sector leaders, cluster

---

* Corresponding Author's Email: horak@mail.vstecb.cz.

1. INTRODUCTION

According to Hyblova (Hýblová 2014), farming represents a significant part of the Czech Republic's economy. It secures the production of food and impacts many related processing businesses. Even though the volume of agricultural production and its extent in the gross domestic product has been decreasing, there is tremendous enthusiasm for expanding the exhibition of agribusiness organizations (Veronika Machová and Vrbka 2018). Local farming work productivity is emphatically influenced by the nominal price of rural land and population density (Junga, P., Vrbka, J., & Krulicky 2018). Shockingly, micro-regions are overwhelmed by huge farms performed at lower efficiency levels than micro-regions with divided farm size structure (Ženka et al. 2015).

Conferring to Abdullahi, Sheriff and Mahieddine (Abdullahi, Sheriff, and Mahieddine 2017); Vochozka and Machova (Vochozka and Machová 2018); Machova and Vochozka (V. Machová and Vochozka 2019); Vrbka and Rowland (Vrbka and Rowland 2020), various systems have been applied to the procedures from the utilization of the neural networks, support vector machine, fuzzy logic approach and as of late, the best approach producing quick and magnificent outcomes utilizing the deep learning approach of convolution neural network for image arrangements. According to Test results from Abdullahi, Sheriff and Mahieddine (Abdullahi, Sheriff, and Mahieddine 2017), a 99.58% image recognition accuracy using a convolution neural network was reported. Balducci, Impedovo and Pirlo (Balducci, Impedovo, and Pirlo 2018) observed with ample margins for innovation, companies wishing to employ a sustainable and optimized agriculture industrial business invest in technology, and in knowledge and skilled workforce.

Organic farming has turned into a point that gets an expanding scholastic just as well known consideration. Investigations have indicated that organic agricultural companies outperform conventional companies in the terms of profitability. Be that as it may, their asset turnover is extensively lower (Krause and Machek 2018). Dairy products are the export pillars of Czech agrarian foreign trade, and the dairy business was one of the most significant beneficiaries of public support on innovations from the Rural Development Programme (RDP). Research has shown that innovations, and open help of advancements, empowered dairies to settle their profits and to expand their competitiveness, during the time of financial emergency (Špička, Smutka, and Selby 2015).

Stekla and Grycova (Stekla and Grycova 2016) revealed that for the agriculture sector in the Czech Republic, there is a negative relationship between the short-term debt to the total assets and profitability, between the long-term debt to the total assets and profitability, and between the total debt to the total assets and profitability.

According to Spicka, Boudny and Janotova (Špička, Boudný, and Janotová 2009), current subsidies have an impact on the stability of the farmers' income. Svatos and Smutka (Svatoš and Smutka 2010) reported a dramatic change in terms of commodity structure, territorial, and primarily value structures in the Czech Republic. Most of the progressions is because of essentially the process of the EU enlargement and have resulted in a dominant share of the member countries of the EU 27 in the agricultural trade of the nation.

Technical inefficiency is a significant phenomenon in Czech agriculture. The average level of technical efficiency is around 90% for agricultural companies (Čechura 2010). Naglova and Gurtler (Naglova and Gurtler 2016) proved different impacts of subsidies on agricultural company´s management. Government subsidies influence the medium and large enterprises significantly and positively. Nerudova and Krchniva (Nerudova and Krchniva 2016) conclude that the proportion of explained profitability by the formula factors as defined by the Draft Directive on the Common Consolidated Corporate Tax Base can differ by more than 30% with respect to the sector of economic activity classified by the NACE, whereas in the individual subsectors of the agriculture the difference may amount to 40%. The comparison of return on assets and adjusted return on assets reflecting the elimination of the deferred tax effect reveals that the effect of deferred tax reporting is not so high in the large agricultural holdings in the Czech Republic (Bohušová, Svoboda, and Semerádová 2019).

Kalusova and Badura (Kalusova and Badura 2017) used multiple regression and correlation analysis to point the fact that in addition to the internal corporate factors, the external factors of the macro-environment were also statistically highly significant for certain groups of agricultural enterprises. The paper also points to some differences in the direction and intensity of action of the chosen factors. Puticova, Fronek and Mezera (Putićová, Froněk, and Mezera 2007) utilized the exponential smoothing model and projected a fall of the number of workers and a growth of personal costs in the sector.

Using the Stochastic Frontier Approach, models were assessed as translogarithmic creation capacity. The results pointed out the nearness of critical heterogeneity among agricultural firms in the examined branches and among various parts of the food handling industry (Rudinskaya 2017). The result of Sedlacek, Kourilova and Psencik (Sedláček, Kouřilová, and Pšenčík 2012) analysis is an identification of distortions in reported production power and the value of company property, caused by the yield method based on the matching principle.

Agriculture is significant for the existence of human life on Earth as their survival depends on it for food production. Because the agricultural sector is just obviously overwhelming to the advanced innovation and the awareness of the smart farm concept, it is progressively far-reaching by misusing the Internet of Things (IoT) model applied to natural and recorded data through time-series.

The objective of the contribution is the analysis of the agricultural sector in the Czech Republic using Kohonen networks. Within the analysis, the leaders in the sector will be identified.

2. MATERIALS AND METHODS

For the purposes of this contribution, a data set will be created containing complete financial statement data of 4,201 companies operating in 2016 in the agriculture sector of the Czech Republic. Those are entities whose main activities are classified in Section A of the Classification of the economic activities CZ-NACE. The set of the companies will be generated from Bisnode´s Albertina database.

The data will be entered into an Excel table. Each row will contain financial statement data of a specific company which will be identified by its name and identification number. The data set will not contain the companies that did not perform their main activity during the whole monitored period. This includes the companies that were closed in the aforementioned period (and thus did not influence significantly the direction of this national economy sector), and the companies that started their activity in the monitored period (and similarly, did not affect the direction of the CR agricultural sector). The importance of the companies that started their activity on 1 January 2016 and those who finished their activity on 31 December 2016 could be discussed; it would, however, did not have a significant impact on achieving the objective of this contribution.

Moreover, the data that do not show any dispersion were also excluded.

The data set will be subjected to a cluster analysis using a Kohonen network. For the cluster analysis, Dell´s Statistica software, version 12, will be used, as well as the module Data mining, and Neural networks as a concrete tool. Here, the neural networks without a teacher (Kohonen network) will be used. Data for analysis will be chosen: we will choose a table with a data set from Excel. In all cases, these are continuous predictors. The data set will be divided into three subsets:

- Training data set: it includes 70% of the companies. This set will be used for the creation of the Kohonen network.
- Testing data set: it includes 15% of the companies in the original data set. This set will be used for verification of the created Kohonen network parameters.
- Validation data set: it will also include 15% of the companies in the data set. This set will also be used to verify whether the Kohonen network is applicable or not.

Both the topological length and width of the Kohonen network will be set to 10. The number of calculation repetitions (iteration) is 10,000. However, it must be noted that the level of error is decisive. If there is no improvement in the parameters of the Kohonen network with the new iteration, the training will be finished before the 10,000th iteration is carried out. If the parameters improve even with the 10,000th iteration, the whole process must be repeated and a higher number of required iterations must be chosen to make sure that the results obtained are the best possible ones. The speed of learning will be first set at 0.1, and at 0.02 at the end.

The results, that is, distribution of the companies into 100 clusters, will be entered in the Excel table. Subsequently, the individual clusters will be subjected to the analysis of the absolute indicators and return on equity. Here it is necessary to answer the question of how to identify the sector leader. There are several possible variables to be taken into account, including the following ones:

- Volume of assets;
- Volume of fixed assets;
- Operating earnings;
- Earnings before tax.

Furthermore, it must be determined whether the clusters with significantly high absolute values of the selected variables or the clusters which show the highest average values will be sought.

Within the analysis, we will examine both the average values and absolute values of the individual clusters. This way it will be possible to identify:

- The most successful clusters within the agriculture sector;
- The most successful companies in the agriculture sector.

Return on equity will show, inter alia, the attractiveness of the individual clusters for potential investors.

3. RESULTS

The clusters were created based on the methodology applied. The division of the companies into the individual clusters of the Kohonen map can be seen in Figure 1.

Figure 1 shows a 3D representation of the created Kohonen map and the number of companies in the individual clusters. The figure clearly shows that the highest number of companies is in the cluster (1, 8), followed by the cluster (3, 9), and the imaginary third position is occupied by the cluster (3, 10). A slightly higher number of companies are in the clusters (4, 10) and (5, 10). The number of companies in other clusters is significantly lower. Also, it should be noted that three of the Kohonen map clusters are vacant, namely (2, 3), (3, 1) and (3, 2).

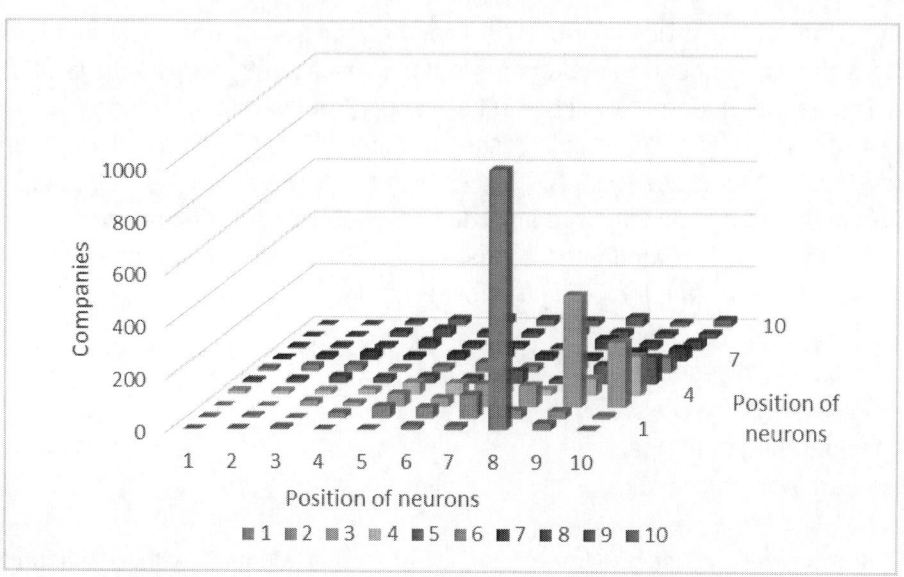

(Source: Own processing)

Figure 1. Division of companies into individual Kohonen map clusters.

Table 1. Number of companies in individual Kohonen map clusters

Network: 1. SOFM 10-100: Samples: Training, testing, validation									
	1	2	3	4	5	6	7	8	9	10
1	1	3	9	2	4	17	16	990	26	4
2	2	7	0	20	44	42	90	30	29	11
3	0	0	18	14	48	32	86	82	427	249
4	13	13	15	19	46	45	37	22	64	150
5	9	14	26	22	27	22	47	15	72	103
6	10	21	24	13	19	37	21	39	55	56
7	6	17	28	17	25	36	23	17	37	48
8	6	10	12	28	17	16	7	40	23	30
9	2	5	19	31	18	19	28	23	18	18
10	1	2	12	24	31	26	21	34	14	26

(Source: Own processing)

To get a clearer picture of the number of companies in the individual clusters, Figure 1 is complemented by concrete values given in Table 1.

The table clearly shows that besides the above-mentioned clusters with a high number of companies (in the table, the cells are colored yellow), no other clusters contain more than a hundred companies.

Further analysis of the companies operating in the agriculture sector, or the analysis of the entire institutional sector of the national economy will be carried out from two perspectives:

- The prism of the average values of companies in the individual clusters. This way it is possible to determine how the companies in the individual clusters are characterized and to what extent they are on average successful in their activities.
- Absolute values for individual clusters. This way it will be possible to identify the influence of the individual clusters on the future development and success of the CR agricultural sector.

3.1. Analysis of Average Values

The first characteristic used is the fixed assets average value of the companies in the same cluster (Figure 2).

In practice, there shall be the marginal rate of substitution of capital for labor, that is, the substitution of fixed assets for workers. In agriculture, this marginal rate of substitution does not have to be absolute, as agriculture is a very specific sector of the national economy, not only due to its strategic importance but also the structure of its production factors. The most important production factor in agriculture is definitely land. Therefore, it is logical that in the case of agriculture companies, fixed assets will create a large share of their assets. Only after subtracting the value of the land from the overall fixed assets of an agricultural company, it will be possible to identify the automation of agricultural production and thus the functioning of the marginal rate of substituting labor for capital. In such a case it could be stated that the companies owning a high volume of fixed assets perform a high number of orders with a lower number of employees. In any case, and especially in the case of the agricultural companies, the volume of the fixed assets predetermines the volume of the sales from the main activity. This is given by the fact that land is a fixed production factor. It is not consumed but is an essential prerequisite for achieving sales. However, it is assumed that it is an operationally necessary asset. In the case of agriculture companies, we have identified one cluster with a very high volume of fixed assets, the cluster (10, 1). On average, the companies of this cluster own the assets worth more than CZK 62 billion. The imaginary second place is occupied by the cluster (10, 2). However, from the graph, it is not possible to estimate the average values of the other clusters. Therefore, the graph in Figure 3 is added.

Unlike the graph in Figure 2, the graph in Figure 3 does not include the clusters (10, 1) and (10, 2). The overview is thus more detailed and it can be stated that the clusters in the section (4, 1), (10, 1) and (10, 5) achieve higher average values. It results from the triangle section of the Kohonen map that the highest average values (besides the aforementioned clusters) are achieved by the clusters (9, 2) and (8, 2). These clusters also achieve significantly higher values in the agriculture sector.

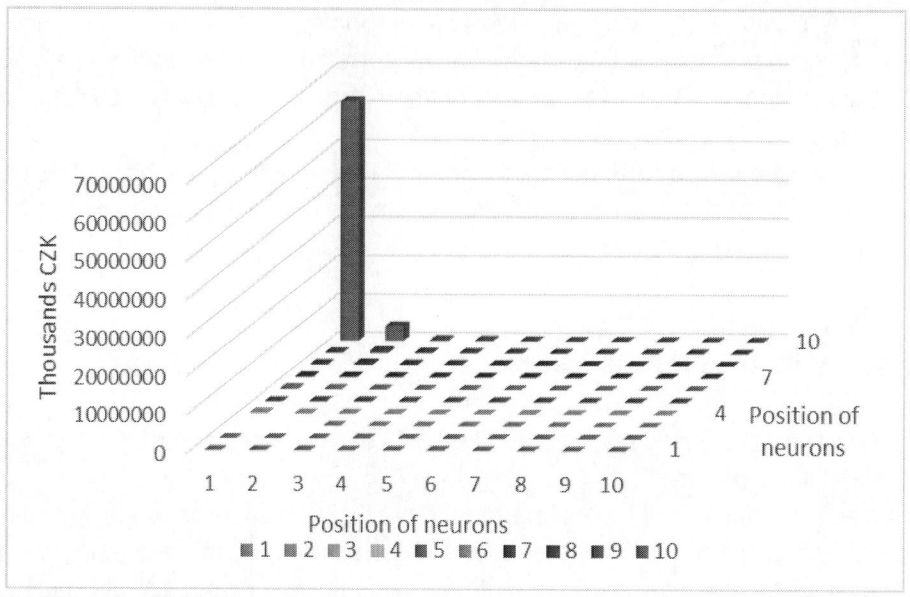

(Source: Own processing)

Figure 2. Fixed assets average values of companies in individual clusters.

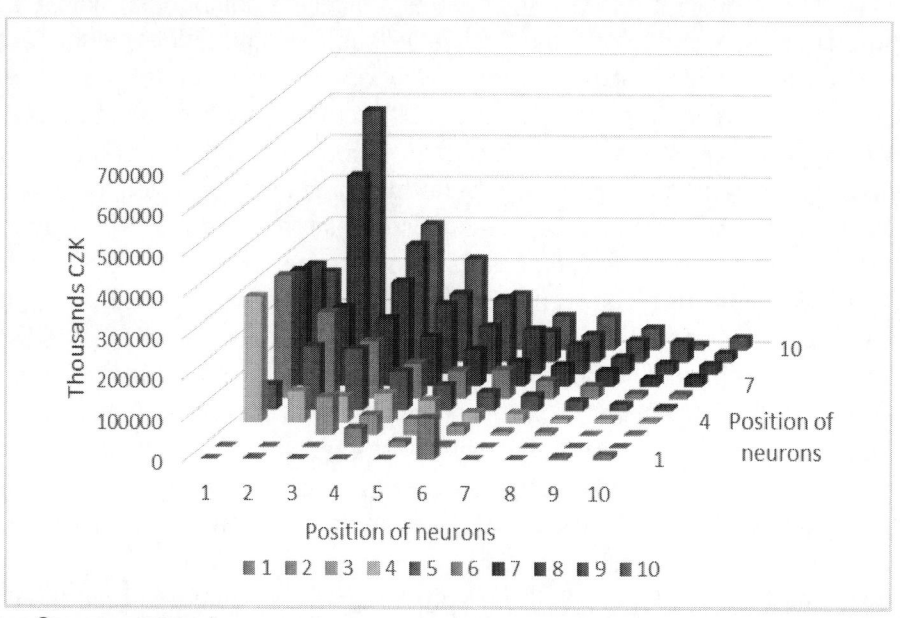

(Source: Own processing)

Figure 3. Average values of companies fixed assets in individual clusters without clusters (10, 1) and (10, 2).

In addition to fixed assets volume, another interesting indicator is the overall assets of an average company in the individual clusters. The volume of the overall assets predetermines the ability of the company to generate results. The overall assets include two of the three production factors – fixed assets and material. The third production factor, human labor, is considered at the moment of its consumption. Similarly to overall assets, higher values are achieved by the clusters (4, 1), (10, 1) and (10, 4). The above-average values are seen in the clusters (9, 2), (8, 2), (8, 1) and (7, 1).

There are two other average values with a great explanatory value: operating earnings and earnings before tax.

The average operating earnings allow comparing the success of the companies in the individual clusters in terms of performing their main activities. The highest average operating earnings are achieved by the companies in the cluster (10, 1), generating more than CZK 6 billion. The cluster is followed by the companies of the cluster (10, 2), generating average operating earnings of nearly CZK 187 million. The operating earnings of other companies are incomparably lower.

A significantly high value of the operating earnings is achieved also by the companies in the clusters (9, 2), (8, 2) and (7, 1). Operating earnings as a variable represent the company's main activity, that is, the level of its success (the vision with which the company was founded) and the potential of the future growth of the company.

The last average variable analyzed is the earnings before tax. A profit that a company generates predetermines the company's success in the eyes of investors. For the purposes of the analysis, the earnings before tax were chosen, as the result of the company activity is not distorted by the tax optimization carried out by the management of the company. Here, the situation is very different. In this case, the highest value is not achieved by the cluster (10, 1), but by the cluster (1, 10). The earnings before tax of an average company of this cluster are more than CZK 140 million. It is followed by the companies in the cluster (1, 2) with the average earnings before tax of nearly CZK 123 million. On the other hand, the clusters (10, 1) and (10, 2) achieve minimum earnings before tax of tens and hundred thousands of CZK. This is in a large disproportion to the operating earnings the companies of both clusters achieved in 2016. Only the companies in the clusters (1, 4), (2, 8) and (9, 1) reported a loss in 2016.

3.2. Analysis of Absolute Indicators

As stated above, the analysis of the absolute indicators will show to what extent the individual clusters of companies are important for the entire agriculture sector of the CR. The same variables as in the case of the average values have been analyzed.

Figure 4 shows the absolute values of fixed assets of the companies in the same cluster.

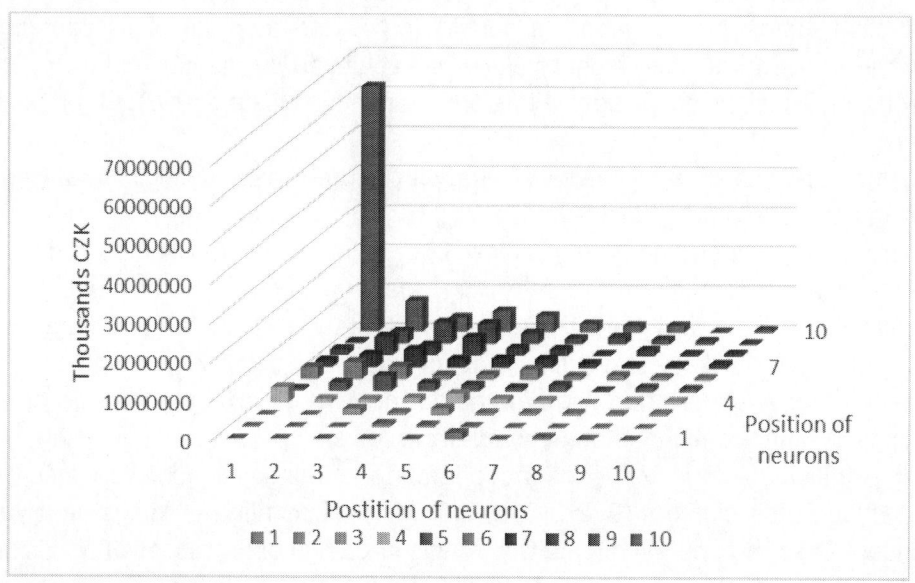

(Source: Own processing)

Figure 4. Volume of assets owned by companies of the same cluster.

It follows from the graph that the largest volume of assets is owned by the cluster (10, 1), which is followed by the clusters (10, 2), (10, 4), (9, 3), (8, 6) and (10, 6). There is also an interesting complementing of the information by the share the individual clusters have on the volume of the owned assets (Figure 5).

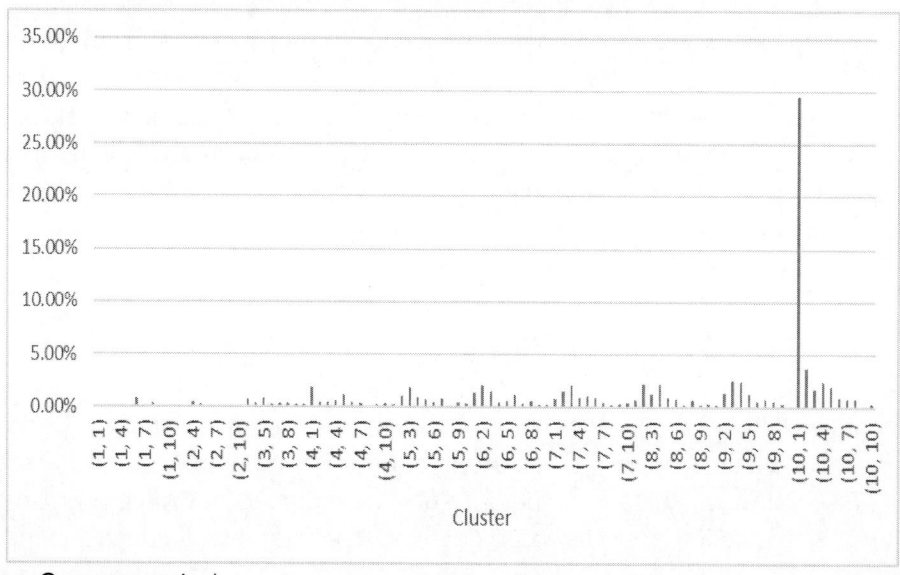

(Source: Own processing)

Figure 5. Individual clusters share on assets owned within the agricultural sector.

As seen from the graph, the companies of the cluster (10, 1) own nearly 23%, and the companies of the cluster (10, 2) own almost 3.18% of all assets in the agriculture sector. No other cluster owns a significant share of the institutional sector assets.

The second variable examined was the volume of fixed assets.

The situation will be better illustrated by the relative comparison of the clusters, or their share on the overall fixed assets owned within the agriculture sector. The fixed assets owned by the companies of the cluster (10, 1) account for almost 30% of the overall fixed assets. The companies of the cluster (10, 2) own a significantly lower share, specifically almost 3.7%. Except for the cluster (10, 1), no cluster can be considered important from this point of view.

Comparing absolute operating earnings indicates that the most successful cluster is (10, 1). Significantly, less successful clusters are the clusters (9, 2), (8, 2), (9, 3) and (6, 3). The cluster (10, 1) generates 35% of the operating earnings of the entire agriculture sector. No other cluster participates significantly in the agriculture sector operating earnings.

An interesting fact is that in terms of profit, the dominant cluster was (10, 1). In the case of earnings before tax (i.e., including financial and extraordinary earnings), the situation is different, with the cluster (1, 9) contributing most to it, generating 4.16% of the earnings before tax for the whole sector. It is followed by the clusters (2, 7), generating 3.74%, and (1, 10) with a 3.29% share on the overall earnings before tax of the sector. It results from the comparison that the importance of the cluster (10, 1) is in the category of the earnings before tax of the agriculture sector insignificant.

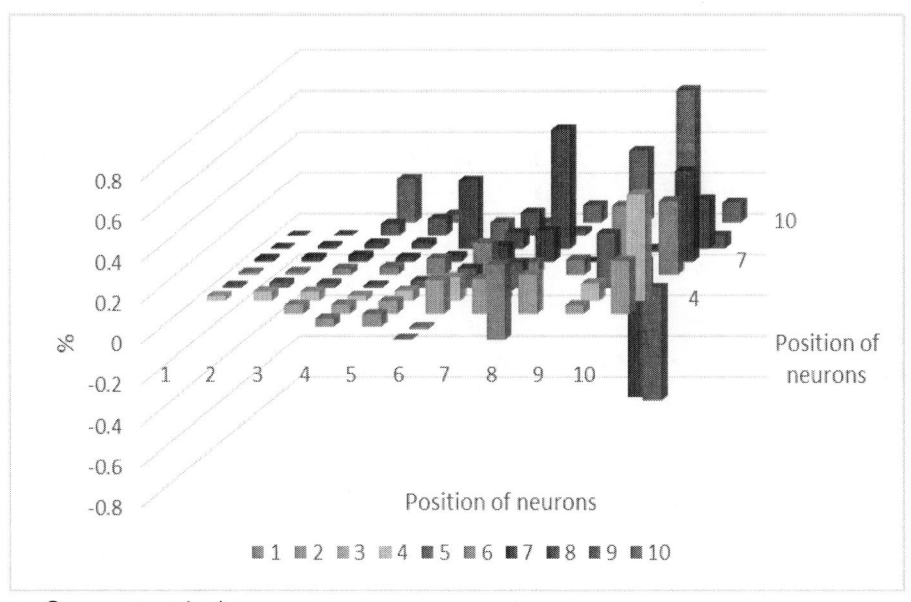

(Source: Own processing)

Figure 6. Comparing ROE of profitable clusters in the interval (-100; +100).

An interesting indicator is the comparison of ROE for individual clusters. It indicates that some clusters achieve extreme values which are often beyond rational range. This applies, for example, to clusters (2, 1) or (1, 4). It was therefore necessary to set a ROE interval for a graph representation. Figure 6 shows only the clusters whose ROE is in the interval (−100% to + 100%).

ROE, or return on equity, provides information on the valuation of the owners' deposit. It is considered one of the most important indicators of a company's success. Its volume is, by default, compared with the profitability of other investment opportunities in the market. The ROE weakness is in not taking into account the investment opportunities level of risk. The figure shows significant differences between the individual clusters. Despite the limited interval for showing the results, it must be stated that the clusters in the figure show very different values both in the negative and positive part of the interval. It is even not possible to identify the most and the least successful clusters. To state this, it would be necessary to examine each of the clusters separately in order to find out whether the result is rational and whether it corresponds to the company's capabilities. For example, negative earnings and negative equity make a positive ROE. The resulting value may thus appear positive; however, it is not rational in the given context. Those are of course disadvantages of ratio indicators in general.

4. Discussion

It follows from the analyses carried out that the most important cluster for the agriculture sector is (10, 1). This cluster consists of one company only; still, it shows the absolute highest volume of assets and fixed assets and generates high operating earnings. What is interesting, however, is that its earnings before tax are minimal and do not correspond to the value of the assets administered and generated operating earnings. It can thus be concluded that the cluster (10, 1) is the most important cluster of the entire agriculture sector in the CR.

Table 2. Leaders of Czech agriculture sector in 2016

Identification	Number of companies in cluster	Assets in total	Fixed assets	Added value	Operating earnings	Earnings before tax
(10, 1)	1	70,337,868	62,152,700	7,831,937	6,356,727	204
(10, 2)	2	9,917,312	7,762,969	1,461,517	373,529	31
(9, 3)	19	7,788,122	5,366,459	532,742	343,579	148,967
(8, 2)	10	7,545,020	4,799,850	1,054,823	471,031	87,385
(9, 2)	5	6,375,225	3,043,443	1,012,858	510,763	8,990
Total	37	101,963,547	83,125,421	11,893,877	8,055,629	245,577
Share in total	0.88%	32.67%	39.45%	31.09%	44.36%	1.42%

(Source: Own processing)

It should be recalled that in 2016, a total of 4,201 companies were operating in the agriculture sector. Taking into account all the analyses carried out, it can be stated that the leaders of the sector are the companies in the clusters (10, 1), (10, 2), (9, 3), (8, 2) and (9, 2). The cluster (1, 9) has been included due to its results expressed in the number of companies included (3). Table 2 shows the overall overview of the most successful clusters.

37 out of 4,201 companies have been identified as agriculture sector leaders. This accounts for 0.88% of all companies operating in the sector in the monitored period. The 37 companies own 32.67% of all assets allocated in the agriculture sector, and 39.45% of all fixed assets in agriculture. The companies generate in total 44.36% of the operating earnings of the whole agriculture sector, which is, however, only 1.42% of the earnings before tax of the entire agriculture sector in the CR.

CONCLUSION

The objective of the contribution was the analysis of the agriculture sector in the Czech Republic by averages of Kohonen networks. Within the analysis, the leaders in the sector have been identified.

The objective of the contribution has been achieved. Kohonen networks were used to carry out a cluster analysis. 4,201 companies operating in the agriculture sector in 2016 were divided into 100 clusters (Kohonen map had been pre-determined by averages of grid topology 10 x 10), or more precisely, into 97 clusters, as the clusters (2, 3), (3, 1) and (3, 2) were vacant. All clusters were subjected to the analysis. The cluster with the highest number of companies was (1, 8). Nevertheless, this cluster cannot be considered essential for the development of the CR agriculture sector. On the contrary, the agriculture sector is strongly influenced by the cluster (10, 1). Although there is only one company in the cluster, the average values, as well as the sum of the examined variables, significantly outweigh all other companies operating in the agriculture sector. Other clusters have a significant impact on the development of the CR agriculture sector, namely (10, 2), (9, 3), (8, 2) and (9, 2). Generally speaking, 37 companies can be considered leaders of the agricultural sector in CR.

It can thus be stated that a relatively small group of companies have a very high impact on the agriculture sector development. Taking more details into consideration, we can state that this group significantly affects the development of the whole national economy. This is due to the nature of this primary national economy sector. Although in terms of the GDP volume agriculture is not among the most important institutional sectors of the national economy, in terms of the character of its products, structure of the production factors used and other factors, it is an absolutely unique strategic sector essential for the functioning of the state and its economy. If the state were not food independent, it would not be able to manage even its own political and economic development.

Following the results obtained, it can be concluded that the future agriculture sector development can be predicted based on the results of 37 companies. Given their number and small impact on the development of the sector, other companies create a breeding ground whose aggregated form will not change much. As a prediction tool, the analysis of the 37 companies appears to be very positive. However, a negative fact is that performance fluctuation (caused by any causes) can result in fluctuation of the whole institutional sector of the national economy.

Further research shall thus be focused on the following:

- We should find out whether the number of companies in the individual clusters will change over time, especially in the clusters of the agriculture sector leaders (both in terms of number and concrete companies, in particular in the case of the cluster (10, 1)).
- We should verify the ability to predict the agriculture sector development based on the analysis of the agriculture sector leaders.

We should find out how possible fluctuations in the leaders´ results affected the development of the agriculture sector (with a particular focus on the cluster (10, 1)).

REFERENCES

Abdullahi, Halimatu Sadiyah, Ray E. Sheriff. & Fatima Mahieddine. (2017). *"Convolution Neural Network in Precision Agriculture for Plant Image Recognition and Classification."* In . https://doi.org/10.1109/intech.2017.8102436.

Balducci, Fabrizio, Donato Impedovo. & Giuseppe Pirlo. (2018). "Machine Learning Applications on Agricultural Datasets for Smart Farm Enhancement." *Machines.* https://doi.org/10.3390/machines6030038.

Bohušová, Hana, Patrik Svoboda. & Lucie Semerádová. (2019). "Deferred Tax for Tax Planning in the Czech Agricultural Companies." *Agricultural Economics (Czech Republic).* https://doi.org/10.17221/312/2018-AGRICECON.

Čechura, Lukáš. (2010). "Estimation of Technical Efficiency in Czech Agriculture with Respect to Firm Heterogeneity." *Agricultural Economics.* https://doi.org/10.17221/23/2010-agricecon.

Hýblová, Eva. (2014). "Analysis of Mergers in Czech Agricultural Companies." *Agricultural Economics (Czech Republic).* https://doi.org/10.17221/15/2014-agricecon.

Junga, P., Vrbka, J. & Krulicky, T. (2018). *"Determining Financial Compensation in the Case of Agricultural Land Expropriation – New Methodology,"* 101–6.

Kalusova, Lenka. & Peter Badura. (2017). "Factors Determining the Financial Structure of Czech and Slovak Agricultural Enterprises." *Agricultural Economics (Czech Republic).* https://doi.org/10.17221/325/2015-AGRICECON.

Krause, Josef. & Ondrej Machek. (2018). "A Comparative Analysis of Organic and Conventional Farmers in the Czech Republic." *Agricultural Economics (Czech Republic)*. https://doi.org/10.17221/161/2016-AGRICECON.

Machová, V. & Vochozka, M. (2019). "Using Artificial Intelligence in Analyzing and Predicting the Development of Stock Prices of a Subject Company." In *Contributions to Economics*. https://doi.org/10.1007/978-3-030-11754-2_18.

Machová, Veronika. & Jaromír Vrbka. (2018). "Value Generators for Businesses in Agriculture." *The 12th International Days of Statistics and Economics*, 1123–32.

Naglova, Zdenka. & Martin Gurtler. (2016). "Consequences of Supports to the Economic Situation of Farms with Respect to Their Size." *Agricultural Economics (Czech Republic)*. https://doi.org/10.17221/191/2015-AGRICECON.

Nerudova, Danuse. & Katerina Krchniva. (2016). "Tax Sharing under the Common Consolidated Corporate Tax Base: Measurement of the Profit Generating Factors in the Agriculture Sector." *Agricultural Economics (Czech Republic)*. https://doi.org/10.17221/222/2015-AGRICECON.

Putićová, Marie, Pavel Froněk. & Josef Mezera. (2007). "Prediction of Labour and Personal Costs Development in the Food Industry Branches in the Czech Republic up to 2013." *Agricultural Economics*. https://doi.org/10.17221/457-agricecon.

Rudinskaya, Tamara. (2017). "Heterogeneity and Efficiency of Food Processing Companies in the Czech Republic." *Agricultural Economics (Czech Republic)*. https://doi.org/10.17221/1/2016-AGRICECON.

Sedláček, Jaroslav, Jindřiška Kouřilová. & Jiří Pšenčík. (2012). "Models of the Realistic Reporting of Subsidies in the Farm Accounting." *Agricultural Economics*. https://doi.org/10.17221/3/2011-agricecon.

Špička, Jindřich, Jan Boudný. & Bohdana Janotová. (2009). "The Role of Subsidies in Managing the Operating Risk of Agricultural Enterprises." *Agricultural Economics*. https://doi.org/10.17221/17/2009-agricecon.

Špička, Jindřich, Luboš Smutka. & Richard Selby. (2015). "Recent Areas of Innovation Activities in the Czech Dairy Industry." *Agricultural Economics (Czech Republic)*. https://doi.org/10.17221/128/2014-AGRICECON.

Stekla, Jana. & Marta Grycova. (2016). "The Relationship between Profitability and Capital Structure of the Agricultural Holdings in the Czech Republic." *Agricultural Economics (Czech Republic)*. https://doi.org/10.17221/232/2015-AGRICECON.

Svatoš, Miroslav. & Luboš Smutka. (2010). "Development of Agricultural Foreign Trade in the Countries of Central Europe." *Agricultural Economics*. https://doi.org/10.17221/22/2010-agricecon.

Vochozka, Marek. & Veronika Machová. (2018). "Determination of Value Drivers for Transport Companies in the Czech Republic." *Nase More*. https://doi.org/10.17818/NM/2018/4SI.6.

Vrbka, J. & Rowland, Z. (2020). "Using Artificial Intelligence in Company Management." In *Lecture Notes in Networks and Systems*, 84, 422–29. Springer. https://doi.org/10.1007/978-3-030-27015-5_51.

Ženka, Jan, Petr Žufan, Luděk Krtička. & Ondřej Slach. (2015). "Labour Productivity of Agricultural Business Companies and Cooperatives in the Czech Republic: A Micro-Regional Level Analysis." *Moravian Geographical Reports*. https://doi.org/10.1515/mgr-2015-0021.

In: Global Challenges of Digital Transformation of Markets ISBN: 978-1-53619-754-9
Editors: E. de la Poza and S. E. Barykin   © 2021 Nova Science Publishers, Inc.

Chapter 13

Tools Making Optimal Management Decisions to Ensure Economic Stability of Economic Entities

Oksana Kulikova[1], Lyudmila Nikitina[1], Svetlana Suvorova[2,*] and NatalyaTropynina[1]

[1]Saint Petersburg State University of Industrial Technologies and Design,
Saint Petersburg, Russia
[2]Peter the Great St.Petersburg Polytechnic University,
Saint Petersburg, Russia

Abstract

Existing approaches to assessing the level of economic stability contain several unresolved problems. Among them, we can highlight the operational monitoring organization of the economic stability level of enterprises and industries. In this study, we developed tools for making optimal management decisions to ensure the economic stability of light industry enterprises based on the linear-quadratic programming model. The solution of the optimization problem for industrial enterprises made it possible to determine the reference values of indicators that ensure their economic stability. Applying the model we proposed within a single company allowed to obtain information about the current level of a single enterprise's economic stability. The developed tools can be used within the boundaries of a group of enterprises to determine the average level of economic stability to implement strategic planning and increase the competitiveness of the industry. This allows to generate positive synergy aimed at developing the material and technical base, resource, human and intellectual potential; ensuring a continuous process of production and sales of products, maintaining the stability

* Corresponding Author's Email: suvorova_sd@mail.ru.

of enterprises in the medium and long term; reorienting professional activities to stimulate and support digital projects.

Keywords: management decisions, economic stability of enterprise, functional blocks, quadratic programming, mathematical model

1. INTRODUCTION

At present, the issues of regular stability monitoring of market entities are particularly relevant, so the development of economic relations should be aimed at the effective management of all production processes. At the same time, economic entities should systematically monitor the effectiveness of production process management, while simultaneously carrying out operational monitoring of the level of economic stability of enterprises and industries. Achieving these goals is impossible without careful study of tools for making optimal management decisions.

Economic entities of the Russian light industry are considered as the object of this article. The subject of the study is the calculation of target indicators for determining benchmarks for the economic stability of industrial enterprises. The objective is to develop tools for making optimal management decisions to ensure the economic stability of light industry enterprises, since high economic and geopolitical risks with insufficient support from the state can lead to inefficient functioning of enterprises in the market and even to bankruptcy (Dvas and Dubolazova 2018; Dermot McAleese n.d.).

At present, the process of maintaining the economic stability level is one of the key purposes for each enterprise. At the present stage in the development of economic relations, enterprises must constantly monitor the effectiveness of management of all production processes. Many researchers who study economic stability strongly believe that such conditions as prolonged economic instability, strong geopolitical risks, and weak incentives for development by the state can lead to inefficient functioning of the enterprise in the market and even to its bankruptcy.

In this regard, there is an increasing need in the Russian economy to assess the impact of various factors on the economic stability of industrial enterprises and to develop practical recommendations for improving production, strategic management, sales policy, and other activities of economic entities in the context of innovative economic development.

The theoretical study of issues related to the concept of economic stability of the enterprise, from the standpoint of the theory of profit maximization, has been researched by outstanding scientists such as J.D. Keynes, A. Marshall, and A. Smith. They identified the stability of the enterprise with the ability to keep profits at a target level. General issues of economic stability of enterprises in the real sector of the economy were considered and explained in the works of Eli Ginzerberg (Ginzberg 2017) and Jean-Herve Lorenzi (Lorenzi et al. 2016); Muhammad Hanif and Sikandar Bilal Khattak (Hanif and Khattak 2017). Approaches to assessing the financial stability of an enterprise were developed by D. Bar and N. Schulze (Baur and Schulze 2009); Cruella, P. Huerta, F. Labondance (Creel, Hubert and Labondance 2015); I.V. Solovyeva, N. G. Tregulova, O. Y. Malinina, S. L. Vasenev (Krivka and Stonkutė 2015). Several authors, such as I.I. Kovalenko, A.S. Sokolitsyn, N.A. Sokolitsyna (Kovalenko, Sokolitsyn and Sokolitsyna 2018) research the dynamics of sustainability indicators under the influence of external and internal risks, taking into account the stages of the enterprise life cycle. The tools for assessing the level of economic sustainability of enterprises were studied by A. Zharov, N. Stashevskaya, L. Petrova (Zharov, Stashevskaya and Petrova 2018).

It should be noted that there are no universal tools for assessing the level of economic stability of enterprises, especially in conditions that limit economic growth, and internal problems associated with a drop in consumer demand and a decrease in the capitalization of Russian companies. The novelty of the study lies in the fact that we suggest using the method of fractional-linear programming to solve the optimization problem of assessing the economic stability of an economic entity based on data from light industry enterprises in Russia and to establish reference values for indicators of economic stability of industry enterprises.

2. MATERIALS AND METHODS

In our opinion, the economic stability of the enterprise is understood as the balanced state of technological, innovative digital, human, financial, and communication resources of the company, formed due to internal and external factors that provide additional competitive advantages and the maximum level of marginality in critical situations as well as in the event of external threats.

To assess the economic stability of enterprises, we use the quadratic programming model to solve the problem of optimizing management decision-making (Ahmed Simi and Talukder 2017; Mokeyev and Vorobiev 2015; Olayinka et al. 2015) with the definition of zonal values.

Objective function:

$$z = \sum_{i=1}^{n}(x_i - c_i)^2 \rightarrow \min(\max) \tag{1}$$

Restrictions:

$$a_i \leq x_i \leq b_i; x_i \geq 0$$

The total standard deviation of all indicators from their average value is selected in the model as an integral indicator since the objective function is a measure of the dispersion of an indicator around its average value.

The indicators that make up the integral indicator can be normalized by applying a formula such as:

$$\frac{x_i - c_i}{b_i - a_i} \qquad (2)$$

In this case, the values of each indicator will be no more than unity.
Reference designations:
n is the number of studied indicators, $i = \overline{1, n}$;
m is the number of surveyed enterprises, $j = \overline{1, m}$;
xij is the value of the ith indicator in the jth enterprise (source data matrix);
xi is the variable (desired) value of the ithindicator;
Z is the integral indicator;
ai is the minimum value of the ith indicator: ai= minj{xij};
bi is the maximum value of the ith indicator: bi = maxj{xij};
ci is the average value of the ith indicator:

$$c_i \sum_{j=1}^{m} \frac{x_{ij}}{m} \qquad (3)$$

We relied on analysis of scientific literature, expert surveys, and the experience of foreign countries to select the key indicators based on generally accepted formulas, which were later grouped into functional blocks. The composition of functional blocks is shown in Figure 1.

The technological block is characterized by the level of technical and technological equipment of the enterprise. A company's focus on advanced technologies in the production and promotion of products can significantly reduce its costs while maintaining a high and constant level of quality. The next fundamental focus of the enterprise's activities is its innovative development in the digital environment. In this regard, the innovative-digital block is of great importance for the study. Creating conditions for the economic stability of enterprises requires to actively implement the innovative development vector (Valitov and Khakimov 2015; Krymov et al. 2019; MacGregor 2006).

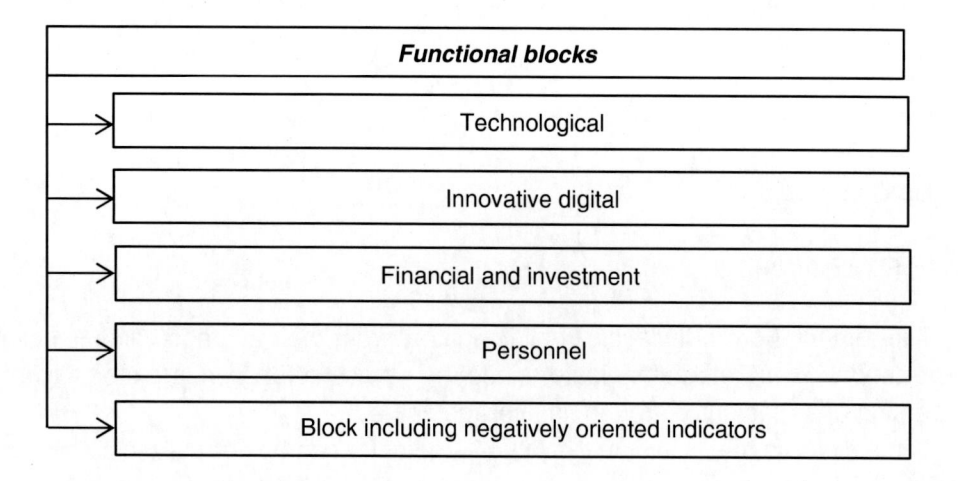

Figure 1. Structure of functional blocks.

Without it, production goes into a stage of stagnation, which ultimately leads to withdrawal from the market. At the moment, issues related to improving the efficiency of using financial resources are undoubtedly relevant to all organizations. The ability to conduct a timely analysis of financial results, identify surpluses and deficits is ensured by constant monitoring of the state of internal resources (Babkin et al. 2017). A clear systematization of tools for analyzing financial and economic activities contributes to the accuracy of assessing the state of the enterprise. This block should be formed bearing in mind the priorities of the company's development. Another important functional block of rapid assessment of the company's stability is the personnel block. Any enterprise conducts its economic activities and develops thanks to human resources. Personnel is a key and very significant factor in the industry, activating all other resources and determining their purpose and productivity.

The formation and filling of functional blocks for assessing the stability of an enterprise is the initial stage of developing an integral indicator that allows you to determine the extreme values of deviations from a given state at any time. It should be noted that in addition to the selected functional blocks, it is also necessary to form a combined block that includes negatively oriented indicators.

3. RESULTS

The proposed tools for optimizing management decision-making to ensure economic stability are universal and can reflect the specifics of enterprises in various sectors of the national economy. In order to test it and calculate an integral indicator for assessing the level of economic stability, we analyzed the activities of the economic entities operating in the Russian textile industry ("Production in the Light Industry" n.d.). The necessary data for solving the quadratic programming problem are presented in Table 1.

Using the data presented in Table 1, let us build integral indicators for each functional block. Technological unit:

$$z_1 = (x_1 - 0.064)^2 + (x_2 - 0.053)^2 + (x_3 - 0.093)^2 + (x_4 - 0.331)^2 + (x_5 - 0.439)^2$$

Innovative digital unit:

$$z_2 = (x_6 - 0.134)^2 + (x_7 - 0.254)^2 + (x_8 - 0.360)^2 + (x_9 - 0.066)^2 + (x_{10} - 0.087)^2$$

Financial and investment unit:

$$z_3 = (x_{11} - 0.516)^2 + (x_{12} - 0.643)^2 + (x_{13} - 1.308)^2 + (x_{14} - 5.209)^2 + (x_{15} - 0.888)^2$$

Table 1. Source data matrix for solving the quadratic programming problem (xij)

Indicators	PNK «Krasnja Nit»	«Saljut»	«Trud»	NPP «ANA»	«Pnkim. Kirova»	«Baltijskajamanufactura»	«Objedinennyevolokna»	«Prjadil'najafabrika «Vereteno»	«Severnyjtekstil»	ShP«Galant»
1. Technological functional unit										
Fixed assets renovation rate (X1)	0.18	0.07	0.06	0.06	0.08	0.03	0.04	0.05	0.07	0.01
Fixed assets increase rate (X2)	0.17	0.06	0.04	0.11	0.05	0.01	0.01	0.01	0.08	0.00
Assortment update ability rate (X3)	0.20	0.18	0.02	0.20	0.07	0.05	0.02	0.07	0.12	0.01
Capital ratio rate (mln rub. per person) (X4)	0.25	0.07	0.70	0.09	4.54	0.01	0.16	0.75	0.15	0.16
Production mechanization and automation rate (X5)	0.48	0.66	0.35	0.44	0.55	0.65	0.30	0.35	0.53	0.08
2. Innovative digital functional unit										
Costs of protecting new technology rate (X6)	0.19	0.21	0.06	0.32	0.23	0.07	0.06	0.04	0.14	0.02
Correlation of new and old technologies rate (X7)	0.45	0.38	0.08	0.36	0.44	0.08	0.11	0.10	0.40	0.14
E-commerce fraction (X8)	0.59	0.56	0.24	0.58	0.64	0.11	0.12	0.14	0.54	0.09

Indicators	PNK «Krasnja Nit»	«Saljut»	«Trud»	NPP «ANA»	«Pnkim. Kirova»	«Baltijskajamanufactura»	«Objedinennyevolokna»	«Prjadil'najafabrika «Vereteno»	«Severnyjtekstil»	ShP«Galant»
Fraction of R&D expenses in revenue (x9)	0.10	0.08	0.01	0.11	0.13	0.05	0.02	0.04	0.11	0.00
Fraction of costs for licenses, patents, know-how (x10)	0.22	0.15	0.02	0.02	0.15	0.02	0.02	0.02	0.12	0.03
3. Financial and investment functional unit										
Autonomy rate (x11)	0.47	0.87	0.88	0.89	0.12	0.10	0.09	0.84	0.80	0.08
Maneuverability rate (x12)	0.54	0.92	0.13	0.97	0.08	1.00	2.06	0.53	0.10	0.10
Absolute liquidity rate (x13)	0.70	2.23	0.49	4.35	2.57	0.82	0.19	0.60	0.71	0.41
Coating rate (x14)	7.51	11.21	2.16	13.16	7.44	1.61	1.97	3.88	1.71	1.45
Profitability on credit rate coefficient (X15)	1.63	0.15	0.78	0.18	1.26	3.32	0.15	0.44	0.75	0.22
4. Personnel functional unit										
Average number of employees (X16)	154.00	109.00	49.0	50.00	388.00	56.00	73.00	56.00	118.00	42.00
Average employee experience (years) (X17)	27.00	25.00	28.0	18.00	20.00	20.00	27.00	24.00	31.00	29.00

Table 1. (Continued)

Indicators	PNK «Krasnja Nit»	«Saljut»	«Trud»	NPP «ANA»	«Pnkim. Kirova»	«Baltijskajamanufactura»	«Objedinennyevolokna»	«Prjadil'najafabrika «Vereteno»	«Severnyjtekstil»	ShP«Galant»
Production and seniority ratio coefficient (X18)	0.11	0.04	0.03	0.10	0.08	0.06	0.02	0.07	0.05	0.02
Employee satisfaction with working conditions rate (X19)	0.80	0.80	0.50	0.90	0.80	0.80	0.40	0.70	0.80	0.30
Percentage of employees with advanced qualifications per year (X20)	0.67	0.54	0.15	0.58	0.35	0.29	0.22	0.38	0.48	0.07
Percentage of employees with Master's degree per year (X21)	0.69	0.66	0.54	0.60	0.40	0.24	0.35	0.58	0.65	0.35
Percentage of employees that speak foreign languages (X22)	0.15	0.21	0.12	0.15	0.09	0.05	0.12	0.11	0.29	0.03
5. Combined unit of indicators with negative orientation										
Fixed assets retirement rate (X23)	0.01	0.03	0.05	0.05	0.06	0.16	0.16	0.13	0.05	0.16
Fixed assets deterioration rate (X24)	0.17	0.29	0.46	0.15	0.17	0.23	0.37	0.44	0.10	0.70

Indicators	PNK «Krasnja Nit»	«Saljut»	«Trud»	NPP «ANA»	«Pnkim. Kirova»	«Baltijskajamanufactura»	«Objedinennyevolokna»	«Prjadil'najafabrika «Vereteno»	«Severnyjtekstil»	ShP«Galant»
Average equipment time of life (years) (X25)	26.00	25.00	28.0	12.00	26.00	29.00	16.00	20.00	27.00	13.00
TAT (turn-around time) innovation indicator (years) (X26)	0.48	0.83	1.00	0.57	0.67	1.25	1.50	1.17	0.75	1.67
Debt to equity ratio rate (X27)	0.91	0.15	1.00	0.12	0.95	1.00	0.84	0.18	0.24	0.93
Staff turnover rate (X28)	0.08	0.06	0.12	0.04	0.01	0.10	0.14	0.08	0.03	0.25
Lost customer increase rate (X29)	0.03	0.02	0.03	0.02	0.03	0.03	0.03	0.03	0.001	0.03

Personnel unit:

$$z_4 = (x_{16} - 110)^2 + (x_{17} - 25)^2 + (x_{18} - 0.060)^2 + (x_{19} - 0.680)^2 + (x_{20} - 0.447)^2 + (x_{21} - 447)^2 + (x_{22} - 0.131)^2$$

Combined unit of indicators with a negative orientation:

$$z_5 = (x_{23} - 0.085)^2 + (x_{24} - 3.076)^2 + (x_{25} - 22.2)^2 + (x_{26} - 0.988)^2 + (x_{27} - 0.631)^2 + (x_{28} - 0.089)^2 + (x_{29} - 0.028)^2$$

For each of the five units, optimal values of the integral indicators can be found by solving the optimization problem. This is a quadratic programming problem since the objective function has a second degree and the constraints are linear (Korchagina et al. 2019; Pereborova et al. 2018; Erik Bajalinov 2003). Moreover, there are no unknown products in the objective function, which greatly facilitates and accelerates its solution. The solution to the optimization problem:

Technological functional unit:

$$\begin{cases} Z_1 = (x_1 - 0.064)^2 + (x_2 - 0.053)^2 + (x_3 - 0.093)^2 + (x_4 - 0.331)^2 + (x_5 - 0.439)^2 \rightarrow max \\ 0.012 \leq x_1 \leq 0.183 \\ 0.004 \leq x_2 \leq 0.171 \\ 0.012 \leq x_3 \leq 0.197 \\ 0.013 \leq x_4 \leq 0.975 \\ 0.080 \leq x_5 \leq 0.656 \end{cases}$$

Innovative digital functional unit:

$$\begin{cases} Z_2 = (x_6 - 0.134)^2 + (x_7 - 0.254)^2 + (x_8 - 0.360)^2 + (x_9 - 0.066)^2 + (x_{10} - 0.087)^2 \rightarrow max \\ 0.018 \leq x_6 \leq 0.321 \\ 0.075 \leq x_7 \leq 0.445 \\ 0.085 \leq x_8 \leq 0.640 \\ 0.001 \leq x_9 \leq 0.125 \\ 0.015 \leq x_{10} \leq 0.215 \end{cases}$$

Financial and investment functional unit:

$$\begin{cases} Z_3 = (x_{11} - 0.516)^2 + (x_{12} - 0.643)^2 + (x_{13} - 1.308)^2 + (x_{14} - 5.209)^2 + (x_{15} - 0.888)^2 \rightarrow max \\ 0.083 \leq x_{11} \leq 0.892 \\ 0.084 \leq x_{12} \leq 2.064 \\ 0.194 \leq x_{13} \leq 4.352 \\ 1.453 \leq x_{14} \leq 13.155 \\ 0.148 \leq x_{15} \leq 3.316 \end{cases}$$

Personnel functional unit:

$$Z_4 = (x_{16}-110)^2+(x_{17}-25)^2+(x_{18}-0.060)^2$$
$$+(x_{19}-0.680)^2+(x_{20}-0.447)^2+(x_{21}-447)^2+(x_{22}-0.131)^2 \to max$$
$$42 \leq x_{16} \leq 388$$
$$18 \leq x_{17} \leq 310$$
$$0.016 \leq x_{18} \leq 0.111$$
$$0.300 \leq x_{19} \leq 0.900$$
$$0.065 \leq x_{20} \leq 0.692$$
$$0.065 \leq x_{21} \leq 0.692$$
$$0.027 \leq x_{22} \leq 0.290$$

5. Technological, innovative digital, financial and investment, personnel, communicative functional units of the enterprise development:

$$Z_5 = (x_{23}-0.085)^2+(x_{24}-0.376)^2+(x_{25}-22.2)^2$$
$$+(x_{26}-0.988)^2+(x_{27}-0.631)^2+(x_{28}-0.089)^2+(x_{29}-0.028)^2 \to min$$
$$0.013 \leq x_{23} \leq 0.162$$
$$0.102 \leq x_{24} \leq 0.701$$
$$12 \leq x_{25} \leq 29$$
$$0.483 \leq x_{26} \leq 1.666$$
$$0.120 \leq x_{27} \leq 0.997$$
$$0.014 \leq x_{28} \leq 0.247$$
$$0.001 \leq x_{29} \leq 0.033$$

In the first four units, the maximum problem is solved.

The objective function of a given view is not bounded from above, so that is why we will search for it at some vertex of the set of admissible values given by the system of data of linear inequalities. The form of the objective function determines that the desired vertex of the set of admissible unknown values will be vertex $(\cdot)$ B (b1, b2, ...bn).

It follows from the conditions that there is one minimum point, $(\cdot)$ C (c1, c2, ...cn), therefore at this point, the objective function of the fifth unit (Z5) reaches the desired minimum.

The results of solving the quadratic programming problem for five blocks are presented in Tables 2 – 6. It should be noted that the absolute maximum of the target function is reached at the values shown in Tables 2 – 5, and the minimum is reached in Table 6.

Zonal indicators included in the technological unit determine the optimal integral value at the level of 3.005.

$$Z_{1max} = 3.005 \quad at \begin{cases} z_1 = 0.696 \\ z_2 = 0.701 \\ z_3 = 0.562 \\ z_4 = 0.669 \\ z_5 = 0.377 \end{cases}$$

Table 2. Results of solving the quadratic programming problem for the technological unit

UNIT 1	max	min	average	rationing			
	b_i	a_i	c_i	$\Delta_i = b_i - c_i$	$v_i = b_i - a_i$	$z_i = (b_i - c_i)/v_i$	$z_{i2} = ((b_i - c_i)/v_i)2$
X1	0.183	0.012	0.064	0.119	0.171	0.696	0.484
X2	0.171	0.004	0.053	0.117	0.167	0.701	0.491
X3	0.197	0.012	0.093	0.104	0.185	0.562	0.316
X4	0.975	0.013	0.331	0.644	0.962	0.669	0.448
X5	0.656	0.080	0.439	0.217	0.576	0.377	0.142

Table 3. The results of solving the quadratic programming problem for the innovative digital unit

UNIT2	max	min	average		rationing		
	b_i	a_i	c_i	$\Delta_i = b_i - c_i$	$v_i = b_i - a_i$	$z_i = (b_i - c_i)/v_i$	$z_{i2} = ((b_i - c_i)/v_i)2$
X6	0.321	0.018	0.134	0.187	0.303	0.617	0.381
X7	0.445	0.075	0.254	0.191	0.370	0.516	0.266
X8	0.640	0.085	0.360	0.280	0.555	0.505	0.255
X9	0.125	0.001	0.066	0.059	0.124	0.476	0.226
X10	0.215	0.015	0.087	0.128	0.200	0.640	0.410

Table 4. The results of solving the quadratic programming problem for the financial and investment unit

UNIT3	max	min	average		Rationing		
	b_i	a_i	c_i	$\Delta_i = b_i - c_i$	$v_i = b_i - a_i$	$z_i = (b_i - c_i)/v_i$	$z_{i2} = ((b_i - c_i)/v_i)2$
X11	0.892	0.083	0.516	0.376	0.809	0.465	0.216
X12	2.064	0.084	0.643	1.421	1.980	0.718	0.515
X13	4.352	0.194	1.308	3.044	4.158	0.732	0.536
X14	13.155	1.453	5.209	7.946	11.702	0.679	0.461
X15	3.316	0.148	0.888	2.428	3.168	0.766	0.587

The zonal values of the innovative digital unit indicators correspond to

$$2.754.Z_{2max} = 2.754 \quad \text{at} \begin{cases} z_6 = 0.617 \\ z_7 = 0.516 \\ z_8 = 0.505 \\ z_9 = 0.476 \\ z_{10} = 0.640 \end{cases}$$

**Table 5. Results of solving the quadratic programming problem
for the personnel unit**

UNIT 4	max b_i	min a_i	average c_i		Rationing		
				$\Delta_i = b_i - c_i$	$v_i = b_i - a_i$	$z_i = (b_i - c_i)/v_i$	$z_i^2 = ((b_i - c_i)/v_i)^2$
X16	388	42	110	278	346	0.803	0.646
X17	31	18	25	6	13	0.462	0.213
X18	0.111	0.016	0.060	0.051	0.095	0.537	0.288
X19	0.900	0.300	0.680	0.220	0.600	0.367	0.134
X20	0.692	0.065	0.447	0.245	0.627	0.391	0.153
X21	0.692	0.065	0.447	0.245	0.627	0.391	0.153
X22	0.290	0.027	0.131	0.159	0.263	0.605	0.365

**Table 6. Results of solving the quadratic programming problem
for the indicators with negative orientation**

UNIT 5	max b_i	min a_i	average c_i	Rationing $v_i = b_i - a_i$	c_i/v_i
X23	0.162	0.013	0.085	0.149	0.570
X24	0.701	0.102	0.376	0.599	0.628
X25	29	12	22.2	17	1.305
X26	1.666	0.483	0.988	1.183	0.835
X27	0.997	0.120	0.631	0.877	0.719
X28	0.247	0.014	0.089	0.233	0.382
X29	0.033	0.001	0.028	0.032	0.875

Zonal values of indicators included in the financial and investment unit have an optimal value of 2.325.

$$Z_{3max} = 2.325 \quad \text{at} \begin{cases} z_{11} = 0.465 \\ z_{12} = 0.718 \\ z_{13} = 0.732 \\ z_{14} = 0.679 \\ z_{15} = 0.766 \end{cases}$$

The zonal values of the personnel unit indicators have an optimal value of 1.306.

$$Z_{4max} = 1.306 \quad at \begin{cases} z_{16} = 0.803 \\ z_{17} = 0.462 \\ z_{18} = 0.537 \\ z_{19} = 0.367 \\ z_{20} = 0.391 \\ z_{21} = 0.391 \\ z_{22} = 0.605 \end{cases}$$

Table 7. Results of applying the quadratic programming model

1. Technological unit	2. Innovative digital unit	3. Financial and investment unit	4. Personnel unit
$Z_{1max} = 3.005$ $at \begin{cases} z_1 = 0.696 \\ z_2 = 0.701 \\ z_3 = 0.562 \\ z_4 = 0.669 \\ z_5 = 0.377 \end{cases}$	$Z_{2max} = 2.754$ $at \begin{cases} z_6 = 0.617 \\ z_7 = 0.516 \\ z_8 = 0.505 \\ z_9 = 0.476 \\ z_{10} = 0.640 \end{cases}$	$Z_{3max} = 1.306$ $at \begin{cases} z_{16} = 0.803 \\ z_{17} = 0.462 \\ z_{18} = 0.537 \\ z_{19} = 0.367 \\ z_{20} = 0.391 \\ z_{21} = 0.391 \\ z_{22} = 0.605 \end{cases}$	$Z_{4max} = 1.306$ $at \begin{cases} z_{16} = 0.803 \\ z_{17} = 0.462 \\ z_{18} = 0.537 \\ z_{19} = 0.367 \\ z_{20} = 0.391 \\ z_{21} = 0.391 \\ z_{22} = 0.605 \end{cases}$
5. Combined unit of indicators with a negative orientation (minimization task)			
$Z_{5min} = 0$ $at \begin{cases} z_{23} = 0.570 \\ z_{24} = 0.628 \\ z_{25} = 1.305 \\ z_{26} = 0.835 \\ z_{27} = 0.719 \\ z_{28} = 0.382 \\ z_{29} = 0.875 \end{cases}$			

The value of an integral indicator for a combined unit that has a negative orientation should tend to 0.

$$Z_{5min} = 0 \quad at \begin{cases} z_{23} = 0.570 \\ z_{24} = 0.628 \\ z_{25} = 1.305 \\ z_{26} = 0.835 \\ z_{27} = 0.719 \\ z_{28} = 0.382 \\ z_{29} = 0.875 \end{cases}$$

The implementation of the proposed quadratic programming model in the practical activities of industry enterprises allowed us to determine the reference values of indicators that ensure the economic stability of economic entities (see Table 7).

The tools that we have developed, which have been tested at light industry enterprises of St. Petersburg, allow to assess the level of economic stability in an industrial enterprise and make management decisions during monitoring.

DISCUSSION

Existing approaches to assessing the level of economic stability contain several unresolved problems. Among them, we can highlight the operational monitoring organization of the economic stability level of enterprises and industries. The functioning of economic entities in the market is impossible without contact with the external environment, which objectively implies constant market fluctuations, for example, the level of interest rates, inflation, unemployment, and business activity. These external factors are outside the zone of influence of companies, so the best solution for business is to maximize the formation and accumulation of the internal resources, which in the future will serve as a guaranteed reserve in the event of adverse external threats.

The analysis of scientific works on this issue, expert survey, and collaboration with highly qualified specialists of the industry allowed us to substantiate the key indicators for assessing the level of economic stability and group them into functional blocks: technological, innovative digital, financial and investment, personnel, and combined units.

The number of indicators in each functional block is optimal for identifying possible threats and the level of stability of economic entities.

Based on the suggested functional blocks, a mathematical model of quadratic programming was constructed to solve the optimization problem of determining zonal values of economic stability. In the model, the total standard deviation of all indicators from their average value is chosen as an integral indicator, since the objective function is a measure of the indicator's dispersion. The developed model makes it possible to assess the enterprises' economic stability by comparing real values of indicators with reference values.

CONCLUSION

The results presented in this paper are highly relevant and have practical value, as confirmed by the enterprises that participated in this study. The enterprises that participated in the study recommended that the Ministry of Industry and Trade of the

Russian Federation use the reference values defined in the article to develop state regulatory policy in the field of light industry. The proposed tools allow to:

- conduct an objective assessment of an industrial enterprise's economic stability;
- develop and make reasonable management decisions to ensure the economic stability of an industrial enterprise
- generate positive synergy aimed at developing the material and technical base as well as resource, human and intellectual potential;
- ensure a continuous process of production and sale of products, maintaining the stability of enterprises in the medium and long term.

It is important to note that this model is convenient and universal for practical use since it excludes the mutual influence of factors, allowing to apply it in various economic sectors for companies that have a short production cycle with a predominance of working capital.

REFERENCES

Ahmed Simi, Farhana and Md. Shahjalal Talukder. 2017. "A New Approach for Solving Linear Fractional Programming Problems with Duality Concept". *Open Journal of Optimization.* https://doi.org/10.4236/ojop.2017.61001.

Babkin, Alexander, Burkaltseva, Diana, Kosten, Dmitri and Vorobev, Yuriy. 2017. "Formation of Digital Economy in Russia: Essence, Features, Technical Normalization, Development Problems". *St. Petersburg State Polytechnical University Journal.* Economics.

Baur, Dirk G. and Schulze, Niels. 2009. "Financial Market Stability-A Test". *Journal of International Financial Markets, Institutions and Money.* https://doi.org/10.1016/j.intfin.2008.06.003.

Bajalinov, Erik. 2003. "*Linear-Fractional Programming Theory, Methods, Applications and Software*". 2003. https://www.researchgate.net/publication/265772549_Linear-Fractional_Programming_Theory_Methods_Applications_and_Software.

Creel, Jérôme, Hubert, Paul and Labondance, Fabien. 2015. "Financial Stability and Economic Performance". *Economic Modelling.* https://doi.org/10.1016/j.econmod.2014.10.025.

Dermot McAleese. n.d. "*Economics For Business: Competition, Macro-Stability & Globalisation 3rd Edition*". Accessed February 4, 2021. https://www.amazon.com/Economics-Business-Competition-Macro-stability-Globalisation/dp/0273683985.

Dvas, Grigory V. and Dubolazova, Yulia A. 2018. "Risk Assessment and Risk Management of Innovative Activity of the Enterprise". In *Proceedings of the 31st International Business Information Management Association Conference, IBIMA 2018: Innovation Management and Education Excellence through Vision 2020.*

Ginzberg, Eli. 2017. *The Illusion of Economic Stability*. The Illusion of Economic Stability. https://doi.org/10.4324/9781315132624.

Hanif, Muhammad and Sikandar Bilal Khattak. 2017. *"Assessment of Economic Factors for Sustainable Construction Industry"*, no. February: 978 - 969. https://www.researchgate.net/profile/Muhammad_Hanif66/publication/315379601_Asse sment_of_Economic_Factors_for_Sustainable_Construction_Industry/links/59e5 b077a6fdcc1b1d96c8e5/Assesment-of-Economic-Factors-for-Sustainable-Construction-Industry.pdf.

Korchagina, Elena, Bochkarev, Andrey, Bochkarev, Pavel, Barykin, Sergey and Suvorova, Svetlana. 2019. "The Treatment of Optimizing Container Transportation Dynamic Programming and Planning". In *E3S Web of Conferences*. https://doi.org/10.1051/e3sconf/201913502016.

Kovalenko, Inna I., Sokolitsyn, Alexander S. and Sokolitsyna, Natalya A. 2018. "The Enterprise's Automated Management Stability System Taking into Account Its Life Cycle Stage". In *Proceedings of the 2018 International Conference "'Quality Management, Transport and Information Security, Information Technologies'"*, IT and QM and IS 2018. https://doi.org/10.1109/ITMQIS.2018.8524966.

Krivka, Algirdas, and Eglė Stonkutė. 2015. "Complex Analysis Of Financial State And Performance Of Construction Enterprises". *Business, Management and Education*. https://doi.org/10.3846/bme.2015.300.

Krymov, Sergei, Kolgan, Maria, Suvorova, Svetlana and Martynenko, Oksana. 2019. "Digital Technologies and Transformation of Modern Retail". In *IOP Conference Series: Materials Science and Engineering*. https://doi.org/10.1088/1757-899X/497/1/012126.

Lorenzi, Jean Hervé, Berrebi, Mickaël, Bacon, Josephine and Giddens, Anthony. 2016. *A Violent World: Modern Threats to Economic Stability*. A Violent World: Modern Threats to Economic Stability. https://doi.org/10.1007/978-1-137-58993-4.

MacGregor, Steven P. 2006. "Strategic Management of Technological Innovation". *Journal of Product Innovation Management,* 23 (1): 102 - 4. https://doi.org/10.1111/j.1540-5885.2005.00184_4.x.

Mokeyev, V. V. and Vorobiev, D. A. 2015. "Analysis of Socio-Economic System Processes Performance with the Help of Eigenstate Models". *Bulletin of the South Ural State University, Series: Mathematical Modelling, Programming and Computer Software,* 8 (1): 66 - 75. https://doi.org/10.14529/mmp150105.

Olayinka, Ibitoye, Atoyebi Kehinde Olusegun, Genevieve Kellikume, and Kadiri Kayode. 2015. "Entrepreneur Decision Making Process and Application of Linear Programming Technique". *European Journal of Business, Economics and Accountancy,* 3 (5): 11 - 15.

Pereborova, N. V., Makarov, A. G., Kozlov, A. A. and Vasil'eva, E. K. 2018. "Development of Integral Optimality Criteria for Mathematical Modeling of Relaxation/Recovery Processes in Polymer Textile Materials". *Fibre Chemistry*. https://doi.org/10.1007/s10692-019-09981-8.

"Production in the Light Industry". n.d. Accessed February 4, 2021. https://promzn.ru/legkaya-promyshlennost.

Valitov, Shamil M. and Khakimov, Almaz Kh. 2015. "Innovative Potential as a Framework of Innovative Strategy for Enterprise Development". *Procedia Economics and Finance*. https://doi.org/10.1016/s2212-5671(15)00682-6.

Zharov, Andrey Nikolaevich, Stashevskaya, Nadezda A. and Petrova, Leila A. 2018. *"Theoretical Approaches of Assessment of Financial Sustainability of an Enterprise"*. 119 (17): 1393 - 97.

In: Global Challenges of Digital Transformation of Markets ISBN: 978-1-53619-754-9
Editors: E. de la Poza and S. E. Barykin   © 2021 Nova Science Publishers, Inc.

Chapter 14

Technological Transformation of the Macroregion Economy as a Result of Digitalization

*Gumar Batov**

Institute of Informatics and Problems of Regional Management, Nalchik, Russia

Abstract

The relevance of the study is that the crisis phenomena, the instability of the economic situation of the subjects of production, sanctions against our country have slowed down the processes connected with using breakthrough technologies. These issues are especially relevant for the regions, which, in terms of their development level, are below the average Russian indicators and are a serious problem for the state. Bearing in mind the state of the studied regions, the most effective way out of the difficult situation may be the implementation of such a technological policy, which will allow more firmly organizing the relationship and interaction between digital and information technologies, on the one hand, and production processes, on the other. The scientific hypothesis of the study is that for problematic and backward regions it is necessary to find ways of development that will allow them to leave the zone of depression and backwardness and embark on the tracks of sustainable development. The purpose of the study is to propose various options for digitalization as a result of studying the state of fixed assets and investments in fixed assets, determining the technological structure of the regional economy, which implies a qualitative change in the way of running a business, which will radically/exponentially increase the productivity of various sectors of the economy and social sphere. The implementation of such a scenario will help the region move to a more progressive technological order.

Keywords: region, investments, digitalization

* Corresponding Author's Email: gumarbatov@mail.ru.

1. INTRODUCTION

Currently, the economy and society of many countries find themselves in a difficult environment. The crisis provoked by the pandemic and the fall in energy prices have led to the fall of the world trade volume, the countries have taken the path of isolation and curtailment of economic and trade projects that were planned in advance. Ordinary citizens also had to go into self-isolation to preserve their health and the health of their loved ones. The main form of work organization has become outside office work, work at home, and remote work.

In these difficult conditions, information and digital technologies turned out to be the main tools for communication and organization of production activities, which made it possible to save some jobs and continue all life processes.

Throughout the world close attention is given to the development and use of digital technologies (Bataev 2018). Despite high costs and sometimes low results, sometimes even negative, many companies are engaged in the implementation of digital technologies in organizational structures and production processes. They are confident that if not now, then in the future they will have an effect, "especially platforms" (Kenney and Zysman 2020). This is in fact correct and cannot be disputed.

Digital technologies are especially useful in Russian conditions, necessary for regions that are noticeably differentiated in terms of human capital, raw materials, state of fixed assets, and climatic conditions. Such a variety of regions makes it necessary to search for a technological policy that will be adapted to the characteristics of this region.

This is what the study conducted by the World Bank experts together with Russian experts on the Russian regions notes: "It cannot be denied that the resource regions, which remain the locomotives of economic growth, experience certain difficulties in ensuring sustainable social and economic development, including changing energy prices and the imposition of sanctions. Taking this into account, it becomes necessary to search for drivers of economic growth on a national scale. Identification of new sources for the national economy's growth can be carried out after a deep and comprehensive analysis of social and economic factors (in addition to natural resources), which determine the development level and productivity of regional economies in Russia " ("Making Best Use of the Economic Potential of Russia ' s Regions Re-Mapping Opportunity" 2018, p. 5).

The semblance of regional unevenness that takes place in the Russian economy is also typical for many European, American and Asian countries.

The depressed regions of the United States include territories from Florida to the North up to the Canadian border, as well as the territory along the West Coast.

In Italy, the depressed regions include the southern regions, especially Calabria.

In Sweden, the depressed cities are Gothenburg, Uddevalla, Landskrona and Malmö, where the private shipyard industry is located and which have found themselves on the verge of bankruptcy due to high competition from Japan and China.

In France, the depressed regions include several areas on the territory of which there are old coal deposits in the Loire river basin, in the Seven mountains, Aquitaine, Auvergne. Rapid scientific and technological progress and corresponding changes in the economic structure have led to an increase in disproportions in the economic development of the country's regions. Industrialized regions of the past such as Lorraine and the Northern Industrial Region have quickly become one of the most critical regions requiring government support.

Among Asian countries, China can be distinguished, where such regions prevail in the western part of the country. Of course, each region, wherever it is located, has different specifics, emphasizing its backwardness, but the common feature for all is that they are a "headache" for each state. It is necessary to invest more funds in such regions to maintain their vital functions. And this is done, as a rule, to the detriment of other regions and industries, which also need investment to develop knowledge-intensive industries and maintain their competitiveness.

Each region has its own "disease", its own problems, but they are united by one main drawback which is that they could not create a technological level corresponding to the requirements of the time, economy, and market, and they lost it. Since they have the same drawback and equal problems, it is possible to offer a general development strategy that will suit the majority, if not everyone. Such a strategy could be the digitalization of production processes that form the basis of the region. It is evident that digitalization is not a panacea, that it has certain drawbacks, but at present, it is difficult to find a more effective tool with which it is possible to solve the problems inherent in lagging regions. In new conditions, with the advent of breakthrough technologies, it becomes possible to solve many problems. One option is using digital technologies and the digitalization of production processes.

Each country is faced with the task of bringing such regions up to the level of average or leaders. In retrospect, each country found some tools that to some extent neutralized the problems of such regions, but they did not completely solve all the problems. For example, in Poland, complex development programs act as the main tool for anti-crisis management in depressed regions, within the framework of which the problems of a particular region, ways of solving them, and the mechanism of their implementation are determined. These programs are developed with the participation of regional representatives, with the participation of central authorities, with the involvement of neighboring regions, a scientific community, local enterprises.

The economic development of the regions largely depends on the technological state and quality of fixed assets, as well as investments in fixed assets. Investments play a major role in the formation of a highly efficient technological base, which must be permanently updated and modernized based on new equipment and new technologies. Only in this case, the region can be efficient and competitive.

2. MATERIALS AND METHODS

The study is based on the application of a systems approach, the theory of technological structures, and the concept of the digital economy. The methods of economic, statistical and trend analysis, scientific abstraction, analogies and scientific generalizations were used. In the course of the development of this paper, the classical and modern works of Russian and foreign scientists, statistical and empirical material prepared in the process of research were used.

The object of the study is the North Caucasian Federal District (NCFD), which is one of the macroregions of the Russian Federation (RF) and belongs to the underdeveloped and lagging regions.

3. RESULTS

Fixed assets (fixed capital) are the main sources of prosperity for the region and the country as a whole. The volume of production, the structure of products, conditions and standard of living of the population depend on their state. The economy and the social sphere depend on the moral and physical state of fixed assets, on the degree of their functioning and on the effect they give; they also determine the level of their stability and development opportunities.

4. DISCUSSION

4.1. The State of Fixed Assets and Investments in Fixed Assets in the Studied Macroregion

An indispensable attribute of fixed assets is the need for their constant renewal, reconstruction, and modernization. Moreover, this activity should be carried out based on modern techniques and new technologies. Without such a procedure, an entity (company, region, country) will be unable to maintain the pace of its development, sustainability, stability and competitiveness. Fixed capital (fixed assets) shows the base on which the production process is carried out. In order to find out the state of the fixed assets and other indicators of the use of fixed capital in the region under study, let us compare its indicators with the average Russian indicators (see Table 1; the data source is the statistical collection "Regions of Russia. Socio-economic indicators", published by Rosstat, 2011, 2019) ("Regions of Russia. Socio-Economic Indicators" n.d.). (The study pays more attention to the state of fixed assets of the material sphere as the basis of the economy).

The main distinguishing feature in the sectoral structure of fixed assets of the Russian Federation and the North Caucasus Federal District is that most of the fixed assets in the Russian Federation are concentrated in the industries, while in the North Caucasus Federal District they are dispersed in industry and agriculture.

The analysis of the general state of the sectoral structure of fixed assets and the introduction of new funds shows that there was an increase in the value of fixed assets used in industrial sectors in the Russian Federation as a whole for the analyzed period, especially in the extraction of minerals. This was facilitated by an increase in the commissioning of fixed assets, which amounted to 41.5%.

There was also a redistribution of fixed assets in the North Caucasus Federal District, but in favor of non-market sectors. At the same time, a sharp increase is observed in agriculture in the structure of input of fixed assets, while their share in the total structure of input of fixed assets decreases. The main investment resources in the Russian Federation are concentrated in industrial sectors, and in the NCFD investments are partially directed to industry and partially to agriculture. At the same time, there is a decrease in investments in industrial sectors and an increase in agriculture. Such a focus of investment cannot but influence the efficiency of production and the rate of its growth.

The main disadvantage of the current investment policy is that it strengthens the existing technological order without contributing to the transition of the entire regional reproduction process to a higher level. However, a radical renewal of production would significantly change the ratio of the main factors of production used in accordance with the achievements of science and technology.

Table 1. Condition and structure of fixed assets of the material sphere of the North Caucasus Federal District, %

Subjects	agriculture		Industrial branches		construction		trade (wholesale and retail)			
	2010	2018	2010	2018	2010	2018	2010	2018	2010	2018
Sectoral structure of fixed assets										
RF	3.1	3.1	25.6	31.4	1.6	1.3	3.3	2.5	27.8	25.2
NCFD	8.6	8.4	16.9	16.1	2.1	2.8	3.7	5.4	27.4	22.7
Structure of commissioning of fixed assets										
RF	5.0	4.7	37.6	41.5	2.4	3.0	4.0	3.7	17.3	20.8
NCFD	7.4	12.9	22.0	15.4	2.0	10.1	8.1	7.2	19.9	13.5
Fixed capital investments by type of economic activity										
RF	3.2	3.5	39.0	46.9	3.9	2.9	3.2	3.2	22.6	22.7
NCFD	6.0	10.7	34.6	27.1	8.9	12.5	1.7	2.2	16.1	16.0

Thus, the structure of fixed assets, the structure of input of fixed assets and investments in fixed assets during the period under study did not change their trends, that is, investments were made in the same industries as before. Naturally, there are no structural changes in the economy. It turns out that the district's economy functions inertially, without any changes.

Based on this analysis, it can be concluded that no attempts were made in the district to change the existing structure of the economy, or all actions were aimed at further consolidating or strengthening the existing structure. The most significant omission is that the share of commissioned fixed assets and investments in industrial sectors is at a low level in the North Caucasus Federal District and tends to decrease.

So far, the district is developing without significant changes, following its traditional agricultural specialization. However, it would be preferable to develop manufacturing and processing industries, where end products with higher added value are typically produced and are industries with increasing returns.

Different types of economic activity react differently to the results of technological progress. According to E. Reinert, "the manufacturing industry means a combination of technological progress, increasing returns and imperfect competition" (Erik Reinert 2008). The most acceptable option for the region under study is a deep and radical technological modernization, which should cover the industries that will form the basis of the region's economy now and in the future. It is the technological modernization of production, which implies the commissioning of new equipment, the improvement of existing equipment based on digital and information technologies, as well as the "digitalization of production processes" (Coyle 2019), that will allow the region to switch to a new technological order.

4.2. General Characteristics and Specific Features of the Macroregion Technological Structure

The technological structure is an important determinant characterizing the technological level of the economy of a region or a country. It is a complex economic category that combines structural features, complex problem-solving techniques, and a technocentric approach.

The works of many foreign and Russian economists are dedicated to the study of technological structures. The modern understanding of the technological order began with the works of N. Kondratyev (King 2000), who laid its theoretical foundations. Considering the long-term fluctuations in the economic environment, Kondratyev reached the conclusion that the main reason for the cyclical nature is the need to renew fixed capital and that progress in society and the economy occurs as a result of (progressive) changes in technology and scientific knowledge.

A notable work by K. Perez, "Technological revolutions and financial capital: the dynamics of bubbles and periods of prosperity" (Cooper and Perez 2003), puts forward the concept of technical and economic paradigms, which is close to the concept of "technological order". Perez's approach is characterized by the fact that the relationship between the real sector and the financial market is established through the prism of technological development, it is noted that economic development is wave-like. Perez develops the ideas of N. Kondratyev and I. Schumpeter (Schumpeter

2013), taking into account the influence of financial capital on the technical and economic paradigm of development.

The majority of Russian researchers developing the topic of the technological order rely on the work of D. Lvov and S. Glazyev "Theoretical and applied aspects of scientific and technological development management" (D. S. Lvov 1985), where they established and described the concept of "technological order".

Another work by S. Glazyev and V. Kharitonov, "Nanotechnology as a key factor in a new technological order in the economy" (Glaz'ev and Kharitonov 2009), describes the elements of the technological order and introduces the concept of "life cycle of a technological order" into economic circulation. The researchers identify the core of the structure, the key factor of production, the organization and method of obtaining scientific knowledge, as well as basic economic institutions. By characterizing each of these factors, it is possible to determine to which technological order this or that economy belongs.

The formation and development of technological structures take place with the direct participation of innovation. J. Schumpeter saw the main reason for the development of society in innovative activities which should be carried out by economic entities, primarily entrepreneurs. His thesis on creative destruction, set out in the monograph "Capitalism, Socialism and Democracy" (Schumpeter 2013), shows how the driving forces of industrial change are formed, that innovations with an innovative basis can ensure long-term economic growth and form a new technological order.

The category "technological order" is a complex structure. Possessing historicism in its development, it characterizes the technogenic development of the economy and society. Each new technological structure forms a new type of economy and reproductive relations, creating a more perfect technological base. The state of subsequent structures is predetermined by the course of scientific and technological progress.

A separate technological paradigm is characterized by a complex internal structure, a certain composition and a set of technologically related industries, which has a relatively uniform technical level, develops synchronously and can be part of the economic system. It is formed by a specific key factor that forms a set of supporting industries that become the foundation of the technological core. The technological structure includes technological chains that cover all technological aggregates of all levels. Technological chains are focused on the corresponding types in the reproductive circuit of the technological order.

Technological structures, as large complexes of technologically related industries, do not appear at once and mature, most often gradually and evolutionarily, but they can be unexpected and revolutionary in certain industries, displacing the previous functional and institutional forms. Structures do not appear in "pure form", they replace each other, compete with each other, coexist with each other, but certainly, one of the structures is dominant, which determines the technological structure of a given economy. As noted by R. Thomson and P.-Ch. Atukorala, "the existing industrial structure of the country largely determines its capabilities for the modernization of the entire economy" (Glaz'ev and Kharitonov 2009).

Each country is characterized by its own technological order but it is not constant, as it changes, modifies, transforms with the advent of new technologies. Currently, many European countries have passed more than half of the fifth order, and the United States has begun to master the sixth technological order.

Russia is still lagging behind other countries, it is on the outskirts of the fifth order, although there are industries that have mastered the fifth. These include aviation, military and rocket and space industries. Nowadays most of the technologies belong to the fourth structure, about 30% to the third.

The third technological order is dominant in the subjects of the North Caucasus Federal District. The third structure includes industries that are engaged in the extraction of minerals, their processing, and the production of wood products, agricultural production, etc. There are productions related to the fourth order in the district. These include chemical production, production of rubber and plastic products and building materials, petroleum products, equipment for the electric power industry, processing industries, etc. In general, the district is characterized by a combination of the third and fourth technological orders with the dominance of the third. The ratio between lifestyles is approximately in the range of 55% to 45% in favor of the third structure.

An original method we developed was used to determine the state of technological structures (TS) in the economy of the subjects of the North Caucasus Federal District. Synthetic indicators of gross domestic product (GDP) for the country's economy and regional domestic product (GRP) for the region were used to identify the technological structure o which the economy belonged. In the applied methodology, other indicators are calculated, besides GDP and GRP. This is the structure of investment in fixed assets by type of economic activity; structure of fixed assets and putting them into operation; the structure of the number of employed by sectors of the economy. In the course of the study, the technological order was calculated according to the proposed indicators and an integral indicator for each of them was determined. Then a summary or general integral indicator was determined, which is the main indicator showing the state of technological orders and which of them dominates.

The developed methodology was used to investigate how the technological structures of the North Caucasus Federal District changed over the period from 2005 to 2018. The analysis showed that there were no significant changes during the studied period. It becomes obvious that the third technological order remains dominant, and it remains relatively stable. Some growth in the technological order, which is observed, is explained by internal changes in the technological order, the growth of production in the metallurgical industry, the commissioning of new capacities in manufacturing, oil refining, the production of machinery and equipment, education and public administration.

The changes are microscopic; in fact, there are no breakthroughs that would allow to move to a higher order. This circumstance is crucial since progressive changes do not occur even given the increase in production efficiency and the change in the quality of the current technological order. In this situation, the digital economy is difficult to build. The main reason, in our opinion, is the conservation of the existing structure of the economy in the constituent entities of the district and even though the products manufactured have rather low quality, they nevertheless find consumers.

This process must be stopped, it is important to stimulate economic growth. Using high technologies and investments in more progressive industries or industries that make up the fourth and fifth technological order will allow the district's economy to move to another level and, accordingly, create a different type of economy (Bailey et al. 2019).

The process of formation of the fourth order in the district may be connected with reindustrialization and intensification of production or introducing a new industrial production, which the Western countries are now engaged in (Vasetskaya and Gaevskaia 2019; Bailey, Glasmeier, and Tomlinson 2019).

Unlike previous eras, when the technical and technological state of production was at a low level and it was problematic to implement such a strategy, there are various options for accelerating such processes in modern conditions. For the regions of the North Caucasus Federal District, the most acceptable is using digital technologies and digitalization of production processes.

4.3. Digitalization as a Way of a Macroregion Economy Technologizing

Digitalization is becoming one of the important tools for increasing labor productivity, competitiveness, a way to transform and diversify the economy. It contributes to creating a new structure of the economy (Schwab 2016).

Digitalization is not a technology or a product; it is an ongoing process that requires a response to constantly emerging digital trends (MIT Sloan Management Review 2018). This is a set of tools for optimizing the workflow by using digital software technologies, which "forms already integral technological environments" habitats "of ecosystems and platforms (Mukhopadhyay and Bouwman 2019).

Many modern efficiently functioning business models have achieved success thanks to the digitalization of processes, however, such companies had to create an organizational structure for this purpose that allows them to quickly implement and use new digital developments. From the standpoint of enterprises, the transformation of all spheres and markets under the influence of digitalization can improve the quality of goods and services while reducing costs. In addition, digitalization is transforming value chains in a variety of ways, opening up new opportunities for increased added value and broader structural change.

J. Burgess and J. Connell state that "technologies are revolutionizing, transforming and changing industries, jobs and skills while shifting the emphasis in trade and industry" (Burgess and Connell 2020).

As an example, we can cite two enterprises of different industries that are located in the territory of the North Caucasus Federal District and have achieved success through the use of software products and digital technologies.

The first enterprise is Sevkavrentgen-D LLC. The company specializes in the production of high-tech X-ray diagnostic equipment and tripod devices for medical purposes. At the enterprise, a full production cycle, from design to service support, is carried out based on electronic control modules, complex technological products are manufactured using digital technologies (3D printing) and software products developed by its own IT service. In connection with the pandemic, the company's products have become especially necessary for medical institutions. The enterprise supplies its products not only to the neighboring countries but has begun to develop the markets of other foreign countries.

The second enterprise is LLC Farm Firma Saturn. It is engaged in the production of dairy products. The company decided to completely renew its activities in order not only to stay on the market but also to increase its competitiveness. It began with developing and updating the product line with the involvement of various experts. Within the framework of this program, the production of several medicinal products began, which were recommended and approved by the Ministry of Health of the Russian Federation.

Attention was paid not only to product updates but also to planning, management, customer and supplier relationships. For this purpose, the company used such software products as ERP, CRM, SCM, and others. The company changed its organizational structure for them. These changes helped to improve competitiveness, reduce costs, and expand the geography of the market. The next step is introducing digital technologies that will effectively plan and manage all flows of information about raw materials, materials, products, services, and customers.

The examples of these enterprises show that many of the problems of the region under study can be solved by digital transformation, which will lead to optimization of production processes, cost reduction, and emergence of new sources of industry income and, ultimately, to a new way of life.

According to G. Litvintseva and S. Petrov, "the digital transformation of the economy and society presupposes a change in the technological order and institutional structure of society, in which it is necessary to take into account the interaction of formal and informal, market and non-market institutions, as well as institutions corresponding to digital processes, non-digital, etc." (Litvintseva and Petrov 2019).

The digitalization process should be preceded by saturating the production processes with innovative technologies. High-tech industries lend themselves to digitalization and transformation most quickly, as stated in the source (Muscio and Ciffolilli 2020). Currently, the transition to a new way of development based on digitalization is not a tribute to some fashion, but a vital necessity.

CONCLUSION

The implementation of the proposed methods and mechanisms will allow lagging regions, wherever they are, to leave this zone and move to a higher technological order. The conclusions obtained based on using this methodology show that it can become the basis for developing a strategy for the development of a region/ regions located in different territories and countries.

New technological, software and digital technologies remain the most important tools and mechanisms for transferring the economy of the constituent entities of the district to another level, to the level of high-tech development. One of the tasks is to increase the number of new technologies used in each economic entity. Otherwise, the district will not be able to leave the zone of depression and will remain at a low level of development. The process of using new technologies cannot be stopped, therefore it is necessary to act in advance.

ACKNOWLEDGMENT

The study was carried out with financial support from the Russian Foundation for Basic Research, project No. 19-010-00287 A "Development of a mechanism for the accelerated development of a problematic macro-region".

REFERENCES

Bailey, David, Dan Coffey, Maria Gavris. & Carole Thornley. (2019). "Industrial Policy, Place and Democracy." *Cambridge Journal of Regions, Economy and Society.* https://doi.org/10.1093/cjres/rsz010.

Bailey, David, Amy Glasmeier. & Philip R Tomlinson. (2019). "Industrial Policy Back on the Agenda: Putting Industrial Policy in Its Place?" *Cambridge Journal of Regions, Economy and Society*, 12 (3), 319–26. https://doi.org/10.1093/cjres/rsz018.

Bataev, A. V. (2018). "Analysis and Development the Digital Economy in the World." In *Proceedings of the 31st International Business Information Management Association Conference*, 61–71.

Burgess, John. & Julia Connell. (2020). "New Technology and Work: Exploring the Challenges." *Economic and Labour Relations Review.* https://doi.org/10.1177/1035304620944296.

Cooper, Richard N. & Carota Perez. (2003). "Technological Revolutions and Financial Capital: The Dynamics of Bubbles and Golden Ages." *Foreign Affairs.* https://doi.org/10.2307/20033522.

Coyle, Diane. (2019). "Do-It-Yourself Digital: The Production Boundary, the Productivity Puzzle and Economic Welfare." *Economica.* https://doi.org/10.1111/ecca.12289.

Lvov, D. S. & Yu. Glazyev, S. (1985). "*Teoreticheskie i Prikladnye Aspekty Upravleniya NTP [Theoretical and Applied Aspects of the Scientific-Technical Progress Management].*" In.

Erik Reinert. (2008). "How Rich Countries Got Rich . . . and Why Poor Countries Stay Poor." *PublicAffairs.* October 7, 2008.

Glaz'ev, S Yu. & Kharitonov, V. V. (2009). "Nanotechnology as a Key Factor in the New Technological Structure of the Economy." *Moscow: Trovant Publ, 10.*

Kenney, Martin. & John Zysman. (2020). "The Platform Economy: Restructuring the Space of Capitalist Accumulation." *Cambridge Journal of Regions, Economy and Society,* 13 (1), 55–76. https://doi.org/10.1093/cjres/rsaa001.

King, J. E. (2000). "Kondratiev and the Dynamics of Economic Development: Long Cycles and Industrial Growth in Historical Context." *History of Political Economy.* https://doi.org/10.1215/00182702-32-2-406.

Litvintseva, G. P. & Petrov, S. P. (2019). "Theoretical Foundations of Digital Transformation of Economy and People's Quality of Life." *Zhurnal Economicheskoj Teorii,* 16 (3), 414–27. https://doi.org/10.31063/2073-6517/2019.16-3.10.

"*Making Best Use of the Economic Potential of Russia's Regions Re-Mapping Opportunity.*" 2018.

MIT Sloan Management Review. (2018). *How to Go Digital: Practical Wisdom to Help Drive Your Organization's Digital Transformation.* Practical Wisdom to Help Drive Your Organization's Digital Transformation.

Mukhopadhyay, Sandip. & Harry Bouwman. (2019). "Orchestration and Governance in Digital Platform Ecosystems: A Literature Review and Trends." *Digital Policy, Regulation and Governance* . https://doi.org/10.1108/DPRG-11-2018-0067.

Muscio, Alessandro. & Andrea Ciffolilli. (2020). "What Drives the Capacity to Integrate Industry 4.0 Technologies? Evidence from European R&D Projects." *Economics of Innovation and New Technology.* https://doi.org/10.1080/10438599.2019.1597413.

"*Regions of Russia. Socio-Economic Indicators.*" n.d. Accessed February 4, 2021. https://rosstat.gov.ru/folder/210/document/13204.

Schumpeter, Joseph A. (2013). *Capitalism, Socialism and Democracy. Capitalism, Socialism and Democracy.* https://doi.org/10.4324/9780203202050.

Schwab, Klaus. (2016). "The Fourth Industrial Revolution: What It Means and How to Respond." *World Economic Forum.*

Vasetskaya, N. & Gaevskaia, T. (2019). "Digitalization as an Instrument for Economic Growth." In *Proceedings of the 33rd International Business Information Management Association Conference, IBIMA 2019: Education Excellence and Innovation Management through Vision 2020.*

Chapter 15

DIGITAL BUSINESS MODEL TRANSFORMATION IN ORDER TO IMPROVE THE EFFICIENCY OF THE COMPANY'S MANAGEMENT PROCESS

Olga Lukina[1], Anna Kurochkina[2] and Anna Karmanova[2,]*

[1]International banking Institute of a name of Anatoly Sobchak,
Saint Petersburg, Russia
[2]Peter the Great St. Petersburg Polytechnic University, Saint Petersburg, Russia

ABSTRACT

In the context of the intensive development of the information society and modern digital technologies, changes are taking place in the economic sphere related to the process of digitalization. The article presents the results of research to determine the essence of digital transformation of business. The definition of the term "digital economy", based on the active development of post-industrial society and the growing importance of information technologies in the 21st century, is considered. Descriptions of approaches to the definition of the concept are given. The purpose of the research is to determine the essence of digital business transformation and research approaches to structured digital transformation of the business model. The object of the research is the digital transformation of business models in order to improve the efficiency of the management process. Digital transformation is seen as the process of integrating digital technologies into all aspects of business processes, which entails the need for fundamental changes in the technology of creating new products and services, operations and culture. Currently, Russia lags behind other countries in the implementation and development of digital technologies. A promising direction is considered to be the cooperation of large corporations in the development of digitalization with private investment in the development of the scientific base and innovation infrastructure. The results of this research are conclusions about the advantages and risks for

* Corresponding Author's Email: aekarmanova@bk.ru.

various companies that digital transformation entails, about the main approaches to implementing business models and the main factors of digital transformation of business models.

Keywords: digital economy, digital transformation, information systems, types of information systems, business model, business

1. INTRODUCTION

In modern conditions, the role of advanced technologies and innovations is steadily growing, allowing to increase the efficiency of production and business processes. The latest technologies penetrate into all new industries and spheres of human life, changing traditional forms and methods of work.

The concept of a digital economy appeared at the end of the twentieth century. The main advantages of the digital economy were virtualization, instant movement and lack of weight of the product. The term "digital economy" is widely changed both in theory and in practice, but experts still cannot come to a consensus on the interpretation. Consider the definition of this term.

The term "digital economy" was first used by American information technology specialist Nicholas Negroponte, who proposed the concept of a digital economy in the form of a transition from the movement of atoms to the movement of bits, contrary to the concepts of weight of raw materials and transport, as attributes of the past, to the concepts of lack of weight of goods and virtuality, as the main elements of the future (Bazzoun 2019).

Obviously, this concept represents an understanding of the term "digital economy," based on the active development of a post-industrial society and the growing importance of information technology in the 21st century. It should be noted that attempts to clarify the term "digital economy" are also made by Russian IT specialists.

Another definition given in the "Strategy for the Development of the Information Society of the Russian Federation for 2017-2030" sounds like this: "The digital economy is an economic activity in which the key factor of production is digital data, the processing of large volumes and the use of the results of analysis of which, compared to traditional forms of business, can significantly increase the efficiency of various types of production, technologies, equipment, storage, sale, delivery of goods and services" (Pavlov et al. 2019; Bataev, Gorovoy, and Mottaeva 2018).

In other words, the digital economy is associated with focusing on the production of digital data, increasing the volume of processed information, optimizing key production processes and providing services. The main elements of the digital economy can be called electronic payments, marketing on social networks, Internet banks, various transactions made using computer networks (Desfonteines Larisa and Semenova Yuliya 2019).

It should be noted that in the Russian Federation the level of knowledge in the field of digital services is currently not at a high level. So, according to a study conducted by the first independent Russian online publication devoted to digital technologies, "3DNews Daily Digital Digital," it was noted that 63% of the Russian population are confident that they know what payments are electronic. But, when answering the question: "What applies to electronic payments?», the opinions of respondents were divided. Only one percent of respondents accurately stated that any payment methods without involving individuals can be attributed to the electronic payment system. Most of the respondents, namely 22% and 20% of respondents, replied that this was, respectively, payment for goods and services using an electronic wallet, as well as payment by bank card. The electronic payment system was equated with Internet banking by 17% of respondents. The survey also revealed that one in 10 Russians never used the electronic payment service (Trofimov 2018; Soluyanov 2014).

There are two approaches to the concept of "digital economy": classical, in which it is presented as an information technology-based economy, working only in the field of electronic goods and services. The second approach: advanced economic production using digital technologies.

The digital economy can be divided into (direct) - net online business and (indirect) - digital activities of mixed enterprises. It should be noted that the digital economy affects almost all aspects of people's lives, even such as health and education (Matrosova, Shtennikov, and Karmanova 2020).

Thus, in the healthcare system, the digital economy poses a number of challenges, consisting of the introduction of new ways of maintaining documentation, the use of telemedicine and the use of information systems for the treatment of patients, the use of mathematical methods and artificial intelligence methods in the processing of medical data (Konttila et al. 2019; Horgan et al. 2020).

In the process of comparing the contribution of the digital economy to Russia's GDP with the display bodies of other countries, it should be noted that Russia occupies lagging positions. According to Table 1 - The contribution of the digital economy to the GDP of Russia in comparison with the indicators of other countries, the final indicator of the size of the digital economy in GDP in percentage ratio is 3.9%, while in the USA or China this indicator is 10.9% and 10%, respectively. At the same time, in Russia, investments by companies in the development of digitalization accounted for a larger share than in China (2.2% and 1.8%, respectively). State expenses on digitalization in Russia remains insignificant compared to other countries.

The national project "Digital Economy" in its program assumes that by 2024, domestic costs for the development of the digital economy at the expense of all sources (in terms of GDP share) will increase by at least 3 times (compared to 2017) (Petrenko et al. 2017; Semyachkov 2018).

Table 1. The contribution of the digital economy to Russia's GDP compared to other countries

Some components of GDP/Countries	USA	China	Some countries of Western Europe	Russian Federation
Investments of companies in the development of digitalization	5	1,8	3,9	2,2
State expenses on digitalization	1,3	0,4	1	0,5
Total:	10,9	10	8,2	3,9

2. MATERIALS AND METHODS

The aim of the study is to determine the essence of the digital transformation of the business and a research of approaches to structured digital transformation of the business model.

Research materials, methods and objects.

Materials: scientific articles and monographs on digital economy, online business, e-commerce, Internet banking; Legislation of the Russian Federation, administrative acts of the Government of the Russian Federation and regulatory documents; public surveys and analytical reviews from the Internet.

The methodology used was analogies and comparisons, analysis of accessibility, completeness and conformity to the validity and completeness of the information provided in the analytical surveys.

The object of the study is the digital transformation of business models in order to increase the efficiency of the management process.

3. RESULTS

In modern realities, with the predominance of the service sector over production, information technologies and the IT sphere as a whole come to the forefront. Now, in order to receive any service, a person faces a much less complex mechanism. The features of modern Internet access, namely its cheapening, provide the consumer with the shortest and easiest way to get what he wants.

The world around us is changing daily along with the development of human civilization. Therefore, the technical and technological development of production is changing. This led to the emergence of a concept such as Industry 4.0, a model that shows how business follows recent events and changes over time. Thus, man, machine and production itself constitute a force in one intelligent and independent network.

Digital transformation is the process of integrating digital technologies into all aspects of business processes, which entails the need for fundamental changes in technology, culture, operations and technology to create new products and services.

That is, digital transformation is not just automation (the introduction of innovative technologies into existing business). It implies a change in the business structure itself, a strategy for business development, a corporate culture and team management, a sales system, as well as radical changes in the creation of completely new products, services and even entire industries (Kotarba 2018).

Digital transformation has been discussed for many years, but there is still no clear definition for digital transformations of business models, approaches to how to use digital transformation of business models, what stages, tools and factors should be considered (Veselovsky et al. 2019).

Digital transformation is the integration of digital technologies into all areas of business, fundamentally changing the process of work. It is also a cultural change that requires organizations to constantly challenge the status quo, experiment and feel comfortable with failures.

Despite the fact that digital transformation is now a popular topic for discussion, the ideas of digital products, services and media were already well understood in the 1990s and 2000s. For example, in retail, media advertising campaigns were considered important digital channels through which it was possible to enter the market in the 1990s and 2000s, despite the fact that purchases were still made mainly in small stores, paid mainly in cash. From 2000 to 2015, an increase in the number of smart devices and social media platforms led to a sharp change in customer-business communication methods, as well as customer expectations for response time and multi-channel. The business began to understand that now it can communicate with customers in digital format on an individual basis and often in real time. The ever-increasing choice of digital payment options, such as PayPal, has also contributed to the expansion of online trading and opportunities for online outlets. Enterprises, using the kinds of personalized customer data that mobile technologies can generate on a mass scale, take advantage of this personalized information and can better adapt their products, communications and interactions to the specific needs of customers.

Digital transformation technologies can be conditionally divided into the following components: people - users who are increasingly using technologies to work together or solve goals and tasks; processes - transforming the business processes themselves; products - they are the results of the success of the introduction of innovative digital technologies and the use of digital tools in development and production. Such digital technologies include 3D printers, digital doubles of products, VR/AR (augmented and virtual reality), open source products (Karmanova 2019).

In 2019, KPMG (the auditing company of the Big Four) in Russia conducted a study on the topic "Digital technologies in Russian companies." It was attended by more than 100 largest Russian companies, the largest industry profiles were banks and financial institutions (23%), FMCG (fast moving consumer goods, everyday goods) (14%) and retail (14%), the most few were telecom (6%) and IT infrastructure (6%). The key conclusion of the study is that large companies have already embarked on the path of digital transformation.

New elements of digital transformation are considered:

- Digital ecosystems - a symbiosis of a team and a technological tool in which there is a high degree of freedom of communication between participants, and current processes are easily adapted and established to the needs of the moment.
- Industry 4.0 technologies are an exponential industrial revolution that makes fundamental changes in production processes. It covers the introduction of cybersystems and the digitalization of industry.
- 3D printing is a software-driven process for creating three-dimensional objects.
- Robotization - the development of automation based on industrial robots.
- The Internet of Things is a complex system of communication of a person with devices and devices with other devices, which allows you to collect, store, process and analyze data arrays.
- Deepening big data analytics -examining data in different contexts and conditions.
- Digital platforms - systems of mutually beneficial algorithmicized relationships of independent participants in the economy, which are carried out in the same information environment.

Preliminary forecasts show that until 2025, the Internet of Things could bring the world economy about 4-11 trillion US dollars annually (Popkova, Ragulina, and Bogovis 2019).

Any business organization requires an information system to ensure that information is collected, stored, processed and issued. An information system is a computer-based system that has a certain practical scope. The introduction of information systems generally helps to automate the routine work of employees, improve the structure of information flows, analyze the document flow system, improve the quality of knowledge and skills of employees, reduce production costs, search and occupy new market niches.

The operation of any information system consists of certain processes operating according to the rules of an open or closed control system. The open information system is characterized by the fact that the consumer uses the received information arbitrarily and there is no feedback. Such a system works autonomously, and the consumer does not affect the purpose of its operation in any way.

The closed information system is distinguished by the presence of feedback between the IS and the consumer. Take into account the response of consumers to the information that they received through the use of feedback channels. The information received is processed and adjusted by the company's employees. The processed information is again sent to the consumer. Such information systems target specific groups of users and take into account their needs and objectives.

4. DISCUSSION

The basis for any information system is the information with which decisions are made or routine tasks are automatically solved. Information systems support typically includes:

- technical support - equipment, computer systems, equipment, all those technical means that are involved in the process of processing and converting information;
- information support - is the methods and means that provide the information base of the system. This can be both encoding information and creating databases;
- Linguistic support - language tools, schemes and decryptions that allow you to work with information;
- mathematical support - mathematical calculations, algorithms and formulas, models of information processing;
- software - programs necessary for automation of operation, providing tasks for computer equipment and solving problems of the organization.

Although information systems are most often understood as computerized work, the staff of the organization participate in the process, depending on the complexity and formalization of the work. Since there are many needs within an organization that a single information system cannot meet, there are different types.

Transaction processing systems are needed to monitor the main work of the business, serve the organizational level. Process management systems monitor and manage the main production processes of the organization, include special programs and product development procedures. Office automation systems provide information support at many levels of the organization. They allow you to solve office routine tasks and transfer information among employees of the organization.

Management information systems allow you to make decisions about managing your organization through information collection and processing. Management is provided with reports summarizing the internal information of the enterprise, on the basis of which decisions are made. Decision support systems calculate, compare and summarize information so that a manager at any organizational level has data to choose the best management decision. Such systems help formulate, model, calculate, compare, predict scenarios (Korchagina, Desfonteines, and Strekalova 2020).

Executive information systems allow performers to access information about the state of the market and the state of the organization. Such information is provided in the form of convenient visual images and allows the manager to make decisions regarding the development of the company. Expert information systems allow, using a certain knowledge base, to replace a human expert. Such systems act as a consultant and provide expert solutions for the needs of users (Kurochkina et al. 2019).

A knowledge management system is needed to develop the competencies of the organization's employees, their knowledge and skills. It provides easy access to the organization's knowledge base. This system supports, creates and disseminates information for employees of the company, which contributes to the growth and development of the general level of competence of employees and, accordingly, to the improvement of the quality of work as a whole.

Strategic information systems enable senior managers to make strategic decisions. They are needed by the organization in order to process information, make decisions about mastering new market segments and gaining a competitive advantage (Voronkova et al. 2017).

Functional business systems are used to ensure and facilitate the routine work of middle managers. In general, these systems are programs that allow you to monitor and manage basic business processes, helping you make decisions and manage work within specific departments.

Any of the listed information systems can be used not only within one entity for which are more targeted, but also within other organizational groups.

If large companies have many opportunities in terms of digitalization, then small and medium-sized businesses, even with a modest budget, can afford a digital transformation. The main thing is to correctly determine the key tasks of this transformation, choose the right digital tools and not get involved in a large number of projects. With digital transformation, small and medium-sized businesses are most likely to implement one project at a time inside a short innovation cycle in 1.5-2 years.

An example of such projects can be the development of chat bots on sites, a mobile application of the tax service, the creation of online banking, blockchain registries in insurance companies, targeted advertising and medical diagnostics when used BigData (big data) and AI (artificial intelligence), streamlining the workflow through optical recognition, as well as the introduction of IoT (Internet of Things) (Dekimpe 2020).

However, if you are not limited to, for example, developing an application or creating a cloud, finding a technology partner is a good option. Small companies will not have enough resources for projects to introduce elements such as artificial intelligence and machine learning. There can be several ways of cooperation, from outsourcing to receiving recommendations, which budget decisions can be used in a specific situation and a specific business.

SMB Group research demonstrates how the transition to digital transformation affects SMB revenues. It was found that compared to competitors who do not use modern development trends, income increased by 18% (SMB Group 2017).

Researchers and practitioners involved in business process reengineering may see similarities between Business Process Reengineering (BPR) and digital transformation. In their frequently cited work, Hammer and Champy (Hammer and Champy 1993) provided a description of BPR. The authors argue that BPR is a rethinking and reengineering of business processes in order to reduce costs and improve products and services. Despite some similarities between BPR and digital transformation, there are also some differences between the two approaches. BPR focuses mainly on automation of rules-based systems. Instead of focusing on rules-based processes, as BPR does, the main goals of digital transformation are to obtain new data and use this data to rethink old rule-based processes. A more data-centric approach allows you to gain new knowledge and, in turn, rethink business models and operations. For example, Airbnb has shifted its focus from processes to data. Airbnb does not own its own physical assets (for example, hotels). Here is an example of how old, rule-based processes in the hotel industry can be completely rethought in a data-driven world. Homeowners of apartments and homeowners who own real estate on Airbnb offer an alternative to hotels and create unique value for guests. How employees interpret newly acquired know-how and use it to improve decision-making capabilities distinguishes digital transformation from other areas of research. All new data sources create newly formed knowledge sources based on these data.

The business model is the main logic of the company, which describes what benefits customers and partners. The business model answers the question of how the provided positive results return to the company in the form of income. The cost created allows you to differentiate from competitors, consolidate relations with customers and achieve a competitive advantage. The business model includes the following components and elements:

- the client dimension includes client segments, communication channels, and customer relationships;
- The favourable dimension includes products, services and values;
- Added cost of measurement includes resources, skills and processes;
- The partnership dimension includes a partner, partner channels, and partnerships;
- financial dimension includes income and expenses.

The goal is to combine the elements of the business model so that they mutually reinforce each other (Wu, Terpenny, and Schaefer 2017). This makes it possible to achieve growth and makes imitation by competitors ineffective (Guo et al. 2021).

Example of Digital Business Model Transformation

ThyssenKrupp is a German industrial group with various divisions. The elevator division produces passenger and cargo elevators, as well as escalators for buildings, residential buildings, hotels, airports, shopping centers and other facilities. In addition to the sale and installation of elevators and escalators, maintenance, repair and modernization services are also offered.

The old business model of the ThyssenKrupp was mainly focused on the production of elevators, their installation and maintenance as necessary. The increase in the number of tall buildings in large cities has led to an increase in demand for high-performance elevators. In addition, customers and users demanded the highest reliability of elevators.

The goal of the elevator business of ThyssenKrupp was to reduce the duration of elevator shutdowns by identifying the causes of potential failures in the prognostic specialist. This would ultimately speed up maintenance and reduce repair time. To solve this problem, the MAX elevator monitoring system, Elevator Monitoring System, was created. Timely identification of potential causes of disconnections requires real-time information that provides key information about the current state of the elevator. To solve this problem, they installed sensors on the components of elevators ThyssenKrupp. These sensors collect information such as cabin speed and engine temperature. This information is then evaluated by predictive analysis and provided to maintenance and technician personnel. These changes allowed ThyssenKrupp to actively carry out maintenance and thereby reduce the downtime of the elevator. In addition, costs, resources and maintenance planning have been improved.

Thus, the MAX elevator monitoring system of ThyssenKrupp is an example of a service-oriented digitization initiative. MAX collects relevant technical and mechanical information using sensors to reduce service backlogs and improve overall ThyssenKrupp service. Simply put, information that was previously ignored is now collected and used to provide value to customers and generate profit for ThyssenKrupp. The customer's maintenance requirements changed and ThyssenKrupp was forced to come up with a solution. The ThyssenKrupp Max system has increased profitability by offering an additional maintenance service that promises to reduce the backlog of maintenance issues.

The firm decision ThyssenKrupp to give preference to the MAX system was probably due to the realization that their internal know-how in the field of maintenance was not used properly.

ThyssenKrupp has digitized its business model by developing an innovative service management system. The company's MAX system ThyssenKrupp created a data-driven maintenance system that gives new benefits to customers and, in turn, provided a new source of revenue.

CONCLUSION

The essence of the digital economy is expressed in the following: digitalization is another stage of economic development, which is reflected in the relationship between business and industrial relations thanks to information technologies, which results in the achievement of significant economic effects.

The digital economy in the Russian Federation is supported by the national program "Digital Economy of the Russian Federation," which aims to create key factors of production, namely the ecosystems of the digital economy. The purpose of this program is also to create the necessary conditions for the development of business, to eliminate possible obstacles to effectively increase the technological effectiveness of businesses.

When studying the prospects for the development of the digital economy in Russia, it should be noted that there is an unconditional increase in digitalization, although Russia lags behind the leaders in some positions. The reason for the lag is the lack of investment, but even with slow growth, it can be said that digitalization helps to improve the business and investment climate, as well as contributes to social and financial involvement of the population, making the availability, quality and convenience of receiving services much higher. The partnership of large corporations in the development of digitalization with private investments in the development of the scientific base and innovative infrastructure, while focusing, rather than on the domestic market, seems promising.

One of the important elements of the company's strategic management is digitalization, so the main approach for the introduction of digital technologies in each company should be the "company-technology" approach. Digital transformation is, in addition to contributing to new technologies, a detailed improvement in products and services, organization structures, development strategies, customer relations and corporate culture.

Digital transformation is certainly a complex process, long-term and costly. Information technology saves not only human resources, but also financial and temporary resources. That is, the process of management in the business begins at the time of creation of the project and ends at the time of receiving feedback from the consumer, which will allow you to track the process completely, make adjustments to it without compromising time and resources, and also make it possible to improve in the future. Introducing digital tools into business, as well as creating places for new professions, is the key to a successful transition to the digital market in the era of the digital economy.

The need for the use of information systems in business is due to the increase in the speed and validity of decisions, increased efficiency of the organization, increased productivity, improved competitiveness of the company, reduced transaction costs, the ability to exchange large amounts of data and simplified operations. However, with the digital transformation of business processes, problems may arise related to threats to cybersecurity, the complexity of estimating the cost of the product being created, and in the future with the release of jobs, which leads to an increase in unemployment.

To effectively implement digital transformation in business processes, it is necessary for the company management to understand that along with digital transformation, it is important to carry out other changes within the company itself, such as synchronizing the improvement of the company's management and the processes of introducing digital technologies into it, and increasing professionalism in the field of digital technology application by the company's leadership.

REFERENCES

Bataev, Alexey V., Alexandr A. Gorovoy. & Angela Mottaeva. (2018). "Evaluation of the Future Development of the Digital Economy in Russia." In *Proceedings of the 32nd International Business Information Management Association Conference, IBIMA 2018 - Vision 2020: Sustainable Economic Development and Application of Innovation Management from Regional Expansion to Global Growth.*

Bazzoun, Mohammed. (2019). "The Digital Economy." *International Journal of Social Science and Economics Invention.* https://doi.org/10.23958/ijssei/vol05-i09/157.

Dekimpe, Marnik G. (2020). "Retailing and Retailing Research in the Age of Big Data Analytics." *International Journal of Research in Marketing.* https://doi.org/10. 1016/j.ijresmar.2019.09.001.

Desfonteines Larisa. & Semenova Yuliya. (2019). "*The Role Of Social Networks In The Political Life Of Society.*" International Business Information Management Association (IBIMA). 2019. https://ibima.org/accepted-paper/the-role-of-social-networks-in-the-political-life-of-society/.

Guo, Chaojie, Russell G. Thompson, Greg Foliente. & Xiang T. R. Kong. (2021). "An Auction-Enabled Collaborative Routing Mechanism for Omnichannel on-Demand Logistics through Transshipment." *Transportation Research Part E: Logistics and Transportation Review.* https://doi.org/10.1016/j.tre.2020.102206.

Hammer, Michael. & James Champy. (1993). "Reengineering the Corporation: A Manifesto for Business Revolution." *Business Horizons.* https://doi.org/10.1016/ S0007-6813(05)80064-3.

Horgan, Denis, Joanne Hackett, C. Benedikt Westphalen, Dipak Kalra, Etienne Richer, Mario Romao, Antonio L. Andreu., et al. (2020). "Digitalisation and COVID-19: The Perfect Storm." *Biomedicine Hub.* https://doi.org/10.1159/000511232.

Karmanova, Anna E. (2019). "Virtual Tourism: Conceptual Problems of Implementation and Prospects for Development." *The International Scientific Journal.* https://doi.org/10.34286/1995-4638-2019-66-3-21-27.

Konttila, Jenni, Heidi Siira, Helvi Kyngäs, Minna Lahtinen, Satu Elo, Maria Kääriäinen, Pirjo Kaakinen., et al. (2019). "Healthcare Professionals' Competence in Digitalisation: A Systematic Review." *Journal of Clinical Nursing.* https://doi.org/ 10.1111/jocn.14710.

Korchagina, Elena, Larisa Desfonteines. & Natalia Strekalova. (2020). "Problems of Training Specialists for Trade in the Conditions of Digitalization." In *E3S Web of Conferences.* https://doi.org/10.1051/e3sconf/202016412014.

Kotarba, Marcin. (2018). "Digital Transformation of Business Models." *Foundations of Management.* https://doi.org/10.2478/fman-2018-0011.

Kurochkina, Anna A., Olga V. Voronkova, Olga V. Lukina. & Tatyana V. Bikezina. (2019). "Management Features of Small and Medium-Sized Business Enterprises." *Espacios*.

Matrosova, Nataliia D., Dmitry G. Shtennikov. & Anna E. Karmanova. (2020). "The Correlation of User's Interaction Activity on the Online Course Forum and User's Educational Achievement." *International Journal of Scientific and Technology Research*.

Pavlov, Boris Petrovich, Ruslan F. Garifullin, Gaziz F. Mingaleev. & Vitalii M. Babushkin. (2019). "Key Technologies of Digital Economy in the Russian Federation." In *Proceedings of the 33rd International Business Information Management Association Conference, IBIMA 2019: Education Excellence and Innovation Management through Vision 2020*.

Petrenko, Sergei A., Krystina A. Makoveichuk, Petr V. Chetyrbok. & Alexey S. Petrenko. (2017). "About Readiness for Digital Economy." In *Proceedings of 2017 IEEE 2nd International Conference on Control in Technical Systems, CTS 2017*. https://doi.org/10.1109/CTSYS.2017.8109498.

Popkova, Elena G., Yulia V. Ragulina. & Aleksei V. Bogovis. (2019). *Industry 4.0: Industrial Revolution of the 21st Century. Studies in Systems, Decision and Control*.

Semyachkov, Konstantin. (2018). "State Management of Russian Regions by Means of Digital Technologies." In *Proceedings of the European Conference on E-Government, ECEG*.

SMB Group. (2017). "*SMB Group ' s 2017 Top 10 SMB Technology Trends*," 1–5. https://www.smb-gr.com/wp-content/uploads/2017/01/2017_top_10_final.pdf.

Soluyanov, Alexey Alexeyevich. (2014). "Payment Systems and the Role of the Central Bank of the Russian Federation." *World Applied Sciences Journal*. https://doi.org/10.5829/idosi.wasj.2014.31.05.14349.

Trofimov, Dmitry V. (2018). "Financial Technologies in the Field of Retail Payments: Current Trends and Perspectives in EU and Russia." *Voprosy Ekonomiki*. https://doi.org/10.32609/0042-8736-2018-3-48-63.

Veselovsky, Mikhail Yakovlevich, Marina Alekseevna Izmailova, Lenar Albertovich Yunusov. & Ildar Albertovich Yunusov. (2019). "Quality of Digital Transformation Management on the Way of Formation of Innovative Economy of Russia." *Quality - Access to Success*.

Voronkova, Olga Vasilevna, Anna Aleksandrovna Kurochkina, Irina Pavlovna Firova. & Tatiana Vasilevna Bikezina. (2017). "Implementation of an Information Management System for Industrial Enterprise Resource Planning." *Espacios*.

Wu, Dazhong, Janis Terpenny. & Dirk Schaefer. (2017). "Digital Design and Manufacturing on the Cloud: A Review of Software and Services." *Artificial Intelligence for Engineering Design, Analysis and Manufacturing: AIEDAM*. https://doi.org/10.1017/S0890060416000305.

In: Global Challenges of Digital Transformation of Markets ISBN: 978-1-53619-754-9
Editors: E. de la Poza and S. E. Barykin   © 2021 Nova Science Publishers, Inc.

Chapter 16

Substantiation of Factors for Assessing the Historical and Cultural Value of the Territories of Settlements Using Digital Technologies

Elena Bykowa[1,*], Irina Dyachkova[1,†], Vilena Zasenko[2,‡] and Petko Monev[3,‖]

[1]Saint Petersburg Mining University, Saint Petersburg, Russia
[2]Peter the Great St. Petersburg Polytechnic University,
Saint Petersburg, Russia
[3]University of Economics, Varna, Bulgaria

Abstract

This article presents the features of the digitalization of the cultural heritage of Russia, substantiates the need for a historical and cultural assessment of the territory to preserve the historical and cultural potential, establish zones for the protection of cultural heritage objects of various categories of settlements, improve information support for urban planning and land management activities, as well as individual and cadastral appraisals of real estate objects. We considered and analyzed the existing methods of such an assessment, described its concept and proposed a list of assessment factors based on the analysis of the experience of performing such assessments in different countries. Within the framework of the study, based on checking the proposed factors for multicollinearity, conclusions

---

[*] Corresponding Author's Email: Bykova_EN@pers.spmi.ru.
[†] Corresponding Author's Email: s195014@stud.spmi.ru.
[‡] Corresponding Author's Email: vikiza@yandex.ru.
[‖] Corresponding Author's Email: mg5ko@abv.bg.

were drawn about the correction of their initial list and the form of the proposed model of the integral indicator of the historical and cultural value of the territory.

Keywords: valuation factors, historical and cultural value, digital technologies, real estate appraisal, cultural heritage objects

1. INTRODUCTION

The pace of development of digital technologies in modern society is amazing. The fruits of digitalization are designed to improve the quality of life of the population, develop the economy and modernize management systems, and therefore modern technologies are being more actively introduced into all areas of human activity (Pirogova and Plotnikov 2020). The modern rates of growth and development of settlements, which the entire world community speaks of, dictate the need for the introduction of innovative products in urban planning activities and land management in settlements (Clark and Mayer 2012; Shojaei et al. 2018). Today, information systems for ensuring urban planning activities, GIS technologies in the cadastre, assessment and land management, FSIS TP, Public cadastral map and much more are being actively developed (Skachkova, Lepihina, and Ignatova 2018). Digital technologies make it possible to solve the problems of information support, accuracy and completeness of data on real estate objects and territories, resolve legal disputes, and support the regulation of land use and protection. The regulation of any processes in urbanized territories has its own characteristics, imposed by the real estate objects located on them. One of the topical and acute problems of the modern settlement is the preservation of historical and cultural monuments.

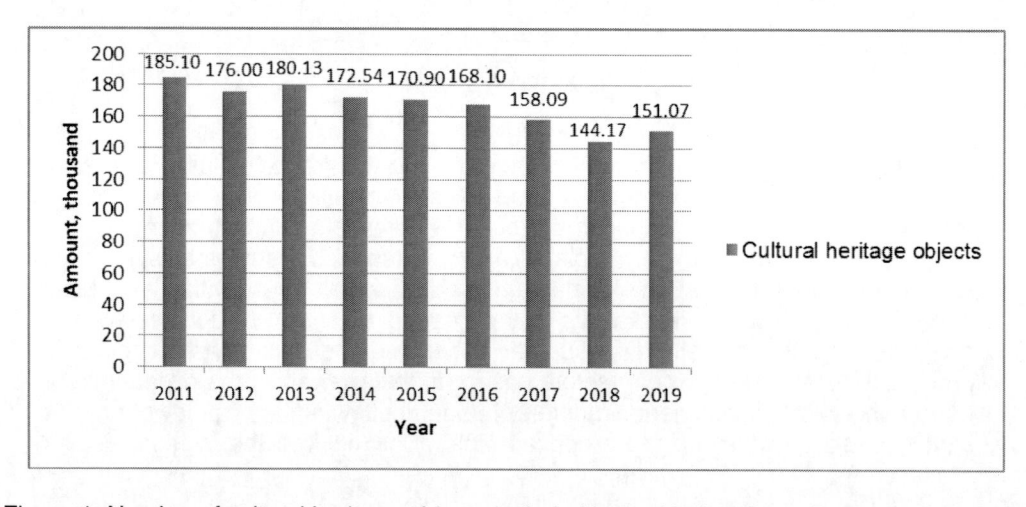

Figure 1. Number of cultural heritage objects included in the Unified State Register of Cultural Heritage Objects, by year.

Russia has a rich historical and cultural heritage. According to the data of the Unified Interdepartmental Information and Statistical System, in 2019 43.8% of the monuments of history and culture in Russia belong to the identified objects of cultural heritage ("EMISS " n.d.). The cultural heritage in the Russian Federation is concentrated in 41 historical settlements of federal significance and 478 historical settlements of regional significance. Preservation of cultural heritage is a priority in the process of any economic activity in cities at any level of government. However, in recent years, there has been a negative trend towards a reduction in the number of valuable objects (see Figure 1).

To ensure the preservation of the historical and cultural heritage in the process of urban planning regulation and the active use of urbanized territories, it is necessary to obtain up-to-date information about their historical and cultural value, i.e., assess the territory in terms of its historical and cultural potential.

Such a comprehensive assessment should be based on a system of accounting for the architectural, natural, recreational, cultural and other features of the territory. Its results can become the basis for establishing and adjusting the protection zones of cultural heritage objects, determining the cadastral and market values of land plots below them and falling within the boundaries of cultural heritage protection zones, determining the costs of restoration of valuable objects, identifying the cultural heritage objects themselves, as well as making investment decisions in relation to these objects.

The need for a historical and cultural assessment of the territory is confirmed in their works by (Scazzosi 2004), Wall and Nuryanti (Wall and Nuryanti 1996), Dimitrovski et. al. (Dimitrovski, Todorović, and Valjarević 2012), Fourie and Santana-Gallego (Fourie and Santana-Gallego 2013). Analysis of historical and cultural features of the territory is an important component of urban planning. In this aspect, it is important to develop and apply a methodology for such evaluation. Kovyazin is engaged in the development of the methodology for assessing the historical and cultural value of the territory (V. F. Kovyazin, Skachkova, and D'yachkova 2021), Scazzosi (Scazzosi 2004), Dimitrovski, Dapkus, Dapkute, Pereira (Dragi Dimitrovski 2012; Dapkus and Dapkute 2015; Pereira 2014), Timothy (Timothy 2009). There are many opinions on the application of different approaches to assessing the historical and cultural value of the territory, which are also studied Ismagilova and others (G. Ismagilova, Safiullin, and Gafurov 2015; Chalhoub 2018; G. N. Ismagilova, Gafurov, and Safiullin 2015), Hribar, Bole, Pipan (Hribar, Bole, and Pipan 2015), as well as RAA SN Scientific Research Institute of Theory and History of Architecture and Urban Planning "Association urban planning and design and State Unitary Enterprise "Research and Development Center of the General Plan of the City of Moscow."

Various approaches to the assessment of the historical and cultural value of urbanized territories, as well as the features of the urban environment that affect the historical and cultural value, were studied by Montella, Angeles, Gandini, Reynard, Ruijgrok (Montella 2015; Angeles 2002; Gandini and Villa 2003; Reynard and Giusti

2018; *Cultural Heritage and Value Creation* 2015; Ruijgrok 2006), Wagner (Wagner 2017), Gumińska (Gumińska 2017).

The analysis of existing methods showed that despite their scientific substantiation and specialization, they have a number of disadvantages, the main of which is a narrow combination of evaluative factors that do not cover the features of development objects, for example, the possibility of economic adaptation of a valuable object, the uniqueness of technical solutions. In this regard, it becomes necessary to develop a universal, but effective methodology for assessing the historical and cultural value of the territory, which will ensure the preservation and adaptation of the historical and cultural environment to modern conditions. Within the framework of this study, the concept of the methodology of historical and cultural assessment is being developed, based on the interpretation of the qualitative and quantitative historical and cultural characteristics of the territory in the form of a list of assessment factors.

Research goal. To substantiate a set of significant evaluative factors of the historical and cultural value of the territory, as well as the type of the assumed model of the dependence of the integral indicator of value on them using digital technologies.

2. MATERIALS AND METHODS

Research methods. To achieve the completeness and accuracy of the results in the selection of evaluation factors, analytical and descriptive research methods, mathematical and statistical methods, including correlation and regression analysis, Gretl and MS Excel software are used.

2.1. The Concept of the Methodology for Assessing the Historical and Cultural Value of the Territory

The developed methodology for the historical and cultural assessment of the territory of settlements is based on the expression of its historical and cultural features in the form of semantic values of the estimated factors with their subsequent transformation into a quantitative value using the theory of fuzzy sets.

The main principles of the methodology are universality, objectivity, openness, scientific character and mathematical validity. In the assessment process, it is necessary to use the data of official and verified sources, as well as to give preference to a more stringent security regime with an ambiguous status of the object. The unit of evaluation is a real estate object, an object of garden and park art, memorial monuments, fountains and other objects that influence the creation of the urban environment. The sequence of actions in the process of historical and cultural assessment according to the developed methodology is shown in Figure 2 (see Figure 2).

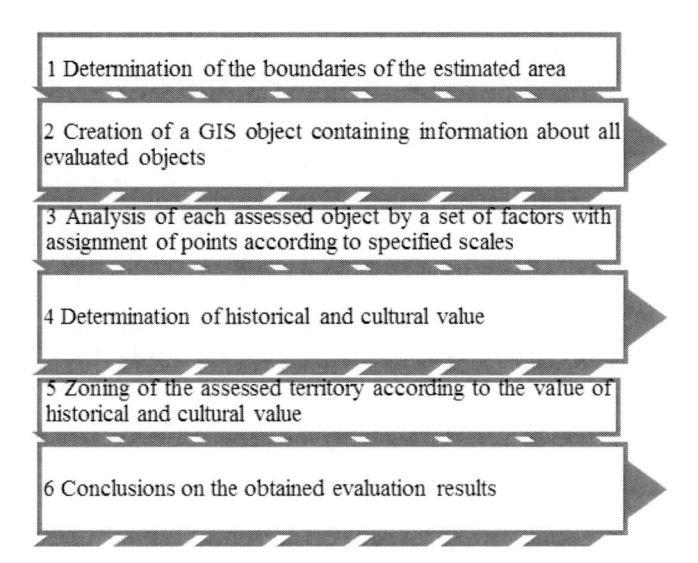

Figure 2. Stages of historical and cultural assessment of the territory.

The results of the historical and cultural assessment of the territory are an important potential object for digital technologies since this methodology assumes that the result is represented in a quantitative form, which creates the possibility of its implementation in various systems and processes. Tarnovsky and Shishovain their work pay attention to the fact that, despite the orientation of modern Russian society towards the active implementation of digital technologies (state program "Digital Economy of the Russian Federation"), little attention is currently paid to the digitalization of cultural heritage in Russia.

The main official source of data on historical and cultural monuments is the portal of the Ministry of Culture of the Russian Federation with Information from the Unified State Register of Cultural Heritage Objects (Historical and Cultural Monuments) of the Peoples of the Russian Federation posted on it, as well as the Unified Interdepartmental Information and Statistical System. The information contained in these services is very limited, there is no information, important from the standpoint of popularization and protection, on the boundaries of territories and zones of protection of cultural heritage objects, the subject of protection. An important step towards the development of digital technologies in the field of cultural heritage protection is the linking of a specific object to an online map and the ability to view it online.

2.2. Selection and Justification of a Preliminary Set of Assessment Factors

The compilation of a preliminary list of factors of historical and cultural assessment is based on the analysis of scientific and practical methods of Russian and foreign researchers, providing for a criterion or factor approach.

Table 1. Classification of development by urban (environment-forming) factor

Name of property	Characteristic	Examples
Architectural dominant, architectural accent (cultural heritage site)	Forms planning, compositional and historical environment in close proximity, closes the street perspective	Cathedral of the Resurrection of Christ Savior on Spilled Blood in St. Petersburg
Valuablecity-formingobject	Positively affects the formation of the historical and cultural environment, maintains the rhythm of space, clearly characterizes the local features of the settlement	Manor-type houses of provincial town in Orenburg
Private (background) object	Preserves the historical and cultural environment, maintains the general appearance of the building	Private houses in Orenburg on the main street
Harmonious object	Fits into the urban environment, disrupts the background building with separate elements	Objects of modern construction
Discordant object	They negatively affect the formation of the historical and cultural environment of the territory, create disharmony in the environment, violate the architectural appearance of the urban environment by its appearance (cladding, style of the building facade), height (number of storeys), functions performed (garage or economic construction near a valuable object)	Long-term construction in the center of Orenburg, shopping center Sennaya in St. Petersburg

The analysis of urbanized territories from the standpoint of historical and cultural potential is reduced to the assessment of objects that form the urban environment. Based on this, an important factor is urban planning, which implies the characteristics of the planning, compositional-spatial, large-scale structure of the historical and urban planning environment (Whitehand and Gu 2010; di Zandieh; Shervin Goodarzian 2014). Emelyanov adheres to the same position, considering the planning organization of the territory as an important assessment characteristic of the historical and urban planning environment. In the assessment of this factor, the definition of the positive, negative or neutral influence of the object on the formation of the appearance of the nearby territory is laid. The urban planning criterion is taken into account in the projects of protection zones for cultural heritage objects and acts of the state historical and cultural expertise of projects for protection zones for cultural heritage objects and is also used in most of the above assessment methods. In terms of assessing the scale and planning organization, the classification of development objects presented in Table 1 is considered.

In any settlement, special attention is paid to the natural carcass; moreover, more than 11% of the territory of settlements in Russia is occupied by green spaces. The cultural heritage monuments are characterized by the presence of gardening art objects on the adjacent territory. For example, noble estates of the 19th century stand out as a separate type of landscape-historical art. Therefore, an important factor in assessing the historical-cultural value is the landscape-environmental factor, which determines the characteristics of the natural landscape (relief, hydrographic network, landscaping). An assessment of whether an object creates an urban landscape, whether it is a part of it, whether there is landscaping in the adjacent territory, or the presence of an object negatively affects the natural composition, allows preserving the natural frame of the city (V. Kovyazin, Romanchikov, and Kitcenko 2020; Kitcenko, Kovyazin, and Romanchikov 2020). At the same time, an important indicator of the development of the recreational and tourist potential of the territory is the presence of recreational and landscaping zones in the nearby territory. The assessment of the accessibility of recreation zones is carried out in accordance with SNiP 2.07.01-89 * Urban planning. Planning and development of urban and rural settlements.

Koroleva and Marcinevskaya emphasize in the importance of the historical landscape in the process of assessing the historical, cultural, and recreational features of the territory. Considering the concept of cultural landscape, which is actively used in Great Britain, Germany, Norway, USA, Poland, one should pay attention to the natural and cultural heritage in aggregate. To do this, it is proposed to evaluate the "uniqueness of the natural landscape and hydrology," taking into account the distance to natural objects, and their uniqueness from a natural point of view.

Assessment of the historical and cultural value of an object cannot fail to include an analysis of the connection of the object with historical events or the activities of famous historical figures, since this may be the tourist and investment potential (Mckercher and Du Cros 2012; Taylor and Lennon 2011; Scazzosi 2004; McKercher and Ho 2006b; 2006a; Piñero et al. 2017).

The concept of historical and cultural value includes the intangible features of an object and territory, which make it possible to characterize attractiveness from the standpoint of cultural development, educational and social life. The participation of Russians in cultural life is growing every year, so by 2019, 88% of Russians have been taking part in cultural events. Consequently, there is a growing demand for the development of cultural sites as investment ones. The cultural factor is an assessment of the impact of an object on the cultural life of the city and (or) the approach to such objects. The factor of participation of the assessed object in the cultural or social life of society implies whether the object is the center of attraction for the city's public life, cultural-social, museum, religious, educational, and other purposes (Wright and Eppink 2016; Montella 2015; Yüceer and Ipekoğlu 2012).

Historical and cultural value as a separate characteristic contains a spiritual component. Possession of educational and spiritual value is assessed in the context of the development of spiritual and (or) educational, patriotic life of the city, district, quarter.

Most of the methods do not consider such a factor as "economic," despite the important component of value in the form of income from the use of the object. Hribar, Bole, and Pipan suggest to include the economic component to the historical and cultural assessment of the territory. In their research, they refer to the fact that the importance of a specific cultural value for the development of the territory is determined by the potentials of economic, environmental, social, and cultural development. Currently, immovable objects located on the territory of historical settlements have moved from objects requiring costs for renovation and reconstruction to a group of objects that are attractive for investment. A significant part of immovable monuments has exhibition value, i.e., may fall into the sphere of interest of tourism firms for the purpose of generating income. The combination of preserving cultural heritage and business development found expression in the program with the code name "Rent of architectural monuments for 1 ruble," approved in the Decree of the Government of the Russian Federation of September 11, 2015 No. 966 ("Program for Renting an OKN for 1 Ruble" n.d.).

To establish the boundaries of the territories of cultural heritage objects, the mental value of the object in the environment is important, therefore, one of the factors is also emotional and artistic. It characterizes the emotional reaction to the external appearance of the object during a field examination, the picturesqueness of the object, the degree of attractiveness of the appearance and interiors.

The historical and cultural value of the territory is increased by objects of cultural heritage and valuable town-forming objects. The protective valuation factor assumes the definition of the category of protection of a cultural heritage object (local, regional, federal significance, a UNESCO World Heritage site, or an identified object), a valuable town-forming or background building object.

Many European countries, within the framework of the preservation and popularization of historical city centers, for example, Austria, adhere to the policy of activating historical centers due to the economic potential revealed in the adaptation of historical objects to modern conditions. Revealing the degree of adaptation of an object to modern conditions will allow obtaining a characteristic of the historical and modern functional use of the object. According to some works (Tuan and Navrud 2008; Smith 2006; G. Ismagilova, Safiullin, and Gafurov 2015; Yuen 2006; Ho and McKercher 2004), the criterion of adaptation of cultural heritage objects is reduced to the assessment of the preservation of the subject of protection: 100% or partial preservation of the subject of protection with modern functional use.

Such scientists as Pavlovsky and Vitvitsky express the opinion that the key in the historical and cultural assessment is artistic and aesthetic virtues and the uniqueness of historical complexes. The belonging of individual buildings or their elements to the widespread architectural style allows one to characterize the architectural and aesthetic component of the historical and cultural value.

The works substantiate the need to characterize engineering and technical solutions (construction and technical factor). The degree of uniqueness of the technical construction of the structure, the latest building materials and technologies, the constructive solution and the degree of preservation of the object are analyzed (the object is completely lost, value has been lost, separate elements have been destroyed, preserved and (or) restored completely).

Thus, a preliminary list of estimated factors of the historical and cultural value of the territory is shown in the Table (Table 2).

Table 2. Preliminary list of assessment factors

№	Factorname	Description
1	Urban planning (environment-forming)	Characteristics of planning, compositional spatial, large-scale structure of the historical and urban planning environment
2	Landscape-environmental	Characteristics of a natural landscape in the context of the urban planning structure
3	Historicalandmemorial	Characteristics of the memorial and event layer
4	Cultural	Characteristics of the cultural and social orientation of the construction
5	Emotional-artistic	The mental value of the environment
6	Economic	Possible income from using the object
7	Guard	Determination of the category of protection (local, regional, federal, UNESCO site, identified or valuable building site)
8	Functional	Degree of adaptation in modern conditions
9	Construction and technical	Uniqueness of the object in terms of value
10	Architectural and aesthetic	
11	Presence of landscaping and recreation areas in the nearby territory	
12	Uniqueness of the natural landscape and hydrology	
13	Possession of educational, patriotic, spiritual and aesthetic value	
14	Degree of uniqueness of the technical construction of the structure, the latest building materials and technologies, the constructive solution	
15	State of preservation of the object	

3. RESULTS

3.1. Checking the Estimated Factors for Multicollinearity and Justifying Their Final List

Before compiling a model of the dependence of the integral value of the value on the factors under consideration, the proposed factors should be checked for multicollinearity, since if it is present in the regression model, it is impossible to judge the effect of regressors (variables) on the function (Bykowa, Bogolyubova, and Simonova 2019). There are several ways to identify the interdependence between factors: analysis of matrices of paired and partial correlation coefficients, the Farrar-Glouber method, the method of additional regressions, closely related to the method of inflationary factors (VIF) (Orlova and Filonova 2015). The last of these methods is considered to be one of the most correct.

Table 3. VIF calculation for factors assessing the historical and cultural value of the territory

№	Name of factors	VIF value
1	Urbanplanning (environment-forming)	14.423
2	Landscape-environmental	4.679
3	Historicalandmemorial	3.035
4	Cultural	2.623
5	Emotional-artistic	3.929
6	Economic	1.366
7	Guard	4.679
8	Functional	1.462
9	Constructionandtechnical	1.823
10	Architecturalandaesthetic	10.673
11	Presence in the nearby territory of landscaping and recreation areas	1.537
12	Uniqueness of the natural landscape and hydrology	1.205
13	Possession of educational, patriotic, spiritual and aesthetic value	1.802
14	Degree of uniqueness of the technical construction of the structure, the latest building materials and technologies, the constructive solution	1.575
15	State of preservation of the object	1.177

The variance inflation factor VIF shows how many times the variance of the regression coefficient increases due to the correlation of the regressors X1 …Xk in comparison with the variance of this coefficient if the regressors were uncorrelated. The variance inflation factor is calculated by formula 1.

$$\mathrm{VIF}_j = 1/\left(1 - R_j^2\right)$$

(1)

where Rj2 is the coefficient of determination of the jth regressor Xj, (j = 1,…, k), k is the number of model factors), for all other regressors.

It is believed that if the variance inflation factor VIF> 10, then this regressor leads to multicollinearity (Bykowa, Bogolyubova, and Simonova 2019).

Having calculated the variance inflation factor VIF for the estimated assessment criteria using the Gretl software product (GNURegressionEconometricsTime-seriesLibrary), which is used to solve the problems of mathematical modeling (Table 3), it should be concluded that factor 1, which is "urban planning," and factor 10, which is "architectural-aesthetic," have a VIF value > 10, that is, they are collinear, which means they cannot be included in the model at the same time.

The factor inflation method allows us to identify multicollinearity correctly, however, as Orlova and Filonova distinguish in their work (Orlova and Filonova 2015), its disadvantage is that in the case of collinearity of several factors, it is impossible to identify which of them should be excluded from the model using this method. In mathematical statistics, there are several methods for eliminating correlating factors, such as t-statistics, Belsley's method, analysis of the matrix of partial correlation coefficients of dependent correlating variables and the resulting indicator. The simplest and most effective way is to identify which of the correlating factors has a greater correlation coefficient with an independent variable, that is, to assess the degree of connection of one feature with one factor, excluding the influence of all other factors.

The analysis of the matrix of partial correlation coefficients showed that factor 1 "urban planning" has a greater impact on the historical and cultural value than factor 10 "architectural and aesthetic" (Table 4).

Table 4. Correlation matrix of dependent factors

	Historical and cultural value	Factor 1	Factor 10
Historical and cultural value	1		
Factor 1	0.924	1	
Factor 10	0.897	0.943	1

Re-analysis of the assessment criteria for multicollinearity with the exclusion of factor 10 "architectural and aesthetic" using the factor inflation method showed that there is no relationship between the assessment factors (Table 5).

Table 5. VIF values for evaluation factors after excluding multicollinearity

№	Name of factors	VIF value
1	Urban planning (environment-forming)	7.366
2	Landscape-environmental	4.645
3	Historical and memorial	3.027
4	Cultural	2.623
5	Emotional-artistic	3.826
6	Economic	1.363
7	Guard	4.677
8	Functional	1.462
9	Construction and technical	1.718
10	Architectural and aesthetic	1.534
11	Presence in the nearby territory of landscaping and recreation areas	1.193
12	Uniqueness of the natural landscape and hydrology	1.785
13	Possession of educational, patriotic, spiritual and aesthetic value	1.535
14	Degree of uniqueness of the technical construction of the structure, the latest building materials and technologies, the constructive solution	1.176

4. DISCUSSION

The absence of multicollinearity between these factors indicates that it is possible to use a linear regression model of dependence when assessing the historical and cultural value of a territory.

Improvement of the methodological apparatus for the assessment of urbanized territories, taking into account their historical and cultural potential, will allow to optimize the elements of the land management model in settlements, in particular, to improve the process of establishing protection zones of cultural heritage objects, to introduce the results of historical and cultural assessment into information provision of urban planning activities (ISOGD), as well as become a tax regulator in the context of individual and cadastral assessments.

CONCLUSION

The selection and justification of criteria for assessing the historical and cultural value of a territory is an important step in the process of developing a methodology for such an assessment since it is the factors that reflect the valuable features of the territory of settlements. As a result of the above studies, we can conclude that the following are analytically and mathematically grounded valuation factors: town-planning (environment-forming); landscape and environmental; historical and memorial; cultural; emotional and artistic; economic; guard; functional; construction and technical; the presence of landscaping and recreation areas in the nearby territory; the uniqueness of the natural landscape and hydrology; possession of educational, patriotic, spiritual and aesthetic value; the degree of uniqueness of the technical construction of the structure, the latest building materials and technologies, the constructive solution, the degree of preservation of the object. This list allows a diversified approach to the historical and cultural assessment of the territory, considering the historical and cultural value of the territory as a comprehensive assessment of the historical and urban planning environment, taking into account its economic, recreational, natural, architectural and social potential.

The results of the historical and cultural assessment of the territory of settlements, obtained in the course of the proposed methodology, will help not only preserve the country's cultural heritage but also develop digital technologies in the field of land management in settlements, which are of particular relevance in modern conditions (Pirogova et al. 2019).

REFERENCES

Angeles, Los. 2002. "Assessing the Values of Cultural Heritage." *Heritage.*

Bykowa, E. N., A. A. Bogolyubova, and D. D. Simonova. 2019. "Analysis of the Water Bodies Zones Influence on the Cadastral Value of Garden and Horticultural Land Plots." In *IOP Conference Series: Earth and Environmental Science.* https://doi.org/10.1088/1755-1315/350/1/012069.

Chalhoub, Michel Soto. 2018. "Cultural Heritage in Sustainable Development." *Journal of Cultural Heritage Management and Sustainable Development.* https://doi.org/10.1108/jchmsd-06-2017-0040.

Clark, Ruth Colvin, and Richard E. Mayer. 2012. *E-Learning and the Science of Instruction: Proven Guidelines for Consumers and Designers of Multimedia Learning: Third Edition. E-Learning and the Science of Instruction: Proven Guidelines for Consumers and Designers of Multimedia Learning: Third Edition.* https://doi.org/10.1002/9781118255971.

Cultural Heritage and Value Creation. 2015. *Cultural Heritage and Value Creation.* https://doi.org/10.1007/978-3-319-08527-2.

Dapkus, Rimantas, and Kristina Dapkute. 2015. "Evaluation of the Regional Tourism Attractiveness." In *Research for Rural Development*.

Dimitrovski, Darko Dragi, Aleksandar Tomislav Todorović, and Aleksandar Djordje Valjarević. 2012. "Rural Tourism and Regional Development: Case Study of Development of Rural Tourism in the Region of Gruţa, Serbia." *Procedia Environmental Sciences*. https://doi.org/10.1016/j.proenv.2012.03.028.

Dragi Dimitrovski, Darko. 2012. "Rural Tourism and Regional Development: Case Study of Development." *Procedia Environmental Sciences*.

Fourie, Johan, and María Santana-Gallego. 2013. "Ethnic Reunion and Cultural Affinity." *Tourism Management*. https://doi.org/10.1016/j.tourman.2012.10.002.

Gandini, G. C., and E. Villa. 2003. "Analysis of the Cultural Value of Local Livestock Breeds: A Methodology." *Journal of Animal Breeding and Genetics*. https://doi.org/10.1046/j.1439-0388.2003.00365.x.

Gumińska, Anna. 2017. "Sustainability Trends Reflected in the Architecture of the European Examples." In *IOP Conference Series: Materials Science and Engineering*. https://doi.org/10.1088/1757-899X/245/6/062027.

Ho, Pamela S.Y., and Bob McKercher. 2004. "Managing Heritage Resources as Tourism Products." *Asia Pacific Journal of Tourism Research*. https://doi.org/10.1080/1094166042000290655.

Hribar, Mateja Šmid, David Bole, and Primož Pipan. 2015. "Sustainable Heritage Management: Social, Economic and Other Potentials of Culture in Local Development." *Procedia - Social and Behavioral Sciences*. https://doi.org/10.1016/j.sbspro.2015.03.344.

Ismagilova, G. N., I. R. Gafurov, and L. N. Safiullin. 2015. "Using Historical Heritage as a Factor in Tourism Development." In *Interdisciplinary Behavior and Social Sciences - Proceedings of the 3rd International Congress on Interdisciplinary Behavior and Social Sciences, ICIBSoS 2014*. https://doi.org/10.1201/b18146-5.

Ismagilova, Gulnara, Lenar Safiullin, and Ilshat Gafurov. 2015. "Using Historical Heritage as a Factor in Tourism Development." *Procedia - Social and Behavioral Sciences*. https://doi.org/10.1016/j.sbspro.2015.03.355.

Kitcenko, A. A., V. F. Kovyazin, and A. Y. Romanchikov. 2020. "Modern Condition and Prospects for the Development of Forest Infrastructure to Improve the Economy of Nature Management." In *Scientific and Practical Studies of Raw Material Issues-Proceedings of the Russian- German Raw Materials Dialogue: A Collection of Young Scientists Papers and Discussion, 2019*. https://doi.org/10.1201/9781003017226-28.

Kovyazin, V., A. Romanchikov, and A. Kitcenko. 2020. "Assessment of Infrastructure of Forest Land." In *IOP Conference Series: Materials Science and Engineering.* https://doi.org/10.1088/1757-899X/817/1/012017.

Kovyazin, V F, M E Skachkova, and I S D'yachkova. 2021. "Historical and Cultural Assessment of Urbanized Territories Is the Part of Cadastral, Land Management and Other Economic Activities." *Geodesy and Cartography* 966: 57–62. https://doi.org/10.22389/0016-7126-2020-966-12-57-62.

Mckercher, Bob, and Hilary Du Cros. 2012. *Cultural Tourism: The Partnership between Tourism and Cultural Heritage Management. Cultural Tourism: The Partnership Between Tourism and Cultural Heritage Management.* https://doi.org/10.4324/9780203479537.

McKercher, Bob, and Pamela S.Y. Ho. 2006a. "Assessing the Tourism Potential of Smaller Cultural and Heritage Attractions." *Journal of Sustainable Tourism.* https://doi.org/10.2167/jost.

———. 2006b. "Assessing the Tourism Potential of Smaller Cultural and Heritage Attractions." *Journal of Sustainable Tourism.* https://doi.org/10.2167/jost620.0.

Montella, Massimo. 2015. "Cultural Value." In *Cultural Heritage and Value Creation: Towards New Pathways.* https://doi.org/10.1007/978-3-319-08527-2_1.

Orlova, I, and E Filonova. 2015. "The Choice of Exogenous Factors in the Regression Model with Multi-Collinear Data." *International Journal of Applied and Basic Research.*

Pereira, A. 2014. "The Cultural Landscape as a Cross-Cutting Resource for Tourism Products in Low-Density Rural Territories: Diagnosis and Guidelines for Alto Minho (NW Portugal)." *WIT Transactions on Ecology and the Environment.* https://doi.org/10.2495/ST140201.

Piñero, Ignacio, José T. San-José, Patricia Rodríguez, and Milagros M. Losáñez. 2017. "Multi-Criteria Decision-Making for Grading the Rehabilitation of Heritage Sites. Application in the Historic Center of La Habana." *Journal of Cultural Heritage.* https://doi.org/10.1016/j.culher.2017.01.012.

Pirogova, Oksana, Marina Makarevich, Olga Ilina, and Vladimir Ulanov. 2019. "Optimizing Trading Company Capital Structure on the Basis of Using Bankruptcy Logistic Models under Conditions of Economy Digitalization." In *IOP Conference Series: Materials Science and Engineering.* https://doi.org/10. 1088/1757-899X/497/1/012129.

Pirogova, Oksana, and Vladimir Plotnikov. 2020. "Management of Enterprise Development Based on Adaptive Value Model in Digital Conditions." In *E3S Web of Conferences.* https://doi.org/10.1051/e3sconf/202016410024.

"*Program for Renting an OKN for 1 Ruble.*" n.d. Accessed February 8, 2021. http://auipik.ru/activity/programma-arendy-okn-za-1-rubl/.

Reynard, Emmanuel, and Christian Giusti. 2018. "The Landscape and the Cultural Value of Geoheritage." In *Geoheritage: Assessment, Protection, and Management.* https://doi.org/10.1016/B978-0-12-809531-7.00008-3.

Ruijgrok, E. C. M. 2006. "The Three Economic Values of Cultural Heritage: A Case Study in the Netherlands." *Journal of Cultural Heritage*. https://doi.org/10.1016/j.culher.2006.07.002.

Scazzosi, Lionella. 2004. "Reading and Assessing the Landscape as Cultural and Historical Heritage." *Landscape Research*. https://doi.org/10.1080/01426390420 00288993.

Shojaei, Davood, Hamed Olfat, Abbas Rajabifard, and Mark Briffa. 2018. "Design and Development of a 3D Digital Cadastre Visualization Prototype." *ISPRS International Journal of Geo-Information*. https://doi.org/10.3390/ijgi7100384.

Skachkova, M. E., O. Y. Lepihina, and V. V. Ignatova. 2018. "Information Support of Monitoring of Technical Condition of Buildings in Construction Risk Area." In *Journal of Physics: Conference Series*. https://doi.org/10.1088/1742-6596/1015/4/042056.

Smith, Laurajane. 2006. *Uses of Heritage. Uses of Heritage*. https://doi.org/10.4324/9780203602263.

Taylor, Ken, and Jane Lennon. 2011. "Cultural Landscapes: A Bridge between Culture and Nature?" *International Journal of Heritage Studies*. https://doi.org/10.1080/13527258.2011.618246.

Timothy, Dallen J. 2009. *Cultural Heritage and Tourism in the Developing World. Cultural Heritage and Tourism in the Developing World*. https://doi.org/10.4324/9780203877753.

Tuan, Tran Huu, and Stale Navrud. 2008. "Capturing the Benefits of Preserving Cultural Heritage." *Journal of Cultural Heritage*. https://doi.org/10.1016/j.culher.2008.05.001.

Wagner, Tomasz. 2017. "Searching for Innovations and Methods of Using the Cultural Heritage on the Example of Upper Silesia." In *IOP Conference Series: Materials Science and Engineering*. https://doi.org/10.1088/1757-899X/245/ 4/042088.

Wall, G., and W. Nuryanti. 1996. "Heritage and Tourism." *Annals of Tourism Research*. https://doi.org/10.1016/0160-7383(95)00062-3.

Whitehand, J. W. R., and Kai Gu. 2010. "Conserving Urban Landscape Heritage: A Geographical Approach." In *Procedia - Social and Behavioral Sciences*. https://doi.org/10.1016/j.sbspro.2010.05.047.

Wright, William C. C., and Florian V. Eppink. 2016. "Drivers of Heritage Value: A Meta-Analysis of Monetary Valuation Studies of Cultural Heritage." *Ecological Economics*. https://doi.org/10.1016/j.ecolecon.2016.08.001.

Yüceer, Hülya, and Başak Ipekoğlu. 2012. "An Architectural Assessment Method for New Exterior Additions to Historic Buildings." *Journal of Cultural Heritage*. https://doi.org/10.1016/j.culher.2011.12.002.

Yuen, Belinda. 2006. "Reclaiming Cultural Heritage in Singapore." *Urban Affairs Review*. https://doi.org/10.1177/1078087406289187.

Zandieh; Shervin Goodarzian, di. 2014. *"Landscape Approach, the Success Factor of Urban Tourism." Bagh-e Nazar*.

"EMISS." n.d. Accessed February 8, 2021. https://www.fedstat.ru/indicator/55126.

In: Global Challenges of Digital Transformation of Markets ISBN: 978-1-53619-754-9
Editors: E. de la Poza and S. E. Barykin   © 2021 Nova Science Publishers, Inc.

Chapter 17

DIGITAL TRANSFORMATION AND NEW ERA OF TECHNOLOGICAL INNOVATIONS OF GLOBAL HOSPITALITY SERVICE MARKETS

Marina Morozova[1,], Pavel Isupov[1] and Liliya Korchevska[2]*

[1]Department of Economics and Finance, North-West Institute of Management,
branch of RANEPA, Saint-Petersburg, Russia
[2]Kherson National Technical University, Kherson, Ukraine

ABSTRACT

Digital transformation has emerged as an essential component of hospitality industry development in conditions of market recession caused by intensive pandemic expansion. Despite the crucial negative consequences of early 2020 pandemic, there is a data analyzed in this paper, which testifies that COVID-19 was some sort of a driver that forced companies of hospitality industry to develop more actively, that likely would not have happened in regular conditions. More interestingly, the positive impact of the recent COVID-19 spread is being observed worldwide in terms of ability of hospitality businesses to adapt and overcome restrictions, limitations, tourist flow decline and become digitalized. An important role of innovative development of markets for the service and hospitality industry is determined in this paper as a key driver of an economic development. Data used in this paper is open source and is available for public access. The result findings and implications of this paper are of interest to both academic and professional purposes.

Keywords: hospitality, innovation, transformation, service, technology, global markets

---

* Corresponding Author's Email: morozova-ma@ranepa.ru.

1. INTRODUCTION

Hospitality and leisure industry that suffer critically from the recent COVID-19 pandemic restrictions and limitations is among the hardest hit along with restaurant and air transportation, experiencing not the greatest period of time. However, the purpose of this study is to propose a theoretical and empirical framework to harness and recover hospitality and leisure industry activity through innovation and digital transformation. Even with all the negative impact done due to recent pandemic, we cannot ignore the fact that this occasion that came out of nowhere forced the hospitality industry to develop, improvise, adapt, find unique solutions and overcome. An outbreak like this already happened before. According to the research, pandemic related to respiratory illness with pneumonia-like symptoms (Severe acute respiratory syndrome - SARS) that progressed almost exactly the same way in 2003 but didn't get the amount of press coverage compared to COVID-19 that appeared in 2019 also had similar economic impact (Chen, Jang, and Kim 2007). This started from 50 percent reduction of arrivals from abroad, and led to a 30 percent decline in tourism industry in less than a month. Two months change in earnings of hotels reflected from 20 to 70 percent decline, which indicates that the tourism and hospitality industries had the most serious impact due to SARS back then in 2003. Main idea is that the hotel stocks were sensitive to the SARS outbreak and the hotel stock performance would react to the occurrence of similar diseases, which is that happened with COVID-19 expansion. As long as we already have a breakdown on how economics behave under influence of such disease spread, we can approximately estimate for how long we are going to remain suspended. There is a two time periods, which can be described as an immediate future in terms of what hotels and restaurants are going to look like over the next 6-12 months and long-term future whether pandemic persists and it changes hospitality industry fundamentally (Martins, Riordan, and Dolnicar 2020).

2. MATERIALS AND METHODS

2.1. Sample and Procedure

The target group was hotels, accommodation facilities and restaurants that operate around the year worldwide. We used data gathered from IATA, UNWTO, STATISTA, SOJERN, TradingView, Bureaus of labor from all over the world (selectively), several National tourism and hospitality statistical agencies as well as several Ministries of Sport and Tourism's registry from all over the world to prepare the sampling frame. Our registry included 54 luxury, 107 high-tier, 488 upper-upscale, 540 mid-tier and 840 economy class companies that operate on market for at least 3 years. The details such as brand names of mid and lower tier are not displayed in this paper purposely in order to prevent possible speculations as long as this study should not be considered as a financial advice nor an open call to action. Another method over than an analysis of statistical and financial data that was used in this paper is an Expert Judgement. We interviewed a target group consisting of general managers of hotels, restaurants, tour operators and affiliates from Russia, United Arab Emirates, Qatar, Kuwait, Saudi Arabia, United States of America, United Kingdom, Canada and Australia. They were invited to discuss their visions and perspectives of hospitality and travel industry future development based on specific set of criteria. A feedback report was formed for every completed and justified interview and the innovations they implemented to remain sustainable are displayed in subsequent paragraphs. Another data set of 250 hotels and accommodation facilities shows how COVID-19 affected the market of labor in Europe and Russia. It was composed manually from National Labor Agencies reports and job aggregators open data and was processed with methods of descriptive statistics, the results of which are presented in the subsequent paragraph.

3. RESULTS

The following results shown below display how different hotel classes were affected by COVID-19 pandemic (see Figure 1).

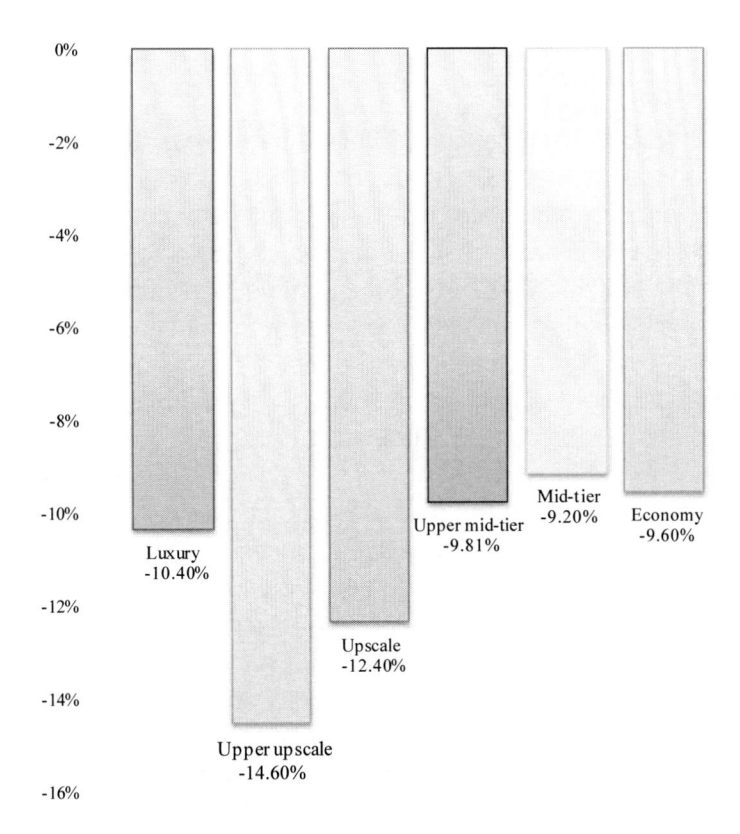

Figure 1. Hotel classes affected by COVID-19 pandemic.

Table 1. Hospitality stock price fluctuations ($ USD)

Stock name	Price at 14 Feb 2020	Price at 20 April 2020	% Change
Marriot Intl.	145.16 $	79.38 $	-45.32%
Hyatt Hotels	88.75 $	54.51 $	-38.58%
Hilton Worldwide	112.75 $	71.43 $	-36.65%
Wyndham Hotels & Resorts Inc.	58.71 $	32.29 $	-45.00%
WYNN Resorts LTD	132.05 $	70.12 $	-46.90%

Source: tradingview.com.

Table 2. Changes in the labor market in the hospitality industry

Hotel Category	Reduction in force	Wage reduction
Luxury	7.49%	9.51%
Upper-Upscale	11.24%	11.81%
Upscale	10.07%	10.34%
Upper mid-tier	9.4%	9.02%
Mid-tier	4.2%	7.3%
Economy	3.1%	15.57%

Source: National Labor Agencies, personal interviews with top management in hospitality industry.

Upper upscale class of hotels was affected in the most dramatic way with a two months loss of the its average value of 14.6%. However, McKinsey research suggested that economy hotels are better able to tap segments of demand that remain relatively healthy despite travel restrictions and expected to return to pre-pandemic levels faster than others ("COVID-19's Effect on the Hotel Industry | McKinsey" n.d.). Our study suggestion is that the luxury segment was not affected due to decrease in demand, but due to both seasonal factor and restrictions on air transportation. Hence, we expect luxury segment of hotels to recover quick on account because of the least susceptibility to market fluctuations. The second important dataset is mostly gathered from American stock markets (NASDAQ/NYSE). The results were taken as a snapshot of stocks daily average price to the date presented (see Table 1).

The results display a significant decline in prices on 2 months' time horizon. This indicates fear, uncertainty and doubt of investors what are selling out their shares in businesses, perhaps caused by the negative expectations regarding of how long this pandemic is going to last. On the other hand, knowing the data that proves this phenomenon is temporary and the economy will eventually recover opens a space to some reasonable financial decisions that may be used as an opportunity to diversify the portfolio of assets. However, even if the consequences are well known due to recent experience, the costs and losses are inevitable and decisions should be made. These decisions are mostly associated with personnel management. In this case, to analyze how structure of the work power changed we analyzed hospitality companies human resource adjustments presented in quantitative units (see Table 2).

The results provided above indicate that hotel industry companies statistically were not able to avoid neither stuff reduction nor wage reduction. This fact is also confirmedby Romir& Gallup International and Antal Russiaresearches of COVID-19 impact on market of labor ("COVID-19: Buyer the Day after Tomorrow. Moods and Expectations I Romir & Gallup International" n.d.). According to these sources, hospitality and leisure industries will lose from ten to thirty percent of their pre-pandemic levels of workforce.

4. DISCUSSION

According to the statistical data and regression models shown in above paragraph, we expect many adjustments to be implemented. Firstly, the amount of labor involved in hospitality and restaurant business will be definitely adjusted either by direct cost of labor reduction or quantitative job cuts. Secondly, the amount of traditional services that can be accessed on offline only basis will mostly be transferred to digital space (Zopiatis and Theocharous 2018). Mobile technology is the most popular innovation that hotels are integrating into their guest experience, which as well is an evidence of increasing role of direct booking, however, so far only large networks can afford that switch in a true momentum. Branded mobile apps are being offered by major hotels like the Marriott, Hilton, Sheraton, IHG, Ritz Carlton, and Hyatt, etc. (Wong and Chi-Yung 2002). where guests are allowed to easily check-in, make pre-check, in requests, communicate with stuff and control several room features (Román and Martín 2016). Thirdly, hotels and accommodation facilities will probably adjust their service policy towards the high-value event industry activities. Fourthly, some hotels that are classified with 4* are expected invest in their infrastructure improvements to obtain a 5* class in order to capture the niche segment, as luxury brands are less affected by crisis or temporarily decline. Fifthly, we expect big market players such as hospitality and real estate property holdings or hedge funds with large share of free cash available in circulation to likely invest in landscapes or purchase real estate assets of smaller players, who are forced to sellout due to both significant revenue reduction caused by lack of ability to cover their current liabilities as a result of decrease in customer flow and value drop of this class of assets caused by pandemic (Barinova 2020; Komkov and Bondareva 2007; Golovanova and Bekaeva 2017). Sixthly, hotels are quickly responding through excellent initiatives including eco-power generation, sourcing local organic produce, adding green areas, installing eco-friendly appliances, partially switch to using solar panels, which is also a positive step towards reducing their own costs (Liao et al. 2017). These marketing innovations are mostly aimed to a portrait of a conscious consumer. Seventhly, pandemic triggered a series of inevitable management decisions, which led to increase in hotels innovative activity (Kim and Park 2017). As an example, COVID-19 related limitations forced to replace the certain amount of room attendants by cleaning robots, which is easily explained due to significant physical and airborne contact reduction. Moreover, cleaning robots are not only available to clean dust, dirt and small garbage, but are also available to manage humidity level, purify the air and adjust the temperature without customer participation (Victorino et al. 2005).

As of temporarily issues some of restaurants bring plastic dividers that goal is to increase the social distance and health security range, others are bringing new seating placement design and planning solutions which are focused on compliance with applicable laws to protect consumers health and experience (Lu and Gursoy 2015; Jensen 2012). However, these actions are significantly reducing the restaurants income because all of them are some sort of slowing down the consumption rate of their main product made (Chou et al. 2020; Laužikas et al. 2015). As a temporary solution, restaurants are forced to develop strategies, which will allow either to increase the space by adjusting the restaurant hall seating spots or to increase the product sales volume by making partnerships with food delivery aggregators, that may lead to increase their market share. Otherwise, to remain on certain level of confidence restaurant businesses will inevitably be forced to adjust their pricing policy.

CONCLUSION

The hospitality and leisure industry must strive to become creative risk-takers who are not afraid of making unique solutions. Due to pandemic spread, hospitality industry was forced to improvise and implement both management and technological innovations at the same time to remain on market and cut the costs. The bigger players impacted the least, but the smaller players are about to get washed away from the competitive market without proper government support. According to the independent experts, the restaurants that is not a developed network are likely to be closed forever with an probability vary from 50 to 90 percent (Baum and Hai 2020). In UAE, hotel occupancy dropped by more than 70% in March 2020 ("COVID-19: Insights on Travel Impact, The Middle East and Africa #48 | Sojern" n.d.). Expedia sold its stake for $1 billion USD that is extremely lower than its real market value. The largest decrease in hotel occupancy is observed in the upper-scale segment. Companies are now actively reducing personnel costs by decreasing the number of employees and reducing the payroll through the digitalization of labor and the use of new technologies, such as: automatic registration, voice assistants, alternative services, the Internet of Things, the growth of outsourced personnel, etc. Despite all the negative trends that we observed in this study, quick recovery of stock markets brings us back to reality and makes us see not only cons but also pros (Gursoy and Chi 2020).

Hospitality industry positive trends:

- decrease in income and drop in the level of employment;
- closing of most hotels;

- direct marketing growth;
- revision of pricing policy (caused by a decrease in trust between OTAs and their customers);
- increase in volume of direct bookings;
- maximizing the role of digital in management and marketing (analytics, big data, customization, innovative and effective online communications) (Lu and Gursoy 2015; Liao et al. 2017).

Hospitality industry negative trends:

- swing of operational impact and mitigation (caused by misunderstanding critical cash points and any breaches of lending covenants);
- financial impact (real estate assets significantly dropped in price and require a lot of time to recover);
- shortsighted stakeholders are selling out their shares in business (as a result the whole business is suffering due to current assets are taken out of circulation).

Restaurant business positive trends:

- supplement growth by 10 times;
- active connection to aggregators, chat bots;
- niche restaurants (do not switch to delivery);
- popular restaurants (complex gastronomic projects, food halls with different culinary concepts);
- reducing the cost of restaurant projects from $0.5-$1 million to $0.05-$0.10 million USD (food halls);
- anti-COVID-19 certification is now possible.

Restaurant business negative trends:

- an increase in the number of couriers, the risk of not being in demand for couriers in the future);
- difficult to switch to online delivery (lack of close interaction with delivery aggregators);
- decrease in effective demand;
- the need for social distance;
- the supply chain are suffering losses due to inability of some suppliers to fulfill their obligations.

Managerial Implications

The most important managerial implication to emerge from this study is the need of preparing to the worst-case scenario situations and to not afraid experimenting with implementing innovations when the company is in the period of sustainable growth and is well developing (Xue, Jo, and Bonn 2020). We recommend monitoring asset structure and adjusting it depending on what is happening on the market. We highly recommend to the managers of hospitality industry companies to reduce the accounts payable and increase the share of free cash to be prepared for any temporarily shut down that could happen in future. The asset structure is recommended to be diversified reasonably as well. At the same time, customer orientation should be used as the core criteria implying for both technological and managerial innovations. Customer oriented marketing solutions such as personalized services with tailored benefits is a reliable strategy to develop and remain or even enhance financial performance of company that operates in hospitality or leisure industries. Business processes should be easily transferable and adjustable if the company at some point is forced to enter new markets and use new tools, while maintaining the existing infrastructure and services (Rhee and Yang 2015). Personnel education and training is essential for successfully overcoming periods of instability, because if employee is able to cover the wide range of tasks and successfully finish them (Denizci Guillet, Mattila, and Gao 2020). These steps will allow everyone in organization to be prepared for a wide range of unforeseen situations, to successfully overcome periods of economic downturn and lack of customers or revenue and finally to remain sustainable developing (Karr-Wisniewski and Lu 2010).

REFERENCES

Barinova, Natalya. 2020. "Innovation Commercialization in Russia and Ways of Overcoming It at the Current Stage of Economy Development." *Vestnik of the Plekhanov Russian University of Economics*, 32-41. https://doi.org/10.21686/2413-2829-2020-2-32-41.

Baum, Tom, and Nguyen Thi Thanh Hai. 2020. "Hospitality, Tourism, Human Rights and the Impact of COVID-19." *International Journal of Contemporary Hospitality Management.* https://doi.org/10.1108/IJCHM-03-2020-0242.

Chen, Ming Hsiang, Soo Cheong (Shawn) Jang, and Woo Gon Kim. 2007. "The Impact of the SARS Outbreak on Taiwanese Hotel Stock Performance: An Event-Study Approach." *International Journal of Hospitality Management.* https://doi.org/10.1016/j.ijhm.2005.11.004.

Chou, Sheng Fang, Jeou Shyan Horng, Chih Hsing Liu, Yung Chuan Huang, and Shu Ning Zhang. 2020. "The Critical Criteria for Innovation Entrepreneurship of Restaurants: Considering the Interrelationship Effect of Human Capital and

Competitive Strategy a Case Study in Taiwan." *Journal of Hospitality and Tourism Management*. https://doi.org/10.1016/j.jhtm.2020.01.006.

"*COVID-19: Buyer the Day after Tomorrow. Moods and Expectations | Romir & Gallup International*." n.d. Accessed February 5, 2021. https://romir.ru/studies/dannye-issledovaniya-covid-19-pokupatel-poslezavtra-nastroeniya-i-ojidaniya-za-20-nedelyu-2020-g.

"*COVID-19: Insights on Travel Impact, The Middle East and Africa #48 | Sojern*." n.d. Accessed February 6, 2021. https://www.sojern.com/blog/covid-19-insights-on-travel-impact-middle-east-and-africa-48/.

"*COVID-19's Effect on the Hotel Industry | McKinsey*." n.d. Accessed February 5, 2021. https://www.mckinsey.com/industries/travel-logistics-and-infrastructure/our-insights/hospitality-and-covid-19-how-long-until-no-vacancy-for-us-hotels.

Denizci Guillet, Basak, Anna Mattila, and Lisa Gao. 2020. "The Effects of Choice Set Size and Information Filtering Mechanisms on Online Hotel Booking." *International Journal of Hospitality Management*. https://doi.org/10.1016/j.ijhm. 2019.102379.

Golovanova, Nataliya, and Anna Bekaeva. 2017. "Problems and risks of commercialization of innovations in the russian economy." *Business Management/Biznes Upravlenie*.

Gursoy, Dogan, and Christina G. Chi. 2020. "Effects of COVID-19 Pandemic on Hospitality Industry: Review of the Current Situations and a Research Agenda." *Journal of Hospitality Marketing and Management*. https://doi.org/10.1080/19368623.2020.1788231.

Jensen, Jan Moller. 2012. "Shopping Orientation and Online Travel Shopping: The Role of Travel Experience." *International Journal of Tourism Research*. https://doi.org/10.1002/jtr.835.

Karr-Wisniewski, Pamela, and Ying Lu. 2010. "When More Is Too Much: Operationalizing Technology Overload and Exploring Its Impact on Knowledge Worker Productivity." *Computers in Human Behavior*. https://doi.org/10.1016/j.chb.2010.03.008.

Kim, Dohee, and Byung Jin (Robert) Park. 2017. "The Moderating Role of Context in the Effects of Choice Attributes on Hotel Choice: A Discrete Choice Experiment." *Tourism Management*. https://doi.org/10.1016/j.tourman.2017.07.014.

Komkov, N. I., and N. N. Bondareva. 2007. "Problems in the Commercialization of Scientific Research and Ways of Addressing Them." *Studies on Russian Economic Development*. https://doi.org/10.1134/S1075700707010029.

Laužikas, Mindaugas, Hailee Tindale, Lukas Tranavičius, and Emilis Kičiatovas. 2015. "Effects of Consumer Behaviour on Innovations in Fast Food Industry." *Entrepreneurship and Sustainability Issues*. https://doi.org/10.9770/jesi.2015.3.1(8).

Liao, Chechen, Hong Nan Lin, Margaret Meiling Luo, and Sophea Chea. 2017. "Factors Influencing Online Shoppers' Repurchase Intentions: The Roles of Satisfaction and Regret." *Information and Management*. https://doi.org/10.1016/j.im.2016.12.005.

Lu, Allan Cheng Chieh, and Dogan Gursoy. 2015. "A Conceptual Model of Consumers' Online Tourism Confusion." *International Journal of Contemporary Hospitality Management*. https://doi.org/10.1108/IJCHM-04-2014-0171.

Martins, Antje, Tyler Riordan, and Sara Dolnicar. 2020. "*A Post-COVID-19 Model of Tourism and Hospitality Workforce Resilience*." https://doi.org/10.31235/osf.io/4quga.

Rhee, Hosung Timothy, and Sung Byung Yang. 2015. "How Does Hotel Attribute Importance Vary among Different Travelers? An Exploratory Case Study Based on a Conjoint Analysis." *Electronic Markets*. https://doi.org/10.1007/s12525-014-0161-y.

Román, Concepción, and Juan Carlos Martín. 2016. "Hotel Attributes: Asymmetries in Guest Payments and Gains - A Stated Preference Approach." *Tourism Management*. https://doi.org/10.1016/j.tourman.2015.08.001.

Victorino, Liana, Rohit Verma, Gerhard Plaschka, and Chekitan Dev. 2005. "Service Innovation and Customer Choices in the Hospitality Industry." *Managing Service Quality*. https://doi.org/10.1108/09604520510634023.

Wong, Kevin K. F., and Lam Chi-Yung. 2002. "Predicting Hotel Choice Decisions and Segmenting Hotel Consumers:A Comparative Assessment of a Recent Consumer Based Approach." *Journal of Travel and Tourism Marketing*. https://doi.org/10.1300/J073v11n01_02.

Xue, Pengsongze, Woo Mi Jo, and Mark A. Bonn. 2020. "Online Hotel Booking Decisions Based on Price Complexity, Alternative Attractiveness, and Confusion." *Journal of Hospitality and Tourism Management*. https://doi.org/10.1016/j.jhtm.2020.08.013.

Zopiatis, Anastasios, and Antonis L. Theocharous. 2018. "PRAXIS: The Determining Element of Innovation Behavior in the Hospitality Industry." *Journal of Hospitality and Tourism Management*. https://doi.org/10.1016/j.jhtm.2017.12.004.

In: Global Challenges of Digital Transformation of Markets ISBN: 978-1-53619-754-9
Editors: E. de la Poza and S. E. Barykin   © 2021 Nova Science Publishers, Inc.

Chapter 18

DIGITAL IMAGE OF A DYNAMIC SALES FUNNEL

S. E. Barykin[1], S. M. Sergeev[1,], I. V. Kapustina[1], Elena de la Poza[2], D. V. Varlamova[3] and N. A. Gviliya[4]*

[1]Peter the Great St. Petersburg Polytechnic University, St. Peterburg, Russia
[2]Center for Economic Engineering (INECO).
Universitat Politècnica de València, Spain
[3]National Research University of Information Technologies,
Mechanics and Optics (ITMO University), St. Peterburg, Russia
[4]Saint Petersburg State University of Economics, St. Peterburg, Russia

ABSTRACT

Commercial activity has always been affected by the competitive environment, and the development of online trading is the next stage of development and the defining trend for the near future. The changes in the business landscape that have occurred under the influence of COVID-19 pose new challenges for marketers and entrepreneurs. It is necessary to use the forced sharp growth of online interaction with consumers. The course on the digital economy requires the use of scientific and mathematical methods to optimize the target indicators of economic activity. Such global changes in business interaction give rise to innovative tools for evaluating the results of commerce and transform the previous methods to meet the new realities of the market This is a basic condition for the sustainability of doing business in any industry. This study is devoted to the development of a theoretical description of the process of multi-stage interaction with the consumer pool. To solve the problem of formalization of this process, a mathematical model has been developed, which is based on digital information interaction from the stage of determining the target audience to the complete completion of a commercial transaction.

* Corresponding Author's Email: sergeev2@inbox.ru.

The article presents the results of the work on modeling salesfunnel as the basis of the software of a modern market analyst using a cross-system approach. In contrast to the classic salesfunnel, the presented algorithms allow using the multidimensional conversionfunnel not only to evaluate the results of the business for the reporting period: thanks to the flow of model arguments in real time, it becomes possible to optimize the commercial process by switching to the concept of leading economic indicators.

In practice, this means that effective business planning can be implemented on digital platforms. The arguments of the mathematical model are Internet statistics, the dynamics of consumer preferences, and the history of the business process accumulated in the big data system. This involves the means of queuing theory, differential calculus, economic and mathematical modeling based on such indicators as KPI (Key Performance Indicators), CTR (click-through), CR (Conversionrate). This allowed us to formulate the concept of a digital double of the commercial process. We have developed mathematical formalisms that are convenient for practical applications. This allows you to provide an acceptable implementation of algorithms describing the conversion funnel for computer programming.

Keywords: sales funnel, conversion funnel, digital marketing

1. Introduction

The retail audit of the first half of 2020 showed that new processes are developing in the field of online commerce. If earlier this channel was used for the purchase of large durable goods and online purchases on the global Internet sites of large aggregators, now the processes of shifting consumer interest towards everyday goods are clearly observed. A sharp increase in consumer activity in the FMCG segment was noted in the Nielsen review and identified as a long-term trend. Among the fundamental changes in the structure of consumer demand, the growth of purchases from mobile devices, cross-border purchases and work on the D2C (direct to customer) model are also highlighted. In 2019, the entire e-commerce segment of the Russian Federation was estimated at RUB 4,172 billion; in the first half of 2020, the volume of online purchases significantly exceeded the level of the same period last year. This is primarily due to the impact of the new reality caused by the COVID-19 pandemic, which simultaneously gave impetus to the expansion of online commerce, and this process continues even after the easing of quarantine measures, as the population has appreciated the advantage of online shopping. The change in consumer behavior is also reflected in Nielsen's data on a 4.2% increase in the level of Internet population coverage. It is noted that the mobile Internet segment has also grown, which is used by 86.2 million people, which is 70.5% of the population of Russia.

The use of a wide range of economic indicators, displayed in digital form, allows you to implement the entire chain of business interaction in the online space. For commercial success and winning in the competition, it is necessary to predict the dynamics of changes in the number of potential consumers. Taking into account the multi-stage nature of transactions, there is a requirement for maximum efficiency of each stage. Now the sales funnel method for monitoring all stages of business processes is well known. The transition of a significant share of business processes to online, transforms this method into a new quality of conversion funnel. The effectiveness of mobile applications requires scientifically based algorithms that use feedback from real-time data on consumer activity. A business built on this approach and information support for management decisions based on leading indicators will provide an advantage in the competition.

A digital ecosystem is a self-organizing, sustainable system based on digital platforms that form a single information environment in which ecosystem members can interact in the absence of rigid functional links between them. The basis of the digital ecosystem is a variety of platform technologies that form a single information environment for all its participants: society, business and the state (S. Y. Barykin, Kapustina, Kirillova, et al. 2020).

It is necessary to consider the issue of training personnel for the digital industry in the context of creating teams in enterprises (Bril, Kalinina, et al. 2020), scientific organizations and universities that have the necessary digital competencies and digital literacy, that is, the ability to use modern methods, experimental and research technologies to develop globally competitive products. This competence becomes an integrator of the technological, ethical, and cognitive aspects of education. In this paradigm, the methodological approach to solving the problem of personnel training is based on a problem-oriented scientific approach, and the model of creating mirror engineering centers is a possible model for scaling competencies, spreading knowledge and developing network interaction (S. Barykin, Borovkov, Rozhdestvenskiy, Tarshin, et al. 2020).

Creation a sustainable supply chain means balancing reliability and flexibility. Decentralized communication is giving way to more precise and modern solutions. The combination of optimization modeling and data analysis is the basic technology that allows you to create a sufficiently detailed model of the real supply chain of its digital counterpart Idea -. The goal of creating a digital twin is to manage risks in supply chains, thereby making them more reliable and resilient in the event of any failures. Modern technologies allow us to collect large amounts of data on supply chains online (S. Y. Barykin, Bochkarev, Kalinina, and Yadykin 2020). It can successfully act as a replacement for expensive field monitoring methods without causing any damage to the physical object. A digital twin is an evolving digital profile of the historical and current behavior of a physical object or process that helps optimize business performance (Kapustina et al. 2020).

Changes in the high-tech sector also oblige enterprises to transform their workforce in order to achieve a sustainable competitive advantage. The introduction of high-tech solutions leads to a change in the format and content of almost any work, as well as to a rethinking of approaches to personnel planning (Bril, Evseeva, et al. 2020).

The process of managing the organization's personnel within the digital ecosystem, while maintaining the basic goal setting, is transformed from an instrumental point of view. The transition from a traditional HR system to a digital one involves a difference between how employees interact with each other and with management. The key factor in the system of digital interaction is the ability of each employee to freely contact the information and analytical center. The digital interaction system also differs from the traditional one by expanding the channels for exchanging information and analytics (Barykin, Kalinina, et al. 2021; Barykin, Kapustina, Sergeev, et al. 2021; Barykin, Bochkarev, et al. 2021; Barykin, Kapustina, Valebnikova, et al. 2021; Barykin, Smirnova, Sharapaev, et al. 2021). Considering the tasks of personnel management in the digital age, it can be shown that the problem of digital personnel management is the scientific search for the features of employee interaction in the new technological structure of Industry 4.0 under the influence of the flow of innovations and changes occurring in it. It includes improvements in performance, reliability, quality, and security (Sergey Barykin, Kalinina, Aleksandrov, Konnikov, et al. 2020).

Over the past decade, technologies and equipment that can radically change the approach to managing the processes of cargo movement and cargo transportation have become widespread. This includes the possibility of machine-readable exchange of information about goods and cargo among themselves. To solve such large-scale problems, the use of scientifically based mathematical models is required. This approach will allow us to use the digital footprint of processes in the logistics network and develop an algorithmic basis for a whole set of software tools for more effective management of the logistics industry (S. Y. Barykin, Kapustina, Sergeev, et al. 2020).

It is necessary to find an economically optimal management of the flows of goods and cargo based on digital information about their movement, taking into account the stochastic nature of the volumes and directions of flows. At the same time, it is necessary to choose and justify the methodology for calculating the DC node terminals that are part of the network structure of logistics activities. The resulting set of mathematical relations allows us to model the operation of a network distribution center as a nodal element of a logistics system operating on the principles of a 3PL operator in the conditions of the stochastic nature of incoming and shipped commodity flows (Shmatko et al. 2021).

2. MAIN CHARACTERISTICS OF THE SALES FUNNEL

The sales funnel is a marketing model that reflects the theoretical path (which, in our opinion, can be called an abstract path) of the client from getting acquainted with the product to concluding a transaction (Borisoglebskaya, Provotorov, et al. 2019). The sales funnel in the ideal embodiment can be represented as a tactical scheme of formalization of the step-by-step path of some ideal consumer. In reality, buyers move along such an abstract path non-linearly, returning to the previous step, rethinking their movement, and possibly losing their purchasing power or need for a particular product.

In any case, the sales funnel is a mandatory element of the marketing concept, as it allows you to find problematic sales stages and eliminate them. (Borisoglebskaya, Provotorova, et al. 2019)The goal of a sales funnel is to turn a potential customer into an actual buyer. The sales funnel consists of external and internal parts: from the beginning of the abstract path, when the audience is not yet familiar with the product (external funnel), to the final point (internal funnel) of interaction between the supplier and the buyer.

The indicators of the sales funnel can be divided into quantitative and qualitative. Quantitative indicators are used to calculate the conversion rate and allow you to find out what percentage of potential customers moved from the previous stage to the next. The conversion rate of a digital sales funnel is calculated as the ratio of the number of customers moving to a new step in the funnel to the number of customers remaining in the previous step (Borisoglebskaya, Provotorova, and Sergeev 2019b). Qualitative indicators allow you to find out the reasons for the loss of customers. The analysis of these indicators also allows you to identify existing problem points and organize work aimed at eliminating them.

To analyze the bottlenecks of the sales funnel, a consistent assessment of the impact on the profit of each of the metrics can be carried out: the number of informed customers at the top of the funnel, the conversion of informed customers into order-takers and end users (Sergey Krasnov, Sergeev, Titov, et al. 2019). Conversion losses depend on the convenience of the site, the terms of purchase, the value offer or discount program, the ill-considered conduct of the potential customer from the choice of the product to the payment method, delivery, and then to the after-sales service.

The site's sales funnel allows you to manage the trading process. The process of establishing a flow of interested buyers is a lead generation (leads –site visitors who are interested in purchasing a product, left their application or at least contact information). A pre-developed scenario of interaction with the client, starting from the moment of greeting and ending with the execution of the transaction, is a sales script (there are scripts for an incoming call and scripts for an outgoing call of a call center).

According to the hierarchical model of communication, the sales funnel, in order to sell something, it is necessary to go through the stages of communication with the client from attracting attention to the proposed product to making sure that the right choice will lead to a purchase, while the number of potential customers at each stage is reduced. In the hundred years that have passed since the introduction of this term, the principles of selling have remained unchanged.

"A real sales consultant should be a good marketer, looking at everything through the eyes of the buyer and able to prepare the buyer for the purchase" - these are the words of William Townsend, who proposed the marketing model "sales funnel"in 1924 in the development of the AIDA model (Attention – attention, Interest – interest, Desire – desire, Action – action), developed by Elias Lewis in 1896(Sergey Krasnov, Sergeev, Zotova, et al. 2019).

Peterson A. in 1959 published a visual image of the sales funnel in the book "Sales in pharmaceuticals, "detailing" and sales training". Describing the importance of moving from the general to the particular, the author noted: "This can be compared to the movement of matter through a funnel or a V-shaped percolator." This movement he called the funnel of progression. The variant of the classical model is modified by many modern authors. A step-by-step plan for attracting potential customers via the Internet was developed by Smith. Friedman reveals the methods of turning potential buyers into those who actually buy.

The specific, detailed version of the sales funnel can be different for different types of businesses, depending on what problems need to be solved. A typical sales funnel in internet marketing is called a conversion funnel. Internet technologies allow you to control the quantitative indicators of conversion rates at various stages.

Psychology considers the sale of goods and services as a reason and a reason for communication that takes place on the basis of the laws of communication.

One of the first hierarchical models of communication was proposed by Elias Lewis, who formulated the slogan "Attract attention, maintain interest, create desire". Later, he added a fourth slogan - "get action." In 1916, the psychologist G. Adams wrote that the psychological states of "sensation, attention, association, fusion, memory, appearance, and action" should be taken into account when advertising and selling.

A person can be controlled with a sufficient set of stimuli. Under the influence of internal and external factors, a person experiences conscious states: attention, interest, desire, action, satisfaction. By correcting external factors, it is possible to facilitate the transition of a person from one state to another and further to the final state of satisfaction.

Later, the communication model was used to predict sales. Currently, the model is also used to guide advertising campaigns aimed at various ways to search for products by the customer on the Internet.

3. STATEMENT OF THE PROBLEM

The forecasting necessary for effective commercial activity should consider many stages of interaction with the consumer pool. The sales funnel representation of the process used in analytics is widely used for evaluating sales results. However, such a tool is designed for offline sales and is nothing more than a convenient abstraction. In addition, the results of using sales funnel are limited by the fact that lagging indicators appear in this model(S. Krasnov et al. 2019). The processes taking place in online trading allow us to radically transform the sales funnel and turn it into a powerful business forecasting tool with the ability to objectively evaluate all stages of commercial interaction. For such a transition, it is necessary to formulate the fundamental differences in its application at the present stage. The initial and final stages - prospective customers, unformed preferences, and product delivery, respectively - reflect basically the same set of consumers, but the sources of information - consumer awareness and loyalty-are completely different. If the sales funnel uses coldcall-type interaction methods, then in online mode it will be landing pages, or landingpage, blogposts, and online tracking services, courier delivery, and online banking, respectively. You can also interpret transitions from offline modes for the following stages: initial contact, determining demand, evaluating a potential purchase, intentions, purchase.

These will be potential customers who have shown interest, clarification of the set of requirements, content sites, targeted marketing, advertising on social platforms, and estimation of potential opportunities. The stages of the offer, the calculation will be the following set: SEO search engine optimization (search engine optimization), SEM search marketing (Search Engine Marketing), viraladvertising (viral marketing), IFO (Irresistible Free Offer). The meeting, discussion of disagreements, objections, the final offer turns into the registration of the client and subscription to the services. Separately, we note the completion of the transaction, which now has the form "product registration system", "Internet banking"(Pilipenko et al. 2019).

The task of this study is to formalize the description of the stages of online interaction, to compile a mathematical model and to find methods for optimizing the commercial process in this paradigm.

Table 1. Comparison of stages of interaction with consumers

Stages of interaction with consumers	Sales Funnel	Conversion Funnel
Initial Contact	Prosepecting Unquualified leads	Landing page targeted page blog posts
Qualification	Qualifying leads Intital meeting	Content, marketing inbound marketing
Develop Solution	Problem/Solution testimonials	Services and/or product information
Presentation	Pricing information	Customer Reference
Evaluation	Make an offer	Search engine
Negotiation	Negotation finalize proposal	Site registration subscribation, supply options
Closing	Closing the deal	System for making orders, online payment

4. MATHEMATICAL MODEL

Since the process of interaction with consumers of goods and services is divided into a number of stages, we will introduce the corresponding axis X. The client moves along this axis, going through the stages of the commercial process from the initiation of his interest to the final transfer of money (Provotorov, Sergeev, and Part 2019). For a quantitative description of the situation in dynamics at each stage along X we will postpone the value Q, numerically equal to such commercial indicators as customer requests, offers made, contracts concluded, etc. A decreasing number of potential consumers move on to each next stage. Thus, we observe a functional dependence $Q(x,t)$ not only on the stage axis X, but also from time to time t. This formalism reflects the level of the request of potential consumers who are at the moment t at the stage $x \in X$ on the offered product or service. If you define a virtual consumer shift with $t = t^*$ along X starting from a certain stage x_1 until the next one x_2, then you can write it down to estimate the losses W potential customers:

$$W = -\frac{Q(x_2,t^*) - Q(x_1,t^*)}{x_2 - x_1}.$$

This indicator is called the bounce rate and is used to determine the effectiveness of commercial services at this stage. Limit values during the transition $x_1 \to x_2$ give an instant value W, numerically equal to the partial derivative: $\lim\limits_{x_2 \to x_1} W = -\frac{\partial Q}{\partial x}\Big|_{x=x_1}$. Thus, the bounce rate level changes along the axis X, and the essence of the variable W it consists in the degree of narrowing of the sales funnel. Physically, this means the ratio of the number of $-\frac{\partial Q}{\partial x}\Big|_{x=x_1} \Delta t$ potential customers, for a period of time Δt per stage x_1, to the reduced number of them $-\frac{\partial Q}{\partial x}\Big|_{x=x_2} \Delta t$ at the exit from x_2. This is expressed by the ratio: $(W(x_1) - W(x_2))\Delta t = -\frac{\partial Q}{\partial x}\Big|_{x=x_1} \Delta t - \left(-\frac{\partial Q}{\partial x}\Big|_{x=x_2} \Delta t\right)$.

This problem arises in a number of applications of queuing theory. Indeed, in this case, mathematical formalisms reflect the process of passing the initial flow through a sequence of service points, in each of which there are losses of its intensity. Such an operation can be represented as a sequence of operations: $T_{q1}, T_{q2}, ..., T_{qN}$, where q_i - the probability of a potential client to move from the stage of the commercial process i the next one. Accordingly, the losses in this case occur with a frequency of $p_i = 1 - q_i$. To be able to apply Renyi's theorem, we change the time scale (Borisoglebskaya et al. 2020). The coefficient on the time scale will be the value of $(q_i)^{-1}$. Then, according to Renyi's theorem, the sequential passage through the stages of commercial interaction is equivalent to the transformation $T_{q1q2...qN}$. In this case, the sequence of such decreasing flows will converge with a high degree of confidence to the Poisson flow. To do this, it is necessary to meet the conditions of uniformity: $\lim\limits_{n\to\infty} q_1 \cdot q_2 \cdot ... \cdot q_n = 0$

, which in practice means similar performance indicators of the stages of commercial interaction. The obtained result allows us to proceed to mathematical modeling of the level of organization of interaction with the consumer at all stages of the sales process of goods and services.

5. ECONOMIC AND MATHEMATICAL MODELING

The resulting mathematical description must be linked to the business quality indicators. To do this, enter the function $g(x)$ to account for the Key Performance Indicator index, which determines the effectiveness of the organization of the commercial process at the stage of $x = x_1, x_2, ..., x_N$, where N - number of interaction stages. This integral indicator reflects both the degree of interest of potential customers, as well as the professionalism of developers of business schemes, mobile applications and the level of use of technological capabilities of online trading. Quality of work at the stage x the higher the higher the value is $g(x)$. When switching to the concept of conversion at the stage x its level is determined from the formula: $g(x)^{-1} \Delta x (Q(x, t_2) - Q(x, t_1)) = g(x)^{-1} \Delta x \Delta Q$.

For formalized accounting of the adverse impact of the competitive environment on the bounce rate level bouncerate W you must also enter the function $D(x,t)$. This integral indicator takes into account the activities of competitors that divert part of the client pool, changes in legislation, and the influence of other market factors. The general equation of dynamics in this case has the form:

$-\dfrac{\partial Q}{\partial x}\bigg|_{x=x_1} \Delta t - \left(-\dfrac{\partial Q}{\partial x}\bigg|_{x=x_2} \Delta t \right) = g_n^{-1} \Delta x (\Delta Q - D(x,t)\Delta t)$, this makes it possible, using the

Lagrange theorem, to write a dynamic model of the process in the form (1):

$$g_n \frac{\partial^2 Q}{\partial t^2} + D(x,t) = \frac{\partial Q}{\partial t} \tag{1}$$

Next, we will link the KPI indicators (Fedotov et al. 2020). To do this, the performance of the means of interaction with consumers is denoted as μ_n, where n - stage number on the axis X. The density of requests at the entrance to the x_n denote as λ_n, the number of communication channels available to clients is equal to m (for example, the degree of performance of software-implemented mobile applications). The conversion rate is calculated using the formula (2):

$$g_n = 1 - \frac{\lambda_n^{m+s}}{m^s \mu_n^{m+s} m!} \left[\sum_{k=0}^{m} \frac{\lambda_n^k}{k! \mu_n^k} + \frac{\lambda_n^{m+1}}{m! \mu_n^{m+1}} \frac{1 - \left(\frac{\lambda_n}{m \mu_n} \right)^s}{m - \frac{\lambda_n}{\mu_n}} \right]^{-1} \tag{2}$$

At the same time, the impact of the competitive environment $D(x,t)$ we take into account losses $v(t)$ potential consumers, calculated by the formula (3):

$$D(x,t) = 1 - \frac{v(t)}{\lambda} \left[\sum_{k=0}^{n} \frac{\alpha_n^k}{k!} + \frac{\alpha_n^m}{m_n!} Y \right]^{-1} \frac{\alpha_n^m}{m!} Y \tag{3}$$

where $\alpha_n = \lambda_n / \mu_n$; $Y = \sum_{s=1}^{\infty} \frac{\alpha_n^s}{\prod_{k=1}^{s} (m + k \frac{v(t)}{\mu_n})}$

6. CALCULATION

To calculate the dynamics of the business process, we calculate the input flow of potential consumers using the Verhulst equation (Provotorov et al. 2020). At the same time $Q_0(t)$ - the volume of potential customers at the beginning of the promotion, Ω - supporting the capacity of the market, θ - dynamics of consumer preferences. We use the ratio: $\frac{dQ_0(t)}{dt} = \theta Q_0(t) \left(1 - \frac{Q_0(t)}{\Omega} \right)$. In the calculation process using a computer, we used an analytical solution of the equation in quadratures of the following form:

$$Q_0(t) = \frac{\Omega Q_0^* e^{\theta t}}{\Omega + Q_0^* (e^{\theta t} - 1)}.$$

It should be noted that this ratio, or logistic S - the function must have a starting value other than zero, which in practice corresponds to the volume of pre-orders for a product or service (Borisoglebskaya, Provotorova, and Sergeev 2019a). Then, taking the first derivative, we immediately get the dynamics of changes in the intensity of the flow of client requests, or the flow at the entrance to the conversion funnel, which is calculated as: $Q_0'(t) = \frac{\theta \Omega Q_0^* e^{\theta t} (\Omega - Q_0^*)}{\left[\Omega + Q_0^* (e^{\theta t} - 1) \right]^2}$.

The discreteness of the process is taken into account not only by the counting set of stages, but also by time. Since the discrete Verhulst equation is transformed into the Feigenbaum map, it is very convenient to use it for practical calculations with the implementation on a computer (Golosnoy et al. 2019).

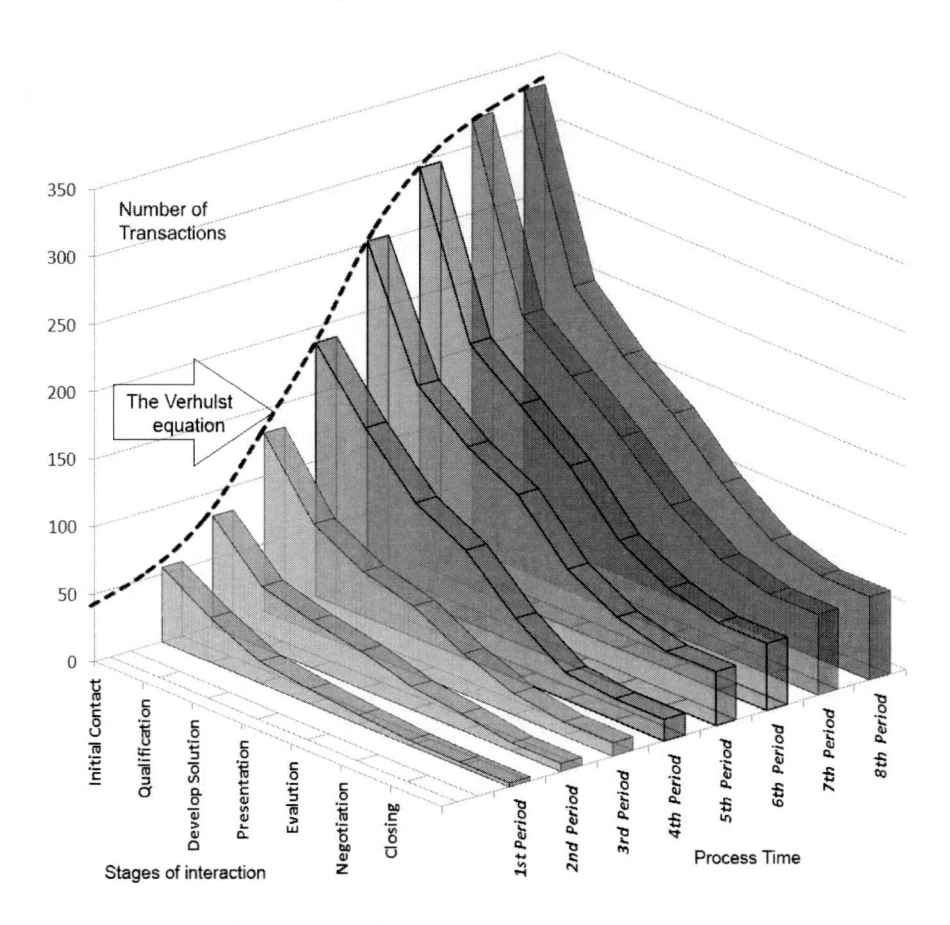

Figure 1. Dynamic sales funnel data slices set.

Table 2. The degree of quality of the commercial service

The level of work of the commercial service	The decrement in N = 8	The decrement in N = 12
Optimal interaction at all stages	0,10	0,08
The commercial process is well organized	0,14	0,12
There are reserves for improving the quality of interaction	0,21	0,18
There are losses of potential customers	0,30	0,22
The commercial service is poorly organized	0,42	0,27
Poor customer service, most consumers refuse goods and services	0,50	0,32

As a result, you can get a set of cross sections of the three-dimensional salesfunnel Figure 1. The initial data corresponds to the Verhulstequation solution with a non-zero initial condition determined by the pre-order level.

The process of online interaction (Figure 1) is calculated using the presented model. This simulation allows you to automate the process and get the result in the form of recommendations to managers. In this case, by setting the optimization criterion, you can program a convenient application for calculating the best business interaction. In our case, the exponential regression decrement index was used in the mathematical model calculation.

The results of the calculations allow us to summarize in Table 2 convenient for practical use data on the quality of the organization of the commercial process.

CONCLUSION

The process of digital transformation of the service sector is a complex process (S. M. Sergeev et al. 2020). Various aspects of digitalization, including social aspects, should be taken into account (S. Sergeev and Kirillova 2019). Sales funnel originated as a method of evaluating the company's work with consumers. At the same time, the use of such a tool is effective for those types of businesses that are characterized by a long sales process, a high level of interaction with potential customers of goods and services is important, and new consumers are actively attracted. In this type of offline trading, the use of salesfunnel is acceptable in the B2B and B2C segments. The qualitative leap in the level of online trading in recent months is accompanied by the transition of the interaction process to the Internet, as well as the expansion of the range of D2C interaction. It is the quality of the development of websites, trade portals, platforms, and integration with other services that determines the degree of conversion of potential consumers during the transition from one stage of interaction to another. Thus, there is a transformation of the process into a conversion funnel. Despite the similarity of the purpose of the processes within these two tools for promoting goods and services, they are fundamentally different. First, it is the transition to digital virtual interaction and real-time work. Secondly, the widespread use of aggregator sites, which provide greater opportunities to reach the client pool. Finally, and most importantly, a commercial enterprise has the opportunity to adjust its strategy of market interaction, optimize all stages of the business process by using algorithms based on leading economic indicators.

The interpretation of the results obtained will be a set of tools that form the basis of software solutions in the form of expert systems for making management decisions in a commercial enterprise. Detailing the successive phases of the conversion funnel allows you to identify the problems of the business organization ahead of time. It is also possible to predict future demand and necessary investments in real time. At the same time, financial and economic planning is carried out on the basis of a scientifically based, balanced analysis with the use of optimization methods.

REFERENCES

Barykin, S., Borovkov, A., Rozhdestvenskiy, O., Tarshin, A. & Yadykin, V. (2020). "STAFF COMPETENCE and TRAINING for DIGITAL INDUSTRY." *IOP*

Conference Series: Materials Science and Engineering, 940 (1). https://doi.org/ 10.1088/1757-899X/940/1/012106.

Barykin, Sergey Yevgenievich, Andrey Aleksandrovich Bochkarev, Sergey Mikhailovich Sergeev, Tatiana Anatolievna Baranova, Dmitriy Anatolievich Mokhorov, and Aleksandra Maksimovna Kobicheva. 2021. "A Methodology of Bringing Perspective Innovation Products to Market." *Academy of Strategic Management Journal* 20 (2): 19. https://www.abacademies.org/articles/a-methodology-of-bringing-perspective-innovation-products-to-market.pdf.

Barykin, Sergey Yevgenievich, Olga Vladimirovna Kalinina, Irina Vasilievna Kapustina, Victor Andreevich Dubolazov, Cesar Armando Nunez Esquivel, Elmira Alyarovna Nazarova, and Petr Anatolievich Sharapaev. 2021. "The Sharing Economy and Digital Logistics in Retail Chains: Opportunities and Threats." *Academy of Strategic Management Journal* 20 (2): 1–14. https://www.abacademies.org/articles/the-sharing-economy-and-digital-logistics-in-retail-chains-opportunities-and-threats.pdf.

Barykin, Sergey Yevgenievich, Irina Vasilievna Kapustina, Sergey Mikhailovich Sergeev, Olga Vladimirovna Kalinina, Viktoriia Valerievna Vilken, Yuri Yevgenievich Putikhin, and Lydia Vitalievna Volkova. 2021. "Developing the Physical Distribution Digital Twin Model within the Trade Network." *Academy of Strategic Management Journal* 20 (1): 1–24. https://www.abacademies.org/articles/developing-the-physical-distribution-digital-twin-model-within-the-trade-network.pdf.

Barykin, Sergey Yevgenievich, Irina Vasilievna Kapustina, Olga Aleksandrovna Valebnikova, Natalia Viktorovna Valebnikova, Olga Vladimirovna Kalinina, Sergey Mikhailovich Sergeev, Marisa Camastral, Yuri Yevgenievich Putikhin, and Lydia Vitalievna Volkova. 2021. "Digital Technologies for Personnel Management: Implications for Open Innovations." *Academy of Strategic Management Journal* 20 (2): 1–14. https://www.abacademies.org/articles/digital-technologies-for-personnel-management-implications-for-open-innovations.pdf.

Barykin, Sergey Yevgenievich, Elena Aleksandrovna Smirnova, Petr Anatolievich Sharapaev, and Angela Bohuovna Mottaeva. 2021. "Development of the Kazakhstan Digital Retail Chains within the EAEU E-Commerce." *Academy of Strategic Management Journal* 20 (2): 1–18. https://www.abacademies.org/articles/development-of-the-kazakhstan-digital-retail-chains-within-the-eaeu-ecommerce-market.pdf.

Barykin, Sergey, Olga Kalinina, Igor Aleksandrov, Evgenii Konnikov, Vladimir Yadikin. & Mikhail Draganov. (2020). "Personnel Management Digital Model Based on the Social Profiles' Analysis." *Journal of Open Innovation: Technology, Market, and Complexity*, 6 (4), 1–20. https://doi.org/10.3390/joitmc6040152.

Barykin, Sergey Yevgenievich, Andrey Aleksandrovich Bochkarev, Olga Vladimirovna Kalinina. & Vladimir Konstantinovich Yadykin. (2020). "Concept for a Supply Chain Digital Twin." *International Journal of Mathematical, Engineering and Management Sciences*, 5 (6), 1498–1515. https://doi.org/10.33889/IJMEMS.2020.5.6.111.

Barykin, Sergey Yevgenievich, Irina Vasilievna Kapustina, Tatiana Viktorovna Kirillova, Vladimir Konstantinovich Yadykin. & Yevgenii Aleksandrovich Konnikov. (2020). "Economics of Digital Ecosystems." *Journal of Open Innovation: Technology, Market, and Complexity*, 6 (4), 1–16. https://doi.org/10.3390/joitmc6040124.

Barykin, Sergey Yevgenievich, Irina Vasilievna Kapustina, Sergey Mikhailovich Sergeev. & Vladimir Konstantinovich Yadykin. (2020). "Algorithmic Foundations of Economic and Mathematical Modeling of Network Logistics Processes." *Journal of Open Innovation: Technology, Market, and Complexity*, 6 (4), 1–16. https://doi.org/10.3390/joitmc6040189.

Borisoglebskaya, L. N., Provotorov, V. V., Sergeev, S. M. & Kosinov, E. S. (2019). "Mathematical Aspects of Optimal Control of Transference Processes in Spatial Networks." *IOP Conference Series: Materials Science and Engineering*, 537 (4). https://doi.org/10.1088/1757-899X/537/4/042025.

Borisoglebskaya, L. N., Provotorova, E. N. & Sergeev, S. M. (2019a). "Commercial Software Engineering under the Digital Economy Concept." *Journal of Physics: Conference Series*, 1399 (3). https://doi.org/10.1088/1742-6596/1399/3/033029.

———. (2019b). "Promotion Based on Digital Interaction Algorithm." *IOP Conference Series: Materials Science and Engineering*, 537 (4). https://doi.org/10.1088/1757-899X/537/4/042032.

Borisoglebskaya, L. N., Provotorova, E. N., Sergeev, S. M. & Khudyakov, A. P. (2019). "Automated Storage and Retrieval System for Industry 4.0 Concept." *IOP Conference Series: Materials Science and Engineering*, 537 (3), 0–6. https://doi.org/10.1088/1757-899X/537/3/032036.

Borisoglebskaya, L. N., Sergeev, S. M., Provotorova, E. N. & Zaslavskiy, A. A. (2020). "Digital Algorithms for Supply Chain Automation of Mechanical Engineering Production." *IOP Conference Series: Materials Science and Engineering*, 862 (4). https://doi.org/10.1088/1757-899X/862/4/042025.

Bril, Alexander, Svetlana Evseeva, Olga Kalinina, Sergey Barykin. & Elena Vinogradova. (2020). "Personnel Changes and Labor Productivity in Regulatory Budget Monitoring." *IOP Conference Series: Materials Science and Engineering*, 940 (1). https://doi.org/10.1088/1757-899X/940/1/012105.

Bril, Alexander, Olga Kalinina, Sergey Barykin. & Anna Burova. (2020). "The Methodological Features of the Economic Evaluation of Personnel Management Operational Projects." In *Innovations in Digital Economy*, edited by Dmitrii Rodionov, Tatiana Kudryavtseva, Mohammed Ali Berawi, and Angi Skhvediani, 143–54. Cham: Springer International Publishing.

Fedotov, A. A., Sergeev, S. M., Provotorova, E. N., Prozhogina, T. V. & Yu Zaslavskaya, O. (2020). "The Digital Twin of a Warehouse Robot for Industry 4.0." *IOP Conference Series: Materials Science and Engineering*, 862 (3), 0–6. https://doi.org/10.1088/1757-899X/862/3/032061.

Golosnoy, A. S., Provotorov, V. V., Sergeev, S. M., Raikhelgauz, L. B. & Ja Kravets, O. (2019). "Software Engineering Math for Network Applications." *Journal of*

Physics: Conference Series, 1399 (4). https://doi.org/10.1088/1742-6596/1399/4/044047.

Kapustina, Irina, Olga Kalinina, Alina Ovchinnikova. & Sergei Barykin. (2020). "The Logistics Network Digital Twin in View of Concept of the Non-Destructive Quality Control Methods." *E3S Web of Conferences*, 157. https://doi.org/10.1051/e3sconf/202015705001.

Krasnov, S., Zotova, E., Sergeev, S., Krasnov, A. & Draganov, M. (2019). "Stochastic Algorithms in Multimodal 3PL Segment for the Digital Environment." *IOP Conference Series: Materials Science and Engineering*, 618 (1). https://doi.org/10.1088/1757-899X/618/1/012069.

Krasnov, Sergey, Sergey Sergeev, Aleksandr Titov. & Yelizaveta Zotova. (2019). "Modelling of Digital Communication Surfaces for Products and Services Promotion." *IOP Conference Series: Materials Science and Engineering*, 497 (1). https://doi.org/10.1088/1757-899X/497/1/012032.

Krasnov, Sergey, Sergey Sergeev, Elizaveta Zotova. & Nadezhda Grashchenko. (2019). "Algorithm of Optimal Management for the Efficient Use of Energy Resources." *E3S Web of Conferences*, 110. https://doi.org/10.1051/e3sconf/201911002052.

Pilipenko, O. V., Provotorova, E. N., Sergeev, S. M. & Rodionov, O. V. (2019). "Automation Engineering of Adaptive Industrial Warehouse." *Journal of Physics: Conference Series*, 1399 (4). https://doi.org/10.1088/1742-6596/1399/4/044045.

Provotorov, V. V., Danilevich, D. V., Fedotov, A. A., Sergeev, S. M. & Ja Kravets, O. (2020). "Digital Management by Supply Networks in Engineering." *IOP Conference Series: Materials Science and Engineering*, 862 (3). https://doi.org/10.1088/1757-899X/862/3/032024.

Provotorov, V. V., Sergeev, S. M. & Part, A. A. (2019). "Solvability of Hyperbolic Systems with Distributed Parameters on the Graph in the Weak Formulation." *Vestnik Sankt-Peterburgskogo Universiteta, Prikladnaya Matematika, Informatika, Protsessy Upravleniya*, 15 (1), 107–17. https://doi.org/10.21638/11702/spbu10.2019.108.

Sergeev, S. & Kirillova, T. (2019). "Information Support for Trade with the Use of a Conversion Funnel." *IOP Conference Series: Materials Science and Engineering*, 666 (1). https://doi.org/10.1088/1757-899X/666/1/012064.

Sergeev, Sergey M., Anna A. Kurochkina, Olga V. Lukina. & Vilena E. Zasenko. (2020). "Interactive Algorithm for Estimating Consumer Demand for Tourism Services for Sustainable Operation of the Transport Industry." *IOP Conference Series: Materials Science and Engineering*, 918 (1). https://doi.org/10.1088/1757-899X/918/1/012219.

Shmatko, Alexey, Sergey Barykin, Sergey Sergeev. & Anuphat Thirakulwanich. (2021). *"Modeling a Logistics Hub Using the Digital Footprint Method — The Implication for Open Innovation Engineering."*

In: Global Challenges of Digital Transformation of Markets ISBN: 978-1-53619-754-9
Editors: E. de la Poza and S. E. Barykin   © 2021 Nova Science Publishers, Inc.

Chapter 19

PREDICTIVE METHODOLOGY FOR ASSESSING PERIODIC MARKET FLUCTUATIONS

S. M. Sergeev[1,], S. E. Barykin[1], A. Yu. Burova[2], L. N. Borisoglebskaya[3], V. L. Buniak[2], Y. L. Gobareva[2] and Bilal Khalid[4]*

[1]Peter the Great St.Petersburg Polytechnic University, Russia
[2]Financial University under the Government of the Russian Federation,
St. Petersburg branch, Russia
[3]Orel State University, Orel, Russia
[4]Business School, King Mongkut's Institute of Technology Ladkrabang,
Bangkok, Thailand

ABSTRACT

The paper presents the results of developing algorithms aimed at optimizing managerial decision-making in commerce. The most difficult task in constructing algorithms for supporting managerial decisions within the Industry 4.0 paradigm is to develop an interface for machine-to-machine interaction between data flows describing the current market demand and software-controlled subsystems of digital logistics platforms. Several problems have to be solved, taking into account diverse criteria. We used methods of stochastic mathematical modeling, queuing theory and the theory of optimal decisions, proposing a procedure for assessing periodic movements of consumer demand with uncertain dynamics of market indicators. A convenient implementation is offered in the form of software for digital logistics platforms, relevant for a wide range of business applications.

Keywords: market, economics, commerce, mathematical model

---

* Corresponding Author's Email: sergeev2@inbox.ru.

1. Introduction

Since the late 1990s, both the business environment and the technologies used to exchange data flows and to manage material flows in supply chains have undergone dramatic changes thanks to innovations in many segments of industry and transport, as well as a number of political decisions and ongoing globalization.

New opportunities, along with wide technological and informational resources have allowed entrepreneurs to achieve their potential much more efficiently in most business sectors. The cross-border exchange of goods and cargo has intensified, both in Europe and between other states. The structure of transport networks has become more complex, and international transport services of all types have become widely available. Creation a sustainable supply chain means balancing reliability and flexibility. Decentralized communication is giving way to more precise and modern solutions. The combination of optimization modeling and data analysis is the basic technology that allows you to create a sufficiently detailed model of the real supply chain of its digital counterpart Idea -. The goal of creating a digital twin is to manage risks in supply chains, thereby making them more reliable and resilient in the event of any failures. Modern technologies allow us to collect large amounts of data on supply chains online (S. Y. Barykin, Bochkarev, Kalinina, and Yadykin 2020). It can successfully act as a replacement for expensive field monitoring methods without causing any damage to the physical object. A digital twin is an evolving digital profile of the historical and current behavior of a physical object or process that helps optimize business performance (Kapustina et al., 2020). There is now an imbalance between the increasingly complex parameters describing the interactions of consumers and producers and decision-making methods applied in management of the logistics infrastructure.

The problem is partially solved by outsourcing (Zhabko, Shindyapin, and Provotorov 2019) some functions to 3PL (Third Party Logistics) and 4PL logistics. In turn, this segmentation of business on the scale of interstate economic unions such as BRICS or EAEU, including the corresponding free trade zones, caused a number of problems associated with the difficulty of predicting the real volume of demand for services in the transport and logistics sector.

Only the adoption of the Web 4.0 concept (Borisoglebskaya et al., 2019) and widespread penetration of high-speed, primarily mobile access to the global Internet brought positive changes. What is more, fundamentally new opportunities appeared for cloud computing and easily accessible cloud platforms with a rich array of functions. These technologies are invariant with respect to software shells, which has been the reason for qualitative changes in a number of industries.

A digital ecosystem is a self-organizing, sustainable system based on digital platforms that form a single information environment in which ecosystem members can interact in the absence of rigid functional links between them. The basis of the digital ecosystem is a variety of platform technologies that form a single information environment for all its participants: society, business and the state (S. Y. Barykin, Kapustina, Kirillova, et al., 2020).

The process of managing the organization's personnel within the digital ecosystem, while maintaining the basic goal setting, is transformed from an instrumental point of view. The transition from a traditional HR system to a digital one involves a difference between how employees interact with each other and with management (Barykin, Kalinina, et al. 2021; Barykin, Kapustina, Sergeev, et al. 2021; Barykin, Bochkarev, et al. 2021; Barykin, Kapustina, Valebnikova, et al. 2021; Barykin, Smirnova, Sharapaev, et al. 2021). The key factor in the system of digital interaction is the ability of each employee to freely contact the information and analytical center. The digital interaction system also differs from the traditional one by expanding the channels for exchanging information and analytics. Considering the tasks of personnel management in the digital age, it can be shown that the problem of digital personnel management is the scientific search for the features of employee interaction in the new technological structure of Industry 4.0 under the influence of the flow of innovations and changes occurring in it. It includes improvements in performance, reliability, quality, and security (Sergey Barykin, Kalinina, Aleksandrov, Konnikov, et al., 2020).

Changes in the high-tech sector also oblige enterprises to transform their workforce in order to achieve a sustainable competitive advantage. The introduction of high-tech solutions leads to a change in the format and content of almost any work, as well as to a rethinking of approaches to personnel planning (Bril, Evseeva, et al., 2020).

It is necessary to consider the issue of training personnel for the digital industry in the context of creating teams in enterprises (Bril, Kalinina, et al., 2020), scientific organizations and universities that have the necessary digital competencies and digital literacy, that is, the ability to use modern methods, experimental and research technologies to develop globally competitive products. This competence becomes an integrator of the technological, ethical, and cognitive aspects of education. In this paradigm, the methodological approach to solving the problem of personnel training is based on a problem-oriented scientific approach, and the model of creating mirror engineering centers is a possible model for scaling competencies, spreading knowledge and developing network interaction (S. Barykin, Borovkov, Rozhdestvenskiy, Tarshin, et al., 2020).

2. MATERIALS AND METHODS

Over the past decade, technologies and equipment that can radically change the approach to managing the processes of cargo movement and cargo transportation have become widespread. This includes the possibility of machine-readable exchange of information about goods and cargo among themselves. To solve such large-scale problems, the use of scientifically based mathematical models is required. This approach will allow us to use the digital footprint of processes in the logistics network and develop an algorithmic basis for a whole set of software tools for more effective management of the logistics industry (S. Y. Barykin, Kapustina, Sergeev, et al., 2020).

It is necessary to find an economically optimal management of the flows of goods and cargo based on digital information about their movement, taking into account the stochastic nature of the volumes and directions of flows. At the same time, it is necessary to choose and justify the methodology for calculating the DC node terminals that are part of the network structure of logistics activities. The resulting set of mathematical relations allows us to model the operation of a network distribution center as a nodal element of a logistics system operating on the principles of a 3PL operator in the conditions of the stochastic nature of incoming and shipped commodity flows (Shmatko et al., 2021).

The mathematical methods currently applied for extrapolating a known set of values to predict the future process are based on trend analysis and regression function. Let us consider the options for constructing trends available in common software packages and assess whether they are applicable to making economic forecasts (Provotorov 2008) for the volumes of demand with complex periodic seasonal dependences. First of all, the exponential, logarithmic, power and particularly linear regression have to be excluded. The reason for this is that all of the given trend lines have a monotonic diagram and cannot simulate complex dependences with multiple outliers and inflections. The polynomial approximation seems to be slightly more suitable. Applying the approximating polynomial can yield a satisfactory approximation to the process considered for a short period (Podvalny, Podvalny, and Provotorov 2017). However, there is little practical benefit from this method. Firstly, the initial data were lagging indicators. Secondly, more importantly, the resulting function cannot be used for any forecasts. Indeed, according to mathematical theory, a polynomial of order n can have no more than $n-1$ extrema (Provotorov, V. V. and Provotorova E. N 2017). This means that continuing the calculations based on the obtained equation for forecasting produces values of plus or minus infinity. It follows, then, that the approximation by a power function is theoretically useless for forecasting and that fundamentally different, more advanced methods for mathematical modeling of complex periodic processes are required.

Our study is based on data flows characterizing the current and projected demand; these flows can be obtained digitally using standard protocols in fully automated mode. Processing in real time primarily serves for constructing diagrams of the variation in the total load of logistics capacities (Artemov et al., 2019). This dependence should take into account the stochastic, uneven nature of the demand, reflecting the seasonal variation with a pronounced annual frequency. We used mathematical analysis and computer processing methods based on applied software (Provotorov, Sergeev, and Part 2019) packages to expand this dependence into a Fourier series, expanding its complex form into a number of harmonic components, each a periodic function. Next, systems of Erlang-type differential equations are formulated to calculate the evolution of demand for the required planning horizon (Volkova, Gnilitskaya, and Provotorov 2014).

3. Main Formalisms of the Mathematical Model

The results are based on the theory of spectral analysis, in particular, Fourier series expansion. The complex dependence of seasonal or periodic demand is regarded as *T*, a periodic function *D(t)* of the continuous time argument *t*. If *D(t)* satisfies the Dirichlet conditions, that is, has a countable number of discontinuities of the first kind (Provotorov, Ryazhskikh, and Gnilitskaya 2017), does not have infinite values, is piecewise-continuous, has a finite number of extrema, then the system of trigonometric functions

$$D(t) = \frac{a_0}{2} + \sum_{n=1}^{\infty}(a_n \cos(\omega_n t) + b_n \sin(\omega_n t)), \tag{1}$$

$$a_n = \frac{2}{T}\int_{-T/2}^{T/2} D(t)\cos(\omega_n t)dt, \quad b_n = \frac{2}{T}\int_{-T/2}^{T/2} D(t)\sin(\omega_n t)dt,$$

$$a_0 = \frac{2}{T}\int_{-T/2}^{T/2} D(t)dt, \quad \omega_n = \delta\omega n = 2\pi n / T$$

forms an orthonormal basis for expanding the periodic dependence *D(t)*.

The concept of demand (Provotorov, V. V. and Provotorova E.N 2017) for goods and services as physically measurable quantities implies that the Dirichlet conditions are fully satisfied. In particular, sharp drops or increases in the consumption of goods or services can act as discontinuities. There are diverse reasons for this, for example, substitute product suddenly appearing on the market, weather anomalies, political events that provoke panic buying or loss of consumer interest (Volkova and Provotorov 2014). For convenient approximation taking into account the seasonal nature of demand processes, we transform expression (1) to the following form:

$$D(t) = A(t) + \sum_{n=1}^{\infty} A_n \cos(2\pi nt / T + \theta_n)$$

This allows to isolate the average component *A(t)* of the process and seasonal fluctuations around it. The ratios of the quantities are determined by the formulas: $\theta_n = arctg(a_n / b_n)$, $A_n = \sqrt{a_n^2 + b_n^2}$. The goal is to determine the unknown expansion coefficients *T*, *A(t)*, *A_n*, θ_n for *n* = 1,2,.... This problem is easily solved by standard add-ons in any mathematical software (Golosnoy et al., 2019) package. Moreover, the depth of expansion determining the accuracy of the approximation can be limited; the values of 3 or 4 harmonics are sufficient for practical purposes, since the influence of *A_n* on the forecasting accuracy decreases rapidly with increasing index *n*.

4. INITIAL DATA OF THE MODEL

The same as with any market value, the internal structure of demand parameters is complex and difficult to describe, characterized by time lags. The problem of statistical evaluation of these parameters (Provotorov et al., 2020) has to be solved. Besides, the statistical processing of objects of non-numerical nature must have the property of consistency in the case of nonparametric estimation of periodic trends in time series. The first step in modeling the demand is to consider the general representation in the form $D^*(t) = D(t) + \lambda(t)$, where the component $D(t)$ is a deterministic function that satisfies the condition $D(t) = D(t + mT) : \forall m = 1, 2, ...$; t is the time; T is the period; $\lambda(t)$ are the random changes due to many factors such as competitive market environment, changes in consumer preferences, economic and other reasons known to the marketer. For mathematical modeling of seasonal demand, it is necessary to process statistical data and estimate the value of T and the values of the elements of the vectors $\{A_0, A_1, A_2, ...\}$ and $\{\theta_1, \theta_2, ...\}$. For this purpose, the functions $D^*(t); D(t); \lambda(t)$ are formally represented over a sufficiently long time interval $t \in [0, t^*]$. Let us introduce additional functions of the form $D_k^*(t) = D^*(t + kT); k = 1, 2, ...$, defined on $t \in [0, T]$. The deviations $\lambda(t)$ are centered random fluctuations. The period T is estimated by introducing the deviation index $\Delta(T, D^*) = \Delta(T, D_1^*(t), D_2^*(t), ...)$ and the estimate of the amplitude $H(T, D^*) = H(T, M[D_k^*(t)])$, where the expected value $M[D_k^*(t)]$ is obtained by calculating the averaged values of the initial functional dependences. To calculate them, we apply expressions for processing statistical series in the following manner:

$$\Delta(T, D^*) = \int_0^1 \max\{|\tilde{D}_i(q) - \tilde{D}_j(q)|dq \; ; \; i, j = 1, 2, ...,$$

where the normalized values are calculated by the formulas:

$$q = t / T,$$

$$\overline{D}^*(q) = M[D^*(t)],$$

$$H(T, D^*) = \int_0^1 \int_0^1 [\overline{D}^*(q) - \overline{D}^*(r)]^2 \, dq dr \; , \; \overline{D}^*(q) = M[D^*(t)].$$

For practical purposes, it is important to obtain an average estimate of the periodic component:

$$\overline{D}^{*} = \int_{0}^{1} \overline{D}^{*}(q)dq$$

and its variation from period to period, which allows to observe long-term trends and is used for forecast planning.

5. ACCOUNTING FOR MARKET UNCERTAINTY

The obtained expansion of the periodic or seasonal load on logistics in a Fourier series in the form

$$D(t) = A(t) + \sum_{n=1}^{\infty} A_n \cos(2\pi n t / T + \theta_n),$$

serves to assess the dependence of the expected value in separable functions under market uncertainty. This makes it possible to formulate the differential equations by analogy with the Erlang system. To do this, we introduce: $v_i(t)$, the periodic functions reflecting the capabilities of the total resources of the logistics industry; $E_K(t)$, the system states and the corresponding probabilities $p_i(t) = \varphi_i(t) + \alpha_i(t)$, where the functions $\phi_i(t)$ are periodic with a period $T/2\pi i$; $\lim_{t \to \infty} \alpha_i(t) = 0$ with all possible i, and $0 \le p_i(t) \le 1$. The meaning of functions $\phi_i(t)$ consists in stationary probabilities of values of $p_i(t)$.

The following sequence is composed to solve the problem:

$$p_{0i}'(t) = -\lambda_i(t)p_{0i}(t) + v_i(t)p_{1i}(t), \quad p_{1i}'(t) = -v_i(t)p_{1i}(t) + \lambda_i(t)p_{0i}(t)$$

and a condition for a full group $\sum_i p_i(t) = 1$ is added. Next, converting to the form

$$p_{0i}'(t) = -\left[\lambda_i(t) + v_i(t)\right]p_{0i}(t) + v_i(t),$$

and defining the initial conditions:

$$p_{0i}(0) = \alpha_i \le 1, \ p_{1i}(0) = 1 - \alpha_i \le 1$$

for any *i* in the range of admissible values, we obtain a system of differential equations integrable by quadratures.

6. MATHEMATICAL MODEL

Let us carry out the required transformations and substitutions. Then the corresponding solution has the following form:

$$p_{0i}(t) = \exp\left\{-\int_0^t [\lambda_i(x) + v_i(x)] dx\right\} \times$$

$$\times \left[\alpha_i + \int_0^t v_i(x) \exp\left\{-\int_0^t [\lambda_i(x) + v_i(x)] dx\right\} dx\right]. \tag{2}$$

Notably, the actual algorithm, underlying expert decision-making systems, is fundamentally changed because the dependence $p_i(t)$ can be expressed analytically. Because the functions $\lambda_i(t)$ and $v_i(t)$ are periodic, we introduce the substitution $\phi_i(t)$ of the form $\varphi_i(t) = \int_0^t [\lambda_i(x) + v_i(x)] dx$, allowing to integrate the system.

Next, to analyze periodic processes, we also denote k, satisfying the inequality: $kT \le t < (k+1)T$. This allows to ultimately obtain the expression for calculating the function $\phi_i(t)$:

$$\varphi_i(t) = ka_i + \int_0^\tau [\lambda_i(z) + v_i(z)] dz$$

The following notation is adopted in this case: $a_i = \int_0^T [\lambda_i(x) + v_i(x)] dx$, $\tau = t - kT$.

Similarly, the functionals entering, reflecting the dynamics of the periodic process, should be expressed to obtain the final solution of the equation. Thus, it is precisely by substituting the expansion of the periodic integral:

$$\int_0^t v_i(x) \exp[\varphi_i(x)] dx =$$

$$= \sum_{l=1}^k \int_{(l-1)T}^{lT} v_i(x) \exp[\varphi_i(x)] dx +$$

$$+ \int_{kT}^t v_i(x) \exp[\varphi_i(x)] dx$$

that we obtain the desired result for $p_{0i}(t)$, i.e., the probabilities found in the following form, convenient for practical applications:

$$p_{0i}(t) = \exp\left[-\varphi_i(\tau)\right]\left[\frac{b_i}{\exp(a_i)-1} + \int_0^{\tau} v_i(x)\exp\left[-\varphi_i(x)\right]dx\right] +$$
$$+ \exp\left[-ka_i - \varphi_i(\tau)\right]\left[\alpha_i - \frac{b_i}{\exp(a)-1}\right].$$

The coefficient b_i corresponds to the value $b_i = \int_0^T v_i(x)\exp\left[\varphi_i(x)\right]dx$.

The multidimensional set of analytically expressed dependences $p_{0i}(t)$ can be used to construct expert systems, where the processes are periodic, with a complex nature.

The result of the analytical solution obtained is the formula for convergence of elementary components (2) of a nonlinear periodic process. In this case, the modeling accuracy depends only on the degree of expansion of any depth.

CONCLUSION

The current market environment is affected by diverse factors generating the overall uncertainty. Solving the problem of making managerial decisions allows to optimize the main economic indicators of commercial activity in all business sectors. Because seasonal conditions affect the consumer demand throughout the year, we obtained algorithms for forecasting periodic demand in the Industry 4.0 paradigm. It was assumed for the algorithms that it is generally possible to obtain instantaneous values of the economic indicators in real time. This option only emerged in recent years due to large-scale digital transformation of all sectors of commercial activity. The model is in demand mainly in transport and logistics, introducing more consistent interaction into logistics outsourcing within the 3PL concept and offering steps towards the more functional 4PL. We obtained an analytical solution in quadratures that is scalable for each of these systems. This expands the potential scope of applications to be found for the results, since superimposing the solutions with the weights corresponding to the initial expansion allows to obtain an integrated dependence, which serves as the basis for making economically optimal decisions in logistics management.

REFERENCES

Artemov, M. A., E. S. Baranovskii, A. P. Zhabko, and V. V. Provotorov. 2019. "On a 3D Model of Non-Isothermal Flows in a Pipeline Network." *Journal of Physics: Conference Series* 1203 (1): 0–9. https://doi.org/10.1088/1742-6596/1203/1/012094.

Barykin, S., A. Borovkov, O. Rozhdestvenskiy, A. Tarshin, and V. Yadykin. 2020. "Staff Competence and Training for Digital Industry." *IOP Conference Series: Materials*

Science and Engineering 940 (1). https://doi.org/10.1088/1757-899X/940/1/012106.

Barykin, Sergey Yevgenievich, Andrey Aleksandrovich Bochkarev, Sergey Mikhailovich Sergeev, Tatiana Anatolievna Baranova, Dmitriy Anatolievich Mokhorov, and Aleksandra Maksimovna Kobicheva. 2021. "A Methodology of Bringing Perspective Innovation Products to Market." *Academy of Strategic Management Journal* 20 (2): 19. https://www.abacademies.org/articles/a-methodology-of-bringing-perspective-innovation-products-to-market.pdf.

Barykin, Sergey Yevgenievich, Olga Vladimirovna Kalinina, Irina Vasilievna Kapustina, Victor Andreevich Dubolazov, Cesar Armando Nunez Esquivel, Elmira Alyarovna Nazarova, and Petr Anatolievich Sharapaev. 2021. "The Sharing Economy and Digital Logistics in Retail Chains: Opportunities and Threats." *Academy of Strategic Management Journal* 20 (2): 1–14. https://www.abacademies.org/articles/the-sharing-economy-and-digital-logistics-in-retail-chains-opportunities-and-threats.pdf.

Barykin, Sergey Yevgenievich, Irina Vasilievna Kapustina, Sergey Mikhailovich Sergeev, Olga Vladimirovna Kalinina, Viktoriia Valerievna Vilken, Yuri Yevgenievich Putikhin, and Lydia Vitalievna Volkova. 2021. "Developing the Physical Distribution Digital Twin Model within the Trade Network." *Academy of Strategic Management Journal* 20 (1): 1–24. https://www.abacademies.org/articles/developing-the-physical-distribution-digital-twin-model-within-the-trade-network.pdf.

Barykin, Sergey Yevgenievich, Irina Vasilievna Kapustina, Olga Aleksandrovna Valebnikova, Natalia Viktorovna Valebnikova, Olga Vladimirovna Kalinina, Sergey Mikhailovich Sergeev, Marisa Camastral, Yuri Yevgenievich Putikhin, and Lydia Vitalievna Volkova. 2021. "Digital Technologies for Personnel Management: Implications for Open Innovations." *Academy of Strategic Management Journal* 20 (2): 1–14. https://www.abacademies.org/articles/digital-technologies-for-personnel-management-implications-for-open-innovations.pdf.

Barykin, Sergey Yevgenievich, Elena Aleksandrovna Smirnova, Petr Anatolievich Sharapaev, and Angela Bohuovna Mottaeva. 2021. "Development of the Kazakhstan Digital Retail Chains within the EAEU E-Commerce." *Academy of Strategic Management Journal* 20 (2): 1–18. https://www.abacademies.org/articles/development-of-the-kazakhstan-digital-retail-chains-within-the-eaeu-ecommerce-market.pdf.

Barykin, Sergey, Olga Kalinina, Igor Aleksandrov, Evgenii Konnikov, Vladimir Yadikin, and Mikhail Draganov. 2020. "Personnel Management Digital Model Based on the Social Profiles' Analysis." *Journal of Open Innovation: Technology, Market, and Complexity* 6 (4): 1–20. https://doi.org/10.3390/joitmc6040152.

Barykin, Sergey Yevgenievich, Andrey Aleksandrovich Bochkarev, Olga Vladimirovna Kalinina, and Vladimir Konstantinovich Yadykin. 2020. "Concept for a Supply Chain Digital Twin." *International Journal of Mathematical, Engineering and*

Management Sciences 5 (6): 1498–1515. https://doi.org/10.33889/IJMEMS .2020.5.6.111.

Barykin, Sergey Yevgenievich, Irina Vasilievna Kapustina, Tatiana Viktorovna Kirillova, Vladimir Konstantinovich Yadykin, and Yevgenii Aleksandrovich Konnikov. 2020. "Economics of Digital Ecosystems." *Journal of Open Innovation: Technology, Market, and Complexity* 6 (4): 1–16. https://doi.org/10.3390/ joitmc6040124.

Barykin, Sergey Yevgenievich, Irina Vasilievna Kapustina, Sergey Mikhailovich Sergeev, and Vladimir Konstantinovich Yadykin. 2020. "Algorithmic Foundations of Economic and Mathematical Modeling of Network Logistics Processes." *Journal of Open Innovation: Technology, Market, and Complexity* 6 (4): 1–16. https://doi.org/10.3390/joitmc6040189.

Borisoglebskaya, L. N., V. V. Provotorov, S. M. Sergeev, and E. S. Kosinov. 2019. "Mathematical Aspects of Optimal Control of Transference Processes in Spatial Networks." *IOP Conference Series: Materials Science and Engineering* 537 (4). https://doi.org/10.1088/1757-899X/537/4/042025.

Bril, Alexander, Svetlana Evseeva, Olga Kalinina, Sergey Barykin, and Elena Vinogradova. 2020. "Personnel Changes and Labor Productivity in Regulatory Budget Monitoring." *IOP Conference Series: Materials Science and Engineering* 940 (1). https://doi.org/10.1088/1757-899X/940/1/012105.

Bril, Alexander, Olga Kalinina, Sergey Barykin, and Anna Burova. 2020. "The Methodological Features of the Economic Evaluation of Personnel Management Operational Projects." In *Innovations in Digital Economy*, edited by Dmitrii Rodionov, Tatiana Kudryavtseva, Mohammed Ali Berawi, and Angi Skhvediani, 143–54. Cham: Springer International Publishing.

Golosnoy, A. S., V. V. Provotorov, S. M. Sergeev, L. B. Raikhelgauz, and O. Ja Kravets. 2019. "Software Engineering Math for Network Applications." *Journal of Physics: Conference Series* 1399 (4). https://doi.org/10.1088/1742-6596/1399/4/ 044047.

Kapustina, Irina, Olga Kalinina, Alina Ovchinnikova, and Sergei Barykin. 2020. "The Logistics Network Digital Twin in View of Concept of the Non-Destructive Quality Control Methods." *E3S Web of Conferences* 157. https://doi.org/10.1051/e3sconf/ 202015705001.

Podvalny, S. L., E. S. Podvalny, and V. V. Provotorov. 2017. "The Controllability of Parabolic Systems with Delay and Distributed Parameters on the Graph." *Procedia Computer Science* 103 (October 2016): 324–30. https://doi.org/10.1016/ j.procs.2017.01.115.

Provotorov, V. V., and Provotorova E.N. 2017. *"Optimal Control of the Linearized Naver-Stokes System in a Netlike Domain,"* 431–43.

Provotorov, V. V., D. V. Danilevich, A. A. Fedotov, S. M. Sergeev, and O. Ja Kravets. 2020. "Digital Management by Supply Networks in Engineering." *IOP Conference Series: Materials Science and Engineering* 862 (3). https://doi.org/10.1088/1757- 899X/862/3/032024.

Provotorov, V. V., V. I. Ryazhskikh, and Yu A. Gnilitskaya. 2017. "Unique Weak Solvability of a Nonlinear Initial Boundary Value Problem with Distributed Parameters in a Netlike Domain." *Vestnik Sankt-Peterburgskogo Universiteta, Prikladnaya Matematika, Informatika, Protsessy Upravleniya* 13 (3): 264–77. https://doi.org/10.21638/11701/spbu10.2017.304.

Provotorov, V. V., S. M. Sergeev, and A. A. Part. 2019. "Solvability of Hyperbolic Systems with Distributed Parameters on the Graph in the Weak Formulation." *Vestnik Sankt-Peterburgskogo Universiteta, Prikladnaya Matematika, Informatika, Protsessy Upravleniya* 15 (1): 107–17. https://doi.org/10.21638/11702/spbu10.2019.108.

Provotorov, V V. 2008. "Eigenfunctions of the Sturm-Liouville Problem on a Star Graph." *Sbornik: Mathematics* 199 (10): 1523–45. https://doi.org/10.1070/sm2008v199n10abeh 003971.

Shmatko, Alexey, Sergey Barykin, Sergey Sergeev, and Anuphat Thirakulwanich. 2021. *"Modeling a Logistics Hub Using the Digital Footprint Method — The Implication for Open Innovation Engineering."*

Volkova, A S, Yu. A Gnilitskaya, and V V Provotorov. 2014. "On the Solvability of Boundary-Value Problems for Parabolic and Hyperbolic Equations on Geometrical Graphs." *Automation and Remote Control* 75 (2): 405–12. https://doi.org/10.1134/S0005117914020192.

Volkova, A S, and V V Provotorov. 2014. "Generalized Solutions and Generalized Eigenfunctions of Boundary-Value Problems on a Geometric Graph." *Russian Mathematics* 58 (3): 1–13. https://doi.org/10.3103/S1066369X14030013.

Zhabko, A. P., A. I. Shindyapin, and V. V. Provotorov. 2019. "Stability of Weak Solutions of Parabolic Systems with Distributed Parameters on the Graph." *Vestnik Sankt-Peterburgskogo Universiteta, Prikladnaya Matematika, Informatika, Protsessy Upravleniya* 15 (4): 457–71. https://doi.org/10.21638/11702/spbu 10.2019.404.

In: Global Challenges of Digital Transformation of Markets ISBN: 978-1-53619-754-9
Editors: E. de la Poza and S. E. Barykin   © 2021 Nova Science Publishers, Inc.

Chapter 20

DIGITAL TRANSFORMATION OF TRADE: OPPORTUNITIES FOR THE DEVELOPMENT OF ONLINE STORES

Irina Krasyuk[1,*], Tatyana Kirilova[1,†], Elmira Nazarova[1,‡],
Olena Chukurna[2,§] and Karina Kkhalaf[3,#]

[1]Peter the Great St. Petersburg Polytechnic University, St. Petersburg, Russia
[2]Odessa national polytechnic university, Odessa, Ukraine
[3]VELTORF LLC, St. Petersburg, Russia

ABSTRACT

This article discusses the prospects for the development of e-commerce in retail chains. E-commerce is a new evolutionary impulse of competition, it makes it more adapted, i.e., more improved in terms of the effectiveness of the business model and attractiveness to consumers. An important role in the development of online commerce is played by online stores, which provide communication interaction with consumers and the organization of the trading process with minimal costs. The digital transformation of retail trade causes fundamental transformations of the shopping landscape caused by the use of modern information technologies. The article defines the features of the development of online stores as the most effective channel for the development of trade. The purpose of the article is to identify the general characteristics and conditions for the development of online stores, to determine the prospects for the development of online commerce. Achieving this goal determined the formulation and solution of the followingtasks of scientific research: to determine the factors affecting the

[*] Corresponding Author's Email: krasyuk_ia@spbstu.ru.
[†] Corresponding Author's Email: kirillova_tv@spbstu.ru.
[‡] Corresponding Author's Email: green.tea.with.mint@yandex.ru.
[§] Corresponding Author's Email: elenachukurna@gmail.com.
[#] Corresponding Author's Email: Guffyrina@mail.ru.

development of online stores by retail chains and customers; to identify the specifics of the formation of business processes; to draw up a portrait of the target audience based on the results of the marketing research; to analyze the dynamics of development. the research methodology is based on a systematic approach, the theory of goal setting and the idea of expediency, which is due to the content of the research logic. In the course of the study, the content of the methodology for studying the development of online stores based on marketing, as a set of scientific theories and ideas, was determined and disclosed. The results obtained allow us to determine who is the main consumer in online stores of networks, what factors influence the dynamics and prospects of their development. The authors believe that the development of online stores will contribute to personalized customer satisfaction. Digitalization of trade processes orients market participants to the development of cooperation. The article concludes with a discussion of the results obtained and the definition of directions for further research.

Keywords: digitalization of trade, online store, marketing, retail chains

1. INTRODUCTION

Digital transformation covers all spheres of life, from the innovation-rich high-tech sector to the retail industry. Successful companies focus their activities only in the digital sphere, creating value through electronic processes (Google, Alibaba). A digital business model based on electronic value creation processes is at the heart of the business strategy. Competitive advantages are largely determined by innovative reformatting of trading activities. The development of innovative business models of trade is based on the concept of Schumpeter's concept (the principle of combination and creative destruction), as well as Christensen's ideas about disruptive innovation - it has a great influence on established (analog) business models. Existing theories and indicators of enterprise value creation were reinterpreted in view of the emergence of e-business. Amit and Zott in 2001 proved that the "business model" construct as a subject of analysis includes the creation of value through multiple sources and is therefore certainly suitable for understanding and defining the fundamental transition from analog to digital technologies. Information technology is a crucial factor in economic and social development in the twenty-first century, since IT innovations and their intelligent use can open up completely new ways of doing business and creating value that go beyond the creation of the porter value chain(Amit and Zott 2001; Kollmann T. 2014). New opportunities for creating value through the systematic collection, processing and application of information - with full or partial independence from physical value chains - led to the emergence of the concept of Net Economy Valua Chain and the emergence of a trend that will shape the overall economic environment of e-business in a new way. The concept of e-business can be considered both from a theoretical and practical point of view. on the one hand, it is the use of information technologies for preparing (information stage), conducting negotiations (communication stage) and implementing business processes (transactional stage) between economic partners through innovative communication networks (theoretical approach), and on the other hand, the use of innovative (Ianenko, Ianenko, Kirillova, et al. 2020; Ianenko, Ianenko, Mironova, et al. 2020; Moon 2015).

E-business is becoming the engine of socio-economic development of society, so it is necessary to identify new ways of organizing and conducting trade activities. The relationship between the development of new products and inter-firm relationships, which allows us to determine the need for key factors for the success of companies, including mutual commitment, mutual trust, mutual adaptation and mutual relationship management. This development trend is becoming particularly relevant in the context of digitalization of trading activities and determines the use of trust marketing tools. The development and complexity of the economy has caused the problem of asynchronous cyclical development, which is based on the statement that the system of macroeconomic indicators is not ideal. The theory of long waves proposed by Kondratiev and the theory of innovative development based on it by Schumpeter require new approaches to describe the cyclical nature of development. A theoretical solution to this problem was found By Mensch in the 1970s. The model of structure change developed by him connects the dynamics of technological and economic processes, which are influenced by two mutual processes of investment and savings, which indirectly affects the development of trade, stimulating purchasing power and the formation of new trade formats.

The following factors can be identified as the growth factors of online trading: innovation, market reach, and professionalization. Innovative trade ideas were transformed into innovative solutions for using the Internet as a sales channel. The spread of tablets and smartphones, the creation of websites and digital platforms led to the creation of online stores, the successful development of a new market potential of this sales channel. Customers began to make higher demands on the reliability and speed of product delivery, data submission and information support of trade operations, and the possibility of return. The growth of competition has led to the evolution of online commerce in relation to unresolved service problems, which contributes to the growth of its scope of activity.

Consumer market is a rapidly evolving and constantly changing branch. It is necessary for trade enterprises to be flexible and adaptive, to reschedule business processes quickly in order to respond to the environment. Nowadays trade is mainly associated with changes. Retailers are becoming digital brokers who supply goods from the warehouse to consumer's home. E-commerce has reached rather high level due to the technical and technological progress and high-qualified staff. Digital transformation of trade influences social life and media archaeology.

Analyzing the theoretic base, we can point out that the aforementioned challenge is poorly studied. So, in what way will digital and analogue phenomena cut each other?

Practical relevance of the methods on theory development lies in the opportunity of applying them in the practical activity of trade enterprises (Roggeveen and Sethuraman 2020; Ianenko, Stepanov, and Mironova 2020; Kapustina et al. 2019).

Determining research objectives means defining a problem by the head of sales department. Exploratory research is a flexible method which allows to define directions of the problem development. Literature searches, secondary data analysis, case studies, review of experience, focus group method are used to define the scope of research. It might be specialized literature as well as business overview. Scientific novelty of the research lies in describing e-commerce development directions based on digitalization of business processes in federal retail chains using marketing tools, which in turn will benefit the integration between online and offline forms of trade. Applying marketing tools at the federal level allows the most important methods of strategic management of retail chains to adapt to the modern economic environment. Digital transformation is changing the attitudes to trading. At the same time, digital transformation does not only create new opportunities for trade network resources or monitor these opportunities in terms of confidentiality and information security. Due to the sense, emotions and intellect of market agents, complex trading operations become possible in control loops, which allows digital transformation to be inbounded in an analogue shell (Wang and Goldfarb 2017; Bhatnagar and Syam 2014; Lo, Lin, and Hsu 2016; Hong and Kim 2012).

2. MATERIALS AND METHODS

2.1. Research Theory and Methodology

The role of digitalization and its impact on the development of trade is growing, because market players need to look for fundamentally new sources of increasing competitiveness. The introduction of innovations into existing business processes helps trade to build momentum and continue its dynamic development. There are many concepts based on the concept of "innovation" and considered their impact on trade and the economy as a whole. Thus, considering "waves of innovative development," Kondratyevcame to the conclusion that the end of the cycle is a crisis, when the productive forces of society will move to a higher level of development. Ref. (Abdolmaleki and Ahmadian 2016) discusses the relationship between the development of new products and intercompany relations, which allows to determine the need for key factors of success of companies, including mutual commitment, mutual trust, mutual adaptation and mutual relationship management. This trend of development becomes especially relevant in the context of digitalization of trade activities and determines the application of trust marketing tools. The development and complication of the economy caused the problem of asynchrony of cyclical development, which is based on the statement that the system of macroeconomic indicators is not ideal. The theory of long waves proposed by Kondratiev, and, based on it,Schumpeter's theory of innovative development requires new approaches to describe the cyclic development. A theoretical solution to this problem was found by Mensch in the 1970s. The model of structure change developed by him connects the dynamics of technological and economic processes influenced by two mutual processes of investment and savings(Troub 1981), which indirectly affects the development of trade, the stimulation of purchasing power and the formation of new trade formats.

The reasons for such "waves" are the need to modernize fixed assets, the emergence of new technologies and industries.

The latter theory led to the conclusion that the economy is most susceptible to innovation during the depression. It is depression that leads to the search for ways to overcome it, which can provide an innovative process (this phenomenon is called the "depression trigger effect") (Troub 1981).

Scientific and technological revolutions are leading to a reassessment of the role of innovation in the development of trade and the economy as a whole. In the modern world, trade players need to look for new ways to survive in the market, they need to build up their competitive advantages. This opportunity is given to them by the digital transformation of trade, namely the development of online stores.

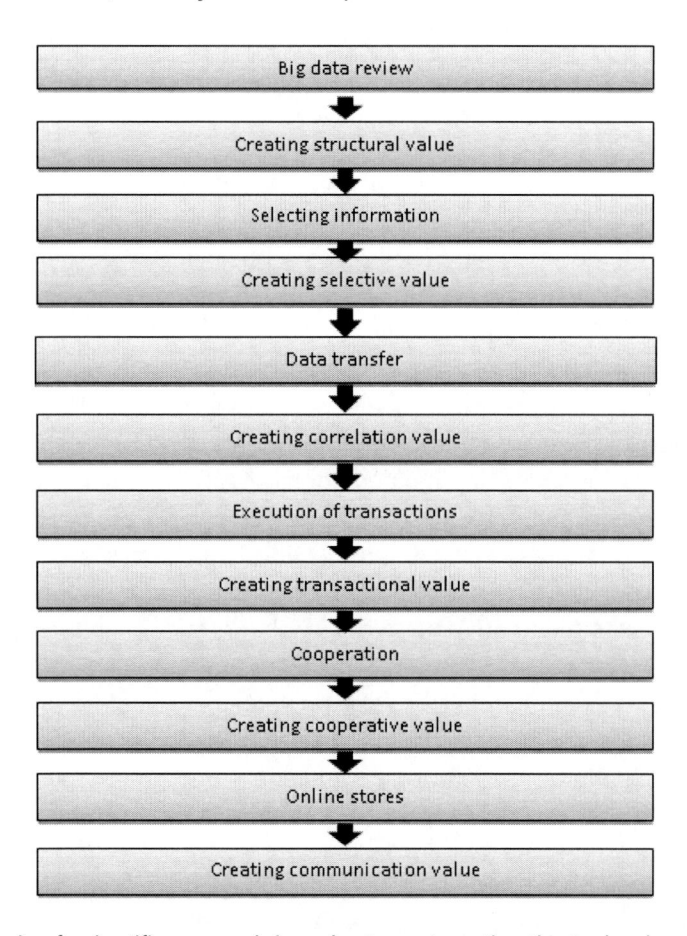

Figure 1. The logic of scientific research in order to systematize the technology of applied research.

The development of online stores contributes to the creation of surplus value through electronic platforms. Electronic offers create electronic surplus value, taking into account the specifics of the enterprise. This allows you to form the logic of scientific research, which can be presented in the form of Figure 1.

In general, electronic platforms are built from three main elements: information, communication and transaction. in order to create individual electronic surplus value for customers, electronic platforms will be needed. Various combinations of electronic surplus value and corresponding electronic platforms are possible. in the network economy, there are electronic supply, electronic store, electronic trading platform, electronic community, electronic company (Kollmann T. 2013).

2.2. Theoretical Foundations

This article is based on information from the following key databases: Scopus, Web of Science, Semantic Scholar, ResearchGate; the reports of the client analysis in federal retail chains conducted by Romir, the largest research holding, specializing in large-scale marketing, cross-media, public, social and economic studies; the data from the official website of the Federal State Statistics Service.

Leading experts of Russian federal retail chains give their opinion on the first results of chains digitalization and its future development. The leading analyst of the international investment company QBF gives a positive assessment of the dynamics and points out that digitalization has covered all processes in retail chains: from operational activities to communication with customers. According to Vashchenko, the head of trade operations department in the Russian stock market at IC Freedom Finance, online stores in retail chains are developing rapidly. This is due to the fact that the costs for developing and building new stores are very high and long-term for pay off. Therefore investing in the development of their websites is much more beneficial for retailers (Asif et al. 2015).

To reach a wider range of customers, trade organizations create online stores through appropriate internet portals as an additional sales channel. Online trading creates conditions for taking advantage of digital transformation by displaying ads and offers tailored to the user's interests, depending on their behavior. online stores usually have a typical design, so customers quickly navigate the structure of the site. The ease of trading operations and access to the services offered make online trading more popular for making purchases. Currently, stationary trading is in a difficult situation, it needs to increase the attractiveness of the offline shopping process. Modern stores should create conditions for comfortable shopping, so that the purchase process creates a good mood and brings pleasure. In order to make customer advice as individual as possible, two areas of development can now be implemented: on the one hand, the increased use of social networks and recommendations from direct customers, and on the other hand, the offer of technological solutions that provide recommendations based on customer behavior and customer profiles in the past and present. Such systems are called recommendation systems (Lund and Manyika 2016).

When creating online stores in addition to stationary outlets, it is important that the sales channels offered to customers are coordinated with each other and thus provide customer support and support. This is known by the terms "omni-channel," "multi-channel," "cross-channel," or "non-linear trading."

This kind of integration into the network is manifested, in particular, in the fact that purchases begin online, and end in offline mode. A full-scale implementation of this process involves identifying the customer in the online store using cookies and fields for login and password can be made relatively simple and already at an early stage of the purchase process, identification in the offline store is made at the end of this process, when the corresponding customer card is used. For example, in an online store, the customer can be provided with individualized information at an early stage, which is not so easy to do in a regular store. However, even here, customer requests go so far that the customer is provided with the most adapted offers and information for him. To realize these opportunities, the digital transformation of the store must be so deep that the individual approach in the form in which it used to take place in small local stores could.

Due to the fact that inexpensive sensors are becoming more advanced, the stationary trading environment will continue to undergo changes in the future. at the same time, sensors and actuators make it possible to port concepts that have already been tried in online trading, such as product selection recommendations or product comparison, to the physical level. at the same time, the advantages of offline trading, which include the social component, can be expanded by digital auxiliary functions. In this regard, it is also important to ensure a direct, individual approach to the client, since mass communication, for example through advertising booklets, has lost its appeal in recent years.

To implement such an individualized approach to the client, it is necessary to collect information about its current context, which can only be done through a networked environment. The collected contextual information can then be processed using individually adapted services and used in adaptive support systems, such as dialog consultants, or to generate context-oriented advertising information.

3. RESULTS

The Federal Law of December 28, 2009 No.381-FZ (amended December 25, 2018) "On the Basics of State Regulation of Trade Activities in the Russian Federation" defines retailing as a type of trading that includes buying and selling goods for private, family, households use, and other purposes not related to entrepreneurial activities. According to this definition, the activity of retail chains is aimed at the end user, and, consequently, the strategy, first of all, is based on the analysis of consumer preferences.

The following factors influence retailers activity: consumer demand, financial solvency, inflation expectations, buyer's intentions and consumption pattern (Prentice, Wang, and Loureiro 2019).

Consumer demand is the main factor not only for the structure of retail trade by product categories, but also for the ways of selling goods to the end consumer.

To save and increase turnover and market share, it is necessary for retail chains to adapt to the changing environment that causes changes in the consumers behavior and preferences.

Figure 2 presents several factors formed by consumers that have led to an increase in e-commerce share in chain stores.

Modern buyer usually does not have much free time for shopping. It is more convenient to choose a good on the Internet and arrange either delivery or customer pickup.

The buyer chooses a good that fully meets his ideas about quality-price ratio. The greatest demand is for goods of the mid-price and economy segment. The prices in the online store are lower than the respective prices in the offline store. This is due to the absence of some costs included in the selling price of the product (for example, store staff salaries, rent, electricity and water supply).

In conditions of heavy traffic and frequent traffic jams, delivery option in an online store is very attractive for buyers. In addition, some buyers do not have their own car, and buying space consuming or heavy goods becomes problematic for them.

The online version of the stores presents the full range of goods that are sold in respective retail chain Retail chains usually divide their suppliers by location. Therefore, range of goods in different shops may vary within one retail chain. E-commerce provides the opportunity for the buyer to choose from a wider range of similar products.

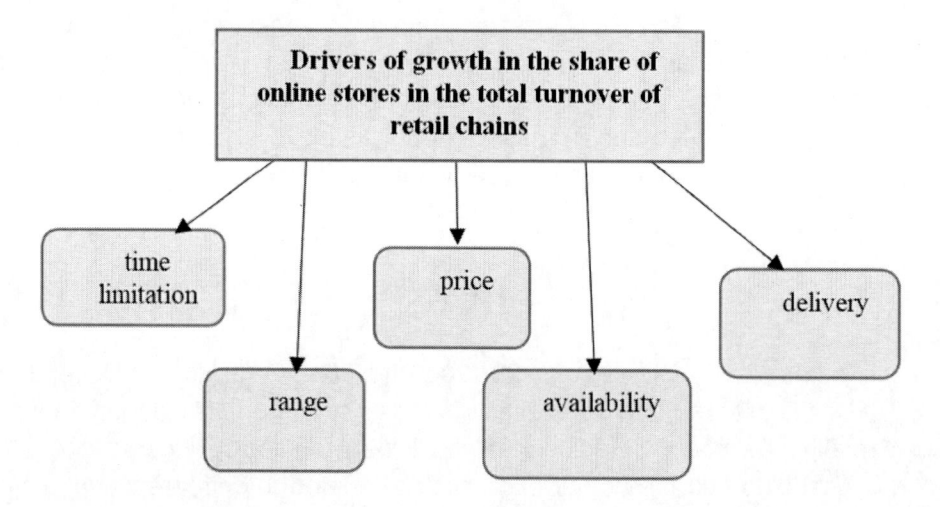

Figure 2. Drivers of growth in the share of online stores in the total turnover of retail chains ("Romir Scan Panel" 2008).

Availability is an important factor for buyers. The full range of goods in the shop is controlled by store staff, who are often not able to understand the store's needs correctly and on time. Delivery of lacking goods takes from three to seven days, and delivery through distribution centers increases this time. E-commerce simplifies this logistic chain, since the warehouse of an online store is much larger than a shop's warehouse, which makes it possible to store more inventories. Besides, there is also an experience of shipping products from the manufacturer himself to the end user directly.

Online stores development is influenced not only by external factors, but by the internal resources of retailers as well. The aim of the trading is to make a profit by increasing either prices or turnover due to the optimization of distribution costs. Reducing the costs for providing services to an individual client allows to minimize the costs of economic activity, as well as maintain attractive prices and, as a result, retain regular customers and attract new ones. E-commerce allows to minimize the risks associated with external factors (for example, the epidemiological situation in the country). Internal drivers of growth of online sales in retail chains are shown in Figure 3:

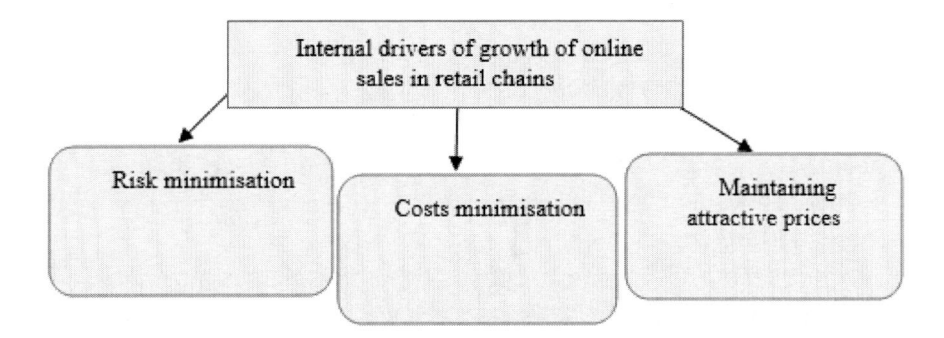

Figure 3. Internal drivers of growth of online sales in retail chains ("Romir Scan Panel" 2008).

Online stores as an exchange for selling goods have their own characteristics that influence business processes in retail chains, are shown in Figure 4:

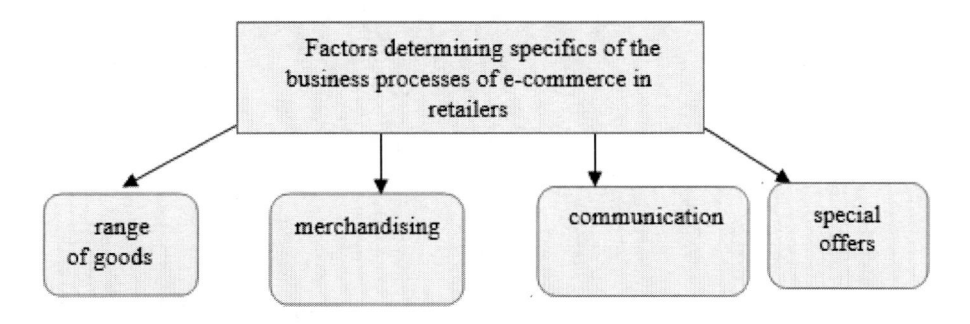

Figure 4. Factors determining specifics of the business processes of e-commerce in retailers ("Romir Scan Panel" 2008).

Due to the fact that a buyer cannot touch a real good when doing online shopping, the main tool to motivate a client to buy is using catalogues and information cards published on the website. They should be full, relevant and up-to date.

In an online store, visualization is a critical factor as it helps the buyer to better orient in the shopping place. Offline stores work carefully with product display, as it is a powerful tool for increasing sales. Shop assistants categorize the goods, taking into consideration priorities. Online stores should be convenient to navigate and designed with a customer in mind.

Online stores do not have the ability to use effective communication as offline stores do (signboards, POS-catalogues, price tags, show windows and leaflets). In this regard, online stores have less effective communication but they can use such communication tools as banners, cross-links, online consultations.

In order to attract as many buyers as possible, online stores should constantly organize advertising campaigns and promotions so that to provide maximum trade information to the buyer.

In order for as many buyers as possible to switch to the "online shopping" mode, the online store must constantly organize advertising campaigns and promotions so that the buyer has the maximum volume of trade information provided.

Customer profile is a set of significant characteristics that helps to identify the target audience, on the basis of which the most interesting content can be chosen.

This is essential since 77% of the buyers perceive content that meets their needs and demands. This means that advertising and links that will pop up when a buyer is in the vastness of an online store must meet the characteristics of the buyer himself: if the bulk of buyers have an average income, then advertising for a product in the middle price segment will work more effectively.

The profile of the end user is an important factor influencing the development strategy of an online store in retail chains.

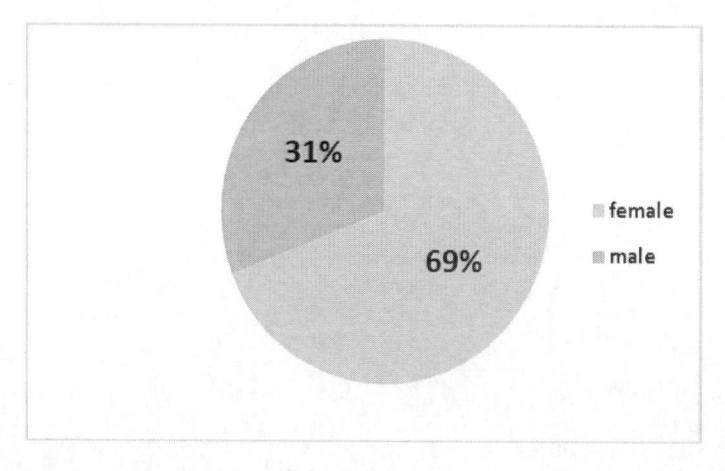

Figure 5. Classification of the customers of online stores in federal chains by gender (Lipiäinen and Karjaluoto 2015).

In April 2019, a field study was conducted, the sample size was more than ten thousand people. The largest federal chains in Russia took part in the survey: Auchan, X5 Retail Group, Leroy Merlin and OBI.

Based on the results of the study of Romir consumer scan panel (2019), we will form a customer profile of online stores of federal chains in Russia.

Figures 5, 6, 7 and 8 present the results of the consumer research by gender, income level, age and family size.

According to Figure 5, more than 50% of the buyers in online stores are women, whereas only 31% of those are men who prefer online service.

Age group is an important element of the customer profile.

According to Figure 6, the majority of the buyers (37%) are aged from 30 to 39 years, and online stores are least popular among youngsters under 19 years.

Another important characteristic of the customer profile is income level, as it determines which price category should be the priority.

There are three groups of income level of the customers: less than RUB 15,000, RUB 15,000- 35,000, and RUB 35,000 and higher).

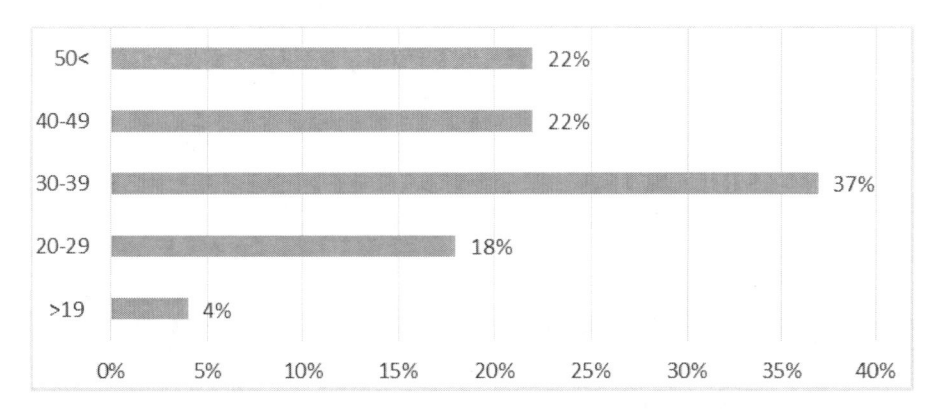

Figure 6. Classification of the customers of online stores in federal chains by age groups (Lipiäinen and Karjaluoto 2015).

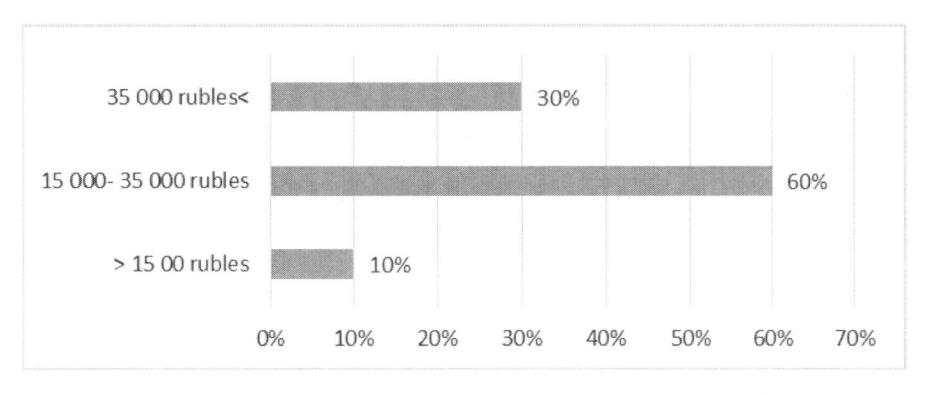

Figure 7. Classification of the customers of online stores in federal chains by income level (Lipiäinen and Karjaluoto 2015).

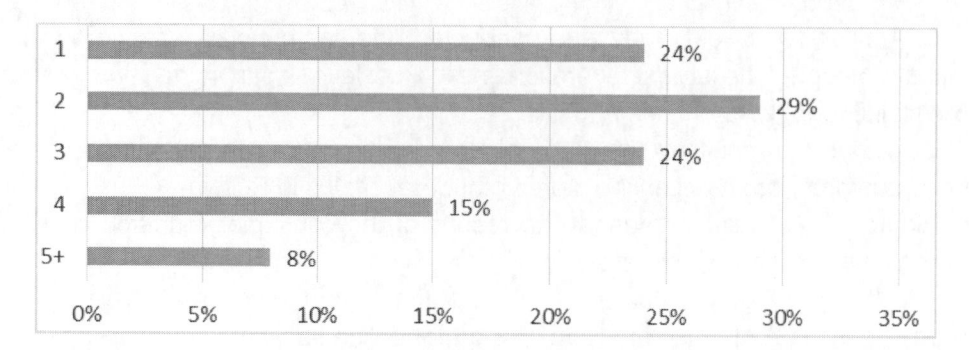

Figure 8. Classification of the customers of online stores in federal chains by family size (Baharev V. V. 2017; Barrot and Sauvagnat 2016).

According to the Romir research scan panel (Figure 7), the majority of the customers who use online stores have an average income level between RUB 15,000 and RUB 35,000 (60%).

The quantity of purchased goods depends on the family size.

The results of the studies presented in Figure 8 show that the majority of people (29%) who purchase goods through online services have two members in their family.

Thus, we can describe our customers as women aged 30-39, with an average income (RUB 15,000-35,000), and their families consist of 2 members.

Based on these indicators, web shops or online stores can choose the content relevant for this category of the customers, which will be an effective tool, since they form the bulk of the sales.

One more important factor in making a purchase is the availability of a device for the customer to make a purchase.

According to Figure 9, we can see that the most popular device is a mobile phone (59.6%), then computers (36.7%), and tablets (3.7%). The website of an online store should be mainly adapted to mobile devices.

The customers of online stores can be categorized by location.

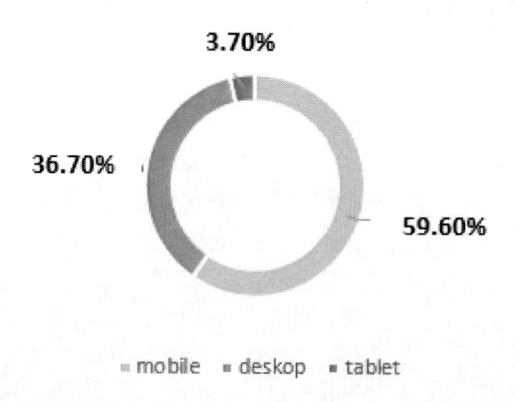

Figure 9. The share of sales of online stores in federal chains according to the device used for 2019 (Bell, Gallino, and Moreno 2018).

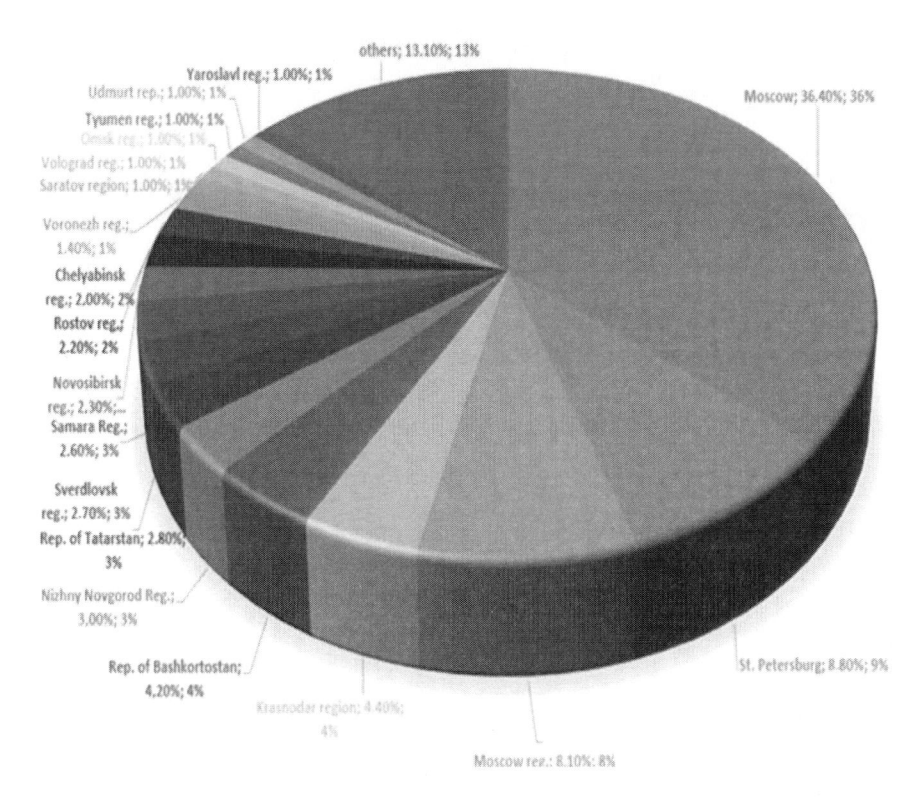

Figure 10. Sales of online stores of federal chains % in 2019 by location (Irina Krasyuk et al. 2019).

According to Figure 10, almost 50% of the total sales of federal retail chains through the online stores belong to Moscow and Moscow region, followed by Saint Petersburg (8.8%).

The share of the other regions is between 2% and 5%.

Such distribution of sales shares between the regions depends on the development of transport and logistics infrastructure, the cost of transport services and low purchasing power in the regions.

In order to objectively assess the dynamics of online stores development in Russian federal chains and determine the opportunities for their further development, it is necessary to analyze such important economic factors as: the share of retail chains in retail trade, the share of sales of retail chains through online stores, and shopping space sufficiency per 1000 people.

Figure 11 shows the dynamics of retail chains turnover in the total retail turnover of the Russian Federation between 2017 and 2019, in%:

Figure 11 shows that the share of retail chains in 2019 increased by 1.5% compared to the previous year, and by 3.5% compared to 2017 (reference year), which is a positive tendency in the development of retail chains in Russia.

Another critical factor is the share of e-commerce in the total turnover.

Next this factor will be considered over 2017-2019 (Figure 12):

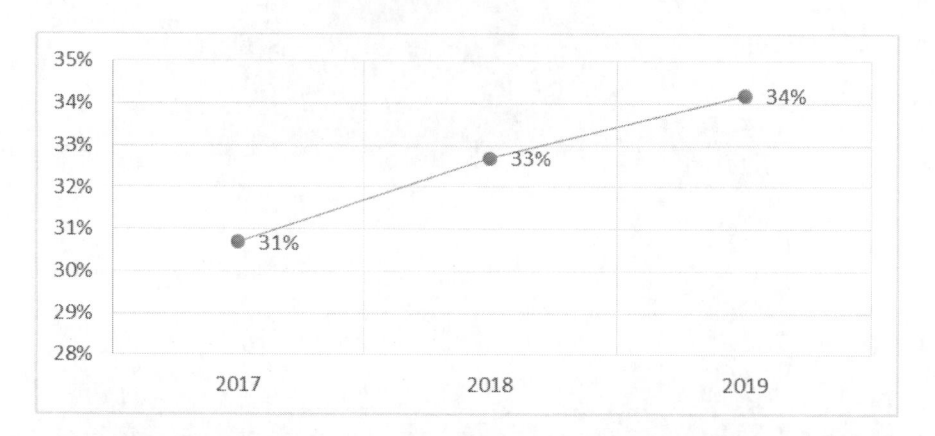

Figure 11. The share of retail chains in retail trade turnover in the Russian Federation in 2017–2019, % (Chang and Taylor 2016; Desfonteines et al. 2019).

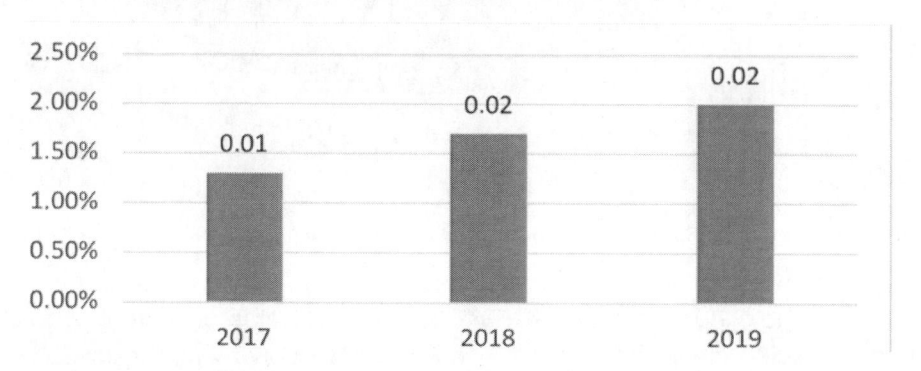

Figure 12. The share of e-commerce in the total turnover of retail chains in 2017-2019, % (Gielens and Gijsbrechts 2018).

The data in Figure 12 shows positive dynamics of the development of online service.

The growth in 2019 was 0.3%.

This may seem an insignificant increase. However, only over the second quarter of 2020 this value increased by almost one and a half times.

The positive dynamics is due to the epidemiological situation in the country, which has shown the importance of e-commerce, starting from the second quarter of 2020.

It is also worth considering the sufficiency of modern shopping space for the population.

Data for the period of 2014-2019 is presented in Figure 13.

This factor should be considered exactly in such a time span.

According to Figure 13, there was a significant increase in the commissioning of new shopping space by retailers from 2014 to 2016: the indicator increased by 16%.

But as from 2017, the growth rate of new space commissioning began to decrease.

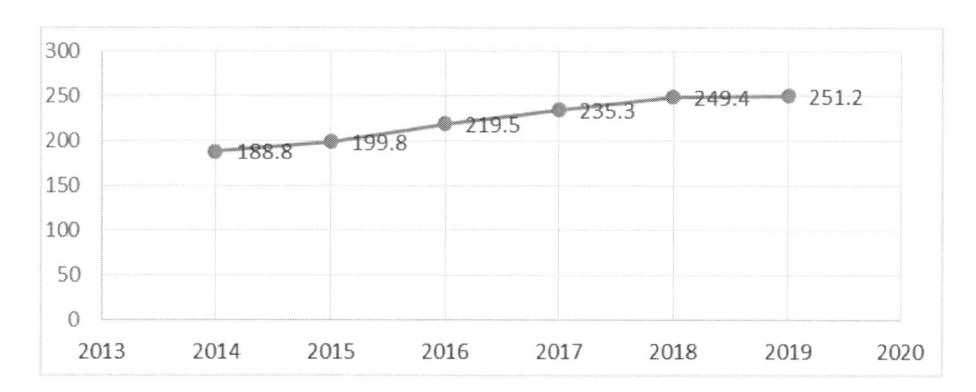

Figure 13. Sufficiency of modern shopping space for the population (per 1000 people, sq. M.) 2014-2019 (Irina Krasyuk, Yanenko, and Nazarova 2020; Goodyer 2012; Graef 2015; Guyt and Gijsbrechts 2014).

In conclusion, nowadays commissioning of new space is decreasing, which is reflected by the factor of sufficiency of shopping space for the population, the share of e-commerce in retail chains is increasing and is becoming a powerful tool for trading at minimal costs (Kazakova K. V. 2014; Chkalova O. 2018; I. Krasyuk and Medvedeva 2019).

4. DISCUSSION

This article examines the consumer goods market of federal retail chains in Russia, evaluates its development with using online shop. The research shows that online stores are one of the leading trends in digitalization of trade(Donaldson 2018).

Retail chains are leaders in the implementation of innovations, in particular, they are actively developing online trading. The work of retail chains is also of interest because they occupy the largest share in the structure of the country's total turnover: in 2019 - 34.20% of the total retail market.

The development and implementation of online stores of retail trade chains has a great information potential, in addition, it is a powerful tool for increasing turnover while minimizing enterprise costs. Despite the fact that the share of online stores is gaining momentum rather slowly (due to the unpreparedness of the Russian market and poor development of logistics supply chains), taking into account the slowdown in the commissioning of new retail space (growth in 2019 decreased by 5% compared to the growth of 2018), in 2020 this indicator will give a significant increase (Fost and Fost 2014; Ianenko, Stepanov, et al. 2019).

According to experts in the field of economics and trade, several factors influence the chain's online stores: time constraints, price, delivery, availability of goods and assortment. Nowadays our life is limited in time and it is sometimes difficult for a buyer to find time to visit a store. Online store services easily solve this problem - the online store has a full range of goods in the required quantity, it is enough to allocate a few minutes to select and place an order, and delivery can be arranged directly to work or home at the required time. In addition, the sale of goods and services through online stores helps chains save money: some cost items (rent of premises, salaries of consultant managers, payments for electricity and water supply) are canceled out. In the context of modern realities, price competition prevails over all other types of competition, and the client, in most cases, chooses products among similar ones, relying on the price factor, taking into account the price-quality ratio. For getting maximum effect, the content of the online store should be customer-oriented.

This is possible due to marketing research and building a client portrait. In April 2019, a field study was conducted, the sample size was more than ten thousand people. The largest federal chains in Russia took part in the survey: Auchan, X5 Retail Group, Leroy Merlin and OBI. More than 10,000 respondents took part in the survey, and as the analysis of the results showed, more than 50% of the respondents are women aged 30-39 with an average income (15,000-30,000 rubles), who have 2 people in their family (Khosiev et al. 2019; Helal 2019; Kotier and Zaltman 1996; Lukyanov and Drapkin 2017).

Thus, the design of the site, the promotion tools used, should be correlated with the buyer who most often turns to the online store: advertising and links should meet the main characteristics of the target segment. This is essential since 77% of the buyers perceive content that meets their needs and demands (Lyamin and Krasyuk 2019; Nilova and Malyutenkova 2020; Nilova et al. 2019).

Digitalization currently covers all spheres of human activity, trade is no exception. To be viable and competitive, retail chains are forced to adjust to changing external conditions and keep pace with the times.

Otherwise, they risk, as once small forms of business, come to naught.

Online stores of retail trade chains are a powerful tool for the development of trade, increasing turnover and minimizing risks and costs, therefore they have a huge potential for development and are the leading trend in digitalization in general (Nolan 2020).

CONCLUSION

In the modern world, with the development of a new technological order, digitalization of trade is a necessary condition for further development, since it affects all areas of activity and, in particular, the trade sector. With the development and implementation of digitalization, the "traditional" type of trade is gradually being replaced by digital forms. The most visible digital transformation of trade business processes is online commerce. A large share of the total retail trade turnover in Russia is occupied by retail chains, for which flexibility and quick response to changing external conditions are the key factors that determine their level of competitiveness. That is why federal chains act as "leaders" in adapting digital processes to their activities and direct resources to the development of their online stores (Ianenko, Ianenko, et al. 2019; Ogonowski et al. 2014; Purdy and Daugherty 2017).

E-commerce in retail chains of Russia is gaining momentum. It is becoming a powerful tool for increasing turnover and minimizing costs and expenses.

The development of online stores of retail chains is influenced by such consumer-related factors as: time limitation, price, range, availability of goods and delivery. Apart from the factors that are determined by the buyer, the development of online services is also influenced by the internal factors of the chains that determine whether they concern over the development of this tool, such as minimizing risks, reducing costs and supporting competitive prices.

Online stores have their own aspects that are determined by the range, merchandising, communications and promotions. Online stores cannot use traditional methods of merchandising, forming range and promotions that are effectively used by offline stores, and should also carefully work on the online patterns and systems of communication with the customers since online stores have no possibility of live consultations.

The online stores of the chains have their own target audience: women aged 30-39, with an average income (RUB 15,000-35,000), whose families consist of 2 members. Online stores use customer profile analysis to form selling content that will satisfy the customer and therefore increase the sales (Sanovich 2019; Sidorova 2018; Strekalova, Korchagina, and Desfonteines 2020).

The share of retail chains in the total retail turnover of the Russian Federation is increasing along with the share of online stores in the structure of sales of retail chains. Despite the fact that traditional stores have also developed, the analysts showed that this growth is slowing down while online shopping is growing fast.

The significance of online stores can hardly be overestimated. Experts agree that the future of trade is focused on the development of e-commerce. It allows retail chains to minimize costs and reduce expenses, which makes it possible to support prices at a competitive level. Price is one of the most important factors for a buyer when choosing a product: a low price level helps the chains to maintain customer loyalty and attract new customers, which directly affects turnover and profits, which is the main target of any business ("The Expert Council Presented Its Vision of the Concept of the 'Digital Economy' Program. Official Website of the Open Government" 2017).

REFERENCES

Abdolmaleki, Kaveh, and Sahar Ahmadian. 2016. "The Relationship between Product Characteristics, Customer and Supplier Involvement and New Product Development." *Procedia Economics and Finance* 36: 147–56. https://doi.org/10.1016/s2212-5671(16)30026-0.

Amit, Raphael, and Christoph Zott. 2001. "Value Creation in E-Business." *Strategic Management Journal* 22 (6–7): 493–520. https://doi.org/10.1002/smj.187.

Asif, Farazee M. A., Amir Rashid, Carmine Bianchi, and Cornel M. Nicolescu. 2015. "System Dynamics Models for Decision Making in Product Multiple Lifecycles."

Resources, Conservation and Recycling 101: 20–33. https://doi.org/10.1016/j.resconrec.2015.05.002.

Baharev V. V., Nekrasov S. S. 2017. "MARKETING OF INNOVATIVE ACTIVITIES OF RETAIL TRADE ENTERPRISES." *Practical Marketing*, no. 1-2 (240-1): 5–8.

Barrot, Jean Noël, and Julien Sauvagnat. 2016. "Input Specificity and the Propagation of Idiosyncratic Shocks in Production Networks." *Quarterly Journal of Economics* 131 (3): 1543–92. https://doi.org/10.1093/qje/qjw018.

Bell, David R., Santiago Gallino, and Antonio Moreno. 2018. "Offline Showrooms in Omnichannel Retail: Demand and Operational Benefits." *Management Science* 64 (4): 1629–51. https://doi.org/10.1287/mnsc.2016.2684.

Bhatnagar, Amit, and Siddhartha S. Syam. 2014. "Allocating a Hybrid Retailer's Assortment across Retail Stores: Bricks-and-Mortar vs Online." *Journal of Business Research* 67 (6): 1293–1302. https://doi.org/10.1016/j.jbusres.2013.03.003.

Chang, Woojung, and Steven A. Taylor. 2016. "The Effectiveness of Customer Participation in New Product Development: A Meta-Analysis." *Journal of Marketing* 80 (1): 47–64. https://doi.org/10.1509/jm.14.0057.

Chkalova O., Tikhonov S. 2018. "Corporate Events to Develop Employees' Higher Cognitive, Social and Emotional Skills and Disseminate Values of Social Responsibility and Sustainability." *7th International Conference on Social Responsibility, Ethics and Sustainable Business* 7: 44–45.

Desfonteines, Larisa, Elena Korchagina, Andrei Varnaev, and Julia Semenova. 2019. "Organizational Culture of Trade Enterprises in the Context of Modern Demographic Challenges and Applying Information Technologies." *IOP Conference Series: Materials Science and Engineering* 497 (1). https://doi.org/10.1088/1757-899X/497/1/012117.

Donaldson, Dave. 2018. "Railroads of the Raj: Estimating the Impact of Transportation Infrastructure." *American Economic Review* 108 (4–5): 899–934. https://doi.org/10.1257/aer.20101199.

Fost, Markus, and Markus Fost. 2014. "Handelsstrukturen von Produzierenden Unternehmen [Trade structures of manufacturing companies]." In *E-Commerce-Strategien Für Produzierende Unternehmen*, 33–51. https://doi.org/10.1007/978-3-658-04988-1_3.

Gielens, Katrijn, and Els Gijsbrechts. 2018. *Handbook of Research on Retailing*. *Handbook of Research on Retailing*. https://doi.org/10.4337/9781786430281.

Goodyer, J. 2012. "On Thin Ice." *Engineering and Technology* 7 (11): 44–47. https://doi.org/10.1049/et.2012.1110.

Graef, Inge. 2015. "Market Definition and Market Power in Data: The Case of Online Platforms." *SSRN Electronic Journal* 38 (4): 473–505. https://doi.org/10.2139/ssrn.2657732.

Guyt, Jonne Y., and Els Gijsbrechts. 2014. "Take Turns or March in Sync? The Impact of the National Brand Promotion Calendar on Manufacturer and Retailer

Performance." *Journal of Marketing Research.* https://doi.org/10.1509/jmr.
14.0193.

Helal, Guida. 2019. *"Social Media, Online Brand Communities, and Customer Engagement in the Fashion Industry."* In: https://doi.org/10.4018/978-1-5225-7344-9.ch007.

Hong, Taeho, and Eunmi Kim. 2012. "Segmenting Customers in Online Stores Based on Factors That Affect the Customer's Intention to Purchase." In *Expert Systems with Applications*, 39:2127–31. https://doi.org/10.1016/j.eswa.2011.07.114.

Ianenko, Marina, Mikhail Ianenko, Dmitriy Huhlaev, and Oksana Martynenko. 2019. "Digital Transformation of Trade: Problems and Prospects of Marketing Activities." In *IOP Conference Series: Materials Science and Engineering.* Vol. 497. https://doi.org/10.1088/1757-899X/497/1/012118.

Ianenko, Marina, Mikhail Ianenko, Tatyana Kirillova, Svetlana Amakhina, and Natalya Nikitina. 2020. "Digital Transformation Strategies of Trade Enterprises: Key Areas, Development and Implementation Algorithms." In *IOP Conference Series: Materials Science and Engineering.* Vol. 940. https://doi.org/10.1088/1757-899X/940/1/012051.

Ianenko, Marina, Mikhail Ianenko, Liubov Mironova, Victoriia Ivanova, and Vladimir Bakharev. 2020. "Innovative Digital Technologies in the Concept Development of Brand Equity Management." In *IOP Conference Series: Materials Science and Engineering.* Vol. 940. https://doi.org/10.1088/1757-899X/940/1/012054.

Ianenko, Marina, Mikhail Stepanov, Mikhail Ianenko, and Svetlana Iliashenko. 2019. "Peculiarities of Product Policy in the Internet of Things." In *IOP Conference Series: Materials Science and Engineering.* https://doi.org/10.1088/1757-899X/497/1/012119.

Ianenko, Marina, Mikhail Stepanov, and Liubov Mironova. 2020. "Brand Identity Development." In *E3S Web of Conferences.* https://doi.org/10.1051/e3sconf/202016409015.

Kapustina, Irina, Tatiana Pereverzeva, Tatiana Stepanova, and Iuliia Rusu. 2019. "Convergence of Institutes of Retail Traditional and Digital Economy." In *IOP Conference Series: Materials Science and Engineering.* https://doi.org/10.1088/1757-899X/497/1/012120.

Kazakova K. V., Pushilin D. V. 2014. "Prospects for the Development of E-Commerce." *Basic Research* 12 (9): 1968–72.

Khosiev, Boris N., Gamlet Y. Ostaev, Gregory R. Kontsevoy, Aleksandr N. Suetin, Vyacheslav A. Sokolov, Petr V. Antonov, and Sergey N. Suetin. 2019. "Development of a Brand Promotion Strategy: Management Accounting and Comprehensive Analysis." *Indo American Journal of Pharmaceutical Sciences* 6 (5): 10060–68.

Kollmann T. 2013. *"E-Business"* 5 (Auflage).

———. 2014. "E-Entrepreneurship." *Springer Gabler* 5 (Auflage).

Kotier, Philip, and Gerald Zaltman. 1996. "Social Marketing: An Approach to Planned Social Change." *Social Marketing Quarterly* 3 (3–4): 7–20. https://doi.org/10.1080/15245004.1996.9960973.

Krasyuk, I., and Y. Medvedeva. 2019. "Resource Support in Business Analytics of Innovative Development of Trade and Technological Systems." In *Proceedings of the 33rd International Business Information Management Association Conference, IBIMA 2019: Education Excellence and Innovation Management through Vision 2020.*

Krasyuk, Irina, Yulia Medvedeva, Vladimir Baharev, and Grigory Chargaziya. 2019. "Evolution of Strategies of Retail and Technological Systems under Broad Digitalization Conditions." *IOP Conference Series: Materials Science and Engineering* 497 (1). https://doi.org/10.1088/1757-899X/497/1/012124.

Krasyuk, Irina, Marina Yanenko, and Elmira Nazarova. 2020. "Conceptual and Strategic Framework for the Digitalization of Modern Retail as Part of Innovative Marketing." *E3S Web of Conferences* 164. https://doi.org/10.1051/e3sconf/202016409006.

Lipiäinen, Heini Sisko Maarit, and Heikki Karjaluoto. 2015. "Industrial Branding in the Digital Age." *Journal of Business and Industrial Marketing* 30 (6): 733–41. https://doi.org/10.1108/JBIM-04-2013-0089.

Lo, Louis Yi Shih, Sheng Wei Lin, and Li Yi Hsu. 2016. "Motivation for Online Impulse Buying: A Two-Factor Theory Perspective." *International Journal of Information Management* 36 (5): 759–72. https://doi.org/10.1016/j.ijinfomgt.2016.04.012.

Lukyanov, Sergei A., and Igor M. Drapkin. 2017. "Global Value Chains: Effects for Integrating Economy." *World Economy and International Relations* 61 (4): 16–25. https://doi.org/10.20542/0131-2227-2017-61-4-16-25.

Lund, Susan, and James Manyika. 2016. "How Digital Trade Is Transforming Globalisation." *E15Initiative. Geneva: International Centre for Trade and Sustainable Development (ICTSD) and World Economic Forum*, no. January.

Lyamin, B. M., and I. A. Krasyuk. 2019. "Features of Investing in Innovative Projects in Actual Economic Conditions." In *Smart Innovation, Systems and Technologies*, 139:388–97. https://doi.org/10.1007/978-3-030-18553-4_49.

Moon, Paul J. 2015. "Brand." *American Journal of Hospice and Palliative Medicine* 32 (1): 119. https://doi.org/10.1177/1049909113501853.

Nilova, Liudmila, and Svetlana Malyutenkova. 2020. "Challenges and Opportunities for Promoting Functional Foods in E-Commerce." In *E3S Web of Conferences*. Vol. 164. https://doi.org/10.1051/e3sconf/202016409012.

Nilova, Liudmila, Svetlana Malyutenkova, Sergey Chunin, and Natalia Naumenko. 2019. "IOT in the Development of Information Support of Food Products for Healthy Nutrition." *IOP Conference Series: Materials Science and Engineering* 497 (1). https://doi.org/10.1088/1757-899X/497/1/012112.

Nolan, Emma. 2020. "Modifying the Conceptual Model of Site Selection in the Organisation of Association Conferences." *Journal of Convention and Event Tourism*, 1–20. https://doi.org/10.1080/15470148.2020.1810188.

Ogonowski, Andrzej, Andrew Montandon, Elsamari Botha, and Mignon Reyneke. 2014. "Should New Online Stores Invest in Social Presence Elements? The Effect of Social Presence on Initial Trust Formation." *Journal of Retailing and Consumer Services* 21 (4): 482–91. https://doi.org/10.1016/j.jretconser.2014.03.004.

Prentice, Catherine, Xuequn Wang, and Sandra Maria Correia Loureiro. 2019. "The Influence of Brand Experience and Service Quality on Customer Engagement." *Journal of Retailing and Consumer Services* 50 (May): 50–59. https://doi.org/ 10.1016/j.jretconser.2019.04.020.

Purdy, Mark, and Paul Daugherty. 2017. "How AI Boosts Industry Profits and Innovation." *Accenture*, 1–28.

Roggeveen, Anne L., and Raj Sethuraman. 2020. "Customer-Interfacing Retail Technologies in 2020 & Beyond: An Integrative Framework and Research Directions." *Journal of Retailing* 96 (3): 299–309. https://doi.org/10.1016/j.jretai. 2020.08.001.

"*Romir Scan Panel.*" 2008. 2008.

Sanovich, Sergey CN-HM742. 2019. "Russia : The Origins of Digital Misinformation." In *Computational Propaganda: Political Parties, Politicians, and Political Manipulation on Social Media.*

Sidorova, Elena A. 2018. "Russia in Global Value Chains." *World Economy and International Relations* 62 (9): 71–80. https://doi.org/10.20542/0131-2227-2018-62-9-71-80.

Strekalova, Natalia, Elena Korchagina, and Larisa Desfonteines. 2020. "Features of Consumer Behavior of Russian Tourists in Duty-Free Shops." *E3S Web of Conferences* 09020 (164). https://doi.org/10.1051/e3sconf /202016409020.

"*The Expert Council Presented Its Vision of the Concept of the 'Digital Economy' Program. Official Website of the Open Government.*" 2017. 2017.

Troub, Roger M. 1981. "Stalemate in Technology: Innovations Overcome the Depression." *Journal of Economic Issues* 15 (3): 806–8. https://doi.org/10.1080/ 00213624.1981.11503897.

Wang, Kitty, and Avi Goldfarb. 2017. "Can Offline Stores Drive Online Sales?" *Journal of Marketing Research* 54 (5): 706–19. https://doi.org/10.1509/jmr.14.0518.

Chapter 21

THE DIGITAL COMMUNICATIONS STRATEGY DEVELOPMENT AS A FACTOR OF THE BRAND IDENTITY PROMOTION

Marina Yanenko[1,*], Mikhail Stepanov[1,†], Liubov Mironova[1,‡],
Karina Kkhalaf[2,§] and Ryszard Pukala[3,∥]

[1]St. Petersburg State University of Industrial Technologies and Design, Saint-Petersburg, Russia
[2]VELTORF LLC, St. Petersburg, Russia
[3]The Bronislav Markiewicz State Higher School of Technology and Economics, Jaroslav, Poland

ABSTRACT

The article analyzes the role of brand identity within the trade and retail sector expressed in increasing the brand equity and subsequent market value. The current conditions and the expanding the application of digital technologies set new requirements for the trading firms' promotion, so the aim of the study is to form a theoretical framework for development of the digital communication strategy that will allow the firms effectively interact with customers in the long term. Therefore, in the article the authors consider the concept of the brand identity which is the semantic foundation of the firms' promotional activities andthe primary factor in uniting communication messages into a single consistent approach, highlight the

---

* Corresponding Author's Email: yanenko_57@mail.ru.
† Corresponding Author's Email: michail.stepanov@gmail.com.
‡ Corresponding Author's Email: obrazts@gmail.com.
§ Corresponding Author's Email: k.khalaf@veltorf.com.
∥ Corresponding Author's Email: ryszard.pukala@interia.pl.

need for effective communication of the brand to the target audience. They reveal the interrelation and mutual influence of the digital communications and the effective promotion of brand identity, the effects on the formation of the loyal customer base and the brand equity, give the characteristics for the main digital communication tools, formulate the principles and present an algorithm for the digital communications strategy development and implementation. This work provides the theoretical foundations for further research related to the study of the digital communications effectiveness in terms of attracting and retaining consumers and increasing the brand equity.

Keywords: brand management, brand identity, promotion, digital marketing tools, brand equity, integrated marketing communications, communication strategy, digital communications

1. INTRODUCTION

Branding is an important activity that has a direct impact on the financial results of organizations. Its role is important in almost all business sectors, however especially so in the highly competitive retail sector which requires constant attraction and retention of customers, employees, suppliers and interaction with other stakeholders. In the trade sector, the brand builds long-term lasting relationships with consumers which forms the basis for the future steady growth of the organization, the possibility of further market extension and profit growth. The development of digital technologies has determined the necessity of new approaches to more efficient interaction of trading firms with their customers and partners using new communication tools. In today's branding, digital communications are becoming the main instrument for enhancing the brand's equity, expressed in terms of brand loyalty, brand awareness, association, perceived quality, related associations, and other assets that contribute to the growth of its market value.

However, despite the wide scientific and practical interest in digital communications, there is still a significant shortcoming of works devoted to their effective usage for the brand identity promotion especially in the trade and retail sector.

This study aims to provide a theoretical framework for the development of a digital communications strategy in order to promote the brand identity more effectively in today's digital world.

To achieve this goal, the authors have analyzed the concept of the brand identity, identified its effects on the brand equity, investigated the relationship and formulated the tasks of digital communications in its promotion and presented an algorithm for the digital communications strategy development.

2. MATERIALS AND METHODS

2.1. Literature Review

The most important aspect of the brand creation is the development of its essence, main idea, design and semantic concept – its identity. The problem of brand identity development has been studied in the works in the scientific works of Aaker (USA), Kapferer (France), Kotler (USA), de Chernatoney (UK), Lambin (France), Pförtsch (Germany), Wheeler(de Chernatony 1999; D. Aaker 1996; D. A. Aaker 2012; Kapferer 2009; Kotler and Pförtsch 2010; Lambin et al. 2012; Wheeler 2009).These works allow to form the conceptual understanding of that term. In modern marketing, brand identity is concept, made up of a unique set of brand associations, ideas, messages and values that developers aspire to create or maintain. There are a variety of complementary approaches to defining the term of brand identity.

Kapferer, who first proposed the concept of brand identity in 1986, characterizes it as the key concept in brand management and defines it as a system of features and qualities of the brand, which ensure its identification and differentiation (Kapferer 2009). According to Aaker, brand identity can be presented as a unique combination of brand associations that the brand developers want to create (D. Aaker 1996). DeChernatonypresents identity as "character, goals and values that reflects the unique differentiation of a brand" (de Chernatony and McDonald 2012). A clear, distinct identity can be considered one of the key traits of an outstanding brand.

Nowadays it is a necessity for trade and retail organizations to build the relationships with their customers and it starts with creating the brand identity. Trade and retail sector has its peculiarities. Different aspects of the effective performance of the organizations in the trade and retail sphere was studied by Krasyuk andNazarova (Krasyuk, Yanenko, and Nazarova 2020), Medvedeva, Baharev and Chargaziya (Krasyuk, Medvedeva, and Baharev 2019), Ianenko et al. (Ianenko, Ianenko, et al. 2019), Stepanov andIliashenko (Ianenko, Stepanov, et al. 2019). The mentioned works discover the features of the activities of the trade organizations and help to take them into account when forming the brand identity.Brand identity helps retailers to differentiate from competitors, to build relationships with customers based on shared values, to set high prices, toeffectively cooperate with different stakeholders including partners and suppliers (Baldwin 2017; Burt and Davies 2010; Sääksjärvi and Samiee 2011).

At the same time, it is not enough to form an attractive brand identity; it is also necessary to break through the "wall of information noise" to get the attention of potential customers, while maintaining the principle of economic expediency and not over inflating the communication budget, to encourage interested individuals to buy and eventually, to transfer random customers into the loyal audience, and relationships with them into long-term productive cooperation. All these tasks cannot be realized without reasonable, constant, organized and carefully planned marketing communications, in which digital tools have acquired significant weight and influence.

All communications of an organization should be unified. Following the concept of Integrated Marketing Communications (IMC) is an essential condition for the effective promotion of the brand identity (Šerić, Ozretić-Došen, and Škare 2020). The concept of IMC was proposed in the early 1990s in the works by Schultz (Keller et al. 2016)and later it was developed in the works of Moriarty (Duncan and Moriarty 1998a), Duncan (Duncan and Moriarty 1998b), Newsom (Newsom 1998), Kliatchko (Kliatchko 2005) and others (Blakeman 2006; Kitchen and de Pelsmacker 2004; Schultz, Patti, and Kitchen 2013; Blech and Blech 2008; Madhavaram, Badrinarayanan, and McDonald 2005).These authors laid the foundation for a modern integrated approach to promotion. Many modern researchers emphasize on its exceptional relevance in the current conditions of the digital technologies' development (Chaihanchanchai and Anantachart 2019; Percy and Percy 2018; Abashidze 2017; Essamri, McKechnie, and Winklhofer 2019; Madhavaram, Badrinarayanan, and McDonald 2005).

Integrated Marketing Communications represents an approach to promotional activities aimed at achieving the synergy effect by means of strategic, systematic planning of communications, the unity and consistency of the messages to customers, the coordination of tools used in order influence both the end-users and various stakeholders of the organization as well as its own employees. One of the most important features of today's IMC, which has been greatly enriched by the introduction of digital technologies, is that they actively engage with consumers and stakeholders and encourage focused dialogue with them on the basis of databases (Sellahvarzi and Mirabi 2014; Madhavaram, Badrinarayanan, and McDonald 2005). It is noteworthy that despite the changes in society caused by the development of technologies, the transition to electronic paperwork, the emergence of social media and their popularity with the major part of society, most scientific papers emphasize the exceptional compliance of IMC with the current market situation, the effectiveness of the integrated approach for the brand identity promotion and the tendency to increasing engagement with the customers for better communication strategy implementation.

The importance of the IMC has increased due to introduction of the new media and digital communications. Despite the fact that digital communications can be used in the implementation of any element of the marketing mix (product; price; place; promotion) in that article we consider on their promotional function. In the framework of promotion, the tasks of digital communications can be identified as: attracting customers attention; strengthening brand awareness; generating sales; increasing conversion; building relationships with consumers; collecting feedback and the others. Despite all of these diverse marketing communication tasks, according to a number of studies, increasing brand awareness is considered as a more important task than immediate sales increases. Moreover, this statement applies to both the B2C and the B2B spheres [32–40].

The active development of digital communications has been reflected in the numerous scientific papers devoted to various aspects of their implementation, such as the works of Ianenko et al. (Ianenko, Stepanov, and Mironova 2020), Teresa, Flávio and Rare (Teresa and Tiago 2012), Ivanov (Eugenia 2012), Oancea and Mihaela

(Olimpia and Mihaela 2015), Kailani (Kailani 2012), Chinedu,IOgba and Emeka (Ogbonnaya, Ogba, and Emeka 2020).

2.2. Theoretical Fundamentals

The development of digital technologies has also affected the marketing communications mix. Initially it consisted of five major elements: advertising, public relations, sales promotion, personal selling, direct marketing. In the modern interpretations of the promotion mix the digital communications are included as a separate independent element.

Within the framework of the IMC concept, the communication activities should be built in accordance with the overall marketing strategy and aimed at achieving marketing targets. At the same time there are a wide range of tools inside any of the elements. The tools used within an element must also be coordinated in a mutually complementary way to cause the synergy effect.

Despite the relevance of the integrated approach in planning of digital communications, there are still particular issues that should be taken into account while developing the digital communications strategy. One of the most important issues is the engagement with the customers which leads to the emergence of the "non-linear marketing" concept and in turn the integration of the brand into the consumers' digital environment and their everyday life (Fraccastoro, Gabrielsson, and Bolman 2020; Rangaswamy et al. 2020).

The key difference between "new media" and traditional communication channels is the ability to conduct bilateral communication through digital technologies. This "two-way" nature of digital communications allows for the establishment of a dialogue between the brand and its potential buyer to create the emotional connection with customers and to allow building long-term cooperation with them.It means they have strategic orientation and implies the digital marketing communications strategy development.

Digital marketing communications can be considered as an element of digital marketing that is a part of traditional marketing (Keller et al. 2016; Fraccastoro, Gabrielsson, and Bolman 2020). Digital marketing is a component of the marketing area focused on promoting and selling goods and services using digital communication channels at all stages of interaction with the customers (Abashidze 2017).

It can be explained as an integrated use of information channels in the virtual space to support the company's marketing activities aimed at generating profit and retaining customers through recognition of the strategic importance of digital technologies and developing an integrated approach to improving the representation of online services in order to best meet the needs of customers and raise and awareness of the company and brand (Batra and Keller 2016).

Digital marketing channels include all technology that can transmit information digitally. In addition to the Internet it includes digital television, local networks, cable networks, mobile devices and interactive displays. All these methods can be used in building brand in the trade and retail sector by means of conveying the brand identity essence.

It is important to understand that different tools are used to perform different tasks as part of the promotion. Table 1 presents the characteristics and potential tasks that a tool can solve.

Table 1. Digital communications tools features

Digital communication tools	Characteristics	Tasks
Website	an internet resource used to provide extended background information about an organization, its brands, products and services	• integration and unification of the used digital tools • delivering messages • promotion of goods • building relationships with stakeholders
Landing page	a webpage focused on collecting the contact data of the target audience	• conversion of visitors into buyers • persuading visitors to take action by completing a transaction in the online trade
Search engine optimization	various techniques which are aimed at increasing the visibility of the website to web search engine users	• increasing conversion rates • corporate website promotion
Web application (or web app)	an application software that provide interaction with the web server and stores data on the server, regardless of its operating system	• sales promotion through push-notification, special programs, discounts and promotions • getting feedback • strengthening loyalty
Online advertising (display ads, search ads, ads in social media apps and mobile ads)	a form of advertising which uses digital technologies to deliver promotional messages to customers	• the attraction of customers' attention • delivering messages • promotion of goods, benefits, values and associations of a brand • raising brand awareness • explanation of product's features • updating needs • sales promotion
Social media marketing	the usage of social platforms for business purposes. Organization and maintenance of company's own communities, corporate blogs, podcasts on different platforms.	• gaining the attention of the target audience • increasing brand awareness • promotion of the brand identity • building relationships with customers

Digital communication tools	Characteristics	Tasks
Dealing with feedback	getting information directly from consumers to improve the service, assortment and performance of a firm in general	• complaint management • increasing brand loyalty • marketing research • improving internal processes
Cooperation with influencers (influencer Marketing)	addressing the target audience through the person who has their credit of trust	• increasing brand awareness • promotion of the key elements of the brand identity • ingraining brand associations into the minds of their target audience
Co-creation	engaging the target audience in the product design process;	• existing product development • new product development • combining target audience coverage
Messaging apps	direct communication with customers through messages	• attracting and nurturing new leads • supplying relevant information • answering questions • converting leads into paying customers • building relationships with clients
Content marketing	an activity focused on creating, publishing and distributing actual and interesting information for the targeted audience online	• attracting attention and generate leads • expanding the customer base • generating or increasing online sales • promoting brand identity • increasing brand awareness • engaging an online community of users • building reputation • displaying professionalism and showing company's competence
Email direct marketing	sending direct commercial messages to potential and actual customers	• direct appeal to the customer • sales promotion • updating needs • supplying relevant information about special offers • maintaining relationships
Organizing and conducting webinars	special online events aimed at building relationships with customers and encouraging them to buy	• updating needs • sales promotion • building relationships • developing reputation • displaying professionalism and showing company's competence

There are certain principles that should be considered while forming digital communication mix. The principles and their features presented in the Table 2 below.

Table 2.The digital communications mix formation principles

Principles	Features
Matching target audience	Digital communications tools should be effective in providing connection with consumers and stakeholders.
Personalization	Careful segmentation and the accurate description of the target audience should be carried out to communicate personally with each consumer using the digital communication tools.
Complementary of used digital tools	The full usage of social platforms and the digital media in order to provide comprehensive coverage of the target audience should be provided.
Consistency of used digital tools	Providing full presence of the organization in the digital space using interrelated structure of the used social platforms, apps, the company's website and other tools.
Regular updates	Regularly updating content for audience engagement.
Attention to the content	The content provided through the digital media tools should have the value for the subscribers and serve to fulfill their informational needs and solve their problems of choice.
Consumer Engagement (interactivity)	The activity aimed at the intentional reaction stimulation.
Customers' data collection	Accumulation of consumers' data allows the company to hold the direct dialogue and effectively interact with them on a mutually convenient and beneficial basis: to provide customized assortment of products and services, which leads to the better customer satisfaction and a persistent emotional connection with the brand.

2.3. The Methodology of the Research

The process of scientific research included several stages which are represented on the Figure 1 below.

To study the concept of the brand identity and for the identification brand identity effects on the brand equity the general methods of thinking such as abstraction, deduction, analysis-synthesis, analogy were used.

The digital communication tools were investigated and classified using the methods of analysis, systemization and comparison. The algorithm for the digital communications strategy were developed using collection, generalization and systematization of facts.

The authors analyze and characterize the basic tools of digital marketing communications and emphasize the importance of the integrated approach in forming a communication strategy. Also, they identify certain principles for the effective the digital communications mix formation, namely: matching target audience; personalization; complementarity of used digital tools; consistency of used digital tools; regular updates; attention to the content; consumer engagement (interactivity); customers' data collection.

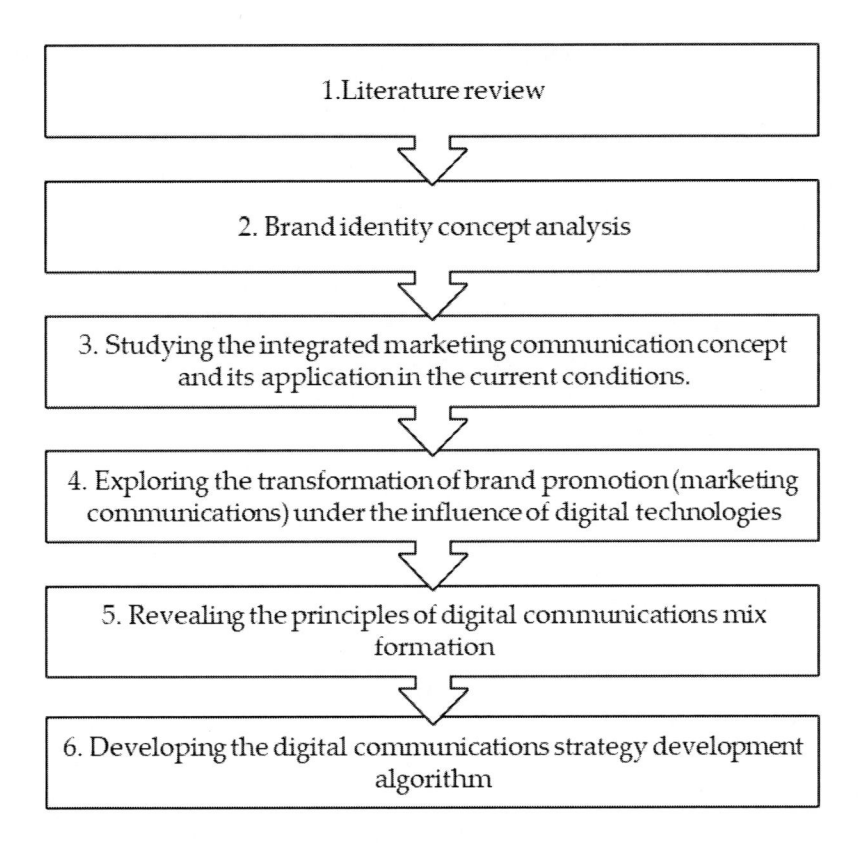

Figure 1. The scientific search process.

3. RESULTS

3.1. Brand Identity

There are a number of reasons why brand identity development is important as a factor of its success, for instance:

1. High level of information noise. Consumers are used to receiving many messages from a diverse range of sources and don't distinguish between them. All the messages blur into one single message about the brand. In these circumstances, it is important that all communications convey coherent ideas regarding the promoted brand. Consistency and clarity of the messages about the brand can improve the efficiency of perception resulting in increased recognition of the brand by consumers.
2. Fierce competition. Branding is one way by which companies differentiate themselves from their competitors in the customer's perception. A carefully designed brand identity allows companies to surround the brand with a halo of unique associations and form a special, exceptional symbolic consumer value.

3. Product standardization and technical availability. Technical innovations can be quickly copied and cannot serve as a competitive advantage for a long period, so differentiation through the formation of a unique brand identity becomes the most important aspect in solving the problem of consumer retention.

These factors show that the brand identity is important as a way of effective interaction with the consumer and as a competitive advantage expressed in the strict determination of the framework of the brand, the statement of its ideas and strengths. Similar to the diversity of definitions of the brand identity, researchers developed models for its creation.

Different brand creation models can be used for the trade and retail firms, for instance, the brand wheel; the Jean-NoelKapferer's Brand Identity Prismand the others.

The most famous and widely used model is the brand wheel. It is based on the formation of a brand around its key idea – the brand essence. The developer transforms the brand essence in its personality, describing the brand in the characteristics of the human beings. The personality doesn't describe the target consumer, it represents the brand as if it was a person who then builds a personal relationship with the buyer or a potential future consumer. A person can be characterized by the presence of basic assumptions and values, similarly values are laid in the foundation of the brand. Any brand must appear in response to the needs of customers and these same needs must be reflected and stated in its identity. All of these aspects are expressed in the attributes of the brand - its visual, tactile and any other manifestations, which simplifies the customer acquaintance with the brand and helps to establish steady relationships.

Jean-NoelKapferer represented the brand identity as a hexagonal prism, which consists of the certain elements, such as physique, personality, culture, relationship, self-image reflection. All these elements should be projected into the minds of the potential consumers in its integrity. Physical facet helps to make the brand recognizable it includes all the attributes of a brand such as logo, corporate design, tone, slogan or colors etc. The personality is the characteristics of a brand in as a human being. It can also be described by the types of relationships prevailing between the buyer and the brand. Culture can be reflected in the company history, its traditions, and the corporate values. Relationship isvery important because it forms foundation for the future of the brand. Self-image acts as the way of self-identification of a buyer. It shows how the customers see themselves and how the brand image can be incorporated into their own identity. Reflection describes a brand's customer base. Companies can use it for promotional purposes, and for the ads and commercials creations. The brand identity should be robust, recognizable and memorable.

Whatever model is chosen, the brand identity can only act as a competitive advantage if its ideas have been effectively conveyed to consumers, stakeholders and the general public through marketing communication tools. Marketing communications have a direct relationship with the development of strong brands. Their functions are to attract the attention of the consumer, to gain their interest, to provide information about the product, to help with the implementation of choice, to stimulate actions, to maintain relationships with them, to get feedback about the product, form a positive public opinion about the activities of the organization, to motivate the employees. The ultimate goals of marketing communications are to increase awareness, strengthen loyalty, and eventually enhance the brand equity. Based on all of the above-mentioned points, a carefully designed brand identity can only contribute to the strong brand development if it is complemented by a consistent marketing communications strategy.

3.2. Integrated Marketing Communications in the Modern Digitalized Environment

The modern digitalized environment has brought about several tendencies. Today's consumers has significantly changed due to ubiquitous adoption of the hand-held devices, increasing use of social media, the growth of shopping channels and the customer trust for online shopping (Dwivedi et al. 2020). They don't want only to consume the product, but also to participate in the process of its creation. They have high demands for feedback, get used to the information overload and become unresponsive for advertising messages. All that sets new challenges for all the firms which works in the current conditions.

Outcomes of the digitalization resulted in a number of positive and negative results for organizations. It has a positive effect on customer retention by means of engagement andconducting the two-way dialogue with them. The negative consequences are that new technologies requires skilled workforce or the special training for current employees. The huge range of communication tools and channels should be organized into the system and itrequiresnot only workforce but also the other recourses.

The customers use different media for activities such as reading the news, researching products and enjoying entertainment and companies can use it for its strategic purposes.

3.2.1. Digital Marketing Communications Strategy

Digital communications are increasingly attracting attention from practitioners and the scientific community because they are relatively accessible, allow for the promotion of goods in a cost-effective manner, facilitate interaction with consumers, speed up information sharing and enable databases to be formed, providing access to the psychographic and behavioral characteristics of the target audience. At the same time, the popularity and dynamic development of digital communications require the adoption of appropriate scientifically sound approaches to shaping their strategy.

In accordance with the analyzed features of the digital communications and the outlined principles of the digital mix formation strategy, the following key stages of the digital communications strategy development can be identified. The stages and tasks within the stages presented in the Table 3.

Table 3. The key stages of the digital communications strategy development

Stages	Tasks
Setting strategic targets of the digital communications	The goals of digital communications are formulated based on the common marketing goals, with the emphasis on the brand identity promotion; aimed at building relationships and engaging with the costumers; taking into account the designed sales funnel.
Targeting	Digital communications are extremely personalized. Targeting in digital communications requires the most accurate definition of criteria, because based on them the selection of the platforms for communication with customers is carried out.
The digital communications mix formation and its integration with other elements of the communication mix	The selected channels and tools should be integrated into a unified system for convenient and continuous interaction with the potential customers. The content should be presented by the information useful for consumers, allowing them to make an informed choice, reflecting the professionalism and key competences of the organization. The content shouldn't look like an advertising message. Digital tools are complemented by traditional.
Choosing performance metrics	Metrics are formed in accordance with the strategic targets, they should allow evaluating the effectiveness of the chosen approaches and the used digital tools.
Implementation, control, adjustments	It is important to monitor the external and internal market situations in order to make required adjustments depending on changes.

The first stage that includes setting the strategic targets should be based on the market situation and must have an analytical justification.The preliminary careful analysis allows the company to avoid mistakes in planning. But, the strategic targets can be corrected depending on the changes in the marketing environment.

The second stage, targeting, helps to catch the attention of the potential customers who the brand is meant for. The main task of targeting is to describe precisely he brand audience. This description later will help to launch campaign the most effective way by means of reducing the price for a contact.

The digital communications mix formation is closely related to the implementation of the whole communication policy of an organization. It is inseparable from the othercomponents of the marketing communication mix, but represents a complete subsystem, which is characterized by both its own strategic goals related to the marketing and statutory goals of a firm, as well as strategic communication goals that affect the overall effectiveness of the business unit.

In order to assess the effectiveness of communications, it is necessary to choose or develop the performance metrics. It will help the firm to evaluate how successful the implementation of the strategy is and allows to make adjustments if necessary, during the implementation period.

4. DISCUSSION

The development of digital technologies encourages innovations in all areas of life. In promotion, it is connected with the changes in the customers' lifestyle and their perception of reality and requires the adaptation of methods, tools and strategies of the promotion to the current conditions. For this reason, the development of a digital communications strategy is an innovative process that requires the development of approaches and methods for its implementation.

It is worthnotingthat the marketing communications strategy is part of the overall marketing strategy of the organization, which consists of stages: external and internal audit, segmentation and selection of the target segment, determination of positioning, brand identity development, shaping policies of the mix marketing elements, establishment of efficiency metrics and the implementation process, control and adjustment. When forming a marketing strategy, it should be taken into account that all elements of the marketing mix carry certain information about brand's unique selling proposition, and therefore all of them convey the brand identity. It means that actually the brand

Thus, the quality of the product, the price as well as used distribution channels should correspond the stated brand identity concept.

The effect of the digital communications is represented not only in the sales increase but also, and more importantly, in enhancing the brand equity represented by the brand awareness, its loyalty, popularity, perceived quality, related associations and other assets that contribute to the growth of its market value.Therefore, the prospective research areas may be related to the study of the effectiveness of the above-presented strategy in terms of attracting and retaining consumers, and other aspects of the brand equity.

CONCLUSION

1. The brand identity - the most important component in the promotional activities of companies, because it provides the semantic unity of communication, allows to convey coherent ideas regarding the promoted brand, to surround the brand with a nimbus of unique associations, to form a special, exceptional symbolic consumer value and finally to retain customers.The consisted brand identity eventually helps to enhance the brand equity represented by the brand awareness, its loyalty, popularity, perceived quality, related associations and other assets that contribute to the growth of its market value.

2. In order to convey the basic ideas of the brand identity, a wide range of the communication mix elements can be used. Recently, the promotion mix has significantly expanded with new digital communication tools, which in some industries have begun to replace traditional ones. All the used communication tools should be integrated into a single system to achieve a synergy effect

following the basic integrated marketing communication principles. A strategic approach to the organization and implementation of digital communications on the principles of the IMC concept contributes to more effective promotion of brand identity, building interactions and long-term relationships with potential consumers.

3. Given the specifics of digital communications, the digital communications mix formation principles can be identified, namely: matching target audience; personalization; complementarity and consistency of used digital tools; regular updates; attention to the content; consumer engagement (interactivity); customers' data collection. Taken into account the above-mentioned principles an algorithm for the digital communications strategy development was presented which includes following stages: setting strategic targets of the digital communications, targeting, the digital communications mix formation and its integration with other elements of the communication mix, choosing performance metrics, implementation, control, adjustments.

REFERENCES

[1]   Aaker, David. 1996. "Building Strong Brands, Free Press, 1996." *Free Press*, 1996. https://doi.org/http://dx.doi.org/10.1007/s00404-015-3641-1.

[2]   Aaker, David A. 2012. "Win the Brand Relevance Battle and Then Build Competitor Barriers." *California Management Review*. https://doi.org/10.1525/cmr.2012.54.2.43.

[3]   Abashidze, Irakli. 2017. "Integrated Marketing Communications in Web 2.0 Environment: Challenges and Opportunities of Online Presence." *Journal of Research in Marketing*. https://doi.org/10.17722/jorm.v8i1.202.

[4]   Baldwin, Jonathan. 2017. "Designing the Brand Identity in Retail Spaces." *The Design Journal*. https://doi.org/10.1080/14606925.2016.1248623.

[5]   Batra, Rajeev, and Kevin Lane Keller. 2016. "Integrating Marketing Communications: New Findings, New Lessons, and New Ideas." *Journal of Marketing*. https://doi.org/10.1509/jm.15.0419.

[6]   Blakeman, Robyn. 2006. *Integrated Marketing Communication: Creative Strategy from Idea to Implementation. IPA Bulletin*.

[7]   Blech, G, and M Blech. 2008. "Advertising and Promotion: An IMC Perspec-tive." In *Advertising and Promotion : An Integrated Marketing Communications Perspective*.

[8]   Burt, Steve, and Keri Davies. 2010. "From the Retail Brand to the Retail-Er as a Brand: Themes and Issues in Retail Branding Research." *International Journal of Retail and Distribution Management*. https://doi.org/10.1108/095905 51011085957.

[9]   Chaihanchanchai, Papaporn, and Saravudh Anantachart. 2019. "Through the Looking Glass: Understanding Thai Academics' Viewpoints on Integrated

Marketing Communications." *Kasetsart Journal of Social Sciences* 40 (2): 402–10. https://doi.org/10.1016/j.kjss.2017.10.003.

[10] Chernatony, Leslie de. 1999. "Brand Management Through Narrowing the Gap Between Brand Identity and Brand Reputation." *Journal of Marketing Management.* https://doi.org/10.1362/026725799784870432.

[11] Chernatony, Leslie de, and Malcolm McDonald. 2012. *Creating Powerful Brands: In Consumer, Service and Industrial Markets. Creating Powerful Brands: In Consumer, Service and Industrial Markets.* https://doi.org/10.4324/9780080476919.

[12] Duncan, Tom, and Sandra E. Moriarty. 1998a. "A Communication-Based Marketing Model for Managing Relationships." *Journal of Marketing.* https://doi.org/10.2307/1252157.

[13] Duncan, Tom, and Sandra E Moriarty. 1998b. "Marketing for Model Managing Relationships." *Journal of Marketing.*

[14] Dwivedi, Yogesh K., Elvira Ismagilova, D. Laurie Hughes, Jamie Carlson, Raffaele Filieri, Jenna Jacobson, Varsha Jain, et al. 2020. "Setting the Future of Digital and Social Media Marketing Research: Perspectives and Research Propositions." *International Journal of Information Management*, no. May: 102168. https://doi.org/10.1016/j.ijinfomgt.2020.102168.

[15] Essamri, Azzouz, Sally McKechnie, and Heidi Winklhofer. 2019. "Co-Creating Corporate Brand Identity with Online Brand Communities: A Managerial Perspective." *Journal of Business Research* 96 (March): 366–75. https://doi.org/10.1016/J.JBUSRES.2018.07.015.

[16] Eugenia, Adelina. 2012. "Emerging Markets Queries in Finance and Business." *Procedia - Social and Behavioral Sciences* 3 (12): 536–42. https://doi.org/10.1016/S2212-5671(12)00192-X.

[17] Fraccastoro, Sara, Mika Gabrielsson, and Ellen Bolman. 2020. "The Integrated Use of Social Media, Digital, and Traditional Communication Tools in the B2B Sales Process of International SMEs." *International Business Review*, no. November: 101776. https://doi.org/10.1016/j.ibusrev.2020.101776.

[18] Ianenko, Marina, Mikhail Ianenko, Dmitriy Huhlaev, and Oksana Martynenko. 2019. "Digital Transformation of Trade: Problems and Prospects of Marketing Activities." In *IOP Conference Series: Materials Science and Engineering.* Vol. 497. https://doi.org/10.1088/1757-899X/497/1/012118.

[19] Ianenko, Marina, Mikhail Stepanov, Mikhail Ianenko, and Svetlana Iliashenko. 2019. "Peculiarities of Product Policy in the Internet of Things." In *IOP Conference Series: Materials Science and Engineering.* https://doi.org/10.1088/1757-899X/497/1/012119.

[20] Ianenko, Marina, Mikhail Stepanov, and Liubov Mironova. 2020. "Brand Identity Development." In *E3S Web of Conferences.* https://doi.org/10.1051/e3sconf/202016409015.

[21] Kailani, Camelia Mihart. 2012. *"Modelling the Influence of Integrated Marketing Communication on Consumer Behaviour : An Approach Based on Hierarchy of Effects Concept"* 62: 975–80. https://doi.org/10.1016/j.sbspro.2012.09.166.

[22] Kapferer, Jean-Noël. 2009. "Kapferer's Brand-Identity Prism Model." *EURIB - European Institute for Brand Management.*

[23] Keller, Kevin Lane, Don E. Schultz, Heidi F. Schultz, Mike Reid, Sandra Luxton, Felix Mavondo, Barbara Caemmerer, et al. 2016. "Integrated Advertising, Promotion, and Marketing Communications." *International Journal of Advertising.*

[24] Kitchen, Philip J., and Patrick de Pelsmacker. 2004. *A Primer for Integrated Marketing Communications. A Primer for Integrated Marketing Communications.* https://doi.org/10.4324/9780203502860.

[25] Kliatchko, Jerry. 2005. "Towards a New Definition of Integrated Marketing Communications (IMC)." *International Journal of Advertising.* https://doi.org/10.1080/02650487.2005.11072902.

[26] Kotler, Philip, and Waldemar Pförtsch. 2010. *"Basics of Ingredient Branding,"* April. https://doi.org/10.1007/978-3-642-04214-0_2.

[27] Krasyuk, Irina, Yulia Medvedeva, and Vladimir Baharev. 2019. *"Evolution of Strategies of Retail and Technological Systems under Broad Digitalization Conditions Evolution of Strategies of Retail and Technological Systems under Broad Digitalization Conditions."* https://doi.org/10.1088/1757-899X/497/1/012124.

[28] Krasyuk, Irina, Marina Yanenko, and Elmira Nazarova. 2020. "Conceptual and Strategic Framework for the Digitalization of Modern Retail as Part of Innovative Marketing." *E3S Web of Conferences* 164. https://doi.org/10.1051/e3sconf/202016409006.

[29] Lambin, Jean-Jacques, Isabelle Schuiling, Jean-Jacques Lambin, and Isabelle Schuiling. 2012. "The Market Orientation Concept." In *Market-Driven Management.* https://doi.org/10.1007/978-0-230-36312-0_2.

[30] Madhavaram, Sreedhar, Vishag Badrinarayanan, and Robert E. McDonald. 2005. "Integrated Marketing Communication (Imc) and Brand Identity as Critical Components of Brand Equity Strategy: A Conceptual Framework and Research Propositions." *Journal of Advertising.* https://doi.org/10.1080/00913367.2005.10639213.

[31] Newsom, Doug. 1998. "Driving Brand Value: Using Integrated Marketing to Manage Profitable Stakeholder Relationships." *Public Relations Review.* https://doi.org/10.1016/s0363-8111(98)80025-8.

[32] Ogbonnaya, Chinedu, Ike-elechi Ogba, and Ernest Emeka. 2020. *"Examining the Effect of Customers' Perception of Bank Marketing Communication on Customer Loyalty"* 8: 4–11. https://doi.org/10.1016/j.sciaf.2020.e00383.

[33] Olimpia, Oancea, and Elena Mihaela. 2015. "The Influence of The Integrated Marketing Communication on The Consumer Buying Behaviour." *Procedia*

Economics and Finance 23 (October 2014): 1446–50. https://doi.org/10.1016/S2212-5671(15)00446-3.

[34] Percy, Larry, and Larry Percy. 2018. "Introduction to IMC." In *Strategic Integrated Marketing Communications*. https://doi.org/10.4324/9781315164342-1.

[35] Rangaswamy, Arvind, Nicole Moch, Claudio Felten, Gerrit van Bruggen, Jaap E. Wieringa, and Jochen Wirtz. 2020. "The Role of Marketing in Digital Business Platforms." *Journal of Interactive Marketing* 51: 72–90. https://doi.org/10.1016/j.intmar.2020.04.006.

[36] Sääksjärvi, Maria, and Saeed Samiee. 2011. "Relationships among Brand Identity, Brand Image and Brand Preference: Differences between Cyber and Extension Retail Brands over Time." *Journal of Interactive Marketing*. https://doi.org/10.1016/j.intmar.2011.04.002.

[37] Schultz, Don E., Charles H. Patti, and Philip J. Kitchen. 2013. *The Evolution of Integrated Marketing Communications: The Customer-Driven Marketplace. The Evolution of Integrated Marketing Communications: The Customer-Driven Marketplace*. https://doi.org/10.4324/9781315872728.

[38] Sellahvarzi, Solmaz, and Vahid Reza Mirabi. 2014. "*Management Science Letters*" 4: 1415–20. https://doi.org/10.5267/j.msl.2014.6.027.

[39] Šerić, Maja, Đurđana Ozretić-Došen, and Vatroslav Škare. 2020. "How Can Perceived Consistency in Marketing Communications Influence Customer–Brand Relationship Outcomes?" *European Management Journal* 38 (2): 335–43. https://doi.org/10.1016/j.emj.2019.08.011.

[40] Teresa, Maria, and Flávio Tiago. 2012. "*Revisiting the Impact of Integrated Internet Marketing on Firms' Online Performance : European Evidences*" 5: 418–26. https://doi.org/10.1016/j.protcy.2012.09.046.

[41] Wheeler, Alina. 2009. *Designing Brand Identity. Journal of the Electrochemical Society*. Vol. 129.

In: Global Challenges of Digital Transformation of Markets ISBN: 978-1-53619-754-9
Editors: E. de la Poza and S. E. Barykin © 2021 Nova Science Publishers, Inc.

Chapter 22

DIGITAL TRANSFORMATION OF THE RUSSIAN VENTURE ECOSYSTEM UNDER THE IMPACT OF THE COVID-19

Bilal Khalid[1] and Elena Naumova[2,]*

[1]KMITL Business School, King Mongkut's Institute of technology Ladkrabang,
Bangkok, Thailand
[2]Saint Petersburg State Maritime Technical University, Saint-Petersburg, Russia

ABSTRACT

The article analyzes current trends in the digital transformation of the Russian venture ecosystem and the impact of the Covid-19 pandemic on the venture ecosystem in the context of innovative development of Russian regions. The purpose of the study is to identify key areas of development of the domestic venture ecosystem in the pre-pandemic period and under the influence of the Covid-19 pandemic. The problem of the functioning of mechanisms for the development of the innovation process has recently become of increasing interest to specialists in various scientific fields. As in the global venture capital market, the domestic venture ecosystem has faced typical challenges in the context of the Covid-19. In the context of the pandemic and in the post-pandemic period, the most startups have been canceled or postponed at least until the end of 2020 or 2021. The forced pause in the work of innovative enterprises during the pandemic had a very negative impact on their financial condition – even large, stable enterprises operating in the market found it difficult to bear constant expenses without an influx of income. As a result of the research, the main directions of transformation of the domestic venture ecosystem and prospects for innovative development of Russian regions are identified. Firstly, the trend to optimize investment portfolios inspires a reduction in the number of venture transactions. Secondly, there has been a significant transformation in the structure of the

---

* Corresponding Author's Email: elenanaumova@mail.ru.

venture capital market. Finally, there is a rush of interest in startups in both healthcare and biotechnology.

Keywords: venture financing, venture ecosystem, pandemic, investing, digital startups

1. INTRODUCTION

Currently, one of the most significant difficulties for the domestic scientific and technical sphere is the gap that exists in the Russian system of developing innovations and their commercial development. Thus, regarding the digital transformation the question arises of the need to ensure effective interaction of various participants in the process of commercial development of innovations.

Organizations that regularly generate new entrepreneurial and scientific-technical ideas and consolidate their own and attracted resources to create, develop, and bring new products, services, and technologies to the market achieve success in a highly competitive market.

As you know, the key participants in the modern innovation process today are the state, fundamental and applied science, and business. The quality of implementation of the innovation process directly depends on the level of coherence of their interaction. Venture financing is a way to bring together representatives of science and business on a mutually beneficial basis, which brings a significant effect in the context of the development of the world and national economy.

The problem of the functioning of mechanisms for the development of the innovation process has recently become of increasing interest to specialists in various scientific fields.

In particular, Rakhaeva and Mizyueva consider the essence and characteristic features of venture financing and its role in the modern practice of project financing (Rakhaeva and Mizyureva 2020).

Eexplore the essence of venture financing in modern conditions in relation to small businesses in various industries in works (Engel 2011; Gurkov 2004; Dezhina, Medovnikov, and Rozmirovich 2019).

Evaluate the spread of venture financing of innovative business in various regions of the world, comparing it with the economic development of these regions we can see in works (Sprague 2015; Fedirko 2017; Sieradzka 2017; Hmeleva and Terekhina 2019).

Modern formats of venture financing of innovations (Kuppuswamy and Bayus 2015; Jean Sébastien Lantz, Sahut, and Teulon 2011; Jean Sebastien Lantz and Sahut 2010; Golder, Mitra, and Kuppuswamy 2018).

Some authors analyzes the impact of the venture market on the development of domestic innovative entrepreneurship and predicts the importance of such entrepreneurship for the modern Russian economy (Hellmann and Puri 2000; Ferrary and Granovetter 2009; Ahlstrom and Bruton 2006; De Bernardi and Azucar 2020; Bonini and Capizzi 2019) and pay special attention to the stages of development of innovative startups and the peculiarities of attracting venture financing at different stages of startup development (Davila, Foster, and Gupta 2003; Ewens and Marx 2018; Köhn 2018).

Bonini and Capizzi focus on the role of venture capital in the development of the national and global economy, understanding it as a catalyst for innovative and technical development of individual States and the whole world (Bonini and Capizzi 2019).

Chan also believes that venture financing contributes to the promotion and industrial development of innovations, thereby contributing to global scientific and technological progress (Chan 2020).

Iyer explores the role of venture financing of innovative enterprises in the scientific, technical and economic development of India (Veena Iyer 2020).

Park and LiPuma consider the classification of modern formats of venture financing of innovative startups, identifying the role of individual formats of venture business in the dissemination of technical innovations (Park and LiPuma 2020).

Brown, Rocha and Cowling investigate the impact of the Covid-19 pandemic on the British venture capital market, assessing the scale of the crisis in the venture business and the direction of exit from them (Brown, Rocha, and Cowling 2020).

Liu and Park they pay special attention to the transformation of venture business in modern conditions, when there is a change in the needs of startups in resources and financing (Liu and Park 2020).

Some works cover the project features in the digital economy (Schislyaeva et al. 2019; Ilin, Kalinina, and Barykin 2018; Vilken et al. 2019; Aleksander Bril, Kalinina, and Levina 2018; Alexander Bril, Kalinina, and Valebnikova 2016). Thus, today we can distinguish a wide range of scientific papers devoted to the topic of venture financing in the context of innovative development of the economy as a whole, as well as the regional economy.

2. MATERIALS AND METHODS

The innovation process is a long-term algorithm of a complex nature, within which an innovative idea is transformed into a commercially demanded product. In other words, the innovation process is aimed at improving the economic efficiency and competitiveness of a particular organization by creating an innovation and its successful implementation in the tactical activities and strategy of the organization. Within the existing innovation process models, it is customary to allocate some consecutive stages: basic research, applied research, development works, production and marketing activities, and distribution.

Innovation in modern conditions should be understood as a certain set of processes that are aimed at creating and improving a variety of new products, technologies and services, as well as their introduction and mass distribution on the market, among consumers. In addition, innovation as a process concerns not only various products, technologies and services, but also raw materials, materials, algorithms and methods of production and management activities.

In recent years, the concept of "startup" has become firmly established in the scientific discourse, as well as in professional slang and everyday life. The startup is based on an innovative idea that determines the competitive advantage and demand for the manufactured product, technology, and service on the market. At the same time, a startup operates in conditions of extreme market uncertainty: it is an innovation-based business that is at the initial stage of development and is characterized by insufficient funds.

Currently, startups are created in order to develop innovative products, technologies and services, bring them to the market and implement them. In other words, the goal of creating a startup is to conduct technological entrepreneurship. The mobility of startups due to their small size, flexibility and ability to quickly respond to changing environmental conditions determines their competitive advantage compared to large enterprises. At the same time, the startup is extremely limited in resources – financial, material, and human.

A startup is an innovative project that is currently at the earliest, pre-investment stage of development. At the same time, for startups, this pre-investment stage is divided into the following three micro-stages or stages of development of innovative enterprises: seeding, start-up, and early growth.

According to the national venture capital Association of the United States, "venture capital investments are financial resources provided by professional investors to young, rapidly growing organizations that have the potential to become companies that make a significant contribution to the economy" ("What Action Was Positively Affected by the Epidemic Coronavirus I Vedomosti" n.d.). Venture capital financing generally involves the investor making long-term investments in various high-risk companies, aimed at future income generation as a result of the sale of the investor's share in the capital of a funded organization at the moment when this organization is successful in the market.

The current venture capital market includes the following segments: the institutional venture capital segment, the informal venture capital segment, and the corporate segment. Each of the selected segments of the venture market has a specific set of distinctive characteristics that distinguish these segments from each other ("Consumers Boost Shares of Coronavirus Essentials I Financial Times" n.d.).

The venture market performs an accumulating function through the financing of innovative companies, through which the financial resources of venture market participants and the state are directed to stimulate and develop scientific and technological progress, commercialization and dissemination of innovative technologies ("VCs Warn Coronavirus Will Impact Fundraising for the next 2 Quarters I TechCrunch" n.d.).

The venture market also performs an integration function, in which the pool of financial resources of investors and intellectual resources of the founders of innovative enterprises is combined into one pool. The economic effect of this Association is clearly seen in the accelerated renewal of traditional industries for the national and global economy, the opening of new technological niches and new market niches.

In addition, the venture capital market performs a motivational function, encouraging participants in traditional markets to increase their competitiveness by investing in the development of scientific and technical potential. The high level of uncertainty of innovative business and its instability in a competitive environment determines the need for startups in venture investments. This format of attracting financial resources to an innovative project leads to the fact that the participation of a venture investor in the project implementation contributes to its success in the market. The investor provides the startup founders with management and business experience, a set of skills, and helps them form useful connections in the business community. Thus, venture investments help the startups that attracted them to overcome a set of problems that are typical for new enterprises in conditions of high market competition and increased turbulence of the external environment.

In addition, the high level of risk when implementing innovative projects makes it difficult for startups to obtain financial resources for development from generally accepted sources, which include Bank lending, issuing equity and debt securities. This adds to the need for startups to make venture capital investments, which are provided by investors to startups without requiring collateral obligations or any guarantees. The only condition for providing venture financing is the investor's participation in the future profit of the startup or in the share of the future value of the enterprise (Park and LiPuma 2020).

Thus, the idea of venture financing of innovative projects is to get a high premium for high risk: financing a risky startup, if it is successful, brings the investor income that is many times higher than the initial investment of the investor.

Providing an innovation project with financial resources at an early stage of the life cycle reduces the risk of rejection of innovation by the market and increases its effectiveness.

3. RESULTS

Venture ecosystem in Russia includes the issuance of grants and the performance of venture deals. The parameters of the venture ecosystem functioning in 2017-2019 are presented in Table 1.

Table 1. Parameters of the Russian venture ecosystem functioning

Directions	Indicators	2017	2018	2019
Venture deals	Number of transactions	205	195	229
	Total volume of transactions, million USD	243.7	433.7	548.1
Grants	Number of grants issued	4558	3995	4357
	Amount of grants issued, million USD	88.5	99.3	106.4
The total volume of the market		412.1	661.9	747.7

In 2017, the number of venture transactions was 205, and the total volume of venture transactions was 243.7 million USD. In 2017, 4558 grants were issued for a total of 88.5 million USD. The total volume of the venture capital market in 2017 was 412.1 million USD. 2018 is characterized by a slight reduction in the number of venture capital transactions – up to 195. At the same time, the total volume of venture transactions amounted to 433.7 million USD. 3995 grants worth 99.3 million USD were issued in 2018. The total volume of the venture capital market was 661 million USD in 2018. In other words, it increased by more than 50% compared to 2017. In 2019, there were 229 venture capital transactions worth 548.1 million USD. Thus, both the number of transactions and their total amount exceed the figures for 2018. In 2019 4357 grants were issued in the amount of 106.4 million USD. The total volume of the venture capital market in 2019 was 747.7 million USD, exceeding the market volume for 2018. Thus, during the study period, there is a stable growth of all the resulting indicators of the functioning of the domestic venture ecosystem.

The most active grant-giving Fund was the Foundation for the promotion of small forms of enterprises in the scientific and technical sphere (the innovation promotion Fund, or the Bortnik Foundation). Figure 1 shows the distribution of venture capital investments by stage of company development.

The volume of investment in Russian startups at the seed stage in 2017 amounted to 18.4 million USD. In 2018, the volume of investment in start-UPS at the seed stage increased to 34.8 million USD ("How a Startup Can Attract Investment in a Crisis I Vedomosti" n.d.). The result of 2019 is slightly higher than the result of last year, amounting to 39.1 million USD.

The volume of investment in enterprises at the start-up stage is also growing. So, in 2017, 16.6 million USD was invested in companies that are at the "startup" stage. In 2018, the volume of investments in companies at the startup stage increased to 20.7 million USD, and in 2019, the volume of investments exceeded the total figure of the previous year and amounted to 28.7 million USD.

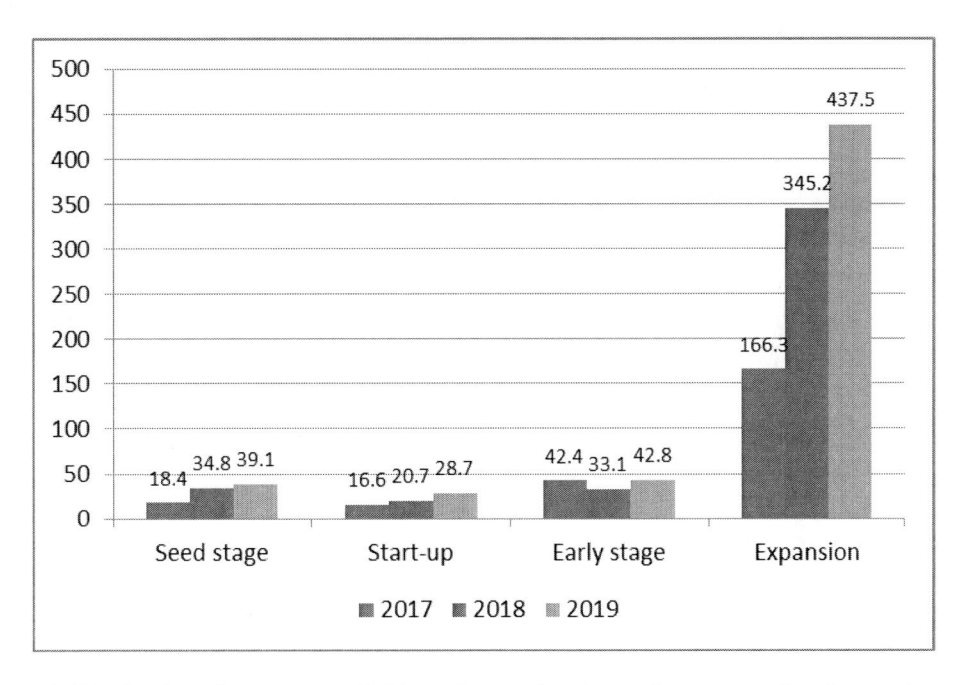

Figure 1. Distribution of venture capital investments by stage of company development, million USD.

The volume of venture capital investments in companies that are at the early stage of development is slightly higher than the volume of investments in companies at the "startup" stage. So, in 2017, the volume of investments in companies at the early development stage amounted to 42.4 million USD, in 2018 it decreased to 33.1 million USD, and in 2019 it increased to 42.8 million USD.

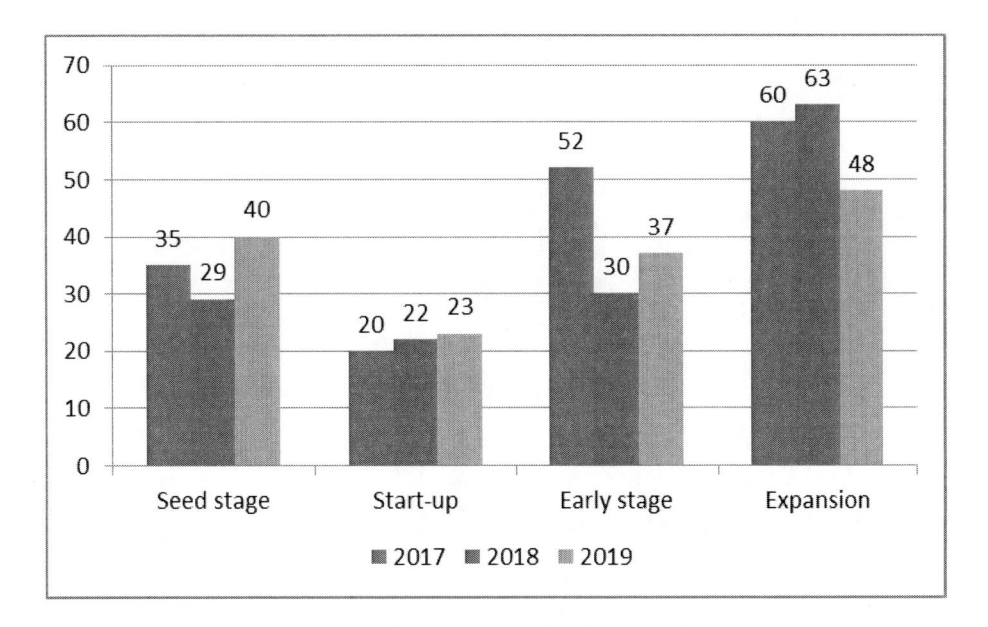

Figure 2. Distribution of the number of venture transactions by company development stages.

The maximum amount of venture capital investment is attracted by companies that are at the stage of expansion. Thus, in 2017, the volume of investments in companies at the expansion stage amounted to 166.3 million USD. In 2018, investments in companies under expansion totaled 345.2 million USD. Finally, the volume of investments in companies at the expansion stage in 2019 amounted to 437.5 million USD. Figure 2 illustrates the distribution of the number of transactions by stage of development of companies.

Companies that are at the seed stage carry out a fairly large number of venture capital investment transactions. So, in 2017, 35 venture investment transactions were made by companies at the seed stage, in 2018 the number of venture investment transactions of companies at the seed stage decreased to 29, and in 2019 it increased to 40 transactions. Companies that are at the "startup" stage in 2017 completed 20 transactions on venture financing. In 2018, the number of transactions on venture financing of companies at the startup stage increased to 22. in 2019, 23 transactions on venture financing of companies at the startup stage were completed. Early-stage venture capital investment was very active in 2017, when 52 transactions were completed. In 2018, the number of venture capital financing deals for early-stage companies decreased to 30, while in 2019, 37 deals were made with early-stage companies. The maximum activity of venture financing in 2017-2018 was observed for companies at the expansion stage – in 2017, 60 transactions were made on venture financing of companies at the expansion stage, in 2018 – 63 transactions. 2019 is characterized by a reduction in the number of venture financing transactions for companies at the expansion stage – only 48 transactions were made. Figure 3 shows the average amount of a venture transaction for the period. In 2017, the average size of a venture transaction was 1.5 million USD. In 2018, the average transaction size doubled to 3.0 million USD. In 2019, the average transaction size increased to 3.1 million USD.

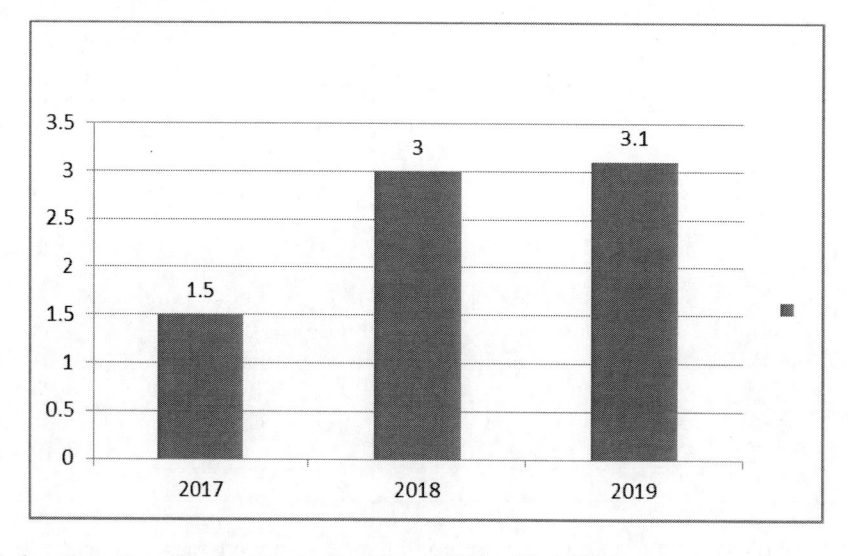

Figure 3. Average size of a venture transaction, USD million USD.

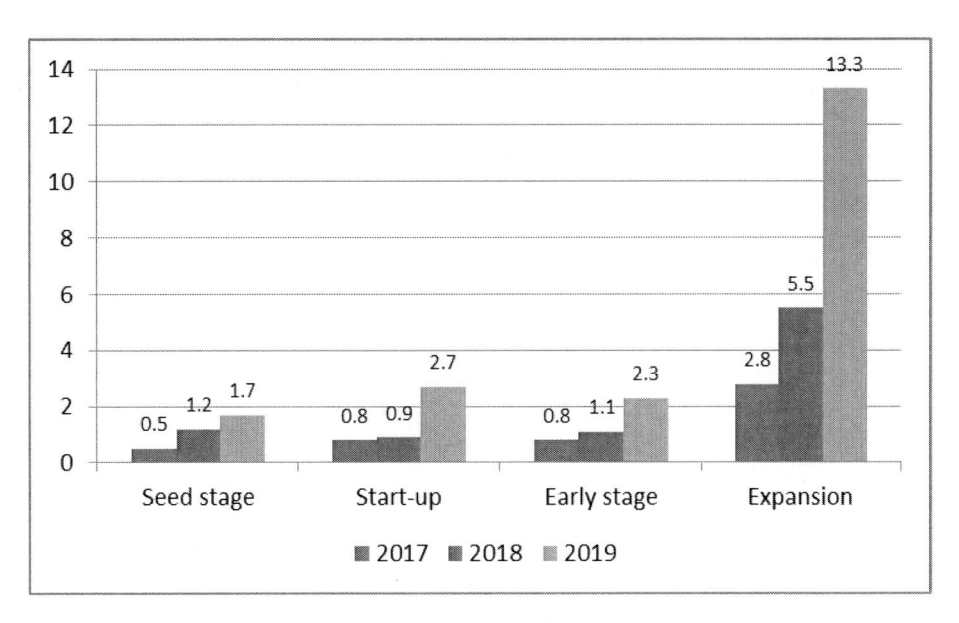

Figure 4. Average size of a venture transaction by stage of company development, million USD.

Figure 4 illustrates the average size of a venture transaction by company development stage.

For companies that are at the seed stage of development, the size of the venture transaction is minimal – in 2017 it was 0.5 million USD, in 2018 it increased to 1.2 million USD. and in 2019, it reached 1.7 million USD. The size of a venture transaction for companies at the start-up stage and at an early stage of development differs slightly. So, for companies at the "startup" stage in 2017, the average transaction size was 0.8 million USD, in 2018 it increased to 0.9 million USD. and in 2019, it reached 2.7 million USD. For early-stage companies, the average transaction size was also 0.8 million USD in 2017, which increased to 1.1 million USD in 2018. and in 2019, it amounted to 2.3 million USD. The maximum size of a venture transaction is typical for companies at the stage of expansion – in 2017 it amounted to 2.8 million USD, in 2018 it increased to 5.5 million USD. and in 2019, it rose sharply to 13.3 million USD. Figure 5 illustrates the dynamics of investors ' exits from investment projects.

In 2017, there were 30 exits of investors from investment projects, the amount of exits from investment projects amounted to 79.9 million USD. Thus, the average amount of exits left 2.7 million USD. In 2018, the number of investors exits from investment projects increased slightly to 32. At the same time, the amount of investor withdrawals from investment projects increased significantly and amounted to 128.9 million USD. Thus, the average amount of output in 2018 was 4.0 million USD. In 2019, there were 27 exits of investors from investment projects worth 135.4 million USD. The average output in 2019 was 5.0 million USD. Figure 6 illustrates the distribution of venture capital investment by economic sector. The largest volume of venture capital investments is attracted by the it sector. Thus, in 2017, the it sector attracted investments in the amount of 205.3 million USD. Investments in the biotechnology sector amounted to 14.7 million USD in 2017, and investments in the industrial technology sector - 23.7 million USD. In 2018, investment in the it sector increased to 409 million USD. At the same time, investments in biotechnologies and industrial technologies decreased to 12.8 and 11.9 million USD respectively.

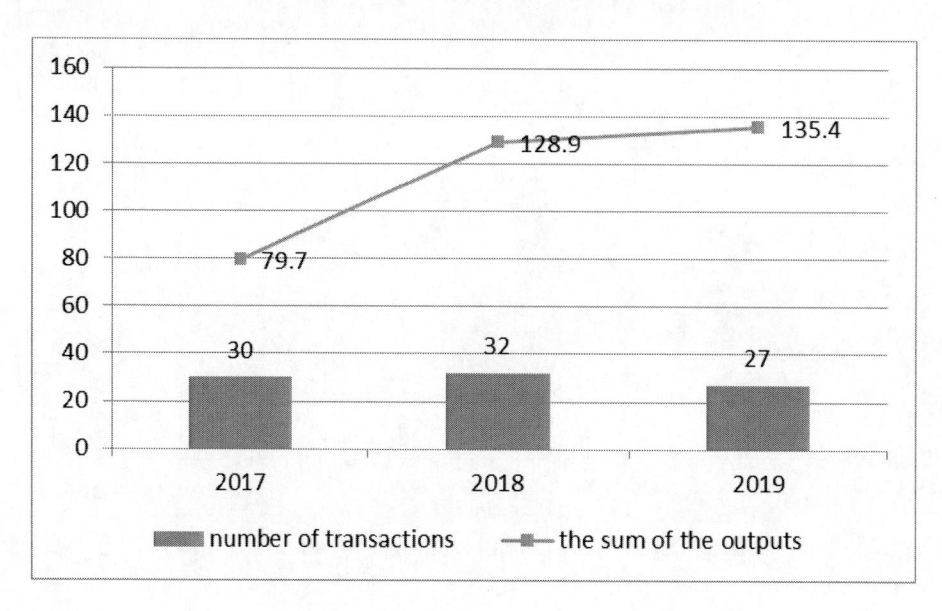

Figure 5. Dynamics of investor exits, million USD.

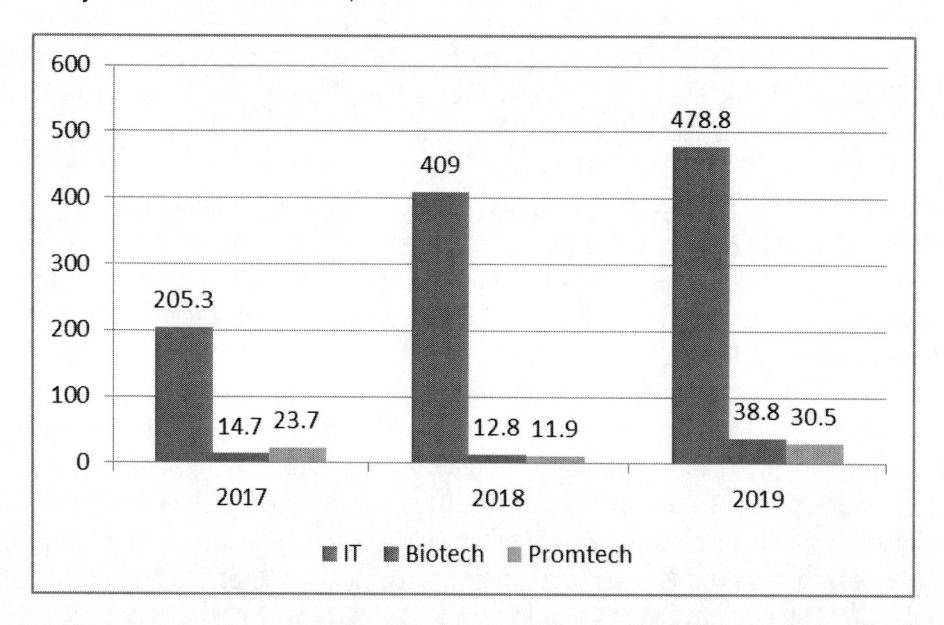

Figure 6. Distribution of venture capital investments by economic sector, million USD.

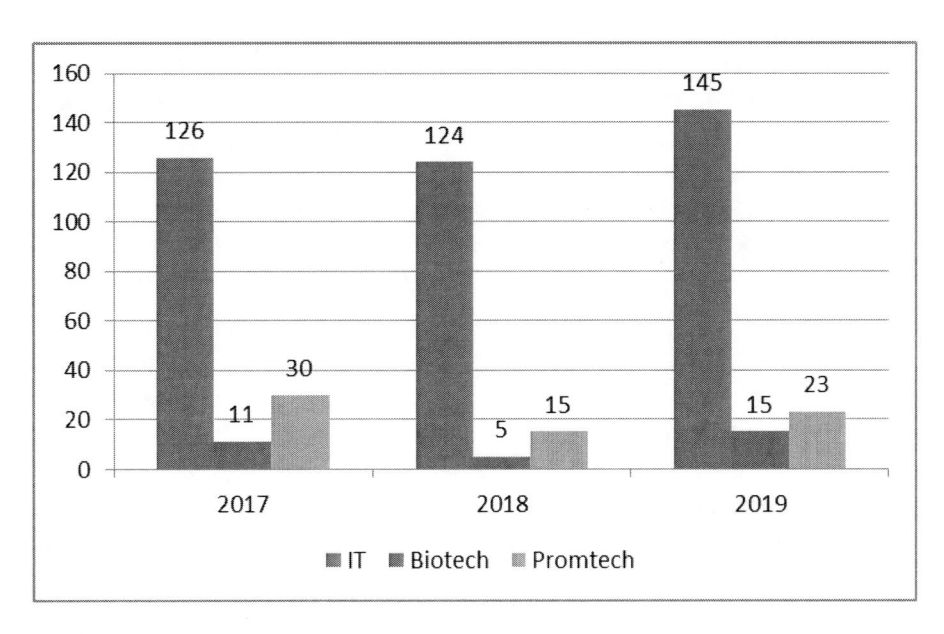

Figure 7. Distribution of the number of venture transactions by economic sector.

In 2019, the volume of investments in the it sector amounted to 478.8 million USD. Investments in the biotechnology sector amounted to 38.8 million USD, and in the industrial technology sector - 30.5 million USD, which is 90% more than in the entire previous year. Figure 7 illustrates the distribution of the number of venture transactions by sector.

Most venture capital financing deals are made in relation to companies in the it sector. Thus, in 2017, there were 126 transactions on venture financing of it companies, 11 transactions with companies in the biotechnology sector and 30 transactions on financing of companies in the industrial technology sector. 2018 is characterized by a decrease in investor interest in the biotechnology and industrial technology sectors. So, in 2018 there were 124 deals on venture investment in it companies, 5 deals on investment in companies in the biotechnology sector and 15 deals on investment in companies in the industrial technology sector. 2019 is characterized by stable investor interest in the it sector and growing interest in the industrial technology and biotechnology sectors. Thus, the number of transactions on venture financing of it companies was 145, 15 transactions on venture financing of companies in the biotechnology sector and 23 transactions in the industrial technology sector were made.

Thus, we can talk about the stable growth of the venture ecosystem of the Russian Federation in the last 3 years. There was an increase in the volume of investment and the number of transactions, the amount of transactions on venture investment increased. The it sector is the most interesting for investors. interest in the biotechnology and industrial technology sectors was growing even before the Covid-19 pandemic.

When the Covid-19 epidemic began to spread rapidly around the world, it turned out that the world economy was not ready for such a shock. In the regions that were affected by the Covid-19 epidemic, manufacturing and service enterprises were closed, which led to the rapid collapse of many supply chains around the world. The huge economic damage suffered by various sectors of the economy caused large-scale changes in the value of shares on the stock market and, accordingly, led to a transformation of investor behavior. As a result, on March 12, the UK stock market fell by 10%, while in the US, the Dow Jones and S&P 500 indices fell to the level of 1987 ("What Action Was Positively Affected by the Epidemic Coronavirus I Vedomosti" n.d.).

In the situation of the epidemic Covid-19 the most stable and economically promising for investors were companies that worked in healthcare, biotechnology, as well as enterprises manufacturing products or providing services essential to many people, forcibly locked in their homes. In particular, there was a rapid increase in the market value of the shares of "canned soup manufacturer Campbell Soup, manufacturer of disinfectant wipes Clorox, manufacturer of clothing for medical workers and hygiene products Kimberly-Clark". Worldwide, there was a massive transfer of many office employees to remote work, as a result, this "led to a jump in the popularity of the Zoom video conferencing service — during February, the company's securities increased in price by almost 50%" ("What Action Was Positively Affected by the Epidemic Coronavirus I Vedomosti" n.d.).

Many venture capital investors and global venture funds have taken a wait-and-see approach to the market as the Covid-19 pandemic spreads. In the face of extreme uncertainty in the global economy, the vast majority of venture capital investors were forced to start the process of optimizing their investment portfolios. Since the beginning of the Covid-19 pandemic and in the near future, venture investors and venture funds will focus on projects with a minimum level of risk, allowing you to get a guaranteed profit. Accordingly, startups after the conditional end of the first wave of the Covid-19 pandemic and in the situation of waiting for the second wave are unlikely to expect increased interest from investors ("VCs Warn Coronavirus Will Impact Fundraising for the next 2 Quarters I TechCrunch" n.d.).

As in the global venture capital market, the domestic venture ecosystem has faced typical challenges in the context of the Covid-19 pandemic. Firstly, this is the already mentioned trend to optimize investment portfolios, which inspires a reduction in the number of venture transactions, a reduction in the volume of transactions. Secondly, there has been a significant transformation in the structure of the venture capital market: currently, there is an increased interest in companies in the Life Science sector and in biomedical technologies. This makes it even more difficult to attract external financing for companies from other sectors. Thirdly, the forced pause in the work of innovative enterprises during the pandemic had a very negative impact on their financial condition – even large, stable enterprises operating in the market found it difficult to bear constant expenses without an influx of income. Finally, in the context of the pandemic and in the post-pandemic period, the opportunities for pitching startups to investors are extremely limited – most exhibition events have been canceled or postponed at least until the end of 2020 or 2021.

At the same time, to solve the latter problem, participants in the modern investment market began to look for workarounds for investment pitching. "One of the solutions was first presented by the tech investor Sequoia China, which held its annual demo day in an online format. Traditional face-to-face meetings of Chinese entrepreneurs with potential sponsors were replaced with three-hour virtual sessions, during which about 30 startups presented their projects to 50 investors". Investment pitching in the online format is not a fundamentally new solution today – projects such as Pitching StartupBlink and GlobalPitch carried out investment pitching in the online format long before the start of the pandemic. However, the beginning of the Covid-19 pandemic has contributed to the active development of investment pitching practices in the online format. It is expected that in the future these practices will remain popular, thus increasing the availability of investment pitching for regional startups that have problems presenting their projects at Moscow and international offline exhibitions, conferences and events. Thus, circumventing the restrictions of the pandemic can act as a driver for the spread of venture investment of innovative entrepreneurship in Russian regions.

4. DISCUSSION

With the beginning of the Covid-19 pandemic, experts assumed that many markets – in particular, the restaurant market, the tourist market, and the entertainment market- would experience long-term stagnation in the near future, due to the outflow of financial resources. However, the needs of modern society for delicious and varied food, entertainment and experiences are now basic, and they cannot disappear as a result of the pandemic. While maintaining basic needs and changing norms of social interaction, the forms and methods of customer service and the configuration of logistics chains are transformed. Accordingly, businesses need to adopt new hybrid practices of production, logistics and customer service that combine offline and online activities in the new environment. Thus, startups that operate through such hybrid practices have good prospects in the venture capital market.

You can also note the favorable prospects for startups, whose goal is to reduce the dependence of business and production on the presence of a person. For example, before the start of the Covid-19 pandemic, it was necessary to convince investors of the feasibility of reducing the human factor in agricultural production. At present, investors do not need to explain why an agricultural robot can reduce the dependence of agricultural production on the well-being of workers and thus increase the reliability of performing key work in the production of agricultural products.

A separate issue is startups in the field of biotechnology, healthcare, and Life Science. Venture funds that work primarily with companies in these sectors are currently in a relatively better position compared to funds that focus on other sectors. Against the background of the spread of the Covid-19 pandemic, there was an increase in investor interest in new technologies in such areas as healthcare, biotechnology, Biomedicine, and telemedicine. Accordingly, not only global venture funds, but also domestic venture funds that invest in companies in the Life Science sector, now have a unique chance to attract funds from new investors interested in new technologies, as well as to replenish their investment portfolios with new high-quality assets.

At the same time, it should be noted that this is a key condition for the development of the domestic venture financing market and the large-scale spread of venture financing practices for innovative entrepreneurship to the regions of the Russian Federation (Barykin, Kalinina, et al. 2021; Barykin, Kapustina, Sergeev, et al. 2021; Barykin, Bochkarev, et al. 2021; Barykin, Kapustina, Valebnikova, et al. 2021; Barykin, Smirnova, Sharapaev, et al. 2021). It is necessary to implement a state policy aimed at supporting venture investment. Within the framework of this policy, it is necessary to solve a set of legal problems of the venture market, as well as to form a venture infrastructure.

CONCLUSION

It can be concluded that the main task of all participants in the venture capital market is to invest and assist in the development of such companies that produce various kinds of high-tech products and provide high-tech services. Subsequently, it is these innovative companies that set internationally accepted standards for the level of technological development and quality of life. Thus, by financing innovative companies, venture market participants largely determine the course of technological development and innovative development of all sectors of the national and global economy.

The Covid-19 pandemic has caused two multidirectional trends in the venture capital market. On the one hand, investors are extremely cautious in the face of increased uncertainty and unpredictability of the economic environment. On the other hand, there is a rush of interest in startups operating in the sectors of healthcare, biotechnology, and Life Science. In the future, favorable prospects in the venture capital market are expected for startups that will master a hybrid model of production and service based on a combination of online and offline activities.

REFERENCES

Ahlstrom, David. & Garry D. Bruton. (2006). "Venture Capital in Emerging Economies: Networks and Institutional Change." *Entrepreneurship: Theory and Practice.* https://doi.org/10.1111/j.1540-6520.2006.00122.x.

Barykin, Sergey Yevgenievich, Andrey Aleksandrovich Bochkarev, Sergey Mikhailovich Sergeev, Tatiana Anatolievna Baranova, Dmitriy Anatolievich Mokhorov, and Aleksandra Maksimovna Kobicheva. 2021. "A Methodology of

Bringing Perspective Innovation Products to Market." *Academy of Strategic Management Journal* 20 (2): 19. https://www.abacademies.org/articles/a-methodology-of-bringing-perspective-innovation-products-to-market.pdf.

Barykin, Sergey Yevgenievich, Olga Vladimirovna Kalinina, Irina Vasilievna Kapustina, Victor Andreevich Dubolazov, Cesar Armando Nunez Esquivel, Elmira Alyarovna Nazarova, and Petr Anatolievich Sharapaev. 2021. "The Sharing Economy and Digital Logistics in Retail Chains: Opportunities and Threats." *Academy of Strategic Management Journal* 20 (2): 1–14. https://www.abacademies.org/articles/the-sharing-economy-and-digital-logistics-in-retail-chains-opportunities-and-threats.pdf.

Barykin, Sergey Yevgenievich, Irina Vasilievna Kapustina, Sergey Mikhailovich Sergeev, Olga Vladimirovna Kalinina, Viktoriia Valerievna Vilken, Yuri Yevgenievich Putikhin, and Lydia Vitalievna Volkova. 2021. "Developing the Physical Distribution Digital Twin Model within the Trade Network." *Academy of Strategic Management Journal* 20 (1): 1–24. https://www.abacademies.org/articles/developing-the-physical-distribution-digital-twin-model-within-the-trade-network.pdf.

Barykin, Sergey Yevgenievich, Irina Vasilievna Kapustina, Olga Aleksandrovna Valebnikova, Natalia Viktorovna Valebnikova, Olga Vladimirovna Kalinina, Sergey Mikhailovich Sergeev, Marisa Camastral, Yuri Yevgenievich Putikhin, and Lydia Vitalievna Volkova. 2021. "Digital Technologies for Personnel Management: Implications for Open Innovations." *Academy of Strategic Management Journal* 20 (2): 1–14. https://www.abacademies.org/articles/digital-technologies-for-personnel-management-implications-for-open-innovations.pdf.

Barykin, Sergey Yevgenievich, Elena Aleksandrovna Smirnova, Petr Anatolievich Sharapaev, and Angela Bohuovna Mottaeva. 2021. "Development of the Kazakhstan Digital Retail Chains within the EAEU E-Commerce." *Academy of Strategic Management Journal* 20 (2): 1–18. https://www.abacademies.org/articles/development-of-the-kazakhstan-digital-retail-chains-within-the-eaeu-ecommerce-market.pdf.

Bernardi, Paola De. & Danny Azucar. (2020). "Funding Innovation and Entrepreneurship." In *Contributions to Management Science*. https://doi.org/10.1007/978-3-030-33502-1_8.

Bonini, Stefano. & Vincenzo Capizzi. (2019). "The Role of Venture Capital in the Emerging Entrepreneurial Finance Ecosystem: Future Threats and Opportunities." *Venture Capital*. https://doi.org/10.1080/13691066.2019.1608697.

Bril, Aleksander, Olga Kalinina. & Anastasia Levina. (2018). "Two-Stage Commercial Evaluation of Engineering Systems Production Projects for High-Rise Buildings." In *E3S Web of Conferences*. https://doi.org/10.1051/e3sconf/20183303004.

Bril, Alexander, Olga Kalinina. & Olga Valebnikova. (2016). "Innovation Venture Financing Projects in Information Technology." In *Lecture Notes in Computer Science (Including Subseries Lecture Notes in Artificial Intelligence and Lecture Notes in Bioinformatics)*. https://doi.org/10.1007/978-3-319-46301-8_67.

Brown, Ross, Augusto Rocha. & Marc Cowling. (2020). "Financing Entrepreneurship in Times of Crisis: Exploring the Impact of COVID-19 on the Market for Entrepreneurial Finance in the United Kingdom." *International Small Business Journal: Researching Entrepreneurship.* https://doi.org/10.1177/0266242620937464.

Chan, Vincent. (2020). "A Disruptive and Creative Venture." *IEEE Communications Magazine.* https://doi.org/10.1109/MCOM.2020.8999415.

"Consumers Boost Shares of Coronavirus Essentials | Financial Times." n.d. Accessed February 11, 2021. https://www.ft.com/content/842ea58c-5f34-11ea-8033-fa40a0d65a98.

Davila, Antonio, George Foster. & Mahendra Gupta. (2003). "Venture Capital Financing and the Growth of Startup Firms." *Journal of Business Venturing.* https://doi.org/10.1016/S0883-9026(02)00127-1.

Dezhina, Irina G., Dan S. Medovnikov. & Stanislav D. Rozmirovich. (2019). "State Support of Small Innovative Companies by the Fund for Assistance to Innovations." *Sotsiologicheskie Issledovaniya.* https://doi.org/10.31857/S013216250007447-4.

Engel, Jerome S. (2011). "Accelerating Corporate Innovation: Lessons from the Venture Capital Model." *Research Technology Management.* https://doi.org/10.5437/08953608X5403007.

Ewens, Michael. & Matt Marx. (2018). "Founder Replacement and Startup Performance." *Review of Financial Studies.* https://doi.org/10.1093/rfs/hhx130.

Fedirko, Oleksandr. 2017. "Forms of Supporting Local Innovative Business Activity in European Countries." *International Economic Policy.*

Ferrary, Michel. & Mark Granovetter. (2009). "The Role of Venture Capital Firms in Silicon Valley's Complex Innovation Network." *Economy and Society.* https://doi.org/10.1080/03085140902786827.

Golder, Peter, Debanjan Mitra. 7 Venkat Kuppuswamy. (2018). "A Review of Crowdfunding Research and Findings." In *Handbook of Research on New Product Development.* https://doi.org/10.4337/9781784718152.00028.

Gurkov, Igor. (2004). "Business Innovation in Russian Industry." *Post-Communist Economies.* https://doi.org/10.1080/1463137042000309548.

Hellmann, Thomas. & Manju Puri. (2000). "The Interaction between Product Market and Financing Strategy: The Role of Venture Capital." *Review of Financial Studies.* https://doi.org/10.1093/rfs/13.4.959.

Hmeleva, Galina. & Darya Terekhina. (2019). "Results and Prospects of Developing Innovation Aerospace Cluster in Samara Region." *Vestnik Volgogradskogo Gosudarstvennogo Universiteta. Ekonomika.* https://doi.org/10.15688/ek.jvolsu.2019.3.6.

"How a Startup Can Attract Investment in a Crisis | Vedomosti." n.d. Accessed February 11, 2021. https://www.vedomosti.ru/management/blogs/2020/08/14/836643-kak-startapu-privlech-investitsii.

Ilin, Igor, Olga Kalinina. & Sergei Barykin. (2018). "Financial Logistics Innovations in IT Project Management." In *MATEC Web of Conferences.* https://doi.org/10.1051/matecconf/201819305062.

Köhn, Andreas. (2018). "The Determinants of Startup Valuation in the Venture Capital Context: A Systematic Review and Avenues for Future Research." *Management Review Quarterly.* https://doi.org/10.1007/s11301-017-0131-5.

Kuppuswamy, Venkat. & Barry L. Bayus. (2015). "A Review of Crowdfunding Research and Findings." *SSRN Electronic Journal.* https://doi.org/10.2139/ssrn.2685739.

Lantz, Jean Sebastien. & Jean Michel Sahut. (2010). "Corporate Venture Capital and Financing Innovation." *Problems and Perspectives in Management.* https://doi.org/10.2139/ssrn.1762247.

Lantz, Jean Sébastien, Jean Michel Sahut. & Frdric Teulon. (2011). "What Is the Real Role of Corporate Venture Capital?" *International Journal of Business.*

Liu, Yu. & Haemin Park. (2020). "The Changing Resource Needs of New Ventures and Venture Capital Syndicate Expertise Diversity." *Academy of Management Proceedings* 2020: 14876. https://doi.org/10.5465/AMBPP.2020.14876abstract.

Park, Sarah. & Joseph A. LiPuma. (2020). "New Venture Internationalization: The Role of Venture Capital Types and Reputation." *Journal of World Business.* https://doi.org/10.1016/j.jwb.2019.101025.

Rakhaeva, V. & Mizyureva, V. (2020). "Russia in International Ratings and the Impact of Coronavirus on Its Economy." *Buhuchet v Sel'skom Hozjajstve (Accounting in Agriculture).* https://doi.org/10.33920/sel-11-2007-06.

Schislyaeva, Elena, Olga Saychenko, Sergey Barykin. & Irina Kapustina. (2019). "International Energy Strategies Projects of Magnetic Levitation Transport." In *Advances in Intelligent Systems and Computing.* https://doi.org/10.1007/978-3-030-19868-8_32.

Sieradzka, Katarzyna. (2017). "Sources of Financing for Innovative Business Activities in Poland." *Central European Review of Economics & Finance.* https://doi.org/10.24136/ceref.2017.025.

Sprague, Carolyn. (2015). *Venture Capital & the Finance of Innovation. Venture Capital & the Finance of Innovation -- Research Starters Business.*

"VCs Warn Coronavirus Will Impact Fundraising for the next 2 Quarters | TechCrunch." n.d. Accessed February 11, 2021. https://techcrunch.com/2020/03/07/vcs-warn-coronavirus-will-impact-fundraising-for-the-next-2-quarters/.

Veena Iyer, S. (2020). "Venture Debt: A Catalyst for Indian Entrepreneurship." *Venture Capital.* https://doi.org/10.1080/13691066.2020.1801141.

Vilken, Viktoria, Olga Kalinina, Sergei Barykin. & Elizaveta Zotova. (2019). "Logistic Methodology of Development of the Regional Digital Economy." In *IOP Conference Series: Materials Science and Engineering.* https://doi.org/10.1088/1757-899X/497/1/012037.

"What Action Was Positively Affected by the Epidemic Coronavirus | Vedomosti." n.d. Accessed February 11, 2021. https://www.vedomosti.ru/finance/articles/2020/03/07/824697-aktsii-polozhitelno-koronavirusa.

In: Global Challenges of Digital Transformation of Markets ISBN: 978-1-53619-754-9
Editors: E. de la Poza and S. E. Barykin   © 2021 Nova Science Publishers, Inc.

Chapter 23

THE EFFICIENCY OF SERVICE SECTOR ORGANIZATIONS ON THE BASIS OF CUSTOMER SATISFACTION

Olga Chkalova[1,*], Marina Efremova[1,†], Tatyana Muranova[1,‡], Andrey Kazaev[1,§] and Julya Valeeva[2,‖]

[1]Lobachevsky State University of Nizhni Novgorod, Nizhni Novgorod, Russia
[2]Kazan State Power Engineering University, Kazan, Russia

ABSTRACT

It is shown that in a traditional client-oriented management performance indicators, based on the measurement of the volume of sales and market share are losing relevance. Changing of the efficiency estimation paradigm requires certain measurement procedures. The aim of this article is to analyze, summarize and organize the existing indicators for measuring customer satisfaction. For analysis, it uses the most notable publications by European, American and Russian authors on the topic of customer-oriented business and measuring customer satisfaction of recent years. The authors identified existing approaches and indicators to measure satisfaction. We would like to highlight that depending on the context and purpose of analysis, there can be different methods and indicators for measuring customer satisfaction.

The methodological approach we suggest is based on a system of indicators, allowing to measure customer satisfaction of different customer groups according to their loyalty: established customers, new customers, customers ready to go to a competitor, because keeping them requires different tools and techniques. In

* Corresponding Author's Email: ochkalova@iee.unn.ru.
† Corresponding Author's Email: emvnki@mail.ru.
‡ Corresponding Author's Email: muranovatd@mail.ru.
§ Corresponding Author's Email: andrey-kazayev@yandex.ru.
‖ Corresponding Author's Email: valis2000@mail.ru.

order to be able to interpret the efficiency of a service-sector organization's performance from the perspective of customer satisfaction taking into account the nature of the sector, the retail sector has been chosen as the target of research. The given system of indicators will allow to conduct regular monitoring of customer satisfaction, to use various tools for their retention, as well as to predict socio-economic results of the customer-oriented organization.

Keywords: customer-service organizations, satisfaction, performance indicators, customer, monitoring of customer satisfaction

1. INTRODUCTION

The development of modern society is characterized by accelerated growth of the service sector, which today contributes nearly 60% to the Russian GDP. In most countries in the USA, Western Europe, Japan the share of the service sector in GDP has already reached 65% or even exceeded this level. The service sector includes various lines of business: trade, accommodation, restaurant business, transport, communications, finance, education, healthcare and other fields of business connected with customer service. The efficiency of such organizations can be evaluated on the basis of their position on the market, investment attractiveness and internal resources. But the efficiency of all service sector organizations depends on one crucial factor – customer satisfaction. The founder of Marketing F. Kotler emphasizes that "marketing is meeting needs profitably" (Kotler 2012). This idea is shared by American experts F. Reichheld and U. Sasser (F. F. Reichheld and Sasser 1990) who state that customer loyalty in "service-profit chains" is the main element of profitability and long-term growth.

Satisfied customers provide a series of positive factors for a service sector organization. They would prefer it over its competitors, come back to this organization and recommend it to their acquaintances. Their average purchase amount will grow steadily because regular customers are less price sensitive and buy more products, including the new ones, selling which requires promotional efforts. Having regular customers is a lot more cost-effective for an organization than winning new ones, as it does not require advertising costs and other means of communication. These statements are confirmed by scientific research in the USA and Europe. For instance, a University of Michigan professor K. Fornell has established a relation between the growth of Customer Satisfaction Index (CSI) and large market capitalization: a 1% CSI growth leads to a 3% large market capitalization growth (Customer Satisfaction Fundamental basis of business survival, 2005). For a typical American selling organization, purchases made by regular customers account for nearly 70% of their turnover. The costs of attracting a new customer are 5-10 times higher than the costs of retaining a loyal customer. The costs of winning back a lost customer are 50-100 times higher than regular customer costs.

In the world science and practice, the strategy of development of services companies where customer satisfaction is a priority is called customer-oriented strategy (Grönroos 1994; Narver and Slater 1990; Saxe and Weitz 1982). Research analysis in this field shows that scientific interest in this problem has been growing rapidly since the beginning of 1980s (Coltman, Devinney, and Midgley 2011; Smirnova, Rebiazina, and Frösén 2018; Webster, Malter, and Ganesan 2011). Customer-oriented development of service sector organizations is currently one of the most burning topics for foreign and Russian researchers dealing with issues connected with the development of the service sector (Frambach, Fiss, and Ingenbleek 2016; Gebauer and Kowalkowski 2012; Peter Fader 2012). Most Western companies have already gone through an active transition period from the system of mass production to customer-oriented value creation (Giannikas, McFarlane, and Strachan 2019). In Russia this kind of situation is only starting to develop, especially in organizations where competition for customers is the most fierce: in the banking, insurance and telecommunications sectors.

In the context of client-oriented business, the efficiency measurement vector shifts from product to customer and is based not on sales and market share, but on customer satisfaction. Customer equity is becoming the main asset of a sales chain, and customer satisfaction – a priority efficiency criterion for customer-oriented organizations. There is a number of scientific publications devoted to this topic, with eloquent titles, like for example, The Myth of Market Share. Why Market Share is the Fool's Gold of Business (Pennington 2004), Manage for Profit, no for Market Share: A Guide to Greater Profits in Highly Contested Markets (Simon, Bilstein, and Luby 2012).

Changing of the efficiency estimation paradigm requires certain measurement procedures (Bloemer and Kasper 1995; Gronroos 1984; Oliver 1980).

The development of business Analytics of trading operations, the ability to assess the results of customer satisfaction are among the main issues, since they have a direct impact on the formation of not only financial indicators of trading companies, but also on the image component of their activities (Wirtz and Bateson 1999; Beerli, Martín, and Quintana 2004; "The Service Profit Chain: How Leading Companies Link Profit and Growth to Loyalty, Satisfaction and Value" 1999).

The results of the research show that the issues connected with measuring customer satisfaction are the focus of attention for many scientists (Angilella et al., 2014; Bouranta, Siskos, and Tsotsolas 2015; Drosos et al., 2018).

In many countries of the world (Sweden, Germany, the USA, Israel etc.), National Customer Satisfaction Indexes (NCSI) are used to measure customer satisfaction (Anderson, Fornell, and Lehmann 1994; Fornell et al., 1996; Hom 2000). In some European countries (Portugal, Belgium, Denmark, Spain, Finland, France, Greece, Iceland, Italy, Great Britain, Sweden and Switzerland) a European CSI has been introduced since 1998. CSI is multi-sector quantitative estimation of customer satisfaction and the principal organizations' efficiency factors through regular collection of data throughout the country, performed by an independent organization. As a rule, the survey method is used for evaluation, according to the selected scale. For instance, the American National Index (ACSI) uses a scale from 1 to 10; and the European Customer Satisfaction Index (ECSI) – from 0 to 100. The object of evaluation can be the quality of product (service), like, for example, in Sweden, or, in addition to that – customer loyalty.

The aim of this article is to analyze, summarize and organize the existing indicators for measuring customer satisfaction. For analysis, it uses the most notable publications by European, American and Russian authors on the topic of customer-oriented business and measuring customer satisfaction of recent years (I. Krasyuk and Medvedeva 2019; I. A. Krasyuk and Medvedeva 2019).

As a result of the analysis, other indicators describing customer satisfaction have been revealed. For instance, a consulting company Temkin Group (USA) has developed TLR (Temkin loyalty rating) to calculate repeat purchases in one organization within 60 days.

In order to measure customer satisfaction for organizations that work with customer calls, foreign researchers have suggested a methodology, based on observing the behavior of office staff in call-centers during a call. The principal criterion is first contact resolution rate (FCR) for calls with successful results for a customer after the first call (when the customer wasn't transferred to another office worker or was transferred the fewest number of times). The applied rating scale is from 1 to 7.

Another indicator for measuring customer satisfaction is the rate of recency, frequency and monetary value of purchase (RFM) (Yeh, Yang, and Ting 2009).

- Recency (R) is the time passed since the last order placed by the customer, in days;
- Frequency (F) is the total number of orders placed by the customer during the observed period;
- Monetary value of purchase (M) is the sum of money spent by the customer while being a loyal customer of a particular organization.

This indicator describes the value of this customer to the organization on the basis of the analysis of the period of time passed since the last purchase, frequency of purchase throughout the customer's interaction period with the organization and the total amount of purchase.

Another widespread indicator is net promoter score (NPS) suggested by a researcher F. Reichheld (F. Reichheld 2006). This indicator measures the degree of probability that the customer will recommend the service company that he/she liked to his/her friends and acquaintances. This methodology is based on a ten-point rating scale. Customers are asked two questions: "How much chance is there that you will recommend this company to a friend or colleague?" and an open clarifying question, giving respondents an opportunity to formulate the reason for their loyalty (refusal): "Elaborate on the main reason for your appraisal."

As a result of the survey, the customers were divided into three groups:

1. Those who gave the company a rating of 9, 10 points: the "promoters" group. They are ready to keep buying products and services from the company, as well as recommend it to their friends and relatives.
2. Those who gave the company a rating of 8, 7 points: the "neutrals" group. In general, they are satisfied with the organization and sometimes recommend it to their friends and colleagues. But this is a group that can easily go to a competitor if they have more tempting offers.
3. Those who gave the company a rating of 6-1 points: the "detractors" group. These are customers who are not loyal to the sales chain and give negative feedback about it.

Table 1. Indicators for measuring customer satisfaction

Indicator Set	Single Indicators
Keeping and increasing the number of established customers	**– Customer equity of a sales chain** – NPS/ net promoter score – CSI/CDI – customer satisfaction/delight index – RFM – recency, frequency and monetary value – Share of regular customers in the total number of customers – Increase in the share of repeat visits – The amount of single purchases made by a regular customer – Average purchase amount of existing customers – Average frequency of visits to the shop – Customer retention rate – Customer retention costs **– CLV customer lifetime value**
Attracting new customers	– ROIC return on investment in customer – Average frequency of visits to the shop – Average purchase amount of new customers – Costs of attracting new customers to 1 RUB revenue – Share of newly attracted customers in the total number of customers – Share of revenue from new customers – Rate of growth of the number of new customers – Rate of growth of the amount of purchases made by new customers – Rate of growth of turnover from new customers.
Planning the leaving of some regular customers	– defection rate – retention rate – the number of claims and complaints from customers.
Increase of an average check	– Impulse-sales turnover – Cross-sales turnover.
Good Will–business reputation	– Tri*M (measuring, management, monitoring) managing the interrelations of all the groups interested in the activities of the sales chain – The degree of brand awareness in the target market.

Net Promoter Score is determined by calculating the difference between the number of promoters and detractors (1):

$$NPS = \% \text{ promoters} - \% \text{ detractors} \tag{1}$$

These and other customer satisfaction indicators revealed are shown in Table 1.

In Russia, the term CSI was introduced during the preparation for entering the WTO. However, the methods of calculating this indicator have not been determined during the research we carried out. This type of research is just starting to develop in Russian science. The majority of indicators developed by Russian researchers are a modification of the above mentioned indicators (Smirnova, Rebiazina, and Frösén 2018). In Russia today there is no clear system of measuring customer satisfaction allowing graded evaluation of clients on the basis of the level of their loyalty to the organization.

2. MATERIALS AND METHODS

The methodological approach we suggest is based on a system of indicators, allowing to measure customer satisfaction of different customer groups according to their loyalty: established customers, new customers, customers ready to go to a competitor, because keeping them requires different tools and techniques. In order to be able to interpret the efficiency of a service-sector organization's performance from the perspective of customer satisfaction taking into account the nature of the sector, the retail sector has been chosen as the target of research. Let us consider the following hypotheses:

1. Revenue, profit and efficiency are determined by the number of customers and the average check of 1 customer;
2. Revenue, profit and efficiency of a selling organization are provided by regular customers who have already had some positive experience working with this sales chain, as well as newly attracted customers;
3. In the group of regular customers, there are always those who are ready to go to a competitor after some time. It has been established by some foreign research that for even the most loyal customers it takes 7 years maximum to change their preferences and go to a competitor;
4. Average check includes the major check and additional check. The major check is determined by a sum of planned purchases, the additional check – by impulse purchases, including cross purchases.
5. Business reputation of the sales chain (Good will) is determined by the number of customers ("word of mouth") (Figure 1)

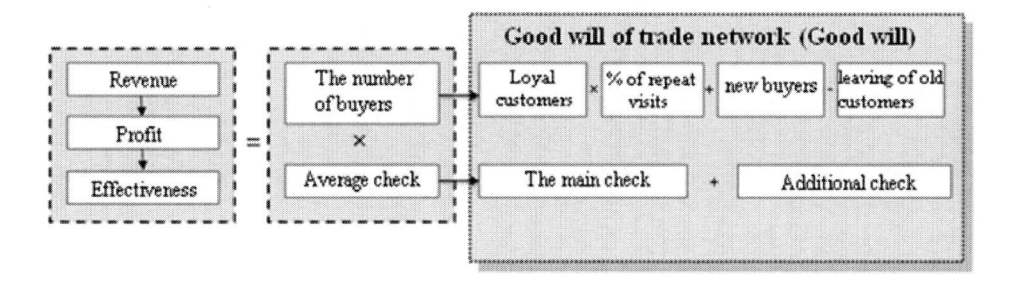

Figure 1. Assessing the performance of a sales chain on the basis of customer satisfaction.

3. RESULTS

Based on the above hypotheses, let us differentiate the indicators for measuring customer satisfaction into the following sets:

1. keeping and increasing the number of established customers,
2. attracting new customers,
3. planning the leaving of some regular customers,
4. increase of an average check, including the additional check,
5. business reputation of the sales chain (GoodWill).

To evaluate each set of indicators, we have suggested single indicators, received as a result of summarizing foreign and Russian professional literature. Besides, the table shows indicators which were adapted by us for measuring customer satisfaction: the amount of single purchases made by an established (new) customer, costs of keeping the existing customers (attracting new customers), the share of established (new) customers in the total number of customers, average amount of purchase made by established (new) customers, the return on customer investment, etc. (Table 1).

4. DISCUSSION

Let us describe some indicators:

Customer Equity of a sales chain is a sum of CLV of all its existing and potential customers. The sources of information are the following: average purchase frequency indicators, average check, average length of the period during which the customer stays loyal to the sales chain.

CLV (customer lifetime value) is net discounted customer value, a discounted cash flow created during the period of collaboration with the customer. As a result, single actions designed to attract customers gradually develop into customer assets of the company, consisting of customers who thanks to their loyalty provide a source of steady long-term cash flow coming from purchases made by them.

CLV equals average revenue per customer throughout the period less costs (product costs, maintenance costs and marketing costs).

Planning customers' leaving (2) is carried out on the basis of defection rate, i.e., the percentage of customers who refused to buy products or services of the sales chain during one year.

$$PLV = CUR \times [IMIP + CLV] - CANC \tag{2}$$

PLV - Planning customers' leaving (RUB), CUR - Customer Attraction Rate (%), IMIP - Initial margin of the initial purchases (RUB), CLV - Customer lifetime value (RUB), CANC - Costs of attracting a new customer (RUB).

To calculate the additional check, the following indicators can be suggested:

Impulse Sales, i.e., the number of additional products, bought by a customer during a certain period of time;

Cross Sales, i.e., the number of additional products, cross-displayed and bought by the customer during a certain period of time. The sources of information are the following: records of purchase history, price, and purchase analysis in the consumer basket.

The degree of brand awareness in the target market can be measured through the number of recommendations given by existing customers, helping to attract new customers.

The scale of awareness includes a number of levels:

1. Highest awareness. The customer associates the need with a product or a brand;
2. "Uninduced awareness" when the customer is aware of the product or brand, but does not associate it directly with the need;
3. "Induced awareness" when the customer is hardly aware of the product or brand and does not associate it with the need;
4. "Lack of awareness" when the customer is not aware of the product or brand, and does not associate it with the need.

CONCLUSION

Using the suggested methodological approach and system of indicators allows to focus our attention not on the market share, but on measuring customer satisfaction. While measuring customer satisfaction, it is necessary to consider the consumer experience of both the established and new customers and plan the leaving of established customers, which is always inevitable. This approach takes into account the average check, including the additional check, depending on the level of sales chain's staff competence and merchandizing. According to this approach, it is necessary to assess the business reputation of a customer-oriented organization, which depends on customer loyalty.

Thus, this approach allows to tackle the measurement of customer satisfaction of each group of customers from different angles and evaluate the efficiency of a customer-oriented service-sector organization on the basis of its results.

In our research, we would like to highlight that depending on the context and purpose of analysis, there can be different methods and indicators for measuring customer satisfaction. The existing methodological approaches differ from each other in a number of aspects, many of them keep developing. Therefore the methodological approach suggested in this research cannot be considered as the final version. Nevertheless, we believe it to be quite up-to-date, as it takes into account the sector peculiarities of a selling organization and allows to perform a detailed analysis of different groups of customers depending on the level of their loyalty. This system of indicators will allow to monitor customer satisfaction on a regular basis, use various tools for keeping customers, as well as forecast social and economic results of a customer-oriented organization.

REFERENCES

[1]   Anderson, Eugene W., Claes Fornell, and Donald R. Lehmann. 1994. "Customer Satisfaction, Market Share, and Profitability: Findings from Sweden." *Journal of Marketing.* https://doi.org/10.1177/002224299405800304.

[2]   Angilella, Silvia, Salvatore Corrente, Salvatore Greco, and Roman Słowiński. 2014. "MUSA-INT: Multicriteria Customer Satisfaction Analysis with Interacting Criteria." *Omega (United Kingdom).* https://doi.org/10.1016/j.omega.2013.05. 006.

[3]   Beerli, Asunción, Josefa D. Martín, and Agustín Quintana. 2004. "A Model of Customer Loyalty in the Retail Banking Market." *European Journal of Marketing.* https://doi.org/10.1108/03090560410511221.

[4]   Bloemer, José M. M. M., and Hans D. P. Kasper. 1995. "The Complex Relationship between Consumer Satisfaction and Brand Loyalty." *Journal of Economic Psychology.* https://doi.org/10.1016/0167-4870(95)00007-B.

[5]   Bouranta, Nancy, Yannis Siskos, and Nikos Tsotsolas. 2015. "Measuring Police Officer and Citizen Satisfaction: Comparative Analysis." *Policing.* https://doi.org/ 10.1108/PIJPSM-01-2015-0008.

[6]   Coltman, Tim, Timothy M. Devinney, and David F. Midgley. 2011. "Customer Relationship Management and Firm Performance." *Journal of Information Technology.* https://doi.org/10.1057/jit.2010.39.

[7]   Drosos, Dimitris, Nikos Tsotsolas, Michalis Skordoulis, and Miltiadis Chalikias. 2018. "Patient Satisfaction Analysis Using a Multi-Criteria Analysis Method: The Case of the NHS in Greece." *International Journal of Productivity and Quality Management.* https://doi.org/10.1504/IJPQM.2018.096091.

[8]   Fornell, Claes, Michael D. Johnson, Eugene W. Anderson, Jaesung Cha, and Barbara Everitt Bryant. 1996. "The American Customer Satisfaction Index: Nature, Purpose, and Findings." *Journal of Marketing.* https://doi.org/10.2307/1251898.

[9]   Frambach, Ruud T., Peer C. Fiss, and Paul T. M. Ingenbleek. 2016. "How Important Is Customer Orientation for Firm Performance? A Fuzzy Set Analysis of Orientations, Strategies, and Environments." *Journal of Business Research.* https://doi.org/10.1016/j.jbusres.2015.10.120.

[10]   Gebauer, Heiko, and Christian Kowalkowski. 2012. "Customer-Focused and Service-Focused Orientation in Organizational Structures." *Journal of Business and Industrial Marketing.* https://doi.org/10.1108/08858621211257293.

[11]   Giannikas, Vaggelis, Duncan McFarlane, and James Strachan. 2019. "Towards the Deployment of Customer Orientation: A Case Study in Third-Party Logistics." *Computers in Industry.* https://doi.org/10.1016/j.compind.2018.10.005.

[12]   Gronroos, Christian. 1984. "A Service Quality Model and Its Marketing Implications." *European Journal of Marketing.* https://doi.org/10.1108/EUM0000000004784.

[13]   Grönroos, Christian. 1994. "From Marketing Mix to Relationship Marketing." *Management Decision.* https://doi.org/10.1108/00251749410054774.

[14]   Hom, Willard. 2000. "An Overview of Customer Satisfaction Models." *Customer Satisfaction Models.*

[15]   Kotler, Philip. 2012. "Marketing Management/Philip Kotler, Kevin Lane Keller." *Pearson Education International.*

[16]   Krasyuk, Irina and Y. Medvedeva. 2019. "Resource Support in Business Analytics of Innovative Development of Trade and Technological Systems." In *Proceedings of the 33rd International Business Information Management Association Conference, IBIMA 2019: Education Excellence and Innovation Management through Vision 2020.*

[17]   Krasyuk, Irina A., and Yuliya Y. Medvedeva. 2019. "Drives and Obstacle for the Development of Marketing in Russian Retailing." In *Proceedings of the 33rd International Business Information Management Association Conference, IBIMA 2019: Education Excellence and Innovation Management through Vision 2020.*

[18]   Narver, John C., and Stanley F. Slater. 1990. "The Effect of a Market Orientation on Business Profitability." *Journal of Marketing.* https://doi.org/10.1177/002224299005400403.

[19]   Oliver, Richard L. 1980. "A Cognitive Model of the Antecedents and Consequences of Satisfaction Decisions." *Journal of Marketing Research.* https://doi.org/10.1177/002224378001700405.

[20]   Pennington, Malcolm. 2004. " The Myth of Market Share: Why Market Share Is the Fool's Gold of Business20041Richard Miniter. The Myth of Market Share: Why Market Share Is the Fool's Gold of Business . New York, NY: Crown Business 2002. 172 Pp. ." *Journal of Fashion Marketing and Management: An International Journal.* https://doi.org/10.1108/jfmm.2004.8.2.245.1.

[21] Fader, Peter 2012. *"Customer Centricity: Focus on the Right Customers for Strategic Advantage, Second Edition / Wharton Digital Press."* May 15, 2012.

[22] Reichheld, Fred, F., and W. E. Sasser. 1990. "Zero Defections: Quality Comes to Services." *Harvard Business Review.*

[23] Reichheld, Fred. 2006. "Ultimate Question: For Driving Good Profits and True Growth (Hardcover)." *Harvard Business School Press Books.*

[24] Saxe, Robert, and Barton A. Weitz. 1982. "The SOCO Scale: A Measure of the Customer Orientation of Salespeople." *Journal of Marketing Research.* https://doi.org/10.1177/002224378201900307.

[25] Simon, Hermann, Frank F Bilstein, and Frank Luby. 2012. "Optimize Your Marketing Mix to Capture the Highest Additional Profit." In *Harvard Business Press Chapters.*

[26] Smirnova, Maria M., Vera A. Rebiazina, and Johanna Frösén. 2018. "Customer Orientation as a Multidimensional Construct: Evidence from the Russian Markets." *Journal of Business Research.* https://doi.org/10.1016/j.jbusres.2017.10.040.

[27] "The Service Profit Chain: How Leading Companies Link Profit and Growth to Loyalty, Satisfaction and Value." 1999. *Work Study.* https://doi.org/10.1108/ws.1999.07948aae.003.

[28] Webster, Frederick, Alan J. Malter, and Shankar Ganesan. 2011. "The Role of Marketing in the Corporation: A Perpetual Work in Progress." *SSRN Electronic Journal.* https://doi.org/10.2139/ssrn.530882.

[29] Wirtz, Jochen, and John E. G. Bateson. 1999. "Consumer Satisfaction with Services: Integrating the Environment Perspective in Services Marketing into the Traditional Disconfirmation Paradigm." *Journal of Business Research.* https://doi.org/10.1016/S0148-2963(97)00178-1.

[30] Yeh, Cheng I., King Jang Yang, and Tao Ming Ting. 2009. "Knowledge Discovery on RFM Model Using Bernoulli Sequence." *Expert Systems with Applications.* https://doi.org/10.1016/j.eswa.2008.07.018.

In: Global Challenges of Digital Transformation of Markets ISBN: 978-1-53619-754-9
Editors: E. de la Poza and S. E. Barykin   © 2021 Nova Science Publishers, Inc.

Chapter 24

THE STUDY OF THE DYNAMIC SERIES OF ECONOMIC INDICATORS OF ENTERPRISES IN THE HOTEL SECTOR

*Marina Efremova[*], Natalya Baranova, Ludmila Bogatyreva,
Tatiana Zikova, Elena Kochkurova and Nikolai Shimin*
Lobachevsky State University of Nizhniy Novgorod, Nizhniy Novgorod, Russia

ABSTRACT

The research presents the calculation of the main economic performance indicators of the hotels based on official statistics. The forecast threshold values of some statistics describing the state of the sector of collective accommodation facilities in the Russian Federation as a whole are proposed. Based on comparison of indicators of the sector of collective placements with the average Russian proposals on optimization of the number of placements and their economic indicators are formulated. The analysis of statistical data shows the need for increasing the value of the considered indicators, including due to reorganization (optimization) of a control system of the hotel enterprise. Hotel management has to be directly involved in the development of strategic growth, influencing, thus, rendering of services, development of the tourist market, development of the own enterprise. The resources of placement in the hotel business is the choice of the services and the markets offering the best investment opportunities.

Keywords: performance indicators, economic indicators, hotel, activity analysis, hotel market, state of development, development trend

---

[*] Corresponding Author's Email: efremovamv@iee.unn.ru.

1. INTRODUCTION

The analysis of economic indicators of the activity of hotels shows the situation in the market of hotel services. It is very important to understand what factors in the economic situation of the hotel lead to receiving profit.

According to statistical data in Russia, the number of officially registered collective placements in Russia has increased more, than twice for the last 15 years. The main contribution was made by hotels - more, than three times. By more than two times also the number of rooms of the Russian hotels has grown (Romanyuk and Gareev 2019). And other specialized collective placements show smaller dynamics. They include such objects as rest houses; recreation facilities; camping; tourist centers; the public automobiles used as collective placements (tourist trains, cruise vessels, yachts).

Thaw the aim of the study is the calculation of the main economic performance indicators of the hotels based on the data of official statistics. Some researchers show that "results indicated that hotels should closely monitor demand-based pricing, optional product pricing, promotional pricing, and psychological pricing among pricing strategies and length of stay control in non-pricing strategies, as they have a significant relationship with revenue management performance which in turn can provide a competitive advantage in business" (Nair 2019). Pereira asserts that "revenue management is a key tool for hotel managers' decision-making process" (Pereira 2016). In general, it can be argued "the hotel industry to develop more comprehensive performance measurement systems, as hotels are facing increased pressure from stakeholders, including the government and consumers, to follow sustainable practices" (Patiar and Wang 2020). Researchers had asserted "hotel companies, like any other organization, can use financial measures or indicators to generate information for the decision-making process of their managers to improve business performance. The results obtained should allow companies in the hotel industry to promote an adequate return to their shareholders and investors, pay creditors and adequately reward employees, and sustain growth" я (Mucharreira et al. 2019). "In a competitive market, an increase in supply while keeping demand relatively constant would decrease prices and revenues" (Dogru, Mody, and Suess 2019). While the literature suggests that hotels' crisis management capabilities can be improved by evaluating the efficacy of crisis-coping strategies used for a past crisis, a limited number of empirical studies have focused on such assessment (Kim, Roehl, and Lee 2019). "One of the factors of competitiveness of the hotel industry is the financial-economic situation, which may also be called a financially stable position, financial stability, and financial competitiveness" (Baranova and Bogatyreva 2018). Furthermore, "the assessment of financial stability can be described through a system of calculation of indicators that characterize the level of independence judging by the elements of the assets and provide an opportunity to measure how stable the analyzed organization financially is" (Baranova and Bogatyreva 2018).

Recently, the hotel industry has become a stimulus for economic development. This fact is shown in some papers (dos Santos, Méxas, and Meiriño 2017; Elhoushy,

Elbayoumi Salem, and Agag 2020; Gössling 2015) and "within the tourism industry, the hotel sector's vulnerabilities are multi-faceted" (Brown et al. 2017).

2. MATERIALS AND METHODS

The methodological basis of the study was the official data of Russian statistics. The method of comparative analysis of economic indicators of the Russian collective placements made it possible to achieve the goal of the study.

2.1. Activity of Collective Placements

The data of official Russian statistics ("Official Site of Federal State Statistics Service in Russia" n.d.) characterizing dynamics of the hotel market in general and also hotels and similar means of placement during 2015-2019 are presented in Tables 1, 2 and 3.

The results of the calculations concerning three hotels JSC "The Hotel Barnaul," JSC "The Hotel Novorossiysk," JSC "The Tomsk Hotel." The analysis was conducted based on three groups of indicators: assets (the amount of non-current assets, the number of current assets, the total quantity of assets); profit and profitability (the result from operating activities, the net profit, the asset profitability of net income); liquidity (fixed, absolute) (Baranova and Bogatyreva 2018).

3. RESULTS

3.1. Operational Indicators of Activity of Hotels

Consideration and analysis of operational indicators of the activity of hotels are relevant in modern economic conditions.

For assessment of hotel business there are the following economic criteria:

- indicators of profitability of one number,
- total income from each occupied or available number,
- income on one guest or one berth,
- gross operating profit on each room,
- indicators of profitability of the conference areas,
- Food and Beverage (F&B), etc.

Table 1. Indicators of the assets group

Name of the object	2015	2016	2017	2018	2019
		Indicators of the assets group			
		Revenue			
Hotel Barnaul	105 035 000.00	112 856 000.00	131 760 000.00	155 480 000.00	147 931 000.00
Hotel Novorossiysk	86 549 000.00	88 799 000.00	108 259 000.00	94 177 000.00	93 066 000.00
Tomsk Hotel	28 718 000.00	23 412 000.00	17 629 000.00	17 599 000.00	13 550 000.00
Name of the object	2015	2016	2017	2018	2019
		Cost price			
Hotel Novorossiysk	68 641 000.00	71 270 000.00	71 270	88 740 000.00	63 526 000.00
Tomsk Hotel	28 183 000.00	16 419 000.00	14 555 000.00	14 397 000.00	13 186 000.00
	Amount of net income				
Hotel Novorossiysk	487 000.00	-260 000.00	-788 000.00	14 049 000.00	10 882 000.00
Tomsk Hotel	-2 471 000.00	-1 967 000.00	640 000.00	63 000.00	-1 666 000.00

Table 2. Indicators of the profit and profitability group

Name of the object	2015	2016	2017	2018	2019
	Indicators of the profit and profitability group				
Result from operating activities					
Hotel Barnaul	17 205 000.00	11 855 000.00	18 638 000.00	35 152 000.00	28 702 000.00
Hotel Novorossiysk	4 214 000.00	4 057 000.00	5 250 000.00	20 270 000.00	19 310 000.00
Tomsk Hotel	-406 000.00	6 017 000.00	2 175 000.00	2 315 000.00	-450 000.00
	Amount of net income				
Hotel Barnaul	10 277 000.00	7 748 000.00	12 364 000.00	28 893 000.00	22 436 000.00
Hotel Novorossiysk	487 000.00	-260 000.00	-788 000.00	14 049 000.00	10 882 000.00
Tomsk Hotel	-2 471 000.00	-1 967 000.00	640 000.00	63 000.00	-1 666 000.00

Table 3. Indicators of the profit and profitability group

Name of the object	2015	2016	2017	2018	2019
		Indicators of the liquidity			
Current liquidity					
Hotel Barnaul	1.30	2.09	0.53	1.35	0.88
The Hotel Novorossiysk	1.89	1.66	2.85	1.88	1.10
The Tomsk Hotel	1.72	1.68	4.06	4.63	6.50
		Absolute liquidity			
Hotel Novorossiysk	0.22	0.42	1.08	0.54	0.09
Tomsk Hotel	0.02	0.05	0.01	0.11	1.20

From the category of operational efficiency two indicators are the most often used:

The Revenue per available room (RevPAR). The Gross operating profit per available room (GOPPar) (Abrate, Nicolau, and Viglia 2019).

RevPAR calculator computes the revenue per available room and is a performance metric in the hotel industry that is calculated by dividing a hotel's total guestroom revenue by the room count and the number of days in the period being measured (Lea R. Dopson and David K. Hayes 2008).

In world practice, this criterion of efficiency is used as a base for definition and the analysis of the quality of work of hotel and allows to keep track of effectiveness and effective management of the number of rooms. But "RevPAR, as traditionally measured, will not be an adequate measure of performance as it considers only the rooms portion of the hotel asset" (Kimes 2011).

RevPAR indicates the performance of a hotel in terms of rooms inventory management and provides some general market trends. "Hoteliers aim to maximize RevPAR by means of an occupancy and average rate trade-off. Rooms revenue makes up a large portion of total revenue" (Younes and Kett 2003).

RevPar pays off on as follows:

$$RevPar - \frac{Rooms\ Rev}{Rooms\ Ava} \qquad (1)$$

where Room Revenue is the income from the sale of the number of rooms; Rooms Available is the total of rooms in the hotel.

$$RevPAR = ADR * OR\ (Occ), \% \qquad (2)$$

where ADR - average room rate in days; OR or OCC - occupancy ratio.

For hotels that are different in the sizes, the revenue of the number of rooms can vary from 50 to 95% in the absence of, for example, proceeds from the restaurant, SPA, event rooms, etc. RevPAR can be only a reflection of a share of income from the sale of numbers, at the same time doesn't consider other sources of income. But The indicator of RevPar will be better in hotels with the greatest number of rooms, than in small hotels. GOPPar - the indicator reflecting profit on one number.

$$GOPPar = \frac{GOP \ (Gross \ Operating \ Profit)}{Available \ Rooms} \tag{3}$$

GOP (Gross Operating Profit) - gross operating profit on one available number. The GOP pays off as a difference between total sales of the number of rooms, restaurants, cafe, other departments and the sum of a direct operating and other expenses. This indicator allows to reflect better profitability of hotel in general, and not just the number of rooms, therefore, the overall performance of the management of departments and hotel in general.

GOPPar "is defined as total gross operating profit (GOP) per available room per day, where GOP is equal to total revenue less the total departmental and operating expenses." GOPPAR offers an overall more robust performance measure, especially when comparing the financial performances of hotels with different sizes or in different markets (E. Younes n.d.).

GOPPar is a KPI that allows hotels to apply the laws of economics to comprehensively describe the process of Revenue Management with all the details taken into account (Cross, Higbie, and Cross 2009) and make adjustments not only on achieving the top line but aligning it with the bottom line as well. From an ownership perspective, GOPPAR allows seeing what the value of the owner's asset is at any given time.

Issues of evaluating the performance of enterprises focused on the end user can improve the effectiveness of activities. Resourcing provides the basis for long-term planning, which can be used as a tool for KPI (I. A. Krasyuk and Medvedeva 2019; I. Krasyuk and Medvedeva 2019).

It is necessary to remember that larger hotels have big costs of the room service and hotels in general, however, at redistribution on one number, it is much less expense than at small hotels.

Thus:

- the indicator can be used as the efficiency of use, main for assessment, and work of the number of rooms;
- GOPRar will be more correct to be used for assessment of the profitability of the hotel in general taking into account all departments bringing income.

4. DISCUSSION

4.1. The Interpretation of the Results of the Calculation

4.1.1. The Hotel Barnaul

The share of fixed assets in the property at the end of the analyzed period amounted to 73.3%. The company has a "heavy" asset structure. This usually indicates significant overhead. In this case, to maintain financial stability, the company needs to have a high share of equity and long-term borrowed capital in sources of financing.

The profitability of all operations (profit before tax) of the company at the end of the analyzed period amounted to 18.1% and was 1.3% lower than the rate of return on sales (core business). Thus, the hotel Barnaul loses part of its effectiveness due to other activities. The ratio of net profit and sales revenue, that is, the indicator of sales profitability by net profit reflects that part of the revenues that remains at the disposal of the company from each ruble of sales. The value of the indicator in the analyzed period increased from 9.8% to 15.2%. Thus, the company is expanding opportunities to independently finance its working capital, without attracting external sources for these purposes. This ratio has been considered in combination with indicators such as sales and net profit per employee, sales per unit area, etc. For this, it is necessary to further analyze the costing of the enterprise.

4.1.2. The Hotel Novorossiysk

The structure of current assets for the analyzed period has changed significantly. At the same time, in the analyzed period, the bulk of current assets invariably accounted for receivables (46.3%). The proportion of inventories in current assets increased from 8.1% to 42.6%.

The cost of inventories for the analyzed period increased by 2,146,000 thousand rubles (from 1,155,000 to 3,301,000), which is a negative change, as the duration of inventory turnover has increased.

Such a sharp increase in reserves (by 185.8%) makes it necessary to further in-depth analysis of their composition and structure according to analytical accounting. At the same time, the growth rate of reserves (185.8%) for the analyzed period significantly outstripped the growth rate of revenue (7.5%), which immobilized part of the financial resources in the company's working capital.

The return on equity (actual) of the enterprise (determining the effectiveness of investments of owners' funds) throughout the analyzed period was positive and changed sharply, increasing from 2.1% to 68.2%, which indicates the possibility of attracting investment into the company.

The level of return on assets for net profit in the amount of 50.6% at the end of the analyzed period is ensured by a high turnover of assets, which amounted to 4.334 turns per year at the end of the period, with a high (11.7%) return on all operations (on net profit).

Evaluation of the effectiveness of the management of the main activities of the company from the standpoint of profit is given by the profitability indicator calculated based on the results from the main activity. The profitability of production assets (showing how much profit each ruble invested in the production assets of the company) brings at the beginning of the analyzed period was 18.1%, and at the end of the period, it was 96.0%. This value of the profitability indicator consists of the profitability of sales (core business), which at the end of the analyzed period amounted to 20.8%, and the turnover of production assets equal to 4.628 turnover per year.

4.1.3. The Hotel Tomsk

The property structure is characterized by a relatively low share of current assets, which did not change, amounting to 7.8% at the beginning and 9.9% at the end of the analyzed period. The current assets of the Enterprise for the analyzed period remained virtually unchanged, amounting to 6,836,000 thousand rubles at the end of the period. The growth of current assets occurred due to an increase in the following components:

- money;
- other current assets while reducing:
- stocks;
- accounts receivable;
- short-term financial investments.

The structure of current assets for the analyzed period has changed significantly. At the same time, in the analyzed period, the bulk of current assets invariably accounted for receivables (56.6%). The proportion of inventories in current assets decreased from 25.1% to 15.6%. The cost of inventories for the analyzed period decreased by 599,000 thousand rubles (from 1,663,000 to 1,064,000). Such a sharp decrease in stocks may be caused by a reduction in the volume of the company. The share of receivables (short-term and long-term) in current assets decreased from 66.8% to 56.6%. For the analyzed period, the volume of receivables decreased by 550.000 thousand rubles (from 4,419,000 to 3,869,000), which is a positive change and may indicate an improvement in the situation with payment for the company's products and the choice of an appropriate sales policy and the provision of consumer credit to customers. The amount of cash in the analyzed period tended to increase from 67,000 thousand rubles up to 1,261,000 thousand rubles.

The company for the analyzed period reduced the amount of short-term financial investments from 417,000 thousand rubles up to 68,000 thousand rubles, while their share in the structure of current assets decreased from 6.3% to 1.0%. The cost of sales of the company for the analyzed period decreased by 15 124,000 thousand rubles or 51.9% (from 29 124,000 to 14,000.000 thousand rubles). From the implementation of all types of activities at the end of the analyzed period, the company received a loss in the amount of 1,754,000 thousand rubles, which is 25.9% less than the loss at the beginning of the period, which amounted to 2,368,000 thousand rubles. The absence in the analyzed period of the company net profit indicates that it did not have a source of working capital replenishment.

CONCLUSION

The analysis of statistical data shows the need for an increase in the value of the considered indicators, including due to reorganization (optimization) of a control system of the hotel enterprise.

The research results allow to note the following conclusions. Forming a strategy to achieve certain sizes of profitability, the enterprise management must consider it not as passively received income, but as a result of conquest. Profitability, earned through the initiative, will be the result of innovation, the absence of fear of risk, the rational use of funds, the forward-looking debt policy. In most cases, profitability is at the same time received, earned and allowed. At the same time, it is important, especially in conditions of financial instability, that all measures are taken by the enterprise to increase profitability (when using all the opportunities) contribute to the achievement of the set goals.

Justification of the target size of profitability may include the following activities:

1. Determination of the volume of trade at which it is possible to obtain target profitability;
2. Development of pricing policies and strategies;
3. Formation of assortment policy (determination of the optimal commodity-group structure corresponding to the demand of the population and ensuring the achievement of the chosen goal);
4. Formation of a resource policy (commodity support, labor, material and financial resources);
5. Gross income management;
6. Using the possibilities of effective allocation of money;
7. Management of distribution costs;
8. Conformity assessment of profitability opportunities to its target value, etc.

Thus, assessing the effectiveness of the policy of selling products (works, services), special attention should be paid to the analysis of the effectiveness of the top management of the enterprise, without decisions and operational actions of which such a financial situation of the enterprise could not have developed.

To ensure a reliable future and a successful way out of crisis situations, constant work is needed to optimize business processes in the areas listed below that ensure the survival of the enterprise.

For this reason, the following measures need to be taken:

- improvement of logistics;
- periodic analysis of the business sustainability of the enterprise;
- improvement of the management structure and technological processes;
- development of computer systems.

Optimization of the use of fixed assets, including:

- analysis of the degree of use of space equipment, the ability to sell or rent excess;

- conservation of unused equipment;
- optimization of the use of each room;
- use of outsourcing.

Measures should be taken to accelerate the turnover of funds, which includes:

- checking the creditworthiness of customers, maintaining the purchasing and payment history of customers;
- if possible, analysis and evaluation of the financial stability of customers;
- the introduction of criteria for the solvency of customers and the establishment for different customers of the relevant criteria for the limits of permissible commodity credit and installment period;
- introducing the dependence of managers' remuneration on receipt of payments from customers;
- active use of factoring operations;
- the introduction of customer incentives in advance payments or in timely repayment of debts with an attractive system of discounts and incentives.

Besides, it is necessary to optimize cash outflows by the following measures:

- optimization of volumes and terms of orders of goods, materials and services for themselves;
- coordination with suppliers of payment methods that are most convenient in terms of time and with minimal premiums for using a loan;
- changing the investment schedule so that cash outflow does not impair the ability to make regular payments.

Inventory optimization by the following activities:

- periodic analysis and sorting of goods into ABC and XYZ groups, reduction in the inventory of groups that do not affect the sales volume or satisfaction of demand;
- reduction of insurance stocks due to optimization of volumes and terms of sending orders for replenishment of stocks;
- sale of illiquid assets for nothing;
- optimization of the execution of production operations and workflow.

Cost optimization using:

- optimization of labor costs: the introduction of bonus payment schemes for qualitative indicators of labor results instead of quantitative;

- review of the organizational structure to optimize management and reduce labor costs;
- reduction of general business expenses.

Optimization of cash flow control:

- daily reconciliation of cash balance;
- the introduction of a system of applications for the allocation of funds, which are subject to approval by management weekly or daily;
- empowerment to permit the allocation of funds of only one or two managers;
- an order to control payments for goods and services delivered to one manager.

Improving the quality of management:

- creation of a personnel reserve;
- taking measures to train department heads in modern management;
- clarification of competencies - the introduction of job requirements for professional qualifications of specialists;
- increased control detail and reporting frequency;
- the transition from rewards for quantitative indicators to rewards for the positive dynamics of qualitative indicators;
- promoting quality workmanship and the ability to find innovative solutions.

Management of the hotel has to be directly involved in the development of strategy, influencing, thus, rendering of services, development of the tourist market, development of the enterprise, absorption of competitors and creation of strategic alliances.

REFERENCES

Abrate, Graziano, Juan Luis Nicolau, and Giampaolo Viglia. 2019. "The Impact of Dynamic Price Variability on Revenue Maximization." *Tourism Management*. https://doi.org/10.1016/j.tourman.2019.03.013.

Baranova, Natalia, and Liudmila Bogatyreva. 2018. "The Financial and Economic Aspect of Assessing the Competitiveness of the Hospitality Industry." *PEOPLE: International Journal of Social Sciences*. https://doi.org/10.20319/pijss.2018.41. 0109.

Brown, Nancy A., Jane E. Rovins, Shirley Feldmann-Jensen, Caroline Orchiston, and David Johnston. 2017. "Exploring Disaster Resilience within the Hotel Sector: A Systematic Review of Literature." *International Journal of Disaster Risk Reduction*. https://doi.org/10.1016/j.ijdrr.2017.02.005.

Cross, Robert G., Jon A. Higbie, and David Q. Cross. 2009. "Revenue Management's Renaissance: A Rebirth of the Art and Science of Profitable Revenue Generation." *Cornell Hospitality Quarterly.* https://doi.org/10.1177/ 1938965508328716.

Dogru, Tarik, Makarand Mody, and Courtney Suess. 2019. "Adding Evidence to the Debate: Quantifying Airbnb's Disruptive Impact on Ten Key Hotel Markets." *Tourism Management.* https://doi.org/10.1016/j.tourman.2018.11.008.

E. Younes, R. Kett. n.d. *"Refining the Anomalies out of RevPAR. | Semantic Scholar."* Accessed February 3, 2021. https://www.semanticscholar.org/paper/ Refining-the-anomalies-out-of-RevPAR.-Younes-Kett/8fcbcc336a76f04ed11b75 ea5516dea786f4a234.

Elhoushy, Sayed, Islam Elbayoumi Salem, and Gomaa Agag. 2020. "The Impact of Perceived Benefits and Risks on Current and Desired Levels of Outsourcing: Hotel Managers' Perspective." *International Journal of Hospitality Management.* https://doi.org/10.1016/j.ijhm.2019.102419.

Gössling, Stefan. 2015. "New Performance Indicators for Water Management in Tourism." *Tourism Management.* https://doi.org/10.1016/j.tourman.2014.06.018.

Kim, Minsun, Wesley Roehl, and Seul Ki Lee. 2019. "Effect of Hotels' Price Discounts on Performance Recovery after a Crisis." *International Journal of Hospitality Management.* https://doi.org/10.1016/j.ijhm.2019.04.006.

Kimes, Sheryl E. 2011. "The Future of Hotel Revenue Management." *Journal of Revenue and Pricing Management.* https://doi.org/10.1057/rpm.2010.47.

Krasyuk, I., and Y. Medvedeva. 2019. "Resource Support in Business Analytics of Innovative Development of Trade and Technological Systems." In *Proceedings of the 33rd International Business Information Management Association Conference, IBIMA 2019: Education Excellence and Innovation Management through Vision 2020.*

Krasyuk, Irina A., and Yuliya Y. Medvedeva. 2019. "Drives and Obstacle for the Development of Marketing in Russian Retailing." In *Proceedings of the 33rd International Business Information Management Association Conference, IBIMA 2019: Education Excellence and Innovation Management through Vision 2020.*

Lea R. Dopson and David K. Hayes. 2008. *"Maagerial Accounting for the Hospitality Industry."* Wiley. 2008.

Mucharreira, Pedro Ribeiro, Marina Godinho Antunes, Nuno Abranja, Maria Rosário Texeira Justino, and Joaquín Texeira Quirós. 2019. "The Relevance of Tourism in Financial Sustainability of Hotels." *European Research on Management and Business Economics.* https://doi.org/10.1016/j.iedeen.2019.07.002.

Nair, Girish K. 2019. "Dynamics of Pricing and Non-Pricing Strategies, Revenue Management Performance and Competitive Advantage in Hotel Industry." *International Journal of Hospitality Management.* https://doi.org/10.1016/j.ijhm. 2018.10.007.

"Official Site of Federal State Statistics Service in Russia." n.d. Accessed February 3, 2021. https://rosstat.gov.ru/.

Patiar, Anoop, and Ying Wang. 2020. "Managers' Leadership, Compensation and Benefits, and Departments' Performance: Evidence from Upscale Hotels in Australia: Leadership, Compensation and Performance." *Journal of Hospitality and Tourism Management.* https://doi.org/10.1016/j.jhtm.2019.11.005.

Pereira, Luis Nobre. 2016. "An Introduction to Helpful Forecasting Methods for Hotel Revenue Management." *International Journal of Hospitality Management.* https://doi.org/10.1016/j.ijhm.2016.07.003.

Romanyuk, Anton V., and Roman R. Gareev. 2019. "Hospitality Industry in Russia: Key Problems and Solutions." *Journal of Environmental Management and Tourism.* https://doi.org/10.14505/jemt.v10.4(36).09.

Santos, Rodrigo Amado dos, Mirian Picinini Méxas, and Marcelo Jasmim Meiriño. 2017. "Sustainability and Hotel Business: Criteria for Holistic, Integrated and Participative Development." *Journal of Cleaner Production.* https://doi.org/10.1016/j.jclepro.2016.04.098.

Younes, By Elie, and Russell Kett. 2003. "GOPPAR, a Derivative of RevPAR." *HVS International*, no. March: 1-6.

In: Global Challenges of Digital Transformation of Markets ISBN: 978-1-53619-754-9
Editors: E. de la Poza and S. E. Barykin   © 2021 Nova Science Publishers, Inc.

Chapter 25

IMPACT OF DIGITALIZATION ON THE IMAGE AND OVERALL NUMBER OF VISITORS OF SHOPPING CENTERS

Valeriy V. Nikishkin[*] and Vadim V. Tsimbaev[†]
Plekhanov Russian University of Economics, Moscow, Russia

ABSTRACT

The main aim of this work is to analyze the latest digital trends so that they could be used by shopping centers to achieve their goals. We have conducted a survey of buyers of shopping centers to study how the usage of technological solutions provided by digitalization may affect how they perceive the image of a mall and its overall number of visitors. The solutions suggested were chatbots in shopping centers' mobile apps, beacons and push-notifications, a separate pick-up point of goods from the stores inside a mall, "smart route" feature on the basis of cloud computing and the concept of "smart stores," AR-elements and robots in the shopping area, digital payments via a shopping center's app. The survey enabled us to find out that the suggested solutions are more effective as instruments to form an image of a shopping center rather than as instruments to directly affect the overall number of visitors. The most effective instruments, according to the survey, were a separate pick-up point and AR-elements in the shopping area. Hence, we have proven that the technological solutions used by retail chains can be adapted for shopping centers and be used to increase their ability to compete with rivals, as well as making moving forward to the next stage of shopping centers' evolution as "smart malls."

Keywords: shopping centers, digitalization, marketing management

---

[*] Corresponding Author's Email: valeriynik@yandex.ru.
[†] Corresponding Author's Email: v.v.tsimbaev@mail.ru.

1. INTRODUCTION

Digital economy transforms our society and economic relations. In the decree of the President of Russian Federation dated 09.05.2017 №203 it is defined as an economic activity that has digital data, big data processing and usage of the results of the analysis as key factors of production, enabling it to significantly increase the efficiency of different types of production, technologies, equipment, storage sales, delivery of products and services in comparison with traditional economic activities. This definition enables us to underline how digital economy changes different aspects of national economy, including its commercial side.

Digital economy and the elements of its ecosystem provide a basis for an interaction within economic framework that changes the way how goods and services are bought and consumed, making it multivariate. Hence, the enterprises have to emphasize their focuses on the future and form their images accordingly, promoting positive associations with the brand and stimulating repeating purchases. Image is an artificial abstract form of an object that defines attitude towards the mentioned perceived object (Chapman and Sadd 2014; Barich and Kotler 1991; Aksu, Pektaş, and Eseoğlu 2011). Thereby it can be stated that an image of a company is its artificial abstract image that defines attitudes of third parties (especially, consumers and buyers of its goods and services) towards it.

Shopping centers and retail chains are currently at the forefront of the introduction of new technologies. They play an active role in the process of digitalization of the society. Fung Business Intelligence agency has analyzed the current situation and chosen the following trends as those affecting different spheres of the life of society the most: integration of artificial intelligence, internet of things, cloud computing, realization of the concept of "smart stores," usage of augmented reality, robots and digital payments (Renne 2018). Each solution provided can be analyzed and illustrated.

A concept of artificial intelligence (AI) was a topic of serious discussions between professionals and experts. AI can be divided into Strong AI and Weak AI. A concept of Strong AI (a fully independent intelligence) is mostly used in science fiction whereas examples of realization of the concept of Weak AI have already been implemented by some enterprises to fulfill certain tasks, given they are simple, for some time (Tegmark 2019; Spyros 2017). Some examples of those tasks can be planning, problem-solving, object manipulation, perception and many others (Heath 2018).

In the first half of 2020 individuals were installing a mobile app called Replika that was serving as their digital companion, helping them to avoid the feelings of discomfort and lone lines during the period of lockdown. One of the features of the app was that it was constantly learning from its users to become a better interlocutor. In April (2020) half a million of people downloaded the app (Metz 2020). This fact is a proof that a concept of AI is interesting for large groups of people.

Retail chains do not ignore this trend and try to follow it. For example, a Chinese company Alibaba has created a number of Ais to achieve their goals. One of them,

Tmall Smart Selection, allows consumers to get tailored recommendations based on their online behavior. At the same time, the same AI analyses data on demand for chosen goods, enabling the company to make better forecasts on which goods are more likely to become more popular among consumers than the others. Another example is an AI-powered chatbot, Dian Xiaomi, that can process 90% of customer enquiries and serve 3,5 million of buyers every day, decreasing the amount of time and resources spent for those tasks within the company in the process (Marr 2018).

A term of Internet of Things (IoT) is used to refer to a number of technologies that enable physical objects to interact with other objects using special sensors in a number of ways (Xu 2012; Mansfield-Devine 2018; Illingworth 2001). This field of work is so popular among retail chains that the spending on it in 2018 accounted to $670 million, and by the end 2020 it is forecasted to increase up to $2,5 billion ("Retail Spend on 'IoT' to Reach $2.5bn by 2020" n.d.). "Beacon" technologies, Radio-Frequency Identification and "Click and Collect" services are viewed as the most promising ones.

"Beacons" are objects that use Bluetooth and similar technologies to send information to potential consumers' gadgets nearby. Having a smart device with a turned-on Bluetooth, a potential customer may receive a notification, informing him or her about special opportunities available at a store nearby. One of the surveys indicated that 73% of buyers believe the content sent via this technology may affect their desire to buy goods and services (PR Newswire 2014; Milnes 2015). Push-notifications are not the only way to utilize this technology for the companies. American retailer Target has "beacons" to direct visitors inside their stores and collect data on their movement to later analyze it and change the inner environment to effectively achieve goals of the company (Tode 2017; Allurwar, Nawale, and Patel 2016). Other enterprises (such as Neiman Marcus) may use this technology to inform their loyal customers about events in certain stores to stimulate an increase of number of customers participating in them (Forsey 2018).

Radio-Frequency Identification (RFID) is a technology that enables companies to manage their stocks efficiently. Using special tags, retail chains can locate their goods within their supply chain and distribution network allowing the seller to precisely know how many units of certain goods have been taken from the shelf in a certain store. This technology can be used to actively influence the image of the enterprise. This technology was used by the Denim Manufacturer Levi's in the USA to control the number of goods on the shelves maintaining the number of them so that the number of cases when the shelves were empty was minimized ("LEVI'S & INTEL – RFID PILOT AT LEVI'S - Digital Innovation and Transformation" n.d.). Hence, RFID enables the company to avoid the situation of deficit within a store that may lead to a negative impact on the image of the brand that could have resulted from buyers believing that the company does not care about them by leaving the shelves empty. Using this technology Levi's maintained the level of its customer service and decreased costs, associated with the storage of the goods.

"Click and Collect" services enable customers to receive goods they have bought online at the chosen pick-up points or stores. Those pick-up points may cooperate with different retail chains, creating an opportunity for buyers to collect goods from several suppliers from one place, decreasing the amount of time spent. If several "Click and Collect" service suppliers are located in one shopping center that is located conveniently, it may lead to an increase of number of consumers visiting the mentioned mall. What is more those people may not only pick-up the goods they have ordered via internet but also purchase from the stores located inside the commercial center.

Cloud Computing that was an unusual instrument for retail chains at some point is now more affordable due to corporations like Google, IBM and others providing enterprises with technological resources that they could not use before. One of example of such cooperation between an IT-Giant and a retailer is the partnership of American Pharmacy Chain Walgreens and IBM. Using technologies and resources of the latter, Walgreens managed to analyze what goods were the most demanded in its store and what number of personnel specializing on what products was needed in each shop (Wilson 2017). In the future popularization of Cloud Computing via IT-giants' infrastructure might enable enterprises of different sizes and industries to analyze big data, changing the whole approach towards greater inclusion of analysis and marketing in everyday tasks.

Another trend that is getting popular lately is "smart stores." Those stores are operating offline but employ a wide range of technologies, reshaping shopping experience the way it seemed impossible before. Amazon Go's way of integrating offline stores into its business model may be considered a good example. In the stores of this company buyers do not have to pay for the goods purchased at the cashiers' desks. Instead, they install a special app that conducts the payment process, while the customer does not actively participate in it. He or she just picks the goods and exits the store and money is debited from the account automatically. This model works due to a number of cameras and scanners and usage of other technologies checking if a particular product was taken away or not (Ives, Cossick, and Adams 2019; Thompson 2018; Susan Fourtané 2018). This system might seem vulnerable but its subsystems ensure that no one can leave without paying for the goods one way or another. That was demonstrated in June 2020 when marauders, using the chaos created by riots in the USA, tried to rob an Amazon Go store in Seattle. The criminals were charged for the goods "stolen" after the system identified where they were taken and who were the "buyers" ("Looted Amazon Go Store Reportedly Bills the Looters Automatically - Gizmochina" n.d.).

Virtual Reality (VR) in our everyday life was a topic of heated discussions in the middle of the 2010s. Those discussion are still underway, however experts are more and more often pointing out Augmented Reality (AR) as a technology that has great potential when it comes to working with customers. Although only 5% of retail chains' representatives stated that they were using this technology at the moment, 76% of them were planning to employ it in the next 2 years (Williams 2019). AR enables companies to achieve various goals, among them (Scholz and Smith 2016; McKone, Haslehurst, and Steingoltz 2016; Bodhani 2013):

- improves conversion rates and reduces the percentage of goods returned;
- optimizes warehouse space;
- combines traditional retail experience and e-commerce;
- enhances brand recognition with gamification;
- empowers advertising campaigns;
- allows customers to "try" before they buy with a 3D product preview;
- displays additional information about products.

AR technology provides companies with an opportunity to enhance customer experience, drastically changing it by providing buyers with more information that may affect their decision-making and adding an element of a game and novelty. This way enterprises may achieve greater competitive ability and improve the value proposed. It comes as no surprise that 75% of consumers that participated in the survey expect retailers to integrate AR into their operations in the nearest future (Afshar n.d.).

Another opportunity to enrich customer experience is the usage of special robots. Robots in retail can be used in 2 different ways: as tools used for interaction with buyers in stores and in logistics (e.g., in warehouses, etc.). Many operations in the latter are rather simple and repetitive they recur repeatedly. When human personnel is employed at such tasks it may result in their (personnel's) decrease in efficiency, caused by exhaustion (both physical and mental) and loss of motivation, in the long-run. However when companies employ robots they avoid this situation, as robots are created for the purpose of fulfilling repetitive tasks. This idea was brought to life by a Walmart retail chain that deployed robots in more than 350 automatized systems of inventory management in 2019 . Amazon has also followed the trend and built a fully automatic warehouse in New Jersey with a minimum number of personnel (Bogue 2009; Kamei et al. 2010; Bogue 2019).

In stores robots are more commonly used to interact with customers. For example, a robot made by Softbank Robotics (model "Pepper") was deployed in one of B8TA' stores (B8TA is a company that sells electronics). As a result, a number of visitors of that shop was increased by 70%. Of course, partially it was caused by an interest of consumers of seeing an "artificial worker." Similar humanoid-like robots may interact with customers using their artificial intelligence, identify human emotions, move objects and collect data for further analysis and processing (Au-Yong-Oliveira, Garcia, and Correia 2020). Robots along with "smart stores" may change the whole business model of commerce, decreasing the number of personnel and improving efficiency.

Digital payments are not a completely new technology in the market. However in the situation of coronavirus pandemic it has become obvious that this technology is very beneficial for the society. Digital payments are executed with special chips on the bankcards or with special apps in users' devices. This way of payment creates a situation when the transaction is taking place without a physical contact between a buyer and a seller. What is more, in the case of an app a consumer does not need to bring cards with him as smart devices are able to "save" several cards (even in case of a robbery an original owner may block the phone and/or delete all the data including information on the cards from home). Currently digital payments are widely used in China where 35,2% of users of smart devices utilize them and an average sum of transaction per user was $1,162,7 in 2019. Russian market is different, as a share of those who use digital payments and their spending is less (8,8% and $194,2, accordingly) (Sudha. G, Sornaganesh.V, Thangajesu Sathish. M 2020; Nasution et al. 2020). However, there are reasons to believe that the numbers might improve in the future.

Mentioned trends shape not only retail chains but also directly affect companies from other industries. One of the examples is the market of services of shopping centers that are currently suffering from the pressure of new formats of trade organization and, as a result, their key performance indicators decrease (in 2018 the number of visitors of shopping centers reduced by 7.6% and it lead to an increase of number of unoccupied tenant spaces by 9.4% in 2019 (Frost-Norton 2005; Ram 2017; Statista 2020)).

It is important to clarify that shopping centers are providing their services to two different groups of customers: their tenants and buyers. In fact, to operate efficiently malls have to use a system that takes into account needs of both groups and enables the company to approach them the best way suitable for each one. One of the solutions may be a two-circuit marketing management system of shopping centers. Both circuits include diverse groups of buyers and tenants. For example, the latter can be divided into 2 sub-circuits: a sub-circuit of actual tenants (tenants that are already working in a shopping center) and a sub-circuit of potential tenants (those who are not using a specific mall's services but may do it in the future). Hence, the process of integrating innovations has to be implemented in both circuits the way that will enable the shopping center to use all the benefits of working with representatives of each circuit.

One of possible applications of AI in malls is the usage of chatbots in mobile apps. This solution may be interesting for shopping centers as it can be used to manage the working process with both circuits (although, it must be noted that the chatbots for 2 circuits will be different and be used to achieve different goals). In the case of the circuit of buyers, chatbots in mobile apps may be used to reply to customer inquiries as well as collecting data that might be used later to customize the services offered. Chatbots for tenants might be more effective in automatization of business processes like coordination of repair works and logistics. Instead of signing many forms and getting all the needed permits tenants could just log into an app and do all the necessary "paperwork" without having to spend hours on it. This solution may not only affect the image of a shopping center and optimize the way standard business processes are conducted but also increase a value of a product provided by the shopping centers in the form of its services.

IoTmay be efficiently integrated in operations within the circuit of buyers. Beacon technologies can be used to inform buyers about special offers in the shopping centers as well as events and new arrivals in the stores of tenants. They can also be used to track the way buyers move inside the mall to collect valuable data and improve customer experience as well as to change the routes used by visitors if needed. For example, data collected can be analyzed and if certain areas of a shopping center are more "crowded" and others are not, the pricing for tenants can be changed to compensate for a different number of buyers available to avoid the situation when customers (tenants) pay the same amount for different level of service (in the form of number of visitors being available in area).Also most crowded areas may have more inner advertising helping tenants that are far from the flow of buyers to reach their potential customers better. What is more a logical and well-argumented pricing together with wide range of ad options in optimal places can help to form an image of a shopping center that is very professional in its field of work, helping to retain tenants in the long-run.

Currently pick-up points can be seen in shopping centers, enabling buyers to collect all the ordered goods in one place. However,one step further would be a pick-up point of shopping centers that may enable buyers to collect the goods from the tenants of the center in one place without having to spend time going from one store to another. If a mall is able to create a digital infrastructure that stores data on the goods ready to be bought in the shopping center and the data can be "delivered" to the buyer efficiently, this concept may become a reality with a pick-up point organized on the territory of the mall. What is more this pick-up point of goods from all the stores can become a kind of an attraction for the buyers becoming an area visited by many buyers. This tool can be used to change the flow of visitors and provide tenants who are far from the anchor tenants with potential buyers.

The concept of "smart store" can be adapted for the needs of shopping centers and become a concept of "smart mall." One of the possible ways to implement it is to provide visitors with a service that can create a "smart" route within the mall. A visitor may choose stores he or she wants to visit as well as goods he wants to buy and the algorithm backed-up by cloud computing suggests the most effective route and offers that might be the most interesting for the buyer. This concept might seem too futuristic but the same was said about AI and robots in retail years ago. Shopping centers that will find new ways to help buyers to manage their scarce resources (including time) will get a competitive advantage over their rivals (Krasyuk and Medvedeva 2019). If many visitors use a shopping center's infrastructure every day the mentioned solution may also provide the managers of the company with an instrument to direct the flow of buyers in real-time, adjusting the way they move using the "smart" route feature.

The solution mentioned above cannot be implemented without the analysis if big data using cloud computing. Shopping centers can cooperate with IT-companies to gain access to their resources. By analyzing data, malls can process information that can be later used to customize the product offered to buyers and tenants and increase the value already proposed. There are malls that have overwhelming number of visitors like "Evropeyskiy" in Moscow that can be offer access to its infrastructure for 6 million of people per month (like it was in December 2019). In other words, it welcomed roughly 200 thousand visitors every day in its peak month. By collecting different data, the administration of the mall could have managed the flow of buyers so that the queues could have been decreased and all tenants could have had access to an even greater number of visitors if their movement within the building was directed using cutting-edge technologies. The physical infrastructure (elevators, escalators, etc.) might also be used more efficiently if the mentioned direction of the visitor flows was conducted with the aid of cloud computing.

AR is a tool that can be effectively used to work within the circuit of buyers. For example, it can be used to simplify the process of navigating in the shopping space using an app of the mall. By using the camera of user's device, a shopping center can provide buyer with a projection of information that might be useful for a visitor like arrows pointing where he should go next or showing which stores are scheduled to open in the nearest future. Another opportunity is to use holograms to display how clothes and other goods may look in real life. Knowing that there is a model that fits the user, he may consider visiting a shopping center that can offer it.

Buyers may not always be aware what kind of stores are located in the shopping center or what goods can be bought there. It must also be noted that not all the consumers have the same degree of proficiency when it comes to using mobile apps, websites and other instruments of communication with a company that involves using modern technologies. Sometimes buyers may enter a store just to ask where he or she can buy a product that is offered by another tenant of the mall without an intention of actually buying goods from the store entered. This problem is often solved with interactive navigation terminals, however robotic assistants can also be used to help visitors. They may give instructions on how to get to a certain store, explain how to use elements of interactive navigation or just welcome a buyer and wish him a good day, setting up good mood for shopping.

In addition, other robots located in the stores may be used to collect data on the process of interaction with visitors and their number. Later, after analyzing it, shopping centers can use this information to improve certain aspects of their work to ensure an even better customer experience, including, among other, improvements in the pool of tenants and their assortment as well as managing the flow of visitors.

Digital payments are an important element of trading at the moment. They enable companies to reduce the risks associated with the health of their personnel and consumers, as well as, time needed to pay for the goods and services. By encouraging tenants to accept digital payments, shopping centers can improve the overall level of the service and minimize the mentioned risks. Another way a mall can achieve it is by providing buyers with an opportunity to pay via its mobile app. Digital payments within an app can also encourage customers to spend more if they can get incentives for doing so. As a result buyers might visit the mall that implemented such a system more often and, hence, increase the overall attendance and as a result the value of partnership with a mall for tenants.

Shopping centers have to find the ways to use the latest cutting-edge technologies for their benefit, as it may help them to form the image needed to attract buyers and tenants, as well as improving the efficiency with which they conduct their day-to-day operations such as logistics, managing the flow of visitors, analyzing the enquiries of tenants, collecting data on buyers, reducing the workload of personnel and creating new advertising products for tenants within the mall. Of course, there are companies in the industry that are already effectively using latest technologies to achieve their goals like mobile apps, scanners to control the flow of visitors, etc. (Krasyuk and Medvedeva 2019). However in order to make a step forward towards the "smart mall" concept becoming massively represented in our lives companies need to integrate solutions mentioned above in their business models and every day operations. Following latest trends, shopping centers will be able to keep their competitiveness and effectively protect their market share in terms of both the circuit of tenants and the circuit of buyers.

2. MATERIALS AND METHODS

The solutions suggested above seem interesting and useful for shopping centers in the future. However in order to prove whether those solutions would be of use for the companies we have conducted a quantitative research of mall visitors.

To assess how the solutions proposed may affect the formation of the image of a shopping center and the number of visitors (also known as the traffic of a shopping center), two questions were chosen. The first one was whether a solution might affect how a visitor perceives a shopping center. The answers to be chosen from were: it will positively affect my opinion on the mall; it will negatively affect my opinion of the mall; it will not affect my opinion on the mall; I find it difficult to answer. The other question was whether an implementation of solution might affect how a buyer visits a mall. The answers to be chosen from were: yes, it might positively affect how often I visit the mall; yes, it might negatively affect how often I visit the mall; no, it will not affect how often I visit the mall; I find it difficult to answer. The survey in question was conducted in 2020, 203 buyers offour malls in Moscow (among others "Evropeyskiy," "Moskovskiy") have participated in it.

The following technical solutions were included: chatbots integrated into mobile apps of malls; beacons in the shopping area that can send push-up notifications on special offers in stores; a separate pick-up point for goods of tenants of the shopping center; "smart route" feature for visitors (based on the combination of cloud computing and the concept of "smart stores"); AR-elements and robots in the shopping area; digital payments via mobile app.

In order to make it clear for the respondents what each solution included we decided to add a brief explanation of each of them. Those explanations can be seen in Table 1 (the original explanations were in Russian, however they were translated for the Table 1).

Table 1. Explanation of each solution of the survey

Technological solution	Brief explanation
A chatbot in a shopping center's mobile app	If a visitor has any questions about the shopping center, he or she can use a chat with an AI to get the answers (e.g., about working hours, discounts in certain shops, dates of special events).
Beacons and push-notifications based on IoT and Bluetooth technology	If a visitor has a turned on Bluetooth on his or her smartphone he or she can receive push-notifications about discounts and other special offers in stores he walks by inside the mall.
A separate pick-up point of goods from the stores of a mall	A buyer can choose goods he or she is interested in via the website of the mall, add it to his or her online "basket" (as in the case of online shops) and after that can visit one place inside a mall to pay for and pick up the chosen goods.
"Smart route" feature	Before visiting a shopping center an individual can choose the stores he or she plans to visit using a special "navigator" at the website or in the app of the mall, then a special algorithm will create a route that will include all the chosen stores and enable him or her to spend a minimum amount of time at the mall (reducing time spent inside).
AR-elements in the shopping area	There are several ways AR-elements can be used in shopping centers: firstly, this technology can be used to "try" clothes (for example, from home via the camera of a smart device with a shopping center's app), secondly, to make it easier to navigate inside a mall (directions are shown on the screen of a smart device).
Robots assisting visitors in the most crowded areas	Visitors sometimes have problems with finding certain stores in malls, robots with AI and speakers can be placed in crowded areas to help with it by answering questions and giving directions.
Digital payments via a shopping center's mobile app	A user's bankcard's information is added into the mobile app, then he or she can use an app to pay for goods and services in the mall, receiving bonuses in the process.

3. RESULTS

The survey has shown how certain solutions could have affected the image of a shopping center. It must be stated that all the proposed solutions were stated to have a positive impact on the image of a shopping center by the majority of respondents, if implemented. The percentages of respondents believing that solution may positively affect how they perceive the image of a shopping center can be seen in Table 2.

It can be stated that 2 solutions that have the greatest impact on a shopping center's image (according to the survey) are separate pick-up point of goods from stores inside a mall and AR-elements in the shopping area. Another "popular" solutions are chatbots and a "smart route" feature. Hence, the four mentioned solutions may be considered as the ones with the greatest potential in terms of improving a shopping center's image.

Respondents were mostly choosing "...positive..." and "...will not affect..." answers. Only 3 proposed solutions were referred to as possibly having a negative effect on the image and they are beacons (18%), robots (9%) and digital payments (also 9%). It can be concluded that these 4 solutions are questionable in terms of having a positive effect on the image of a shopping center as it may both affect it positively and negatively.

Respondents have also answered whether the chosen innovative solutions may affect the way they visit a shopping center. It must be noted that the impact of the proposed solutions in terms of formation of image is greater than in terms of affecting the overall number of visitors. Table 3 contains the data of what share of respondents believe that proposed solutions may affect the likelihood of them visiting a mall.

Table 2. Percentage of respondents that believe that the implementation of chosen solutions may have a positive impact on the image of a shopping center

Technological solution	Percentage of respondents that believe that the implementation the solution in question may have a positive impact on the image of a shopping center
A chatbot in a shopping center's mobile app	82%
Beacons and push-notifications based on IoT and Bluetooth technology	73%
A separate pick-up point of goods from the stores of a mall	100%
"Smart route" feature	82%
AR-elements in the shopping area	91%
Robots assisting visitors in the most crowded areas	73%
Digital payments via a shopping center's mobile app	64%

Table 3. Percentage of respondents that believe that proposed solutions may affect the likelihood of them visiting a mall

Technological solution	"Positive" answers (%)
A chatbot in a shopping center's mobile app	27%
Beacons and push-notifications based on IoT and Bluetooth technology	45%
A separate pick-up point of goods from the stores of a mall	73%
"Smart route" feature	45%
AR-elements in the shopping area	73%
Robots assisting visitors in the most crowded areas	27%
Digital payments via a shopping center's mobile app	18%

We analyzed the answers given and summarized data from both Tables 2 and 3 in Table 4 to have a clear understanding of how the solutions affect the image of a shopping center and a likelihood of it being visited by buyers, according to the survey.

Table 4. Impact of the solution on the image of a shopping center and the likelihood of visiting a mall from the point of view of the respondents

Technological solution	Impact on image	Impact on the likelihood of visiting a mall
A chatbot in a shopping center's mobile app	Positive impact	Almost no impact
Beacons and push-notifications based on IoT and Bluetooth technology	Can have both positive and negative impact	Can have both positive and negative impact
A separate pick-up point of goods from the stores of a mall	Strong positive impact	Positive impact
"Smart route" feature	Positive impact	Moderate positive impact
AR-elements in the shopping area	Strong positive impact	Positive impact
Robots assisting visitors in the most crowded areas	Can have both positive and negative impact	Almost no impact
Digital payments via a shopping center's mobile app	Can have both positive and negative impact	Almost no impact

Although integration of chatbots into shopping centers' mobile apps may create opportunities of improving image for a considerably large share of potential buyers (82% of respondents have indicated that), they are not as effective when it comes to affecting the overall number of visitors as only a quarter of respondents believe that the implementation of this solution might have a positive effect for them. In other words, only 1 buyer out of 4 participants of the survey have stated that chatbots will affect how often they visit a mall. This instrument may be considered a good tool of improving the image of the company but that is not the case of its number of visitors.

Beacons, on the other hand, are completely different. The ratio of the positive answers on the first question (regarding the image) to the positive answers on the second question (number of visitors) is 1,6 to 1. Hence, more than a half of those who considered beacons as an instrument that can positively affect the image of a shopping center actually stated that they may also affect the attendance. 45% of respondents have also noted that this solution may have no effect while 10% stated that it might have a negative impact. Beacons as a technological solution that can be used by shopping centers may affect the overall traffic of a shopping center both positively and negatively. Despite positive effect being 4-5 times greater than the negative one, it must be taken into account that beacons can have a negative effect and that may be a problem in the future if the solution is implemented.

A separate pick-up point of goods that can be bought in the stores of the mall as a solution for shopping centers was chosen by the majority of respondents as an instrument that may have a positive effect on the overall number of visitors. 100% of respondents believed that it will have a positive effect on the image of a shopping center as well. That means that this solution may be the most interesting for shopping centers in terms of image formation and overall number of visitors, making it an instrument with the greatest potential among the ones included in the survey.

"Smart route" feature was also a solution that was stated to influence the image of a shopping center however respondents did not believe it to make a string impact on the overall number of visits. At the same time, the fact that almost a half of respondents chose it as affecting the chances of them visiting a shopping center means that a further research can be conducted to study whether this solution is of use for shopping centers or not to achieve the goals of malls.

AR-elements in the shopping area along with a separate pick-up point were mentioned by respondents as a possible instrument of impacting the traffic of malls. It can be stated that this solution has a potential to be considered a valuable tool for shopping centers both in terms of image formation and improving the number of visitors.

Only a quarter of respondents noted that robotic assistants is a factor that may have positively influenced their will to visit a shopping center. Together with 73% of respondents stating that this feature may positively influence the image of a mall that means that robots are more of an image formation instrument rather than an instrument of improving the overall number of visitors.

Digital payments through the mobile app of a shopping center had the least number of "votes for" as an instrument affecting the number of visitors (only 1 respondent out of 5 stated that this instrument may affect the chances of buyers visiting a shopping center). This solution also had the least number of "positive" answers on the first question. Hence, we have to admit that this instrument may not be effective in terms of both image formation and improving the number of visitors. However it might be effective as an instrument aimed at increasing an average sum of money spent in the mall and stimulating purchases, however a further research might be needed.

DISCUSSION

Although integration of chatbots into shopping centers' mobile apps may create opportunities of improving image for a considerably large share of potential buyers (82% of respondents have indicated that), they are not as effective when it comes to affecting the overall number of visitors as only a quarter of respondents believe that the implementation of this solution might have a positive effect for them. In other words, only 1 buyer out of 4 participants of the survey have stated that chatbots will affect how often they visit a mall. This instrument may be considered a good tool of improving the image of the company but that is not the case of its number of visitors.

Beacons, on the other hand, are completely different. The ratio of the positive answers on the first question (regarding the image) to the positive answers on the second question (number of visitors) is 1,6 to 1. Hence, more than a half of those who considered beacons as an instrument that can positively affect the image of a shopping center actually stated that they may also affect the attendance. 45% of respondents have also noted that this solution may have no effect while 10% stated that it might have a negative impact. Beacons as a technological solution that can be used by shopping centers may affect the overall traffic of a shopping center both positively and negatively. Despite positive effect being 4-5 times greater than the negative one, it must be taken into account that beacons can have a negative effect and that may be a problem in the future if the solution is implemented.

A separate pick-up point of goods that can be bought in the stores of the mall as a solution for shopping centers was chosen by the majority of respondents as an instrument that may have a positive effect on the overall number of visitors. 100% of respondents believed that it will have a positive effect on the image of a shopping center as well. That means that this solution may be the most interesting for shopping centers in terms of image formation and overall number of visitors, making it an instrument with the greatest potential among the ones included in the survey.

"Smart route" feature was also a solution that was stated to influence the image of a shopping center however respondents did not believe it to make a string impact on the overall number of visits. At the same time, the fact that almost a half of respondents chose it as affecting the chances of them visiting a shopping center means that a further research can be conducted to study whether this solution is of use for shopping centers or not to achieve the goals of malls.

AR-elements in the shopping area along with a separate pick-up point were mentioned by respondents as a possible instrument of impacting the traffic of malls. It can be stated that this solution has a potential to be considered a valuable tool for shopping centers both in terms of image formation and improving the number of visitors.

Only a quarter of respondents noted that robotic assistants is a factor that may have positively influenced their will to visit a shopping center. Together with 73% of respondents stating that this feature may positively influence the image of a mall that means that robots are more of an image formation instrument rather than an instrument of improving the overall number of visitors.

Digital payments through the mobile app of a shopping center had the least number of "votes for" as an instrument affecting the number of visitors (only 1 respondent out of 5 stated that this instrument may affect the chances of buyers visiting a shopping center). This solution also had the least number of "positive" answers on the first question. Hence, we have to admit that this instrument may not be effective in terms of both image formation and improving the number of visitors. However it might be effective as an instrument aimed at increasing an average sum of money spent in the mall and stimulating purchases, however a further research might be needed.

CONCLUSION

In conclusion we would like to point out the main findings of our work:

1. Technological innovations are actively affecting the process of image formation of a shopping center in the minds of buyers (when working with their circuit). Image formation is an important function of a shopping center that enables it to effectively compete with its rivals and retain its competitive advantages.

2. Due to the development of infrastructure of digital economy, new technological solutions are emerging. And those solutions may be of use for the shopping centers to work with the circuit of buyers. Most of the solutions suggested can be effective at image formation, as noted by the respondents of the survey due to the fact that respondents stated that they (solutions) may positively affect how they perceive the image of shopping centers.

3. At the same time, it cannot be stated that all the technological solutions suggested may be equally effective at improving the number of visitors of shopping centers. Only two innovations (a separate pick-up point with goods from stores of the mall and AR-elements in the shopping area) were chosen by the overwhelming majority of respondents as those having the greatest positive impact on traffic of the shopping center, according to the results of the survey. Another solution that shopping centers may find interesting is a "smartroute" feature due to the fact that it has a potential to be effective at achieving goals associated with improving the services of a shopping center and managing the flow of visitors.

4. In the future when digital technologies become more affordable for companies of different budgets, shopping centers may proceed to the next stage of their development. This stage that may be called "smartmalls" will be more technology-reliant and be able to provide consumers with a greater level of tailored service.

REFERENCES

[1] Afshar, Vala. n.d. *"New Rules of Customer Engagement: Key Findings from Global Research - Salesforce.Com."* Accessed March 4, 2021. https://www.salesforce.com/resources/articles/customer-engagement/?bc= OTH.

[2] Aksu, Mustafa, Güzide Öncü Eroğlu Pektaş, and Merve Eseoğlu. 2011. "Fashion Phenomenon in Postmodern Marketing Applications and Effects on the Marketing Components." In *Procedia - Social and Behavioral Sciences*. https://doi.org/10.1016/j.sbspro.2011.09.126.

[3] Allurwar, Navalkrushna, Balasaheb Nawale, and Swapnesh Patel. 2016. "Beacon for Proximity Target Marketing." *International Journal Of Engineering And Computer Science*. https://doi.org/10.18535/ijecs/v5i5.08.

[4] Au-Yong-Oliveira, Manuel, Jacinta Garcia, and Cristina Correia. 2020. "Innovation and Robots in Retail - How Far Away Is the Future?" In *Advances in Intelligent Systems and Computing*. https://doi.org/10.1007/978-3-030-45691- 7_65.

[5] Barich, H., and P. Kotler. 1991. "A Framework for Marketing Image Management." *Sloan Management Review*.

[6] Bodhani, A. 2013. "Getting a Purchase on AR." *Engineering & Technology*. https://doi.org/10.1049/et.2013.0408.

[7] Bogue, Robert. 2009. "The Role of Robots in the Food Industry: A Review." *Industrial Robot*. https://doi.org/10.1108/01439910910994588.

[8] ———. 2019. "Strong Prospects for Robots in Retail." *Industrial Robot*. https://doi.org/10.1108/IR-01-2019-0023.

[9] Chapman, Laura, and Debbie Sadd. 2014. "Events as Strategic Marketing Tools in Shopping Centers." *Event Management*. https://doi.org/10.3727/152599514X13989500765925.

[10] Forsey, Caroline. 2018. "7 Innovative Ways Retailers Are Using Beacon Technology." *HubSpot*. 2018.

[11] Frost-Norton, Tammie. 2005. "The Future of Mall Research: Current Trends Affecting the Future of Marketing Research in Malls." *Journal of Consumer Behaviour*. https://doi.org/10.1002/cb.8.

[12] Heath, Nick. 2018. "What Is AI? Everything You Need to Know about Artificial Intelligence." *ZDNet*. 2018.

[13] Illingworth, Nicola. 2001. "The Internet Matters: Exploring the Use of the Internet as a Research Tool." *Sociological Research Online*. https://doi.org/10.5153/sro.600.

[14] Ives, Blake, Kathy Cossick, and Dennis Adams. 2019. "Amazon Go: Disrupting Retail?" *Journal of Information Technology Teaching Cases*. https://doi.org/10.1177/2043886918819092.

[15] Kamei, Koji, Kazuhiko Shinozawa, Tetsushi Ikeda, Akira Utsumi, Takahiro Miyashita, and Norihiro Hagita. 2010. "Recommendation from Robots in a Real-World Retail Shop." In *International Conference on Multimodal Interfaces and the Workshop on Machine Learning for Multimodal Interaction, ICMI-MLMI 2010*. https://doi.org/10.1145/1891903.1891929.

[16] Krasyuk, Irina A., and Yuliya Y. Medvedeva. 2019. "Drives and Obstacle for the Development of Marketing in Russian Retailing." In *Proceedings of the 33rd International Business Information Management Association Conference, IBIMA 2019: Education Excellence and Innovation Management through Vision 2020*.

[17] "*LEVI'S & INTEL – RFID PILOT AT LEVI'S - Digital Innovation and Transformation*." n.d. Accessed March 4, 2021. https://digital.hbs.edu/platform-digit/submission/levis-intel-rfid-pilot-at-levis/.

[18] "*Looted Amazon Go Store Reportedly Bills the Looters Automatically - Gizmochina*." n.d. Accessed March 4, 2021. https://www.gizmochina.com/2020/06/09/looted-amazon-go-store-reportedly-bills-the-looters-automatically/.

[19] Mansfield-Devine, Steve. 2018. "Open Source and the Internet of Things." *Network Security*. https://doi.org/10.1016/S1353-4858(18)30016-3.

[20] Marr, Bernard. 2018. "*The Amazing Ways Chinese Tech Giant Alibaba Uses Artificial Intelligence And Machine Learning*." 2018. https://www.forbes.com/sites/bernardmarr/2018/07/23/the-amazing-ways-chinese-tech-giant-alibaba-uses-artificial-intelligence-and-machine-learning/?sh=495d6981117a.

[21] McKone, Dan, Robert Haslehurst, and Maria Steingoltz. 2016. "Virtual and Augmented Reality Will Reshape Retail." *Harvard Business Review*.

[22] Metz, Cade. 2020. "*Riding Out Quarantine With a Chatbot Friend: 'I Feel Very Connected' - The New York Times*." 2020. https://www.nytimes.com/2020/06/16/technology/chatbots-quarantine-coronavirus.html.

[23] Milnes, Hilary. 2015. "Elle Uses Beacon Technology to Drive 500,000 Retail Store Visits." *Digiday*. 2015.

[24] Nasution, Muhammad Irwan Padli, Nurbaiti Nurbaiti, Nurlaila Nurlaila, Tri Inda Fadhila Rahma, and Kamilah Kamilah. 2020. "Face Recognition Login Authentication for Digital Payment Solution at COVID-19 Pandemic." In *2020 3rd International Conference on Computer and Informatics Engineering, IC2IE 2020*. https://doi.org/10.1109/IC2IE50715.2020.9274654.

[25] PR Newswire. 2014. "Swirl Releases Results of Retail Store Beacon Marketing Campaigns." *PR Newswire*, 2014.

[26] Ram, Sangeeth. 2017. "Meeting Millennials Where They Shop : Shaping the Future of Shopping Malls." *McKinsey & Company*.

[27] Renne, Chan. 2018. "Trends Shaping the Future of Retail." *Rila.Org*, no. December. http://www.rila.org/sustainability/future/Documents/04 Trends Shaping the Future of Retail.pdf.

[28] "*Retail Spend on 'IoT' to Reach $2.5bn by 2020*." n.d. Accessed March 4, 2021. https://www.juniperresearch.com/press/press-releases/retail-spend-on-iot-to-reach-2-5bn-by-2020.

[29] Scholz, Joachim, and Andrew N. Smith. 2016. "Augmented Reality: Designing Immersive Experiences That Maximize Consumer Engagement." *Business Horizons*. https://doi.org/10.1016/j.bushor.2015.10.003.

[30] Spyros, Makridakis. 2017. "The Forthcoming Artificial Intelligence (AI) Revolution: Its Impact on Society and Firms." *Futures*.

[31] Statista. 2020. "ECommerce Report 2020: Statista Digital Market Outlook." *Statista*.

[32] Sudha. G, Sornaganesh.V, Thangajesu Sathish. M, Chellama. A. V. 2020. "Impact of Covid-19 Outbreak in Digital Payments." *Peer-Reviewed, Refereed, Indexed Journal with IC*.

[33] Susan Fourtané. 2018. "The Amazon Effect: Amazon Go Stores and The Future of Retail." *Intresting Engineering*. 2018.

[34] Tegmark, Max. 2019. "Benefits & Risks of Artificial Intelligence." *Future of Life Institute*.

[35] Thompson, Ben. 2018. "Amazon Go and the Future." *Stratechery*.

[36] Tode, Chantal. 2017. "*Target Innovates In-Store Beacon Marketing with Newsfeed-like Content Stream / Retail Dive*." 2017. https://www.retaildive.com/ex/mobilecommercedaily/target-innovates-in-store-beacon-marketing-with-newsfeed-like-content-stream.

[37] Williams, Robert. 2019. "*52% of Retailers Feel Ill-Prepared to Support Emerging Mobile Tech, Study Says / Retail Dive*." 2019. https://www.retaildive.

com/news/52-of-retailers-feel-ill-prepared-to-support-emerging-mobile-tech-study-s/561005/.

[38] Wilson, Matthew. 2017. *"Walgreens Taps Retail Analytics on IBM Cloud to Improve Efficiency."* 2017. https://www.ibm.com/blogs/cloud-computing/2017/09/25/walgreens-retail-analytics-ibm-cloud/.

[39] Xu, Xiangxuan. 2012. "Internet of Things in Service Innovation." *Amfiteatru Economic.*

In: Global Challenges of Digital Transformation of Markets ISBN: 978-1-53619-754-9
Editors: E. de la Poza and S. E. Barykin   © 2021 Nova Science Publishers, Inc.

Chapter 26

IMPLEMENTATION OF INTEGRATED DIGITAL SOLUTIONS IN THE PASSENGER CAR MARKET

Olga Kotomenkova[1,*], Anna Vinogradova[1],
Valentina Milova[2], Katsiaryna Bahrantsava[3]
and Chaudhari Prashant[4]

[1]Peter the Great St. Petersburg Polytechnic University,
St. Petersburg, Russia
[2]St. Petersburg State University of Aerospace Instrumentation,
St. Petersburg, Russia
[3]Belarusian Trade and Economics University of Consumer Cooperatives,
Gomel, Belarus
[4]Dr. D.Y. Patil's School of Engineering,
Lohegaon, Pune, India

ABSTRACT

One of the integrated digital solutions on the passenger car market, based on the choice of alternatives and criteria, is the methodology for assessing the quality and safety of passenger car functional units, based on pneumatic tires as an integral part of the car. To this end, a nomenclature of quality and safety indicators was developed, including complex indicators and single indicators of the first and second levels; a selection of indicators of quality and safety for their evaluation was made, weighting coefficients of indicators of quality and safety were determined, and expert qualification evaluation of tires based on a complex quality indicator was conducted.

The results of a comprehensive assessment of the quality and safety of pneumatic tires of famous brands within their dimensional segments made it possible to analyze and interpret them in order to develop a set of preventive and corrective measures, as well as proposals and recommendations to normative and

---

* Corresponding Author's E-mail: kot-og@yandex.ru.

technical documentation and regulatory acts to improve the range of products, their quality, safety and competitiveness.

Keywords: Car Market, Quality and Safety, The Nomenclature of Indicators, Car Tires, Digitalization

1. INTRODUCTION

The car industry is one of the fastest growing sectors of the national economy. The improvement of the range of products, materials and components is mainly due to the introduction and development of a large number of innovations in mechanical engineering (Zhgulev et al. 2018; Bozhuk and Pletneva 2018). At the same time, the problem of preserving and improving the quality and safety of products is currently quite acute, including when assessing the risks of innovative enterprises (Pukała 2016).

It is clear that in the era of "Industry 4.0", individualized demand and small-scale customized production will become a trend that requires strong customer orientation and quick response capabilities (Lu et al. 2020). For example, unmanned cars (Deore et al. 2020), cars with voice support and an obstacle detector for disabled people (Gulati, Ishaan and Dass 2020), cars with height-adjustable suspension for comfortable driving of a particular driver (Kwon, Hyun and Yi 2020) and others are actively promoted in the passenger car market.

It is expected that the traditional role of cars as means of transport will now undergo major changes as a result of the emerging smart car industry, in which connection to the Internet can not only improve road safety by allowing passengers to drive independently, but also entertain them (Park, Nam and Kim 2019), including through the concept of breakthrough technologies, providing a new basis for innovative products for emerging mass (Ray and Kanta Ray 2011) and premium markets (Stylidis et al. 2020).

The quality and safety of car industry products are strictly controlled and regulated by relevant guidance and approved regulatory documents. At the same time, the existing quality and safety assessment methods need to be improved, taking into account current production conditions (Kalinina et al. 2020) and product requirements (Chernikova et al. 2017), which necessitate the introduction of integrated digital solutions in the passenger car market.

The integration of digital solutions in the passenger car market contributes to the modernization of their systems and functional components.

A separate niche in this segment is car tires. Tires - are one of the most important components of car safety (Egaji, Chakhar and Brown 2019). Innovative approaches to optimising qualitative and quantitative characteristics led to monitoring failures of irreversible changes in car tire design (Fedorko et al. 2019), studying the magnetism of car wheels with pneumatic radial tires (Brol and Szegda 2018), real-time forecasting of pneumatic tire characteristics using an improved tire and ice interface model

(Jimenez and Sandu 2019), electronic regulation of an automatic tire pressure monitoring system (Sandoni and Ringdorfer 2006), the development of an autonomous pressure sensor (Qian, Kim and Lee 2018), creation of a new test stand to evaluate the effectiveness of brakes and pneumatic wheels (Cantoni et al. 2020) and other solutions.

Classic and innovative solutions in passenger cars, units and structures are monitored for quality and safety at all stages of the product life cycle. It should be noted that emphasis is currently being placed on the assessment of indicators and criteria that are not regulated by regulatory and technical documentation, for example, the assessment and selection of an optimized solution in the development of the car body (Choudry et al. 2018), the life cycle assessment of the internal combustion engine and electric car (Pero, Delogu and Pierini 2018), the assessment of thermal comfort parameters (Ravindra, Agarwal and Mor 2020) and air quality in the car interior (Szczurek and Maciejewska 2016), the assessment of risks of advanced driver assistance systems (Sini and Violante 2020) and others. However, we have not found a universal mechanism (methodology, algorithm) to assess the quality and safety performance of individual functional systems, units and components of passenger cars.

2. MATERIALS AND METHODS

The implementation of integrated digital solutions in the passenger car market involves the development of an algorithm (methodology) to assess the quality and safety of both products as a whole and individual parts, assemblies and components.

The methodology for evaluating product quality and safety involves several stages, including: identification of key indicators, determination of indicator weights, evaluation of actual indicator values, aggregation of indicators, data interpretation, and development of a set of measures.

A graphical model of the methodology is provided in Figure 1.

3. RESULTS

3.1. Selection of Alternatives and Criteria for Evaluation

The development of a methodology for assessing the quality and safety of passenger cars was adopted as a separate functional unit.

The selection of alternatives and criteria for assessing the quality and safety of the individual functional unit of a vehicle was carried out using an analytical hierarchical procedure method (Kotomenkova O. and Vinogradova A. 2019).

The following were accepted as alternatives to the quality and safety of passenger cars: passenger car body, passenger car internal combustion engine, passenger car transmission, passenger car running gear, passenger car control mechanism, passenger car electrical equipment.

The following criteria were adopted as quality and safety criteria for passenger cars: reliability (fail-safety, durability, repairability, maintainability), safety.

The results are provided in Tables 1-3.

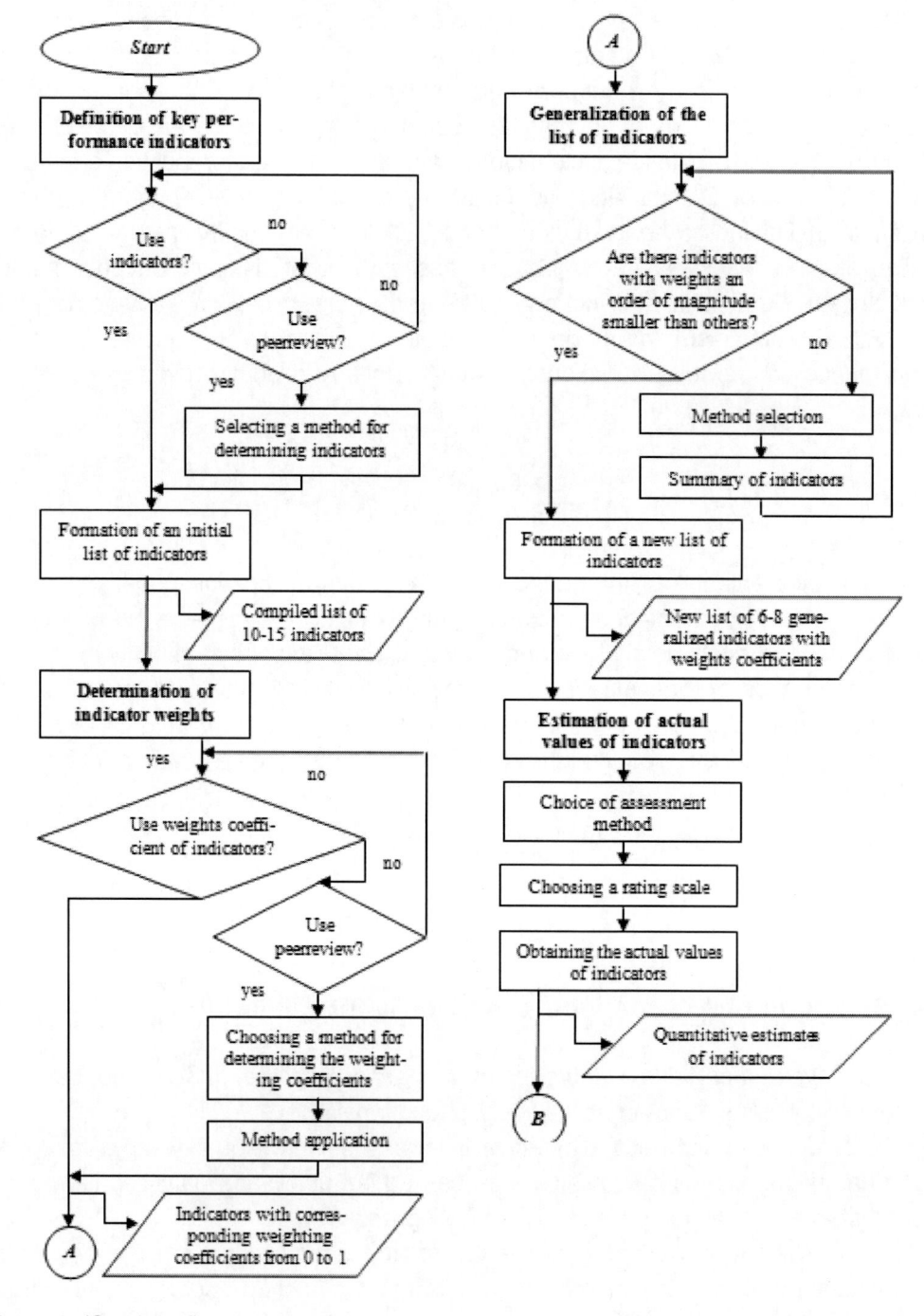

Figure 1. (Continued)

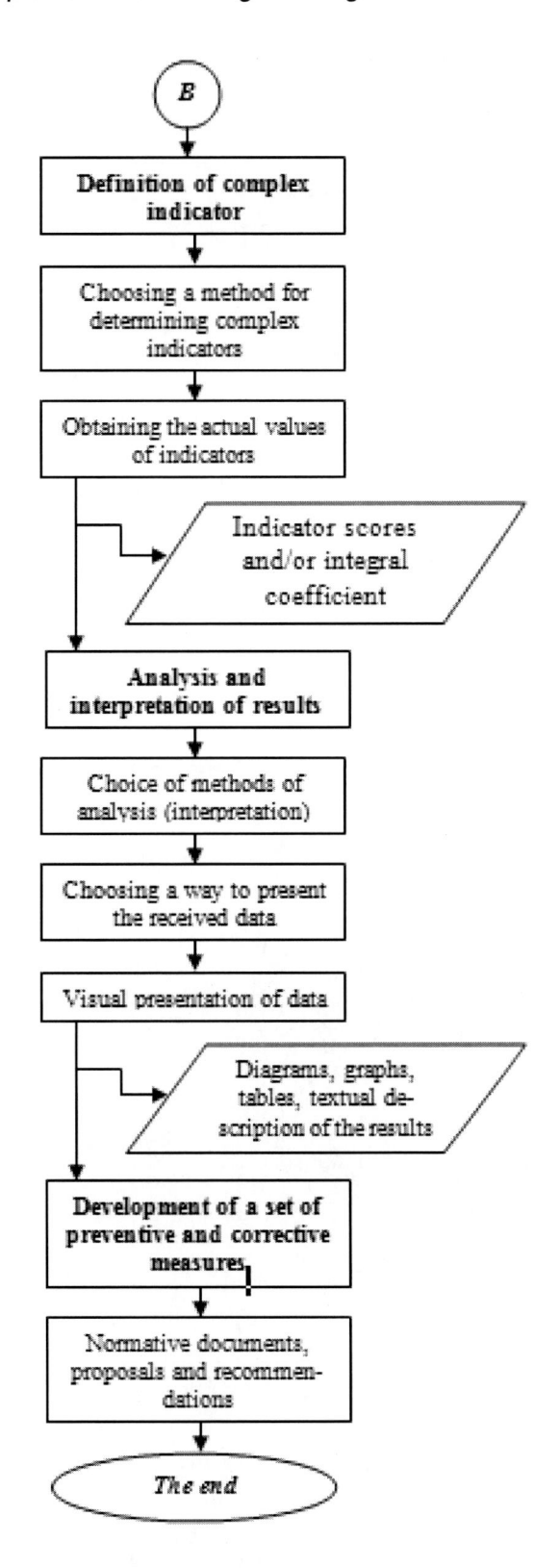

Figure 1. Algorithm for assessing the quality and safety product.

Table 1. Results of paired comparisons of alternatives by "reliability" criterion

	Car body	Internal combustion engine	Transmission	Running gear	Control mechanism	Electrical equipment	Total	
							by sum	rationed amount
Car body	1.00	0,25	0,50	0,25	0,50	2.00	4,50	0.076
Internal combus-tion engine	4.00	1.00	5.00	1.00	4.00	5.00	20.00	0,334
Transmission	2.00	0.20	1.00	0.20	1.00	2.00	6.40	0.107
Running gear	4.00	1.00	5.00	1.00	4.00	5.00	20.00	0.334
Control mechanism	2.00	0.25	1.00	0.25	1.00	1.00	5.50	0.092
Electrical equipment	0.50	0.20	0.50	0.20	1.00	1.00	3.40	0.057
							59.80	1.000

Table 2. Results of paired comparisons of alternatives by "safety" criterion

Alternatives	Car body	Internal combustion engine	Transmission	Running gear	Control mechanism	Electrical equipment	Total	
							by sum	rationed amount
Car body	1.00	4.00	4.00	1.00	1.00	4.00	15.00	0.257
Internal combus-tion engine	0.25	1.00	1.00	0.20	0.25	1.00	3.70	0.063
Transmission	0.25	1.00	1.00	0.20	0.25	0.50	3.20	0.055
Running gear	1.00	5.00	5.00	1.00	2.00	5.00	19.00	0.326
Control mechanism	1.00	4.00	4.00	0.50	1.00	2.00	12.50	0.214
Electrical equipment	0.25	1.00	2.00	0.20	0.50	1.00	4.95	0.085
							58.35	1.000

3.2. Development of a Nomenclature of Quality and Safety Indicators

The selection of quality and safety indicators for use in the methodology being developed was based on the following requirements:

Table 3. Final assessment of alternatives by criteria

Alternatives	Criteria		Total
	Reliability	Safety	
Car body	0.076	0.257	0.333
Car internal combustion engine	0.334	0.063	0.397
Car transmission	0.107	0.055	0.162
Car running gear	0.334	0.326	0.66
Car control mechanism	0.092	0.214	0.306
Car electrical equipment	0.057	0.085	0.142

quality assessment can be used to compare products of the same type produced by different manufacturers and marketed by different suppliers;

the assessment can be used to calculate the competitiveness of products;

the indicators to be assessed must be identical to the main product characteristics declared by the manufacturers or suppliers (sellers).

The choice of customer groups for which the products to be evaluated are intended was based on an analysis of the current market situation of the products under investigation and the requirements for them.

The range of quality indicators for car pneumatic tires was developed in accordance with current regulatory documents. Table 4 presents complex and individual indicators of the quality and safety of pneumatic tires for passenger cars.

3.3. Selection of Quality and Safety Indicators for Car Pneumatic Tires

On the basis of the developed range of indicators and taking into account the characteristics of tire manufacturers, a list of indicators of quality and safety of passenger car pneumatic tires was drawn up for evaluation by means of pair comparison. The matrix of paired comparisons is presented in Table 5.

In order to select quality and safety indicators for pneumatic tires for passenger cars, experts were asked to compare the indicators in pairs. The experts did not quantify the advantage of one parameter over another or the degree of importance of the parameters, but used the concepts of "more", "less" and "equal".

The results of the assessment were recorded in the form of a square matrix of matching paired comparisons (1):

$$\begin{cases} 1, if \ x_i > x_j \\ 0, if \ x_i = x_j \\ -1, if \ x_i < x_j \end{cases} \tag{1}$$

where x_i– column number, x_j– line number.

Table 4. Quality and safety indicators of pneumatic tires for passenger cars

| Complex indicators | Single indicators | |
	1st level	2nd level
Indicators of appointment	Tire dimensions	
	Double thickness, mm	
	Tire weight, kg	
	Dimension deviation, %, from nominal	Profile width
		Outside diameter
Reliability indicators	Resistance to shear of the bead of a tubeless tire from the rim shelf, kN (kg·s)	
	Tire reliability tests depending on load and speed	
	trouble-free operation depending on load and speed	No tread delamination, plys delamination, cord delamination or cord breaks
		The outer diameter of the tire, measured 6 hours after testing
Indicators of economical use of raw materials, materials, fuel, energy, labor resources	Tire tread rubber hardness	
Ergonomic performance	Rolling noise level, dB	
Manufacturability indicators	Rolling resistance coefficient	
Environmental performance		
Safety indicators	Tightness of tubeless tire or tube	
	Static unbalance of tubeless tires (tube type tires)	
	Dynamic unbalance of the tire	
	Radial and lateral run out of the tire, mm	

Complex indicators	Single indicators		2nd level
	1st level		2nd level
	Fluctuations in radial and lateral forces due to tire non-uniformity and taper effect		
	Wear indicator height, mm		
	Wet Grip Index		
Aesthetic indicators	The indicator of the perfection of the design solution, point		

Table 5. Matrix of paired comparisons

	x_1	x_2	x_3	...	x_n
x_1	x_1/x_1	x_2/x_1	x_3/x_1	...	x_n/x_1
x_2	x_1/x_2	x_2/x_2	x_3/x_2	...	x_n/x_2
x_3	x_1/x_3	x_2/x_3	x_3/x_3	...	x_n/x_3
...	...	...	...	...	...
x_n	x_1/x_n	x_2/x_n	x_3/x_n	...	x_n/x_n

3.4. Determining the Weighting Factors for the Quality and Safety of Car Pneumatic Tires

A preference method was used to implement the method, where the expert group numbered the importance score of the quality and safety indicators of pneumatic tires for passenger cars in order of their importance: the least important property is assigned to property 1, the most important property -– 2 and further on in ascending order.

The reference (complex) property importance factor is one (2):

$$\sum_{i=1}^{n} q_i = 1 \tag{2}$$

where q_i– the weighting factor of the i-th quality and safety indicator; n – number of assessed quality and safety indicators.

On the basis of the expert assessments received, importance coefficients were calculated for all ranked indicators, where the expert group directly assessed the importance of each property on a scale of relative importance with a range of values from 1 to 10. It was acceptable to assign both whole and fractional values to the properties. The same values were allowed for indicators of equal importance.

The value of importance factors was calculated using a formula (3):

$$q_i = \frac{p_i}{\sum_{i=1}^{n} p_i} \tag{3}$$

where qi– the weighting factor of the i-th quality and safety indicator; pi– the rank (assessment) of the significance of the quality and safety indicator by an expert; n – number of assessed quality and safety indicators.

The accuracy of expert evaluations was determined by the consistency of expert opinions. The degree of coincidence of the experts' assessments was calculated using a concordance coefficient (4):

$$W = \frac{12 \cdot S}{m^2(n^3 - n)} \tag{4}$$

where W – concordance factor; S – squared deviation of the ranks or scores of the quality and safety indicator from the arithmetic mean; n – number of assessed quality and safety indicators; m – number of experts.

The sum of squares of rank deviations from the arithmetic mean for all quality and safety indicators and the experts were calculated using the formula (5):

$$S = \sum_{i=1}^{n} (\sum_{j=1}^{m} p_{ij} - \frac{\sum_{i=1}^{n} \sum_{j=1}^{m} p_{ij}}{n})^2 \tag{5}$$

where S – squared deviation of the ranks or scores of the quality and safety indicator from the arithmetic mean; pij – score in ranks given to the i-th quality and safety indicator by the j-th expert; n – number of assessed quality and safety indicators; m – number of experts.

The results of determining the importance factors for the quality and safety indicators of pneumatic tires for passenger cars by the expert group are provided in Table 6.

3.5. Qualimetric Evaluation of Pneumatic Car Tires

The products of 13 of the most popular brands of manufacturers were selected for the qualification evaluation of pneumatic tires for passenger cars, among others: Michelin (France), Goodyear (USA), Pirelli (Italy), Hankook (Korea), Continental (Germany), Nokian (Finland), Yokohama (Japan), Bridgestone (Japan), Dunlop (Great Britain), Toyo (Japan), Kumho (Korea), Nitto (USA), КАМА (Russia).

The quality and safety rating scale includes three levels: excellent (3), good (2), satisfactory (1) and bad (0).

The importance factor was calculated using the formula (6):

$$Q_i = q_i \times a_i, \tag{6}$$

where Qi – a single quality indicator of the i-th property, taking into account the weighting factor a_i; qi – single absolute indicator of quality of the i-th property; ai – the weighting factor of the i-th property.

Table 6. Weights coefficient of indicators quality and safety of pneumatic tires for passenger cars

Indicators quality and safety	Weights coefficient of indicators										$\sum_{j=1}^{m} p_j$
	Expert										
	№ 1		№ 2		№ 3		№ 4		№ 5		
	p_j	q_i	p_j	q_i	p_j	q_i	p_j	q_i	p_j	q_i	
Load index	7	0.13	7	0.13	7	0.13	8	0.15	8	0.15	37
Speed index	6	0.11	6	0.11	6	0.11	6	0.11	7	0.13	31
Rolling resistance	5	0.09	5	0.09	4	0.07	5	0.09	5	0.09	24
Wet grip	9	0.16	8	0.15	8	0.15	7	0.13	6	0.11	38
Rolling noise level, dB.	4	0.07	4	0.07	5	0.09	3	0.05	3	0.05	19
Height of the tread wear indicator, mm.	8	0.15	9	0.16	9	0.16	9	0.16	9	0.16	44
Shore hardness of rubber, u.	2	0.04	3	0.05	1	0.02	4	0.07	4	0.07	14
Tire weight, kg	1	0.02	2	0.04	3	0.05	2	0.04	2	0.04	10
Tightness of tubeless tire or tube	10	0.18	10	0.18	10	0.18	10	0.18	10	0.18	50
Perfection of design solution (tread pattern)	3	0.05	1	0.02	2	0.04	1	0.02	1	0.02	8
Total	55	1.0	55	1.0	55	1.0	55	1.0	55	1.0	275

In general, the quality and safety of tires were rated the high by experts throughout the size range (Figure 2).

4. DISCUSSION

Thus, the conclusion should be that it is necessary to develop a methodology for assessing the quality and safety of the running gear of passenger cars as a whole, or of individual units, parts and components (table 3).

The range of quality and safety indicators developed for pneumatic tires can be used in their qualification evaluation (table 4).

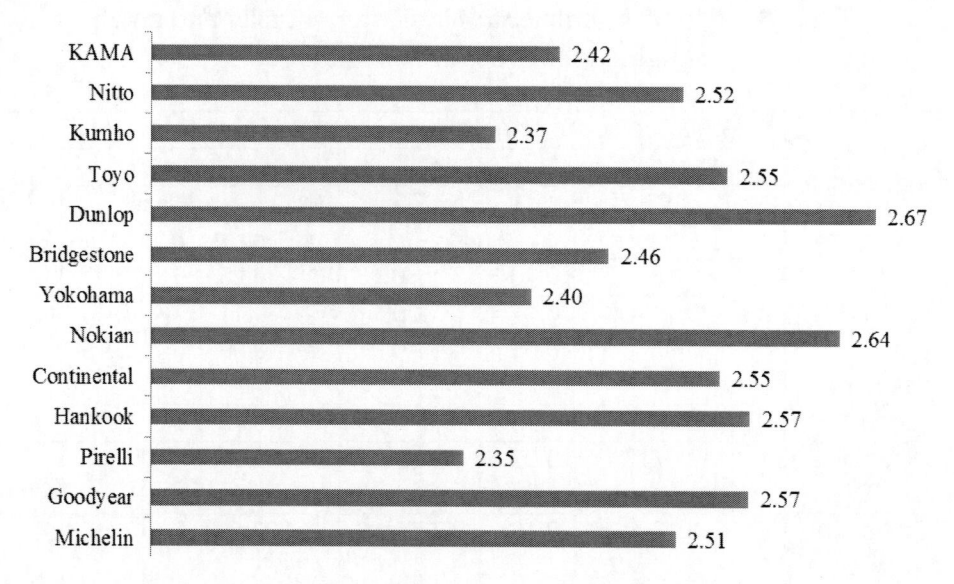

Figure 2. Comprehensive index for the quality and safety of pneumatic passenger car tires.

For the qualimetric evaluation, the experts selected 10 indicators of quality and safety of pneumatic tires for passenger cars by means of a method of paired comparisons, including: rolling noise level, dB; rolling resistance; level of the wear indicator, mm; wet grip; speed index; load index; Shore hardness of rubber, units; tire weight, kg; tightness of tubeless tire or tube; perfection of artistic and design solution (tread pattern).

An analysis of Table 6 shows that, in the opinion of experts, the greatest importance is attached to such indicators as the tightness of the tubeless tire or tube and the height of the wear indicator in mm (the average importance coefficients are 10.0 and 8.8 respectively); the least– perfect design solution (tread pattern) and the tire weight in kg (the average weight coefficients are 2.0 and 1.6 respectively).

Experts' opinions are conditioned by the particular importance in terms of safety of the tightness of the tubeless tire or tube and the height of the wear indicator.

The tubeless tire's tightness index exists in two types:

the tire is airtight, which is due to the tire's full tight fit with the car disc, no air is released in the connection of the two planes, thus, thanks to the right pressure (kg/cm2 or psi), which is indicated by the manufacturer of the car itself in the documentation, the driver can be confident on the road, feel the feedback from the car (information), for example, where the wheels are turned, etc., reduce the load on the vehicle's suspension, improve dynamics and save fuel, eliminating the risk of uneven tire wear.

the tire is not airtight; this can be caused by factors such as a lack of tread, side cuts, punctures, corrosion on the disc and wear of the tire itself in the areas adjacent to the disc. It is categorically impossible to use such a wheel.

This threatens traffic safety and can lead to consequences such as an explosion of the wheel, the 'unrolling' of the tire from the rim, severe tire wear and a noticeable reduction in car handling.

The height of the wear indicator is the indicator that currently marks the tires produced for passenger cars in millimetres and characterises the residual tread used by the car pneumatic tire manufacturer to drive safely at all permitted speeds, weather conditions and road situations. The smaller the rubber tread, the greater the vehicle's brake way, the worse its traction in the rain, the less resistant it is to the "aquaplaning" effect, the worse the handling and the greater the likelihood of the over/understeer.

The height of the wear indicator is the indicator that currently marks the tires produced for passenger cars in millimetres and characterises the residual tread used by the car pneumatic tire manufacturer to drive safely at all permitted speeds, weather conditions and road situations. The smaller the rubber tread, the greater the vehicle's brake way, the worse its traction in the rain, the less resistant it is to the "aquaplaning" effect, the worse the handling and the greater the likelihood of the over/understeer.

The weight of a vehicle's tire has a greater impact on the vehicle's fuel consumption, acceleration and maximum speed, since general purpose tires, which are only used on public roads and not on motorways, are considered to be lightweight for experts who assessed their quality and safety.

Every person, including an expert, has his or her own opinion about such an indicator as the perfection of an art and design solution, but this indicator has very little impact on the safety of cars in general, which results in a low average importance factor when assessing the expert group's opinions.

The consistency of expert opinions can be assessed as high: $W = 0.943$.

An analysis of Table 6 shows that, in the opinion of experts, the greatest importance is attached to such indicators as the tightness of the tubeless tire or tube and the height of the wear indicator in mm (the average importance coefficients are 10.0 and 8.8 respectively); the least - perfect design solution (tread pattern) and the tire weight in kg (the average weight coefficients are 2.0 and 1.6 respectively).

Experts' opinions are conditioned by the particular importance in terms of safety of the tightness of the tubeless tire or tube and the height of the wear indicator.

The results obtained are due, firstly, to the fact that 13 of the most popular tire brands were selected for the survey, which were proven themselves over many years to be reliable in terms of quality and safety; secondly, all the tires studied have quality certificates, which indicates that the indicators meet the requirements of regulatory documents, including a number of properties assessed by the expert group.

It was advisable to analyze the results of a comprehensive quality and safety assessment of pneumatic tires for passenger cars within their dimensional segments. For example, based on the results of a comprehensive assessment of all the tire brands studied by experts, the highest scores were given to products size 185/60R14 (average score 34.722), the lowest scores were given to products size 205/55R16 and 215/65R16 (respectively, 31.540 and 31.604 scores) and tires size 225/65R17 and 195/65R15 received average scores (respectively, 32.682 and 32.374 scores).

In addition, it should be noted that in each size range, the tires of different manufacturers received the highest rating from experts, on the basis of which it can be concluded that in the conditions of tough non-price competition representatives of different brands try to occupy their market segment in a certain size range, while maintaining relatively high quality products in other size segments.

CONCLUSION

The search for integrated digital solutions in the passenger car market on the basis of this research led to the following conclusions:

1. Quality and safety control of products in the passenger car market– is an important component of a balanced approach in an innovative economy. A particular attention should be paid to improving methods and mechanisms for assessing the quality of products, parts, assemblies and components in terms of obtaining quantitative values in various categories. The choice of alternatives and criteria for assessing the quality and safety of passenger cars demonstrated the need to develop a methodology for assessing the quality and safety of the running gear of passenger cars as a whole, or individual units, parts and components.
2. The paper proposes a methodology for assessing the quality and safety of the functional components of a passenger car using the example of pneumatic car tires, which are an integral part of the vehicle. A nomenclature of tire quality and safety indicators was developed for this purpose, including comprehensive indicators and single indicators of the first and second levels. In addition, tire quality and safety indicators were selected for evaluation, weighting coefficients for tire quality and safety indicators were determined, and expert qualification evaluation of tires was carried out based on a comprehensive quality indicator.
3. The results of a comprehensive assessment of the quality and safety of pneumatic tires of 13 brands within their dimensional segments made it possible to analyze and interpret them in order to develop a set of preventive and corrective measures, as well as proposals and recommendations to normative and technical documentation and regulatory acts to improve the range of products, their quality, safety and competitiveness.

REFERENCES

Bozhuk, Svetlana, and Pletneva, Natal'ya. 2018. "The Problems of Market Orientation of Russian Innovative Products (Electric Cars as a Case Study)". In *Advances in Intelligent Systems and Computing*. https://doi.org/10.1007/978-3-319-70987-1_132.

Brol, S. and Szegda, A. 2018. "Magnetism of Automotive Wheels with Pneumatic Radial Tires". *Measurement: Journal of the International Measurement Confederation*. https://doi.org/10.1016/j.measurement.2018.05.034.

Cantoni, C., Gobbi, M., Mastinu, G. and Meschini, A. 2020. "Brake and Pneumatic Wheel Performance Assessment – A New Test Rig". *Measurement: Journal of the*

International Measurement Confederation. https://doi.org/10.1016/j.measurement. 2019.107042.

Chernikova, Anna, Golovkina, Svetlana, Kuzmina, Svetlana and Demenchenok, Tatiana. 2017. "Supplier Selection Based on Complex Indicator of Finished Products Quality". In *IOP Conference Series: Earth and Environmental Science.* https://doi.org/10.1088/1755-1315/90/1/012045.

Choudry, Saphir A., Müller, Steffen, Alber, Uwe, Riedel, Frank and Landgrebe, Dirk. 2018. "A Multidimensional Assessment and Selection Methodology: Optimized Decision-Making of Joining Technologies in Automobile Body Development". In *Procedia Manufacturing.* https://doi.org/10.1016/j.promfg.2018.02.122.

Deore, Harshal, Akshat Agrawal, Vivek Jaglan, Pooja Nagpal and Mayank Mohan Sharma. 2020. "A New Approach for Navigation and Traffic Signs Indication Using Map Integrated Augmented Reality for Self-Driving Cars". *Scalable Computing: Practice and Experience.* https://doi.org/10.12694/scpe.v21i3.1742.

Egaji, Oche Alexander, Chakhar, Salem and Brown, David. 2019. "An Innovative Decision Rule Approach to Tyre Pressure Monitoring". *Expert Systems with Applications.* https://doi.org/10.1016/j.eswa.2019.01.051.

Fedorko, Gabriel, Molnar, Vieroslav, Dovica, Miroslav, Toth, Teodor, Soos, Lubomir, Fabianova, Jana and Pinosova, Miriama. 2019. "Failure Analysis of Irreversible Changes in the Construction of Car Tyres". *Engineering Failure Analysis.* https://doi.org/10.1016/j.engfailanal.2019.05.035.

Gulati, Ujjwal, Ishaan, and Rajeshwar Dass. 2020. "Intelligent Car with Voice Assistance and Obstacle Detector to Aid the Disabled". In *Procedia Computer Science.* https://doi.org/10.1016/j.procs.2020.03.383.

Jimenez, Emilio, and Sandu, Corina. 2019. "Towards a Real-Time Pneumatic Tire Performance Prediction Using an Advanced Tire-Ice Interface Model". *Journal of Terramechanics.* https://doi.org/10.1016/j.jterra.2018.04.004.

Kalinina, Olga, Firova, Snezhana, Barykin, Sergey and Kapustina, Irina. 2020. "Development of the Logistical Model for Energy Projects' Investment Sources in the Transport Sector". In *Advances in Intelligent Systems and Computing.* https://doi.org/10.1007/978-3-030-19756-8_29.

Kotomenkova, O. and Vinogradova, A. 2019. "Formation of the Nomenclature of Quality and Safety Indicators of Collagen-Based Shampoos and Their Qualimetric Assessment|International Business Information Management Association (IBIMA)". In *Madrid.* https://ibima.org/accepted-paper/formation-of-the-nomenclature-of-quality-and-safety-indicators-of-collagen-based-shampoos-and-their-qualimetric-assessment/.

Kwon, Baek Soon, Young Jin Hyun and Kyongsu Yi. 2020. "Mode Control of Electro-Mechanical Suspension Systems for Vehicle Height, Levelling and Ride Comfort". *Proceedings of the Institution of Mechanical Engineers, Part D: Journal of Automobile Engineering.* https://doi.org/10.1177/0954407019851028.

Lu, Chao, Feifan Chang, Ke Rong, Yongjiang Shi and Xiaoyu Yu. 2020. "Deprecated in Policy, Abundant in Market? The Frugal Innovation of Chinese Low-Speed EV

Industry". *International Journal of Production Economics*. https://doi.org/ 10.1016/ j.ijpe.2019.107583.

Park, Jiyoun, Changi Nam and Hye jin Kim. 2019. "Exploring the Key Services and Players in the Smart Car Market". *Telecommunications Policy*. https://doi.org/ 10.1016/j.telpol.2019.04.003.

Pero, Francesco Del, Delogu, Massimo and Pierini, Marco. 2018. "Life Cycle Assessment in the Automotive Sector: A Comparative Case Study of Internal Combustion Engine (ICE) and Electric Car". In *Procedia Structural Integrity*. https://doi.org/10.1016/j.prostr.2018.11.066.

Pukała, Ryszard. 2016. "Use of Neural Networks in Risk Assessment and Optimization of Insurance Cover in Innovative Enterprises". *Engineering Management in Production and Services*. https://doi.org/10.1515/emj-2016-0023.

Qian, Jingui, Dong Su Kim and Dong Weon Lee. 2018. "On-Vehicle Triboelectric Nanogenerator Enabled Self-Powered Sensor for Tire Pressure Monitoring". *Nano Energy*. https://doi.org/10.1016/j.nanoen.2018.04.022.

Ravindra, Khaiwal, Neha Agarwal and Suman Mor. 2020. "Assessment of Thermal Comfort Parameters in Various Car Models and Mitigation Strategies for Extreme Heat-Health Risks in the Tropical Climate". *Journal of Environmental Management*. https://doi.org/10.1016/j.jenvman.2020.110655.

Ray, Sangeeta and Pradeep Kanta Ray. 2011. "Product Innovation for the Peoples Car in an Emerging Economy". *Technovation*. https://doi.org/10.1016/ j.technovation.2011.01.004.

Sandoni, Germano and Ringdorfer, Martin. 2006. "Electronic Regulation of an Automated Car Tyres Pressure Control System". In *IFAC Proceedings Volumes (IFAC-PapersOnline)*. https://doi.org/10.3182/20060912-3-de-2911.00090.

Sini, Jacopo, and Violante, Massimo. 2020. "A Simulation-Based Methodology for Aiding Advanced Driver Assistance Systems Hazard Analysis and Risk Assessment". *Microelectronics Reliability*. https://doi.org/10.1016/j.microrel.2020. 113661.

Stylidis, Kostas, Al-Saidi, Elias, Erinjery, Arun Thomas, Lindkvist, Lars, Wickman, Casper and Söderberg, Rikard. 2020. "Design of the Top Tether Component for the Premium Car Market Segment: Case Study of Volvo Cars". In *Procedia CIRP*. https://doi.org/10.1016/j.procir.2020.02.160.

Szczurek, Andrzej and Maciejewska, Monika. 2016. "Categorisation for Air Quality Assessment in Car Cabin". *Transportation Research Part D: Transport and Environment*. https://doi.org/10.1016/j.trd.2016.08.015.

Zhgulev, Evgenii, Bozhuk, Svetlana, Evdokimov, Konstantin and Pletneva, Natalia. 2018. "Analysis of Barriers to Promotion of Electric Cars on Russian Market". In *Engineering for Rural Development*. https://doi.org/10.22616/ERDev2018.17. N377.

In: Global Challenges of Digital Transformation of Markets ISBN: 978-1-53619-754-9
Editors: E. de la Poza and S. E. Barykin   © 2021 Nova Science Publishers, Inc.

Chapter 27

DETERMINING WAYS TO IMPROVE THE COMPANY'S BUSINESS PROCESSES BASED ON THE ASSESSMENT OF THE PROBABILITY OF BANKRUPTCY IN THE DIGITAL ECONOMY

Sergey Borisov* and Sergey Yashin

National Research Nizhny Novgorod State University n. a. N. I. Lobachevsky,
Nizhny Novgorod, Russia

ABSTRACT

The purpose of this work is to identify areas for improving the business processes of an industrial company in the digital economy. To achieve this goal, we propose to use an integrated approach, including the simultaneous use of various models for assessing the likelihood of bankruptcy and determining the directions for improving the financial and economic activities of a company.

To identify the most preferable ways to improve the business processes of the company, we propose to highlight the key indicators of the financial and economic efficiency of the company, the formation of a system of complex integral indicators and the formation of a list of recommendations for improving the business of the company based on them.

The results obtained include the values of integral indicators characterizing the degree of probability of bankruptcy, the consistency of the results in accordance with various Russian and foreign models, as well as the development of a system of recommendatory measures aimed at improving the efficiency of the company in modern economic conditions.

Based on the conducted research, we have determined that indicators that are integral components in models for assessing the likelihood of bankruptcy of a company can be considered as key indicators of the efficiency of business

---

* Corresponding Author's Email: ser211188@yandex.ru.

processes. Based on these indicators, it is possible to form complex indicators for assessing the likelihood of bankruptcy, which serves as the basis for the formation of a set of recommendations for making management decisions.

Keywords: bankruptcy, business processes, assessment of the firm, digital economy

1. Introduction

In modern economic conditions, a process approach to management is gaining special relevance, a distinctive feature of which is the identification of key indicators (KPI) responsible for the performance of certain business processes taking place in the company. In accordance with the results of the latest research conducted by foreign colleagues, the main accents in applying the process management model are the initial definition of key performance indicators, and then the description of key business processes using various notations. A special place among these is held by the Scrum methodology (Wannes and Ghannouchi 2019; D. Mogilko et al. 2019; D. Y. Mogilko et al. 2020; Gromova 2019). Also, in accordance with the results of recent studies, it can be concluded that an essential aspect in the application of the process approach in management is not only a qualitative description of business processes and the determination of factors affecting the efficiency of their implementation but also the quantitative assessment of such factors. Furthermore, considerable attention is paid to the assessment of the quality of the business process model and its modernization in the field of the 'input' parameters of the model (Galimova et al. 2019; Rudskoy et al. 2019; Drotár et al. 2019; E. S. Balashova and Gromova 2017; E. Balashova et al. 2019; Sharipova et al. 2020).

When identifying key performance indicators of business processes (KPI) in research work and in real business practice, an approach based on the works of R. Norton and D. Kaplan devoted to the development of a balanced scorecard (BSC) is often used ("Balanced Scorecard Institute" n.d.; Avduevskaia, Kuporov, and Chepikova 2018; Kuladzhi, Babkin, and Murtazaev 2018). At the same time, the authors of this work divide all indicators into four groups: financial and economic indicators; indicators related to personnel training and development; indicators characterizing the efficiency of business processes, as well as a group of indicators characterizing relationships with customers. The main aim of the balanced scorecard is to build an enterprise management system to increase the values of financial and economic indicators based on changes in three projections, not directly related to finance. Thus, it is the financial and economic indicators that, as a rule, act as the resulting indicators of the entire BSC system, which depend on the implementation of the remaining perspectives (cross-sections) of the system. Accordingly, the total efficiency of the system is determined by the values of financial and economic indicators. This circumstance allows saying that for the development of measures to improve the efficiency of business processes, it is possible to use models related to the assessment and interpretation of integral indicators based on private financial and economic indicators of the company's performance.

Given this circumstance, we propose to use Russian and foreign models for assessing the likelihood of bankruptcy to determine the current level of efficiency in the implementation of business processes and the development of measures aimed at increasing the effectiveness of the financial and economic activities of the enterprise.

Fouzia Kahloun and Sonia Ayachi Ghannouchi note in (Kahloun and Ghannouchi 2018) that the problem of assessing the likelihood of bankruptcy has been known for a long time in science, but until now it has gained extremely high importance. A particular aggravation of this problem occurs during periods of political and economic instability caused by wars, natural disasters such as floods, fires, as well as challenges in the area of health protection. So, for the world community, 2020 marked by the impact of the COVID-19 pandemic, which has significantly changed the practice of doing business, has become the reason for the bankruptcy of many global companies that have a long history. Such events in many respects increase the interest in the use and improvement of the crisis-forecasting methods and determining the ways out of the crisis.

An interesting approach to the problem of bankruptcy, associated with the issue of effective use of a legal instrument necessary for financial restructuring of a 'sick' business, converting debt into equity capital, is considered in the research materials of Jaka Cepec, Peter Grajzl (Cepec and Grajzl 2020).

It is important to note that the procedure for assessing the likelihood of bankruptcy is becoming more accessible from a technical point of view due to the significant development of information technologies and various software products for financial and economic calculations. The importance of the digital economy and business platforms operating within the framework of this methodology is considered in the studies presented in the article (Curtis and Mont 2020).

To assess the likelihood of bankruptcy of an enterprise and to develop ways for improving the business processes of a company, the authors of this study propose a comprehensive use of various Russian and foreign techniques discussed below. It should be noted that the approbation of the application of these models was previously applied by the authors in relation to one of the large industrial enterprises in Nizhny Novgorod, Red Anchor Plant JSC (the main activity is the production of chains, except for hinged ones) (Chernichenko and Kotov 2020).

2. MATERIALS AND METHODS

As part of the study, another industrial enterprise, Russian Aircraft Corporation MiG, associated with the production of helicopters, airplanes and other aircraft, was also considered as an object for approbation. Further, it will be shown that the complex methodology proposed by the authors is confirmed by calculations of the performance indicators of financial and economic activities of this enterprise, which means that its effectiveness and versatility are shown for various enterprises. A set of models that will be used to assess the likelihood of bankruptcy and identify ways to improve the business processes of the company is presented in Figure 1. It should be noted that for the convenience of performing calculations according to the models under consideration, computer support is of great importance, which is an essential component of the digital economic system. So, to achieve these goals, various software can be used, from classic Office software packages to specialized mathematical programs such as MATLAB with specialized thematic modules built into them.

Let us consider the theoretical foundations of the models, their functionality, scope and limitations, as well as the application of these models in practice to assess the probability of bankruptcy of a large Nizhny Novgorod industrial enterprise, JSC Russian Aircraft Corporation MiG.

To assess the likelihood of bankruptcy of an enterprise, it is necessary, first of all, to assess its solvency. The most popular method for assessing solvency is the Altman model, which shows the likelihood of future bankruptcy, and the indicators that are involved in the model characterize the company's potential and performance for the reporting period.

Altman's two-factor model. Due to the dependence on only two factors, this model is the most simple and intuitive. The indicators used are the liquidity ratio and the share of borrowed funds in the company's liabilities (1).

$$Z = -0.3877 - 1.0736 * Kcl + 0.579 * (BC / L) \tag{1}$$

where Kcl is the current liquidity ratio; BC is the borrowed capital; L is the liabilities.

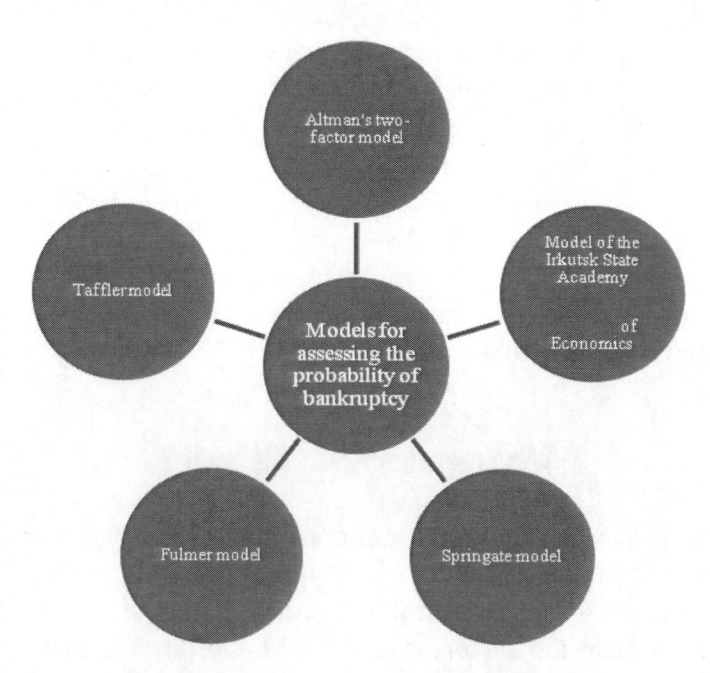

Figure 1. Project proposed for developing a smart contracting system.

Table 1 shows the values of the Z-score, which make it possible to determine the likelihood of bankruptcy of an enterprise (Wardayanti et al. 2017; Plotnikova, Bataev, and Byraeva 2018).

The disadvantage of Altman's model is that it does not take into account the specifics of the activities of individual enterprises. Industry specificities and other individual parameters of companies can negate the result obtained using Altman's model, and companies that were, according to it, a step away from bankruptcy will survive, while the financially stable ones will go bankrupt.

Like other methods of forecasting bankruptcy, the model of the British economist Richard Taffler is based on taking into account internal factors that characterize the financial condition of the enterprise. The probability of bankruptcy, according to the Taffler model, is estimated, as a rule, for open joint-stock companies. He developed a linear regression model based on four coefficients. This four-factor model was derived from the analysis of financial performance and financial health of 46 UK firms that went bankrupt and 46 firms that were financially stable from 1969 to 1975.

$$Zscore = 0.53 * X1 + 0.13 * X2 + 0.18 * X3 + 0.16 * X4 \tag{2}$$

where X1 = Profit from sales/Current liabilities; X2 = Current assets/(Current liabilities + Long-term liabilities); X3 = Long-term liabilities/Total assets; X4 = Total assets/Sales revenue.

The boundaries for determining the probability of bankruptcy in accordance with the Taffler model are presented in Table 2 (Kuznetsova 2019).

The disadvantages of the model include: applies only to joint-stock companies whose shares are quoted on the stock market; the final Z-score is difficult to interpret; the model cannot be used for the Russian economy, since Taffler could not take into account the specific factors of the Russian market.

Table 1. Z-score value for a two-factor assessment model

Z value	Bankruptcy probability
Z < 0	Low probability of bankruptcy, decreases with decreasing Z value
Z > 0	High probability of bankruptcy, increases with increasing Z value
Z = 0	Bankruptcy probability 50/50

Table 2. Value of the Z-score when assessed by the Taffler model

Z value	Bankruptcy probability
Z > 0.3	Low probability of bankruptcy, "green zone"
Z < 0.2	High probability of bankruptcy, "red zone"
From 0.2 to 0.3	"Gray zone" of uncertainty

The next model for predicting bankruptcy is the G. Springate model. It was created by Canadian scientist Gordon Springate at Simon Fraser University. It is very similar to Altman's model, as since Springate borrowed part of the coefficients from the American scientist:

$$Zscore = 1.03*X1 + 3.07*X2 + 0.66*X3 + 0.4*X4 \qquad (3)$$

where X1 = Working capital/Assets; X2 = (Profit before tax + Interest payable)/Assets; X3 = Profit before tax/Current liabilities; X4 = Revenue/Assets.

It can be noted that the first two coefficients have already been used in Altman's model, the coefficient X3 has a specific weight of 0.66 and, accordingly, has more weight in determining the Z-score. Profit before tax is used in the calculation of X3, which means that the determining factor in the final assessment of the probability of bankruptcy according to the Springate model will be sales profit. Table 3 shows the boundaries of the Z-score value according to the Springate model.

In 1984, the American scientist J. Fulmer developed his own model for assessing the bankruptcy of an enterprise. This model is distinguished by the multiplicity of factors on which the final Z-score depends: there are nine of them (4).

$$Z = 5.528*X1 + 0.212*X2 + 0.073*X3 + 1.27*X4 + 0.12*X5$$
$$+ 2.235*X6 + 0.575*X7 + 1.083*X8 + 0.984*X9 - 3.075 \qquad (4)$$

where X1 = Retained earnings of previous years/Assets; X2 = Sales revenue/Assets; X3 = (Profit before tax + Interest payable)/Equity; X4 = Cash flow/(Current + Long-term liabilities); X5 = Long-term liabilities/Assets; X6 = Current liabilities/Assets; X7 = Lg (Tangible assets); X8 = Working capital/(Long-term + Current liabilities); X9 = Lg((Profit before tax + Interest payable)/Interest payable)

Table 4 shows the boundaries of the Z-score according to the Fulmer model.

Table 3. Z-score value when assessed by the Springate model

Z value	Bankruptcy probability
Less than 0.862	Enterprise bankruptcy is likely
More than 0.862	Enterprise bankruptcy is unlikely

Table 4. Z-score value assessed by the Fulmer model

Z value	Bankruptcy probability
Less than 0	Enterprise bankruptcy is likely
More than 0	Enterprise bankruptcy is unlikely

Since Fulmer uses nine coefficients, the model certainly has a high forecast accuracy - it is 98% for a year ahead, and 81% for two years. Moreover, one of all, it uses the size of the enterprise as one of the factors in assessing the likelihood of bankruptcy. This is quite important since the financial position of large companies and small businesses can be assessed in different ways.

All the above models were created by foreign scientists and cannot fully take into account the factors of the Russian economic environment. The domestic market has its own characteristics, taking into account which it is necessary to assess the likelihood of bankruptcy.

In 1997, scientists from the Irkutsk State Academy of Economics (ISAE) developed a model to assess the likelihood of bankruptcy of companies. According to the authors, the ISAE model, due to the rejection of the shortcomings inherent in foreign approaches, should have higher accuracy in predicting the bankruptcy of an enterprise for domestic companies. Based on a survey of business representatives conducted by researchers, indicators were identified that are most often used by managers to assess the financial condition of an enterprise: net profit, revenue, costs of creating and selling finished goods, the amount of equity, and the amount of own and total capital (5).

$$R = 8.38 * K1 + K2 + 0.054 * K3 + 0.63 * K4 \qquad (5)$$

where К1 is the efficiency ratio of using own asset; К2 is the profitability coefficient; К3 is the turnover ratio; К4 is the rate of return.

The critical (boundary) values of the R-index when assessed by the ISAE model are presented in Table 5.

The most important advantage of this model is its applicability in Russian conditions. Note that the first coefficient of the K1 model is also taken from Altman's model, the K3 coefficient was used in the Taffler bankruptcy model. Nevertheless, the rest of the financial ratios from the model have not been previously used in foreign approaches to assessing bankruptcy. It is worth paying attention to the fact that the first coefficient has a disproportionately large specific weight of 8.38. In other words, one way or another, almost all models are united by the large value of the dependence of the probability of bankruptcy on the use of the own assets of companies at risk.

Table 5. Value of the R-index assessed by ISAE model

R value	Bankruptcy probability
Less than 0	Maximum
From 0 to 0.18	High
From 0.18 to 0.32	Average
From 0.32 to 0.42	Low
More than 0.42	Minimum

3. RESULTS

Within the framework of practical testing, the authors used the classic software tool Microsoft Excel, which, on the one hand, is very convenient to use, and on the other hand, a fairly functional product that is quite suitable for solving the problem. Let us consider the application of these models to assess the likelihood of bankruptcy of a large Russian industrial enterprise - Russian Aircraft Company MiG. Based on the data of the accounting statements of this enterprise for 2018-2019, the aggregated asset and liability of the balance sheet were compiled. They are presented in Tables 6, 7.

Table 6. Aggregated asset balance of the Russian Aircraft Company MiG

Class	Name	At the beginning of the reporting period		At the end of the reporting period	
		rub	%	rub	%
A1	Most liquid assets	17831743	8.7%	10108066	4.6%
A2	Quick assets	68956440	33.7%	97245076	43.8%
A3	Slow assets	50064629	24.5%	43665313	19.7%
A4	Sticky assets	67902767	33.2%	70987751	32.0%
Balance		204755579	100%	222006206	100%

Table 7. Aggregated liability of the balance sheet of the Russian Aircraft Company MiG

Class	Name	At the beginning of the reporting period		At the end of the reporting period	
		rub	%	rub	%
L1	Maturing liabilities	64259528	31.4%	90028572	40.55%
L2	Short-term liabilities	45840341	22.4%	64513338	29.06%
L3	Long-term liabilities	123000708	60.1%	88319786	39.78%
L4	Permanent liabilities	-28344998	-13.8%	-20855490	-9.39%
Balance		204755579	100%	222006206	100%

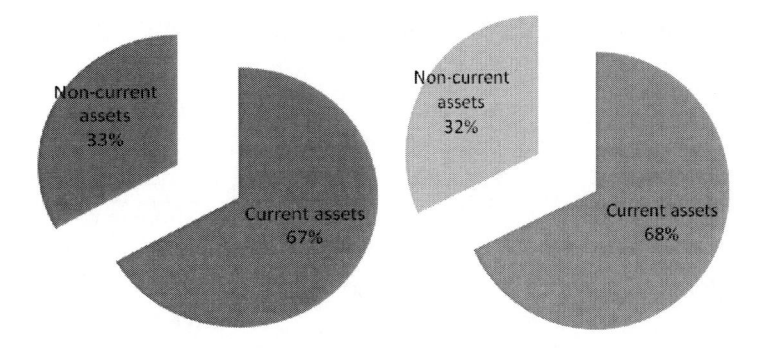

Figure 2. Ratio of current and non-current assets at the beginning and end of the period.

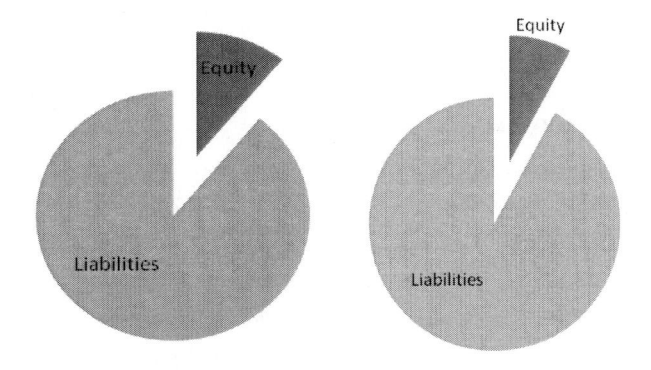

Figure 3. Ratio of liabilities and equity at the beginning and end of the period.

For clarity of presentation of data presented in the aggregated balance sheet of the company, we use pie charts to display the ratio of current and non-current assets at the beginning and end of the year (Figure 2) and liabilities and equity at the beginning and end of the year (Figure 3).

Let us present the results of calculations and their interpretation according to the considered models using the example of assessing the probability of bankruptcy at a large industrial enterprise - JSC Russian Aircraft Manufacturing Company MiG in Table 8.

4. Discussion

Thus, we can conclude that, according to foreign concepts of assessing the likelihood of bankruptcy, the insolvency of an enterprise is unlikely or absent at all. However, the dynamics of changes in integral indicators corresponding to foreign models indicates that there is a deterioration in the state of the enterprise and the likelihood of bankruptcy increases. But, at the same time, the value of the probability of bankruptcy does not leave the 'low zone.'

**Table 8. Summary table with the results of assessing the probability
of bankruptcy**

Model name	Calculated value of the integral indicator		Bankruptcy probability assessment	
	2018	2019	beginning of period	end of period
Altman's two-factor model	-1.06	-0.80	low	low
Fulmer model	1.89	1.34	low	low
Springate model	0.54	0.39	average	average
Taffler model	0.67	0.62	low	low
ISAE model	1.06	-0.25	Minimum	Maximum

At the same time, according to the domestic ISAE model, $R > 0$ in 2018, which indicates a low degree of probability of bankruptcy of the enterprise, but in 2019, $R < 0$, which indicates a high probability of bankruptcy in 2019. It is interesting to note here that the first indicator in the domestic ISAE model is similar to the first indicator in the Springate model, and it goes from a positive value in 2018 to a negative area in 2019 because current assets in 2018 exceed short-term liabilities, and in 2019, current assets are becoming insufficient to cover short-term liabilities.

When forming a generalized conclusion, it is better to rely more on Russian developments, since they more accurately describe the real state of domestic enterprises, and one should use them as reference when planning the company's activities. Moreover, the integral indicators that correspond to Western models also indicate a deterioration in the financial and economic condition of the enterprise. In this regard, the enterprise needs to start developing anti-crisis management measures and turn to risk management methods for managing and resolving a crisis situation.

CONCLUSION

The following should be noted as recommendations that should be made to improve the business processes of the enterprise analyzed in the research material:

1. Since the enterprise has insufficient funds at the beginning and end of the period (8.7% and 4.6%, respectively), it is necessary to increase the amount of funds, especially since the level of funds decreases by the end of the period. At the same time, we see that the volume of accounts receivable increases in absolute and percentage terms (growth from 33.7% to 43.8%) - accordingly, the company starts selling more on credit. Such a high level of accounts receivable, together with a high share of short-term liabilities (31.4% and 40.55% at the beginning and at the end of the year, respectively), means that the company needs to improve its financial and credit policy and to a lesser

extent provide products to their counterparties on credit since the enterprise does not have enough cash.

2. The company should introduce stricter control over accounts receivable, reduce the time it takes to sell the company's products on credit, modernize the schedule of financial receipts from buyers and the cost of repaying the company's loans - the receipt of funds should precede loan payments.

3. The company should recommend an additional issue of shares to increase the amount of equity capital, which is negative at the beginning and end of the period.

4. It is necessary to attract additional funds, including private investors, to reduce the negative value of equity capital. On the one hand, JSC Russian Aircraft Manufacturing Company MiG reduces the negative share of equity capital from -13.8% at the beginning of the period to -9.39% in the balance sheet liability at the end of the period. However, the amount and share of equity capital remain negative, which indicates a low degree of liquidity and solvency of the company.

5. The company should start a financial recovery procedure to get out of the crisis.

ACKNOWLEDGMENTS

The study was carried out within the framework of the basic part of the state assignment of the Ministry of Education and Science of the Russian Federation, project 0729-2020-0056 "Modern methods and models for diagnosing, monitoring, preventing and overcoming crisis phenomena in the economy in the context of digitalization as a way to ensure the economic security of the Russian Federation."

REFERENCES

Avduevskaia, Ekaterina A., Yurii Y. Kuporov, and Evgenia M. Chepikova. 2018. "Estimation of the Efficiency of Investment by Households in Financial Instruments and Human Capital." In *Proceedings of the 32nd International Business Information Management Association Conference, IBIMA 2018 - Vision 2020: Sustainable Economic Development and Application of Innovation Management from Regional Expansion to Global Growth.*

"*Balanced Scorecard Institute.*" n.d. Accessed February 4, 2021. https://balancedscorecard.org/.

Balashova, Elena, Inna Krasovskaya, Elena Schislyaeva, and Felix Shamrai. 2019. "Calculation and Analytical Instrumentarium for Estimating the Economic Efficiency of the Digital Technologies Development Process." In *IOP Conference*

Series: Materials Science and Engineering. https://doi.org/10.1088/1757-899X/497/1/012107.

Balashova, Elena S., and Elizaveta A. Gromova. 2017. "Russian Experience of Integrating Modern Management Models." *Espacios.*

Cepec, Jaka, and Peter Grajzl. 2020. "Debt-to-Equity Conversion in Bankruptcy Reorganization and Post-Bankruptcy Firm Survival." *International Review of Law and Economics.* https://doi.org/10.1016/j.irle.2019.105878.

Chernichenko, Svetlana, and Roman Kotov. 2020. "Methodological Tools for Diagnosing Insolvency (Bankruptcy) of Organizations in the Anti-Crisis Management System." *Food Processing: Techniques and Technology.* https://doi.org/10.21603/2074-9414-2020-4-588-601.

Curtis, Steven Kane, and Oksana Mont. 2020. "Sharing Economy Business Models for Sustainability." *Journal of Cleaner Production.* https://doi.org/10.1016/j.jclepro.2020.121519.

Drotár, Peter, Peter Gnip, Martin Zoričak, and Vladimír Gazda. 2019. "Small- and Medium-Enterprises Bankruptcy Dataset." *Data in Brief.* https://doi.org/10.1016/j.dib.2019.104360.

Galimova, Margarita, Tatiana Gileva, Nataliya Mukhanova, and Ludmila Krasnuk. 2019. "Selecting the Path of the Digital Transformation of Business-Models for Industrial Enterprises." In *IOP Conference Series: Materials Science and Engineering.* https://doi.org/10.1088/1757-899X/497/1/012071.

Gromova, Elizaveta A. 2019. "Agile Project Management as a Catalyst for the Russian Industry Development." In *AIP Conference Proceedings.* https://doi.org/10.1063/1.5092938.

Kahloun, Fouzia, and Sonia Ayachi Ghannouchi. 2018. "Improvement of Quality for Business Process Modeling Driven by Guidelines." In *Procedia Computer Science.* https://doi.org/10.1016/j.procS.2018.07.207.

Kuladzhi, Tamara, Aleksandr Babkin, and Said Alvi Murtazaev. 2018. "Matrix Tool for Efficiency Assessment of Production of Building Materials and Constructions in the Digital Economy." In *Advances in Intelligent Systems and Computing.* https://doi.org/10.1007/978-3-319-70987-1_141.

G. V. Kuznetsova. 2019. "The Anti-Crisis Management of Industrial Enterprises on the Basis of Formation of Mechanism for Strategic Controlling." *Business Inform.* https://doi.org/10.32983/2222-4459-2019-2-348-353.

Mogilko, D., V. Iliashenko, V. Chantsev, and A. C. F. M. Von Schmit. 2019. "Data Management in the Business Processes System." In *Proceedings of the 33rd International Business Information Management Association Conference, IBIMA 2019: Education Excellence and Innovation Management through Vision 2020.*

Mogilko, Dmitry Yu, Igor V. Ilin, Victoria M. Iliashenko, and Sergei G. Svetunkov. 2020. "BI Capabilities in a Digital Enterprise Business Process Management System." In *Lecture Notes in Networks and Systems.* https://doi.org/10.1007/978-3-030-34983-7_69.

Plotnikova, Ekaterina V., Alexey V. Bataev, and Zarina Sh Byraeva. 2018. "Bankruptcy of Credit Organizations in Russian Federation: Causes and Prevention." In *Proceedings of the 32nd International Business Information Management Association Conference, IBIMA 2018 - Vision 2020: Sustainable Economic Development and Application of Innovation Management from Regional Expansion to Global Growth.*

Rudskoy, Andrey, Alexey Borovkov, Pavel Romanov, and Olga Kolosova. 2019. "Reducing Global Risks in the Process of Transition to the Digital Economy." In *IOP Conference Series: Materials Science and Engineering*. https://doi.org/10.1088/1757-899X/497/1/012088.

Sharipova, Sabina R., Elena R. Schislyaeva, Elena S. Balashova, and Olga A. Saychenko. 2020. "The Mechanism of Creating a Strategy of Sustainable Development of Company in the Eco-System of the Digital Economy." In *Advances in Intelligent Systems and Computing*. https://doi.org/10.1007/978-3-030-39319-9_14.

Wannes, Aicha, and Sonia Ayachi Ghannouchi. 2019. "KPI-Based Approach for Business Process Improvement." In *Procedia Computer Science*. https://doi.org/10.1016/j.procs.2019.12.182.

Wardayanti, Ari, Wahyudi Sutopo, Muh Hisjam, and Amran Rasli. 2017. "Bankruptcy Prediction Using Altman Z-Score Model and 5w + 1h Approach to Elaborate Strategy (Case Study: Spin off Company)." *Advanced Science Letters*. https://doi.org/10.1166/asl.2017.9948.

In: Global Challenges of Digital Transformation of Markets ISBN: 978-1-53619-754-9
Editors: E. de la Poza and S. E. Barykin   © 2021 Nova Science Publishers, Inc.

Chapter 28

INFLUENCE OF DIGITAL ECONOMY ON THE TRANSFORMATION OF BANKING FOR BUSINESS

Elena Generalnitskaia[1,] and Natalya Loginova[2]*
[1]Dar-Cosmetic Ltd., Saint-Petersburg, Russia
[2]Russian Customs Academy the St.-Petersburg branch named after Vladimir
Bobkov, Saint-Petersburg, Russia

ABSTRACT

The article describes the importance of digitalization for the Russian economy not only because of the expectation of GDP growth and economic efficiency increase but because it could provide each company of business sector equal access to banking services. In this article, we prove the problem of Russian banking system asymmetry. We consider the number of banking infrastructure institutions per 1 million inhabitants and their structure (proportion of head offices, branches, supplementary and operational offices). Next, we point out seven trends of business and banking sector interaction in order to point out its features and reveal existing problems. Trend 1 ascertains broad digital transformation of the banking sector. Trend 2 claims that the Internet became the main communication channel of electronic exchange between the business and banking sectors. Trend 3 states that the business sector shows the low development of technical infrastructure. Trend 4 declares the growth of legal entities accounts for Internet access in the total number of accounts opened by them. Trend 5 indicates increase in the number of orders (payment orders) transmitted in electronic form by legal entities. Trend 6 claims improvement of information security of banking transactions. And finally trend 7 indicates rapid growth in the number of payment

---

* Corresponding Author's Email: e_generalnitskaya@mail.ru.

cards held by legal entities as well as the number of transactions made by means of them. Analyses of listed trends showed that the business sector falls behind the banking sector that can involve it in digital interaction.

Keywords: Digitalization Trends, Banking Sector, Business Sector, Asymmetry of Russian Banking Sector

1. INTRODUCTION

The Digital revolution has a considerable effect on the national economy. According to the National Research University Higher School of Economics by 2030 GDP growth will be more than half associated with digitalization (1.47% of 2.75% of annual GDP growth) primarily as a result of increased efficiency and competitiveness of all sectors of the economy (Abdrakhmanova et al., 2019). At the same time, according to the McKinsey report, economy digitalization by 2025 may result in 4.1-8.9 trillion rubles growth of GDP, which is equal to 19-34% total GDP increase ("McKinsey Report Digital Russia: New Reality " 2019). One of the most important sectors of the Russian economy that can make a significant contribution to GDP increase is the business sector. In the structure of gross domestic product in 2018, the share of the business sector was 73.8% (Gokhberg et al., 2019).

Because of the problem of asymmetry of the Russian banking sector companies have unequal conditions for development. At the same time, we consider the banking sector as one of the leaders of digitalization in Russia and involves other sectors to its processes (Bataev 2017a). The objectives of the current study were to estimate the asymmetry of the Russian banking sector and availability of banking services, point out digital trends of banking and business sector interaction in order to underline the current situation, the problems facing them, and suggest methods to increase digitalization processes between banking and business sectors (Sergeev, Marikhina, and Rodionov 2018).

2. MATERIALS AND METHODS

In this study, we used statistics from the Bank of Russia available on the official website which is tracking information about the banking sector as well as statistics collected by the National Research University Higher School of Economics (HSE) in their statistic review (Digital Economy Indicators in the Russian Federation) about digitalization level of the Russian economy (Lyukevich, Rodionov, and Kindeeva 2018). The study used tabular and graphical methods, the method of statistical analysis of financial indicators, content analysis of the official websites of Russian banks, an interdisciplinary approach for a comprehensive study of the problem (Barykin, Kalinina, et al. 2021; Barykin, Kapustina, Sergeev, et al. 2021; Barykin, Bochkarev, et al. 2021; Barykin, Kapustina, Valebnikova, et al. 2021), as well as other methods of scientific analysis (Bataev 2017b).

3. RESULTS

Sustainable economic growth depends on the quality and availability of banking services. Digitalization has a significant influence on the increase of availability of banking services but at the same time, the level of business sector digitalization should correspond to some requirements to benefit from it. The Russian banking sector is ahead of the business sector in terms of the scale and degree of digital transformation application. To estimate the current situation and indicate existing problems we are going to point out some important digital transformation trends of interaction between banking and business sector. But before there is important to estimate the level of availability of banking services and asymmetry of the Russian banking sector in order to underline the importance of digitalization.

3.1. Level of Availability of Russian Banking Services

The Bank of Russia policy of rehabilitating the banking sector, commercial banks mergers and acquisitions, the constant increase of online banking services share in the total volume of services provided by commercial banks resulted in a process of reducing the number of commercial banks and their branches (Figure 1).

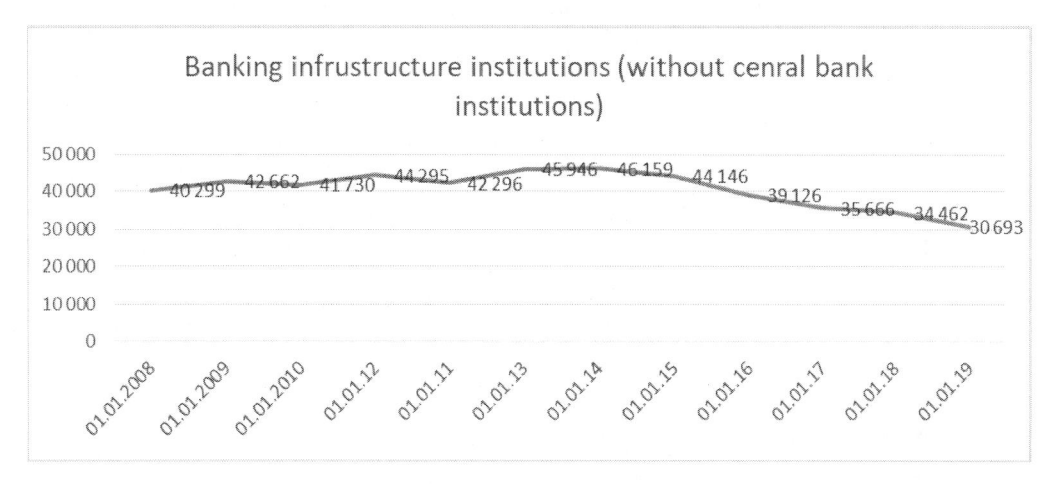

Figure 1. Russian banking infrastructure institutions (without the Bank of Russia institutions).

The latest figure shows that the total number of banking infrastructure institutions (excluding Bank of Russia institutions) has decreased by 28% over the past 10 years.

It could negatively influence on results of business sector companies, which are late in digitalization. Availability of banking services declines for them.

3.2. Asymmetry of the Russian Banking Sector

In order to define the territorial asymmetry development of the Russian banking sector, it is important to consider not only the number of banking infrastructure institutions per 1 million inhabitants (Figure 3) but also their structure (Figure 2). Head offices and branches are full services rather than supplementary and operational offices. They have a number of restrictions on banking services established by the regulations of Bank of Russia.

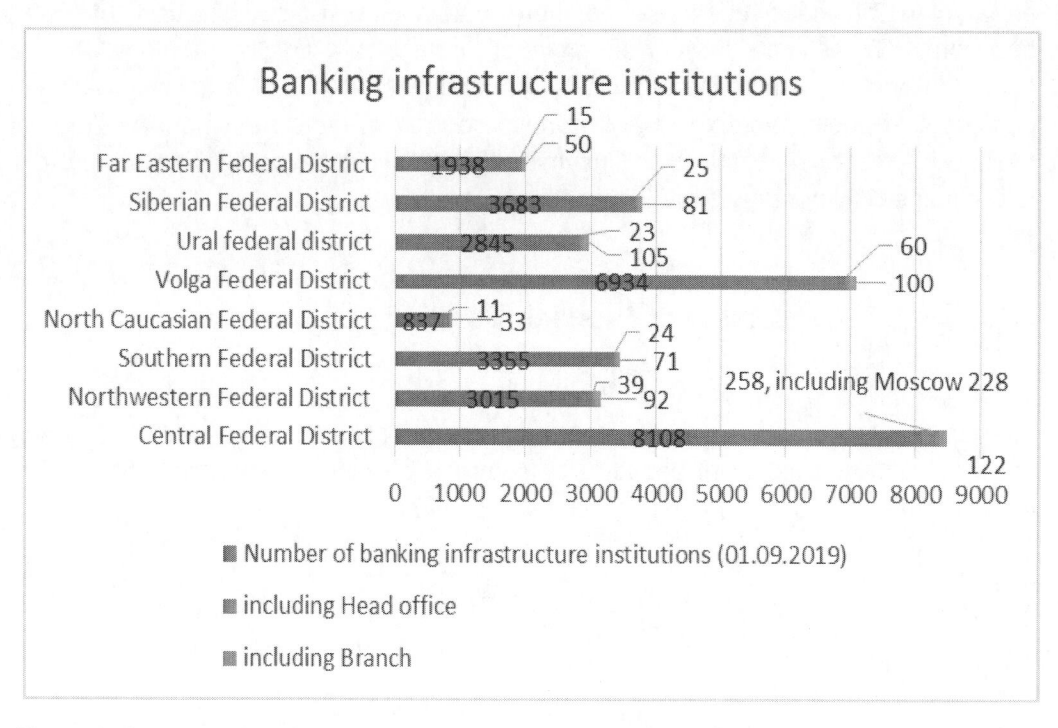

Figure 2. Structure of banking infrastructure institutions (01.09.19).

Figure 2 demonstrates the share of head offices and branches in the total amount of banking infrastructure institutions is 2.8%. The majority (56.7%) of the head offices of commercial banks (258 out of 455) are concentrated in the Central Federal District. Moreover, the share of the head offices of credit institutions registered in Moscow in the total number of credit institutions of Central Federal District amounted to 88.4% (01.09.19) which means it is the largest economic and financial center of the Russian Federation.

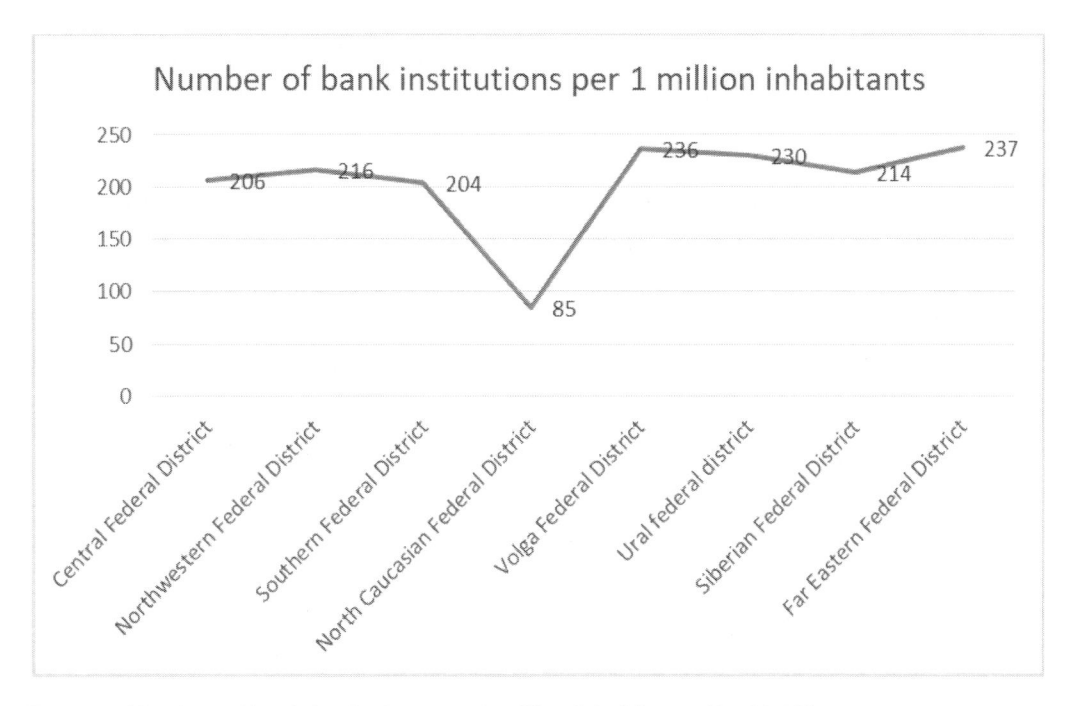

Figure 3. Number of bank institutions per 1 million inhabitants (01.09.19).

Figure 3 gives the evidence that the numbers of bank institutions of all regions apart from the North Caucasian Federal District differ by 15%. The smallest number of banking institutions per 1 million inhabitants is in the North Caucasian Federal District (85 bank institutions). It is 2.5 times lower than the total value of bank institutions per Russian Federation population (209 bank institutions). This likely caused by North Caucasian Federal District regional specifics (based on historical data it demonstrates low lending activity and high overdue debt, which negatively affects the performance of commercial banks).

Summing up Russian banking sector has developmental asymmetry because of head offices and branches concentration in some regions and various numbers of bank institutions per 1 million inhabitants for different regions, especially for North Caucasian Federal District. That means that companies registered in different regions have unequal banking opportunities. Interaction digitalization of business and banking sectors can substantially smooth out inequality.

Next, we are going to turn to digitalization trends of business and banking sector interaction in order to analyze the current situation and reveal existing problems.

3.3. Digitalization Trends of Business and Banking Sector Interaction

3.3.1. Trend 1

Broad digital transformation of the banking sector. We are witnessing a broad digital transformation of the banking sector. It is ahead of other sectors of the economy and involves them in digitalization (Votintseva et al., 2019). Banks adopt the foreign experience, use new technologies (e.g., big data, cloud infrastructure), provide a wide range of online services, become open, agile, flexible, etc. New digital banking models appear, e.g., digital banks set up by large traditional banks, digital subsidiary of a traditional bank, the digital bank itself, banks with digital remote channels (banks created by the model of reselling products of other banks) (Law and Chung 2020). The quality of banking services increases while the cost does not change or even goes down.

There are some other banking sector features caused by digitalization. They do not influence the interaction between the business and banking sector directly but may have some impact.

Digitalization caused the transformation of the organizational structure of credit institutions. In general, the IT department starts expanding gradually and at the same time, other banking departments start decreasing.

Implementing new technologies, distribution of remote banking services, technical progress, and labor productivity growth lead to a reduction in the number of people employed in the banking sector of the Russian Federation. This may bring to structural unemployment as well as banking services cost reduction. According to McKinsey, end-to-end digitalization of key processes in a traditional bank (e.g., sales of new products or services in the branches) can reduce their cost by 40-60% ("McKinsey Report Digital Russia: New Reality" 2019).

3.3.2. Trend 2

The Internet became the main communication channel of electronic exchange between the business and banking sectors. The Internet became the main communication channel for electronic exchange between banks and companies. According to HSE statistic review, 64.2% of Russian companies used the Internet to carry out banking and other financial transactions in 2017. At the same time, only 78.3% of companies used fixed broadband internet (47.4% used mobile broadband internet) (Table 1). That indicates that 82% of the companies connected to fixed broadband Internet carried out banking and other financial transactions using it. The fact that the Internet has become the main communication channel is confirmed in Figure 5. It shows that the share of payment orders of legal entities (bank clients) sent via the Internet in 2018 was 95.8% which 2.5 times more than in 2008.

3.3.3. Trend 3

The business sector shows low development of technical infrastructure.

The analysis of digital technologies of the business sector showed a lack of its technical infrastructure development (Table 1). As stated before, only 78.3% of companies used fixed broadband internet in 2017, among them 29.6% had low Internet distribution level (256 Kbps and lower), that could negatively influence on the development of efficient online interaction with partners. Furthermore, only 22.6% of companies used cloud services (Figure 4), 62.2% of companies used electronic data exchange technologies between own and external systems, 53.7% used software to carry out financial settlements in electronic form. The low digitalization level of the business sector resulted in the low ability to use technologies and services provided them by the banking sector.

Table 1. Digital technologies in the business sector (as a percentage of the total number of organizations in the sector, 2017)

Digital technology	Total (business sector)
Using fixed broad band internet	78.30%
Using mobile broad band internet	47.40%
Distribution by maximum data rate	
Higher 100 Mbps	10.8%
30.1-100 Mbps	21.4%
2.0-30 Mbps	38.2%
256 Kbps	24.4%
Lower 256 Kbps	5.2%
Use of cloud services	22.60%
Use of electronic data exchange technologies between own and external systems	62.20%
Use of software to carry out financial settlements in electronic form	53.7%

Data after HSE review.

Figure 4 shows the dynamics of cloud services use.

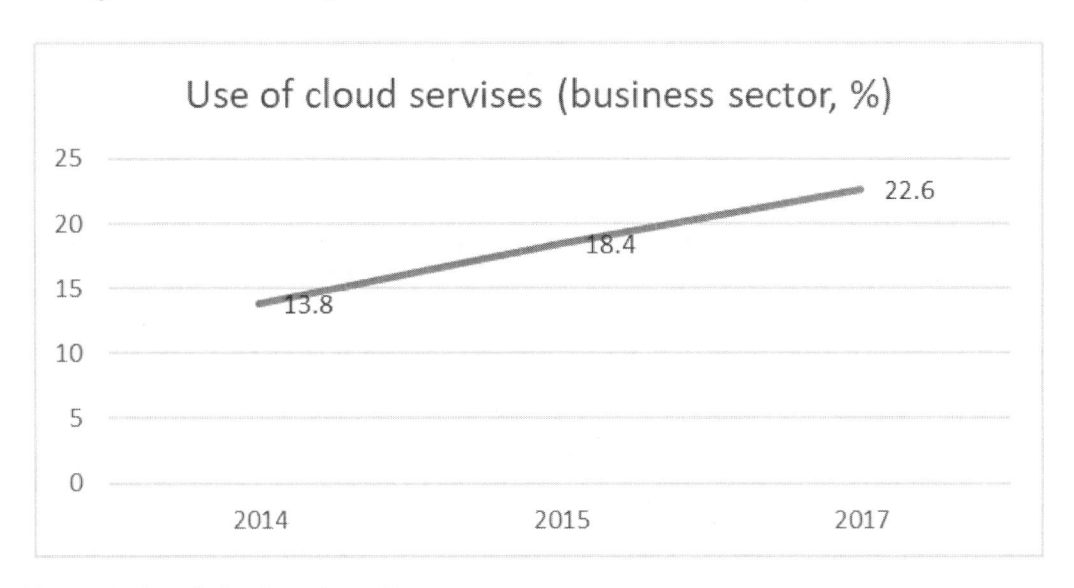

Figure 4. Use of cloud services, %.

Figure 4 shows that 64% more companies began to use cloud services from 2014 to 2017, which indicates the spread of this technology. Mostly cloud services were used in 2017 to store email data (16.3%) (Votintseva et al., 2019), which indicates limited use of cloud services. Implementation of cloud technologies between banking and business sector is constrained by the requirements for the personal data protection, the requirement to provide high information security, lack of clearly described regulatory restrictions on the cloud services use, etc. ("McKinsey Report Digital Russia: New Reality " 2019).

3.3.4. Trend 4

Growth of legal entities accounts with Internet access in the total number of accounts opened by them. Today the overwhelming majority of legal entities accounts have Internet access. Figure 5 demonstrates that the share of accounts of legal entities with remote access grew more than twice times from 42.9% in 2008 to 98.4% in 2019. The expansion of Internet accounts opens the benefits of online banking to legal entities. Banking services became not only more convenient being at hand but also Internet access made it more personal and changed the technical paradigm of interaction.

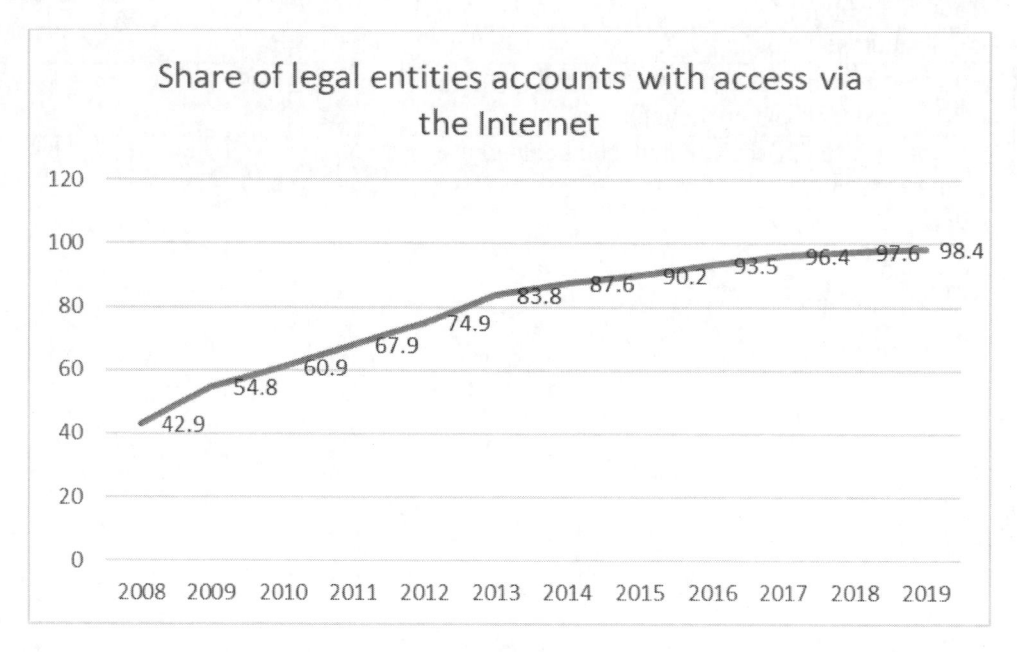

Figure 5. Share of accounts belonging to legal entities (non-credit institutions) with access via the Internet in the total number of accounts opened by legal entities (non-credit institutions).

3.3.5. Trend 5

The number of orders (payment orders) transmitted in electronic form by legal entities increased (Figure 6). The most numerous group of banking settlement documents is payment orders. Therefore, it is enough to consider the share of payment orders on purpose to analyze electronic payments of bank clients. The share of orders (payment orders) in electronic form in the total number of orders received by banks from client legal entities was steadily growing from 62.9% in 2008 to 95.8% in 2018, which indicates an increased digitalization of economic relations between banking and business sector. Almost all orders transmitted in electronic form in 2018 were transmitted using the Internet (93.8%) (Schepinin and Bataev 2019). This indicator increased from 38.0% in 2008 to 93.8% in 2018 that proves that The Internet has become the main channel of data exchange between the banking and business sector (Kudryavtseva, Skhvediani, and Bondarev 2018).

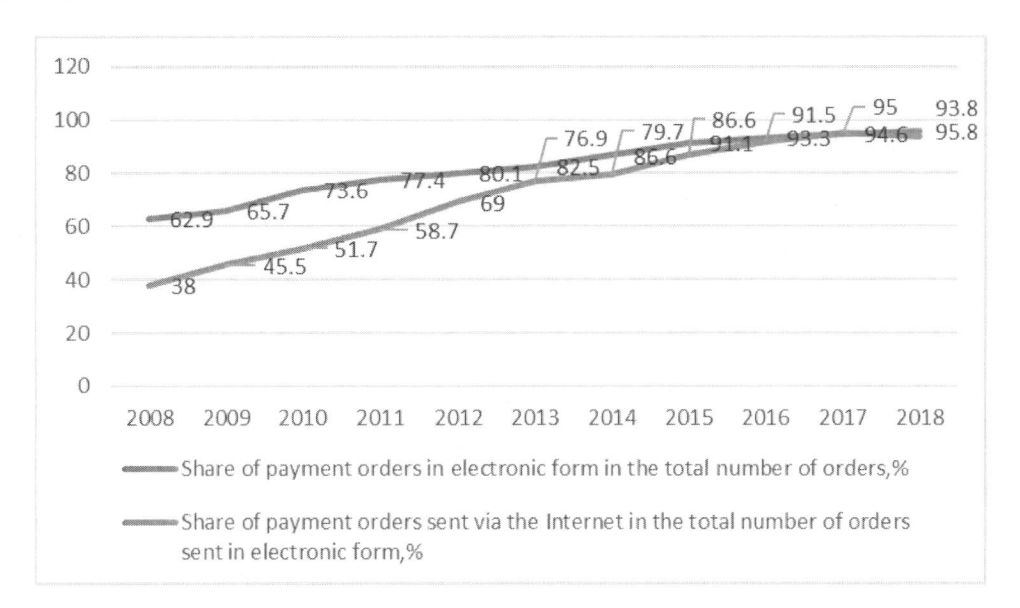

Figure 6. Electronic payments by clients of banks (legal entities) using payment orders.

3.3.6. Trend 6

Improvement of information security of banking transactions. A set of measures provided by the government, Bank of Russia, banking and business sector focused on information security and cyber-stability of the financial system including the application of new technologies (big data, artificial intelligence) resulted in taking fraud in the financial sector under control. According to FinCERT (computer emergency response team of Bank of Russia), the volume of unauthorized transactions from legal entities accounts at the end of 2018 amounted to 1.469 billion rubles (in comparison in 2017 this amounted to about 1.57 billion rubles, in 2016 to 1.89 billion rubles, in 2015 to 3.7 billion rubles) (Fedotova et al., 2019; Romanov 2019).

3.3.7. Trend 7

Rapid growth in the number of payment cards held by legal entities as well as the number of transactions made by means of them. Payment cards have already turned into a digitalization tool. Using them becomes an integral part of business sector payments. Payment cards made a transition from physical to virtual and are used by means of smartphones and smartwatches. Payment cards give an opportunity to use mobile banking apps, mobile wallets (Generalnitskaia 2019). In addition, payment infrastructure accepts both physical payment cards and mobile wallets.

The significant growth in the number of payment cards of legal entities during the last 11 years is illustrated in Figure 7.

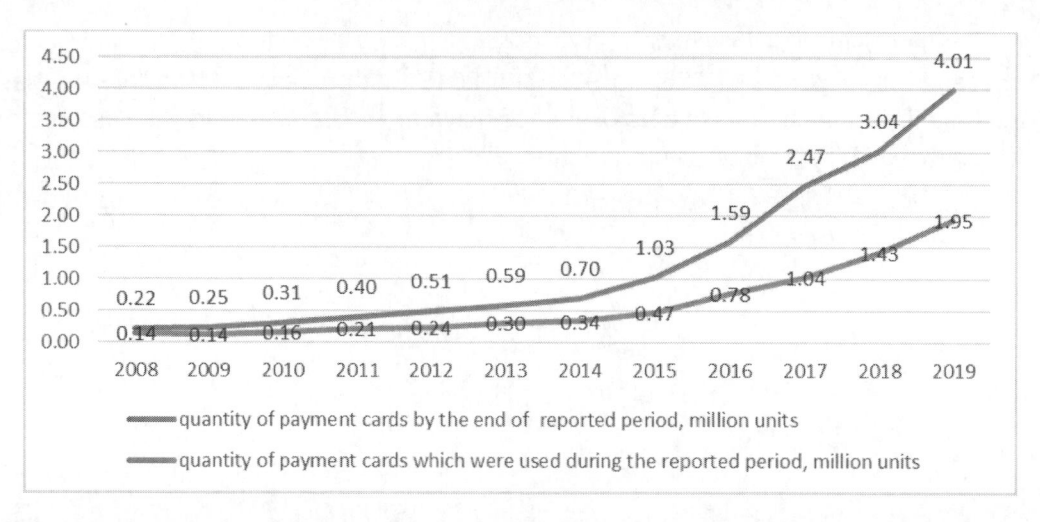

Figure 7. Number of payment cards held by legal entities.

From 2008 to 2019, the number of payment cards increased by nearly 18 times from 223 thousand to 4 million units. It may be caused by the development of cashback services, the attractiveness of personal offers, and service conditions for cardholders. Also nowadays payment infrastructure is developing. For example, Sberbank launched a free service "cash with purchase" in partnership with Mastercard and Visa. That means that clients of any bank can withdraw cash making purchases in the shop cash register that allows such service. Additionally, Bank of Russia has recently stated that it is going to launch a service which will allow to cash in payment cards in the shop cash register. It could help to smooth the asymmetry of the Russian banking sector.

Correspondingly, the number of transactions by legal entities using payment cards showed dramatic growth (Figure 8).

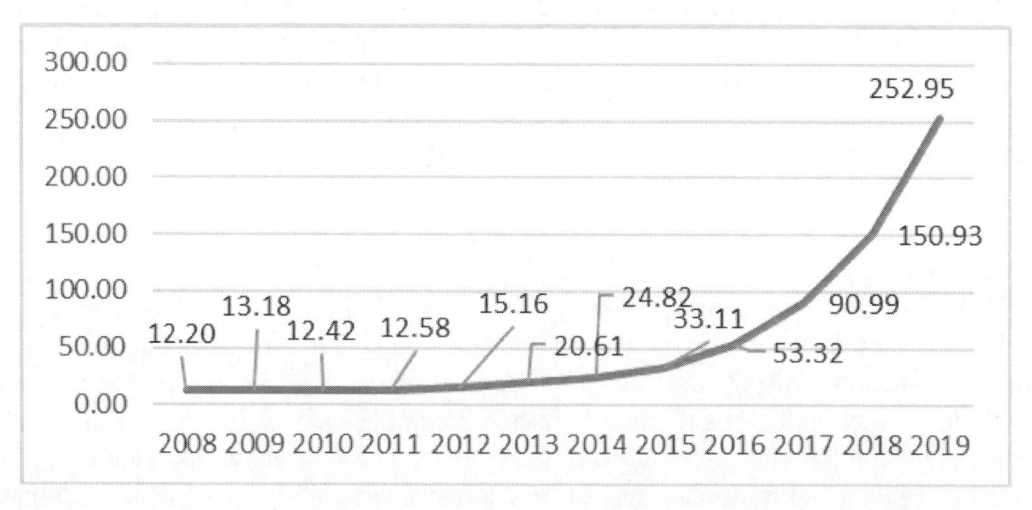

Figure 8. Number of legal entity transactions made by means of payment cards, million units.

It increased by approximately 21 times from 12 million units in 2008 to 252 million units in 2019. According to the Bank of Russia statistics, mostly payment cards were used by legal entities to pay for goods and services.

4. DISCUSSION

Digital interaction between the Russian business sector and the banking sector is of great importance since it can contribute to stable economic growth, which is especially important in the context of the territorial asymmetry of the development of the Russian banking sector. In addition, the COVID-19 experience has proven the importance of online banking in ensuring the sustainability of economic relations in today's business environment.

At the same time, the analysis of digitalization of business and the banking sector, carried out by the authors of this study, showed that their digital interaction is constrained by the low level of digital development of the business sector, which indicates the need for urgent technological modernization of business structures (Bataev, Koroleva, and Gorovoy 2019; Bataev and Plotnikova 2019; Lychkina 2016). Companies in the business sector must implement a digital strategy in the near future to ensure a balanced development policy (Hauptman and Cohen 2011; Ng 2014). Otherwise, it is missing out on the opportunities that the banking sector presents.

It is important to clarify that a key factor in the intensification of interactions between business and the banking sector is the timely tracking of new tools that contribute to improving the efficiency and effectiveness of their joint work (Albertazzi and Gambacorta 2009; Shaikh, Glavee-Geo, and Karjaluoto 2017; Arduini and Morabito 2010). Underestimation by the business sector of the advantages that open up to them through digital interaction with the banking sector may negatively affect the development of both individual business structures and the domestic economy as a whole (Dahlman, Mealy, and Wermelinger 2016; Ng 2014; Skotarenko et al., 2019).

CONCLUSION

Summarizing the identified trends, we can state the following: 1. Banks provide the economy with effective digital services (introduce new digital technologies, create a digital ecosystem, develop new services, increase the speed of transactions, etc.) and attract business. sectors to digitalization processes. 2. The main channel of communication between the banking sector and business in the digital economy is the Internet. 3. The vast majority of those in the business sector with a bank account use a remote access account. 4. The share of digital interaction between banks and businesses, including settlements in electronic form, has increased. 3. The key factor for the development of digital interaction between the business sector and the banking sector is opening a bank account with remote access and gaining access to the Internet.

Hence, an internet connection and a remote access account offer clear benefits of digital banking. It is important to note that the banking sector is in a more advantageous position in organizing digital interaction than the business sector, which is due, for example, to the fact that the latter does not have a bank account, since this is a right, not an obligation, and small businesses use this.

REFERENCES

———. 2017b. "Implementation of Cloud Automated Banking Systems Innovative Way of Financial Institutions." In *Proceedings of the 29th International Business Information Management Association Conference - Education Excellence and Innovation Management through Vision 2020: From Regional Development Sustainability to Global Economic Growth.*

"*McKinsey Report Digital Russia: New Reality.*" 2019. 2019. https://www.mckinsey.com/ru/our-insights#.

Abdrakhmanova, Gulnara, Konstantin Vishnevskiy, Leonid Gokhberg, and Yury Dranev. 2019. *What Is the Digital Economy? Trends, Competencies, Measurement.*

Albertazzi, Ugo, and Leonardo Gambacorta. 2009. "Bank Profitability and the Business Cycle." *Journal of Financial Stability.* https://doi.org/10.1016/j.jfs.2008.10.002.

Arduini, Fabio, and Vincenzo Morabito. 2010. "Business Continuity and the Banking Industry." *Communications of the ACM.* https://doi.org/10.1145/1666420.1666452.

Barykin, Sergey Yevgenievich, Andrey Aleksandrovich Bochkarev, Sergey Mikhailovich Sergeev, Tatiana Anatolievna Baranova, Dmitriy Anatolievich Mokhorov, and Aleksandra Maksimovna Kobicheva. 2021. "A Methodology of Bringing Perspective Innovation Products to Market." *Academy of Strategic Management Journal* 20 (2): 1–19. https://www.abacademies.org/articles/a-methodology-of-bringing-perspective-innovation-products-to-market.pdf.

Barykin, Sergey Yevgenievich, Olga Vladimirovna Kalinina, Irina Vasilievna Kapustina, Victor Andreevich Dubolazov, Cesar Armando Nunez Esquivel, Elmira Alyarovna Nazarova, and Petr Anatolievich Sharapaev. 2021. "The Sharing Economy and Digital Logistics in Retail Chains: Opportunities and Threats." *Academy of Strategic Management Journal* 20 (2): 1–14. https://www.abacademies.org/articles/the-sharing-economy-and-digital-logistics-in-retail-chains-opportunities-and-threats.pdf.

Barykin, Sergey Yevgenievich, Irina Vasilievna Kapustina, Sergey Mikhailovich Sergeev, Olga Vladimirovna Kalinina, Viktoriia Valerievna Vilken, Yuri Yevgenievich Putikhin, and Lydia Vitalievna Volkova. 2021. "Developing the Physical Distribution Digital Twin Model within the Trade Network." *Academy of Strategic Management Journal* 20 (1): 1–24. https://www.abacademies.org/

articles/developing-the-physical-distribution-digital-twin-model-within-the-trade-network.pdf.

Barykin, Sergey Yevgenievich, Irina Vasilievna Kapustina, Olga Aleksandrovna Valebnikova, Natalia Viktorovna Valebnikova, Olga Vladimirovna Kalinina, Sergey Mikhailovich Sergeev, Marisa Camastral, Yuri Yevgenievich Putikhin, and Lydia Vitalievna Volkova. 2021. "Digital Technologies for Personnel Management: Implications for Open Innovations." *Academy of Strategic Management Journal* 20 (2): 1–14. https://www.abacademies.org/articles/digital-technologies-for-personnel-management-implications-for-open-innovations.pdf.

Bataev, Alexey V. 2017a. "Contemporary Approaches to Advancement of the Banking Sector – Virtual Credit Organizations." In *Proceedings of the 30th International Business Information Management Association Conference, IBIMA 2017 - Vision 2020: Sustainable Economic Development, Innovation Management, and Global Growth.*

Bataev, Alexey V., and Ekaterina V. Plotnikova. 2019. "Assessment of Digital Banks' Performance." *Espacios.*

Bataev, Alexey, Lada Koroleva, and Alexandr Gorovoy. 2019. "Innovative Approaches in the Financial Sphere: Assessment of Digital Banks' Performance." In *Proceedings of the European Conference on Innovation and Entrepreneurship, ECIE.* https://doi.org/10.34190/ECIE.19.038.

Dahlman, Carl;, Sam; Mealy, and Martin Wermelinger. 2016. "Harnessing the Digital Economy for Developing Countries." *OECD Development Centre Working Papers.*

Fedotova, Gilyan V., Anastasia A. Gontar, Viktor A. Titov, Arthur K. Kurbanov, and Emma V. Kuzmina. 2019. "Increasing the Economic Security of Information Banking Systems." In *Studies in Computational Intelligence.* https://doi.org/10.1007/978-3-030-13397-9_118.

Generalnitskaia, Elena Igorevna. 2019. "Trends of Economic Relations Transformation in Context of Digital Economy (On the Example of Commercial Banks and Business Sector)." *Krasnoyarsk Science.* https://doi.org/10.12731/2070-7568-2019-4-20-33.

Gokhberg, Leonid, Gulnara Abdrakhmanova, Yury Dranev, and Ekaterina Dyachenko. 2019. *Digital Economy : 2019.*

Hauptman, Hanoch, and Arie Cohen. 2011. "The Synergetic Effect of Learning Styles on the Interaction between Virtual Environments and the Enhancement of Spatial Thinking." *Computers and Education.* https://doi.org/10.1016/j.compedu.2011.05.008.

Kudryavtseva, Tatiana J., Angi E. Skhvediani, and Arseniy A. Bondarev. 2018. "Digitalization of Banking in Russia: Overview." In *International Conference on Information Networking.* https://doi.org/10.1109/ICOIN.2018.8343196.

Law, K. S., and Fu Lai Chung. 2020. "Knowledge-Driven Decision Analytics for Commercial Banking." *Journal of Management Analytics.* https://doi.org/10.1080/23270012.2020.1734879.

Lychkina, Natalya. 2016. "Synergetics and Development Processes in Socio-Economic Systems: Search for Effective Modeling Constructs." *Business Informatics.* https://doi.org/10.17323/1998-0663.2016.1.66.79.

Lyukevich, Igor, Dmitry Rodionov, and Alina Kindeeva. 2018. "Eliminating Multicollinearity and Considering Microeconomic Indicators in a Multifactorial Model for Predicting Bank Bankruptcy." In *Proceedings of the 32nd International Business Information Management Association Conference, IBIMA 2018 - Vision 2020: Sustainable Economic Development and Application of Innovation Management from Regional Expansion to Global Growth.*

Ng, Irene C. L. 2014. "New Business and Economic Models in the Connected Digital Economy." *Journal of Revenue and Pricing Management.* https://doi.org/10.1057/rpm.2013.27.

Romanov, Rashit. 2019. "The Basic Principles of Information Protection in the Russian Federation in the Transition to a Digital Economy." *NBI Technologies.* https://doi.org/10.15688/nbit.jvolsu.2018.3.2.

Schepinin, Vladimir, and Alexey Bataev. 2019. "Digitalization of Financial Sphere: Challenger Banks Efficiency Estimation." In *IOP Conference Series: Materials Science and Engineering.* https://doi.org/10.1088/1757-899X/497/1/012051.

Sergeev, Dmitrii, V. V. Marikhina, and D. G. Rodionov. 2018. "The Impact of Economic and Geopolitical Shocks of 2014 - 2017 on the Modern Banking System of Russia." In *Proceedings of the 32nd International Business Information Management Association Conference, IBIMA 2018 - Vision 2020: Sustainable Economic Development and Application of Innovation Management from Regional Expansion to Global Growth.*

Shaikh, Aijaz A., Richard Glavee-Geo, and Heikki Karjaluoto. 2017. "Exploring the Nexus between Financial Sector Reforms and the Emergence of Digital Banking Culture – Evidences from a Developing Country." *Research in International Business and Finance.* https://doi.org/10.1016/j.ribaf.2017.07.039.

Skotarenko, O., A. Babkin, L. Senetskaya, and S. Bespalova. 2019. "Tools for Digitalization of Economic Processes for Supporting Management Decision-Making in the Region." In *IOP Conference Series: Earth and Environmental Science.* https://doi.org/10.1088/1755-1315/302/1/012147.

Votintseva, Ludmila, Marina Andreeva, Ivan Kovalenin, and Roman Votintsev. 2019. "Digital Transformation of Russian Banking Institutions: Assessments and Prospects." In *IOP Conference Series: Materials Science and Engineering.* https://doi.org/10.1088/1757-899X/497/1/012101.

In: Global Challenges of Digital Transformation of Markets ISBN: 978-1-53619-754-9
Editors: E. de la Poza and S. E. Barykin   © 2021 Nova Science Publishers, Inc.

Chapter 29

POST-COVID MARKETING 2019: LAUNCHING A NEW CYCLE OF DIGITAL DEVELOPMENT

Anastasia Sozinova[1,], Nadezhda Savelyeva[1] and Marina Alpidovskaya[2]*

[1]Vyatka State University, Kirov, Russia
[2]Financial University, Moscow, Russia

ABSTRACT

The goal of this study is to model marketing after the global COVID-2019 pandemic.

We use the following methods of scientific research: classification, problem and comparative analysis, synthesis, method of analysis of cause-and-effect relationships, hypothetical-deductive method, method of expert assessment, formalization and strategizing. We consider the impact of digitalization on marketing development and the variation of the integral marketing indicator in 2016-2019. The research uses the example of the leaders (countries from the top 20) of the World Bank global ranking by the value of the index of "doing business" for 2020.

Post-COVID 2019 marketing scenarios were modeled under the influence of digitalization. They show that digital technology is likely to be used to launch a new cycle of digital marketing development. It has been proved that digital technologies cannot be used as a countercyclical tool for regulating the market situation, since the scenarios indicate the absence of regression dependence, digital technologies in marketing can be used as a tool for launching a new cycle of marketing development, developing countries have a large potential for using digital technologies in marketing since the correlation between the digital competitiveness index and the integral marketing indicator is higher (-92.61% developing countries, -64.34% developed countries).

Keywords: marketing, post-crisis COVID-2019, industry 4.0

---

* Corresponding Author's Email: aa_sozinova@vyatsu.ru.

1. INTRODUCTION

The volatility of global markets in the post-crisis era of COVID-2019 makes it difficult to manage and makes the influence of external factors more and more powerful and less predictable. The state of the market environment gripped by the epidemiological crisis is very alarming, as there has been a critical decline in market concentration, and it is likely to lead to a decrease in natural incentives for marketing activities.

In such conditions, enterprises need regular marketing activities to maintain competitiveness. At the same time, we should take into account significant economic conditions and the nature of doing business for enterprises that are focused on domestic markets and global enterprises that are simultaneously present in different markets and are forced to be more susceptible to the spread of the global COVID 2019 pandemic.

Therefore, despite the general marketing fundamentals for all enterprises, marketing tools that are successfully applied and work in domestic markets, despite the presence of the consequences of COVID-2019, show distorted results in global markets today and turn out to be ineffective. Unlike internally oriented enterprises, global business presupposes a much greater dependence on economic and business cycles, on processes of globalization of the first half of the 20th century, and the forced de-globalization of the first half of 2020.

In addition, the period of COVID-2019 is unique as, unlike previous economic crises, almost all enterprises were forced to move to Industry 4.0. At the same time, the transition to a digital type of business was carried out under the control of states and COVID-2019 set a high speed of digitalization of all business processes, including marketing activities. The new regulated format of the industrial revolution helps to reduce the risks associated with the transition to Industry 4.0 and maximize benefits.

In this regard, the problem of marketing management after COVID-2019 taking into account the influence of digital technologies is becoming highly relevant. This process can have one of two scenarios.

The first scenario involves the launch of a new business cycle after COVID-2019, that is, accelerating the rate of economic growth based on the use of industry 4.0 technologies. The second scenario is related to the prospect of using achievements of Industry 4.0 in business as a countercyclical tool for regulating market conditions, that is, to prevent a crisis after COVID-2019 and stabilize economic systems. Simultaneous implementation of the presented scenarios is difficult. Therefore, they will be considered as an alternative in the research.

The goal of the work is to simulate marketing scenarios under the influence of the global COVID-2019 pandemic.

2. MATERIALS AND METHODS

The development of Industry 4.0 is described by Alpidovskaya and Popkova (Alpidovskaya and Popkova 2019), Belik et al., (Belik et al. 2020), Bozhuk et al., (S. G. Bozhuk, Maslova, et al. 2019). Prospective scenarios for the development of Industry 4.0 considered by Haabazoka et al., (E. Popkova, Haabazoka, and Ragulina 2020), Popkova (E. G. Popkova 2019), Popkova and Gulzat (E. G. Popkova and Gulzat 2020), Popkova and Sergi (E. G. Popkova and Sergi 2020; G. Popkova and Sergi 2018; E. G. Popkova and Bruno 2019). The priorities of the development of society in the conditions of Industry 4.0 are considered by Popkova et al., (E. Popkova, Sozinova, and Menshchikova 2019), Ragulina (Ragulina 2019), Ragulina et al., (Ragulina et al., 2019), Saveleva et al. (Savelyeva et al., 2019). The essential understanding of the role of Industry 4.0 in regional development is devoted by Sergi (B Sergi 2019), Sergi et al., (Bruno Sergi et al., 2019). The causal relationships of the formation of Industry 4.0 and the role of the marketing concept in them are investigated by Sozinova (Anastasia A. Sozinova 2019; 2018b; 2018a), Sozinova et al., (Anastasia A. Sozinova et al., 2019). The role of information and communication technologies as a vector of development is presented by Fokina et al., (Fokina et al., 2018), Zavyalova et al., (Zavyalova, Studenikin, and Starikova 2018).

The research of marketing activities is done by Bozhuk et al. (S. G. Bozhuk, Evdokimov, et al., 2019), Bozhuk and Pletneva (S. Bozhuk and Pletneva 2018), Kataeva et al. (Kataeva et al., 2017). Digital marketing tools research reviewed by Sozinova et al. (Amastasia A. Sozinova, Fokina, and Shchinova 2017), Sozinova and Fokina (Anastasia Andreevna Sozinova and Fokina 2015; 2014), Zhgulev et al. (Zhgulev et al., 2018).

The economic aspects of the COVID-2019 pandemic are explored by Ataguba (Ataguba and Ataguba 2020), Laing (Laing 2020), Dente and Hashimoto (Dente and Hashimoto 2020), Nadrian (Nadrian 2020). gives an economic analysis of the consequences of mandatory self-isolation decisions during COVID-2019. Bentata (Bentata 2020) examine the impact of COVID-2019 and the cyclical nature of economic systems. Certain issues of COVID-2019 have been studied but in general, scenarios for the transformation of marketing under the influence of COVID-2019 and the further development of digitalization are poorly understood and need further research.

For this, the study uses methods of regression and correlation analysis to determine the impact of digitalization. Its indicator is the Digital Competitiveness Index, IMD, (x), on the integral marketing indicator in 2019 (y1), and its variation in 2016-2019 (y2). The integral marketing indicator is calculated as the arithmetic mean of statistical indicators reflecting individual indicators of marketing activity: market size (10th pillar: Market size), the efficiency of product markets (7th pillar: Product market), innovation potential (12th pillar: Innovation capability).

The study uses the example of the leaders (countries from the top 20) of the World Bank global ranking for 2020 according to the value of the index of "doing business" for 2020.

- Hypothesis H1: there is a positive relationship between digitalization and the 2019 Integrated Marketing Indicator, that is, r (x,y1) > 0 (in correlation analysis) and their correlation is quite high, that is, R2(x, y1) > 50% (in regression analysis);
- Hypothesis H2: there is a negative relationship between digitalization and the variation of the Integrated Marketing Indicator in 2016-2019, that is, r (x,y1) < 0 (in correlation analysis) and their correlation is quite high, that is, R2(x, y1) > 50% (in regression analysis).

The statistical basis for the study is presented in Tables 1 (2016–2017 2016; Schwab 2019; Group 2017) and Tables 2 (IMD 2019; Bris and Cabolis 2020).

3. RESULTS

According to data from Table 2, we obtained the following results of correlation analysis (Figure 1) and regression analysis (Tables 3 and 4). At the same time, due to the nature of the studied indicators (reciprocal: IMD: the higher the indicator, the better; the Integral Marketing Indicator: the lower the better), the negative correlation r denotes a direct relationship between the indicators. In the case of the study of the relationship between the Digital Competitiveness Index and the variation of the Integral Marketing Indicator, the correlation is interpreted in the traditional sense.

As can be seen from Figure 1, digitalization affects marketing development to a greater extent in developing countries (-92.61%). In developed countries, the impact of digitalization on marketing development is also quite strong (-64.34%). At the same time, in developing countries, the variation of the Integral Marketing Indicator is significantly reduced under the influence of digitalization (-66.59%). In developed countries, the variation of the Integral Marketing Indicator is increasing under the influence of digitalization (26.55%).

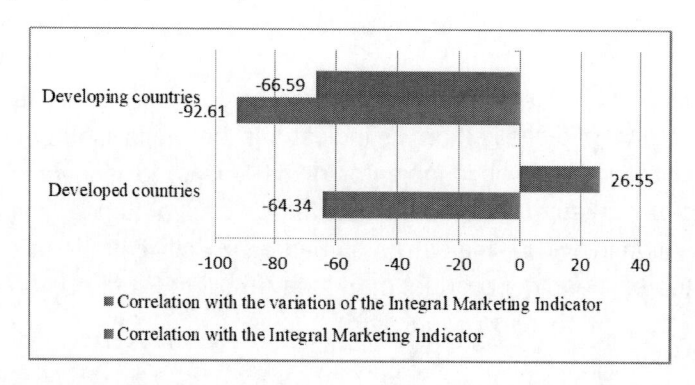

Figure 1. Cross-correlation of digitalization with marketing in developed and developing countries, %. Source: calculated by the authors.

Table 1. Statistics for calculating the Integral Marketing Indicator in 2016-2019, Rank

Year	Position in Doing Business 2020 Ranking	Developed countries (top 10)						Developing countries (top 20)					
	Country	New Zealand	Singapore	Denmark	Republic of Korea	USA	UK	Malaysia	UAE	Thailand	Russia	China	Turkey
2019	10th pillar: Market size	66	27	55	14	2	8	24	32	18	6	1	13
	7th pillar: Product market	3	2	12	59	8	21	20	4	84	87	54	78
	12th pillar: Innovation capability	27	13	11	6	2	8	30	33	50	32	24	49
	Integral Marketing Indicator	32.0	14.0	26.0	26.3	4.0	12.3	24.7	23.0	50.7	41.7	26.3	46.7
2018	10th pillar: Market size	67	27	55	14	2	7	23	28	18	6	1	13
	7th pillar: Product market	4	1	15	67	3	12	24	11	92	83	55	76
	12th pillar: Innovation capability	27	14	12	8	2	7	17	35	51	36	24	47
	Integral Marketing Indicator	32.7	14.0	27.3	29.7	2.3	8.7	21.3	24.7	53.7	41.7	26.7	45.3
2017	10th pillar: Market size	64	35	57	13	2	7	24	29	18	6	1	14
	7th pillar: Product market	5	2	10	73	3	6	26	11	65	60	38	127
	12th pillar: Innovation capability	20	9	10	18	2	12	22	25	50	49	28	69
	Integral Marketing Indicator	29.7	15.3	25.7	34.7	2.3	8.3	24.0	21.7	44.3	38.3	22.3	70.0
2016	10th pillar: Market size	64	37	58	13	2	9	24	27	18	6	1	17
	7th pillar: Product market	6	2	13	77	4	5	24	11	71	49	39	126
	12th pillar: Innovation capability	23	9	10	20	4	13	22	25	54	56	30	71
	Integral Marketing Indicator	31.0	16.0	27.0	36.7	3.3	9.0	23.3	21.0	47.7	37.0	23.3	71.3

Table 2. Statistics of the Integral Marketing Indicator and digital competitiveness in the top 20 countries

Position in Doing Business 2020 Ranking	Country	IMD, Digital Competitiveness Index	Integral Marketing Indicator, rank				
			2016	2017	2018	2019	Variation
		x	-	-	-	y1	y2
Developed countries (top 10)	New Zealand	86.026	31	29.7	32.7	32	3.60
	Singapore	99.373	16	15.3	14	14	5.81
	Denmark	95.225	27	25.7	27.3	26	2.52
	Republic of Korea	91.297	36.7	34.7	29.7	26.3	12.86
	USA	100	3.3	2.3	2.3	4	24.17
	UK	88.691	9	8.3	8.7	12.3	16.63
Developing countries (top 20)	Malasia	82.39	23.3	24	21.3	24.7	5.44
	UAE	90.295	21	21.7	24.7	23	6.23
	Thailand	68.434	47.7	44.3	53.7	50.7	7.11
	Russia	70.406	37	38.3	41.7	41.7	5.23
	China	84.292	23.3	22.3	26.7	26.3	7.66
	Turkey	59.793	71.3	70	45.3	46.7	21.16
Average	-	84.685	-	-	-	27.31	9.87
Standard deviation	-	12.067	-	-	-	13.31	6.85

As it can be seen from Tables 3 and 4, the relationship between digitalization (x) and variation of the Integral Marketing iIdicator (y1) is very small (R2 = 5.9%), but the impact of digitalization (x) on the Integral Marketing iIdicator (y) is very high (R2 = 88,8%).

Based on the calculations presented, we have carried out modeling of marketing scenarios. The results are shown in Table 5.

Table 3. Results of regression analysis for impact of digitalization on the Integral Marketing Indicator in developed and developing countries

Regression statistics									
Multiple R	0.888436123								
R-square	0.789318745								
Normalized R-square	0.768250619								
Standard error	6.694309644								
Observations	12								
Analysis of variance									
	df	SS	MS	F	Value of F				
Regression	1	1678.951351	1678.951	37.46507	0.000113				
Rest	10	448.137816	44.81378						
Total	11	2127.089167							
	Coefficients	Standard error	t-statistics	P-value	Bottom 95%	Top 95%	Bottom 95,0%	Top 95,0%	
Y-intersection	110.3175131	13.6986537	8.053165	1.11E-05	79.79501	140.84	79.79501	140.84	
Variable X 1	-0.980209204	0.160142099	-6.12087	0.000113	-1.33703	-0.62339	-1.33703	-0.62339	

Table 4. Results of regression analysis for impact of digitalization on the variation of the Integral Marketing Indicator in developed and developing countries

Regression statistics									
Multiple R	0.059430423								
R-square	0.003531975								
Normalized R-square	-0.096114827								
Standard error	7.492175562								
Observations	12								

Table 4. (Continued)

Analysis of variance								
	df	SS	MS	F	Value of F			
Regression	1	1.989620157	1.989620157	0.035444943	0.854432013			
Rest	10	561.3269465	56.13269465					
Total	11	563.3165667						
	Coefficients	Standard error	t-statistics	P-value	Bottom 95%	Top 95%	Bottom 95,0%	Top 95,0%
Y-intersection	12.72587224	15.3313372	0.830056249	0.425878998	-21.43447582	46.8862203	-21.43447582	46.8862203
Variable X 1	-0.033743087	0.179228746	-0.188268274	0.854432013	-0.433089618	0.365603445	-0.433089618	0.365603445

Table 5. Marketing scenarios influenced by digitalization

Characteristics of Scenario	Accelerating digitalization scenario	Scenario of counter cyclical regulation of market conditions
Consequence of digitalization	Launching a new cycle of digital technologies in marketing	Using digital technologies in marketing as a counter cyclical tool for regulating market conditions
Independent variable	IMD, Index of Digital Competitiveness	
Dependent variable	Integral Marketing Index (y)	Variation of the Integral Marketing iIndicator over 4 years (y1)
Average of the dependent variable	13.31	6.85
Regression dependence	y = 110.32-0.98x	y = 12.73-0.034x
Consequences of rising / falling independent variable	If the independent variable changes by 1%, the dependent variable improves / worsens its performance by 0.98.	If the independent variable changes by 1%, the dependent variable practically does not change its indicators (change by 3.4%)
Conclusion	High probability of scenario realization	Low probability

4. DISCUSSION

As you can see from the Table 5, the use of digital technologies in marketing as a counter cyclical tool for market regulation is unlikely. The scenario of launching a new cycle of development of digital technologies in marketing has a very high probability of implementation. Therefore, we can expect an increase in the introduction of digital technologies in marketing.

CONCLUSION

We have come to the following conclusions. First, digital technologies, most likely, cannot be used as a counter cyclical tool for regulating market conditions, since the scenarios indicate the absence of regression dependence.

Secondly, digital technologies in marketing can be used as a tool to launch a new marketing development cycle. The compiled regression model confirms it. Nevertheless, digital technologies in marketing should not be the only measure of marketing development, since their influence on the variation of the Integral Marketing Indicator is very small (-5.9%).

Thirdly, developing countries have a more pronounced potential for using digital technologies for marketing development, since the correlation between the Digital Competitiveness Index and the Integral Marketing Indicator is higher (-92.61% developing countries, -64.34% developed countries).

Thus, digital technologies influence marketing, possibly changing it. It should be studied in future research.

REFERENCES

[1] 2016–2017, Global Competitiveness Report. 2016. "Global Competitiveness Report 2016–2017." *World Economic Forum Reports 2016*.

[2] Alpidovskaya, Marina L., and Elena G. Popkova. 2019. "Marx and Modernity: A Political and Economic Analysis of Social Systems Management (Advances in Research on Russian Business and Management)." *Advances in Research on Russian Business and Management*. August 1, 2019. https://www.amazon.com/Marx-Modernity-Political-Economic-Management/dp/1641137495.

[3] Ataguba, Ochega A., and John E. Ataguba. 2020. "Social Determinants of Health: The Role of Effective Communication in the COVID-19 Pandemic in Developing Countries." *Global Health Action*. https://doi.org/10.1080/16549716.2020.1788263.

[4] Belik, Elena B., Elena S. Petrenko, Georgy A. Pisarev, and Anna A. Karpova. 2020. "Influence of Technological Revolution in the Sphere of Digital Technologies on the Modern Entrepreneurship." In *Lecture Notes in Networks and Systems*. https://doi.org/10.1007/978-3-030-32015-7_27.

[5] Bentata, Yassamine. 2020. "COVID 2019 Pandemic: A True Digital Revolution and Birth of a New Educational Era, or an Ephemeral Phenomenon?" *Medical Education Online*. https://doi.org/10.1080/1087 2981.2020.1781378.

[6] Bozhuk, S. G., K. V. Evdokimov, T. D. Maslova, and N. A. Pletneva. 2019. "Problems and Perspectives of Sustainable Marketing Development on the Russian Food Market." In *IOP Conference Series: Materials Science and Engineering*. https://doi.org/10.1088/1757-899X/666/1/012040.

[7] Bozhuk, S. G., T. D. Maslova, N. A. Pletneva, and K. V. Evdokimov. 2019. "Improvement of the Consumers' Satisfaction Research Technology in the Digital Environment." In *IOP Conference Series: Materials Science and Engineering*. https://doi.org/10.1088/1757-899X/666/1/012055.

[8] Bozhuk, Svetlana, and Natal'ya Pletneva. 2018. "The Problems of Market Orientation of Russian Innovative Products (Electric Cars as a Case Study)." In *Advances in Intelligent Systems and Computing*. https://doi.org/10.1007/978-3-319-70987-1_132.

[9]   Bris, and Cabolis. 2020. "IMD World Talent Ranking 2020." *IMD.*

[10] Dente, S. M.R., and S. Hashimoto. 2020. "COVID-19: A Pandemic with Positive and Negative Outcomes on Resource and Waste Flows and Stocks." *Resources, Conservation and Recycling.* https://doi.org/10.1016/j.resconrec. 2020.104979.

[11] Fokina, Olga V., Lyudmila A. Fufacheva, Anastasia A. Sozinova, Aleksey V. Sysolyatin, and Lev L. Bulychev. 2018. "Information and Communication Technologies as a New Vector of Development of Modern Global Economy." *Espacios.*

[12] G. Popkova, Elena, and Bruno S. Sergi. 2018. "Will Industry 4.0 and Other Innovations Impact Russia's Development?" In *Exploring the Future of Russia's Economy and Markets.* https://doi.org/10.1108/978-1-78769-397-520181004.

[13] Group, World Bank. 2017. *Global Investment Competitiveness Report 2017/2018. Foreign Investor Perspectives and Policy Implications.*

[14] IMD. 2019. "IMD World Digital Competitiveness Ranking 2019." *IMD World Competitiveness Center.*

[15] Kataeva, Natalia N., Irina V. Marakulina, Marina A. Sanovich, Anastasia A. Sozinova, and Natalia Vasilyuk. 2017. "Transformation of Approach to Market Segmentation within Crisis Management of Global Entrepreneurship." *Contributions to Economics.* https://doi.org/10.1007/978-3-319-60696-5_62.

[16] Laing, Timothy. 2020. "The Economic Impact of the Coronavirus 2019 (Covid-2019): Implications for the Mining Industry." *Extractive Industries and Society.* https://doi.org/10.1016/j.exis.2020.04.003.

[17] Nadrian, Haidar. 2020. "COVID-2019 Is Still Rapidly Spreading in Iran; Isn't It the Time to Call for International Action?" *Health Promotion Perspectives.* https://doi.org/10.34172/hpp.2020.16.

[18] Popkova, Elena G. 2019. "Preconditions of Formation and Development of Industry 4.0 in the Conditions of Knowledge Economy." In *Studies in Systems, Decision and Control.* https://doi.org/10.1007/978-3-319-94310-7_6.

[19] Popkova, Elena G., and Sergi S. Bruno. 2019. *Digital Economy : Complexity and Variety vs . Rationality.* Springer.

[20] Popkova, Elena G., and Kantoro Gulzat. 2020. "Technological Revolution in the 21st Century: Digital Society vs. Artificial Intelligence." In *Lecture Notes in Networks and Systems.* https://doi.org/10.1007/978-3-030-32015-7_38.

[21] Popkova, Elena G., and Bruno S. Sergi. 2020. "Human Capital and AI in Industry 4.0. Convergence and Divergence in Social Entrepreneurship in Russia." *Journal of Intellectual Capital.* https://doi.org/10.1108/JIC-09-2019-0224.

[22] Popkova, Elena, Lubinda Haabazoka, and Julia Ragulina. 2020. *"Africa 4.0 as a Perspective Scenario for Neo-Industrialization in the Twenty-First Century: Global Competitiveness and Sustainable Development."* In, 275–99. https://doi.org/10.1007/978-3-030-41983-7_19.

[23] Popkova, Elena, Anastasia Sozinova, and Vera Menshchikova. 2019. "Managing the Adaptation of Modern Society to the Industry 4.0 Based on Information

Waves and Impulses." *Theoretical and Practical Issues of Journalism.* https://doi.org/10.17150/2308-6203.2019.8(2).438-446.

[24] Ragulina, Yulia V. 2019. "Priorities of Development of Industry 4.0 in Modern Economic Systems with Different Progress in Formation of Knowledge Economy." In *Studies in Systems, Decision and Control.* https://doi.org/10.1007/978-3-319-94310-7_16.

[25] Ragulina, Yulia V., Alexander N. Alekseev, Irina V. Strizhkina, and Arseniy I. Tumanov. 2019. "Methodology of Criterial Evaluation of Consequences of the Industrial Revolution of the 21st Century." In *Studies in Systems, Decision and Control.* https://doi.org/10.1007/978-3-319-94310-7_24.

[26] Savelyeva, Nadezhda K., Andrey V. Kuklin, Irina P. Lapteva, and Natalia V. Malysheva. 2019. "The Investment Attractiveness of a Regional Market of Educational Services as the Basis of Its Global Competitiveness in Industry 4.0." *On the Horizon.* https://doi.org/10.1108/OTH-07-2019-0042.

[27] Schwab, Klaus. 2019. "Global Competitiveness Report 2019 | World Economic Forum." *World Economic Forum.* 2019.

[28] Sergi, B. 2019. *"Tech, Smart Cities, and Regional Development in Contemporary Russia."* In.

[29] Sergi, Bruno, Elena Popkova, Aleksei Bogoviz, and Tatiana Litvinova. 2019. *Understanding Industry 4.0: AI, the Internet of Things, and the Future of Work.* https://doi.org/10.1108/9781789733112.

[30] Sozinova, Amastasia A., Olga V. Fokina, and Raisa A. Shchinova. 2017. "Marketing Tools for Increasing Company's Reorganization Effectiveness." In *Contributions to Economics.* https://doi.org/10.1007/978-3-319-60696-5_40.

[31] Sozinova, Anastasia A. 2018a. "Effectiveness or Reorganization: Application of Information Technologies in Solving Marketing Problems of Modern Companies." *Espacios.*

[32] ———. 2018b. "Marketing Concept of Managing the Reorganization of Entrepreneurial Structures Using the Latest Information Technologies." *Quality - Access to Success.*

[33] ———. 2019. "Causal Connections of Formation of Industry 4.0 from the Positions of the Global Economy." In *Studies in Systems, Decision and Control.* https://doi.org/10.1007/978-3-319-94310-7_13.

[34] Sozinova, Anastasia A., Aleksei A. Nabokikh, Aleksandra V. Ryattel, and Marina A. Sanovich. 2019. "Analysis of 'Underdevelopment Whirlpools' as a Tool of Managing the Regional Market of Education in the Conditions of Industry 4.0." *On the Horizon.* https://doi.org/10.1108/OTH-07-2019-0034.

[35] Sozinova, Anastasia Andreevna, and Olga Vasilevna Fokina. 2014. "Study of Economic and Technological Factors Influencing Development of Services Market." *Life Science Journal.*

[36] ———. 2015. "Special Aspects of Studying the Internet as a Marketing Communication Channel of the Service Industry." *Mediterranean Journal of Social Sciences.* https://doi.org/10.5901/mjss.2015.v6n4s1p139.

[37] Zavyalova, Elena, Nikolay Studenikin, and Evgeniya Starikova. 2018. "Business Participation in Implementation of Socially Oriented Sustainable Development Goals in Countries of Central Asia and the Caucasus Region." *Central Asia and the Caucasus*.

[38] Zhgulev, Evgenii, Svetlana Bozhuk, Konstantin Evdokimov, and Natalia Pletneva. 2018. "Analysis of Barriers to Promotion of Electric Cars on Russian Market." In *Engineering for Rural Development*. https://doi.org/10.22616/ERDev2018.17.N377.

In: Global Challenges of Digital Transformation of Markets ISBN: 978-1-53619-754-9
Editors: E. de la Poza and S. E. Barykin   © 2021 Nova Science Publishers, Inc.

Chapter 30

RFID System as a Modern Trend in the Field of Digitalization of Russian Retail

Olga Lukina[1], Anna Kurochkina[2]
and Anna Karmanova[2],*

[1]International banking Institute of a name of Anatoly Sobchak,
Saint Petersburg, Russia
[2]Peter the Great St.Petersburg Polytechnic University,
Saint Petersburg, Russia

Abstract

Lorem ipsum dolor sit amet, consectetuer adipiscing elit. Maecenas porttitor congue massa. Fusce posuere, magna sed pulvinar ultricies, purus lectus malesuada libero, sit amet commodo magna eros quis urna. Nunc viverra imperdiet enim. Fusce est. Vivamus a tellus. Pellentesque habitant morbi tristique senectus et netus et malesuada fames ac turpis egestas. Proin pharetra nonummy pede. Mauris et orci.

The retail industry is one of the most receptive to various innovations. In Russian retail, there is a constant increase in the pace of digitalization. The goal of the study is to determine the essence of RFID technologies as a promising innovative trend in the digitalization of Russian retail. The article provides a general overview of the main characteristics of the RFID technology system based on contactless or radiofrequency automatic identification of objects. The study describes the advantages and disadvantages of this technology, evaluates the effectiveness of its use in trade. Currently, RFID technologies are actively used in various fields. Comparative analysis of the RFID system with the traditional bar-coding system allows us to assess the prospects for using this method in the market. Promising areas of use of RFID technologies can be called: security systems, payment systems, systems for optimizing factory work, etc. The areas of

---

* Corresponding Author's Email: aekarmanova@bk.ru.

implementation and application of RFID technologies are expanding. The final section presents the main findings on the research topic.

Keywords: object identification, scanning, readers, digitalization of Russian retail, bar coding, RFID tags, marking

1. INTRODUCTION

An innovative breakthrough in the field of high-tech systems has produced a kind of information and technology revolution. Modern outside of automated systems made it possible to significantly reduce, but not completely exclude, human labor costs. The information breakthrough made it possible to fundamentally change life in society. However, no one canceled the human factor, and therefore the right to mistake. However, no one canceled the human factor, and therefore the right to mistake. In this regard, it is a person who is an inhibitory element that does not completely solve the problem of collecting, processing, analyzing and entering data into the program for managing any processes. It became necessary to organize work in automatic mode. Scientists helped solve this problem using the experience of specialists from the Second World War who used the principles of the radio frequency identification system to determine enemy aircraft. Today, such sensors are installed on all aircraft, and since the beginning of the 80s of the twentieth century, such a technique has gained great popularity in the field of animal husbandry - by order of state authorities, reading sensors have been used to identify animals in order to prevent the spread of rabies. This technique is actively used to this day both in animal husbandry, in industrial production, medicine and even in librarianship. Similar microcircuits are also integrated into security identification tokens, installed on car windscreens for auto-payment of road duties and attached to packages for logistics simplification (Debouzy and Perrin 2012) and (Veselovsky et al., 2019; Dobrolyubova, Alexandrov, and Yefremov 2017).

In Western countries, since 1997, microchips with antennas for transmitting information have been actively used. For example, Procter & Gamble began to use such a system for the first time. Table 1 shows the periods of popularization of the use of this technique.

Note that the technology of radio frequency identification already exists, but is not currently massively used. The origins came from Western countries, and in Russia, the first use of the technique is dated 2012, when the company MediaMarkt first began to use such a system to transfer information. A year later, the system was also operational during the implementation of the Future Stores project, based on the use of information transmission sensors in retail networks (Lim, Bahr, and Leung 2013; Finkenzeller 2010; Tajima 2007).

Table 1. Use of radio frequency identification systems

First used	Use purpose
Early 1940s	Wartime specialists introduce a system for identification of enemy aircraft
1980s	Cattle are chipped to transmit information to prevent the spread of rabies
1997	Procter & Gamble uses a system to transmit information about products in high demand
2004	Metro Group uses a system to transmit information about consumed goods
2005	Wal-Mart uses a system to transmit information about consumed goods
2012	For the first time, a Russian company uses a system to transfer information about the goods required, MediaMarkt
2013	The chain based on X5 Retail Group stores launches a pilot project in the grocery sector, "Stores of the Future"

The retail sector has been and remains one of the most perceptive of various innovations. In Russian retail, as in the world, a constant increase in the rate of digitalization is given. Key trends that have changed the global retail market, namely Big Data, artificial intelligence, advanced reality, blockchain, are already actively affecting Russian realities. Developments are being actively modernized and new methodologies are being introduced. To improve the profitability of retail networks, it would be useful not only to implement systems for counting and analyzing visitor behavior, but also to review requirements for staff and improve productivity. With digital technologies, it is possible to increase the efficiency of operational activities and, accordingly, reduce the cost of goods and make them more accessible in the market. One of the modern innovative technologies is RFID system (Elgendy and Elragal 2016; Dekimpe 2020; Fisher and Raman 2018; Kurochkina et al., 2019).

RFID (Radio Frequency Identification) technology is an automatic object identification technique in which written-off information is transmitted using radio signals (or electromagnetic waves, as in the case of LF and HF band labels). To carry out the transmission, devices called RFID tags or RFID tags consisting of a silicon chip and an antenna that allows sending the signal requested from the RFID transceiver are required. RFID tags can be placed on an object, animal, or human.

The RFID system in trade is a tag consisting of a passive device with an antenna, a capacitor and a small semiconductor chip. Today's technologies allow these components to be combined on an acrylic substrate, reducing the cost of RFID devices and allowing manufacturers to tag products in the same way as conventional labels. RFID tags do not require batteries or maintenance. They are powered by a scanner using inductive coupling or electromagnetic capture techniques.

Information from RFID tags is read using stationary or portable RFID readers. In all cases, RFID allows you to create an "electronic passport" with any information necessary in the work about the object or subject, to track its further movement. One of the main tasks of the RFID system is to increase the efficiency of automated operations, reduce the share of "manual" labor and eliminate errors on the part of personnel (Krasnov et al., 2019; Basker 2012; Bundin et al., 2019; Semyachkov 2018).

2. MATERIALS AND METHODS

The goal of the study is to determine the essence of RFID technologies as a promising innovative development in the field of digitalization of Russian retail.

To achieve the goal, the following objectives were set and achieved:

- study of basic characteristics of RFID system;
- identification of positive and negative trends related to the use of RFID technologies;
- comparing RFID technology with a previously known and popular barcoding technique;
- assessment of the development prospects of the system;
- summarizing the results of the study.

The research object is RFID technology.

The subject of the study is the characteristic features of the system that determine the further prospects for its use.

Comparative, descriptive and statistical methods of research, as well as the method of analysis, were used to solve the tasks.

The initial information for the study was provided by scientific data on the subject under study, analytical reviews from the Internet, publications by domestic and foreign specialists.

3. RESULTS

There is always a situation in society in which when new technologies appear, there will be supporters who will treat it with extreme distrust and criticism. Any new methodology must prove itself before the opinion about it changes. A similar situation was formed when the RFID system appeared on the market. Despite various comments, the spread of the RFID tag system, including in food retail, is a matter of time. It is necessary to remember how the barcode with which any consumer is familiar was introduced. The situation was similar today. In order to spread the system of barcoding goods everywhere, joint efforts of the state and entrepreneurs were needed. Back in 1981, an order was issued in the United States, according to which defense products were required to be supplied strictly with a barcode. Three years later, Wal-

Mart made a similar demand to its suppliers. Note that the media at that time constantly reported that the barcode system will never pay off, even though it helps to improve the quality of service (Watson 2011; Business Encyclopedia 2018).

The RFID system can be considered as a logical continuation of the development of the barcoding system, a technology that is designed to meet the needs of its time. Previously, all necessary information was hidden in barcodes and it was provided in full. Today, that was not enough; suppliers and retailers required detail, clarification and personalization. The barcode system cannot meet these requirements. RFID technology can fully meet these needs. Also using this technique, all information is behind-coded in tags that are reliably protected from counterfeits, which is also an undeniable competitive advantage.

The chip of RFID is something that reminds the barcode, but at the same time there is an ability to transfer information to the programmed reader in big sizes, at long distances and under different conditions. Printed barcodes are typically read by a laser skink that requires direct visibility to determine and retrieve information. When using RFID technology, the scanner can read encoded information, even when the tag is hidden - for example, built into the body of the product or sewn into clothes. A tiny RFID tag can contain much more information than a barcode. Moreover, unlike barcodes, RFID tags can transmit data from various packages, for example, from a buyer's trolley or from boxes of goods.

In addition to these advantages, the RFID system has a number of advantages, which makes it more competitive compared to the barcoding technique. Table 2 shows the comparative characteristics of the RFID system theme and barcoding technology.

The table shows the main characteristics of the systems, by which it can be concluded that the RFID system is a unique technique by which information can be obtained even from moving objects, in the absence of visibility of the label, at a distance of more than 1 m. At the same time, data can be read from several objects simultaneously and when exposed to decaying factors (dirt, chemical effects, etc.). RFID labels can be overwritten, reused (AB&R 2007). Until recently, RFID systems were more expensive than non-contact identification barcode systems. However, technological progress in the field of tags has led to the fact that they began to be used in areas in which only the barcode was previously used. Currently, tag systems successfully compete with bar code. The cost of tag systems is reduced, they become more accessible to wide circles. The production of tag systems is gaining momentum, which is due to the increase in demand (Bibi et al., 2017; Schmidt, Thoroe, and Schumann 2013).

4. DISCUSSION

Taking into account all the positive characteristics that the RFID system possesses, today there are opponents of these devices. American-Canadian and European consumer protection unions believe that the use of RFID technologies in retail can harm consumers themselves, as manufacturers will have the opportunity to monitor customer taste preferences, which will entail a violation of confidentiality. The RFID system also has proponents who believe that this technique will entail an increase in the quality of service. A single standard has not yet been adopted, but many trading enterprises and product manufacturers have already begun to use the latest technologies.

Table 2. Comparative characteristics of RFID system and barcoding technology

Description of characteristic	System RFID	Barcoding technology
Ability to read information without direct contact	Reading hidden tags	Reading is impossible without visible contact
Memory size	High	Insignificant
Ability to overwrite information, reuse	Opportunity is available	Opportunity is absent
Simultaneous identification of multiple objects	yes	no
Ability to read information more than 1m away	yes	no
Possibility of correct operation at various negative impact factors - mechanical, temperature, chemical effects, high humidity, high level of pollution	High resilience	Low resilience
Service life	Long-term use	Short-term use (label integrity violation, poor-quality printing)
Recording of information in "non-stop" mode	yes	no
Reading information from moving objects; possibility of sewing an animated creature into the body to obtain data	yes	no
Cost	high	low
Security for others, protection against counterfeiting	yes	no
Multiple simultaneous reading	possible	impossible
Reading speed	low	high

According to the latest data, the demand for RFID systems is currently experiencing a kind of boom, the results of which can seriously affect the development of many areas of technological progress (Ilin, Voronova, and Knykina 2019; Borisoglebskaya et al., 2019).

In Western countries, RFID technologies are actively used to inform consumers about prices, shelf life and other characteristics of goods of interest. Obviously, RFID systems could well be used in modern grocery stores and in Russia, but there were nuances. For different products, different tags are needed, and it is not always profitable for the seller to independently equip them with goods. There are weight goods, goods from cold or hot shops, foiled goods, canned goods in metal cans, etc. This makes the marking process difficult and in some cases impossible. A more correct solution to this problem is the labeling of products by the manufacturer: it works with one type and can choose the optimal label or place of application on its products. The tags may be in the form of labels, tags, cards, bracelets, tokens, labels with fabric ropes or plastic clips; tags can be housed, that is, enclosed in a protective body. There are also unusual marks in the form of bolts, glass flasks, epoxy rods. The media also provided information about edible tags. They are planned to be put on products so that the consumer is sure that the goods he purchases are absolutely safe for use.

Mobile phone manufacturer Nokia presents a set that allows you to turn a regular phone into an RFID scanner. After several years, mobile phones and handheld PCs capable of scanning RFID tags on goods will give consumers the opportunity to automatically access information contained in computer networks without the need to dial an address on the Internet. A person can simply scan the RFID tag of any physical object to immediately access text and audio-visual information about this object, for example, product description, detailed instructions, museum excursions, video materials, music, and others (Hinings, Gegenhuber, and Greenwood 2018; Peng, Peursum, and Li 2012).

The use of RFID systems allows you to solve a number of tasks at the same time. Let's take a closer look at them:

1. Reduce the inventory process from a few days to several hours - the information is read from all packaged goods through the scanner's nose.
2. Fast tracking of goods - with the help of built-in antennas, a report to the reader on the amount of goods transferred is instantly received.
3. Significantly reduced customer service time in the cash area - labels are read from several goods at the same time.
4. Acceleration of warehouse logistics: the receipt of goods is possible without opening packages.
5. Introduction of the system of "smart shelves": information from the shelves of the trading room is sent using sensors to the device, where the quantity of a particular product is reflected, as well as its location.
6. Using "smart fitting": the buyer has the opportunity to find out all the information about the product, and the manufacturer: to get information about consumer preferences.

7. Protection against theft: anti-theft RFID gates instantly from-control the signal to the security post.
8. Introduction and use of cards of regular customers - a possibility of tracking regular customers who possess the special card with the built-in tag that will give an idea of consumer preferences and tastes.
9. Employee Performance Monitoring - Personal Badges will provide complete information on the quality of staff performance (Korchagina, Desfonteines, and Strekalova 2020; Sergeev and Kirillova 2019).

Contactless information systems based on RFID technology are currently used when there are needs:

− reducing the cost of processing a large amount of data with elimination of errors related to manual input;
− in fast recording of information;
− operational management of high-tech automated complexes (storage areas, transport bases);
− improving quality control in production, warehousing and transportation operations;
− in reduction of labor costs (Sergeev and Kirillova 2019; Korchagina and Desfonteines 2019).

RFID technologies are already actively used in such areas as public transport, gas stations, pass systems based on the use of club cards, electronic documents (passport, driver-driver certificate, etc.).

Promising uses of RFID technologies include the following:

− access systems for residential buildings, hotels;
− protection systems for vehicles;
− plant works optimization systems;
− organization of parking areas operation;
− payment systems on motorways;
− car service services;
− Technical support for mass cultural and sporting events;
− protection of computer systems;
− protective systems.

The fields of implementation and application of RFID-technologies are steadily expanding. THe authors could suggest for future research taking into account RFID technolodies the development of economic and mathematical analytical models of digital processes in logistics such as in works (Barykin, Kalinina, et al. 2021; Barykin, Kapustina, Sergeev, et al. 2021; Barykin, Bochkarev, et al. 2021; Barykin, Kapustina, Valebnikova, et al. 2021).

CONCLUSION

According to the results of the study, we can answer the question: "Why is it necessary to abandon the usual inexpensive barcode systems for goods in favor of the new-fashioned RFID system?" The answer is obvious: RFID is a technology based on a radio frequency information transmission system that was used in wartime. Unlike the conventional barcode system, RFID tags can be read from long distances and from multiple objects at the same time. The information on the labels could be overwritten and corrected, allowing them to be reused. The system has a high level of hacking resistance and is capable of operating under any negative impact factors.

The use of the RFID system in trade or other areas significantly speeds up the data processing process, reduces the level of manual labor, and also minimizes the possibility of errors. Identification of objects is possible even in a movable state and does not require visual contact.

Using the identification method in question allows you to:

- perform control at each stage of operation,
- extend the minimum amount of time and human resources,
- improve the quality of customer service,
- Improve the information processing system,
- minimize the possibility of error tolerance during inventory,
- reduce the number of thefts,
- optimize statistical reporting (Voronkova et al., 2017; Morozova and Gurov 2017; Andrey V. and Alexander S. 2018).

Until recently, the relatively high cost of the RF tag was the main deterrent to the implementation of RFID technology.

The only major obstacle to the introduction of RFID technology remains the resistance of the public fighting for consumer rights. But as the experience of introducing modern technologies into our lives shows, a promise will definitely be found. Moreover, RFID technology, eliminating the weakest link in automated control systems, will probably produce in the near future a real revolution in the industry, agriculture, transport, and other fields, including in special equipment. Currently, given the development prospects of RFID technology, there are no serious competitors.

Effectively manage the supply chain, monitor inventory in warehouses, monitor the movement of goods in the trading room in real-time mode and successfully prevent store theft - these are the realities for a business using RFID technologies.

REFERENCES

AB&R. 2007. "What Is RFID and How Does RFID Work?" *Ab&R.*

Andrey V., Nuykin, and Kravtsov Alexander S. 2018. "Using RFID Technology in the IoT Ecosystem." *Nanoindustry Russia*. https://doi.org/10.22184/1993-8578.2018. 82.313.

Barykin, Sergey Yevgenievich, Andrey Aleksandrovich Bochkarev, Sergey Mikhailovich Sergeev, Tatiana Anatolievna Baranova, Dmitriy Anatolievich Mokhorov, and Aleksandra Maksimovna Kobicheva. 2021. "A Methodology of Bringing Perspective Innovation Products to Market." *Academy of Strategic Management Journal* 20 (2): 1–19. https://www.abacademies.org/articles/a-methodology-of-bringing-perspective-innovation-products-to-market.pdf.

Barykin, Sergey Yevgenievich, Olga Vladimirovna Kalinina, Irina Vasilievna Kapustina, Victor Andreevich Dubolazov, Cesar Armando Nunez Esquivel, Elmira Alyarovna Nazarova, and Petr Anatolievich Sharapaev. 2021. "The Sharing Economy and Digital Logistics in Retail Chains: Opportunities and Threats." *Academy of Strategic Management Journal* 20 (2): 1–14. https://www.abacademies.org/articles/the-sharing-economy-and-digital-logistics-in-retail-chains-opportunities-and-threats.pdf.

Barykin, Sergey Yevgenievich, Irina Vasilievna Kapustina, Sergey Mikhailovich Sergeev, Olga Vladimirovna Kalinina, Viktoriia Valerievna Vilken, Yuri Yevgenievich Putikhin, and Lydia Vitalievna Volkova. 2021. "Developing the Physical Distribution Digital Twin Model within the Trade Network." *Academy of Strategic Management Journal* 20 (1): 1–24. https://www.abacademies.org/articles/developing-the-physical-distribution-digital-twin-model-within-the-trade-network.pdf.

Barykin, Sergey Yevgenievich, Irina Vasilievna Kapustina, Olga Aleksandrovna Valebnikova, Natalia Viktorovna Valebnikova, Olga Vladimirovna Kalinina, Sergey Mikhailovich Sergeev, Marisa Camastral, Yuri Yevgenievich Putikhin, and Lydia Vitalievna Volkova. 2021. "Digital Technologies for Personnel Management: Implications for Open Innovations." *Academy of Strategic Management Journal* 20 (2): 1–14. https://www.abacademies.org/articles/digital-technologies-for-personnel-management-implications-for-open-innovations.pdf.

Basker, Emek. 2012. "Raising the Barcode Scanner: Technology and Productivity in the Retail Sector." *American Economic Journal: Applied Economics*. https://doi.org/10.1257/app.4.3.1.

Bibi, Fabien, Carole Guillaume, Nathalie Gontard, and Brice Sorli. 2017. "A Review: RFID Technology Having Sensing Aptitudes for Food Industry and Their Contribution to Tracking and Monitoring of Food Products." *Trends in Food Science and Technology*. https://doi.org/10.1016/j.tifs.2017.01.013.

Borisoglebskaya, L. N., E. N. Provotorova, S. M. Sergeev, and A. P. Khudyakov. 2019. "Automated Storage and Retrieval System for Industry 4.0 Concept." In *IOP Conference Series: Materials Science and Engineering*. https://doi.org/10.1088/1757-899X/537/3/032036.

Bundin, Mikhail, Aleksei Martynov, Nadezhda Biyushkina, and Pavel Kononov. 2019. "Digital Law for Russia. Nearest Future or Only a Science Fiction?" In

Communications in Computer and Information Science. https://doi.org/10.1007/978-3-030-13283-5_15.

Business Encyclopedia. 2018. "Barcode Definition - What Is Barcode." *Shopify.* 2018.

Debouzy, Jean Claude, and Anne Perrin. 2012. "RFID." In *Electromagnetic Fields, Environment and Health.* https://doi.org/10.1007/978-2-8178-0363-0_7.

Dekimpe, Marnik G. 2020. "Retailing and Retailing Research in the Age of Big Data Analytics." *International Journal of Research in Marketing.* https://doi.org/10.1016/j. ijresmar.2019.09.001.

Dobrolyubova, Elena, Oleg Alexandrov, and Alexey Yefremov. 2017. "Is Russia Ready for Digital Transformation?" In *Communications in Computer and Information Science.* https://doi.org/10.1007/978-3-319-69784-0_36.

Elgendy, Nada, and Ahmed Elragal. 2016. "Big Data Analytics in Support of the Decision Making Process." In *Procedia Computer Science.* https://doi.org/10.1016/j.procs.2016.09.251.

Finkenzeller, Klaus. 2010. *RFID Handbook: Fundamentals and Applications in Contactless Smart Cards, Radio Frequency Identification and near-Field Communication. RFID Handbook: Fundamentals and Applications in Contactless Smart Cards, Radio Frequency Identification and near-Field Communication.* https://doi.org/10.1002/9780470665121.

Fisher, Marshall, and Ananth Raman. 2018. "Using Data and Big Data in Retailing." *Production and Operations Management.* https://doi.org/10.1111/poms.12846.

Hinings, Bob, Thomas Gegenhuber, and Royston Greenwood. 2018. "Digital Innovation and Transformation: An Institutional Perspective." *Information and Organization.* https://doi.org/10.1016/j.infoandorg.2018.02.004.

Ilin, Igor, Olga Voronova, and Tatyana Knykina. 2019. "Improvement of the Business Model of Network Retail in FMCG Sector." In *Proceedings of the 33rd International Business Information Management Association Conference, IBIMA 2019: Education Excellence and Innovation Management through Vision 2020.*

Korchagina, Elena, and Larisa Desfonteines. 2019. "Internal Resources of Increasing Retail Efficiency." *Intellectual Economics.* https://doi.org/10.13165/IE-19-13-2-03.

Korchagina, Elena, Larisa Desfonteines, and Natalia Strekalova. 2020. "Problems of Training Specialists for Trade in the Conditions of Digitalization." In *E3S Web of Conferences.* https://doi.org/10.1051/e3sconf/202016412014.

Krasnov, Sergey, Sergey Sergeev, Aleksandr Titov, and Yelizaveta Zotova. 2019. "Modelling of Digital Communication Surfaces for Products and Services Promotion." In *IOP Conference Series: Materials Science and Engineering.* https://doi.org/10.1088/1757-899X/497/1/012032.

Kurochkina, Anna A., Olga V. Voronkova, Olga V. Lukina, and Tatyana V. Bikezina. 2019. "Management Features of Small and Medium-Sized Business Enterprises." *Espacios.*

Lim, Ming K., Witold Bahr, and Stephen C.H. Leung. 2013. "RFID in the Warehouse: A Literature Analysis (1995-2010) of Its Applications, Benefits, Challenges and

Future Trends." In *International Journal of Production Economics*. https://doi.org/10.1016/j.ijpe.2013.05.006.

Morozova, Tatyana V., and Valeriy V. Gurov. 2017. "Research in RFID Vulnerability." In *Proceedings of the 2017 IEEE Russia Section Young Researchers in Electrical and Electronic Engineering Conference, ElConRus 2017*. https://doi.org/10.1109/ElConRus.2017.7910601.

Peng, En, Patrick Peursum, and Ling Li. 2012. "Product Barcode and Expiry Date Detection for the Visually Impaired Using a Smartphone." In *2012 International Conference on Digital Image Computing Techniques and Applications, DICTA 2012*. https://doi.org/10.1109/DICTA.2012.6411673.

Schmidt, Malte, Lars Thoroe, and Matthias Schumann. 2013. "RFID and Barcode in Manufacturing Logistics: Interface Concept for Concurrent Operation." *Information Systems Management*. https://doi.org/10.1080/10580530.2013.773801.

Semyachkov, Konstantin. 2018. "State Management of Russian Regions by Means of Digital Technologies." In *Proceedings of the European Conference on E-Government, ECEG*.

Sergeev, S., and T. Kirillova. 2019. "Information Support for Trade with the Use of a Conversion Funnel." In *IOP Conference Series: Materials Science and Engineering*. https://doi.org/10.1088/1757-899X/666/1/012064.

Tajima, May. 2007. "Strategic Value of RFID in Supply Chain Management." *Journal of Purchasing and Supply Management*. https://doi.org/10.1016/j.pursup.2007.11.001.

Veselovsky, Mikhail Yakovlevich, Marina Alekseevna Izmailova, Lenar Albertovich Yunusov, and Ildar Albertovich Yunusov. 2019. "Quality of Digital Transformation Management on the Way of Formation of Innovative Economy of Russia." *Quality - Access to Success*.

Voronkova, Olga Vasilevna, Anna Aleksandrovna Kurochkina, Irina Pavlovna Firova, and Tatiana Vasilevna Bikezina. 2017. "Implementation of an Information Management System for Industrial Enterprise Resource Planning." *Espacios*.

Watson, Bartholomew C. 2011. "Barcode Empires: Politics, Digital Technology, and Comparative Retail Firm Strategies." *Journal of Industry, Competition and Trade*. https://doi.org/10.1007/s10842-011-0109-2.

In: Global Challenges of Digital Transformation of Markets ISBN: 978-1-53619-754-9
Editors: E. de la Poza and S. E. Barykin   © 2021 Nova Science Publishers, Inc.

Chapter 31

POST-PURCHASE DISSONANCE IN ONLINE AND OFFLINE CONSUMER BEHAVIOR IN HANDMADE INDUSTRY

Nataliia Krasnostavskaia[1,], Marina Chigir[2,†] and Tatiana Maslova[2,‡]*

[1]Peter the Great St. Petersburg Polytechnic University,
Saint Petersburg, Russia
[2]Saint Petersburg Electrotechnical University "LETI",
Saint Petersburg, Russia, Russia,

ABSTRACT

Consumers in various business areas are becoming more and more demanding of the quality of goods and services, service both in offline and online stores. The handmade industry is one of the specific areas of activity, a way of self-awareness, a type of leisure and business. Post-purchase dissonance has a significant impact on the behavior of consumers of goods and services after purchase, determines their attitude to the brand and the possibility of repeat purchases. The object of the study was offline and online consumers of handmade goods. The subject of the research was the post-purchase dissonance experienced by them when making purchases. The goal of the study was to establish the features of post-purchase dissonance when making online purchases of handmade goods in comparison with offline purchases. The research methodology is based on the idea that a number of resource and situational factors influence the post-purchase dissonance in online and offline purchases of handmade goods. The points of view on the concept of post-purchase dissonance,

* Corresponding Author Email: marketrek@yandex.ru.
† Corresponding Author Email: mvchigir@yandex.ru.
‡ Corresponding Author Email: mtd777@mail.ru.

approaches to its definition, factors contributing to the emergence of post-purchase dissonance, and the effects caused by post-purchase dissonance, features of consumer behavior when making online purchases of handmade goods are investigated. A study of consumers of handmade goods showed that there are features of post-purchase dissonance when shopping for handmade goods online as compared to offline purchases. The data obtained is essential for the development of marketing strategies for brands in the handmade industry.

Keywords: post-purchase dissonance, cognitive dissonance, purchase regret, consumer behavior, decision-making process, purchase decision, handmade goods, handmade products, handmade industry, electronic commerce, e-commerce, internet marketing, marketing

1. INTRODUCTION

Currently, the development of digital technologies contributes to the translation of many business processes into a digital environment. In certain areas of business, the priority of online trading over offline trading has already been firmly established. The digital economy transforms consumer experience in making decisions about purchases, expands the boundaries of consumption, changes the mechanism of consumer choice of goods and services (Bozhuk, Krasnostavskaia, et al. 2019; Bozhuk, Maslova, et al. 2019). Research shows the need to develop effective solutions in modern management and economics (Goncharova, Degtereva, and Sopilko 2018; Rudskaya and Rodionov 2018; Selentyeva, Ivanova, and Kulibanova 2018; Skhvediani and Kudryavtseva 2018; Dvas and Dubolazova 2018). The new opportunities provided by the digital environment are taking competition to a whole new level. As a result, there is a need to understand and effectively use the differences in online and offline consumer decision-making processes about the choice of goods and services, taking into account the new needs of society and digital trends (Aleksandrov, Fedorova, and Parshukov 2020).

Marketing pays special attention to the study of consumer behavior. There are three stages in the purchasing decision-making process: pre-purchase stage, purchase stage and post-purchase stage. Emotions, knowledge and experience of use, arising from the consumer after the purchase, have an impact on the ability to re-purchase the product and the formation of the consumer's attitude and loyalty to the brand. Also, the consumer influences the making of other consumers' purchases, since he can express his positive or negative opinion about the purchase made by him. As a consequence, the post-purchase stage is of particular value to the researcher of consumer behavior.

The handmade industry is the sale of products and services of a wide range. These products are the implementation of finished works (works created by a master of the handmade industry and ready for use by end users, as well as work blanks designed for the end consumer to use them for their personal needs), conducting offline and online masterclasses (video broadcast in real time, as well as recorded, without real-time mode), the sale of products (finished goods, to the creation of which the master is not involved), the provision of services not related to conducting masterclasses.

The need to study the features of post-purchase dissonance that occurs when shopping for handmade goods on the Internet determined the purpose of the study and its relevance. The goal of the study was to establish the features of post-purchase dissonance in online purchases of handmade goods in comparison with offline purchases.

To achieve this goal, research objectives were defined:

- research of points of view on the concept of post-purchase dissonance and identification of existing approaches to its definition;
- study of the factors contributing to the emergence of post-purchase dissonance, and the effects caused by post-purchase dissonance;
- research of points of view on the features of consumer behavior when making online purchases of handmade goods;
- research of consumers of handmade goods to determine the features of post-purchase dissonance when shopping online for handmade goods in comparison with offline purchases.

1.1. Post-purchase Dissonance: Factors and Effects

Post-purchase dissonance is based on Festinger's theory of cognitive dissonance (Festinger 1957). This theory explains the conflict situations that arise in the cognitive structure of a person. The state of cognitive dissonance appears as a reaction to a certain situation, the actions of individuals or an entire society.

Post-purchase dissonance is the uncomfortable state a consumer experiences after making a purchase. Discomfort manifests itself in different ways: doubt, regret, disappointment, guilt or anxiety about the correctness of the purchase.

The changing role of the consumer in the market has led to the need to consider all factors in the purchasing decision-making process. Olejniczak (Olejniczak 2017) noted that the qualitative and quantitative growth of market offers led to an increase in the importance of buyers in the market and changed their expectations in a short period of time. The role of the consumer has changed from a begging to a strong actor with high demands on producers and service providers. The strong consumer position has sparked increased research interest in post-purchase behavior. Many consumer behavior patterns distinguish between two types of consumer reaction after a purchase - satisfaction, when expectations are met, or dissonance after a purchase, when expectations are not met and the buyer has doubts about the purchase.

The consumer, in the decision-making process, and especially after the purchase, when he receives the result of his efforts, involves cognitive and affective abilities. Walchli, Landman (Walchli and Landman 2003) linked counterfactual thinking and post-purchase affects. Counterfactual thinking is the process of imagining what could have been, that is, comparing reality with alternative possibilities. The authors in the study showed that consumer regret increased with both top-down and bottom-up counterfactual thinking. Upward counterfactual thinking focuses on the fact that the situation could be better, while top-down counterfactual thinking focuses on the fact that the situation could be even worse. Kim, Yang (Kim and Yang 2018), using the example of HMR products, investigated the influence of counterfactual thinking on post-purchase behavior, which causes regret of consumers when choosing and buying.

Post-purchase hesitation affects the likelihood of buying a brand in the future. Keaveney, Huber, Herrmann (Keaveney, Huber, and Herrmann 2007), using the example of luxury car buyers, determined that the consequences of buying regret include a decrease in the intention to buy a particular brand or buy from a particular dealership. Customers who change brands experience more regret than customers who don't change brands.

Post-purchase dissonance can lead to cardinal decisions - abandoning a purchase and returning a product. Lee (D. H. Lee 2015) examined consumer take-back behavior in terms of post-purchase dissonance and environmental marketing. The author noted that consumers are increasingly choosing product returns over other options to deal with their dissonance.

Regret influences consumer brand decisions. Dawetas, Diamantopoulos (Dawetas and Diamantopoulos 2018) investigated regret in post-purchase behavior when choosing global and local brands.

The consumer may experience regret for two reasons: the product purchased as a result and the process of making a decision to purchase the product. Das, Kerr (Das and Kerr 2010) noted that regret is a key negative emotion that consumers try to avoid when making decisions. The authors examined the concept of regret arising simultaneously from both the purchased product and the decision-making process. Lee, Cotte (S. H. Lee and Cotte 2009) from the standpoint of regret about the result highlighted regret due to missed alternatives and regret due to a change in significance, from the standpoint of regret about the process, the authors highlight regret due to underestimation and overestimation during decision-making. The authors present a scale for measuring this construction of regret (PPCR). M'Barek, Gharbi (M'Barek and Gharbi 2012) studied the factors that determine customer regret after purchase. The authors have shown that regret is a multidimensional concept, the components of which are the result obtained and the process by which the result is obtained. Das, Joffe (Das and Joffe 2012) confirmed the need to simultaneously evaluate regret both in the decision-making process and in relation to the product after an adverse decision outcome during the post-purchase evaluation.

Regret is common when people buy products with new features. Jiang, Narasimhan, Turut (B. Jiang, Narasimhan, and Turut 2017) showed that consumers can anticipate their potential regret after purchase and make their current choices to mitigate or minimize it. That is, the expected regret of the consumer can significantly influence his purchase decision. The analysis showed that the presence of expected regret can increase or decrease the profit of companies, as well as stimulate or hinder product innovation, depending on whether it makes the consumer segments more or less polarized; in other words.

In consumer decision making, regret is seen as an important factor in consumer satisfaction, post-purchase evaluation, purchase intent and product change decisions. Chen, Jia, He (R. Chen, Jia, and He 2005) determined that the consumer's intention to purchase a product is influenced not only by regret but also by comparison of the expected uncertainty of presentation in alternatives. This power of influence and its direction depend on the consumer's preference for risk and the length of the shopping experience. Salzberger, Koller (Salzberger and Koller 2010) showed that dissonance and satisfaction are complementary constructs describing various aspects of the customer's mental state after the purchase.

Motivation to buy influences post-purchase dissonance. Yang, Chang, Hsu (Yang, Chang, and Hsu 2019), using the example of mobile games, found out what motivation to buy causes the greatest dissonance among consumers of mobile games. The authors found that speculative motivation and impulsive buying motivation cause more dissonance after a purchase.

In the post-purchase dissonance, the emotional component is highlighted. Kurian, Sahay, Misra (Kurian, Sahay, and Misra 2019) studied different consumer purchasing approaches and their relationship to post-purchase behavior using a wide range of products from mobile phones to real estate (Kurian, Sahay, and Misra 2019), taking into account differences in levels of satisfaction after purchase. The authors showed that emotional dissonance ranks highest among post-purchase purchasing behavior.

The authors take into account the features of the digitalization of logistics and trade networks (Barykin, Kalinina, et al. 2021; Barykin, Kapustina, Sergeev, et al. 2021; Barykin, Bochkarev, et al. 2021; Barykin, Kapustina, Valebnikova, et al. 2021). It is important for manufacturers and distributors to reduce post-purchase dissonance, which will translate into increased customer satisfaction. Anitha, Kanimozhi (Anitha and Kanimozhi 2013) evaluated the expectations, perceptions and behavior of buyers after the purchase using the example of two-wheeled vehicles.

Relationship marketing influences the manifestation of post-purchase dissonance in the consumer. Sharifi and Esfidani (Shahin Sharifi and Rahim Esfidani 2014) showed that relationship marketing has resulted in consumers experiencing less post-purchase cognitive dissonance. Because consumers experience less cognitive dissonance, they present more satisfaction and behavioral loyalty. The authors confirmed the mediating role of trust and cognitive dissonance.

Post-purchase dissonance is associated with consumer engagement. Wilkins, Beckenuyte, Butt (Wilkins, Beckenuyte, and Butt 2016), using the example of food products, determined that consumer expectations regarding the filling of the package were positively associated with post-purchase dissonance, and higher dissonance was negatively associated with purchase intentions and positively associated with both perceived visible and invisible negative post-purchase behavior, such as switching to another brand and communicating information to friends to avoid the product. The authors showed that consumers with low product engagement were less likely to buy the brand and were more likely to exhibit visible and invisible negative behaviors.

Post-purchase dissonance affects consumer attitudes towards a brand. Jhamb, Aggarwal, Mittal, Paul (Jhamb et al. 2020), using the example of luxury goods, note that negative consumer experience leads to post-purchase dissonance, unbalanced or distorted attitude towards the brand and other marketing incentives.

Consumer identification with brands influences post-purchase regret. Davvetas and Diamantopoulos (Dawetas and Diamantopoulos 2018) showed that consumer and brand identification attenuates the negative impact of regret on satisfaction and behavioral intentions and enhances the positive impact of satisfaction on repurchase intention and brand recommendation.

Certain marketing incentives can help reduce post-purchase dissonance and increase customer satisfaction with a purchase. Webster, Rennie (Webster and Rennie 2011), using the example of travel, determined that the transmission of information about various types of values before consumption and active reflection help to improve the perception of consumers of their experience, to reduce post-purchase dissonance. The authors determined that the consumer value framework, in addition to being used as a promotional tool to increase customer satisfaction, contributes to product pooling and product benefits.

The use of immediate shopping tactics by retailers increases consumer anxiety. Workman, Lee (Workman and Lee 2019), using the example of fashion, studied the differences between groups of consumers who set fashion trends concerning money and the propensity of consumers to regret buying. The authors found that trendsetters scored higher on quality concerning money and anxiety than later followers. Trendsetters scored more points for not buying than buying. Participants with the highest purchase regret scored higher on strength/prestige, distrust, and anxiety, but not on quality. Participants with high levels of regret not buying scored higher on strength/prestige, quality, and anxiety, but not distrust.

Post-purchase regret is related to the complaint. Tzeng, Shiu (Tzeng and Shiu 2019) determined that regret can positively influence consumer complaints. The authors found that consumers do not complain to third parties without experiencing strong regrets.

Regret, negative emotions and reflections play a role in a consumer's post-purchase behavior. Bui, Krishen, Bates (Bui, Krishen, and Bates 2011) showed that regret lowers consumer satisfaction and increases brand switching intent.

Awareness of purchase alternatives influences post-purchase regret. Lin, Huang (Lin and Huang 2006) studied the influence of ignorance and the effects of ordering on consumer regret in post-purchase evaluation. The authors showed that brands that consumers were not previously aware of do indeed contribute to consumer regret, especially in a post-purchase price comparison situation (versus unknown top-tier brands), this was not the case in a post-purchase comparison situation (vs. with inferior unknown brands).

The rise in daily online promotional offers for the price of transactions and the non-redemption of these coupons by buyers deserves attention from a psychological point of view of non-consumption. Scheinbaum, Shah, Kukar-Kinney, Copple (Scheinbaum et al. 2020) showed that post-purchase regret explains the key reason why trades are not used.

Feelings of guilt are a deterrent to buying and affect the ability to re-purchase a product and recommend it to others. Silva, Martins (Silva and Martins 2017) showed that the feeling of financial guilt as a type of guilt is a precursor to common guilt after a purchase. The authors have shown that including a social cause in a marketing campaign reduces feelings of guilt and regret and increases the likelihood of purchasing and recommending a product.

Post-purchase dissonance has consequences. Keng, Liao (Keng and Liao 2013), using computers, communications and consumer electronics as examples, found that post-purchase dissonance negatively affects post-purchase satisfaction and intent to repurchase and positively influences the intent to file a complaint. Satisfaction positively affects the intent to repurchase and negatively affects the intent to file a complaint. After experiencing post-purchase dissonance, consumers seek external information that mediates the relationship between post-purchase dissonance and satisfaction.

After purchasing a product, price complaints are common. Estelami (Estelami 2003) investigated the frequency and characteristics of various forms of post-purchase price complaints. The author found that one-fifth of all post-purchase consumer complaints were related to prices. Price complaints differ significantly from non-price complaints in terms of frequency and resolution between categories.

Post-purchase hedonic consumption experiences are influenced by price promotions, price promotions. Lee and Tsai (L. Lee and Tsai 2014) found that the time lag between payment and consumption plays an important role in determining the relative strength of these competing effects. The authors have shown that when consumption occurs immediately after payment, discounts make consumption more enjoyable; this pattern changes when consumption is delayed.

After purchase, consumers may find they missed out on a price promotion. Chen, Tsai, Chuang (W. W. Chen, Tsai, and Chuang 2010) studied how consumers perceive price inequities when they learn that they missed a price increase after making a purchase, and examined the associated negative emotions and behavioral responses. Perceived price inequities are more likely to cause anger than disappointment and regret. The timing of a missed price promotion changes the impact of perceived price inequity on regret. Consumers experiencing high levels of anger and frustration complain and spread negative word of mouth communication; consumers experiencing strong regret are inactive.

Sellers promise to refund money to consumers who find lower prices after purchase to prevent regret. Dutta, Biswas, Grewal (Dutta, Biswas, and Grewal 2011) found that the impact of reimbursement on regret depends on how consumers perceive these promises. If consumers view promises as protective tools, then there is minimal regret after return. If consumers view promises as sources of information about a retailer's pricing status, regret persists even after refunds. The authors showed that regret persists among these consumers because seeking a lower price leads to a perceived breach of trust.

Price matching guarantees give consumers the confidence that if they find a lower price elsewhere within a specified period after purchase, the retailer will refund the price difference. Jiang, Kumar, Ratchford (J. Jiang, Kumar, and Ratchford 2017) have shown that price-matching guarantees expand retail demand, but increase price competition.

There is a connection between enduring personality traits and transient affective experiences or states. Mooradian, Olver (Mooradian and Olver 1997) combined these links with recent consumer research models linking consumption-based emotions to consumer satisfaction and post-purchase behavior (including complaints, recommendations, and repeat purchase intentions). The authors confirmed a model linking broad, fundamental personality traits to specific consumer behavior through affective experiences.

Consumers don't always form their post-purchase estimates right away. Mattila (Mattila 2003) showed that consumers may not generate online satisfaction ratings in typical re-consumption situations. The author noted that consumers can only participate in renewal and judgment processes when faced with a post-purchase satisfaction request.

Consumer psychological characteristics influence post-purchase dissonance. Keng, Liao (Keng and Liao 2009), using technological products as an example, demonstrated that constant consumer characteristics (anxiety and general self-confidence) not only directly affect post-purchase dissonance positively and negatively, but are also mediated by temporary consumer feelings (state anxiety and special self-confidence) concerning the buying situation, and then indirectly affect the dissonance after the purchase positively and negatively.

Consumer buying gifts for themselves is associated with the potential for post-purchase regret. David Clarke, Mortimer (David Clarke and Mortimer 2013) studied the identification and relationship of the causes of self-gift, self-gift, and the effect on post-purchase regret. The authors found that regret about buying self-given gifts is observed among consumers with therapeutic and holiday self-gift motivation.

Research looks at post-purchase dissonance across multiple domains. Graff, Sophonthummapharn, Parida (Graff, Sophonthummapharn, and Parida 2012) use the example of mobile phones to determine the main differences between groups of consumers with high and low dissonance.

Dissonance can be measured by measuring individual components. Sweeney, Soutar (A. J. C. Sweeney and Soutar 2006) developed the scale - The Revised Dissonance Scale. This three-dimensional scale consists of 3 subscales and 12 statements: the emotional dimension (5 statements), the purchasing wisdom scale (4 statements), and the transaction anxiety scale (3 statements). The emotional dimension is a person's psychological discomfort after a purchase decision, purchase wisdom is a person's recognition after making a purchase that they may not need a product or could not choose a suitable one, anxiety about a transaction is a person's recognition after making a purchase. that he may have been influenced against his own beliefs by the sales staff (J. C. Sweeney, Hausknecht, and Soutar 2000).

1.2. Post-purchase Dissonance and Impulse Purchases

Post-purchase regret is common with impulse purchases. Do, Usuluddin, Chan (Do, Usuluddin, and Chan 2016) determined that when a consumer has a hedonistic motivation to buy, he is ready to face the consequence - regret, and thought about how to deal with it, even before an impulsive purchase. Saleem, Ali, Ahmad (Saleem, Ali, and Ahmad 2012) found that product engagement and impulse purchases are significant for predicting cognitive dissonance.

The post-purchase consumer experience, rather than the direct purchase experience, enhances or limits future impulse purchases. Spiteri Cornish (Spiteri Cornish 2020) demonstrated that consumers use three types of coping mechanisms to allay post-purchase regret: planned problem solving, positive rethinking, or mental shutdown. Using planned problem solving restricts future impulse buying while using the other two mechanisms leads to increased behavior.

Certain promotion tools affect impulse buying and post-purchase dissonance. Balakrishnan, Foroudi, Dwivedi (Balakrishnan, Foroudi, and Dwivedi 2020) found that coupons have a positive effect on shopping activity and impulse, which further affects post-purchase cognitive dissonance and post-purchase affective dissonance, as well as consumer's intention to re-buy. The authors found that providing additional free coupons reduced the effect of cognitive dissonance, but not affective dissonance.

The site interface stimulates consumer emotions and impulse purchases. Chen, Chen, Lin (W. K. Chen, Chen, and Lin 2020), using the example of clothing, have shown that impulse purchases directly and positively affect the dissonance of consumers in relation to the product, impulse purchases indirectly affect consumers' emotional purchases.

Making impulse purchases online is often accompanied by post-purchase dissonance. Lazim, Sulaiman, Zakuan, Mas'od, Chin, Awang (Lazim et al. 2020) studied the influence of internal and external factors on buying behavior, how consumers overcome regret after making an online purchase. The authors pointed out that sales incentives, credit card payments, visual merchandising, pricing, and online reviews have a significant impact on impulse purchases.

Sellers need effective post-purchase communication to reduce the cognitive dissonance of impulsive consumers. Chang, Tseng (Chang and Tseng 2014) examined the impact of post-purchase arguments on online consumer impulse satisfaction. The authors showed that increasing the number of strong arguments presented after a purchase has a stronger positive effect on online satisfaction than when the arguments are weak. This effect is less pronounced for consumers with a low propensity to regret than for consumers with a high propensity to regret.

1.3. Post-purchase Dissonance and Online Shopping

The concept of cognitive dissonance is also being explored in the field of online shopping. Yap, Gaur (Yap and Gaur 2014) identified key trends in cognitive dissonance research and proposed a further research program to understand consumer dissonance in an online context.

Millennials make up a large proportion of Internet users. It is important for marketers to understand the role that online content plays in their shopping behavior. Gokhale (Gokhale 2019) used smartphones to study the effects of online content (product-related content) on post-purchase behavior in millennials: post-purchase satisfaction and post-purchase dissonance in particular.

In the retail industry, augmented reality (AR) technology is being used as a means of improving customer experience. Romano, Sands, Pallant (Romano, Sands, and Pallant 2020) pointed out that at the time of purchase, AR helps with product development and hedonic value through play. The authors showed that after the purchase AR affects the confidence in the consumer's choice, increases cognitive dissonance.

The cognitive effort a consumer makes to make a decision is associated with post-purchase regret. Park, Hill (Park and Hill 2018) used a laptop as an example to investigate the functions of decision justification and cognitive effort associated with regret in the context of online shopping. The authors determined that regret is greater when the justification for a decision is wasted, and wasted justification for a decision worsens regret when a more cognitive effort is made.

Brand credibility affects post-purchase regret in online shopping. Zulkarnain, Ginting, Novliadi, Siahaan (Zulkarnain et al. 2019) confirmed that brand trust has a significant impact on consumer regret when shopping online. The authors have shown that the brand reliability of an online product is an important factor in reducing consumer regret about the purchase outcome and the purchase process.

Post-purchase regret in online shopping affects the likelihood of a subsequent consumer visit to the seller's site. Rajagopal, Mahajan, Sharma, Udas (Rajagopal et al. 2019) found that post-purchase regret and the discovery that a product is being sold at a lower price on some other portal influences consumer behavior, such as refraining from visiting the site again.

Online reviews are an important source of information when making a purchasing decision. Also, these reviews influence the attitude towards the product after purchase. Zhang, Goh (Zhang and Goh 2020) found in hotels that the number of negative reviews read by consumers after purchase is positively associated with regret and the possibility of cancellation, and this relationship is reinforced by a high rating before buying. The number of hedonic and utilitarian comments and the post-purchase rating collectively affect the cancellation behavior.

Seller ratings also affect post-purchase regret. Tseng (Tseng 2017) showed that the effect of a regretful individual on e-satisfaction is entirely mediated by cognitive dissonance after purchase. The author confirmed the impact of current seller ratings on improving e-satisfaction for regretful consumers.

Post-purchase regret leads to dissatisfaction and refusal to buy again. Liu, Liao, Chang (Liu, Liao, and Chang 2012) investigated the role that search efforts, service attribute assessment, product attribute assessment, and post-purchase price perception play in generating consumer regret and satisfaction in e-commerce. The authors have shown that greater search effort and lower ratings for services, products, and prices lead to greater consumer regret and dissatisfaction.

Webrooming is the consumer practice of searching for products online before purchasing them from a brick-and-mortar store. Webrooming affects post-purchase regret. Arora, Sahney (Arora and Sahney 2019) pointed out that webrooming helps consumers avoid post-purchase regret that they are making sub-optimal offline product choices.

After a purchase, consumers are looking for information about their decision. The use of the Internet makes this process much faster and easier for consumers. Wang, Yang (Wang and Yang 2010) analyzed the psychological activity of search behavior after a purchase. The authors determined that information seeking plays an important role in the transition from "cognitive dissonance" to "balance." Guo, Huang, Lin (Guo, Huang, and Lin 2016) showed that product knowledge has a positive effect on various types of information retrieval and negatively affects post-purchase dissonance. Online pre-purchase and post-purchase searches have a negative impact on post-purchase dissonance.

The complexity of the information presented determines the post-purchase dissonance. Hansen, Thomsen, Beckmann (Hansen, Thomsen, and Beckmann 2013), using information about the health of food as an example, determined that the search for information about the health of a particular product and the complexity of information are positively associated with post-purchase dissonance.

Consumers compare their results to what they would have if they bought earlier or later. Cooke, Meyvis, Schwartz (Cooke, Meyvis, and Schwartz 2001) showed that post-purchase information has a greater impact on satisfaction than pre-purchase information. The authors determined that if consumers who receive information after a purchase want to avoid feelings of regret in the future, they should delay their purchases longer.

1.4. Handmade Industry

Handmade products, made to order according to the individual project of the consumer, can be classified as experiential purchases as opposed to material purchases. Gilovich, Gallo (Gilovich and Gallo 2020) identified the mechanisms underlying the empirical advantage. Van Boven and Gilovich (Van Boven and Gilovich 2003) pointed out that purchases made with the primary intention of gaining life experience make consumers happier than material purchases. The authors have shown that experience makes people happier because they are more open to positive reinterpretation, which is a more significant part of the personality and more conducive to successful social relationships.

In the field of the handmade industry, there is a certain relationship between consumers and sellers. Positive, friendly emotions help develop relationships. The personality of the master, the seller, in the handmade industry contributes to this. Ho (Ho 2012) investigated the influence of buyer-seller friendship on post-purchase customer ratings. The author showed that friendship is beneficial to sellers only when the outcome of the transaction is unfavorable. When buyers and sellers are close friends rather than acquaintances, buyers perceive the adverse outcome as relatively fairer and more satisfying, but this effect does not occur when the outcome is favorable.

Consumers worry about whether the process of consumption suits their psychological needs. Hung, Ho (Hung and Ho 2017) noted that many traditional industries are seeking transformation to have highly personal, unique and emotional experiences. They begin to design and deliver handmade or craft training courses based on their knowledge and methods.

Manufacturing methods (manual or machine) influence consumer response. Frizzo, Dias, Duarte, Rodrigues, Prado (Frizzo et al. 2020) determined that the higher behavioral intentions (probability of purchase and willingness to pay a higher price) attributed to handmade products are related to perceived naturalness and authenticity associated with the method of production.

In some cases, consumers choose handmade work rather than machine-made work. Hsu, Nguyen Ngoc (Hsu and Nguyen Ngoc 2016) have determined that despite the rapid development of automatic machines, products promoted as handmade are popular with consumers for their outstanding performance.

Hof (Hof 2006), using the example of scrapbooking as one of the directions of the handmade industry, investigated how a community of practitioners, which is both a form and a forum of cultural citizenship. This activity offers a way of self-awareness of one's identity as cultural citizens.

Yadav, Mahara (Yadav and Mahara 2019) explored the role of website quality, service and product perception in consumer intent to buy on the Internet using handmade wooden products as an example. Service perception and product perception determine perceived usefulness, while perceived ease of use is determined by site quality and service perception. The authors have shown that trust plays a positive role in determining buying intent. Website quality, service and product perception determine trust, they build consumer confidence in online shopping.

Vanderploeg, Lee (Vanderploeg and Lee 2019) used the theory of values, beliefs, environmental norms to describe the causal influences of pro-ecological behavior in handmade business.

Certain consumers value originality in self-expression. West (West 2010) used greeting cards to show that consumers with higher cultural capital are more likely to favor postcards that are handcrafted, look handmade, or resemble fine art.

Based on the arguments about the factors and effects of post-purchase dissonance, an assumption was made about the existence of features of post-purchase dissonance when shopping online for handmade goods compared to offline purchases. The hypothesis is formulated:

H0: There are no features of post-purchase dissonance in online purchases of handmade goods compared to offline purchases.

An alternative hypothesis is formulated:

H1: There are features of post-purchase dissonance when shopping for handmade goods online versus offline shopping.

As a result of the study, the features of post-purchase dissonance in online purchases of handmade goods compared to offline purchases will be identified or not identified.

2. MATERIALS AND METHODS

The research methodology is based on the idea that a number of resource and situational factors influence the post-purchase dissonance in online and offline purchases of handmade goods.

2.1. Questionnaire Development

To conduct a study of consumers of handmade goods to determine the presence of features of post-purchase dissonance when making online purchases of handmade goods in comparison with offline purchases, a questionnaire was developed - a working document of a customer survey.

The questionnaire contains the following sections:

- information about the experience of online shopping, online and offline shopping for handmade goods:
    - online shopping experience: entry level, intermediate level, high level;
    - experience of online shopping for handmade goods: entry level, intermediate level, high level;
    - experience of offline shopping for handmade goods: entry level, intermediate level, high level;
- scale for the definition of dissonance (The Revised Dissonance Scale), proposed in the work of Sweeney, Soutar (A. J. C. Sweeney and Soutar 2006), used a 7-point bipolar Rensis Likert scale, here 1 corresponds to 'strongly disagree' and 7 to 'strongly agree,' the scale had to be filled out separately online and by offline purchase;
- information about the type of dissonance:
    - regret about the result, used a 7-point bipolar Rensis Likert scale, where 1 corresponds to 'strongly disagree' and 7 to 'strongly agree', the scale had to be filled out separately online and by offline purchase;
    - regret about the decision-making process, used a 7-point bipolar Rensis Likert scale, where 1 corresponds to 'strongly disagree' and 7 to 'strongly agree', the scale had to be filled out separately online and by offline purchase.

2.2. Data Collection

Respondents needed to be able to recall a specific purchase and reproduce details, this placed a limitation on the time frame used. The respondent should have had the experience of online and offline purchases of handmade goods of the same engagement level - an average level of engagement. In order to limit the influence of external factors that are not the objectives of the study, such a factor as the involvement of the consumer in the purchase of the product was excluded from the study model. To do this, consumers previously took a survey to determine the level of their involvement in the purchase of online and offline handmade goods. The survey was conducted according to the questionnaire developed by the author to determine the level of involvement in 2019. The choice of the average level of involvement in online and offline purchases of handmade goods made it possible to avoid a possible impact on the results of determining the presence of features of post-purchase dissonance when making online purchases of handmade goods in comparison with offline purchases.

The type of selection used is a convenient selection.

The study involved 200 respondents who made online and offline purchases of handmade goods at least once over the past year. Period of the survey: 01.03.2020 – 01.05.2020.

The data were analyzed using SPSS software.

3. RESULTS

The main results are presented below.

3.1. Characteristics of the Experience of Online Shopping, Online and Offline Shopping For Handmade Goods

The results of a survey of consumers regarding their experience of making online purchases in various fields and online purchases and offline purchases of handmade goods are presented in Table 1.

Table 1. Characteristics of the experience of online shopping, online and offline shopping for handmade goods

		Online shopping experience		
		beginner level	intermediate level	high level
Experience of online shopping for handmade goods	beginner level	4	32	35
	intermediate level	0	23	51
	high level	0	0	55
Experience of offline shopping for handmade goods	beginner level	3	23	21
	intermediate level	1	27	71
	high level	0	5	49

The data showed that the majority of respondents have an average to high level of online shopping. This has a positive effect on the online shopping experience of handmade goods.

3.2. Characteristics of Dissonance in Online and Offline Purchases of Handmade Goods

The results of a consumer survey regarding the three components of the dissonance that occurs when they make online and offline purchases of handmade goods are presented in Table 2.

**Table 2. Characteristics of dissonance in online and offline purchases
of handmade goods**

		Cognitive measurements					
		Emotional online	Emotional offline	Wisdom of purchase online	Wisdom of purchase offline	Concern over deal online	Concern over deal offline
Online shopping experience	beginner level	5.30	3.82	4.96	3.63	5.24	4.96
	intermediate level	4.00	3.34	4.00	3.26	3.99	2.92
	high level	2.24	1.96	2.11	2.10	2.20	2.16
Experience of online shopping for handmade goods	beginner level	3.80	2.94	3.43	3.07	3.45	3.06
	intermediate level	2.45	2.37	2.45	2.44	2.58	2.44
	high level	1.92	1.64	2.03	1.65	2.09	1.58
Experience of offline shopping for handmade goods	beginner level	4.04	3.17	3.64	3.39	3.74	3.05
	intermediate level	2.61	2.35	2.50	2.40	2.62	2.56
	high level	2.01	1.73	2.19	1.70	2.13	1.63

Comparison of the three components of dissonance for online and offline purchases of handmade goods showed that there are differences and features of post-purchase dissonance in online purchases of handmade goods as compared to offline purchases. The emotional dimension, the measurement of the wisdom of purchase, and the measurement of concern over the deal in the case of offline shopping are lower across all levels of the shopping experience.

3.3. Characterization of Dissonance by the Type of Dissonance: Regret about the Result and Regret about the Decision-Making Process

The results of a consumer survey regarding their experience of online shopping for handmade goods and types of dissonance are presented in Table 3.

Comparison of the levels of regret about objects of regret showed that in the case of online purchases of handmade goods, respondents regret the process of making a decision to purchase more than the result of a purchase, a product.

The results of a consumer survey regarding their experience of making offline purchases of handmade goods and types of dissonance are presented in Table 4.

Comparison of the levels of regret about the objects of regret showed that in the case of offline purchases of handmade goods, respondents regret the process of making a decision to purchase more than the result of the purchase, the product.

Table 3. Characterization of dissonance by the type of dissonance: Regret about the result and regret about the decision-making process of online purchase

		Experience of online shopping for handmade goods		
		beginner level	intermediate level	high level
Purchased product regret online	strongly disagree	23	19	20
	disagree	20	21	12
	somewhat disagree	12	22	23
	neither agree or disagree	9	9	0
	somewhat agree	7	3	0
	agree	0	0	0
	strongly agree	0	0	0
Decision-making process regret online	strongly disagree	0	0	0
	disagree	0	0	0
	somewhat disagree	12	16	17
	neither agree or disagree	9	25	25
	somewhat agree	20	19	13
	agree	13	5	0
	strongly agree	17	9	0

Table 4. Characterization of dissonance by the type of dissonance: Regret about the result and regret about the decision-making process of offline purchase

		Experience of offline shopping for handmade goods		
		beginner level	intermediate level	high level
Purchased product regret offline	strongly disagree	16	34	19
	disagree	20	58	34
	somewhat disagree	11	7	1
	neither agree or disagree	0	0	0
	somewhat agree	0	0	0
	agree	0	0	0
	strongly agree	0	0	0
Decision-making process regret offline	strongly disagree	0	0	0
	disagree	4	11	3
	somewhat disagree	15	24	11
	neither agree or disagree	20	57	40
	somewhat agree	8	7	0
	agree	0	0	0
	strongly agree	0	0	0

4. DISCUSSION

The results of the study showed that in the case of online and offline purchases of handmade goods, there is a post-purchase dissonance. In the case of online purchases of handmade goods, consumers experience post-purchase dissonance at a greater level than in the case of offline purchases of handmade goods. This refuted the null hypothesis and confirmed the hypothesis about the existence of post-purchase dissonance features in online purchases of handmade goods compared to offline purchases.

The revealed results are explained by the specifics of the research object and the specifics of online trade as such.

CONCLUSION

The main findings are presented below.

1. In the theory and practice of consumer behavior, the study of post-purchase processes is important, since the consumer's reaction to a purchase determines the long-term interaction of the consumer with the seller's brand. The post-purchase dissonance arising from the consumer leads to cancellation of purchase, a decrease in brand confidence, and a refusal to purchase again. The research emphasizes that it is necessary to study not only the consumer's post-purchase doubts about the result of the purchase that is goods, but also the consumer's post-purchase doubts about the purchasing decision-making process. In this case, the consumer doubts not about a specific product, but about the chosen ways to solve the problem. Currently, a three-dimensional scale is used to measure dissonance, which allows you to define 3 dimensions: the emotional dimension, the purchase wisdom measurement and the purchase anxiety measurement. This suggests that post-purchase dissonance is a complex and multifaceted concept.

2. Research shows that the emergence of post-purchase dissonance is influenced by the following factors: personal characteristics of the consumer, consumer involvement in the purchasing decision process, availability and search for information about the product after the purchase, purchase motives, reviews and ratings of the product and the seller on the Internet, impulse of purchase, personality of the seller. Post-purchase dissonance negatively affects post-purchase satisfaction, intent to repurchase, and positively influences a consumer's intention to file a complaint.

3. Research shows that building consumer confidence is of great importance when selling handmade goods online. This trust consists of trust in the goods of a particular seller, as in the case of offline sales, and trust in the trading platform where handmade goods are sold. Post-purchase dissonance affects the loss of confidence in the seller's brand and marketplace. There are certain marketing tools that can help prevent and reduce post-purchase dissonance. For example, the correct use of promotions.

4. Research of consumers of handmade goods has shown that there are certain features of post-purchase dissonance when shopping online for handmade

goods in comparison with offline purchases. In the case of online shopping for handmade products, there was an increase in post-purchase dissonance across all dimensions and across all levels of shopping experience. And in the case of online and offline purchases of handmade goods, it is determined that consumers regret more about the purchasing decision process than about the product itself.

The data obtained is essential for the development of marketing strategies and tactics. Sellers need to take a closer look at online shopping and use effective tools to prevent and reduce post-purchase dissonance. The results make it possible to understand the difference between online and offline consumer purchases of handmade goods.

Outside of the marketing research, questions remain regarding the actions that consumers take when faced with post-purchase dissonance when shopping online and offline handmade goods, which also seem interesting. These actions, for example: returning goods to the seller, sending a negative review to the trading platform, word of mouth communications, etc. Actions presumably determine the consequences of post-purchase dissonance and require attention. This topic will be developed in future research.

ACKNOWLEDGMENTS

This research work was supported by the Academic Excellence Project 5-100 proposed by Peter the Great St. Petersburg Polytechnic University.

REFERENCES

Aleksandrov, Igor, Marina Fedorova, and Alexey Parshukov. 2020. "E-Commerce in Russian Rural Areas as a Tool for Regional Development." In *E3S Web of Conferences.* https://doi.org/10.1051/e3sconf/202017513046.

Anitha, R., and V. Kanimozhi. 2013. "A Study on Post Purchase Behaviour with Special Reference to Mahindra Two Wheelers." *Indian Journal of Marketing.* https://doi.org/10.17010/ijom/2013/v43/i6/36390.

Arora, Sourabh, and Sangeeta Sahney. 2019. "Examining Consumers' Webrooming Behavior: An Integrated Approach." *Marketing Intelligence and Planning.* https://doi.org/10.1108/MIP-05-2018-0152.

Balakrishnan, Janarthanan, Pantea Foroudi, and Yogesh K. Dwivedi. 2020. "Does Online Retail Coupons and Memberships Create Favourable Psychological Disposition?" *Journal of Business Research.* https://doi.org/10.1016/j.jbusres.2020.05.039.

Barykin, Sergey Yevgenievich, Andrey Aleksandrovich Bochkarev, Sergey Mikhailovich Sergeev, Tatiana Anatolievna Baranova, Dmitriy Anatolievich Mokhorov, and Aleksandra Maksimovna Kobicheva. 2021. "A Methodology of Bringing Perspective Innovation Products to Market." *Academy of Strategic Management Journal* 20 (2): 19. https://www.abacademies.org/articles/a-methodology-of-bringing-perspective-innovation-products-to-market.pdf.

Barykin, Sergey Yevgenievich, Olga Vladimirovna Kalinina, Irina Vasilievna Kapustina, Victor Andreevich Dubolazov, Cesar Armando Nunez Esquivel, Elmira Alyarovna Nazarova, and Petr Anatolievich Sharapaev. 2021. "The Sharing Economy and Digital Logistics in Retail Chains: Opportunities and Threats." *Academy of Strategic Management Journal* 20 (2): 1–14. https://www.abacademies.org/articles/the-sharing-economy-and-digital-logistics-in-retail-chains-opportunities-and-threats.pdf.

Barykin, Sergey Yevgenievich, Irina Vasilievna Kapustina, Sergey Mikhailovich Sergeev, Olga Vladimirovna Kalinina, Viktoriia Valerievna Vilken, Yuri Yevgenievich Putikhin, and Lydia Vitalievna Volkova. 2021. "Developing the Physical Distribution Digital Twin Model within the Trade Network." *Academy of Strategic Management Journal* 20 (1): 1–24. https://www.abacademies.org/articles/developing-the-physical-distribution-digital-twin-model-within-the-trade-network.pdf.

Barykin, Sergey Yevgenievich, Irina Vasilievna Kapustina, Olga Aleksandrovna Valebnikova, Natalia Viktorovna Valebnikova, Olga Vladimirovna Kalinina, Sergey Mikhailovich Sergeev, Marisa Camastral, Yuri Yevgenievich Putikhin, and Lydia Vitalievna Volkova. 2021. "Digital Technologies for Personnel Management: Implications for Open Innovations." *Academy of Strategic Management Journal* 20 (2): 1–14. https://www.abacademies.org/articles/digital-technologies-for-personnel-management-implications-for-open-innovations.pdf.

Boven, Leaf Van, and Thomas Gilovich. 2003. "To Do or to Have? That Is the Question." *Journal of Personality and Social Psychology.* https://doi.org/10.1037/0022-3514.85.6.1193.

Bozhuk, Svetlana, Natalia Krasnostavskaia, Tatyana Maslova, and Natalia Pletneva. 2019. "The Problems of Innovative Merchandise Trade in the Context of Digital Environment." In *IOP Conference Series: Materials Science and Engineering.* https://doi.org/10.1088/1757-899X/497/1/012115.

Bozhuk, Svetlana, Tatyana Maslova, Nelli Kozlova, and Natalia Krasnostavskaia. 2019. "Transformation of Mechanism of Sales and Services Promotion in Digital Environment." In *IOP Conference Series: Materials Science and Engineering.* https://doi.org/10.1088/1757-899X/497/1/012114.

Bui, My, Anjala S. Krishen, and Kenneth Bates. 2011. "Modeling Regret Effects on Consumer Post-Purchase Decisions." *European Journal of Marketing.* https://doi.org/10.1108/03090561111137615.

Chang, Chia Chi, and Ai Hua Tseng. 2014. "The Post-Purchase Communication Strategies for Supporting Online Impulse Buying." *Computers in Human Behavior.* https://doi.org/10.1016/j.chb.2014.05.035.

Chen, Rong, Jian Min Jia, and Feng He. 2005. "Dynamic Impact of Regret on Consumer Choice Intention." *Xitong Gongcheng Lilun Yu Shijian/System Engineering Theory and Practice.*

Chen, Wei Wei, Dungchun Tsai, and Han Chia Chuang. 2010. "Effects of Missing a Price Promotion after Purchasing on Perceived Price Unfairness, Negative Emotions, and Behavioral Responses." *Social Behavior and Personality.* https://doi.org/10.2224/sbp.2010.38.4.495.

Chen, Wen Kuo, Chien Wen Chen, and Yu Chun Lin. 2020. "Understanding the Influence of Impulse Buying toward Consumers' Post-Purchase Dissonance and Return Intention: An Empirical Investigation of Apparel Websites." *Journal of Ambient Intelligence and Humanized Computing.* https://doi.org/10.1007/s12652-020-02333-z.

Cooke, Alan D.J., Tom Meyvis, and Alan Schwartz. 2001. "Avoiding Future Regret in Purchase-Timing Decisions." *Journal of Consumer Research.* https://doi.org/10.1086/319620.

Das, Neel, and Brad Joffe. 2012. "The Interactive Effects of Decision-Making and Expertise on the Experience of Regret." *Journal of Applied Business Research.* https://doi.org/10.19030/jabr.v28i3.6953.

Das, Neel, and Anthony Kerr. 2010. "'woulda, Coulda, Shoulda': A Conceptual Examination of the Sources of Postpurchase Regret." *Journal of Marketing Theory and Practice.* https://doi.org/10.2753/MTP1069-6679180205.

David Clarke, Peter, and Gary Mortimer. 2013. "Self-Gifting Guilt: An Examination of Self-Gifting Motivations and Post-Purchase Regret." *Journal of Consumer Marketing.* https://doi.org/10.1108/JCM-05-2013-0566.

Dawetas, Vasileios, and Adamantios Diamantopoulos. 2018. "'Should Have i Bought the Other One?' Experiencing Regret in Global versus Local Brand Purchase Decisions." *Journal of International Marketing.* https://doi.org/10.1509/jim. 17.0040.

Do, Ben Roy, Usuluddin, and Chi Ning Chan. 2016. "Exploring the Relationship among Hedonic Shopping Motivation, Impulse Buying, Post-Purchase Regret, and Coping." *International Journal of Information and Management Sciences.* https://doi.org/10.6186/IJIMS.2016.27.4.2.

Dutta, Sujay, Abhijit Biswas, and Dhruv Grewal. 2011. "Regret from Postpurchase Discovery of Lower Market Prices: Do Price Refunds Help?" *Journal of Marketing.* https://doi.org/10.1509/jm.10.0271.

Dvas, Grigory V., and Yulia A. Dubolazova. 2018. "Risk Assessment and Risk Management of Innovative Activity of the Enterprise." In *Proceedings of the 31st International Business Information Management Association Conference, IBIMA 2018: Innovation Management and Education Excellence through Vision 2020.*

Estelami, Hooman. 2003. "Sources, Characteristics, and Dynamics of Postpurchase Price Complaints." *Journal of Business Research.* https://doi.org/10.1016/S0148-2963(01)00224-7.

Festinger, Leon. 1957. "A Theory of Social Cognitive Dissonance." *Human Relations.*

Frizzo, Francielle, Helison Bertoli Alves Dias, Nayara Pereira Duarte, Denise Gabriela Rodrigues, and Paulo Henrique Muller Prado. 2020. "The Genuine Handmade: How the Production Method Influences Consumers' Behavioral Intentions through Naturalness and Authenticity." *Journal of Food Products Marketing.* https://doi.org/10.1080/10454446.2020.1765936.

Gilovich, Thomas, and Iñigo Gallo. 2020. "Consumers' Pursuit of Material and Experiential Purchases: A Review." *Consumer Psychology Review.* https://doi.org/10.1002/arcp.1053.

Gokhale, Nilesh. 2019. "Online Content and Post-Purchase Behavior a Study of Millennials." *Media Watch.* https://doi.org/10.15655/mw/2019/v10/Spl/49615.

Goncharova, N., V. Degtereva, and N. Sopilko. 2018. "Contradictions in Regional Innovative Activity and Ways to Overcome Them." In *Proceedings of the 31st International Business Information Management Association Conference, IBIMA 2018: Innovation Management and Education Excellence through Vision 2020.*

Graff, Jens, Kittipong Sophonthummapharn, and Vinit Parida. 2012. "Post-Purchase Cognitive Dissonance - Evidence from the Mobile Phone Market." *International Journal of Technology Marketing.* https://doi.org/10.1504/IJTMKT.2012.046433.

Guo, Jasmin Chia Wei, Eugenia Y. Huang, and Shu Chiung Lin. 2016. "Investigating the Effect of Pre-Purchase Search and Ongoing Search on Post-Purchase Dissonance." In *AMCIS 2016: Surfing the IT Innovation Wave - 22nd Americas Conference on Information Systems.*

Hansen, Torben, Thyra Uth Thomsen, and Suzanne C. Beckmann. 2013. "Antecedents and Consequences of Consumers' Response to Health Information Complexity." *Journal of Food Products Marketing.* https://doi.org/10.1080/10454446.2013.739553.

Ho, Hillbun Dixon. 2012. "Does Friendship Help in Personal Selling? The Contingent Effect of Outcome Favorability." *Psychology and Marketing.* https://doi.org/10.1002/mar.20506.

Hof, Karina. 2006. "Something You Can Actually Pick up: Scrapbooking as a Form and Forum of Cultural Citizenship." *European Journal of Cultural Studies.* https://doi.org/10.1177/1367549406066078.

Hsu, Yi, and Anh Nguyen Ngoc. 2016. "The Handmade Effect: What Is Special about Buying Handmade?" *International Review of Management and Business Research.*

Hung, Kuo Che, and Ming Chyuan Ho. 2017. "Communication in Craft Experience Design." In *Proceedings of the 2017 IEEE International Conference on Applied System Innovation: Applied System Innovation for Modern Technology, ICASI 2017.* https://doi.org/10.1109/ICASI.2017.7988427.

Jhamb, Deepika, Arun Aggarwal, Amit Mittal, and Justin Paul. 2020. "Experience and Attitude towards Luxury Brands Consumption in an Emerging Market." *European Business Review.* https://doi.org/10.1108/EBR-09-2019-0218.

Jiang, Baojun, Chakravarthi Narasimhan, and Özge Turut. 2017. "Anticipated Regret and Product Innovation." *Management Science.* https://doi.org/10.1287/mnsc.2016.2555.

Jiang, Juncai, Nanda Kumar, and Brian T. Ratchford. 2017. "Price-Matching Guarantees with Endogenous Consumer Search." *Management Science.* https://doi.org/10.1287/mnsc.2016.2513.

Keaveney, Susan M., Frank Huber, and Andreas Herrmann. 2007. "A Model of Buyer Regret: Selected Prepurchase and Postpurchase Antecedents with Consequences for the Brand and the Channel." *Journal of Business Research.* https://doi.org/10.1016/j.jbusres.2006.07.005.

Keng, Ching Jui, and Tze Hsien Liao. 2009. "Consequences of Postpurchase Dissonance: The Mediating Role of an External Information Search." *Social Behavior and Personality.* https://doi.org/10.2224/sbp.2009.37.10.1327.

———. 2013. "Self-Confidence, Anxiety, and Post-Purchase Dissonance: A Panel Study." *Journal of Applied Social Psychology.* https://doi.org/10.1111/jasp.12116.

Kim, Young Ei, and Hoe Chang Yang. 2018. "The Effect of Counterfactual Thinking on Post-Purchase Behavior of Retail Management." *Journal of Distribution Science.* https://doi.org/10.15722/jds.16.2.201802.25.

Kurian, Dr. Shaji, Saurav Sahay, and Dr. Siddharth Misra. 2019. "Post Purchase Evaluation: A Behavioral Study." *International Journal of Psychosocial Rehabilitation.* https://doi.org/10.37200/ijpr/v23i3/pr190378.

Lazim, Nur Adibah Md, Zuraidah Sulaiman, Norhayati Zakuan, Adaviah Mas'od, Thoo Ai Chin, and Siti Rahmah Awang. 2020. "Measuring Post-Purchase Regret and Impulse Buying in Online Shopping Experience from Cognitive Dissonance Theory Perspective." In *2020 6th IEEE International Conference on Information Management, ICIM 2020.* https://doi.org/10.1109/ICIM49319.2020.244662.

Lee, Dong Hwan. 2015. "An Alternative Explanation of Consumer Product Returns from the Postpurchase Dissonance and Ecological Marketing Perspectives." *Psychology and Marketing.* https://doi.org/10.1002/mar.20757.

Lee, Leonard, and Claire I. Tsai. 2014. "How Price Promotions Influence Postpurchase Consumption Experience over Time." *Journal of Consumer Research.* https://doi.org/10.1086/673441.

Lee, Seung Hwan, and June Cotte. 2009. "Post-Purchase Consumer Regret: Conceptualization and Development of the PPCR Scale." In *Advances in Consumer Research.*

Lin, Chien Huang, and Wen Hsien Huang. 2006. "The Influence of Unawareness Set and Order Effects in Consumer Regret." *Journal of Business and Psychology.* https://doi.org/10.1007/s10869-006-9030-9.

Liu, Chuang Chun, Chechen Liao, and I. Cheng Chang. 2012. "An Overall Purchasing Process Model of Internet Buyers: The Role of Regret in Electronic Commerce." In *18th Americas Conference on Information Systems 2012, AMCIS 2012.*

M'Barek, Melika Ben, and Abderrazak Gharbi. 2012. "Les Déterminants Du Regret Post Achat." In *Innovation and Sustainable Competitive Advantage: From Regional Development to World Economies - Proceedings of the 18th International Business Information Management Association Conference.*

Mattila, Anna S. 2003. "The Impact of Cognitive Inertia on Postconsumption Evaluation Processes." *Journal of the Academy of Marketing Science.* https://doi.org/10.1177/0092070303031003006.

Mooradian, Todd A., and James M. Olver. 1997. "'I Can't Get No Satisfaction:' The Impact of Personality and Emotion on Postpurchase Processes." *Psychology and Marketing.* https://doi.org/10.1002/(SICI)1520-6793(199707)14:4<379::AID-MAR5>3.0.CO;2-6.

Olejniczak, Tomasz. 2017. "Post-Purchase Dissonance - A Difficult Area of Research in Poland." *Polish Journal of Natural Sciences.*

Park, Jisook, and W. Trey Hill. 2018. "Exploring the Role of Justification and Cognitive Effort Exertion on Post-Purchase Regret in Online Shopping." *Computers in Human Behavior.* https://doi.org/10.1016/j.chb.2018.01.036.

Rajagopal, K., Vaishali Mahajan, Pankaj Sharma, and Akshay Udas. 2019. "Effects on Consumer Behavior Due to Post Purchase Regret Associated with Online Shopping." *International Journal of Innovative Technology and Exploring Engineering.* https://doi.org/10.35940/ijitee.K1092.09811S19.

Romano, Beatrice, Sean Sands, and Jason I. Pallant. 2020. "Augmented Reality and the Customer Journey: An Exploratory Study." *Australasian Marketing Journal.* https://doi.org/10.1016/j.ausmj.2020.06.010.

Rudskaya, Irina Andreevna, and Dmitry Grigorievich Rodionov. 2018. "Comprehensive Evaluation of Russian Regional Innovation System Performance Using a Two-Stage Econometric Model." *Espacios.*

Saleem, Muhammad Abid, Rao Akmal Ali, and Saeed Ahmad. 2012. "Post Purchase Cognitive Dissonance : Impact of Product Involvement, Impulse Buying and Hedonic Consumption Tendencies Pakistan." *Interdisciplinary Journal of Contemporary Research in Business.*

Salzberger, Thomas, and Monika Koller. 2010. "Investigating the Impact of Cognitive Dissonance and Customer Satisfaction on Loyalty and Complaint Behaviour." *Revista Brasileira de Marketing.* https://doi.org/10.5585/remark.v9i1.2148.

Scheinbaum, Angeline C., Pratik Shah, Monika Kukar-Kinney, and Jacob Copple. 2020. "Regret and Nonredemption of Daily Deals: Individual Differences and Contextual Influences." *Psychology and Marketing.* https://doi.org/10.1002/mar.21324.

Selentyeva, Tamara, Marina Ivanova, and Valeriia Kulibanova. 2018. "Improvement of Approaches to Evaluating the Results of Innovative Clusters Development." In *Proceedings of the 31st International Business Information Management*

Association Conference, IBIMA 2018: Innovation Management and Education Excellence through Vision 2020.

Shahin Sharifi, Seyed, and Mohammad Rahim Esfidani. 2014. "The Impacts of Relationship Marketing on Cognitive Dissonance, Satisfaction, and Loyalty." *International Journal of Retail & Distribution Management.* https://doi.org/10.1108/ijrdm-05-2013-0109.

Silva, Susana Costa e., and Carla Carvalho Martins. 2017. "The Relevance of Cause-Related Marketing to Post-Purchase Guilt Alleviation." *International Review on Public and Nonprofit Marketing.* https://doi.org/10.1007/s12208-017-0183-1.

Skhvediani, A. E., and T. Y. Kudryavtseva. 2018. "The Socioeconomic Development of Russia: Some Historical Aspects." *European Research Studies Journal.* https://doi.org/10.35808/ersj/1114.

Spiteri Cornish, Lara. 2020. "Why Did I Buy This? Consumers' Post-Impulse-Consumption Experience and Its Impact on the Propensity for Future Impulse Buying Behaviour." *Journal of Consumer Behaviour.* https://doi.org/10.1002/cb.1792.

Sweeney, Associate Jillian C, and Geoffrey N Soutar. 2006. "A Short Form of Sweeney, Hausknecht and Soutar's Cognitive Dissonance Scale." *Proceedings of the 20th Annual Conference of the Australian and New Zealand Academy of Management. Ed. / J. Kennedy; L. Di Milia. Vol. CDROM Yeppoon, Queensland, Australia.*

Sweeney, Jillian C., Douglas Hausknecht, and Geoffrey N. Soutar. 2000. "Cognitive Dissonance after Purchase: A Multidimensional Scale." *Psychology and Marketing.* https://doi.org/10.1002/(SICI)1520-6793(200005)17:5<369::AID-MAR1>3.0.CO;2-G.

Tseng, Aihua. 2017. "Why Do Online Tourists Need Sellers' Ratings? Exploration of the Factors Affecting Regretful Tourist e-Satisfaction." *Tourism Management.* https://doi.org/10.1016/j.tourman.2016.08.017.

Tzeng, Shian Yang, and Jerry Yuwen Shiu. 2019. "Regret Type Matters: Risk Aversion and Complaining in a Multidimensional Post-Purchase Regret Framework." *Asia Pacific Journal of Marketing and Logistics.* https://doi.org/10.1108/APJML-10-2018-0452.

Vanderploeg, Jennifer, and Seung Eun (Joy) Lee. 2019. "Factors Influencing Pro-Environmental Behaviors in Craft Businesses." *Clothing and Textiles Research Journal.* https://doi.org/10.1177/0887302X18800394.

Walchli, Suzanne B., and Janet Landman. 2003. "Effects of Counterfactual Thought on Postpurchase Consumer Affect." *Psychology and Marketing.* https://doi.org/10.1002/mar.10057.

Wang, Qianyu, and Xuecheng Yang. 2010. "Psychological Research on Information Searching Behavior of Post-Purchase." In *2010 2nd International Conference on Communication Systems, Networks and Applications, ICCSNA 2010.* https://doi.org/10.1109/ICCSNA.2010.5588867.

Webster, Cynthia M., and Vanessa A. Rennie. 2011. "Pursuing Pleasure: Consumer Value in Leisure Travel." *International Journal of Culture, Tourism and Hospitality Research*. https://doi.org/10.1108/17506181111174673.

West, Emily. 2010. "A Taste for Greeting Cards: Distinction within a Denigrated Cultural Form." *Journal of Consumer Culture*. https://doi.org/10.1177/1469540510376908.

Wilkins, Stephen, Carina Beckenuyte, and Muhammad Mohsin Butt. 2016. "Consumers' Behavioural Intentions after Experiencing Deception or Cognitive Dissonance Caused by Deceptive Packaging, Package Downsizing or Slack Filling." *European Journal of Marketing*. https://doi.org/10.1108/EJM-01-2014-0036.

Workman, Jane E., and Seung Hee Lee. 2019. "Fashion Trendsetting, Attitudes toward Money, and Tendency to Regret." *International Journal of Retail and Distribution Management*. https://doi.org/10.1108/IJRDM-03-2019-0081.

Yadav, Rohit, and Tripti Mahara. 2019. "An Empirical Study of Consumers Intention to Purchase Wooden Handicraft Items Online: Using Extended Technology Acceptance Model." *Global Business Review*. https://doi.org/10.1177/0972150917713899.

Yang, Shu Chen, Rui Min Chang, and Chia Jung Hsu. 2019. "Post-Purchase Dissonance of Mobile Games Consumer." In *Communications in Computer and Information Science*. https://doi.org/10.1007/978-981-15-1758-7_8.

Yap, Sheau Fen, and Sanjaya Singh Gaur. 2014. "Consumer Dissonance in the Context of Online Consumer Behavior: A Review and Research Agenda." *Journal of Internet Commerce*. https://doi.org/10.1080/15332861.2014.934647.

Zhang, Yimiao, and Kim Huat Goh. 2020. "Impact of Online Reviews on Consumer Post-Purchase Attitude Change and Transaction Failure." In *40th International Conference on Information Systems, ICIS 2019*.

Zulkarnain, Zulkarnain, Eka Dj Ginting, Ferry Novliadi, and Surya Siahaan. 2019. "Outcome or Process Regret in Online Purchasing: Consequences of Brand Trust to Consumer Purchase Regret." *International Journal of Supply Chain Management*.

In: Global Challenges of Digital Transformation of Markets ISBN: 978-1-53619-754-9
Editors: E. de la Poza and S. E. Barykin   © 2021 Nova Science Publishers, Inc.

Chapter 32

DIGITAL TRENDS OF THE SHARING ECONOMY IN THE FIELD OF TOOL RENTAL

Natalia Kireeva[*], *Dmitry Zavyalov, Olga Saginova and Nadezhda Zavyalova*

Plekhanov Russian University of Economics, Moscow, Russia

ABSTRACT

The digitalization of the economy is manifested by the development of completely new markets based on the sharing of goods. The rental market is getting a new development and is becoming interesting not only for end users (on P2P platforms), but also for retail chains, which also use its capabilities. Digital platforms influence consumer behaviour and promote ideas for the sharing of goods that have "unused capacity," i.e., which are not permanently in use, such as construction tools. In our study, we compared Google.Trends searches over 5 years for "equipment rental," "tool rental," "tool for hire" and related queries around the world. The results showed that users are looking for rental tools based on their location, trading network, or P2P platform. The search for a tool for hire has a pronounced seasonality. The limitation of the study was the large scale of information presentation without detailing regional features, as well as the fact that only queries in English and Russian were studied, which makes it possible to analyse the results of queries only in English and Russian-speaking countries. The research is of interest to companies looking for new markets for products with reusability and "excess capacity."

Keywords: digitalization, retail, consumer behaviour, equipment, rental business

---

[*] Corresponding Author's Email: nskireeva@gmail.com.

1. Introduction

1.1. Sharing Economy

Sharing has long been known under the guise of renting goods, which were provided both by organizations and individuals (Belk 2010; Ertz, Durif, and Arcand 2016). However, with the advent of digital platforms, temporary use has taken absolutely new meaning. A new socio-economic model has emerged based on the temporary use of property (Böckmann 2013; Trenz, Frey, and Veit 2018; Botsman and Rogers 2010).

The volumes of the sharing economy have been growing for over ten years (Zvolska, Voytenko Palgan, and Mont 2019; Frenken and Schor 2017; Acquier, Daudigeos, and Pinkse 2017). Following the trends, the forecasts are extremely promising. So, from $ 15 billion in 2015 by 2025 revenues of the five main sectors of the sharing economy will grow to $ 335 billion (PricewaterhouseCoopers 2016).

The authors highlight different key aspects in the sharing economy. Some believe that the main thing here is temporary access to resources with underutilized capacities as an alternative to permanent ownership, and balancingthe available resources and consumer needs (Kathan, Matzler, and Veider 2016; Frenken et al., 2015; Lamberton and Rose 2012; Narasimhan et al., 2018). Others talk about the mandatory component of the sharing economy, i.e., digitalization (Barykin, Kalinina, et al. 2021; Barykin, Kapustina, Sergeev, et al. 2021; Barykin, Bochkarev, et al. 2021; Barykin, Kapustina, Valebnikova, et al. 2021; Barykin, Smirnova, Sharapaev, et al. 2021).

1.2. Digitalization

Digitization allows creating the sharing market through intermediary technology platforms. The main task of such platforms is to facilitate exchange in a network of peer-to-peer economic actors.

The sharing economy is seen as an important type of digital economy, where data is used as a key production factor. This data is used to provide temporary access to tangible and intangible resources.

Digitalization allows us to bring together users for their shared access to diverse and disparate resources, which reduces duplication and ineffective consumptionof resources (Hamari, Sjöklint, and Ukkonen 2016; Pomering 2017; Zervas, Proserpio, and Byers 2020; Belk 2010). In turn, the pooling of resources and their consumers on digital platforms reduces economic costs and helps preserve the environment. This is especially pronounced when sharing equipment and tools, when the user's need for their use is, as a rule, not permanent, and is short-term.

1.3. Tool Rental

With their "excess capacity,"tools have been leased for a long time. The leased toolsare used to reduce construction costs, since in some cases the cost of equipment and tools is up to 40% of the cost of construction (Tenepalli, Asadi, and Sai Kala 2017). Authors of the work (Xia et al., 2017) argue that many industries are increasingly relying on rented equipment and machinery.

Of course, rented equipment is subject to certain risks of damage, but the tools are being developed which design prevent financial losses for lessors. For example, work (Hung, Tsai, and Chang 2017) proposes a general strategy for preventive maintenance of leased equipment in order to minimize costs of lessors.

Lessees also bear certain risks of receiving a non-working tool. Here, digital platforms are able to generalize all available experience and provide protection for both lessors and lessees when transferring equipment for temporary use.

1.4. Search Query Statistics

Digitalization allows us to receive large amounts of information about consumer behaviour, because all user actions are recorded. This is a huge field for obtaining scientific results for researchers. One can obtain data from social networks (Geissinger et al., 2019), conduct an interpretive content analysis of interviews with participants in commodity exchange (Gurău and Ranchhod 2020), and obtain data based on the statistics of search queries.

For example, works (Charalampopoulos, Nastos, and Didaskalou 2017; Simionescu and Zimmermann 2017; Kristoufek 2013; Chumnumpan and Shi 2019) are based on the analysis of search queries. The authors managed to study tourist flows, the promotion of new products to the market, the unemployment rate, and cryptocurrency.

In our work, we will also rely on statistics of search queries to identify the level of user interest in renting tools as an indicator of the development of the sharing economy and the redistribution of consumer flows.

The objective of our research is to identify the nature and the desired method of obtaining the service of "tool rental" by Internet users.

The purpose of the study is to show digital trends in the sharing economy in the field of tool rental.

2. MATERIALS AND METHODS

We used the Google.Trends service to determine the statistics of search queries. The service allows us to determine the popularity of individual words and phrases entered by users into the Google search bar on different topics, in different regions, in different languages, for different periods.

Due to its high updateability, the data helps researchers to identify trends (Askitas 2015; Mavragani, Ochoa, and Tsagarakis 2018).

However, the use of this method has several limitations. First, the data is only available in a summary form. Secondly, the meaning of a keyword can change over time and in different regions due to the fact that Google.Trends uses a sampling method every time it generates a report (Askitas 2015; Choi and Varian 2012).

The data sample was obtained on August 30, 2020. The period of the data under consideration is the last 5 years. The popularity of search queries "equipment rental," "tool rental," "tool for hire," "arendainstrumenta," "prokatinstrumenta" (the last two expressions are for Russian-speaking users) was compared. Comparison by regions was not carried out as when analysing search query data, a restriction was imposed in the form of a national language (only English-speaking and Russian-speaking countries). In our case, we looked at the regional level of queries to identify the most global trends among English-speaking and Russian-speaking Google users.

We studied and analysed similar search queries provided by the service to identify trends in the development of tool rental services. The analysis was carried out using keywords that users use together with the studied phrases "equipment rental," "tool rental," "tool for hire," "arendainstrumenta," "prokatinstrumenta."

3. RESULTS

The overall assessment of the popularity of those search queries revealed their pronounced seasonality. (Figure 1).

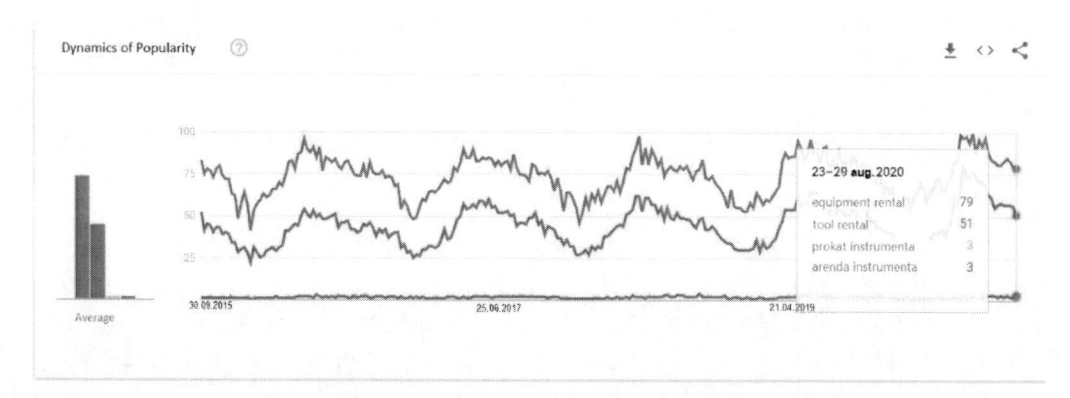

Figure 1.Trends in the popularity of search queries "equipment rental," "tool rental," "tool for hire," "arendainstrumenta," "prokatinstrumenta" over the past 5 years (30.08.2015-30.08.2020).

The demand for rental of tools increases in summer and reaches its minimum values during the New Year holidays. This is primarily due to the seasonality of the work carried out. Most of the tools that users need are used for construction,housekeeping and gardening work.

Construction work, especially related to the construction of country houses and the arrangement of adjacent territories, is mainly carried out in the summer, because most of the English and Russian-speaking countries included in the Google.Trends report are located in the temperate climate zone.

For companies that provide tools for rent, this means that the demand for construction tools is well predicted, and this allows planning capacity utilization.

As the study showed, there is a demand for tool rental not only in the construction industry, but also in medicine, the entertainment industry, and cargo transportation. Among the similar queries offered by the Google.Trends service, in addition to construction equipment and tools for minor home repairs, users are looking for medical equipment, audio and video equipment, and catering equipment.

Table 1 shows similar queries that have gained the most popularity among users.

Table 1. Related searches identified by Google.Trendsservice for the keywords "equipment rental" and "tool rental"

«Equipment rental»	«Tool rental»
Medical equipment rental near me	Tool rental center at the Home Depot
Audio visual equipment rental service	Uhaul near me
Heavy equipment rental near me	Tool rental near me now
Lawn equipment rental near me	Medela rental tool
Herc rentals	Tool rentals near me
Compact power equipment rental	Lowes tool rental near me
Equipment rental near me	Rental near me
Tools rental near me	Lowes near me
Home Depot near me	Home Depot near me
United rentals near me	Home Depot truck rental
Equipment rentals near me	Tool rental near me
Party rental equipment near me	Home Depot tool rental near me
Equipment rental places near me	Rental Stores near me
Rentals near me	Equipment rental near me
Tool rental near me	Rentals near me
Small equipment rental near me	Tool rentals at Home Depot
Equipment rental stores near me	Tool rental companies near me
Construction rental equipment near me	Tool rental places near me
Rental places near me	Sunbelt tool rental near me
Rental stores near me	Power tool rental near me
Herc equipment rental	Truck rentals near me
Rental companies near me	Home Depot rental center
Equipment rental companies near me	Rental places near me
Compact equipment rental	United tool rental near me
Equipment rental agency	Home Depot tool rental centre

4. DISCUSSION

Attention is drawn to the fact that queries indicating a specific company that provide tools for rent are extremely popular. The most popular is the largest American company Home Depot, which sells tools and building materials. Out of 50 similar queries, the company is mentioned in 8 queries (16% of the total number of similar queries and 47% of the total number of mentions of companies).

Among the companies mentioned there is Herc,which is a company that rents out climatic and compressor equipment, power generators, earth-moving machines, and cargo handling equipment. United Rentals is a group of tool retailers that provide users with tools and shop equipment. Party rental is a company that provides catering equipment, reception desks, bar counters, and other equipment that is used for various events from conferences to birthdays. U-haul is a company engaged in moving service (trucks and temporary warehouses for hire). Medela is a company focused on young mothers with babies. It leases professional breast pumps and other infant care equipment. Lowes is a home improvement retail chain. Sunbelt is a construction equipment sales company.

In addition, users also query abstract companies and sites where tools and equipment can be rented (for example, "rental places," "rental stores," "rental companies").

As a rule, users are looking for equipment rental based on their location. Almost all queries contain "near me." However, adding Google fills in the search string automatically when a user enters a search query. The user can choose from a number of proposed options, among which, as a rule, "near me" is in the first place.

The user chooses this query in order to receive equipment in the shortest possible time and with minimal delivery costs; therefore, digitalization of the tool rental market has great prospects. Thanks to digitalization, any user can get the best offers from various companies, a wider selection of equipment and tools, and also to track rental periods.

For queries in Russian, the number of proposed options for similar queries is much lower. Obviously, the motives that drive users are the same as those of users who made inquiries in English.

There is a regional peculiarity of Russian speakers: instead of "near me," users prefer to indicate their location more extensively, i.e., within the city. The search queries "prokatinstrumenta" ("tool for hire") and "arendainstrumenta"("tool rental") were specified by the search words "Omsk," "Gomel," "Ufa," "Grodno," "Chelyabinsk," "Ivanovo," "Krasnodar," or "Almaty."

The search queries were also supplemented by the indication of the companies "Oma" (Belorussia) and "Petrovich" (Russia). The number of similar queries included the Leroy Merlin Company and the Avito P2P platform.

It should be expected that the development of the rental tool market will follow the path of digitalization. With more choice, users will be more willing to take advantage of the sharing economy and increasingly rent rather than purchase the property they only need for a short period of time.

The development of smartphone apps is also driving the development of the sharing economy. With information on the available goods or services at hand, users will increasingly order food from the app, easily book accommodation or rent a car, use a tool or any other property they need for a short while.

The results of the study showed that the market for renting out instruments is quite mature, there are large players here (36% of queries contained the name of a particular company), which will be difficult for new companies to squeeze. However, digital transformation can capture the attention of users through the use of convenient applications that solve user problems.

CONCLUSION

We analysed the search queries "equipment rental," "tool rental," "tool for hire," "prokatinstrumenta" and "arendainstrumenta" and similar queries, which showed us that users are primarily interested in the quickest use of the tools with the lowest delivery costs. 76% of the queries from among similar queries contained the refinement for the keywords using the wording "near me."

Most of the users are looking for certain companies that have established themselves in the tool rental market. 36% of the queries contained the name of the company.

Tool rental is in demand in many industries, from medicine to the entertainment industry. However, their share is not large among the total number of queries: most queries are formulated around the rental of construction and garden tools. 92% of the queries concerned, in one way or another (directly, with the indication of the company or without specifying other specifics), the tool used in the construction or home improvement, and also in transportation.

When formulating queries, regional specificity appears. So, for Russian-speaking Internet users, it is typical to formulate queries indicating a wider location (city scale), while English-speaking users use geolocation and use search near their location.

Undoubtedly, digitalization will allow solving all the problems of users: obtaining the necessary equipment in the shortest possible time with minimal costs. The best way to attract user attention to new services will be the creation of digital platforms, including at the P2P level, which can compete with large trading companies.

Thus, we have solved the problem posed in the study which is to identify the nature and the desired method of obtaining the service "tool rental" by Internet users.

ACKNOWLEDGMENTS

The paper was prepared as part of the state assignment of the Ministry of Science and Higher Education No. FSSW-2020-0009 "Development of a methodology for managing the competitiveness of enterprises in the field of commodity circulation in the digital economy."

REFERENCES

Acquier, Aurélien, Thibault Daudigeos, and Jonatan Pinkse. 2017. "Promises and Paradoxes of the Sharing Economy: An Organizing Framework." *Technological Forecasting and Social Change.* https://doi.org/10.1016/j.techfore.2017.07.006.

Nikolaos Askitas. 2015. "Google Search Activity Data and Breaking Trends." *IZA World of Labor.* https://doi.org/10.15185/izawol.206.

Barykin, Sergey Yevgenievich, Andrey Aleksandrovich Bochkarev, Sergey Mikhailovich Sergeev, Tatiana Anatolievna Baranova, Dmitriy Anatolievich Mokhorov, and Aleksandra Maksimovna Kobicheva. 2021. "A Methodology of Bringing Perspective Innovation Products to Market." *Academy of Strategic Management Journal* 20 (2): 19. https://www.abacademies.org/articles/a-methodology-of-bringing-perspective-innovation-products-to-market.pdf.

Barykin, Sergey Yevgenievich, Olga Vladimirovna Kalinina, Irina Vasilievna Kapustina, Victor Andreevich Dubolazov, Cesar Armando Nunez Esquivel, Elmira Alyarovna Nazarova, and Petr Anatolievich Sharapaev. 2021. "The Sharing Economy and Digital Logistics in Retail Chains: Opportunities and Threats." *Academy of Strategic Management Journal* 20 (2): 1–14. https://www.abacademies.org/articles/the-sharing-economy-and-digital-logistics-in-retail-chains-opportunities-and-threats.pdf.

Barykin, Sergey Yevgenievich, Irina Vasilievna Kapustina, Sergey Mikhailovich Sergeev, Olga Vladimirovna Kalinina, Viktoriia Valerievna Vilken, Yuri Yevgenievich Putikhin, and Lydia Vitalievna Volkova. 2021. "Developing the Physical Distribution Digital Twin Model within the Trade Network." *Academy of Strategic Management Journal* 20 (1): 1–24. https://www.abacademies.org/articles/developing-the-physical-distribution-digital-twin-model-within-the-trade-network.pdf.

Barykin, Sergey Yevgenievich, Irina Vasilievna Kapustina, Olga Aleksandrovna Valebnikova, Natalia Viktorovna Valebnikova, Olga Vladimirovna Kalinina, Sergey Mikhailovich Sergeev, Marisa Camastral, Yuri Yevgenievich Putikhin, and Lydia Vitalievna Volkova. 2021. "Digital Technologies for Personnel Management: Implications for Open Innovations." *Academy of Strategic Management Journal* 20 (2): 1–14. https://www.abacademies.org/articles/digital-technologies-for-personnel-management-implications-for-open-innovations.pdf.

Barykin, Sergey Yevgenievich, Elena Aleksandrovna Smirnova, Petr Anatolievich Sharapaev, and Angela Bohuovna Mottaeva. 2021. "Development of the Kazakhstan Digital Retail Chains within the EAEU E-Commerce." *Academy of Strategic Management Journal* 20 (2): 1–18. https://www.abacademies.org/

articles/development-of-the-kazakhstan-digital-retail-chains-within-the-eaeu-ecommerce-market.pdf.

Belk, Russell. 2010. "Sharing." *Journal of Consumer Research*. https://doi.org/10.1086/612649.

Böckmann, Marco. 2013. "The Shared Economy: It Is Time to Start Caring about Sharing; Value Creating Factors in the Shared Economy." *1st IBA Bachelor Thesis Conference*.

Botsman, Rachel, and Roo C N - O'Neill Library Stacks (STACK) HC79 .C6 B68 2010 Rogers. 2010. "The Rise of Collaborative Consumption." In *What's Mine Is Yours: How Collaborative Consumption Is Changing the Way We Live*.

Charalampopoulos, Ioannis, Panagiotis Nastos, and Eleni Didaskalou. 2017. "Human Thermal Conditions and North Europeans' Web Searching Behavior (Google Trends) on Mediterranean Touristic Destinations." *Urban Science*. https://doi.org/10.3390/urbansci1010008.

Choi, Hyunyoung, and Hal Varian. 2012. "Predicting the Present with Google Trends." *Economic Record*. https://doi.org/10.1111/j.1475-4932.2012.00809.x.

Chumnumpan, Pattarin, and Xiaohui Shi. 2019. "Understanding New Products' Market Performance Using Google Trends." *Australasian Marketing Journal*. https://doi.org/10.1016/j.ausmj.2019.01.001.

Ertz, Myriam, Fabien Durif, and Manon Arcand. 2016. "Collaborative Consumption or the Rise of the Two-Sided Consumer." *The International Journal of Business & Management*.

Frenken, Koen, Toon Meelen, Martijn Arets, and Pieter B van de Glind. 2015. "Smarter Regulation for the Sharing Economy." *The Guardian*.

Frenken, Koen, and Juliet Schor. 2017. "Putting the Sharing Economy into Perspective." *Environmental Innovation and Societal Transitions*. https://doi.org/10.1016/j.eist.2017.01.003.

Geissinger, Andrea, Christofer Laurell, Christina Öberg, and Christian Sandström. 2019. "How Sustainable Is the Sharing Economy? On the Sustainability Connotations of Sharing Economy Platforms." *Journal of Cleaner Production*. https://doi.org/10.1016/j.jclepro.2018.09.196.

Gurău, Călin, and Ashok Ranchhod. 2020. "The Sharing Economy as a Complex Dynamic System: Exploring Coexisting Constituencies, Interests and Practices." *Journal of Cleaner Production*. https://doi.org/10.1016/j.jclepro.2019.118799.

Hamari, Juho, Mimmi Sjöklint, and Antti Ukkonen. 2016. "The Sharing Economy: Why People Participate in Collaborative Consumption." *Journal of the Association for Information Science and Technology*. https://doi.org/10.1002/asi.23552.

Hung, Wei Ting, Tzong Ru Tsai, and Yen Chang Chang. 2017. "Periodical Preventive Maintenance Contract for Leased Equipment with Random Failure Penalties." *Computers and Industrial Engineering*. https://doi.org/10.1016/j.cie.2017.09.031.

Kathan, Wolfgang, Kurt Matzler, and Viktoria Veider. 2016. "The Sharing Economy: Your Business Model's Friend or Foe?" *Business Horizons*. https://doi.org/10.1016/j.bushor.2016.06.006.

Kristoufek, Ladislav. 2013. "BitCoin Meets Google Trends and Wikipedia: Quantifying the Relationship between Phenomena of the Internet Era." *Scientific Reports.* https://doi.org/10.1038/srep03415.

Lamberton, Cait Poynor, and Randall L. Rose. 2012. "When Is Ours Better than Mine? A Framework for Understanding and Altering Participation in Commercial Sharing Systems." *Journal of Marketing.* https://doi.org/10.1509/jm.10.0368.

Mavragani, Amaryllis, Gabriela Ochoa, and Konstantinos P. Tsagarakis. 2018. "Assessing the Methods, Tools, and Statistical Approaches in Google Trends Research: Systematic Review." *Journal of Medical Internet Research.* https://doi.org/10.2196/jmir.9366.

Narasimhan, Chakravarthi, Purushottam Papatla, Baojun Jiang, Praveen K. Kopalle, Paul R. Messinger, Sridhar Moorthy, Davide Proserpio, Upender Subramanian, Chunhua Wu, and Ting Zhu. 2018. "Sharing Economy: Review of Current Research and Future Directions." *Customer Needs and Solutions.* https://doi.org/10.1007/s40547-017-0079-6.

Pomering, Alan. 2017. "Marketing for Sustainability: Extending the Conceptualisation of the Marketing Mix to Drive Value for Individuals and Society at Large." *Australasian Marketing Journal.* https://doi.org/10.1016/j.ausmj.2017.04.011.

PricewaterhouseCoopers. 2016. "The Sharing Economy. Consumer Intelligence Series, Http://Www.Pwc.Com/Cis." *PwC,* 1–30.

Simionescu, Mihaela, and Klaus F Zimmermann. 2017. "Big Data and Unemployment Analysis." *GLO Discussion Paper.*

Tenepalli, Saikumar, S. S. Asadi, and K. Sai Kala. 2017. "A Model Study on Comparative Cost Analysis of Equipment Management in Construction Companies in Tirupati Region." *International Journal of Civil Engineering and Technology.*

Trenz, Manuel, Alexander Frey, and Daniel Veit. 2018. "Disentangling the Facets of Sharing: A Categorization of What We Know and Don't Know about the Sharing Economy." *Internet Research.* https://doi.org/10.1108/IntR-11-2017-0441.

Xia, Tangbin, Lifeng Xi, Ershun Pan, Xiaolei Fang, and Nagi Gebraeel. 2017. "Lease-Oriented Opportunistic Maintenance for Multi-Unit Leased Systems under Product-Service Paradigm." *Journal of Manufacturing Science and Engineering, Transactions of the ASME.* https://doi.org/10.1115/1.4035962.

Zervas, Georgios, Davide Proserpio, and John W. Byers. 2020. "A First Look at Online Reputation on Airbnb, Where Every Stay Is above Average." *Marketing Letters.* https://doi.org/10.1007/s11002-020-09546-4.

Zvolska, Lucie, Yuliya Voytenko Palgan, and Oksana Mont. 2019. "How Do Sharing Organisations Create and Disrupt Institutions? Towards a Framework for Institutional Work in the Sharing Economy." *Journal of Cleaner Production.* https://doi.org/10.1016/j.jclepro.2019.02.057.

In: Global Challenges of Digital Transformation of Markets ISBN: 978-1-53619-754-9
Editors: E. de la Poza and S. E. Barykin   © 2021 Nova Science Publishers, Inc.

Chapter 33

REGRESSION IMPACT ANALYSIS IN DIGITAL PAYMENT SYSTEMS

Irina A. Bolotova[1,], Jerome Van Herpe[2,†] and Viacheslav P. Shkodyrev[1]*

Peter the Great St. Petersburg Polytechnic University, St. Petersburg, Russia
Network International LLC, Dubai, United Arab Emirates

ABSTRACT

In the era of the fastest growing e-commerce market, digital trade promises new opportunities but barriers in providing robust continuous delivery of improvements. Digital transformation of payment infrastructure leads to modifications in software systems used by financial institutions. Unexpected impact due to changes in such complex environments might be not properly assessed and have a negative impact on critical phases of data processing that can lead to online or financial impact. The current approach of the paper aims to minimize the risk and decrease time spent on testing by highlighting only impacted elements of the system during the release delivery. The regression impact analysis system as a solution is proposed in the paper. The JSON-based web API allows passing metadata with the recent changes info, such as functional area, type of element, classification of the system. The regression impact is implemented as a dependency tree with the sub-elements connected to the parent element. If the child element was modified then only the parent element should be tested that will help to minimize the recourses required for the testing. As an output visualization,

---

* Corresponding Author's Email: irenebolotova@gmail.com.
† Corresponding Author's Email: jerome.vanherpe@gmail.com.

the graph models are being used, which is readable for testers and release managers for better analytics and testing.

Keywords: regression impact, payment system, continuous integration, continuous delivery

1. INTRODUCTION

The regression testing is one of the most important and complex software testing methods (Chechik et al., 2009), in financial institutions even a minor change in the software may require rerunning all the set of test cases and as well as test cases designed for that particular change (Sajeev and Wibowo 2003). The main resource usage that is planned to be minimized during the regression testing is the allowable time budget (Orso, Apiwattanapong, and Harrold 2003). All test cases covering the changed components and its affected components must be retested to gain confidence in provided services and lower risk of financial loss (Stachová et al., 2020; Glukhov and Tukkel 2019; Starodubtsev and Starodubstev 2019).

The main goal of the proposed algorithm is to identify and test the part of the software that is affected by the specified change. To visually represent the dependency tree of related elements a software architecture modeling tool "Structurizr" is being used. It is a tool for interactive graphic presentation of elements and its relationships, views, documentation, and decision models (Brown 2015).

The purpose of this study was to developan impact analysis solution that can be used across a variety of systems. At this stage in the research, metrics, stages of the implementation process, workflow, software that was used for practical implementation were proposed.

1.1. Research Problem Coverage

As an example, functional areas in the payment industry can be like Card Embossing, Card Issuance or Account On boarding and many others. If any logic in the functional area is modified then the entire functional process should be tested to avoid any failure during processing. If that particular functional area does not have any downwards dependency to other functional areas then testing time can be shortened up to the time of current functional area testing only, reducing both cost and time to market.

On the other hand, the regression impact can be highlighted not only among functional areas but on dependent elements of the automated processing workflow.

As a sequence of processing steps, starting from data preparation, conversion, analysis and reporting, one change in the process could lead to a bug in the system. As an example, can be given the change in the number of input files from the client which could lead to the failures of at least 3 steps in related systems – transferring, loading, transaction processing. To avoid failures of the working mechanism, regression impact analysis should be known.

1.2. Worldwide Statistic

As a sphere of research is the Middle East and Africa (MEA) financial market as one of the largest and fast-developing markets in the digital payments industry. Nowadays it has an overall structural migration from cash to digital payments. The global number of digital transactions has grown from 326 billion in 2012 to 504 billion in 2017. As a proportion, the number of transactions in MEA in 2017 was 14 per cent, which is expected to increase to 20 per cent. in 2022. Compared to the world's market, it is still the lowest global proportion of digital transactions as North America and Europe with 74 per cent. and 51 per cent. digital transactions, respectively (Brown 2015).

MEA region has the fewest number of cards per adult, and has a growth potential (defined as the population-weighted average of North America and Europe divided by the MEA metric) of nine times its current number. The MEA region has the fewest POS and ATM transactions per adult per annum, with a growth potential of 22 times its current number (Edgar 2016).

1.3. Digital Payment Transformation

In addition to non-traditional payment systems, the digital payments market is characterized by rapid technological change, the introduction of new products and services, including e-commerce services, mobile payment applications, alternative payment systems, prepaid services, changing industry standards, changing consumer needs and the emergence of unconventional competitors or consolidation of solutions across geographies. These projects carry risks associated with any development effort, including cost overruns, delivery delays, performance issues, and market rejection of new or innovative services. Any delay in the provision of new services or failure to differentiate services or accurately predict and meet market demand could lead to its services being less desirable to customers or perhaps even obsolete (Verevka, Gutman, and Shmatko 2019; Wang et al., 2016; Bataev 2018; Afonasova 2018).

In addition, new or innovative services are designed to process complex transactions and provide information about these transactions, all in very large volumes and at very high processing speeds. Any failure to provide an efficient and secure service, or any performance issue that occurs when using a new or innovative product or service, could result in significant processing or reporting errors or other losses (Mei et al., 2009; Liu et al., 2012; Zhai, Jiang, and Chan 2014).

2. MATERIALS AND METHODS

2.1. System Description

Given a complex multi-application system based on different components, each of those developed by vendor organizations. Applications are managed by different teams to complete the implementation of new requirements or bug fixing. But since each developer has only knowledge of its area of development, once his part is completed, it is critical to identify the regression impact and any dependent changes that should be done in other related applications. A solution for this challenge can be envisioned as a dependency meta-data driven system that provides the regression impact analyses.

To define the scope of testing, our innovation in the current study is the placement of JSON codebase annotations in a commit message that can be used to create, store, and manage a graph model of the system's program elements. The article (Pektor, Walek, and Martinik 2020) also describes the hierarchical competency model data model and the mapping process to/from JSON format. The proposed approach uses the technique of dynamic data structures. In our study, a hierarchical competency model is used to create a regression analysis of the impact on a changed element of the system.

Visualization through oriented graph modeling has been selected for better understanding, ease of use and reporting to less technical parties. A node represents a functional area and other components in the system. Meta-data of the node gives additional information about the application the item belongs to, type of the component and description of its functionality.

The tool relies on analytics of any recent code changes to identify impacted functionality of the system. This method highlights all the changed areas of the software system which could be affected by the modification. The method then annotates parts of hybrid multi applications solution by marking recent code changes and propagating the impact of these recent changes. It then creates a change impact graph to determine what areas might have been affected by certain changes to help maintainers rapidly establish a testing plan or pinpoint the source of a bug given the reported location of a failure. The maintainer needs to only examine the marked-up functions instead of going through all the functions.

2.2. Version Control

Git is a widely used version control system that allows users to interactively track changes to code or files. Software engineers can use Git to make new edits with the ability to revert to any previous version of the code. This way, all other developers working on the same project can view the development history and see the changes made (Zhao et al., 2019). The required set commit message contains the Atlassian Jira ticket number for the associated management task and a description of done development changes that can be written whenever the user commits a new version of the code. In addition, Git is a distributed revision control system that allows each team member to facilitate collaboration between developers and merge changes from different branches into releases to perform testing and deliver release artifacts to production.

Historical changes to a function can be modeled as a sequence, where each element corresponds to the source code of the function after each particular change. Tracking the impact of historical code changes on each step of development can improve the testing by highlighting the elements that were modified. In the described system, the tracking is done by Bitbucket Server "Stash" that is a combination of Git server and web interface product. It allows users review, merge code, while controlling read and write access to the code.

The version control system stores change history of each function ever-present in the system, when it was added, modified, and deleted. Information on the developers who have performed these actions is stored as well. Impact-annotations can be very useful in these situations. Right after the change is committed, certain developers can be informed that the code they are responsible for could be affected by such commit, and they might be more inclined to check it for correctness. Further, this information is handled to the testing team that can perform all levels of testing.

2.3. Functional Area

A functional area is defined as a software feature implementing a particular set of business requirements (e.g., a report, an incoming interface, a business logic). The set of functional area covers the organization business offering and serves multiple purposes such as system documentation, sales material and impact analysis.

2.4. Codebase Annotation

While efficient code writing can be considered self-documented at developer level, at organizational level this is severely insufficient. Annotating code blocks such as functions and scripts can achieve better results. Below is given the template of such annotation.

```
{
"ni_impact":{
"name":<package name>,
"functional_area":[<List of functional areas related to code block>],
"regression_impact":[<Placeholder for regression impact - Can be used for documenting unobvious use of the code block>]
}
}
```

JSON notation was used to simplify the development of the downwards system using this information. Example:

```
{
"ni_impact":{
"name":"CUST_CARD_INFO",
"functional_area":["Card Production","CardEmbossing","Virtual Card Creation"],
"regression_impact":[]
}
}
```

Linking code blocks to specific functional area provides several benefits, such as increased code quality (one code block achieves one purpose), increased code maintainability through documentation and simplified future change impact analysis.

2.5. Use Case Description

When a developer commits a change, the meta-data surrounding the modified block of code is provided in the commit message, entering the version control system (VCS). Using built-in VCS commands, the collection of commits between two versions can be obtained, providing the list of all impacted areas. This list is then passed through the dependency model for enrichment and visualization by Structurizr.

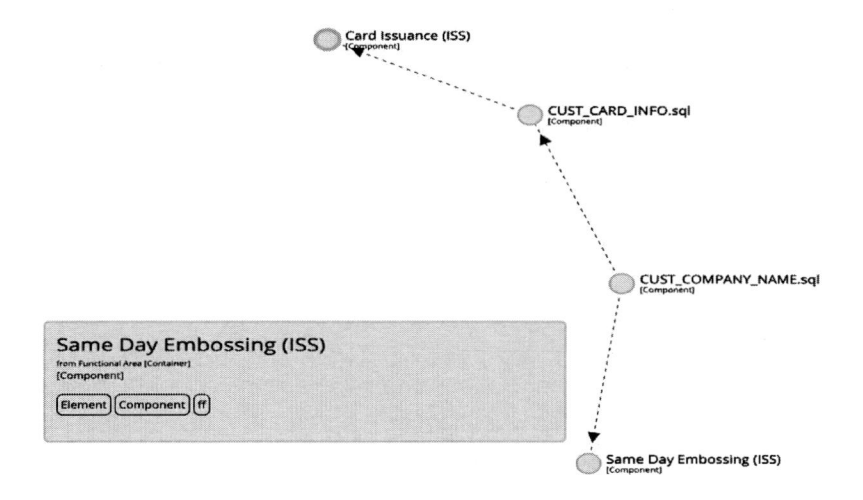

Figure 1. A figure represents components dependencies of the release that need to be tested.

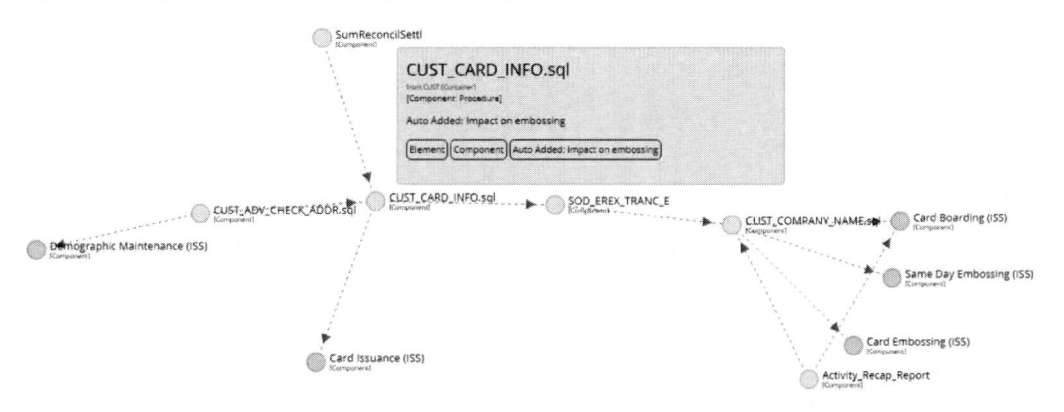

Figure 2. A figure represents the dependency graph model created automatically based on the JSON description.

Created diagrams reflect real structures and the mapping between elements of the system. From the backend the mapping and element's description are written in JSON format. And as Structurizr is a "software as a service," it provides a web-based platformfor publishing software architecture diagrams via a JSON-based web API, or a modelling UI (see Figure 1).

2.6. Dependency Model

Formally, for a function F we define set of parameters F(f1,f2,..fk) that can be annotated with metadata about the change such as a functional area, type of element, classification of the system where it is being used. The number of characteristics can be extended based on the requirements (see Figure 2).

As a relationship parameter mentioned type of the dependency it can be a functional area relation that links functional areas with the item or the impact relationship - the link of another item that has a regression effect on the modification. The regression impact link works in both directions - from the sub-element to the parent element. If the child element was modified then only the parent element should be tested. If the parent element has its own parent dependency then it should be tested as well - it will grow the graph tree till the head of sequence dependency.

3. RESULTS

As a visual demonstration the graph models were involved in the process of better understanding of impact. Data visualization is readable for testers and release managers, allowing to provide safe and valuable positive input in the digitalization of trade networks and global markets (see Figure 3).

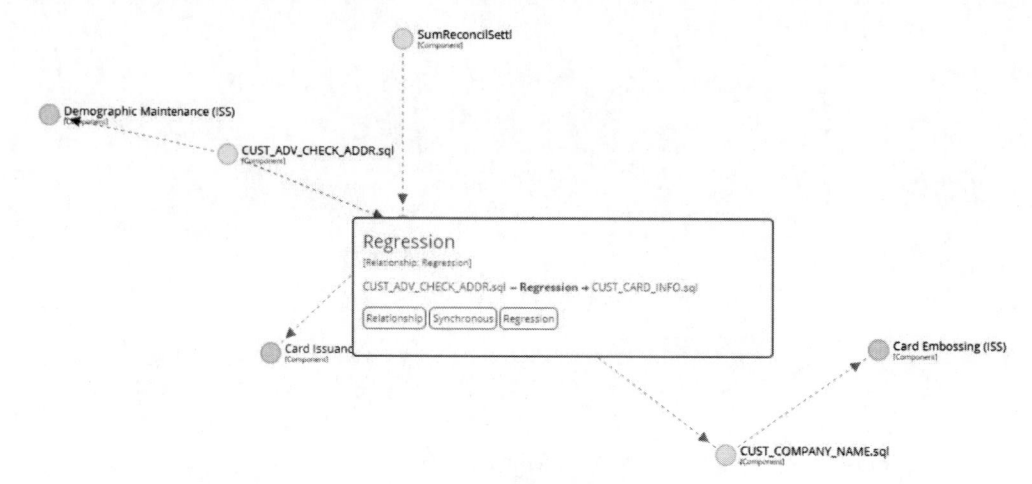

Figure 3. A figure represents the dependency graph model created automatically based on the JSON description.

4. DISCUSSION

The problem of regression impact analysis is a worldwide area of interest in various application areas. Since all systems are unique various solutions can be proposed to analyze the impact of changes that help prioritize test cases for regression testing. One of them is a method for identifying multidimensional dependencies based on cutting off processes. Process slicing can handle multidimensional dependencies efficiently. The proposed algorithm handles cases where any change in one action leads to a change in two or more artifacts. The time budget for regression testing is usually less, so it is impractical to rerun all the tests of the old software along with additional tests for the changed part. The level of detail considered in the studies refers to the method level. This is one of the empirical studies that is directly related to cost-benefit analysis (Park, Kim, and Bae 2009). Another option can be a framework that helps define root cause analysis and change impact analysis for configuration management databases (CMDB) (Krasyuk et al., 2019; Ortu et al., 2020; Parashar, Bhatia, and Kalia 2011). CMDB is used to store various types of information such as hardware, software and services provided by an organization. All necessary information is recorded for each component (Wang et al., 2015). The proposed structure serves to find the root cause of component failure and to identify the set of components that are affected by a change in a particular component (Nadi et al., 2009). In the study, an algorithm was proposed that consistently works with a hierarchical structure and determines the importance of the module for the system using the acyclic graph (Ma and Zhao 2008).

CONCLUSION

Changes in complex financial systems might lead to issues caused by unexpected regression impact or incomplete testing coverage resulting in financial or reputational losses for the organization. To minimize the risk and decrease time spent on testing, an analytic system highlighting the relations between elements of the system assistingthe regression impact analysis was proposed. The metrics proposed in this study, tools for the data analytics and graphical representations have the valuable impact on discovering the relationship between elements and to complete regression testing accordingly. The current research can be expanded by applying the algorithm to programs of different sizes, types and complexity.

REFERENCES

[1] Afonasova, Margarita A. 2018. "Digital Transformation of the Entrepreneurship: Challenges and Prospects." *Journal of Entrepreneurship Education.*

[2] Bataev, Alexey V. 2018. "Analysis and Development the Digital Economy in the World." In *Proceedings of the 31st International Business Information Management Association Conference, IBIMA 2018: Innovation Management and Education Excellence through Vision 2020.*

[3] Brown, Simon. 2015. *"Software Architecture Diagrams Should Be Maps of Your Source Code - DZone Integration."* 2015. https://dzone.com/articles/software-architecture-diagrams-should-be-maps-of-y.

[4] Chechik, Marsha, Winnie Lai, Shiva Nejati, Jordi Cabot, Zinovy Diskin, Steve Easterbrook, Mehrdad Sabetzadeh, and Rick Salay. 2009. "Relationship-Based Change Propagation: A Case Study." In *Proceedings - International Conference on Software Engineering.* https://doi.org/10.1109/MISE.2009.5069890.

[5] Edgar, Dunn. 2016. *"Advanced Payments Report."*

[6] Glukhov, Vacslav V., and I. L. Tukkel. 2019. "The Northern Dimension: The Problem of Spatial Development and the Capabilities of Online Technology." In

IOP Conference Series: Earth and Environmental Science. https://doi.org/10. 1088/1755-1315/302/1/012075.

[7]   Krasyuk, Irina, Yulia Medvedeva, Vladimir Baharev, and Grigory Chargaziya. 2019. "Evolution of Strategies of Retail and Technological Systems under Broad Digitalization Conditions." In *IOP Conference Series: Materials Science and Engineering*. https://doi.org/10.1088/1757-899X/497/1/012124.

[8]   Liu, Heng, Yongnian Zhou, Zheng Jiang, Songqi Gu, Xiangjun Wei, Yuying Huang, Yang Zou, and Hongjie Xu. 2012. "QXAFS System of the BL14W1 XAFS Beamline at the Shanghai Synchrotron Radiation Facility." *Journal of Synchrotron Radiation*. https://doi.org/10.1107/S0909049512038873.

[9]   Ma, Zengkai, and Jianjun Zhao. 2008. "Test Case Prioritization Based on Analysis of Program Structure." In *Proceedings - Asia-Pacific Software Engineering Conference, APSEC*.

[10] Mei, Lijun, Zhenyu Zhang, W. K. Chan, and T. H. Tse. 2009. "Test Case Prioritization for Regression Testing of Service-Oriented Business Applications." In *WWW'09 - Proceedings of the 18th International World Wide Web Conference*. https://doi.org/10.1145/1526709.1526830.

[11] Nadi, Sarah, Ric Holt, Ian Davis, and Serge Mankovskii. 2009. "DRACA: Decision Support for Root Cause Analysis and Change Impact Analysis for CMDBs." In *Proceedings of the 2009 Conference of the Center for Advanced Studies on Collaborative Research, CASCON '09*. https://doi.org/10.1145/1723028. 1723030.

[12] Orso, Alessandro, Taweesup Apiwattanapong, and Mary Jean Harrold. 2003. "Leveraging Field Data for Impact Analysis and Regression Testing." In *Proceedings of the ACM SIGSOFT Symposium on the Foundations of Software Engineering*. https://doi.org/10.1145/940071.940089.

[13] Ortu, Marco, Giuseppe Destefanis, Daniel Graziotin, Michele Marchesi, and Roberto Tonelli. 2020. "How Do You Propose Your Code Changes? Empirical Analysis of Affect Metrics of Pull Requests on GitHub." *IEEE Access*. https://doi.org/10.1109/ACCESS.2020.3002663.

[14] Parashar, Prem, Rajesh Bhatia, and Arvind Kalia. 2011. "Change Impact Analysis: A Tool for Effective Regression Testing." In *Communications in Computer and Information Science*. https://doi.org/10.1007/978-3-642-19423- 8_17.

[15] Park, Seunghun, Hyeonjeong Kim, and Doo Hwan Bae. 2009. "Change Impact Analysis of a Software Process Using Process Slicing." In *Proceedings - International Conference on Quality Software*. https://doi.org/10.1109/QSIC. 2009.54.

[16] Pektor, Ondrej, Bogdan Walek, and Ivo Martinik. 2020. "An Approach for Creating Data Structure of a Hierarchical Competency Model." In *Advances in Intelligent Systems and Computing*. https://doi.org/10.1007/978-3-030-51974-2_11.

[17] Sajeev, A. S. M., and Bugi Wibowo. 2003. "Regression Test Selection Based on Version Changes of Components." In *Proceedings - Asia-Pacific Software*

Engineering Conference, APSEC. https://doi.org/10.1109/APSEC.2003.1254360.

[18] Stachová, Katarína, Zdenko Stacho, Dagmar Cagánová, and Augustín Starecek. 2020. "Use of Digital Technologies for Intensifying Knowledge Sharing." *Applied Sciences (Switzerland).* https://doi.org/10.3390/app10124281.

[19] Starodubtsev, Gennady, and Yuri Starodubstev. 2019. "Quality of Digital Information Resources in Condition of Global Info-Telecommunication System Multifaceted Management." In *IOP Conference Series: Materials Science and Engineering.* https://doi.org/10.1088/1757-899X/497/1/012135.

[20] Verevka, Tatiana V., Svetlana S. Gutman, and Alexey Shmatko. 2019. "Prospects for Innovative Development of World Automotive Market in Digital Economy." In *ACM International Conference Proceeding Series.* https://doi.org/10.1145/3372177.3373320.

[21] Wang, Hongda, Jianchun Xing, Qiliang Yang, Deshuai Han, and Xuewei Zhang. 2015. "Modification Impact Analysis Based Test Case Prioritization for Regression Testing of Service-Oriented Workflow Applications." In *Proceedings - International Computer Software and Applications Conference.* https://doi.org/10.1109/COMPSAC.2015.11.

[22] Wang, Hongda, Jianchun Xing, Qiliang Yang, Wei Song, and Xuewei Zhang. 2016. "Generating Effective Test Cases Based on Satisfiability modulo Theory Solvers for Service-Oriented Workflow Applications." *Software Testing Verification and Reliability.* https://doi.org/10.1002/stvr.1592.

[23] Zhai, Ke, Bo Jiang, and W. K. Chan. 2014. "Prioritizing Test Cases for Regression Testing of Location-Based Services: Metrics, Techniques, and Case Study." *IEEE Transactions on Services Computing.* https://doi.org/10.1109/TSC.2012.40.

[24] Zhao, Ying, Yongnian Zhou, Chun Hu, Xiangzhi Zhang, and Zhaohong Zhang. 2019. "Git-Based Version Control for Beamline Control System at the Shanghai Synchrotron Radiation Facility." In *2018 5th International Conference on Systems and Informatics, ICSAI 2018.* https://doi.org/10.1109/ICSAI.2018.8599515.

In: Global Challenges of Digital Transformation of Markets ISBN: 978-1-53619-754-9
Editors: E. de la Poza and S. E. Barykin   © 2021 Nova Science Publishers, Inc.

Chapter 34

DIAGNOSTICS AND FORECASTING OF BUSINESS PROCESSES IN THE SERVICE SECTOR AS A TOOL FOR STRATEGIC PLANNING AND DEVELOPMENT OF THE CONSUMER MARKET IN THE ECONOMY OF THE REGION

Olga Lukhovskaya, Tatyana Kochetkova[*]
and Yana Zhukova
Plekhanov Russian University of Economic,
Ivanovo branch, Ivanovo, Russia

ABSTRACT

The objective basis for the gradual transition of the society to a qualitatively new state from an industrial to a digital economy is scientific knowledge and information about qualitative changes in business processes in all spheres of society. The article presents the scientific results obtained by the authors in a specific area of commodity-money circulation, to be more concrete, in the consumer market. Revealing the economic matter of the consumer market, the authors give its definition from the process approach position. For effective strategic planning of the regional consumer market development, the authors propose a technique for diagnosing and forecasting its development using information technologies. This technique, in addition to a comprehensive assessment of the state of the consumer market, makes it possible to forecast the development of its business processes and develop recommendations for improving the efficiency of its functioning for enlarged groups of types of economic activities in the service sector. As an example, in the article the forecast of the GRP

[*] Corresponding Author's Email: rumyantsevat@rambler.ru.

of the Ivanovo region was carried out according to one of the cost indicators of the efficiency of the business processes functioning of the consumer market. Forecasting the development of these business processes in the context of the digitalization of the economy is an absolute necessity and an effective tool for regulating the regional consumer market.

Keywords: business processes, digitalization of the economy, regional consumer market, strategic planning

1. INTRODUCTION

The analysis of scientific literature made it possible to identify the following approaches to the definition of the concept of the "consumer market" (Lukhovskaya et al., 2019).

According to the marketing approach, which has a socially-oriented focus, the regional consumer market should be defined as a mechanism for regulating the processes of interaction between consumers, sellers and intermediaries, which is formed depending on the characteristics of consumer preferences and motivations (Kotler and Armstrong 2018).

According to the institutional approach, the regional consumer market is interpreted as a system of institutions that facilitate its functioning. First of all, we are talking about the institution of private ownership of the means of production and the institution of entrepreneurship. The degree of their development allows us to assess the level of their influence on the state of the competitive environment of the consumer market in modern Russia and the role of the trade sphere in its development at the regional level (Cooper, Schiff, and Winters 2003; Bernard and Moxnes 2018; Akkoyunlu 2015).

Within the framework of the reproductive approach, the regional consumer market is considered as a form of organizing the sphere of circulation and ensuring the interconnection of regional production, distribution, exchange and consumption (the classic approach developed by K. Marx) (Aleksandrov, Fedorova, and Parshukov 2020a; 2020b).

According to the economic approach, the consumer market is characterized as "... a system of commodity-money circulations and organizational-economic relations that are formed in the process of sale and purchase. For the development of these relations, there are the most appropriate natural and socio-economic conditions for running business with the aim of meeting the ultimate needs and requirements of the population" (Hoeinghaus et al., 2009; Neretina et al., 2016).

The above mentioned definitions of the concept of "consumer market" indicate its ambiguity in interpretation, whereas they are given on the basis of a certain range of research tasks of scientists-authors.

In the authors' opinion, the regional consumer market should be viewed from the process approach position, identifying business processes in it. The process approach to management has become more and more popular in the recent years, the advantage of its application lies in the continuity of management, which it provides at the junction of individual processes within their system, as well as in their combination and interaction.

The analysis of the scientists-economists' works made it possible to identify more than ten different definitions of a business process, depending on the emphasis of scientists on various properties of the business process.

Initially, the process was understood as "any kind of activity in the work of the organization." This is the definition proposed by W. Deming (Deming 1984).

The next group of scientists (M. Porter, T. Davenport, M. Hammer, J. Champy, EZ Zinder, etc.) are inclined to consider a business process as a system of activities (an ordered set of activities), in which must be "input" (process resources) and "output" (final product for the consumer of the process).

Thus, M. Porter thinks that "a business process is an entity defined through points of input and output, interfaces and organizational devices, partially including the devices of the consumer of services / goods, in which the cost of the produced service / product increases" (Porter 1985b; 1985a).

Nowadays, the generally accepted definition of a business process is given in the international standard of the quality system ISO 9000 "process is a system of interrelated or interacting activities that transform inputs into outputs" (ISO 2015; Teeluckdharry 2008).

According to the authors, within the framework of the process approach to management, the regional consumer market should be defined as a system of business processes in the service sector, representing a system of various types of economic activity, in which the resources used at the input are reproduced in the form of goods and services at the output in order to satisfy the final needs and the needs of the region population within the framework of commodity-money circulation.

Analysis of scientific literature has shown that according to the most common classification, the following types of business processes of an enterprise are distinguished as:

- obligatory processes are processes directly related to the production of products or the providing of services;
- auxiliary processes are processes aimed at ensuring the continuous functioning of the main processes;
- - development processes are processes associated with qualitative changes in the activities of the enterprise and its improvement;
- management processes are aimed at effective control of the above-mentioned business processes of the enterprise.

On the basis of this study, it was also revealed that the issue of classifying business processes in the consumer market is not well developed. Existing scientific works are limited to the selection of business processes of trade enterprises. We want to point out that this area is one of the main segments of the consumer market.

Studying the regional consumer market in terms of the process approach to management, it is necessary to introduce a classification of its business processes (author's edition):

- obligatory processes are processes that generate incomes directly related to the providing of services;
- auxiliary processes are processes that support the infrastructure of the consumer market;
- development processes are processes associated with qualitative changes in the consumer market and its improvement;
- management processes are aimed at efficient control of the above-presented business processes of the consumer market.

On the basis of the proposed classification, it becomes possible to carry out effective diagnostics and strategic planning of the development of the regional consumer market and form business plans of economic objects.

2. MATERIALS AND METHODS

The analysis of scientific literature made it possible to identify the following technique's guidances for assessing the development of the consumer market, which are of greatest interest to the authors.

Demyanenko (Demyanenko 2019) proposes a technique for the study of the local consumer market, the main point of which is the application of the calculational and constructive method in conjunction with multivariate correlation and regression analysis. To justify the regression model of the dependence of the gross regional product (Y, balls) for the analysis such factors as the turnover of the consumer market (X1), the volume of industrial production (X2), the volume of agricultural production (X3), the number of people employed in the economy (X4), security of investments with loans (X5) are taken into consideration (formula 1):

$$Y = -15.4 + 0.21X_1 + 0.159X_2 + 0.262X_3 + 0.443X_4 + 7.484E - 02X_5 \tag{1}$$

R. R. Galieva and V. M. Timiryanova developed a technique for assessing the consumer market and forecasting the retail trade turnover of a trading enterprise (Galieva 2008). The technique involves forecasting the turnover of an enterprise, taking into account changes in the total sectoral volume of turnover in the consumer market in the context of product groups.

The basis of the comprehensive technique for diagnosing the state of the consumer market and assessing its real volume, proposed by A.E. Chusova, is made up of economic-statistical, graphic and mathematical methods (Chusova 2011). The author proposes to diagnose the state of the consumer market based on the assessment: the potential of the consumer market and its security, the competitiveness of domestic goods and manufacturers, food security, etc.

In order to form an assessment system of indicators of business processes in the regional consumer market, the authors reviewed the economic literature on the issue of indicators of the effectiveness of business processes, which showed the lack of a unified approach to the composition of indicators.

Analysis of the existing classifications of the efficiency indicators of enterprise business processes made it possible to identify two ways of their formation. The first way is associated with the allocation of groups of indicators in accordance with the characteristics of the process - cost indicators, time indicators, etc. (V. K. Chaadaev, S. M. Kovalev, V. M. Kovalev, A. S. Kozlov, K. K. Chuprov and others). The second way is associated with the definition of groups of indicators for assessing various elements of the business process - process indicators, product indicators, resource indicators, process satisfaction indicators, etc. (V. G. Eliferov, V. V. Repin, etc.). According to the authors, the most comprehensive system is the system of indicators for assessing the effectiveness of business processes proposed by V. G. Eliferov and V. V. Repin. The authors consider that both components of the assessment of business processes should be used in diagnosing business processes of the regional consumer market.

3. RESULTS

For the effective strategic planning of the regional consumer market development, it is necessary to apply the technique of diagnostics and forecasting of its development proposed by the authors (Siró et al., 2008; Martin and Schouten 2014; Hanson 2005). This technique, in addition to a comprehensive assessment of the state of the consumer market, makes it possible to forecast the development of its business processes and work out the recommendations for improving the efficiency of its functioning for enlarged groups of types of economic activities in the service sector.

The algorithm of such a technique can be represented by consistent implementation of the following stages:

1) structural analysis of the municipality consumer market for enlarged groups of types of economic activities in the service sector;
2) collecting and logical analysis of statistical data in a specifically analyzed group of economic activities in the service sector of business processes types;
3) development of a system for assessing business processes for enlarged groups of types of economic activities in the service sector (differentiated) and the regional consumer market (in general);

4) assessment of the state of business processes of the regional consumer market, identification of business process violations;
5) forecast of the development of business processes of the regional consumer market;
6) the adoption of preventive measures to regulate the business processes of the regional consumer market.

Let us make a more detailed review of the stages of this technique.

Stage 1. Structural analysis of the municipality consumer market for enlarged groups of types of economic activity in the service sector. For example, we are talking about the following groups of the consumer market:

- Transport and communications;
- Trade and commercial activities for the sale of goods and services;
- Hotels and restaurants;
- Operations with real estate, rent;
- Education;
- Health care and social services;
- Other communal, social, personal services.

Stage 2. Collecting and logical analysis of statistical data in a particular analyzed group of economic activity in the service sector by types of business processes: obligatory processes, auxiliary processes, development processes, management processes.

At this stage information on the state of business processes by type of economic activity is collected and processed. Based on the data obtained, the existing structure of business processes is built and their procedures are defined.

Stage 3. Development of a system for assessing business processes of the regional consumer market. This stage is the direct formation of a mechanism for assessing the business processes of the regional consumer market. To conduct a comprehensive assessment of business processes, as mentioned earlier, it is rational to assess them according to various parameters. The authors offer the following assessment parameters: cost, quality, velocity and structure.

Based on the analysis of existing systems for assessing business processes, we have developed a system of indicators designed to assess the effectiveness of business processes in the regional consumer market, presented in the form of a matrix (Table 1). This assessment system is based on an integrated approach and includes:

- assessment of business processes for enlarged groups of types of economic activities in the service sector (differentiated);
- assessment of the regional consumer market (as a whole).

**Table 1. Grouping of the indicators of business process parameters
of the regional consumer market**

Types of business processes of the regional consumer market	Business process parameters			
	cost(C)	quality(Q)	velocity(V)	structure(S)
I. Obligatory business processes (O)	group OC	group OQ	group OV	group OS
II. Auxiliary business processes(A)	group AC	group AQ	group AV	group AS
III. Management business processes (M)	group MC	group MQ	group MV	group RS
IV. Development business processes (D)	group DC	group DQ	group DV	group DS

We want to give you a brief description of each group. Using the indicators of the OC, AC, MC, DC group, the rationality of financial injections into the business processes of the regional consumer market, including the resource intensity and profitability of the process, is assessed.

Based on the indicators of the OQ, AQ, MQ, DQ groups, it is necessary to analyze the achievement of the assigned tasks at various stages of the business processes of the regional consumer market, that is, the quality of services provided by minimizing costs.

Using the indicators of the OV, AV, MV, DV group, the degree of compliance with the established deadlines for completing the stages of business processes of the regional consumer market is assessed.

The OS, AS, MS, DS group includes indicators that characterize various structural aspects of business processes in the regional consumer market. Depending on the goals of assessing the business processes of the regional consumer market, various parameters can be selected as the primary ones. In our opinion, such parameters for assessing business processes as cost, quality, velocity are of the greatest importance for improving the performance of the regional consumer market.

Stage 4. Assessment of the state of business processes in the regional consumer market, identification of business process violations. Initially, at this stage, all the indicators of the matrix are calculated. Then integral indicators are calculated for each type of business process.

The assessment of the state of business processes of the regional consumer market is made according to the selected parameters on the basis of comparing the obtained value of integral indicators with the recommended ones. For this purpose, a scale for assessing the state of business processes by the values of integral indicators is being developed. If the obtained values of the integral indicators are within acceptable limits, then the state of business processes is recognized as acceptable. Then the indicators which values are below the established limits are defined. Further, the reasons for inconsistencies and, therefore, ineffectively performed procedures in the business process are determined.

At the conclusion of the fourth stage, aggregate integral indicators are calculated as a whole for the types of business processes of the consumer market, taking into account the calculated indicators for all enlarged groups of types of economic activities in the service sector. It allows to establish the efficiency (amount) of the functioning of all elements of business processes at the input and output.

Stage 5. Forecast of the development of business processes in the regional consumer market. We propose to forecast business processes using the NeuroShell program, the principle of which is to use neural network technologies, as well as by constructing a regression equation. Forecasting of business processes will allow to describe their expected state in the next cycle (but without taking into account the influence of force majeure circumstances).

Stage 6. Taking some preventive measures to regulate business processes of the regional consumer market. Based on the information obtained in this way, municipal authorities will anticipate the possibility of violations in the business processes of the regional consumer market, which means they will be able to take preventive measures to prevent them.

4. DISCUSSION

At the present stage Russian consumer market has turned into a destructed economic system with disproportions in the level of functioning of its individual elements especially at the regional level. In this connection, the assessment of the efficiency of business processes for enlarged groups of types of economic activities in the service sector carried out locally makes it possible to assess the efficiency of business processes in the consumer market, taking into account the specific indicators characteristic of a given industry (department).

It allows to define the consumer market as a business process and to consider its entity through the points of input and output of a specific system, to assess the efficiency of the reproduction of resources in the form of goods and services and to determine at the output the level of satisfaction of the final needs and needs of the population of the region within the framework of commodity money circulation both for enlarged groups of types of economic activity in the service sector, and in the consumer market as a whole (Koblov, Blinov, and Shiryaev 2005; Blinov and Koblov 2006; Koblov, Shiryaev, and Blinov 2006).

The entity of business processes is also determined through interfaces and organizational devices, partially including the devices of the consumer of services / goods in a specific area of the consumer market. In this case, the efficiency of the business process in each enlarged group and in the consumer market as a whole can be assessed by the volume of "increasing the cost of the produced service / product" in this area and in the region (municipality), respectively.

Profound research and application of modern tools and approaches to assessing the business processes of the regional consumer market by various parameters will make it possible to use the principles of strategic management more fully (Teece 2010; Alvarez 2007).

The use of information technologies in the calculation of the complex system of indicators proposed by the authors, which are used in the technique for diagnosing and predicting the development of business processes in the regional consumer market, will allow to fulfill its effective strategic planning in the context of the digitalization of the economy.

CONCLUSION

Based on the application of this technique, the authors made a forecast of the GRP of the Ivanovo region, this indicator was chosen as a single indicator for assessing the effectiveness of the main(obligatory) business processes by type of economic activity (O) according to the cost parameter (C) - OS group of the proposed matrix.

The forecast was made by constructing a regression equation, where the main processes of the regional consumer market acted as factor indicators, and the GRP of the Ivanovo region was the resultant indicator:

Y - GRP of the Ivanovo region;
X1 - transport and communication services;
X2 - trade and commercial activities for the sale of goods and services;
X3 - hotel and restaurant services;
X4 - operations with real estate, leasing activities;
X5 - educational services;
X6 - health care and social services;
X7 - other utilities, social, personal services.

In this case, the data from the russian federal statistics service were used.

The initial data for the research are presented in Table 2.

The consumer market comprehensive analysis of the Ivanovo region made it possible to come to the following conclusions: during the Soviet period of time the industrially developed Ivanovo region is currently undergoing structural transformations in social production and changes in the organic structure of capital towards an increase in the turnover of the service sector, which clearly demonstrates the diversification of the economic development of the region (Ananiev, Lukhovskaya, and Vasilchuk 2017).

The decline in the volume of material production and the turnover of the industrial infrastructure of the Ivanovo region from 56.7% (2000) to 27.6% (2018) directly affected the decrease in the share of industries producing goods in the GRP structure.

Table 2. Forecast of the development of the main business processes of the consumer market by enlarged groups of economic activity types according to value indicator (GRP)

Years	GRP, billion roubles	Producing service industries	Enlarged economic activity types, %						
			among them						
			Transport and communication services	Trade and commercial activities for the sale of goods and services	Hotel and restaurant services	Operations with real estate, leasing activities	Educational services	Health care and social services	Other utilities, social, personal services
t	Y	Y	X_1	X_2	X_3	X_4	X_5	X_6	X_7
2000	18.09	43.3	6.1	11.9	2.1	14.4	3	4	1.8
2006	55.09	57.9	12.4	15.0	1.0	14.2	5.3	7.4	2.6
2015	170.02	69.9	7.5	25.1	1.4	21.4	5.2	7.1	2.2
2018	164.10	72.4	7.9	24.9	3.2	20.6	5.9	8.2	1.8
Forecasting value indicators									
2020	191.25	76.8	7.2	27.0	4.3	21.9	6.2	8.6	1.7
2021	204.8	78.8	6.7	28.0	4.8	22.5	6.3	8.8	1.6
2022	218.4	81.0	6.3	29.1	5.4	23.2	6.5	9.0	1.6
2023	232.0	83.2	6.0	30.1	5.9	23.8	6.6	9.2	1.5
2024	245.5	85.4	5.6	31.2	6.5	24.5	6.8	9.4	1.5
2025	259.1	87.6	5.3	32.2	7.0	25.1	6.9	9.6	1.4

The application of the techniques for diagnosing and forecasting the development of the consumer market in the context of the use of information technologies will ensure the efficiency of managing social and economic relations at all levels of development of business processes. It is recommended to generate forecast data on the state of the selected business processes of the consumer market based on correlation-regression analysis and neural network technologies. The use of these technologies in the context of the digitalization of the economy is an absolute necessity and an effective tool for developing various scenarios for the development of the regional consumer market, ensuring prevention in its regulation and alignment of interests of all participants in business processes.

REFERENCES

Akkoyunlu, Sule. 2015. "The Potential of Rural–Urban Linkages for Sustainable Development and Trade." *International Journal of Sustainable Development & World Policy*. https://doi.org/10.18488/journal.26/2015.4.2/26.2.20.40.

Aleksandrov, Igor, Marina Fedorova, and Aleksey Parshukov. 2020a. "Development of Farming in Russia Aspiring to Solve Rural Environmental Issues." In *E3S Web of Conferences*. https://doi.org/10.1051/e3sconf/202020305002.

Aleksandrov, Igor, Marina Fedorova, and Alexey Parshukov. 2020b. "E-Commerce in Russian Rural Areas as a Tool for Regional Development." In *E3S Web of Conferences*. https://doi.org/10.1051/e3sconf/202017513046.

Alvarez, Fernando. 2007. "Business Planning." In *Next Generation Business Handbook: New Strategies from Tomorrow's Thought Leaders*. https://doi.org/10.1002/9780470172223.ch42.

Ananiev, M. A., O. K. Lukhovskaya, and E. S. Vasilchuk. 2017. "Food Supply Regional Management System of the Consumer Market in the Modern Russian Economy." In *Contributions to Economics*. https://doi.org/10.1007/978-3-319-55257-6_14.

Bernard, Andrew B., and Andreas Moxnes. 2018. "Networks and Trade." *Annual Review of Economics*. https://doi.org/10.1146/annurev-economics-080217-053506.

Blinov, Alexander B., and Andrey I. Koblov. 2006. "Applying Models to Forecast Mobile Service Market Development." *Proceedings of the 24th International Conference of the System Dynamics Society*.

Chusova, A. E. 2011. "*Consumer Market: Analysis of the State and Theoretical and Methodological Approach to Diagnostics*," 52–55.

Cooper, Richard N., Maurice Schiff, and L. Alan Winters. 2003. "Regional Integration and Development." *Foreign Affairs*. https://doi.org/10.2307/20033699.

Deming, W. Edwards. 1984. "*Out of the Crisis MIT Press*." Reprint, ISBN-13.

Demyanenko, A. E. 2019. "Key Characteristics of Potential of Development of Regional Economy by Supply Chain Strategy." *International Journal of Supply Chain Management*.

Galieva, R. R. 2008. "*Methodology for Assessing the Consumer Market and Forecasting the Retail Turnover of a Trading Enterprise*." 2008. http://www.m-economy.ru/art.php?nArtId=2104.

Hanson, Gordon H. 2005. "Market Potential, Increasing Returns and Geographic Concentration." *Journal of International Economics*. https://doi.org/10.1016/j.jinteco.2004.09.008.

Hoeinghaus, David J., Angelo A. Agostinho, Luiz C. Gomes, Fernando M. Pelicice, Edson K. Okada, João D. Latini, Elaine A.L. Kashiwaqui, and Kirk O. Winemiller. 2009. "Effects of River Impoundment on Ecosystem Services of Large Tropical Rivers: Embodied Energy and Market Value of Artisanal Fisheries." *Conservation Biology*. https://doi.org/10.1111/j.1523-1739.2009.01248.x.

ISO. 2015. "*Quality Management Systems - Fundamentals and Vocabulary*." English.

Koblov, Andrey I., Alexander B. Blinov, and Vladimir I. Shiryaev. 2005. "Mobile Service Market Model of the Region." *Proceedings of the 23rd International Conference of the System Dynamics Society*.

Koblov, Andrey I., Vladimir I. Shiryaev, and Alexander B. Blinov. 2006. "Firm Behavior Optimal Control on Mobile Service Market." In *Proceedings of the 24th International Conference of the System Dynamics Society*.

Kotler, Philip, and Gary Armstrong. 2018. *Kotler & Armstrong, Principles of Marketing | Pearson*. Pearson.

Lukhovskaya, O. K., O. Y. Guryeva, V. I. Perov, I. V. Malova, and T. S. Kochetkova. 2019. "Conceptual Approaches to Determining, Diagnostics, and Forecasting the Region's Consumer Market." In *Specifics of Decision Making in Modern Business Systems*. https://doi.org/10.1108/978-1-78756-691-020191020.

Martin, Diane M., and John W. Schouten. 2014. "Consumption-Driven Market Emergence." *Journal of Consumer Research*. https://doi.org/10.1086/673196.

Neretina, E. A., E. V. Soldatova, N. S. Komleva, N. O. Kolchina, and E. G. Shcherbakova. 2016. "Program-Targeted Regulation of the Regional Consumer Market." *European Research Studies Journal*. https://doi.org/10.35808/ersj/557.

Porter, Michael E. 1985a. "Competitive Strategy: Creating and Sustaining Superior Performance." *Creating and Sustaining Competitive Advantage*.

———. 1985b. "Technology and Competitive Advantage." *Journal of Business Strategy*. https://doi.org/10.1108/eb039075.

Siró, István, Emese Kápolna, Beáta Kápolna, and Andrea Lugasi. 2008. "Functional Food. Product Development, Marketing and Consumer Acceptance-A Review." *Appetite*. https://doi.org/10.1016/j.appet.2008.05.060.

Teece, David J. 2010. "Business Models, Business Strategy and Innovation." *Long Range Planning*. https://doi.org/10.1016/j.lrp.2009.07.003.

Teeluckdharry, Krita. 2008. "ISO 9000: Quality Systems Handbook." *Biomedical Instrumentation & Technology*. https://doi.org/10.2345/0899-8205(2008)42 [23:iqsh]2.0.co;2.

In: Global Challenges of Digital Transformation of Markets   ISBN: 978-1-53619-754-9
Editors: E. de la Poza and S. E. Barykin   © 2021 Nova Science Publishers, Inc.

Chapter 35

Influence of the Evolution of Institutions in the Digital Retail Environment on the Transformation of Consumer Behavior

Tatiana Pereverzeva[1,], Tatiana Stepanova[1], Ruslan Ikramov[1], Vladimir Ulanov[1] and Natallya Snytkova[2]*

[1]Peter the Great St. Petersburg Polytechnic University, St. Petersburg, Russia
[2]Belarusian Trade and Economics University of Consumer Cooperatives, Gomel, Belarus

Abstract

The article examines the issues of the evolution of institutions of the traditional and digital retail environment and their impact on changes in consumer behavior in connection with radical transformations in the conditions of sales and the nature of interaction between retail and consumers. The main stages of the evolution of institutions are identified, the main features of the current stage are identified - the development of multichannel positioning by retailers, blurring the boundaries between online and offline trade, increasing the importance of digital marketing, social networks, and geolocation. The directions of transformation of the institutional matrices of retail and consumer behavior are shown. The influence of the diversity of institutions of the traditional and digital retail economy on the change in consumer behavior patterns is emphasized. It is noted that the use of various omnichannel business models by retail is accompanied by the saving of consumers' free time. A methodological approach is presented for assessing the success of the functioning of digital institutions by determining the congruence of institutions used by business entities in the trade industry, or the consistency of

---

* Corresponding Author's Email: aterina30@rambler.ru.

norms and rules among themselves using the example of institutions that form an omnichannel path – the institution of personalized offers, the institution of recommended shopping lists, the institution of navigation in the trading floor, which allows to ensure optimal institutional and socio-economic development of retail.

Keywords: digital retail, consumer behavior, institutional development, quality of life, digital transformation

1. INTRODUCTION

The starting point for considering the institutions of the digital retail environment is the study of the technological structure, which can be represented as a single technical process of production vertically and horizontally using resources based on the existing scientific and technical potential with adequate organizational, economic and institutional relations (Thelen 2009; "The Tools of Government: A Guide to the New Governance" 2002). The importance of studying the activation of the innovative direction of Russia's development is due to the need to implement a national innovation strategy that permeates all levels and spheres of the national economic system of Russia (Bahauovna and Bahauovna 2016; Scherbakov et al. 2020).

The study of institutional relations of the digital retail environment is of particular relevance not only to ensure the successful development of the retail industry, which is closest to the consumer, but also to ensure a new quality of consumption. The institutional environment of retail reflects the established order, norms and rules that determine the development of economic entities in the trade industry at a certain point in time, and we are talking about both the external institutional environment that determines the order of relations between retail and public authorities in accordance with the law, which control trade in order to protect consumer rights, and the internal institutional environment that determines the flow of business through the rules of accounting policy, Finance, budgeting, pricing, planning. Williamson gives the most General definition, describing the institutional environment as the sum of the main political, social and legal norms that are the basis for production, exchange and consumption (O. E. Williamson 1973; O. Williamson, Wachter, and Harris 2012).

The study of consumer institutions covers a wide range of historical social relations and interactions of social groups, i.e., social relations. Institutions in this case are considered as systems of certain and inevitable connections between members of society, conditioned by external conditions of social survival. Thus, institutions form a kind of skeleton of society, ensuring its historical stability and reproduction as a social integrity (Aidis, Estrin, and Mickiewicz 2008), the so-called "institutional matrix". At the same time, institutions are manifested and implemented both at the formal level – in the form of the Constitution, legislation, legal regulation, etc. and at the informal level – as norms of relationships, behavior, habits, customs, traditions, and historically stable value systems (Copeland and Taylor 1995; Duchin, Lange, and Kell 1995).

The era of digital transformation imposes its own restrictions on the development of these institutions, which are manifested in increasingly developed and civilized forms, while maintaining their specific characteristics (Barykin, Kalinina, et al. 2021; Barykin, Kapustina, Sergeev, et al. 2021; Barykin, Bochkarev, et al. 2021; Barykin, Kapustina, Valebnikova, et al. 2021; Barykin, Smirnova, Sharapaev, et al. 2021). Retail and consumer institutions are interdependent and together form a certain version of the institutional system.

2. MATERIALS AND METHODS

The evolution of retail institutions in retrospect goes through a number of stages:

- The appearance of the first supermarkets. The starting point of the modern relations of the digital revolution is considered to be the twenties of the twentieth century. The first supermarkets quickly gained a significant market share. Retailers focused on promotion tools inside the store, organization of shelves, and planograms for product placement.
- The second stage of the evolution of institutions is associated with the emergence of hyperformat in the sixties of the twentieth century, which was a radical step in terms of space use, productivity, efficiency and cost management. Significantly increased value for buyers, thanks to lower prices and more choice. The main features of this phase are: own brands, multi-format offers, and a more complex retail supply chain.
- The third stage in the evolution of institutions is associated with the emergence of electronic Commerce in the nineties of the twentieth century. The first online stores are gradually increasing their market share. Traditional retailers have started to go online.
- The fourth stage of the evolution of institutions began at the turn of 2010 and continues at the present time, characterized by continued growth of e-Commerce, primarily mobile Commerce. In the international market, online sales account for a larger share of retail turnover. Sales in the e-Commerce segment in the United States in 2018 accounted for about 10% of total retail turnover, in Russia – 4%, in China online sales account for 35% of total retail turnover (Eurostats 2020; eMarketer 2019). Despite the digital revolution in retail, physical stores are still the main place to shop. Global digital retail leaders such as Amazon and Aliexpress are focusing on integrating the consumer experience in offline stores into their digital ecosystem. High-quality omnichannel service is an essential component of the retailer's competitiveness (I. Krasyuk et al. 2019; Ianenko, Ianenko, et al. 2019).

Retailers are developing multi-channel positioning, blurring the lines between online and offline trading. Digital marketing, social networks, and geolocation are becoming more important (I. Krasyuk, Yanenko, and Nazarova 2020; I. A. Krasyuk and Medvedeva 2019; Aleksandrov, Fedorova, and Parshukov 2020). There are new institutions in the digital environment, in particular, figital, representing the integration of physical and digital media store, which in essence means the convergence of traditional institutions and the digital economy (Kapustina et al. 2019). Self-service and electronic payment systems are being further developed. There is an institution of dynamic pricing that affects the interests of both retailers and consumers. The new Institute for digitalization of operations aims to improve the efficiency of the storage and supply chain.

As for the current stage of institutional development of retail, we can distinguish the main, basic groups of institutions that reflect the main digital realities, and additional ones. Among the basic institutions, first of all, we should mention such groups of institutions as intelligent marketing, digitalization of operations and the must-win strategy. Moreover, the structure of the designated groups of institutions can be considered according to the scheme: identification of institutions-characteristics of institutions-positive features for retail – retailers applying this group of institutions.

If we consider a group of intellectual marketing institutes, its content can be described as follows:

- the Institute of dynamic pricing is characterized by convenient electronic price tags, connecting displays to a Central system that can change prices at any time. The positive features of this Institute for retail are an increase in customer experience, more accurate tracking of price elasticity, which leads to an increase in profits. This Institute is implemented by companies such as MiuMiu, Dixie, Biedronka (Poland).
- the Institute of personal recommendations, characterized by the fact that the client receives an offer specifically for their needs. It is based on their age, social group, previous purchases, and so on. The positive features of this Institute are an increase in revenue for the retailer, as well as an increase in customer satisfaction. This Institute is implemented by companies such as Lenta, Metro C&C, and Perekrestok.
- the geolocation-based offer Institute is characterized by the fact that geolocation services send notifications to users who are nearby to attract them or remind them of a delivery. The positive features of this Institute are an increase in traffic and revenue, which is implemented by Walmart.
- the "infinite shelves" Institute is characterized by the fact that a special terminal is located inside the store, allowing people to search for and order models and colors that are not presented in the store. The positive features of this Institute are an increase in customer satisfaction. This Institute is implemented by M. Video and Dixons retail.
- the Institute "Robot consultants" is characterized by the fact that special robots are used to deliver advertising leaflets and inform customers about sales, offers and events. The positive features of this Institute are an interesting

experience of working with clients, increasing the effectiveness of promotions, implemented by the companies Decathlon, Lenta.

If we consider the group of institutions for digitalization of operations, its structure looks like this:

- the Institute of personnel schedule management is characterized by the integration of the personnel schedule planning system, which predicts the workload and optimizes employee employment plans. The positive features of this Institute for retail are a reduction in the total number of employees of the organization. this Institute is implemented by such companies as Metro C&C (Europe), IKEA (Spain).
- the Institute of automation of employee task setting is characterized by application, primarily in the field of logistics in the store, this system tells employees how to build their activities in an optimal way. The positive features of this Institute for retail are optimized operations that lead to lower labor costs. This Institute is implemented by companies such as X5, O'key, Metro C&C.
- the Institute of customer tracking is characterized by the identification and tracking of the movement of customers and staff through cameras in the store, the use of a customer"Heat map". The positive features of this Institute for retail are the identification of time losses (by personnel) for further optimization. This Institute is implemented by companies such as Globus, Aldi (Germany), Lidl (Germany).

If we consider the group of institutions of the Must-win strategy, its structure looks like this:

- the Institute of supply chain digitalization is characterized by the fact that the components of the supply chain are practically combined in a variety of ways to determine the optimal organization in order to increase efficiency and utilization. The positive features of this Institute for retail are reduced logistics costs, a more efficient, clear and transparent supply chain, implemented by companies such as IKEA, Lidl, Ahold.
- the Institute for automated location search is considered as an electronic tool that analyzes a huge number of possible locations, taking into account many details, such as the volume of traffic of current visitors, etc. The positive features of this Institute for retail are the choice of optimal geolocations for business needs. This Institute is implemented by companies such as PocztaPolsaka, Zachodni WBK.
- the so-called "fijital" Institute is characterized by the integration of all (online and offline) business channels, so that consumers can buy a product anywhere and using any device. The positive features of this Institute for retail are the variety of ways to provide services, which leads to a significant increase in the

income of retailers. This Institute is implemented by companies such as IKEA, Smyk, Dixons Carphone.

Retail's use of the diversity of traditional and digital economy institutions affects the behavior of consumers who have to make digital choices and implement digital preferences. The study of digital consumer preferences raises a number of questions - how the use of digital devices affects consumer behavior in the store, how easy access to digital information affects both sales in digital format, and the total sales of retailers, and consumer behavior – we are talking about the so-called "digital influence" and, to a large extent, on changing consumer behavior patterns. In particular, in the expanded model of consumer behavior in the "black box of the buyer's consciousness", the process of making a purchase decision is accelerated, since the main prerequisites for its implementation have already been prepared by the retail, meaning the information block. In addition, considering the motivating factors of marketing in the form of such a tool as price, allows you to note the exceptional mobility of this tool in connection with various promotions, which has a stimulating effect on the decision to buy.

Speaking about various types of consumer behavior, it is impossible not to mention such a model of consumer behavior as the use of consumer schemes and stereotypes in the procedures for purchasing goods in the digital economy, including in the conditions of convergence of traditional and digital economy institutions.

In addition, the procedures for implementing various models of consumer behavior form individual standards of requirements for retailers and their products, which in itself means building an institutional field of consumer behavior, more precisely, an institutional space (Kapustina et al. 2020).

In this area, we can observe a certain phenomenon of the digital gap between retail representatives who use digital technologies and their corresponding institutions to a greater or lesser extent, as well as the phenomenon of the digital gap between consumers in terms of, on the one hand, the mentality and the possibility of using appropriate technologies, and, on the other hand, in terms of the implementation of various options for digital behavior. At the same time, in Russia, Internet penetration is 72.8% of the total population. At the same time, Russians have not only fully mastered the Internet, but also have a high purchasing power online. 55% of Russian consumers make online purchases at least once a month, and the average number of orders per year is 6.2 (Semerikova 2019). In addition, the effectiveness of retail development is largely determined by the use of various omnichannel business models (Ianenko, Stepanov, et al. 2019; Olleros, Zhegu, and Vezzoso 2016) – in terms of using personalized offers, as you make purchases and fill out your personal profile, the app analyzes your shopping habits and generates personalized recommendations for products, which is accompanied by the creation of a General shopping list directly in the app. This type of business process significantly reduces the time to search and study products. If consumers use the payment and order delivery options built into the app, they will save time in this segment. Omni-channel can be supplemented by such processes as navigation in the store's sales area, information on request, choosing a convenient payment method, etc. which together results in saving the buyer's free time.

Thus, digitalization is accompanied by significant changes in consumer behavior and the implementation of digital choice by consumers using specific institutions of retailers.

While significant problems of institutional evolution of retail is not the use of digital technologies, and the lack of a digital culture and skills of functioning in a digital format of the retail industry, emphasizing the need for careful study of the composition of digital and traditional institutions of politics, economics, sociology, and their structural changes. Companies need a visionary senior Executive to manage the changes that digitization brings.

In addition, the issue of digital instability and, accordingly, the assessment of digital product risks is of interest in the implementation of institutional planning of retail organizations and the selection of the most effective and cost-effective products and services (Veselovsky et al. 2017; Popkova et al. 2020; Parakhina, Boris, and Midler 2015; Pogodaeva, Baburina, and Dmitrieva 2018). Moreover, in some situations, as an indicator of digital stability, we can consider the sales volume of retailers as a reaction of consumers to the digital offer.

One of the methodological approaches to assessing the success of certain digital institutions can be considered to determine the congruence of institutions used by business entities in the trade industry, in other words, the consistency of norms and rules among themselves. In particular, an example of this kind of congruent institutions can be the institutions that form the omnichannel path - the Institute of personalized offers, the Institute of recommended shopping lists, the Institute of navigation in the trading floor, and so on. The presence of congruence between institutions allows us to obtain their convergence, that is, their joint use with ensuring optimal institutional and socio-economic development (Samuels 1984; Rutherford 2001; Stephen 2018). At the same time, there is a positive convergence, which consists in the convergence of formal and informal norms based on a trend leading to the optimum; negative convergence, which takes the form of a General trend to an ineffective result; static, which assumes a situation in which formal and informal norms complement each other; evolutionary, which implies the convergence of norms of dynamic progress; and hybrid, associated with the mutual influence of formal and informal norms ("Online Shopping in Numbers: Home Statistics I Shopolog.Ru" n.d.).

The mention of congruence of institutions implies at the same time a clarification of the definition of "incongruence" of institutions, which means a complete mismatch of formal and informal norms of economic entities.

Such assessments help to identify congruent institutions, determine their composition and structure, and ensure effective socio – economic development of retail. The corresponding calculations can be made by constructing a matrix of institutional development of the enterprise and determining the coefficients of congruence and non-congruence of norms using a sociological approach (Kapustina et al. 2019) and considering the opinion of respondents on this issue. The respondents may include consumers of retail products and services.

Research of possible digital segment institutions and identification of the most effective ones for specific companies should be included in the institutional policy of retailers and taken into account in the procedures of institutional planning of enterprises.

In addition, the institutional design of enterprises is considered along with other circumstances as a factor of investment attractiveness and, as a result, investment activity of organizations (Vercueil 2014; Klochikhin 2013), which is crucial for the socio–economic development of territories and improving the quality of life of their population.

3. RESULTS

Qualitative transformations of material assets and labor resources of retailers in connection with the digital revolution form the institutional prerequisites for the dynamics of the institutional environment of the retail industry (Afonasova et al. 2019; Sanovich 2019; Bataev, Gorovoy, and Mottaeva 2018), including the external and internal institutional environment, and a radical transformation of the institutional matrices of economic entities aimed at taking into account the characteristics of consumer behavior.

Careful monitoring of the digital environment institutions used, as well as digital environment institutions together with traditional institutions, allows us to identify the most effective directions for the development of retailers (Barbaruk, Krasyuk, and Medvedeva 2019).

Moreover, the detailed identification of the institutional array used allows us to establish the features of the application of economic and social institutions, their specificity and significance for consumers of goods and services of retailers.

The application of the methodology for evaluating the effectiveness of digital institutions by determining the congruence of institutions used by retailers allows us to identify the most optimal combinations of institutions and use coordinated groups of institutions, as well as ensure their convergence, in this context, optimal institutional and socio-economic development, which ultimately has a positive impact on the financial results of retailers.

In addition, the use of institutions with a high coefficient of congruence has a beneficial effect on the formation of a modern model of consumer behavior, in particular, on building an omnichannel way of selling goods and services.

Ineffective institutions identified in the course of institutional analysis should be replaced with more effective ones, which should be reflected in institutional trade policy.

Thus, monitoring of institutions used by retailers gives an idea of the institutional content of the digital retail environment, allows you to structure existing institutions by types of institutional environment, plan on this basis for institutional changes and thereby improve the efficiency of the retail business.

4. DISCUSSION

The subject of discussion of the studied problem is the interpretation of the concept of "institutional environment" of economic entities. Thus, Williamson provides the most general definition, characterizing the institutional environment as the sum of the basic political, social and legal norms that are the basis for production, exchange and consumption (Barbaruk, Krasyuk, and Medvedeva 2019).

At the same time, in our opinion, the definition of "institutional environment of retail" needs some clarification. This refers, first of all, to the need to differentiate the institutional environment into external and internal, which makes it possible to more fully present the tools for institutional regulation of trade business.

The institutional environment of retail reflects the established order, norms and rules that determine the development of economic entities in the trading industry at a certain point in time, and we are talking about an external institutional environment that determines the order of relationships between retail and government authorities in accordance with the legislation that control trade with the purpose of protecting consumer rights, and the internal institutional environment that determines the course of business through the rules of accounting policy, finance, budgeting, pricing, planning.

The inclusion of the internal environment in institutional analysis and institutional planning allows business entities in the trade industry to make prompt management decisions in those areas of the economy that primarily come into contact with consumers of goods and services, determine their purchasing choices and, ultimately, the volume of sales and financial results retail.

CONCLUSION

Institutional monitoring of retailers allows us to determine the specifics of their institutional development and shows the presence of digital gaps due to different degrees of use of elements of the digital environment, which, in turn, creates prerequisites for the transformation of certain segments, considered as "weak links".

Monitoring of institutional relations of retail in the digital environment and the digital environment together with institutions of traditional economy is the basis for further planning of institutional changes in order to ensure the greatest financial results of economic entities in the trade industry and the formation of new consumer behavior models that improve the quality of life of the population.

This kind of indicator, illustrating the improvement of the quality of life of the population, can be considered as saving the buyer's free time, which can be formed at all stages of creating an omnichannel consumer path - personalized offers, creating a General shopping list in the app, creating recommended shopping lists, using payment and order delivery options built into the app, etc.

Thus, the study of the institutions of the digital environment of retailers together with the institutions of the traditional economy allows us to improve the quality of life of the population and level the institutional gaps of consumers as users of the digital offer of retailers.

ACKNOWLEDGMENT

This paper was financially supported by the Ministry of Education and Science of the Russian Federation on the programm to improve the competitiveness of Peter the Great St. Petersburg Polytechnic University (SPbPU) among the world's leading research and education centers in the 2016–2020.

REFERENCES

Afonasova, Margarita A., Elena E. Panfilova, Marina A. Galichkina. & Beata Ślusarczyk. (2019). "Digitalization in Economy and Innovation: The Effect on Social and Economic Processes." *Polish Journal of Management Studies.* https://doi.org/10.17512/pjms.2019.19.2.02.

Aidis, Ruta, Saul Estrin. & Tomasz Mickiewicz. (2008). "Institutions and Entrepreneurship Development in Russia: A Comparative Perspective." *Journal of Business Venturing.* https://doi.org/10.1016/j.jbusvent.2008.01.005.

Aleksandrov, Igor, Marina Fedorova. & Alexey Parshukov. (2020). "E-Commerce in Russian Rural Areas as a Tool for Regional Development." In *E3S Web of Conferences.* https://doi.org/10.1051/e3sconf/202017513046.

Bahauovna, Mottaeva Angela. & Mottaeva Asiyat Bahauovna. (2016). "Basic Priorities of Innovative Development Russian Regions." *International Journal of Applied Engineering Research.*

Barykin, Sergey Yevgenievich, Andrey Aleksandrovich Bochkarev, Sergey Mikhailovich Sergeev, Tatiana Anatolievna Baranova, Dmitriy Anatolievich Mokhorov, and Aleksandra Maksimovna Kobicheva. 2021. "A Methodology of Bringing Perspective Innovation Products to Market." *Academy of Strategic Management Journal* 20 (2): 19. https://www.abacademies.org/articles/a-methodology-of-bringing-perspective-innovation-products-to-market.pdf.

Barykin, Sergey Yevgenievich, Olga Vladimirovna Kalinina, Irina Vasilievna Kapustina, Victor Andreevich Dubolazov, Cesar Armando Nunez Esquivel, Elmira Alyarovna Nazarova, and Petr Anatolievich Sharapaev. 2021. "The Sharing Economy and Digital Logistics in Retail Chains: Opportunities and Threats." *Academy of Strategic Management Journal* 20 (2): 1–14. https://www.abacademies.org/

articles/the-sharing-economy-and-digital-logistics-in-retail-chains-opportunities-and-threats.pdf.

Barykin, Sergey Yevgenievich, Irina Vasilievna Kapustina, Sergey Mikhailovich Sergeev, Olga Vladimirovna Kalinina, Viktoriia Valerievna Vilken, Yuri Yevgenievich Putikhin, and Lydia Vitalievna Volkova. 2021. "Developing the Physical Distribution Digital Twin Model within the Trade Network." *Academy of Strategic Management Journal* 20 (1): 1–24. https://www.abacademies.org/articles/developing-the-physical-distribution-digital-twin-model-within-the-trade-network.pdf.

Barykin, Sergey Yevgenievich, Irina Vasilievna Kapustina, Olga Aleksandrovna Valebnikova, Natalia Viktorovna Valebnikova, Olga Vladimirovna Kalinina, Sergey Mikhailovich Sergeev, Marisa Camastral, Yuri Yevgenievich Putikhin, and Lydia Vitalievna Volkova. 2021. "Digital Technologies for Personnel Management: Implications for Open Innovations." *Academy of Strategic Management Journal* 20 (2): 1–14. https://www.abacademies.org/articles/digital-technologies-for-personnel-management-implications-for-open-innovations.pdf.

Barykin, Sergey Yevgenievich, Elena Aleksandrovna Smirnova, Petr Anatolievich Sharapaev, and Angela Bohuovna Mottaeva. 2021. "Development of the Kazakhstan Digital Retail Chains within the EAEU E-Commerce." *Academy of Strategic Management Journal* 20 (2): 1–18. https://www.abacademies.org/articles/development-of-the-kazakhstan-digital-retail-chains-within-the-eaeu-ecommerce-market.pdf.

Barbaruk, A., Krasyuk, I. & Medvedeva, Y. (2019). "The Impact of Business Intelligence on Improving the Management of Trade and Technological Processes." In *Proceedings of the 33rd International Business Information Management Association Conference, IBIMA 2019: Education Excellence and Innovation Management through Vision 2020*.

Bataev, Alexey V., Alexandr A. Gorovoy. & Angela Mottaeva. (2018). "Evaluation of the Future Development of the Digital Economy in Russia." In *Proceedings of the 32nd International Business Information Management Association Conference, IBIMA 2018 - Vision 2020: Sustainable Economic Development and Application of Innovation Management from Regional Expansion to Global Growth*.

Copeland, Brian R. & Scott Taylor, M. (1995). "Trade and the Environment: A Partial Synthesis." *American Journal of Agricultural Economics*. https://doi.org/10.2307/1243249.

Duchin, Faye, Glenn Marie Lange. & Georg Kell. (1995). "Technological Change, Trade and the Environment." *Ecological Economics*. https://doi.org/10.1016/0921-8009(95)00014-Z.

eMarketer. (2019). "E-Commerce Share of Total Global Retail Sales from 2015 to 2021." *Statista*.

Eurostats. (2020). "E-Commerce Statistics for Individuals - Statistics Explained." *December 2020*.

Ianenko, Marina, Mikhail Ianenko, Dmitriy Huhlaev. & Oksana Martynenko. (2019). "Digital Transformation of Trade: Problems and Prospects of Marketing Activities." In *IOP Conference Series: Materials Science and Engineering*. https://doi.org/10.1088/1757-899X/497/1/012118.

Ianenko, Marina, Mikhail Stepanov, Mikhail Ianenko. & Svetlana Iliashenko. (2019). "Peculiarities of Product Policy in the Internet of Things." In *IOP Conference Series: Materials Science and Engineering*. https://doi.org/10.1088/1757-899X/497/1/012119.

Kapustina, Irina, Tatiana Pereverzeva, Tatiana Stepanova. & Grigoriy Chargazia. (2020). "Formation Features of Institutional Space of Economic Agents in Trade in the Conditions of Digital Transformation." In *IOP Conference Series: Materials Science and Engineering*. https://doi.org/10.1088/1757-899X/940/1/012063.

Kapustina, Irina, Tatiana Pereverzeva, Tatiana Stepanova. & Iuliia Rusu. (2019). "Convergence of Institutes of Retail Traditional and Digital Economy." In *IOP Conference Series: Materials Science and Engineering*. https://doi.org/10.1088/1757-899X/497/1/012120.

Klochikhin, Evgeny a. (2013). "Public Policy in (Re)Building National Innovation Capabilities: A Comparison of S&T Transitions In China and Russia." *Toxicological Sciences : An Official Journal of the Society of Toxicology*.

Krasyuk, Irina A. & Yuliya Y. Medvedeva. (2019). "Drives and Obstacle for the Development of Marketing in Russian Retailing." In *Proceedings of the 33rd International Business Information Management Association Conference, IBIMA 2019: Education Excellence and Innovation Management through Vision 2020*.

Krasyuk, Irina, Yulia Medvedeva, Vladimir Baharev. & Grigory Chargaziya. (2019). "Evolution of Strategies of Retail and Technological Systems under Broad Digitalization Conditions." In *IOP Conference Series: Materials Science and Engineering*. https://doi.org/10.1088/1757-899X/497/1/012124.

Krasyuk, Irina, Marina Yanenko. & Elmira Nazarova. (2020). "Conceptual and Strategic Framework for the Digitalization of Modern Retail as Part of Innovative Marketing." In *E3S Web of Conferences*. https://doi.org/10.1051/ e3sconf/202016409006.

Olleros, F., Majlinda Zhegu. & Simonetta Vezzoso. (2016). "Competition Policy in a World of Big Data." In *Research Handbook on Digital Transformations*. https://doi.org/10.4337/9781784717766.00027.

"*Online Shopping in Numbers: Home Statistics / Shopolog.Ru*." n.d. Accessed February 7, 2021. https://www.shopolog.ru/metodichka/analytics/onlayn-shoping-v-cifrah-glavnaya-statistika/.

Parakhina, V. N., Boris, O. A. & Midler, E. A. (2015). "Evaluation of Innovative Regional Development Russia." *Asian Social Science*. https://doi.org/10.5539/ass.v11n5p201.

Pogodaeva, Taisya, Natalia Baburina. & Anna Dmitrieva. (2018). "Bank Financing and Innovative Development of Russian Circumpolar Area." *International Journal of Social Economics*. https://doi.org/10.1108/IJSE-08-2016-0227.

Popkova, Elena, Alexander N. Alekseev, Svetlana V. Lobova. & Bruno S. Sergi. (2020). "The Theory of Innovation and Innovative Development. AI Scenarios in Russia." *Technology in Society.* https://doi.org/10.1016/j.techsoc.2020.101390.

Rutherford, Malcolm. (2001). "Institutional Economics: Then and Now." *Journal of Economic Perspectives.* https://doi.org/10.1257/jep.15.3.173.

Samuels, Warren J. (1984). "Institutional Economics." *Journal of Economic Education.* https://doi.org/10.1080/00220485.1984.10845074.

Sanovich, Sergey C N - HM742. (2019). "Russia : The Origins of Digital Misinformation." In *Computational Propaganda: Political Parties, Politicians, and Political Manipulation on Social Media.*

Scherbakov, V. N., Dubrovsky, A. V., Makarova, I. V., Shchennikova, V. N., Nozdrin, V. S. & Anokhin, S. A. (2020). "Strategic Guidelines and Priorities of Russia's Industrial Transformation." *International Journal of Management.* https://doi.org/10.34218/IJM.11.5.2020.086.

Semerikova, Ekaterina. (2019). "Payment Instruments Choice of Russian Consumers: Reasons and Pain Points." *Journal of Enterprising Communities.* https://doi.org/10.1108/JEC-09-2019-0089.

Stephen, Frank. (2018). "New Institutional Economics." In *Law and Development.* https://doi.org/10.4337/9781784718213.00009.

"The Tools of Government: A Guide to the New Governance." 2002. *Choice Reviews Online.* https://doi.org/10.5860/choice.40-2422.

Thelen, Kathleen. (2009). "Institutional Change in Advanced Political Economies." *British Journal of Industrial Relations.* https://doi.org/10.1111/j.1467-8543.2009.00746.x.

Vercueil, Julien. (2014). "Could Russia Become More Innovative? Coordinating Key Actors of the Innovation System." *Post-Communist Economies.* https://doi.org/10.1080/14631377.2014.964464.

Veselovsky, Mikhail Yakovlevich, Alla Vladimirovna Nikonorova, Natal'ya L.vovna Krasyukova, Inna Vladimirovna Bitkina. & Aleksandr Annayarovich Stepanov. (2017). "The Development of Innovative Startups in Russia: The Regional Aspect." *Academy of Strategic Management Journal.*

Williamson, Oliver E. (1973). "Organizational Forms and Internal Efficiency Markets and Hierarchies: Some Elementary Considerations." *American Economic Review.*

Williamson, Oliver, Michael Wachter. & Jeffrey Harris. (2012). "Understanding the Employment Relation: The Analysis of Idiosyncratic Exchange." In *The Economic Nature of the Firm: A Reader, Third Edition.* https://doi.org/10.1017/CBO9780511817410.017.

In: Global Challenges of Digital Transformation of Markets ISBN: 978-1-53619-754-9
Editors: E. de la Poza and S. E. Barykin   © 2021 Nova Science Publishers, Inc.

Chapter 36

MODEL TOOLS FOR MANAGING REGIONAL BUSINESS PROCESSES IN THE ERA OF DIGITALIZATION

Yulia Granitsa[*]

National Research Lobachevsky State University of Nizhny Novgorod,
Nizhny Novgorod, Russia

ABSTRACT

Effective management of regional systems involves the analysis of information about business processes and a long-term forecast of the state of the regional structure, taking into account the scenarios of its development, which in turn is determined by the values of the parameters of business processes. A promising direction in this regard is the use of statistical, computational-constructive and economic-mathematical methods of data analysis. The aim of the study is to study the methodological tools for analyzing regional business processes to improve the quality of predictive analytics at the stage of developing forecasts. The study substantiates the development of a decision-making system based on the construction of simulation flow models, describes the key functional blocks of the proposed tools, defines the place of methods for obtaining predicted values of indicators in the management of regional development. In the work, a panel regression model is built, illustrating the relationship between regional economic indicators; Garch-models describing the dynamics of revenues, expenses and regional budget deficits; simulation models of consumer growth and a model of the production system of the Central Federal District, based on four differential equations characterizing the state of four phase variables. The tools for constructing models were the free econometric package Gretl, the program for the

---

[*] Corresponding Author's Email: ygranica@yandex.ru.

implementation and visualization of engineering calculations Mathcad Prime 6.0 and the platform for simulation Anylogic.

Keywords: buisness process, Garch-model, decision support system, dynamicmodel, forecast, region, simulation modeling

1. INTRODUCTION

The socio-economic system of the region by its nature is a complex, multidimensional and multipurpose system, which includes many elements and heterogeneous relationships in all spheres of society.

Due to its heterogeneity, caused, on the one hand, by differences in resource, scientific, and technical potential, on the other hand, by the imperfection of the distribution mechanism of budgetary funds, it is rightfully the most sensitive to financial and social shocks.

Assessment of the impact of shocks on the development of regional systems with unstable market institutions in the period of global recession is of particular relevance.

In this regard, an objective condition for the formation of an effective economic policy is the widespread use of science-based management tools.

Research in the development of an effective strategy for managing regional processes is presented in the works of Ayvazyan (Makarov et al. 2016), Beklaryan (Beklaryan 2018; Beklaryan and Akopov 2019; Akopov and Beklaryan 2014), Chernyakhovskaya (L. Chernyakhovskaya and Nizamutdinov 2019), Makarov (Makarov et al. 2016), Aleksandrov et al. (Aleksandrov, Fedorova, and Parshukov 2020).

The process of managing regional systems is presented in the form of the following diagram (Figure 1).

Obviously, the model for managing regional business processes is based on a goal-setting block. Indicators for assessing the state and development of business processes are selected depending on the type of business processes and management goals identified by the person making the management decision.

The issues of choosing economic indicators for the purpose of analysis and subsequent forecasting of the state of the regional system are analyzed in the works of Beklaryan (Beklaryan 2018), Granitsa (Granitsa 2020a; 2020b), MalkinaM (Malkina and Balakin 2019), Shakleina, and Midov (Shakleina and Midov 2019).

Typical variants of predictors for assessing economic processes are the growth rate of investment in fixed assets, the growth rate of average wages, the dynamics of prices for natural resources, the birth rate, cash income per capita, the level of budgetary expenditures, the amount of tax and non-tax revenues of the consolidated budget.

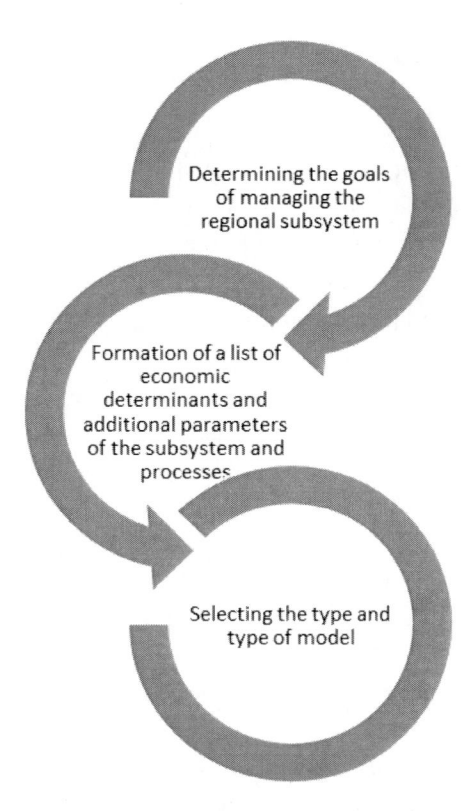

Figure 1. Regional business process management model.

In the works of Sevastyanova (Sevastyanova 2017) and another authors (Ablaev 2015; Glebova and Kotenkova 2014; Glinskiy et al. 2016; Bagautdinova et al. 2012; Mayorova et al. 2018; Maurseth 2003; Semyachkov 2018) regions of the resource type with a high share of the mineral resource complex were investigated, and the level of production of hydrocarbons, oil per capita, the rate of growth of prices for minerals were identified as additional determinants of the development of the regional system at the next stage, the choice of a model for assessing the state and development of the business process of the regional subsystem is carried out, which will be the justification for making a well-grounded management decision

2. MATERIALS AND METHODS

We will investigate the classes of economic and mathematical models for the analysis of regional business processes, we will determine the purpose and role of each class in the management decision support system.

2.1. Regression Models

Regression models, including logistic and panel regressions, have been successfully applied in the works of Zemtsov et al. (Zemtsov et al. 2016), Ejdys (Ejdys 2020; 2018). The authors note that models of this type allow one to build point and interval forecasts, thus, various types of regression models make it possible for a decision maker to analyze scenarios for the development of regional subsystems by setting the changes of some factors of interest to him and getting an assumption about how this will affect others. factors.

The logit models we constructed showed the greatest impact on the stability of the economic development of the regions of a number of indicators of the public and private sectors of the regional economy. The principal component analysis made it possible to single out economic indicators common to all federal districts that make the greatest contribution to the total dispersion of financial indicators, namely, gross regional product, per capita income and government debt.

2.2. Autoregressive Models

Socio-economic forecasting is based on statistical methods for constructing time series models such as ARIMA and GARCH. Forecasting the development of processes and systems using autoregressive models has been successfully demonstrated in the works of Granitsa (Granitsa 2020b), Kopnova, and Rodionova (Kopnova and Rodionova 2020).

The construction of time series analysis models is preceded by a harmonic analysis of the model determinants, which involves the construction of a periodogram and spectral density in order to assess the variability of the determinants characterizing the business process at different frequencies.

We have carried out a harmonious analysis of the monthly revenues of the regional budget to identify hidden periodicities. The results of the spectrum analysis lead us to the conclusion about the significant influence of long-term variability, as evidenced by the peak of the spectral frequency in the period in March 2020, thus, let us formulate the assumption that it was the pandemic that contributed to the fluctuations in the amount of budget revenues.

The result of performing the procedures for analyzing the variability of income and expenditure is the first-order autoregressive model we have constructed, which serves as a tool for forecasting the consolidated budget deficit (Figure 2).

Analysis of the presented model allows us to conclude that the budget deficit in 2020 tends to decrease. However, to assess the quality of the model, it is necessary to additionally construct graphs of conditional variances of the residual income and expenses. We depict them in Figures 3 and 4.

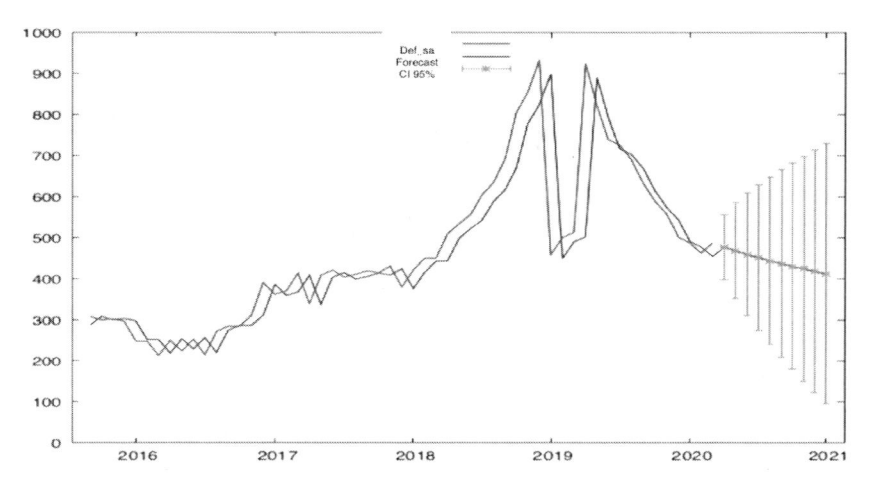

Figure 2. Generalized model for forecasting the budget deficit of the constituent entities of the Russian Federation with conditional autoregressive heteroscedasticity.

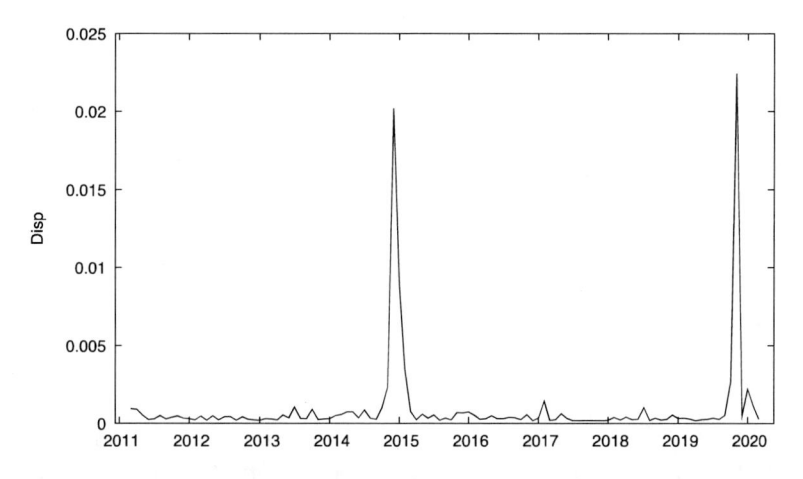

Figure 3. The Graph of conditional variance of errors of the growth dynamics model regional budget revenues.

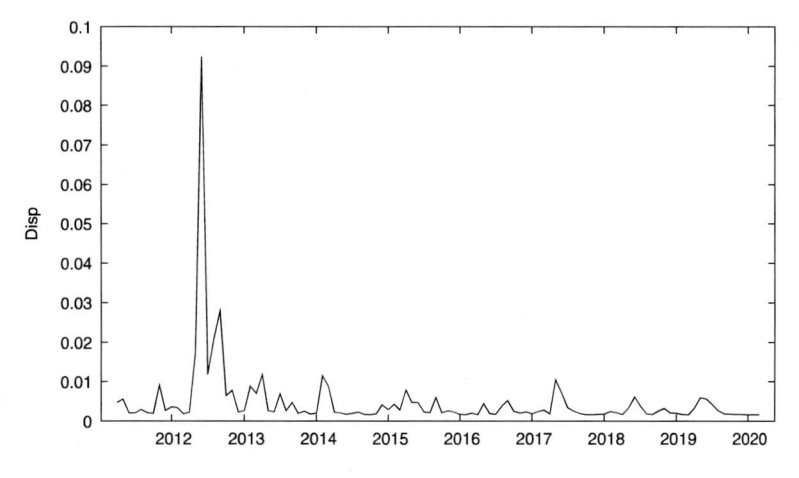

Figure 4. The graph of the conditional variance of errors of the model of the dynamics of the increase in expenditures of regional budgets.

The tool for building and visualizing models with conditional hetero-scedasticity in our work is the free econometric package Gretl.

From the analysis of the information in Figures 3 and 4, we conclude that in 2019 there is a jump in the variance of the errors of the autoregressive model of income, which indicates a possible significant deviation of the predicted value of the regional budget income, and as a consequence, the budget deficit from the actual values.

2.3. Simulation Models

The most difficult task in the field of modeling is associated with the definition of internal relationships between the determinants of business processes of regional subsystems.

A region as a multi-level and multi-aspect dynamic system is characterized by the following properties:

- nonlinear behavior of operations and processes in the system and subsystems;
- memory of previous events;
- the presence of cause-and-effect relationships with the simultaneous complexity, and sometimes the impossibility of establishing a relationship between numerous variables and parameters.

Such features of regional processes determine the circumstance that analytical decisions are poorly suited for the implementation of a decision support system at the regional level, and methods of simulation modeling are replacing analytical models. A simulation model is understood as a model based on the idea of sequential adaptation to a change in the economic situation, not only of the goals and behavior of individual agents and their strategies, but also the parameters of functioning subsystems.

The process of constructing simulation models for various regional subsystems is described in the works of Akopov et al. (Akopov, Beklaryan, and Saghatelyan 2017), Nizamutdinov et al. (L. Chernyakhovskaya and Nizamutdinov 2019; L. R. Chernyakhovskaya et al. 2019; Bakhtizin, Nizamutdinov, and Oreshnikov 2019), Kazakov, and Mikheenko, Makarov et al. (Kazakov and Mikheenko 2020).

The correspondence between the types of simulation and regional business processes is presented in Table 1.

To create a simulation model, we used the Anylogic platform, where a combination of discrete-event, agent-based and system dynamics approach can be successfully implemented.

Figure 5 shows the dynamic model of consumer growth in the market for goods, works, services; the forecast period is from September 01, 2020 to July 31, 2026.

Another simulation model built by us belongs to the group of systems dynamics models and describes the production system of the Central Federal District, which we have chosen as the most advanced and promising of all federal districts of Russia.

Table 1. Types of simulation models in business process management

Comparison criteria	Agent based modeling	System dynamics method	Discrete Event Modeling
Description of the situation in which the model can be applied	There is no information about the behavior of the system as a whole, but the development of individual processes is known. Agent - any object, the behavior of the agent is set by the state diagram	The modeled system is considered as a closed structure that determines its own behavior. The presence of feedback loops.	The simulated system is a sequence of operations performed by agents
Examples of regional processes- objects of modeling	Dynamics of consumers in various markets, dynamics of macroeconomic indicators (GDP)	The spread of the pandemic, the development of innovation spheres, education, the dynamics of indicators of the consolidated budget of the constituent entities	Analysis of the activities of individual industries (healthcare, transport, communications)

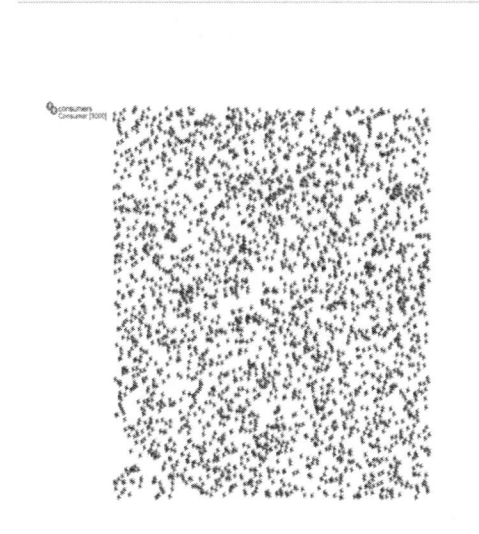

Figure 5. Manufacturing consumer growth model.

The model is based on the idea of the region as an aggregated production structure that produces a homogeneous product flow. A similar perception of the regional system is presented in the works of Naumov, and Trynov (I. V. Naumov, Trynov, and Safonov 2020; Il'ya Naumov and Trynov 2019), Kravchenko et al. (Kravchenko et al. 2018), Baranov et al. (2017; 2018), Vilken et al. (Vilken et al. 2019), Rytova, Gutman (Rytova and Gutman 2019).

In the study, the set of rules by which the production system passes from one state to another is described by differential equations.

In the course of the study, a dynamic model presented by a system of four differential equations was developed, the variables of which characterize changes in the values of flows of material and financial resources.

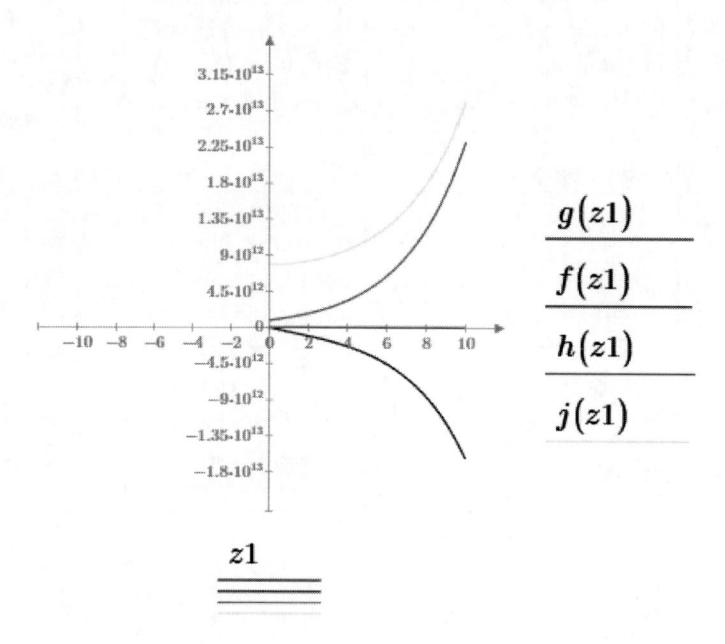

Figure 6. Oscillograms reflecting the change in phase variables over time.

We have chosen as economic determinants characterizing the state of the production system:

- volume of production of goods, works, services (g),
- funds of enterprises (h),
- monetary funds of the population (j),
- product release rate (f)
- z1 - time parameter

To determine the direction of the dynamics of the production system, we will use the solver of the system of differential equations "odesolve" in the program for the implementation and visualization of engineering calculations Mathcad Prime 6.0.

Let's build oscillograms - graphs of changes in phase variables over time, taking into account changes in additional parameters of the model, such as the consumption rate, the degree of equipment depreciation, the volume of exports, profitability, the cost of fixed assets, investments in fixed assets, accounts receivable (Figure 6).

A dynamic analysis of the development of the production system showed that over time, economic agents get richer - the amount of money increases both among organizations and among the population, however, the production rate remains unchanged or decreases, the volume of shipped goods of own production decreases significantly in both cases. All this is obviously due to the fact that funds are redistributed to other regional subsystems and markets.

3. RESULTS

Our research led to the following conclusions:

- Models of linear, logistic, panel regression are applicable to assess the relationship of absolute, relative, standardized values of economic indicators, as well as using such models to assess the likelihood of financial instability in the region in the forecast period, however, the forecast in such models is based on retrospective data, which significantly limits the reliability of the result.
- Autoregressive models with conditional heteroscedasicity provide a significant result for determining the predicted values of economic determinants for any regional subsystem. The main disadvantage of models of this type is the limited amount of data - statistics for a maximum of twenty years are used to forecast most socio-economic indicators, while most of the macroeconomic indicators are presented with a breakdown by year. In addition, a distinctive feature of regional statistics is a significant delay in actual data, which obviously negatively affects the quality of forecast estimates.
- The proposed dynamic simulation model of the production system provides the ability to predict the demand and consumption of products, works, services, depending on the value of controlled additional parameters such as consumption level, export volume, investment in fixed assets, economic profitability.
- The results obtained when building a model of a regional production system allow decision-makers to draw conclusions regarding interrelated business processes related to several subsystems at the regional level.

4. DISCUSSION

In the course of the study, we built a regional production model based on the balance of management of material, labor and financial resources.

In order to take into account regional peculiarities, it is proposed to include in the model additional characteristics reflecting the peculiarities of the functioning of each region, influencing the export indicators, consumption rates, capital intensity of industries.

The development of the proposed model is to expand the composition of indicators of socio-economic processes characterizing the spheres of education, development of innovation, regional finance.

In calculating the indicators, an attempt should be made to apply alternative methods based on the use of the theory of fuzzy sets (Rytova and Gutman 2019).

CONCLUSION

The study shows the possibility of using a model tool for making science-based decisions in the management of regional subsystems.

At the present stage, there are objective prerequisites for improving the currently used model tools due to the wider use of simulation methods, conducting scenario experiments, taking into account the objective capabilities and limitations of regions, and all this is due to the existence and continuous improvement of software that allows building statistical, mathematical, econometric models.

ACKNOWLEDGMENTS

The study was carried out within the framework of the basic part of the state assignment of the Ministry of Education and Science of the Russian Federation, project 0729-2020-0056 2 "Modern methods and models for diagnosing, monitoring, preventing and overcoming crisis phenomena in the economy in the context of digitalization as a way to ensure the economic security of the Russian Federation."

REFERENCES

Ablaev, Ildar. 2015. "Innovation Clusters in the Russian Economy: Economic Essence, Concepts, Approaches." *Procedia Economics and Finance*. https://doi.org/10.1016/s2212-5671(15)00605-x.

Akopov, Andranik S., and Gayane L. Beklaryan. 2014. "Modelling the Dynamics of the 'Smarter Region.'" In *IEEE/IAFE Conference on Computational Intelligence for Financial Engineering, Proceedings (CIFEr)*. https://doi.org/10.1109/CIFEr.2014.6924074.

Akopov, Andranik S., Levon A. Beklaryan, and Armen K. Saghatelyan. 2017. "Agent-Based Modelling for Ecological Economics: A Case Study of the Republic of Armenia." *Ecological Modelling.* https://doi.org/10.1016/j.ecolmodel.2016.11.012.

Aleksandrov, Igor, Marina Fedorova, and Aleksey Parshukov. 2020. "Development of Farming in Russia Aspiring to Solve Rural Environmental Issues." In *E3S Web of Conferences.* https://doi.org/10.1051/e3sconf/202020305002.

Bagautdinova, Nailya, Ilshat Gafurov, Nataliya Kalenskaya, and Aida Novenkova. 2012. "The Regional Development Strategy Based on Territorial Marketing (The Case of Russia)." *World Applied Sciences Journal.* https://doi.org/10.5829/idosi. wasj.2012.18.120030.

Bakhtizin, Albert R., Marsel M. Nizamutdinov, and Vladimir V. Oreshnikov. 2019. "Approach to the Problem of Strategic Management of the Regional Development Based on Adaptive Simulation Model." *Vestnik Sankt-Peterburgskogo Universiteta, Prikladnaya Matematika, Informatika, Protsessy Upravleniya.* https://doi.org/10.21638/11702/spbu10.2019.306.

A. O. Baranov, Z. B. D. Dondokov, K. P. Dyrkheev, and V. N. Suslov. 2017. "Building a Budgetary Block of the Dynamic Input-Output Model and Problems of the Republic of Buryatia Budget Forming." *World of Economics and Management.* https://doi.org/10.25205/2542-0429-2017-17-4-94-106.

A. O. Baranov, Z. B.-D. Dondokov, and V. N. Pavlov. 2018. "Experience of Using a Dynamic Input-Output Model with Fuzzy Parameters for Forecasting the Economy of Buryatia." *World of Economics and Management.* https://doi.org/10. 25205/2542-0429-2018-18-3-104-116.

Beklaryan, Gayane L. 2018. "Decision Support System for Sustainable Economic Development of the Far Eastern Federal District." *Business Informatics.* https://doi.org/10.17323/1998-0663.2018.4.66.75.

Beklaryan, Gayane L., and Andranik S. Akopov. 2019. "Modelling the Efficiency of the Use of Production and Investment Resources at the Regional Level: The Case of Russia." *International Journal of Economics and Business Administration.*

Chernyakhovskaya, Lilia R., Marsel M. Nizamutdinov, Vladimir V. Oreshnikov, and Alsouy R. Atnabaeva. 2019. "Approach to the Organization of Decision Support in the Formulation of Innovative Regional Development Strategies Based on Adaptive-Simulation Model." *Business Informatics.* https://doi.org/10.17323/1998-0663.2019.3.20.34.

Chernyakhovskaya, Liliya, and Marsel Nizamutdinov. 2019. "Development of Knowledge Base for Intellectual Decision Support in the Process of Innovative Project Management." In *Proceedings - 2019 21st International Conference & quot;Complex Systems: Control and Modeling Problems & quot;, CSCMP 2019.* https://doi.org/10.1109/CSCMP45713.2019.8976758.

Ejdys, Joanna. 2018. "Building Technology Trust in ICT Application at a University." *International Journal of Emerging Markets.* https://doi.org/10.1108/IJoEM-07-2017-0234.

————. 2020. "Trust-Based Determinants of Future Intention to Use Technology." *Foresight and STI Governance*. https://doi.org/10.17323/2500-2597.2020.1.60. 68.

Glebova, Irina, and Svetlana Kotenkova. 2014. "Evaluation of Regional Innovation Potential in Russia." *Procedia Economics and Finance*. https://doi.org/10.1016/ s2212-5671(14)00706-0.

Glinskiy, Vladimir, Lyudmila Serga, Ekaterina Chemezova, and Kirill Zaykov. 2016. "Clusterization Economy as a Way to Build Sustainable Development of the Region." In *Procedia CIRP*. https://doi.org/10.1016/j.procir.2016.01.050.

Granitsa, Y. V. 2020a. "*Analysis of the Interrelations of Economic Indicators as a Tool for Predicting Regional Financial Instability*." In https://doi.org/10.2991/ aebmr.k.200312.394.

————. 2020b. "Some Approaches to the Selection of Regional Financial Instability Determinants." In *IOP Conference Series: Materials Science and Engineering*. https://doi.org/10.1088/1757-899X/753/8/082035.

Kazakov, Oleg D., and Olga V. Mikheenko. 2020. "Transfer Learning and Domain Adaptation Based on Modeling of Socio-Economic Systems." *Business Informatics* 14 (2): 7-20. https://doi.org/10.17323/2587-814X.2020.2.7.20.

Kopnova, Elena D., and Lilia A. Rodionova. 2020. "Modeling Globalization Processes Taking into Account Structural Changes, Using Algeria as an Example." *Business Informatics*. https://doi.org/10.17323/2587-814X.2020.1.62.74.

Kravchenko, Tatiana K., Nikolay I. Golov, Aleksey V. Fomin, and Aleksey Y. Lipatnikov. 2018. "Verification of Requirements for the Simulation Model of a Production Enterprise." *Business Informatics*. https://doi.org/10.17323/1998-0663.2018.2.65.78.

Makarov, Valery, Sergey Ayvazyan, Mikhail Afanasyev, Albert Bakhtizin, and Ashkhen Nanavyan. 2016. "Modeling the Development of Regional Economy and an Innovation Space Efficiency." *Foresight and STI Governance*. https://doi.org/ 10.17323/1995-459X.2016.3.76.90.

Malkina, M. Yu., and R. V. Balakin. 2019. "Contribution of Economic Sectors and Their Determinants to Tax Revenues of Consolidated Budgets in Subjects of the Russian Federation." *Region: Economics and Sociology*, no. 2. https://doi.org/10. 15372/reg20190202.

Maurseth, Per Botolf. 2003. "Divergence and Dispersion in the Russian Economy." *Europe - Asia Studies*. https://doi.org/10.1080/0966813032000141079.

Mayorova, Albina Nikolaevna, Svetlana Viktoronva Panasenko, Alexander Fedorovich Nikishin, Gennady Gennadjevich Ivanov, and Elena Aleksandrovna Mayorova. 2018. "Analyzing Regional Differences in the Condition and Development of Trade in Russia." *Entrepreneurship and Sustainability Issues*. https://doi.org/10.9770/ jesi.2018.6.2(30).

Naumov, I. V., A. V. Trynov, and A. O. Safonov. 2020. "Scenario Modelling for Reproducing Investment Potential of Institutional Sectors in the Regions of the

Siberian Federal District." *Finance: Theory and Practice*. https://doi.org/10.26794/2587-5671-2020-24-6-19-37.

Naumov, Il'ya, and Aleksandr Trynov. 2019. "Modeling the Investment Attractiveness of the Types of Economic Activities in the Region with the Use of the Matrix of Financial Flows." *Economic and Social Changes: Facts, Trends, Forecast* [Экономические и Социальные Перемены: Факты, Тенденции, Прогноз]. https://doi.org/10.15838/esc.2019.4.64.4.

Rytova, Elena, and Svetlana Gutman. 2019. "Assessment of Regional Development Strategy in the Context of Economy Digitization on the Basis of Fuzzy Set Method." In *IOP Conference Series: Materials Science and Engineering*. https://doi.org/10.1088/1757-899X/497/1/012060.

Semyachkov, Konstantin. 2018. "State Management of Russian Regions by Means of Digital Technologies." In *Proceedings of the European Conference on E-Government, ECEG*.

Sevastyanova, A. E. 2017. "Creating the Conditions for Innovation Development of Resource-Based Regions." *Regional Research of Russia*. https://doi.org/10.1134/S2079970517010075.

Shakleina, Marina, and Aslan Midov. 2019. "Strategic Classification of Regions According to the Level of Financial Self-Sufficiency." *Economic and Social Changes: Facts, Trends, Forecast* [Экономические и Социальные Перемены: Факты, Тенденции, Прогноз]. https://doi.org/10.15838/esc.2019.3.63.3.

Vilken, Viktoria, Olga Kalinina, Sergei Barykin, and Elizaveta Zotova. 2019. "Logistic Methodology of Development of the Regional Digital Economy." In *IOP Conference Series: Materials Science and Engineering*. https://doi.org/10.1088/1757-899X/497/1/012037.

Zemtsov, Stepan, Alexander Muradov, Imogen Wade, and Vera Barinova. 2016. "Determinants of Regional Innovation in Russia: Are People or Capital More Important?" *Foresight and STI Governance*. https://doi.org/10.17323/1995-459X.2016.2.29.42.

In: Global Challenges of Digital Transformation of Markets ISBN: 978-1-53619-754-9
Editors: E. de la Poza and S. E. Barykin   © 2021 Nova Science Publishers, Inc.

Chapter 37

DEVELOPMENT OF METHODOLOGY FOR ASSESSING EFFECTIVENESS OF ONLINE STORE PROMOTION TOOLS

Angi Skhvediani[1], Alexander Plotnikov[2,†],*
Alexey Ivanov[3,‡] and Lilia Sargu[4,§]
[1]Peter the Great St. Petersburg Polytechnic University,
Saint – Petersburg, Russia
[2]Ltd. "Mercury", Saint – Petersburg, Russia
[3]Ltd. "Petrus", Saint – Petersburg, Russia
[4]University of European Studies of Moldova, Chişinău, Moldova

ABSTRACT

Digital technologies are developing, permeating different spheres of economy. One example is a gradual transition of enterprises from traditional sales to sales through online shops. Development of promotion tools used in digital marketing allows businesses to increase their efficiency through direct communication with the consumer. Thus, development of the methodology for assessing the effectiveness of online store promotion tools becomes relevant. In the current study, the authors present the results of the analysis of five main promotion tools: SEO promotion, contextual advertising, media and banner advertising, SMM, content marketing. Furthermore, a scheme for interaction of these tools with each other is presented. To assess the effectiveness of the promotion tools used, the authors propose a system of indicators, consisting of three categories: economic, synthetic, and business indicators. This system is tested on the example of a small enterprise that sells systems for wine filling on the markets of St. Petersburg and

* Corresponding Author's Email: shvediani_ae@spbstu.ru.
† Corresponding Author's Email: plotnikov_ai_00@mail.ru.
‡ Corresponding Author's Email: silveruan@yandex.ru.
§ Corresponding Author's Email: lsargu@mail.ru.

Moscow in 2017 - 2018. Following the results of the analysis, it is concluded that, thanks to contextual, SMM, and media and banner advertising, it was possible to increase the number of visitors of the website. The use of content marketing allowed increasing loyalty of the target audience for the online store. Additionally, ineffective aspects of using these tools were identified. Thus, the developed system of indicators can be used by enterprises to track and analyze the effectiveness of online marketing tools.

Keywords: marketing, brand, electronic commerce, wine

1. INTRODUCTION

For many years, the Internet has not been regarded by commercial enterprises as a platform for promotion due to its relatively narrow target audience compared to traditional mass media (Chaffey and Ellis-Chadwick 2019; Klimin, Tikhonov, and Efimov 2017; Viktor P Semenov, Sokolitsyn, and Sokolitsyna 2018; Fejling et al. 2019). Active development of the Russian Internet, the rapid spread of mobile gadgets with access the Internet - all this has made digital marketing one of the most effective and at the same time affordable means of promotion with the possibility of deep targeting of communication messages (Klykovskaia 2013; Bataev 2018; Dubgorn, A.; Abdelwahab, M. N.; Borremans, A.; Zaychenko 2019; V P Semenov et al. 2017).

The Internet, with its ability of almost instant communication, allows companies to reach a completely new level of interaction not only with their current, but also with potential customers(Rodionov, Konnikov, and Konnikova 2018; Balashova and Gromova 2017; Shkurkin et al. 2017). A company can tell about itself, its new product or service, identify its weaknesses, create a positive image for its target audience (Kotler, Kartajaya, and Setiawan 2016; Taiminen and Karjaluoto 2015; Makrides, Vrontis, and Christofi 2019; Belov 2019).

Thus, the relevance of the topic is connected with popularization of digital marketing in promoting goods and services via the Internet. With correct configuration, multiple tests, and proper maintenance, this source of sales can become the main or one of the most effective (Yasmin, Tasneem, and Fatema 2015; Khan and Siddiqui 2013; Kostin 2016; Ratilainen 2018).

The purpose of this paper is to develop methodology for assessing effectiveness of online store promotion tools and to assess effectiveness of the use of online store promotion tools by the example of systems for wine filling, sold by small businesses in the markets of St. Petersburg and Moscow.

2. LITERATURE REVIEW

There can be distinguished five main promotion tools that can be used by enterprises working in the field of e-commerce: SEO-promotion, contextual advertising, media and banner advertising, SMM, content marketing.

2.1. SEO-Promotion

When using this method, target audience is attracted to the website through search engines. In order for a web resource to be noticed, it must be at the top of the search results for certain search queries. In order to obtain the necessary effect,SEO optimization of the website is carried out, during which a unique and valuable content is created with the inclusion of popular queries (Zilincan 2015; Saura, Palos-Sánchez, and Cerdá Suárez 2017; Helsen 2019; Bizhanova et al. 2019).

With a comparatively small budget for promotion, it is possible to bring the site to the top of the search results on low-competitive queries.

This will lead to increased target traffic and increased confidence in the website not only from search engines, but also from users. The effect of SEO promotion of the website is long-term.

The main advantages: increased website traffic, low promotion costs, high conversion of website visitors to buyers, a minimum of negative effect of hard selling to a customer, simplification of finding the target audience.

The main disadvantages: the need to constantly monitor the content of the website to meet the requirements of search engines, timely updating the content of the website for search engine queries, not the shortest time to achieve the results of the campaign, the need to adjust the same website to the criteria of different search engines.

2.2. Contextual Advertising

When quick results are needed, promotion through contextual advertising is used. This is an effective tool for promoting goods and services, brands, companies, and websites. A distinctive feature of such online advertising is that the ads are shown to interested users. To see contextual advertising, consumers should initially show interest in the topic to which your site is dedicated, to similar goods or services (Yoo and Eastin 2017; Charlesworth 2014; Kapoor, Dwivedi, and Piercy 2016).

The main advantages: mainly only the target audience and "warm" customers, advertising can be seen immediately in the search results, there are no conditions for mandatory optimization of the website to the requirements of search engines, remarketing: when a potential client who, for some reason, left the website, is "pursued" by contextual advertising on third-party resources, the ability to track expenditures. Payment is not for displays by quantity or time, but for the visits of potential customers to the site, a quick effect. Unlike the work of SEO, you can feel the work of the context in a shorter time. Usually, you can already see dynamics during the first week of the campaign.

The main disadvantages: a small number of visits from ads (depending on the subject of the website), the effect of advertising and obtrusiveness, not a fixed cost of display, the auction system, the budget is much higher than in SEO.

2.3. Media and Banner Advertising

Media advertising and banners are intended to attract attention through visual impact. The company's potential clients are shown bright multimedia ads that immediately arouse people's interest and cause response. With proper organization of an advertising campaign, this way can effectively promote new products and services, popular brands, special offers. The authors take into account the features of digitalization of the trade networks and physical distribution (Barykin, Kalinina, et al. 2021; Barykin, Kapustina, Sergeev, et al. 2021; Barykin, Bochkarev, et al. 2021; Barykin, Kapustina, Valebnikova, et al. 2021; Barykin, Smirnova, Sharapaev, et al. 2021).

Also, advertising aims perfectly to form a positive image of a company or a brand (Obal and Lv 2017; Sokolova and Titova 2019; Tamilmani, Rana, and Dwivedi 2020; Chaffey and Ellis-Chadwick 2019).

The main advantages: the ability to influence the subconscious of websitevisitors depending on certain factors (gender, age, area of work, etc.), successful banners are memorable, the ability to analyze the audience coverage. The more visitors go to the website where the media advertising is placed, the greater the coverage is, the most effective tool to increase brand awareness.

The main disadvantages: large budget, not always high conversion of visitors into customers.

2.4. SMM

Promotion in social networks, not perceived as spam, but still has the necessary effect.

The main advantages: a live interactive audience, no costs for advertising in social networks if it is not promotion for money, the ability to quickly work with proposals and objections of customers, formation of thepool of regular customers who will monitor development of the company, changes, promotions, etc. (Dwivedi, Kapoor, and Chen 2015; Keegan and Rowley 2017; Knoblich et al. 2017; Stephen 2016; Felix, Rauschnabel, and Hinsch 2017).

The main disadvantages: not always the target audience, not all "topics" are promoted in social networks equally well. Usually, SMM works well for b2c, c2c, but with b2b it's not that simple, a lot of time is spent on community. Social networks need constant attention, if you do not show up for a long time - people forget, value your reputation. By making a few not the most effective posts, you can ruin your reputation for a long time and lose loyalty of subscribers, there is tough competition. Everyone tries to get to the top, and there is constant struggle for the right to be the best.

2.5. Content Marketing

For search engines, an indicator of the website quality is the level of its value and usefulness to people. Users prefer those websites that can offer them interesting information on a particular topic, news, useful documents, and recommendations. Promoting a site with content is considered to be very profitable and effective in today's conditions (Baltes 2015; Pulizzi 2013; Holliman and Rowley 2014; Ho, Pang, and Choy 2020).

The main advantages: the ability to quickly gain the trust of readers. Even the first article can make one famous and lead to the top in search engines, recognition. With each new publication an impression of yourself, your resource, and your product is formed, customers memorize, excellent interaction with SEO. There is a great chance to increase traffic by writing the content that will work in SEO, a good text does not look like advertising and does not annoy subscribers.

The main disadvantages: you need good copywriters and text authors, you need time to write these texts, not always high conversion of readers into customers.

3. MATERIALS AND METHODS

For promotion on the markets of St. Petersburg and Moscow in 2018, the authors used 5 promotion tools for wine filling systems. Their functional interdependence is shown in Figure 1.

The following types of links can be seen in the scheme of interaction of promotion tools.

SEO is responsible for the semantic core of the website, all other promotion tools are configured according to it.

Contextual advertising is a driver of attracting the target audience and forms an entry point for users.

Media and banner advertising expand coverage of "cold" and near-target audiences through visual elements. Along with contextual advertising, it is the main transfer to attract new visitors.

Content marketing is responsible for informativeness and usefulness of the content, instilling trust in the website, converting "cold" customers into "warm" ones and carrying a security element to the purchase. Contextual and media advertising form the main pool of potential customers. There is a mutually complementary relationship with SMM due to similarity of the functions of these tools.

SMM is needed to increase visitor return and engage cold and near-target audiences by forming a social networking community. Communication with users can speed up a decision-making process.

SMM and content marketing improve effectiveness of media and banner advertising as well as contextual advertising by working with a "cold" audience.

All tools are interconnected with one another and can function effectively only if properly configured and optimized for the semantic core of an online store.

Relying on the analysis of the literature (Balashova and Gromova 2017; Charlesworth 2014; Dwivedi, Kapoor, and Chen 2015; Khan and Siddiqui 2013), the authors developed a system of indicators and divided them into three groups: economic, synthetic, and business indicators. The system is presented in Table 1.

Table 1. System of indicators for assessing effectiveness of using online store promotion tools

Group	Indicator	Indicator description
Economic indicators	goods turnover	revenue for each promotion tool, RUB
	orders	number of orders for a promotion tool, pcs.
	costs	sum of money spent on a promotion tool, RUB
	grossrevenue	revenue defined as the difference between the final revenue and the total purchase value for each promotion tool, RUB
	specific gross revenue in goods turnover	Share of gross revenue in total goods turnover, share
	specific cost amount in goods turnover	Share of costs in the total volume of goods turnover, share
Synthet icindicators	visits	number of all visitors of the online store, first-time and returned, pcs.
	visitors	show the number of unique visitors, people
	viewing depth	number of pages viewed by visitors, pages
	time spent on a website	The average time a visitor spends on the website, minutes
	refusals	visitors who spent less than 15 seconds on the website, %
	share of visitors with 1 visit	visitors with one visit, %
	share of visitors who returned after 1 day	visitors returned in a day, %
	share of visitors who returned after 2-7 days	visitors who returned within 2-7 days, %
	share of visitors who returned after 8-31 days	visitors who returned within 8-31 days, %
	days between visits	show the average gap between visits, days
	CTR (click-through rate)	shows the conversion of clicks to the number of ad impressions, %
	CPC (cost per click)	click cost, defined as the ratio of the cost of a promotion tool to the total number of clicks, RUB per 1 click
Business indicators	CPO (cost per order)	cost of order conversion for a promotion tool, defined as the ratio of costs to the number of orders for the promotion tool, RUB per 1 click
	ROI (return on investments)	return on investment of a promotion tool, expressed as a ratio of the difference in gross revenue and costs to the costs of a promotion tool, %
	AOV (average order value)	average bill of an order for a certain promotion tool, RUB

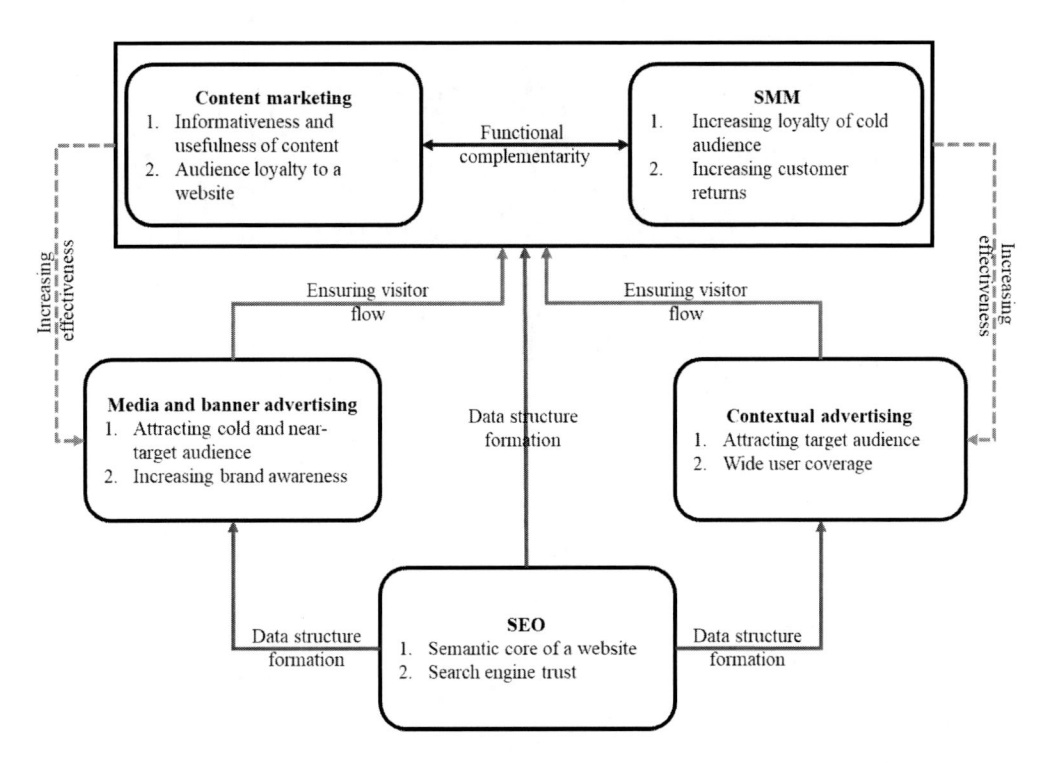

Figure 1. Scheme of functional dependence of promotion tools used by the small business in 2018.

Using these indicators together will make it possible to assess effectiveness of individual promotion tools and the marketing company as a whole. Effectiveness will be evaluated from in terms of increasing the target audience of the online store.

4. RESULTS

Tables 2-3 present the results of the analysis for the effectiveness of using promotion tools in 2017-2018, as well as relative changes in the results for the ratio of 2018 to 2017. Color correction was used to assess the results for easy visualization of the data, as the indicators are presented in different measurement units: rubles, pieces, pages, minutes, percentage, days. Moreover, in the relative changes of the indicators there are both positive and negative changes, but the minus sign does not indicate that the dynamics of the indicator is negative. For example, the CPC indicator for SEO was 10.22 rubles in 2017, while in 2018 it became 3.05 rubles. Relative change is 70.15%, but this indicator has positive dynamics since it shows that the cost per click became cheaper by 70.15%, which is a very good rate in the dynamics of changes.

The results show the dynamics of changes occurring due to internal and external factors (changes in trade mark-ups, the impact of competition, an increase in retail prices and changes in spending on promotion tools.)

Table 2. Relative change in KPI indicators for 2018 compared to 2017 for the promotion tools of SEO and content marketing

Indicators / Year	Promotion tools	SEO 2017	SEO 2018	Change, %	Content marketing 2017	Content marketing 2018	Change, %
Economic indicators	Goods turnover, RUB	807463	561523	-30.46	2173662	2000425	-7.97
	Orders, pcs.	28	24	-14.29	67	76	13.43
	Costs, RUB	15000	10000	-33.33	28000	44000	57.14
	Gross revenue, RUB	109088	67069	-38.52	502550	434656	-13.51
	Specific gross revenue in goods turnover, share	0.135	0.119	-11.85	0.231	0.217	-6.06
	Specific cost amount in goods turnover, share	0.019	0.018	-5.26	0.013	0.022	69.23
Synthetic indicators	Visits, pcs.	1467	3276	123.31	3183	5425	70.44
	Visitors, pcs.	792	2159	172.60	2480	4379	76.57
	Viewing depth, pages	1.91	1.88	-1.57	2.3	2.47	7.39
	Time spent on a website, minutes	0:02:08	0:02:05	-2.34	0:02:15	0:02:23	5.93
	Refusals, %.	13.7	21.8	59.12	11.7	13.3	13.68
	Share of visitors with 1 visit, %.	49.1	61	24.24	77	79.8	3.64
	Share of visitors who returned after 1 day, %.	19.1	15.4	-19.37	8.77	8.09	-7.75
	Share of visitors who returned after 2-7 days, %.	27.7	19.8	-28.52	11.2	8.72	-22.14
	Share of visitors who returned after 8-31 days, %.	3.34	2.92	-12.57	2.17	2.03	-6.45
	Days between visits, days	2.66	2.72	2.26	3.66	5.39	47.27
	CTR, %	19.68	18.77	-4.62	24.78	16.52	-33.33
	CPC, RUB	10.22	3.05	-70.16	8.8	8.11	-7.84
Business indicators	CPO, RUB	535.71	416.67	-22.22	417.91	578.95	38.53
	ROI, %	627	571	-8.93	1695	888	-47.61
	AOV, RUB	28838	23397	-18.87	32443	26321	-18.87

Color legend in the table for the "Change" column: red is negative dynamics, dark green is positive dynamics. Color legend in the table for the rest of the columns: blue is the worst indicator for all promotion instruments in a given period (year); green is the best indicator for all promotion tools in a given period (year).

Table 3. Relative change in KPI indicators for 2018 compared to 2017 for the promotion tools of contextual advertising, media and banner advertising, SMM

Promotion tools / Indicator		Contextual advertising		Change, %	Media and banner	Undefined	SMM
Year		2017	2018		2018	2018	2018
Economic indicators	Goods turnover, RUB	3795798	3989151	5.09	1299691	457407	231628
	Orders, pcs.	93	124	33.33	42	17	9
	Costs, RUB	82685	172155	108.21	128650	67000	36000
	Gross revenue, RUB	1476195	1434476	-2.83	434398	107169	46208
	Specific gross revenue in goods turnover, share	0.389	0.36	-7.46	0.334	0.234	0.199
	Specific cost amount in goods turnover, share	0.022	0.043	95.45	0.099	0.146	0.155
Synthetic indicators	Visits, pcs.	3318	5864	76.73	4607	3252	4385
	Visitors, pcs.	2866	5495	91.73	4355	2717	4249
	Viewing depth, pages	1.63	1.64	0.61	1.51	1.72	1.54
	Time spent on a website, minutes	0:01:06	0:01:00	-9.09	0:01:03	0:01:22	0:00:49
	Refusals, %.	23.4	31.8	35.90	18.4	27.3	26.2
	Share of visitors with 1 visit, %.	84.9	92.2	8.60	92.2	67.4	96.8
	Share of visitors who returned after 1 day, %.	8.59	5.27	-38.65	3.34	19.2	0.84
	Share of visitors who returned after 2-7 days, %.	5.12	1.47	-71.29	3.21	10.8	0.82
	Share of visitors who returned after 8-31 days, %.	1.12	0.51	-54.46	0.74	1.72	0.59
	Days between visits, days	3.1	4.53	46.13	5.11	2.59	5.8
	CTR, %	7.48	6.22	-16.84	2.19	2.82	5.7
	CPC, RUB	24.92	29.36	17.82	27.92	20.6	8.21
Business indicators	CPO, RUB	889.09	1388.35	56.15	3063.1	3941.18	4000
	ROI, %	1685	733	-56.50	60	60	28
	AOV, RUB	40815	32171	-21.18	26906	26906	25736

Color legend in the table for the "Change" column: red is negative dynamics, dark green is positive dynamics. Color legend in the table for the rest of the columns: blue is the worst indicator for all promotion instruments in a given period (year); green is the best indicator for all promotion tools in a given period (year).

Analyzing Tables 2-3, the following conclusions can be drawn:

In 2017, SEO gathered 6 out of 9 indicators with the worst results in the group of economic and business indicators. But in the group of synthetic indicators, SEO took 5 of the 12 best positions and showed the worst results only in 2. We can conclude that in terms of economic efficiency, this tool is not very expedient, but it is one of the best in terms of return of clients.

In 2018, SEO strengthened its position in the synthetic group of indicators and also became a leader in 5 out of 12 indicators, significantly improved the number of visits by 123.31% and the number of visitors by 172.6%, which is almost equal to other tools, and by CPC it became a leader, but there was a strong drop in rejection rate by 59.12%, which may lead to a deterioration of indexing in search engines. In economic and business groups, 6 out of 9 indicators dropped from -9.02% to -38.52%, which worsened the turnover by 30.46%. But in terms of cost of attracting a client it took the first place, having improved its own result by 22.22% compared to 2017. In 2017, content marketing in the group of economic indicators was the best only in terms of specific cost volume, but in business indicators was leading in terms of cost of attracting customers and investment efficiency, which is the main conversion results. And to keep the audience and content informativeness, this tool is also among the leaders in terms of viewing depth, time spent on the website, and refusals.

In 2018, content marketing remained the leader in terms of viewing depth, time spent on the website, and refusals, even slightly improving last year's results by 7.39% and 5.93% respectively. Return on customers fell by an average of 9%, but given the coverage of visitors from the "cold" audience, this is an excellent result and indicates that segmentation of target audiences and the articles written for them were relevant. And the visits and visitors showed positive dynamics of 70.44% and 76.57% respectively. In economic and business groups, it remained the leader only in the efficiency of investments, although the indicator dropped by -47.61%, which indicates a strong influence of external factors.

Contextual advertising in 2017 is the dominant promotion tool in economic indicators, but in terms of costs and specific cost amount showed the worst performance due to the high cost of using this tool. This is also reflected by business indicators, in which the cost of attracting a client was the worst indicator but in terms of the average bill became a leader and approached the leader in investment efficiency. In synthetic terms, this tool took 9 out of the 12 worst indicators, beating only the number of visits and visitors. This indicates its low relevance to the demands of visitors and lack of segmentation by target groups.

In 2018, contextual advertising strengthened the leading position in the economic group, showing positive dynamics in terms of goods turnover and the number of orders by 5.09% and 33.33%, respectively, which, even under the influence of external factors negatively affected only costs and specific cost amount in goods turnover for this promotion tool. 9 out of 12 synthetic indicators declined from -8.6% to -71.29%, which indicates poor optimization of ads for target groups of the "cold" audience. Of course, visits and visitors increased by 76.73% and 91.73% respectively, but the cost of attracting a client increased by 56.15%, and investment efficiency fell by -56.49%.

Overall, the average bill fell by 18.87% to 21.18% due to a decrease in trade mark-ups and an increase in the number of accessories and system components in orders.

The best promotion tool among the new ones was media and banner advertising, which showed proportional results in terms of gross revenue with content marketing with fewer orders but much higher promotion costs. Viewing depth and CTR were the worst of all promotion tools in 2018. Good rates of the average bill, visits, visitors, and refusals indicate that the effectiveness of the tool is not poor, but the cost of attracting a client and low investment efficiency indicate the need for optimization of this tool and for moderate use.

SMM was the worst in almost all groups of indicators, taking the last place in 11 out of 21 indicators. The number of visits and visitors can be called good results.

5. Discussion

The semantic core of a website (SEO) in the format of the goal set for 2018, namely to increase the audience coverage, resulted in a 123% increase in visits, which worsened other synthetic KPI indicators by a quarter. This means that the "cold" audience was unable to determine necessity and usefulness of the content. Goods turnover decreased by 30%, which led to a 9% decrease in the investment efficiency of the promotion tool, which, given the negative changes in the external environment, is not a bad result.

Content marketing allowed increasing loyalty of the covered audience, as well as showed positive changes in the increase of visits by 70%, even having the improved viewing depth and time spent on the website by 7% and 6% respectively, but having slightly worsened other synthetic indicators. But taking into account the overall coverage and audience expansion, this is an excellent result and shows excellent optimization and maximum relevance of content to user requests. Gross revenue and turnover decreased by 13% and 8% respectively, but these changes were only due to the negative changes in the external environment.

Contextual advertising was able to attract the largest number of visitors and end customers, increasing order conversion by 33% and goods turnover by 5% with a negative external environment, which proves a dominant position when using this promotion tool. Obviously, costs increased by 108% due to increased competition, and the synthetic group of KPI indicators dropped by 30-35% on average, but the economic efficiency remains at its maximum in the total profit of the organization.

Media and banner advertising were able to attract an additional pool of the "cold" and near-target audience through visual elements converting effectiveness into additional 1.3 million rubles, but the cost of promotion, the average investment efficiency, and high cost of an order indicates the need for selective and more careful use of this tool. Synthetic indicators show good optimization and adjustment of the tool.

SMM due to direct contact with the audience and the formation of brand and product loyalty was able to attract additional 4385 visitors, which is a high result, but the rest of the group of KPI indicators were at an extremely low level, indicating poor optimization and poor relevance to the selected target audience. The economic and business performance was the worst overall, even considering the changes in the external environment, which proves that the tool was not used effectively.

As a future direction of research, the authors plan to expand the methodology of assessing effectiveness of promotion tools through conducting a factor analysis.

CONCLUSION

Looking at the summary indicators of SEO, content marketing, and contextual advertising in the dynamics of 2018 by the results of 2017, we can say that in the group of economic and business indicators, all the results have negative dynamics, except for the number of orders. SEO slightly improved the cost indicators and the cost of attracting orders, and contextual advertising improved goods turnover by 5%. The number of orders provides positive dynamics, so the goal for 2018 was fulfilled correctly, taking into account the intervening external factors.

In the group of synthetic indicators, 4 have positive dynamics directly related to the coverage of "cold" audience. Positive dynamics of the viewing depth says that informativeness and usefulness of the content increased, even taking into account the sharply increased refusal rate. 8 out of 12 indicators showed negative dynamics, which influenced indexation in the Yandex search engine, the website fell from 2-3 to 5-7 places, but in Google, 1 place remained unchanged. This was affected by the number of refusals and an increase in visitor return time.

New promotion tools, media and banner advertising and SMM showed different results in relation to the main tools. Consequently, media and banner advertising in 4 out of 6 indicators in the economic group have good average results, in the groups of synthetic and business indicators, only 3 out of 15 have good results. SMM has good results in only 3 out of 21 indicators, which indicates extremely ineffective use of this tool.

The "Undefined" tool gives mixed results, which makes it impossible to divide it into contextual and media advertising, and remains difficult to measure and distorts effectiveness of indicators of contextual and media advertising.

As a result, the goal set for 2018 was fulfilled, new promotion tools selected to solve the problems of 2017 were tested, the "cold" and "near-target" audiences of this category of products were covered, which surely slightly worsened the synthetic KPI indicators, but increased the inflow of new visitors and total goods turnover with a strong change in the external environment. Net profit of the organization decreased by 8%, but profit from sales increased by 0.18%.

Within the framework of this paper, the authors presented an analysis of five promotion tools used by online stores: SEO-promotion, contextual advertising, media and banner advertising, SMM, content marketing. Based on the analysis of theoretical literature and the results of practical use of these tools, the scheme of interaction between these tools was presented. To assess effectiveness of the tools, the authors developed a system that includes economic, synthetic, and business indicators. This system was tested on the example of a small enterprise supplying systems for wine filling to the markets of St. Petersburg and Moscow in 2017 - 2018. Generally, the developed system of indicators can be used by enterprises to track and analyze effectiveness of using internet marketing tools.

ACKNOWLEDGMENTS

This research work was supported by the Academic Excellence Project 5-100 proposed by Peter the Great St. Petersburg Polytechnic University

REFERENCES

Balashova, Elena S, and Elizaveta A Gromova. 2017. "Russian Experience of Integrating Modern Management Models." *Espacios* 38 (53): 31.

Baltes, Loredana Patrutiu. 2015. "Content Marketing-the Fundamental Tool of Digital Marketing." *Bulletin of the Transilvania University of Brasov. Economic Sciences. Series V* 8 (2): 111.

Barykin, Sergey Yevgenievich, Andrey Aleksandrovich Bochkarev, Sergey Mikhailovich Sergeev, Tatiana Anatolievna Baranova, Dmitriy Anatolievich Mokhorov, and Aleksandra Maksimovna Kobicheva. 2021. "A Methodology of Bringing Perspective Innovation Products to Market." *Academy of Strategic Management Journal* 20 (2): 19. https://www.abacademies.org/articles/a-methodology-of-bringing-perspective-innovation-products-to-market.pdf.

Barykin, Sergey Yevgenievich, Olga Vladimirovna Kalinina, Irina Vasilievna Kapustina, Victor Andreevich Dubolazov, Cesar Armando Nunez Esquivel, Elmira Alyarovna Nazarova, and Petr Anatolievich Sharapaev. 2021. "The Sharing Economy and Digital Logistics in Retail Chains: Opportunities and Threats." *Academy of Strategic Management Journal* 20 (2): 1–14. https://www.abacademies.org/articles/the-sharing-economy-and-digital-logistics-in-retail-chains-opportunities-and-threats.pdf.

Barykin, Sergey Yevgenievich, Irina Vasilievna Kapustina, Sergey Mikhailovich Sergeev, Olga Vladimirovna Kalinina, Viktoriia Valerievna Vilken, Yuri Yevgenievich Putikhin, and Lydia Vitalievna Volkova. 2021. "Developing the Physical Distribution Digital Twin Model within the Trade Network." *Academy of Strategic Management Journal* 20 (1): 1–24. https://www.abacademies.org/articles/developing-the-physical-distribution-digital-twin-model-within-the-trade-network.pdf.

Barykin, Sergey Yevgenievich, Irina Vasilievna Kapustina, Olga Aleksandrovna Valebnikova, Natalia Viktorovna Valebnikova, Olga Vladimirovna Kalinina, Sergey Mikhailovich Sergeev, Marisa Camastral, Yuri Yevgenievich Putikhin, and Lydia Vitalievna Volkova. 2021. "Digital Technologies for Personnel Management: Implications for Open Innovations." *Academy of Strategic Management Journal* 20 (2): 1–14. https://www.abacademies.org/articles/digital-technologies-for-personnel-management-implications-for-open-innovations.pdf.

Barykin, Sergey Yevgenievich, Elena Aleksandrovna Smirnova, Petr Anatolievich Sharapaev, and Angela Bohuovna Mottaeva. 2021. "Development of the Kazakhstan Digital Retail Chains within the EAEU E-Commerce." *Academy of Strategic Management Journal* 20 (2): 1–18. https://www.abacademies.org/articles/development-of-the-kazakhstan-digital-retail-chains-within-the-eaeu-ecommerce-market.pdf.

Bataev, A. V. 2018. "Analysis and Development the Digital Economy in the World." In *Proceedings of the 31st International Business Information Management Association Conference*, 61–71.

Belov, F. D. 2019. "Monetization Model of Digital Products: Economic and Marketing Efficiency." In *1st International Scientific Conference" Modern Management Trends and the Digital Economy: From Regional Development to Global Economic Growth"(MTDE 2019)*. Atlantis Press.

Bizhanova, Kenzhegul, Arafat Mamyrbekov, Ilkhom Umarov, Akmaral Orazymbetova, and Aziza Khairullaeva. 2019. "Impact of Digital Marketing Development on Entrepreneurship." In *E3S Web of Conferences*, 135:4023. EDP Sciences.

Chaffey, Dave, and Fiona Ellis-Chadwick. 2019. *Digital Marketing*. Pearson UK.

Charlesworth, Alan. 2014. *Digital Marketing: A Practical Approach*. Routledge.

Dubgorn, A.; Abdelwahab, M. N.; Borremans, A.; Zaychenko, I. 2019. "Analysis of Digital Business Transformation Tools." In *Proceedings of the 33rd International Business Information Management Association Conference*, 9677–82.

Dwivedi, Yogesh K, Kawaljeet Kaur Kapoor, and Hsin Chen. 2015. "Social Media Marketing and Advertising." *The Marketing Review* 15 (3): 289–309.

Fejling, Tatiana, Elena Torosyan, Olga Tsukanova, and Olga Kalinina. 2019. "Special Aspects of Digital Technology-Based Brand Promotion." *IOP Conference Series: Materials Science and Engineering* 497 (1). https://doi.org/10.1088/1757-899X/497/1/012027.

Felix, Reto, Philipp A Rauschnabel, and Chris Hinsch. 2017. "Elements of Strategic Social Media Marketing: A Holistic Framework." *Journal of Business Research* 70: 118–26.

Helsen, Kristiaan. 2019. *"Digital Marketing in the Global Marketplace: Latest Developments."*

Ho, John, Christopher Pang, and Crisann Choy. 2020. "Content Marketing Capability Building: A Conceptual Framework." *Journal of Research in Interactive Marketing.*

Holliman, Geraint, and Jennifer Rowley. 2014. "Business to Business Digital Content Marketing: Marketers' Perceptions of Best Practice." *Journal of Research in Interactive Marketing* 8 (4): 269–93.

Kapoor, Kawaljeet Kaur, Yogesh K Dwivedi, and Niall C Piercy. 2016. "Pay-per-Click Advertising: A Literature Review." *The Marketing Review* 16 (2): 183–202.

Keegan, Brendan James, and Jennifer Rowley. 2017. "Evaluation and Decision Making in Social Media Marketing." *Management Decision* 55 (1): 15–31.

Khan, Fawad, and Kamran Siddiqui. 2013. "The Importance of Digital Marketing. An Exploratory Study to Find the Perception and Effectiveness of Digital Marketing amongst the Marketing Professionals in Pakistan." *Journal of Information Systems & Operations Management*, 1.

Klimin, A. I., D. V. Tikhonov, and A. M. Efimov. 2017. "Evaluation of the Effectiveness of Marketing Communications in Russian Business Using the Example of St. Petersburg Enterprises." In *Proceedings of the 30th International Business Information Management Association Conference*, 1465–82.

Klykovskaia, Irina. 2013. "*How to Make Finnish Products and Services More Popular among Russian Customers: The Analysis of the Existing Digital Advertising Campaigns of Finnish Companies in Russia.*"

Knoblich, Stephan, Andrew Martin, Robert Nash, and Paul Stansbie. 2017. "Keys to Success in Social Media Marketing (SMM)–Prospects for the German Airline Industry." *Tourism and Hospitality Research* 17 (2): 147–64.

Kostin, K. 2016. "Global Potential of E-Marketing: Comparing the United States, Russian Federation and the European Union." *AIMS International Journal of Management (AIJM)* 10 (3): 155–73.

Kotler, Philip, Hermawan Kartajaya, and Iwan Setiawan. 2016. *Marketing 4.0: Moving from Traditional to Digital*. John Wiley & Sons.

Makrides, Anna, Demetris Vrontis, and Michael Christofi. 2019. "The Gold Rush of Digital Marketing: Assessing Prospects of Building Brand Awareness Overseas." *Business Perspectives and Research*, 2278533719860016.

Obal, Michael W, and Wen Lv. 2017. "Improving Banner Ad Strategies through Predictive Modeling." *Journal of Research in Interactive Marketing* 11 (2): 198–212.

Pulizzi, Joe. 2013. *Epic Content Marketing: How to Tell a Different Story, Break through the Clutter, and Win More Customers by Marketing Less*. McGraw-Hill Education.

Ratilainen, Saara. 2018. "Digital Media and Cultural Institutions in Russia: Online Magazines as Aggregates of Cultural Services." *Cultural Studies* 32 (5): 800–824.

Rodionov, Dmitriy Grigorievich, Evgenii Alexandrovich Konnikov, and Olga Anatolievna Konnikova. 2018. "Approaches to Ensuring the Sustainability of Industrial Enterprises of Different Technological Levels." *The Journal of Social Sciences Research*, 277–82.

Saura, José Ramón, Pedro Palos-Sánchez, and Luis Manuel Cerdá Suárez. 2017. "Understanding the Digital Marketing Environment with KPIs and Web Analytics." *Future Internet* 9 (4): 76.

Semenov, V. P., E. V. Budrina, I. K. Soldatov, A. G. Budrin, A. V. Soldatova, and E. A. Eniushkina. 2017. "Factor Analysis of the Results of Digital Technology Applications in the Company's Marketing Activities." In *2017 XX IEEE International Conference on Soft Computing and Measurements (SCM)*, 879–82. IEEE.

Semenov, Viktor P., Alexander S. Sokolitsyn, and Natalya A. Sokolitsyna. 2018. "Marketing Activity Management Improvement for Small-Series Production Enterprises." In *2018 IEEE International Conference" Quality Management, Transport and Information Security, Information Technologies"(IT&QM&IS)*, 382–84. IEEE.

Shkurkin, Dmitry V., Irina A. Krasyuk, Sergey M. Krymov, Irina G. Kazantseva, and Grigory N. Zakharenko. 2017. "Sales Policy and Sales Marketing System." *International Journal of Applied Business and Economic Research* 15 (12): 203–13.

Sokolova, N. G., and O. V. Titova. 2019. "Digital Marketing as a Type: Concept, Tools and Effects." In *1st International Scientific Conference" Modern Management Trends and the Digital Economy: From Regional Development to Global Economic Growth"(MTDE 2019)*. Atlantis Press.

Stephen, Andrew T. 2016. "The Role of Digital and Social Media Marketing in Consumer Behavior." *Current Opinion in Psychology* 10: 17–21.

Taiminen, Heini Maarit, and Heikki Karjaluoto. 2015. "The Usage of Digital Marketing Channels in SMEs." *Journal of Small Business and Enterprise Development* 22 (4): 633–51.

Tamilmani, Kuttimani, Nripendra P. Rana, and Yogesh K. Dwivedi. 2020. "Multi-Channel Digital Marketing Strategy in an Emerging Economy: The Case of Flintobox in India." In *Digital and Social Media Marketing*, 239–48. Springer.

Yasmin, Afrina, Sadia Tasneem, and Kaniz Fatema. 2015. "Effectiveness of Digital Marketing in the Challenging Age: An Empirical Study." *International Journal of Management Science and Business Administration* 1 (5): 69–80.

Yoo, Seung-Chul, and Matthew S. Eastin. 2017. "Contextual Advertising in Games: Impacts of Game Context on a Player's Memory and Evaluation of Brands in Video Games." *Journal of Marketing Communications* 23 (6): 614–31.

Zilincan, Jakub. 2015. "Search Engine Optimization." In *CBU International Conference Proceedings*, 3:506–10.

In: Global Challenges of Digital Transformation of Markets ISBN: 978-1-53619-754-9
Editors: E. de la Poza and S. E. Barykin   © 2021 Nova Science Publishers, Inc.

Chapter 38

THE IMPACT OF MARKETING INCENTIVES ON ONLINE AND OFFLINE IMPULSE BUYING BEHAVIOR IN HANDMADE INDUSTRY

Nataliia Krasnostavskaia[1,], Marina Chigir[2,†], Tatiana Maslova[2,‡] and Petko Monev[3,§]*

[1]Peter the Great St. Petersburg Polytechnic University,
Saint Petersburg, Russia
[2]Saint Petersburg Electrotechnical University "LETI",
Saint Petersburg, Russia,
[3]University of Economics - Varna, Varna, Bulgaria

ABSTRACT

In connection with the development of digital technologies, it becomes necessary to develop modern marketing programs that meet the new needs of society and digital trends. The specificity of handmade goods necessitates the integration of marketing communications. The object of the study was offline and online buyers of handmade goods who made impulse purchases. The subject of the study was marketing incentives that influence online and offline impulse purchases of handmade goods. The aim of the study was to study the possibility of the influence of marketing incentives on making impulse purchases in an online environment compared to an offline environment, and determined the purpose of the study and its relevance. The research methodology is based on the idea that a number of marketing incentives influence the making of impulse online and offline purchases of handmade goods. The factors contributing to online and offline

[*] Corresponding Author's Email: marketrek@yandex.ru.
[†] Corresponding Author's Email: mvchigir@yandex.ru.
[‡] Corresponding Author's Email: mtd777@mail.ru.
[§] Corresponding Author's Email: mg5ko@abv.bg.

impulse purchases have been investigated. A study of consumers of handmade goods showed that there is a predominant opportunity for marketing incentives to influence impulse purchases in an online environment compared to an offline environment. The data obtained is essential for the development of marketing strategies for brands in the handmade industry.

Keywords: impulse buying behavior, buying behavior, consumer behavior, decision-making process, purchase decision, handmade goods, handmade products, handmade industry, electronic commerce, e-commerce, internet marketing, marketing incentives, marketing

1. INTRODUCTION

The development of digital technologies is one of the driving forces for the development of society and the economy. The digital economy is transforming the consumer experience of shopping, consumers are becoming more independent in their choice and demanding of the quality of the services provided (S. Bozhuk, Krasnostavskaia, et al. 2019; S. Bozhuk, Maslova, et al. 2019). Research shows the need to develop effective solutions in modern management and marketing (S. G. Bozhuk and Krasnov 2017; Goncharova, Degtereva, and Sopilko 2018; Kapustina et al. 2019; Krasyuk, Yanenko, and Nazarova 2020; Rudskaya and Rodionov 2018; Selentyeva, Ivanova, and Kulibanova 2018; Aleksandrov, Fedorova, and Parshukov 2020; Krasyuk et al. 2019; Skhvediani and Kudryavtseva 2018; Dvas and Dubolazova 2018). The emerging transformations of social environment models and business environment require new solutions from companies (Barykin, Kalinina, et al. 2021; Barykin, Kapustina, Sergeev, et al. 2021; Barykin, Bochkarev, et al. 2021; Barykin, Kapustina, Valebnikova, et al. 2021; Barykin, Smirnova, Sharapaev, et al. 2021). As a result, it becomes necessary to develop modern marketing programs that meet the new needs of society and digital trends.

Consumers in the process of making a purchase decision are influenced by a variety of factors. Manufacturers and sellers of goods specifically design measures to facilitate impulse purchases by consumers. Impulse purchases can be not only goods of impulse demand, but also other goods that attract the attention of consumers through a directed affective and cognitive influence.

The spread of digital technologies exacerbates competition between representatives of the handmade industry: craftsmen and international trading Internet platforms. This forces the artisans and companies to carefully engage in the development of communications with customers and other interested parties. The specificity of handmade goods necessitates the integration of marketing communications, which is impossible without knowledge of the factors that influence the decision-making process to purchase handmade goods.

The need to study the possibility of the influence of marketing incentives on impulse purchases in the online environment as compared to the offline environment determined the purpose of the study and its relevance. The aim of the study was to establish the existence of prevailing opportunities for the influence of marketing incentives on impulse purchases in the online environment as compared to the offline environment.

To achieve this goal, research objectives were defined:

- research of factors contributing to offline impulse purchases;
- research of factors contributing to online impulse purchases;
- research of consumers of handmade goods to determine the particularities of the influence of marketing incentives when making online impulse purchases of handmade goods in comparison with offline impulse purchases.

1.1. Impulse Buying Behavior

Making impulse purchases is determined not only by a variety of internal psychological factors, but is also influenced by external, market stimuli. Iyer, Blut, Xiao, Grewal (Iyer et al. 2020) determined that character traits (desire for sensations, inclination to impulse purchases), motives (utilitarian, hedonistic), consumer resources (time, money) and marketing incentives become key triggers impulse purchases. Self-control of consumers and their moods mediate and explain the affective and cognitive psychological processes associated with impulse buying.

A sudden desire to make a purchase is caused by external, market incentives and internal psychological factors. Parsad, Prashar, Vijay (Parsad, Prashar, and Vijay 2019) showed that the relationship between two personality traits (extraversion and neuroticism) and the propensity to impulse purchases does not depend on the product category. The authors noted that the impact of conscientiousness on impulse buying propensity varies by product category. Fenton-O'Creevy, Furnham (Fenton-O'Creevy and Furnham 2020) have shown that people with high levels of neuroticism and extraversion and people with low levels of consciousness are more likely to be impulse shoppers.

Corporate social responsibility practices (environmental well-being, social well-being, and economic well-being) can influence impulse buying behavior. Hayat, Jianjun, Zameer, Iqbal (Hayat et al. 2020) determined that environmental well-being has a constructive relationship with trust, which further leads to impulse purchases, and economic well-being is directly related to impulse purchases. However, social welfare actions do not affect impulsive consumer buying behavior.

Consumer motivation is one of the factors influencing the relationship between store and impulse buying. Hashmi, Shu, Haider (Hashmi, Shu, and Haider 2020) have shown that shopping pleasure mediates the influence of store atmosphere on impulse shopping behavior. The authors found that hedonic buying motives soften the relationship between store atmosphere and impulse buying.

Certain factors in retailers influence impulse purchases. Vinish, Pinto, Hawaldar, Pinto (Vinish et al. 2020) have shown on the example of clothing stores that store layout, atmosphere and employees are highly positively correlated with impulse shopping behavior. The authors found that store headcount and sales skills are critical aspects of impulse buying in the apparel business and real assets for a retail organization.

Stores need to offer the latest fashions, provide discounts on certain fashions, and create an inviting in-store atmosphere for shoppers to enjoy their shopping. Rahadhini, Wibowo, Lukiyanto (Rahadhini, Wibowo, and Lukiyanto 2020), using the example of fashionable goods, revealed that the hedonistic value of purchases indirectly influences impulse purchases through positive emotions.

Price stocks affect impulse buying. Hajipour, Zadeh, Shafiee, Hosseini (Hajipour et al. 2020) showed that price promotions and service innovations positively influence impulse buying behavior.

One way to influence impulse purchases is to attract celebrities. Parmar, Mann, Ghuman (Parmar, Mann, and Ghuman 2020) found that the presence of celebrities in advertising at the point of sale enhances customer momentum. The authors found it to be more effective for high-engagement products than for low-engagement products.

The atmosphere of a store influences impulse shopping. Jose, Peter Kumar, Joseph (Jose, Peter Kumar, and Joseph 2019) identified the influence of design (lighting, music, color) and social factors (staff appearance, staff behavior and other store visitors) of store atmosphere on impulse shopping behavior.

Visual merchandising is one of the tools for influencing impulse purchases. Pratiwi, Rusfian (Pratiwi and Rusfian 2019) found that visual merchandising chandising has a significant impact on impulse purchases, and the determining factor that has the greatest influence on impulse purchases in the store is the store interior design and layout.

The post-purchase experience of a product plays a role in encouraging impulse buying behavior. Spiteri Cornish (Spiteri Cornish 2020) showed that, regardless of the importance of the buying experience, negative post-purchase experiences lead to post-purchase regrets, which limits future impulse buying, and positive post-buy experiences reinforce impulse buying.

1.2. Online Impulse Buying Behavior

A significant portion of online shopping is associated with impulse purchases. Wu, Chiu, Chen (Wu, Chiu, and Chen 2020) showed an important connection between three specific problems of impulse purchases on the Internet: the perceived risk for e-shops, e-store design, and the psychological state of the online shopper.

Impulse buying is influenced by certain factors. Lazim, Sulaiman, Zakuan, Mas'od, Chin, Awang (Lazim et al. 2020) found that sales incentives, credit card payments, visual merchandising, pricing, and online reviews significantly influence impulse purchases.

There is a link between website functionality and visuals and impulse buying. Bismo, Putra, Sarjono, Nasrul (Bismo et al. 2020) using the example of discount group sites showed that the functional usability of the website and the visual pleasure of using the website have a positive and significant effect on impulse buying due to positive emotional affect as a mediating variable.

Lifestyle is one of the factors influencing impulse purchases. Ittaqullah, Madjid, Suleman (Ittaqullah, Madjid, and Suleman 2020) found that mobile marketing and discounts do not have a significant impact on impulse shopping for consumers on the online marketplace, and lifestyle has a significant positive impact on impulse buying behavior.

Emotional reactions influence impulse buying. Chen, Chen, Lin (W. K. Chen, Chen, and Lin 2020) found that pleasure directly and positively influences the impulsive purchase of consumers.

Companies can benefit from abandoning price competition and instead satisfy buyers by making them less boring. Sundström, Hjelm-Lidholm, Radon (Sundström, Hjelm-Lidholm, and Radon 2019) using the example of fashionable items revealed that impulse purchases of fashionable items on the Internet by young consumers are often motivated by boredom. The authors noted that when consumers are bored, it is easy to provoke incentives such as price, easy access and free shipping, and perceived as easy to get rid of boredom.

Impulse purchases are influenced by information quality factors. Liu, Song, Yang, Cheng, Li (Liu et al. 2020) have shown that the variety, brightness and reliability of information on a website positively affects consumer satisfaction, while pleasure and excitement positively affects impulse buying behavior.

Social media users tend to follow tags, likes, and comments posted by others for products and services, leading to impulse behavior. Nuseir (Nuseir 2020) highlighted the role of Facebook, a social media platform that encourages and creates impulse buying opportunities.

Website quality affects impulse purchases. Hayu, Su-rachman, Rofiq, Rahayu (Hayu et al. 2020) have confirmed that the quality of websites influences impulse online shopping behavior. Tariq, Wang, Akram, Tanveer, Sohaib (Tariq et al. 2020) have shown that high-media websites increase impulse decisions and convert purchase intent.

The streaming marketing sector is working to improve the interaction and understanding between a product, its brand and the user. Gong, Ye, Liu, Wu (Gong et al. 2020), using the example of live streaming platforms, revealed that self-efficacy and psychological belonging of consumers have a synchronous and chain mediating effect on the relationship between the appearance of the platform and impulse buying.

Mobile commerce fosters impulse buying behavior for consumers. Zheng, Men, Yang, Gong (Zheng et al. 2019) found that hedonistic web browsing directly and positively influences consumer impulse buying.

Online impulse shopping has attracted the attention of researchers in various fields, especially in the emerging field of social commerce. There are enough impulse buying stimulants in this interactive environment. Abdelsalam, Salim, Alias, Husain (Abdelsalam et al. 2020) noted that most of the existing studies use the stimulus-organism-response solution.

Social interactions and self-control influence impulse buying. Xu, Zhang, Zhao (Xu, Zhang, and Zhao 2020) used social commerce sites to show that source authority, observational learning, and perceived utility positively influence impulse buying, while self-control negatively affects impulse buying behavior.

Social commerce gives consumers access to product recommendations. Chen, Lu, Wang, Pan (Y. Chen et al. 2019) determined that impulse buying motivation is determined by affective trust in the recommender and attachment to the recommended product, which are influenced by signals related to recommendations (quality and similarity of information) and signals, product-related (indirect expression and aesthetic appeal).

Social commerce tools influence impulse buying. Ab-delsalam, Alias, Salim, Husain (Abdelsalam et al. 2020) showed that the processes of social influence (consent, internalization and identification), individual needs and satisfaction from the use of social networks (purposeful value, entertainment, self-knowledge, social development and maintenance of inter- personal interaction) have a positive effect on the impulse buying behavior of consumers on the Internet on social commerce sites.

The video blog presents various incentives that encourage viewers to make an impulse purchase. Arviansyah, Dhaneswara, Hidayanto, Zhu (Arviansyah et al. 2018) found that the urgency of impulse purchases is influenced by parasocial interaction and perceived utility.

Online reviews contain important information that influences consumer behavior when shopping online. Zhang, Xu, Zhao, Yu (Zhang et al. 2018) showed that the perceived utilitarian and hedonistic value of reading online reviews by consumers improves their browsing behavior, and viewing has a positive effect on consumers' desire to make impulse purchases.

1.3. Handmade Industry

Manufacturing methods (manual or machine) influence consumer response. Frizzo, Dias, Duarte, Rodrigues, Prado (Frizzo et al. 2020) have shown that higher behavioral intentions (probability of purchase and willingness to pay a higher price) attributed to handmade products are related to the perceived naturalness and authenticity associated with the method of production.

In some cases, consumers choose handmade work rather than machine-made work. Hsu, Nguyen Ngoc (Hsu and Nguyen Ngoc 2016) have determined that despite the rapid development of automatic machines, products promoted as handmade are popular with consumers for their outstanding performance.

Certain consumers value originality in self-expression. West (West 2010) used greeting cards to show that consumers with higher cultural capital are more likely to favor postcards that are handcrafted, look handcrafted, or resemble fine art.

Based on the analysis of the factors that determine the performance of impulse purchases in the offline environment, the following marketing incentives were identified:

- product display;
- store layout;
- lighting;
- music;
- assortment;
- price promotions;
- personnel.

Based on the analysis of the factors that determine the performance of impulse purchases in the online environment, the following marketing incentives were identified:

- websiteusability;
- assortment;
- price promotions;
- recommendation mechanism;
- customer reviews;
- social recommendations;
- payment method.

Based on the analysis of the factors that determine the performance of impulse purchases in offline and online environments, an assumption was made about the existence of prevailing opportunities for making impulse purchases in the online environment as compared to the offline environment.

The null hypothesis is formulated:

H0: There is no predominant opportunity for marketing incentives to influence impulse buying of handmade goods in an online environment versus an offline environment.

An alternative hypothesis is formulated:

H1: There are predominant opportunities for impulse buying of handmade goods in an online environment versus an offline environment that marketing incentives can influence.

As a result of the study, the prevailing possibilities of the influence of marketing incentives on making an impulse purchase of handmade goods in an online environment as compared to an offline environment will or may not be identified.

2. MATERIALS AND METHODS

The research methodology is based on the idea that a number of marketing incentives affect the performance of impulse online and offline purchases of handmade goods.

2.1. Questionnaire Development

To conduct a study of consumers of handmade goods to determine the presence of prevailing opportunities for making impulse purchases in an online environment compared to an offline environment, a questionnaire was developed - a working document of a customer survey.

The questionnaire contains the following sections:

- information about the environment of perfect impulse purchases: offline environment, online environment;
- information on marketing incentives that influenced perfect impulse purchases, 7-point, bipolar Rensis Likert scale, 1 - completely not influential, 2 - mostly not influential, 3 - somewhat not influential, 4 - neither not influential nor influential, 5 - somewhat influential, 6 - mostly influential, 7 - completely influential, the scale had to be filled in separately for offline and online purchases.

Determining the impact of product display consists in determining the impact of point-of-sale materials, product packaging, corporate identity, etc.

Determination of the influence of the store layout consists in determining the influence of the location of showcases, points of display of goods, signs, etc.

Determining the influence of the assortment consists in determining the influence of the assortment width, assortment depth, assortment balance, etc.

Determining the impact of price shares is to determine the impact of price offers to consumers.

Determining the influence of personnel consists in determining the influence of establishing and maintaining contact, offering additional products, being informed about the range, motivation, etc.

Determining the impact of website usability consists of determining the impact of navigation, design, ease of use, content, and the like.

Determining the influence of the recommendation engine is to determine the influence of website tools aimed at sales promotion, for example, "people buy with this product," "viewed products," "similar products," "featured products," "best-selling products," "accessories," etc.

Determining the impact of customer reviews consists of determining the impact of review texts and product ratings.

Determining the impact of social recommendations is to determine the impact of recommendations from social networks.

Determining the influence of the payment method consists in determining the influence of the possibility of payment with a bank card.

2.2. Data Collection

The respondents had to be able to recall a particular impulse purchase and reproduce the details, this imposed a limitation on the time interval used. The respondent should have had experience of online and offline shopping for handmade goods.

The type of selection used is a convenient selection.

The study involved 400 respondents who made impulse online and offline purchases of handmade goods at least once over the past year. Period of the survey: 01.02.2020 - 01.04.2020.

Data was analyzed using SPSS software.

3. RESULTS

The main findings are presented below.

3.1. Impact of Marketing Incentives on Impulse Purchases of Handmade Goods in Offline Environment

The results of a consumer survey regarding the impact of marketing incentives on impulse purchases of handmade goods in an offline environment are presented in Table 1. The cells with the maximum number of positive responses from respondents on how the incentive affects impulse purchases are highlighted in color.

Table 1. Impact of marketing incentives on impulse purchases of handmade goods in offline environment

Marketing incentive	Impact assessment							Average score
	1	2	3	4	5	6	7	
Product display	5	21	32	94	136	58	54	4.8125
Store layout	14	43	115	121	70	26	11	3.7800
Lighting	64	97	125	61	23	19	11	2.9575
Music	73	98	153	38	21	15	2	2.7225
Assortment	2	7	14	16	135	168	58	5.5275
Price promotions	1	4	65	83	157	67	23	4.7100
Personnel	23	42	96	101	71	38	29	3.9625

The data showed that the display of the goods is somewhat influential, the layout of the room is neither not influential nor influential, the lighting is somewhat not influential, the music is somewhat not influential, the range is mostly influential, the price action is somewhat influential, the staff is neither not influential nor influential for consumers when making impulse purchases handmade goods in an offline environment.

3.2. Impact of Marketing Incentives on Impulse Purchases of Handmade Goods in the Online Environment

The results of a consumer survey regarding the influence of marketing incentives on impulse purchases of handmade goods in the online environment are presented in Table 2. The cells with the maximum number of positive responses from respondents on how the incentive affects impulse purchases are marked by color.

Table 2. Impact of marketing incentives on impulse purchases of handmade goods in the online environment

Marketing incentive	Impact assessment							Average score
	1	2	3	4	5	6	7	
Website usability	5	19	46	65	104	93	68	4.9875
Assortment	1	5	11	18	20	22	323	6.5225
Price promotions	1	2	15	20	70	147	145	5.9425
Recommendation mechanism	11	17	56	102	115	53	42	4.5200
Customer reviews	17	79	81	98	73	32	20	3.7675
Social recommendations	11	14	27	92	129	65	62	4.8925
Payment method	23	67	75	97	71	43	24	3.8775

The data showed that the usability of the website is somewhat influential, the range is completely influential, the price shares are mostly influential, the recommendation mechanism is somewhat influential, the customer reviews are neither not influential nor influential, the social recommendations are somewhat influential, the payment method is neither not influential nor influential for consumers with making impulse purchases of handmade goods in an offline environment.

3.3. Comparison of the Impact of Marketing Incentives on Impulse Purchases of Handmade Goods in Offline and Online Environments

The results of comparing the impact of marketing incentives on impulse purchases of handmade goods in offline and online environments are presented in Table 3.

Table 3. Comparison of the impact of marketing incentives on impulse purchases of handmade goods in offline and online environments

Marketing incentive	Average score	
	Offlineenvironment	Onlineenvironment
Product display	4.8125	-
Store layout	3.7800	-
Lighting	2.9575	-
Music	2.7225	-
Personnel	3.9625	-
Assortment	5.5275	6.5225
Price promotions	4.7100	5.9425
Website usability	-	4.9875
Recommendation mechanism	-	4.5200
Customer reviews	-	3.7675
Social recommendations	-	4.8925
Payment method	-	3.8775
Average score	4.0675	4.9300

The data showed that marketing incentives for impulse purchases of handmade goods present in the online environment have a significant impact on impulse purchases. The average score of the impact of marketing incentives for impulse purchases of handmade goods present in the offline environment is 4.0675. The average score of the impact of marketing incentives for impulse purchases of handmade goods present in the online environment is 4.9300.

4. DISCUSSION

The results of the study showed that in the case of online and offline impulse buying of handmade goods, there is an influence of marketing incentives. The composition of marketing incentives affecting impulse purchases of handmade goods differs between online and offline environments. In the case of impulse purchases of handmade goods in the online environment, consumers experience the influence of marketing incentives at a predominant level than in the case of impulse purchases in the offline environment. This refuted the null hypothesis and confirmed the hypothesis of the existence of predominant opportunities for the influence of marketing incentives on impulse purchases in the online environment as compared to the offline environment.

The revealed results are explained by the specifics of the research object and the specifics of online commerce as such.

CONCLUSION

The main findings are presented below.

1. Research shows that impulse buying by consumers is influenced by the following factors: personal characteristics of the consumer (for example, propensity for impulse purchases), purchase motives (for example, utilitarian motives), consumer resources (for example, time), marketing incentives from the manufacturer, and seller (for example, price). Self-control and consumer mood also determine the affective and cognitive processes associated with impulse buying.
2. Research identifies various marketing incentives that influence online and offline impulse purchases. Online impulse purchases are influenced by product display, room layout, lighting, music, assortment, price promotions and staff. Offline impulse purchases are influenced by website usability, assortment, price promotions, recommendation engine, customer reviews, social recommendation, and payment method. Evaluation of the purchase made affects post-purchase regret. Negative post-purchase experiences lead to post-purchase regrets, which limits future impulse purchases, while positive post-purchase experiences reinforce impulse purchases.
3. Research shows that the Internet provides a variety of opportunities to influence impulse purchases. Mobile and social commerce promotes impulse shopping behavior. impulse buying motivation is determined Affective trust in the recommender and attachment to the recommended product positively influence impulse buying behavior of consumers. There are certain marketing tools to facilitate impulse shopping. For example, the use of video blogs and product reviews.
4. A study of handmade consumers who made impulse purchases showed that there are predominant opportunities for the influence of marketing incentives on impulse purchases in an online environment compared to an offline environment.

The data obtained is essential for the development of marketing solutions. Sellers need to use marketing incentives that have an increased impact on impulse purchases.

These tools are assortment website recommendations, social recommendations, and price promotions. The results provide an insight into the differences between marketing incentives influencing online and offline impulse purchases of handmade goods by consumers.

Outside of the marketing research, questions of measuring the importance of social interaction in social networks influencing impulse buying behavior in the handmade industry remain, which also seem interesting. Social interaction determines the possibility of making impulse purchases and requires attention, which will develop in future studies.

ACKNOWLEDGMENTS

This research work was supported by the Academic Excellence Project 5-100 proposed by Peter the Great St. Petersburg Polytechnic University.

REFERENCES

Abdelsalam, Samah, Naomie Salim, Rose Alinda Alias, and Omayma Husain. 2020. "Understanding Online Impulse Buying Behavior in Social Commerce: A Systematic Literature Review." *IEEE Access.* https://doi.org/10.1109/ACCESS.2020.2993671.

Aleksandrov, Igor, Marina Fedorova, and Alexey Parshukov. 2020. "E-Commerce in Russian Rural Areas as a Tool for Regional Development." In *E3S Web of Conferences.* https://doi.org/10.1051/e3sconf/202017513046.

Arviansyah, Adhika Pradipta Dhaneswara, Achmad Nizar Hidayanto, and Yu Qian Zhu. 2018. "Vlogging: Trigger to Impulse Buying Behaviors." In *Proceedings of the 22nd Pacific Asia Conference on Information Systems - Opportunities and Challenges for the Digitized Society: Are We Ready?, PACIS 2018.*

Barykin, Sergey Yevgenievich, Andrey Aleksandrovich Bochkarev, Sergey Mikhailovich Sergeev, Tatiana Anatolievna Baranova, Dmitriy Anatolievich Mokhorov, and Aleksandra Maksimovna Kobicheva. 2021. "A Methodology of Bringing Perspective Innovation Products to Market." *Academy of Strategic Management Journal* 20 (2): 19. https://www.abacademies.org/articles/a-methodology-of-bringing-perspective-innovation-products-to-market.pdf.

Barykin, Sergey Yevgenievich, Olga Vladimirovna Kalinina, Irina Vasilievna Kapustina, Victor Andreevich Dubolazov, Cesar Armando Nunez Esquivel, Elmira Alyarovna Nazarova, and Petr Anatolievich Sharapaev. 2021. "The Sharing Economy and Digital Logistics in Retail Chains: Opportunities and Threats." *Academy of Strategic Management Journal* 20 (2): 1–14. https://www.abacademies.org/articles/the-sharing-economy-and-digital-logistics-in-retail-chains-opportunities-and-threats.pdf.

Barykin, Sergey Yevgenievich, Irina Vasilievna Kapustina, Sergey Mikhailovich Sergeev, Olga Vladimirovna Kalinina, Viktoriia Valerievna Vilken, Yuri Yevgenievich Putikhin, and Lydia Vitalievna Volkova. 2021. "Developing the Physical Distribution Digital Twin Model within the Trade Network." *Academy of Strategic Management Journal* 20 (1): 1–24. https://www.abacademies.org/articles/developing-the-physical-distribution-digital-twin-model-within-the-trade-network.pdf.

Barykin, Sergey Yevgenievich, Irina Vasilievna Kapustina, Olga Aleksandrovna Valebnikova, Natalia Viktorovna Valebnikova, Olga Vladimirovna Kalinina, Sergey Mikhailovich Sergeev, Marisa Camastral, Yuri Yevgenievich Putikhin, and Lydia Vitalievna Volkova. 2021. "Digital Technologies for Personnel Management: Implications for Open Innovations." *Academy of Strategic Management Journal* 20 (2): 1–14. https://www.abacademies.org/articles/digital-technologies-for-personnel-management-implications-for-open-innovations.pdf.

Barykin, Sergey Yevgenievich, Elena Aleksandrovna Smirnova, Petr Anatolievich Sharapaev, and Angela Bohuovna Mottaeva. 2021. "Development of the Kazakhstan Digital Retail Chains within the EAEU E-Commerce." *Academy of Strategic Management Journal* 20 (2): 1–18. https://www.abacademies.org/articles/development-of-the-kazakhstan-digital-retail-chains-within-the-eaeu-ecommerce-market.pdf.

Bismo, Aryo, Sukma Putra, Haryadi Sarjono, and Lessya Nasrul. 2020. "Effect of Functional Convenience and Representational Delight on Positive Emotional Effect and Impulse Buying of Discount Group Site Users in Indonesia." *Pertanika Journal of Social Sciences and Humanities.*

Bozhuk, Svetlana G., and Aleks S. Krasnov. 2017. "Methodics of Research of Consumers Psychographic Characteristics in the Internet." In *Proceedings of the 2017 International Conference "Quality Management, Transport and Information Security, Information Technologies", IT and QM and IS 2017.* https://doi.org/10.1109/ITMQIS.2017.8085790.

Bozhuk, Svetlana, Natalia Krasnostavskaia, Tatyana Maslova, and Natalia Pletneva. 2019. "The Problems of Innovative Merchandise Trade in the Context of Digital Environment." In *IOP Conference Series: Materials Science and Engineering.* https://doi.org/10.1088/1757-899X/497/1/012115.

Bozhuk, Svetlana, Tatyana Maslova, Nelli Kozlova, and Natalia Krasnostavskaia. 2019. "Transformation of Mechanism of Sales and Services Promotion in Digital Environment." In *IOP Conference Series: Materials Science and Engineering.* https://doi.org/10.1088/1757-899X/497/1/012114.

Chen, Wen Kuo, Chien Wen Chen, and Yu Chun Lin. 2020. "Understanding the Influence of Impulse Buying toward Consumers' Post-Purchase Dissonance and Return Intention: An Empirical Investigation of Apparel Websites." *Journal of Ambient Intelligence and Humanized Computing.* https://doi.org/10.1007/s12652-020-02333-z.

Chen, Yanhong, Yaobin Lu, Bin Wang, and Zhao Pan. 2019. "How Do Product Recommendations Affect Impulse Buying? An Empirical Study on WeChat Social Commerce." *Information and Management*. https://doi.org/10.1016/j.im.2018.09.002.

Dvas, Grigory V., and Yulia A. Dubolazova. 2018. "Risk Assessment and Risk Management of Innovative Activity of the Enterprise." In *Proceedings of the 31st International Business Information Management Association Conference, IBIMA 2018: Innovation Management and Education Excellence through Vision 2020*.

Fenton-O'Creevy, Mark, and Adrian Furnham. 2020. "Money Attitudes, Personality and Chronic Impulse Buying." *Applied Psychology*. https://doi.org/10.1111/apps.12215.

Frizzo, Francielle, Helison Bertoli Alves Dias, Nayara Pereira Duarte, Denise Gabriela Rodrigues, and Paulo Henrique Muller Prado. 2020. "The Genuine Handmade: How the Production Method Influences Consumers' Behavioral Intentions through Naturalness and Authenticity." *Journal of Food Products Marketing*. https://doi.org/10.1080/10454446.2020.1765936.

Goncharova, N., V. Degtereva, and N. Sopilko. 2018. "Contradictions in Regional Innovative Activity and Ways to Overcome Them." In *Proceedings of the 31st International Business Information Management Association Conference, IBIMA 2018: Innovation Management and Education Excellence through Vision 2020*.

Gong, Xiaoxiao, Zuoliang Ye, Kuo Liu, and Na Wu. 2020. "The Effects of Live Platform Exterior Design on Sustainable Impulse Buying: Exploring the Mechanisms of Self-Efficacy and Psychological Ownership." *Sustainability* (Switzerland). https://doi.org/10.3390/su12062406.

Hajipour, Ebrahim, Fatemeh Haghverdi Zadeh, Majid Mohammad Shafiee, and Seyed Hasan Hosseini. 2020. "The Effect of Price Promotions on Impulse Buying: The Mediating Role of Service Innovation in Fast Moving Consumer Goods." *International Journal of Business Information Systems*. https://doi.org/10.1504/ijbis.2020.10027452.

Hashmi, Hammad Bin Azam, Chengli Shu, and Syed Waqar Haider. 2020. "Moderating Effect of Hedonism on Store Environment-Impulse Buying Nexus." *International Journal of Retail and Distribution Management*. https://doi.org/10.1108/IJRDM-09-2019-0312.

Hayat, Khizar, Zhu Jianjun, Hashim Zameer, and Shahid Iqbal. 2020. "Understanding the Influence of Corporate Social Responsibility Practices on Impulse Buying." *Corporate Social Responsibility and Environmental Management*. https://doi.org/10.1002/csr.1898.

Hayu, Rina Suthia, Surachman, Ainur Rofiq, and Mintarti Rahayu. 2020. "The Effect of Website Quality and Government Regulations on Online Impulse Buying Behavior." *Management Science Letters*. https://doi.org/10.5267/j.msl.2019.11.015.

Hsu, Yi, and Anh Nguyen Ngoc. 2016. "The Handmade Effect: What Is Special about Buying Handmade?" *International Review of Management and Business Research.*

Ittaqullah, Nurul, Rahmat Madjid, and Nursaban Rommy Suleman. 2020. "The Effects of Mobile Marketing, Discount, and Lifestyle on Consumers' Impulse Buying Behavior in Online Marketplace." *International Journal of Scientific and Technology Research.*

Iyer, Gopalkrishnan R., Markus Blut, Sarah Hong Xiao, and Dhruv Grewal. 2020. "Impulse Buying: A Meta-Analytic Review." *Journal of the Academy of Marketing Science.* https://doi.org/10.1007/s11747-019-00670-w.

Jose, Neethu, F. J. Peter Kumar, and Merlin B. Joseph. 2019. "Influence of Design and Social Factors of Store Atmospherics on Impulse Buying Behavior in Sports Goods Retailing." *International Journal of Recent Technology and Engineering.* https://doi.org/10.35940/ijrte.B1204.0982S1119.

Kapustina, Irina, Tatiana Pereverzeva, Tatiana Stepanova, and Iuliia Rusu. 2019. "Convergence of Institutes of Retail Traditional and Digital Economy." In *IOP Conference Series: Materials Science and Engineering.* https://doi.org/10.1088/1757-899X/497/1/012120.

Krasyuk, Irina, Tatyana Kirillova, Vladimir Bakharev, and Boris Lyamin. 2019. "Life Cycle Management in Network Retail Enterprise Based on Introduction of Innovations." In *IOP Conference Series: Materials Science and Engineering.* https://doi.org/10.1088/1757-899X/497/1/012125.

Krasyuk, Irina, Marina Yanenko, and Elmira Nazarova. 2020. "Conceptual and Strategic Framework for the Digitalization of Modern Retail as Part of Innovative Marketing." In *E3S Web of Conferences.* https://doi.org/10.1051/e3sconf/202016409006.

Lazim, Nur Adibah Md, Zuraidah Sulaiman, Norhayati Zakuan, Adaviah Mas'od, Thoo Ai Chin, and Siti Rahmah Awang. 2020. "Measuring Post-Purchase Regret and Impulse Buying in Online Shopping Experience from Cognitive Dissonance Theory Perspective." In *2020 6th IEEE International Conference on Information Management, ICIM 2020.* https://doi.org/10.1109/ICIM49319.2020.244662.

Liu, Beilei, Mengmeng Song, Guanhua Yang, Shi Cheng, and Mengli Li. 2020. "Stimulus Organism Response Model Based Analysis on Consumers' Online Impulse Buying Behavior." *International Journal of Electrical Engineering Education.* https://doi.org/10.1177/0020720920940585.

Nuseir, Mohammed T. 2020. "The Extent of the Influences of Social Media in Creating 'impulse Buying' Tendencies." *International Journal of Business Innovation and Research.* https://doi.org/10.1504/IJBIR.2020.105925.

Parmar, Yadvinder, Bikram Jit Singh Mann, and Mandeep Kaur Ghuman. 2020. "Impact of Celebrity Endorser as In-Store Stimuli on Impulse Buying." *International Review of Retail, Distribution and Consumer Research.* https://doi.org/10.1080/09593969.2020.1781229.

Parsad, Chandan, Sanjeev Prashar, and T. Sai Vijay. 2019. "Comparing between Product-Specific and General Impulse Buying Tendency: Does Shoppers' Personality Influence Their Impulse Buying Tendency?" *Asian Academy of Management Journal*. https://doi.org/10.21315/aamj2019.24.2.3.

Pratiwi, Ayu Agustina, and Effy Zalfiana Rusfian. 2019. "The Effect of Visual Merchandising toward Impulse Buying at MINISO Mall Artha Gading Jakarta." *International Journal of Innovation, Creativity and Change*.

Rahadhini, Marjam Desma, Edi Wibowo, and Kukuh Lukiyanto. 2020. "The Role of Positive Emotion in Hedonic Shopping Value Affecting Consumers" Impulse Buying of Fashion Products." *International Journal of Scientific and Technology Research*.

Rudskaya, Irina Andreevna, and Dmitry Grigorievich Rodionov. 2018. "Comprehensive Evaluation of Russian Regional Innovation System Performance Using a Two-Stage Econometric Model." *Espacios*.

Selentyeva, Tamara, Marina Ivanova, and Valeriia Kulibanova. 2018. "Improvement of Approaches to Evaluating the Results of Innovative Clusters Development." In *Proceedings of the 31st International Business Information Management Association Conference, IBIMA 2018: Innovation Management and Education Excellence through Vision 2020*.

Skhvediani, A. E., and T. Y. Kudryavtseva. 2018. "The Socioeconomic Development of Russia: Some Historical Aspects." *European Research Studies Journal*. https://doi.org/10.35808/ersj/1114.

Spiteri Cornish, Lara. 2020. "Why Did I Buy This? Consumers' Post-Impulse-Consumption Experience and Its Impact on the Propensity for Future Impulse Buying Behaviour." *Journal of Consumer Behaviour*. https://doi.org/10.1002/cb.1792.

Sundström, Malin, Sara Hjelm-Lidholm, and Anita Radon. 2019. "Clicking the Boredom Away – Exploring Impulse Fashion Buying Behavior Online." *Journal of Retailing and Consumer Services*. https://doi.org/10.1016/j.jretconser.2018.11.006.

Tariq, Anum, Changfeng Wang, Umair Akram, Yasir Tanveer, and Muhammad Sohaib. 2020. "Online Impulse Buying of Organic Food: Moderating Role of Social Appeal and Media Richness." In *Advances in Intelligent Systems and Computing*. https://doi.org/10.1007/978-3-030-21255-1_45.

Vinish, P., Prakash Pinto, Iqbal Thonse Hawaldar, and Slima Pinto. 2020. "Impulse Buying Behavior among Female Shoppers: Exploring the Effects of Selected Store Environment Elements." *Innovative Marketing*. https://doi.org/10.21511/im.16(2).2020.05.

West, Emily. 2010. "A Taste for Greeting Cards: Distinction within a Denigrated Cultural Form." *Journal of Consumer Culture*. https://doi.org/10.1177/1469540510376908.

Wu, Ing Long, Mai Lun Chiu, and Kuei Wan Chen. 2020. "Defining the Determinants of Online Impulse Buying through a Shopping Process of Integrating Perceived Risk, Expectation-Confirmation Model, and Flow Theory Issues." *International*

Journal of Information Management. https://doi.org/10.1016/j.ijinfomgt.2020. 102099.

Xu, Haiqin, Kem Z. K. Zhang, and Sesia J. Zhao. 2020. "A Dual Systems Model of Online Impulse Buying." *Industrial Management and Data Systems.* https://doi.org/10.1108/IMDS-04-2019-0214.

Zhang, Kem Z. K., Haiqin Xu, Sesia Zhao, and Yugang Yu. 2018. "Online Reviews and Impulse Buying Behavior: The Role of Browsing and Impulsiveness." *Internet Research.* https://doi.org/10.1108/IntR-12-2016-0377.

Zheng, Xiabing, Jinqi Men, Feng Yang, and Xiuyuan Gong. 2019. "Understanding Impulse Buying in Mobile Commerce: An Investigation into Hedonic and Utilitarian Browsing." *International Journal of Information Management.* https://doi.org/ 10.1016/j.ijinfomgt.2019.02.010.

Chapter 39

TRENDS AND FACTORS OF HIGHER EDUCATION DEVELOPMENT IN DIGITAL ECONOMY

*Julia Grinevich, Anna Vinogradova**
and Elena Letiagina
Lobachevsky State University of Nizhni Novgorod,
Nizhny Novgorod, Russia

ABSTRACT

At the present stage of social development, the attention of the scientific community is focused on the study of the most important issues connected with human capital development and efficient education system formation. It is necessary to modernize educational programs and training systems to prepare students for the skills important for the digital economy. It is required to promote digital literacy not only among students and specialists working in the field of information and communication technologies but also among the entire population. The aging population, the growing middle class and high quality of healthcare lead to the growing number of socially, physically and mentally active people. So, this issue is becoming more relevant. The digital transformation of society and innovations in the IT sphere require changes in the pedagogical approaches, methods and technologies that have been developed for decades. The purpose of the article is to systematize modern scientific research in the field of higher education, to study the approaches to the development of education in the world and to identify the causes of deviations in the development of higher education in Russia from current international trends. We consider the impact of current trends on the formation of human capital in the digital economy. This article is devoted to the study of current scientific views on demand for educational services, current

---

* Corresponding Author's Email: avv21@yandex.ru.

trends and approaches in higher education and their impact on the development of human capital in the context of digitalization of the economy.

Keywords: digital economy, crisis, education system, higher education, social sphere, demand for education, economic growth

1. Introduction

The crisis in global and national economies caused by the coronavirus pandemic lockdown in 2020 shows that it is more devastating for the labor market in comparison with previous ones, and the recovery process will be much longer. The coronavirus epidemic has also become a powerful challenge for the digital economy, and new demands are being made on the quality of human resources in the context of digitalization.

At present, the digitalization of economy and its innovative orientation has become a guide for the development of most countries of the world. Under these conditions, the development of the education system has become the fundamental factor, which allows supporting the innovative way of economic development. Now the economic growth, the country's sustainable development, and human development depend on the level of education (Avelar, Silva-Oliveira, and Pereira 2019), (Parkes, Buono, and Howaidy 2017). The papers of Suwanwela (Suwanwela 2011) are devoted to the study of the problems of adaptation of labor resources in the digital economy.

The educational level of the population largely determines the sectorial structure of the national economy. The professionalism and quality of the labor force, the level and quality of life contribute to the socio-economic development of the country.

Educational policy should be aimed at expanding opportunities for teachers who improve their skills, promote alternative means of developing non-cognitive skills, adapting training programs to the requirements of the labor market in the frame of a digital economy.

2. Materials and Methods

The research of regional development of higher education is reflected in many scientific articles. Some authors analyzed the bottlenecks in the development of higher education in China. Shin investigated the influence of Western University ideas and the socio-cultural tradition of Confucianism on the economic development of Korea (Shin 2012). Qazi, Raza, & Sharif studied the relationship between the development of higher education and unemployment in Pakistan (Qazi, Raza, and Sharif 2017).

The works of Chen are devoted to the issues of integration and optimization of higher education resources, embodied in the concept of resource conservation and development (L. Chen 2017).

The ideas of environmental sustainability harmonization and higher education development deserve attention (X. Chen 2019). The following theoretical methods were used by authors: description, analysis and synthesis, additive method, econometric modeling, functional analysis and synthesis.

3. RESULTS

An important factor determining the long-term socio-economic development of the state is the educational level of the population, which is largely determined by the number of students enrolled in higher education programs.

The percentage ratio of people with higher education in different countries is shown in Figure 1 (see Figure 1).

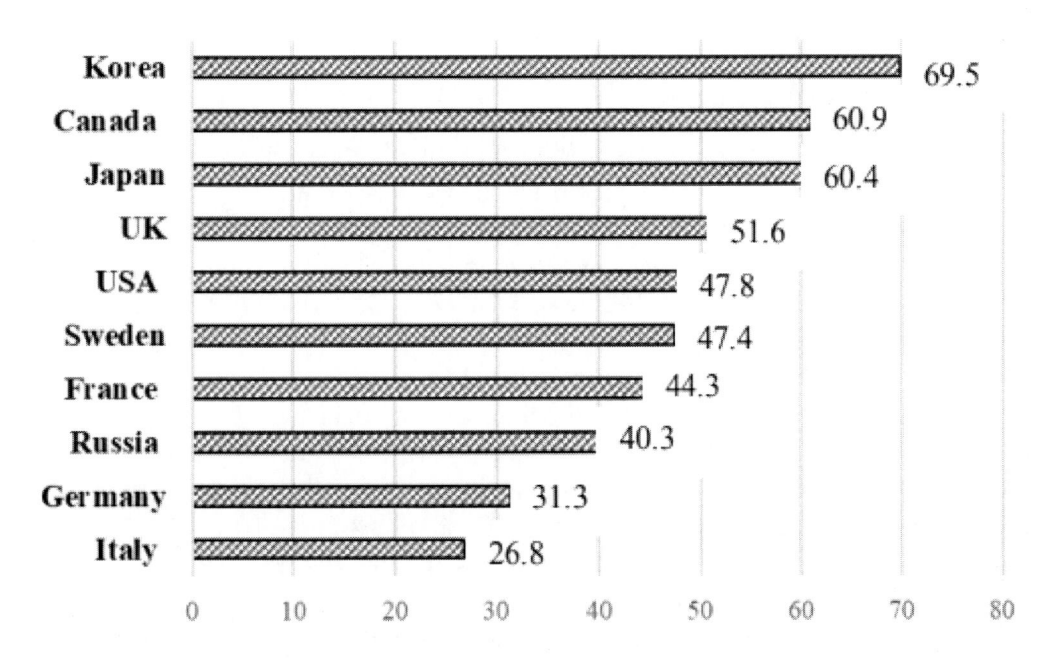

Figure 1. Proportion of young people (25 to 35 years old) with higher education in developed countries, %.

Despite the identified international trends in the education system development, there has been an annual decline in demand for higher education in recent years in Russia, which has become the reason for further research. The fall in real incomes in 2020 and the increased unemployment rate will have a negative impact on the number of students in the future.

Figure 2 shows a decrease in the number of students enrolled in higher education programs in Russia (see Figure 2).

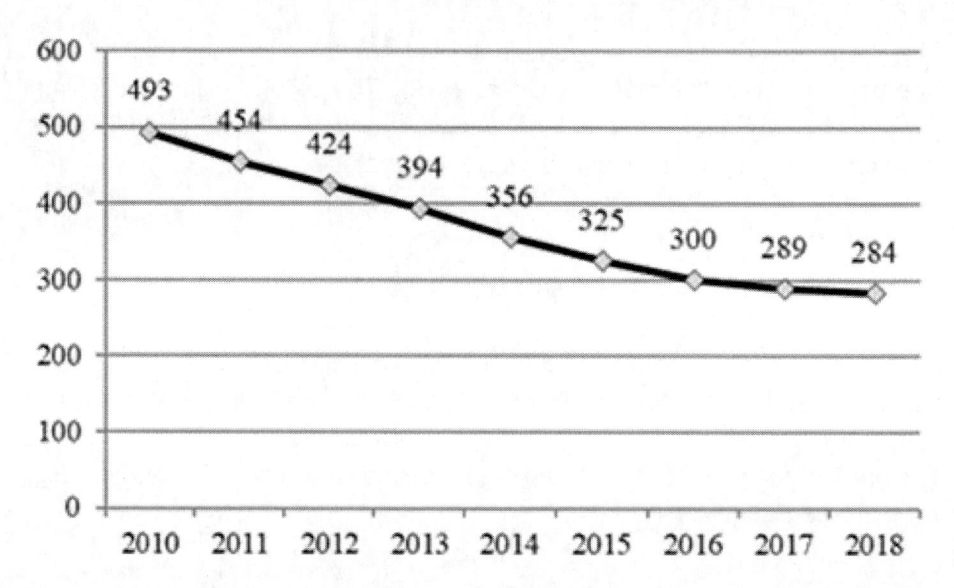

Figure 2. Number of students enrolled in educational programs of higher education in Russia in 2010-2018, per 10,000 population.

When we selected the parameters for establishing a relationship with the number of students in different countries of the world, we used data from surveys where respondents were asked the question "Why didn't you go to university?." In Russian studies, the main answer was as follows: "It is too difficult to enroll, but it is expensive to study" ("Falling Demand for Higher Education I Official Site. Komsomolskaya Pravda" 2019).

State programs focused on supporting higher education are playing an important role in the frame of crisis. Accordingly, the first factor reflects the living standard in the country, and the second the funds that the state is ready to finance for the development of education. Recently, the demographic situation in Russia has been given great importance (maternity capital for the birth of the 2nd child (from 01.01.2007) and for the first (from 01.01. 2020)), the number of young people (as potential consumers of higher education service) was chosen as the third factor.

For further analysis, we used statistical data that determined the above trends in the development of higher education in five countries of the world, among which the most significant factors affecting the number of students enrolled in higher education programs were identified (Table 1).

Table 1. Research results

	Finland	Japan	Korea	USA	Russia
b1	0.64	0.72*	1.65**	0.75**	0.02
b2	1.51*	0.37	4.43***	0.58*	1.50
b3	13.63**	12.36***	10.74***	6.61***	6.68***
R2	0.83	0.98	0.98	0.95	0.97
DW	1.2	1.28	1.96	1.57	1.64

As a result of the remaining significant factors, a three-factor linear model was constructed:

$$Y = a + b1X1 + b2X2 + b3X3 + \in \tag{1}$$

X1 is the GDP per capita, thousand US dollars, X2 is the expenses for higher education per 1 student, thousand US dollars, X3 is the number of young people, % of the population. Y is the number of students of higher education per 1000 population.

The results of the study showed that the most significant parameter for all countries, including Russia, is the number of young people.

Thus, the demographic situation and the stimulation of fertility rate in countries is a very important factor for the further development of education. So, if the share of young people in Russia grows by 1 percent, then the number of students per 1,000 population increases by 6.68 people.

The highest accuracy of the obtained research results can be observed in South Korea. If GDP per capita grows by $ 1,000, the number of students per 1,000 population increases by 1.65 people. If the state's expenses on higher education per 1 student grow by $ 1,000, the number of students per 1,000 population increases by 4.43 people. This country has the largest share of people with higher education (see Figure 1).

4. DISCUSSION

The digital economy creates additional business opportunities and huge consumer benefits. However, at the same time, the new system of organizing economic relations will disrupt the existing production, technological and managerial ties, lead to increased competition, change the requirements for the qualification of employees, and lead to the loss of jobs in some sectors of the national economy. It is impossible to solve these problems without changing the educational policy.

The results obtained in this study are confirmed by a number of trends in the educational sphere.

The number of people who strive to get higher education is increasing (Management and Education 2007; Cheek, Santos, and Vaillant 2015). So the educational level of the population is growing in developed and especially in developing countries. This tendency allows us to talk about the potential increase of their income and welfare, the structure of the population's needs is changing (including material ones) and determines the development of production and stimulates GDP growth (Goksu and Goksu 2015; Ovchinnikova and Ovchinnikova 2017). Many authors note that the return on human capital is higher than on physical, in particular in the United States; the return on higher education is 10-15% (Education 2011; Marginson 2016; Geiger and Heller 2012). At the same time, there are significant obstacles and inequalities in opportunities to obtain higher education (Sánchez and Singh 2018).

There is an increase in the number of higher education institutions and in the proportion of people with higher education between 2000 and 2018. The Russian Federation is one of the leaders in the world in terms of the share of the population with higher education (54%), the similar indicator can be observed in Canada and, in the USA (44%), in most European countries it ranges from 42 in the UK to 27 in Germany ("Education at a Glance: OECD Indicators. OECD 2015, 2016, 2017, 2018" n.d.).

It should be noted the annual growth in demand for education by 6% ("ENIC Russia Official Site. National Information Center for Academic Recognition and Mobility" n.d.). If we consider the share of the population with higher education in the age group of 24-35 years in different countries, this indicator in Finland increased from 38.7 to 41.3% during the period 2000-2018, and in Mexico from 17.5 to 45.8%. Moreover, significant growth is observed both in developed countries and in countries with economies that are developing along a transformational path, such as Turkey, Poland, Hungary, and Slovakia (David and Amey 2020; "Education Resources - Education Spending - OECD Data" n.d.).

In most developed European countries, the number of students per 1,000 population varies between 30 and 50, while in South Korea and the United States it exceeds 60 (Federal State Statistic Service of Russian Federation). At the same time, 17% of graduates in the UK find highly paid jobs quickly, in the United States, France and the Netherlands, the same indicator ranges from 10% to 15%, and in Japan, it is only 7%.

There were considerable changes in the demographic structure of the world's population. A decrease in the share of the young population is observed, for example, in recent years there was a decrease in the share in the EU countries from 16.7% in 2003 to 15.6% in 2016, while in the 50s it was 25%, and in the US was from 29.5% in 1950 to 19.1% in 2014, in Russia from 27.5 to 16.1 for the same period. At the same time, the following trends are observed such as population aging, increasing life expectancy, reducing fertility rates in Europe and the USA, strengthening of migration processes in developed countries, these changes have a significant impact on the educational services market (David and Amey 2020; Rogojanu and Badea 2012).

A knowledge society is being formed, that leads to the use of new approaches in the development of education: the use of modern educational technologies, the active introduction of innovations in education, both in terms of disciplines, educational programs, and in the interaction of educational institutions and various enterprises, the use of information technologies, the use of an interdisciplinary approach (Vorontsov and Vorontsova 2015), and the use of modern approaches to financing the educational system.

The system of financing higher education institutions has experienced some changes. At the moment there are several main financing options in the world practice (Salmi and Hauptman 2019; Abankina et al., 2012; Salmi 2009; Goksu and Goksu 2015).

The first option is the traditional one (offer-based financing), it's associated with state financing of the education system, in particular, the state provides universities with block grants to cover most of the costs (Lung(Moladovan), IoanMoldovan, and Alexandra 2012). In recent years expenses per student have been increasing in most countries, for example in Germany from 13 to 17 thousand dollars from 2005 to 2015 (David and Amey 2020), which becomes a significant burden on the budget. This approach is mostly implemented in European countries, such as Norway, Sweden, Germany, Iceland, Switzerland (Ansell 2008; Busemeyer 2012; David and Amey 2020), while the possibility of using other funding mechanisms is not excluded.

The second option is typical for the current stage (demand-based financing), it involves paying for tuition by students themselves or their families, or providing funds not to Universities but to potential consumers of services, i.e., students, who determine to which educational institutions they will allocate them. This approach is implemented in the form of soft loans to students, vouchers, etc., and allows you to stimulate competition in the educational services market. This financing scheme is developing in the United States, South Korea, and Japan. The government in these countries prefers to spend most of its funds on research grants (Huang 2018).

The third option is called a transformational scenario, which includes elements of the first and second, and it is typical for most countries of the world, in particular for countries of Eastern Europe (Erina and Erins 2015). For example, the UK has moved from a system of public funding for education to a mixed type of public-private (Marginson 2018), which has led to the sustainability and effectiveness of the education system (Marginson 2018).

Each approach has its advantages and disadvantages, in particular, the first approach creates more stability for educational institutions, but at the same time reduces their effectiveness, and the second approach increases competition, but there is a high risk of closing universities that do not meet the expectations of potential students.

It should be noted a direct correlation between the financing of the higher education system and the level of economic development of the state (Bräuninger and Vidal 2000; Ovchinnikova and Ovchinnikova 2017). Some authors also point to the relationship between educational policy, inequality, and economic growth, pointing to the higher efficiency of private financing than public funding (Eckwert and Zilcha 2015). At the same time, the social effect of investments in human capital is higher with state funding than with private financing (Eckwert and Zilcha 2015).

Globalization and internationalization of the educational services market lead to faster exchange of information, increasing the competition between universities and at the same time increasing and changing the direction of financial and human flows, as well as improving the quality and accessibility of education. The number of foreign students and teachers is growing, the number of programs in foreign languages is growing as well, universities are actively involved in international scientific and educational projects, sharing knowledge and technologies are engaged in the convergence of educational programs and assessment systems (Ardakani et al.,

2011). World educational hubs are being actively formed and attract financial resources and students. India is one of the world's leading educational centers in the field of IT (Yeravdekar and Tiwari 2014). In many countries, a significant part of the training is switched to distance learning, and countries are focusing on the concept of lifelong learning (Aleandri and Refrigeri 2013). Countries in Southeast Asia and Oceania have been actively entering the world education market in recent years (Jacob, Neubauer, and Ye 2018).

In 2003, about 2.0 million people received education in all forms, and in 2015 there were more than 4 million international students [1.8% of all students], in 2025 about 7.3 million people are expected to be international students. In 2017, 18% of international students studied in the US, 10% in the UK, 7% in Australia, 7% in Germany, and 7% in France. This is followed by Canada — 5%, Russia – 4%, Spain – 2% ("ENIC Russia Official Site. National Information Center for Academic Recognition and Mobility" n.d.). At the same time, some countries are reconsidering their position regarding foreign students; in particular, previously closed Japan opened its borders in 2015 and set a goal to attract 300 thousand foreign students annually (Ovchinnikova and Ovchinnikova 2017).

Strengthening the processes of liberalization both in the management of the education system and in financing it leads to an increase in the efficiency of education and economic growth of the state as a whole. Universities are given more autonomy in dealing with financial and economic issues while maintaining quality control of education.

Development of the educational process in the context of the accelerated digital transformation of business, industry, economy and society is connected with the accelerated development of technologies and the growing complexity of global markets and management systems.

Formation of an efficient quality assurance system in higher education institutions is focused on the development of an institutional quality, culture and modern approaches to the formation of accreditation systems, independent certification systems.

The impact of global ranking on higher education research and knowledge production as well as the creation of global educational platforms and the emergence of open universities are very important (Letiagina et al., 2020).

Furthermore, it is necessary to take into consideration the emergence of major research and education markets in Asian countries, formed as a result of large-scale urbanization and targeted investment in human capital.

Thus, higher education institutions are becoming increasingly important for the economy. They act as disseminators and creators of new knowledge and contribute to the growth of income, needs, production volumes, etc. Increasing the number of students is a fundamental task for most higher education institutions.

CONCLUSION

The article describes the results of research on the main global trends in the development of higher education, which show global changes affecting universities around the world in the context of human capital formation and digitalization. We believe that despite an aging population and an increase in life expectancy, the national demand for higher education is primarily determined by the number of young people in the country. Therefore, the demographic policy is crucial for the long-term development of education. The formation of the digital skills needed in the digital economy should begin at an early age.

The results of the study are of practical significance for the development of higher education in different countries and can be taken into account in the strategic planning of human capital development and social policy. Future research should further develop and support these initial findings. Moreover, these conclusions do not contradict research that shows that the development of human capital is determined primarily by investments in education and vocational training. Nowadays education is becoming continuous, universal, and personality-oriented, and the transformation of education is a tool for influencing the world market, business, and economic growth.

ACKNOWLEDGMENT

The study was carried out within the framework of the basic part of the state assignment of the Ministry of Education and Science of the Russian Federation, project 0729-2020-0056 "Modern methods and models for diagnosing, monitoring, preventing and overcoming crisis phenomena in the economy in the context of digitalization as a way to ensure the economic security of the Russian Federation.

REFERENCES

Abankina, Irina, Tatiana Abankina, Liudmila Filatova, Elena Nikolayenko, and Eduard Seroshtan. 2012. "The Effects of Reform on the Performance of Higher Education Institutions." *Journal of Applied Research in Higher Education*. https://doi.org/10.1108/17581181211230612.

Aleandri, G., and L. Refrigeri. 2013. "Lifelong Learning, Training and Education in Globalized Economic Systems: Analysis and Perspectives." *Procedia - Social and Behavioral Sciences*. https://doi.org/10.1016/j.sbspro.2013.10.022.

Ansell, Ben W. 2008. "University Challenges: Explaining Institutional Change in Higher Education." *World Politics*. https://doi.org/10.1353/wp.0.0009.

Ardakani, Fatemeh Behjati, Mohammad Hossein Yarmohammadian, Ahmad Ali Foroughi Abari, and Koroush Fathi. 2011. "Internationalization of Higher Education

Systems." In *Procedia - Social and Behavioral Sciences*. https://doi.org/10.1016/j.sbspro.2011.03.353.

Avelar, Aline Bento Ambrosio, Keilla Dayane da Silva-Oliveira, and Raquel da Silva Pereira. 2019. "Education for Advancing the Implementation of the Sustainable Development Goals: A Systematic Approach." *International Journal of Management Education*. https://doi.org/10.1016/j.ijme.2019.100322.

Bräuninger, Michael, and Jean Pierre Vidal. 2000. "Private versus Public Financing of Education and Endogenous Growth." *Journal of Population Economics*. https://doi.org/10.1007/s001480050143.

Busemeyer, Marius R. 2012. "Inequality and the Political Economy of Education: An Analysis of Individual Preferences in OECD Countries." *Journal of European Social Policy*. https://doi.org/10.1177/0958928712440200.

Cheek, Dennis W., Joel Santos, and Nicolas Vaillant. 2015. "Education and Economic Growth." In *International Encyclopedia of the Social & Behavioral Sciences: Second Edition*. https://doi.org/10.1016/B978-0-08-097086-8.92058-0.

Chen, Lu. 2017. "Idea of Resource Saving Higher Education Development on the Integration and Optimization of Educational Resources." *Eurasia Journal of Mathematics, Science and Technology Education*. https://doi.org/10.12973/ejmste/78731.

Chen, Xiaoxia. 2019. "Harmonizing Ecological Sustainability and Higher Education Development: Wisdom from Chinese Ancient Education Philosophy." *Educational Philosophy and Theory*. https://doi.org/10.1080/00131857.2018.1501677.

David, Miriam E., and Marilyn J. Amey. 2020. "Education at a Glance." In *The SAGE Encyclopedia of Higher Education*. https://doi.org/10.4135/9781529714395.n163.

Eckwert, Bernhard, and Itzhak Zilcha. 2015. "The Role of Government in Financing Higher Education." In *The Economics of Screening and Risk Sharing in Higher Education*. https://doi.org/10.1016/b978-0-12-803190-2.00006-6.

"*Education at a Glance: OECD Indicators. OECD 2015, 2016, 2017, 2018.*" n.d. Accessed February 8, 2021. https://www.oecd-ilibrary.org/.

Education, Higher. 2011. *Higher Education : Students at the Heart of the System. Higher Education*.

"*Education Resources - Education Spending - OECD Data.*" n.d. Accessed February 8, 2021. https://data.oecd.org/eduresource/education-spending.htm.

"*ENIC Russia Official Site. National Information Center for Academic Recognition and Mobility.*" n.d. Accessed February 8, 2021. http://www.russianenic.ru/.

Erina, Jana, and Ingars Erins. 2015. "Assessment of Higher Education Financing Models in the CEE Countries." *Procedia - Social and Behavioral Sciences*. https://doi.org/10.1016/j.sbspro.2015.02.379.

"*Falling Demand for Higher Education I Official Site. Komsomolskaya Pravda.*" 2019. November 18, 2019. https://www.spb.kp.ru/daily/27056.5/4123425/.

Geiger, Roger, and Donald Heller. 2012. "Financial Trends in Higher Education: The United States." *Voprosy Obrazovaniya*. https://doi.org/10.17323/1814-9545-2012-3-5-29.

Goksu, Alper, and Gonca Gungor Goksu. 2015. "A Comparative Analysis of Higher Education Financing in Different Countries." *Procedia Economics and Finance.* https://doi.org/10.1016/s2212-5671(15)00945-4.

Huang, Futao. 2018. "Higher Education Financing in Japan: Trends and Challenges." *International Journal of Educational Development.* https://doi.org/10.1016/j.ijedudev.2016.12.010.

Jacob, W. James, Deane Neubauer, and Huiyuan Ye. 2018. "Financing Trends in Southeast Asia and Oceania: Meeting the Demands of Regional Higher Education Growth." In *International Journal of Educational Development.* https://doi.org/10.1016/j.ijedudev.2016.11.001.

Letiagina, Elena N., Yury V. Trifonov, Elena Y. Trifonova, Alexander N. Vizgunov, and Julia A. Grinevich. 2020. "Methodological Approach to Analysis of Management Systems Using the Graph Theory in the Digital Economy." In *Lecture Notes in Networks and Systems.* https://doi.org/10.1007/978-3-030-32015-7_16.

Lung(Moladovan), Maria, IoanMoldovan, and Nistor Lung Alexandra. 2012. "Financing Higher Education in Europe: Issues and Challenges." *Procedia - Social and Behavioral Sciences.* https://doi.org/10.1016/j.sbspro.2012.08.266.

Management, Institutional, and Higher Education. 2007. "Higher Education Management and Policy." *Journal Oj the Programme on Institutional Management Шm Higher Education.*

Marginson, Simon. 2016. "High Participation Systems of Higher Education." *Journal of Higher Education.* https://doi.org/10.1353/jhe.2016.0007.

———. 2018. "Global Trends in Higher Education Financing: The United Kingdom." *International Journal of Educational Development.* https://doi.org/10.1016/j.ijedudev.2017.03.008.

Ovchinnikova, O. P., and N. E. Ovchinnikova. 2017. "Financing of Higher Education in Developed Countries and Russia: An Analysis of Contemporary Trends." *Finance and Credit.* https://doi.org/10.24891/fc.23.38.2305.

Parkes, Carole, Anthony F. Buono, and Ghada Howaidy. 2017. "The Principles for Responsible Management Education (PRME): The First Decade – What Has Been Achieved? The next Decade – Responsible Management Education's Challenge for the Sustainable Development Goals (SDGs)." *International Journal of Management Education.* https://doi.org/10.1016/j.ijme.2017.05.003.

Qazi, Wasim, Syed Ali Raza, and Arshian Sharif. 2017. "Higher Education Development and Unemployment in Pakistan: Evidence from Structural Break Testing." *Global Business Review.* https://doi.org/10.1177/0972150917710344.

Rogojanu, Angela, and Liana Badea. 2012. "Higher Education from the Perspective of Demographical Evolution: Obstacles and Solutions." *Procedia - Social and Behavioral Sciences.* https://doi.org/10.1016/j.sbspro.2012.06.295.

Salmi, Jamil. 2009. "*Scenarios for Financial Sustainability of Tertiary Education.*" In . https://doi.org/10.1787/9789264075375-12-en.

Salmi, Jamil, and Arthur M. Hauptman. 2019. *"Appendix – Innovations in Tertiary Education Financing: A Comparative Evaluation of Allocation Mechanisms."* In . https://doi.org/10.1142/9789813278752_0011.

Sánchez, Alan, and Abhijeet Singh. 2018. "Accessing Higher Education in Developing Countries: Panel Data Analysis from India, Peru, and Vietnam." *World Development.* https://doi.org/10.1016/j.worlddev.2018.04.015.

Shin, Jung Cheol. 2012. "Higher Education Development in Korea: Western University Ideas, Confucian Tradition, and Economic Development." *Higher Education.* https://doi.org/10.1007/s10734-011-9480-5.

Suwanwela, Charas. 2011. "The Role of Universities amid the Challenges of the Knowledge Society." In *The Emergent Knowledge Society and the Future of Higher Education: Asian Perspectives.* https://doi.org/10.4324/9780203145906-15.

Vorontsov, Andrey, and Elena Vorontsova. 2015. "Innovative Education in Russia: The Basic Tendencies Analysis." *Procedia - Social and Behavioral Sciences.* https://doi.org/10.1016/j.sbspro.2015.11.731.

Yeravdekar, Vidya Rajiv, and Gauri Tiwari. 2014. "Internationalization of Higher Education and Its Impact on Enhancing Corporate Competitiveness and Comparative Skill Formation." *Procedia - Social and Behavioral Sciences.* https://doi.org/10.1016/j.sbspro.2014.11.023.

Chapter 40

ASSESSMENT OF INVESTMENTS IN HUMAN RESOURCES

Elena Shishkina[1,], Zoya Lavrova[1,†], Alexander Zorin[1,‡], Aleksey Parshukov[2,§] and Vivek Pandey[3,#]*

[1]St. Petersburg State University of Economics, St. Petersburg, Russia
[2]Peter the Great St. Petersburg Polytechnic University, Saint Petersburg, Russia
[3]University of Allahabad, Prayagraj, India

ABSTRACT

A practical research was done by the authors, they analyzed various indicators that can be taken into account when analyzing the effectiveness of investments in human capital of company employees and optimizing employee performance. The result of the work of the authors was the development of a new methodology for calculating and assessing the effectiveness of investments in the human capital of company employees. This research result was proposed in the form of a mathematical and economic formula. This formula takes into account the differentiation and ratio of planned and actual expenditures of time, finance and knowledge available to the employee. It allows the company's management to assess how profitable certain investments in the human capital of their employees will be. Checking the profitability of the formula developed by the authors was carried out using the data of the company "Alternativa" after the conclusion of agreement of non-disclosure of internal data of the company. In this company, various internal real data were used for calculations and the profitability of the implementation of the proposed settlement tool was proven. The practical significance of this article lies in the presentation of a mathematical and economic

* Corresponding Author's Email: dctu@bk.ru.
† Corresponding Author's Email: zoyal@ya.ru.
‡ Corresponding Author's Email: asspb_hleb@inbox.ru.
§ Corresponding Author's Email: flowprof@gmail.com.
# Corresponding Author's Email: vivek.pandey@hmritm.ac.in.

tool, a method for evaluating certain activities related to investing company funds in personnel and optimizing the work of employees.

Keywords: human capital, calculation of the efficiency of investments in human resources, work optimization of HR

1. INTRODUCTION

Initially, it is necessary to introduce terminology, for example, proposed by Theodor Schultz (Schultz, 1971) and later developed by Gary Becker (GARY S. BECKER, 1976). He was one of the first to propose the designation of human capital through an individualized pool of knowledge, skills and abilities of a company employee, which are inherent in him and which he can use to meet his own needs and the needs of society. The authors of the article use this term in the meaning of a set assigned to a specific person. The ability to express the effectiveness (Kendrick J., 1978) of investments in the human capital (Ritchie-Calder, 1970) (*Intangible Investment and Human Resources*, n.d.) of the company's employees through economic indicators becomes possible thanks to the use of the approach developed by the authors of the article to the organization of the company's human resources.

The importance of employee training is indisputable and is one of the most popular areas in the distribution of the company's budget, at the same time, it is the least justified cost item and is also difficult to calculate(McConnell K. R., 1992). It is important to note that the human capital of each employee is inseparable from himself (Tonhäuser & Seeber, 2015), just as the human capital of the company is inseparable from the employees who work for it at the moment.

The variability of the directions where the company's funds can be invested within the very concept of human capital is wide (Shishkina E. V. & Lavrova Z. I., 2015) (Prikhach A. Yu. et al., 2015). Investments in human capital also entail changes in employee motivation. Thus, with competent investments in employee training (Shishkina E. V. & Lavrova Z. I., 2016) (Borshcheva Y. A., 2011), that is, in increasing the level of knowledge of a specific employee, the employer, who acts as an investor, can positively affect the employee's motivation and loyalty (Kalinina et al., 2018) to the company. For the employer, such investments will be obtaining an additional profession or organizing the retraining of their employees, stimulating the acquisition of higher education in general, covering the costs of specialized events such as conferences, continuing education and retraining courses, as well as paying for specialized professional literature, access to professional resources and payment for materials. studying or working with which can raise awareness and professionalism of the employee.

2. Materials and Methods

2.1. Research Methods and Materials

For further research, it is necessary to divide investment in human capital into separate forms. The research method was an analytical method, collection and classification of data, a mathematical method.

In this regard, it is necessary to consider in more detail the concept of human capital. Human capital is a stock of skills (Brand et al., 1974), skills, knowledge that can be called "benefits" (Rachlin & Rachlin, 2019), their accumulation through the input of investments (*Investment in Human Resources--A Dilemma?*, n.d.) leads to the desired result, brings income not only to its carrier (carriers, if we consider a group of people), but also to those who produced investments, i.e., "Investors".

Each person in one way or another possesses the above qualities. As a tool for assessing the effectiveness of investment (Becker, 1964), you can use labor rationing (Novikov et al., 2019), i.e., dividing the work process into separate elements and element-by-element control over the work of employees.

Investment in human capital (Torosyan et al., 2020) (Zhilenkova et al., 2019) cannot be measured unequivocally (Dyatlov S. A., 1994) (Bondarenko G. I., 2005), but it is possible to assess their impact on the financial side of the company's activities (increase in net profit), reduce time spent on work as well as development of technological innovations on the part of employees.

2.2. Typification of Investments in Human Capital

For convenience and specification of investments in human capital by type, the authors proposed to divide them into the following subgroups.

A group of investments in the training of company employees. This group of investments includes any investments in the company's personnel that are aimed at developing new knowledge and skills or at strengthening and improving the existing ones. Examples of such investments can be full or partial payment for higher education, a loan for it, an interest-free student loan from a company, payment for courses, payment for retraining and professional development, purchase of materials necessary for self-study and payment for lectures.

Group of investments in health care of company employees (Csath, 2019). This group of investments includes all possible financial investments in improving the health and quality of life of employees, thereby increasing their human capital and affecting the company (Rudskaia & Rodionov, 2018). Examples of such investments include providing additional vaccinations for employees, providing supplementary health insurance (VHI), as well as life insurance for an employee, organizing food payments or covering the cost of playing sports. In addition to such obvious investments (Milana, 2014), this group also includes investments in improving the quality of the workplace, organizing the prevention of occupational diseases (*Relation of Investing in Human Resources and the Results*, n.d.) and measures aimed at reducing (*Succeed with Automation: Invest in Human Resources*, n.d.) the level of injuries at work, as well as measures aimed at reducing occupational burnout and occupational deformation.

An investment group that aims to improve employee mobility. This group will include any investments that are aimed at increasing the mobility of an employee, organizing the relocation (dislocation) of an employee and his family, all kinds of compensation from the employer that are aimed at covering the costs of moving an employee (expenses for covering gasoline, operating personal vehicles, expenses per driver, car rental). In addition to the above investments, this group includes the coverage of the costs of obtaining a driver's license, as well as e-commerce (Aleksandrov & Fedorova, 2020).

Coverage of expenses for religious funds, rent or provision of working equipment (for example, a laptop) is also included in this group of expenses, although they are not directly related to the employee's mobility.

Group of investments in the loyalty of company employees This group can include all the costs of the company that are aimed at retaining an employee, increasing his motivation to work for the good of the company. In this context, the term "tactical slavery" can be used, which characterizes the desire to win the favor of a company employee in order to maximize loyalty to the company by satisfying its needs.

This group of investments is more represented in the form of investments of the state or a company in an employee than it is represented by self-investment in own human capital on the part of an employee.

An example of investing in the loyalty of company employees can be corporate gifts, preferential vacation trips, preferential vouchers for the employee's family and children, giving gifts to his children, compensation for any items of his expenses, expenses for corporate team building, etc.

3. RESULTS

3.1. Method and Formula for Calculating Investment in Human Resources

Investments in human capital must be considered from different angles; for this, the concept of "human capital" itself will be considered in more detail below.

Thus, human capital is a set of benefits that, when used, bring benefits to both the employee (the bearer of human capital) and the "investor" (employer). The investor does not have to be the direct employer. Such an investor can be the carrier of human capital itself, which will be self-investment, as well as the state, non-state funds, a pension fund, and even rates from the labor exchange.

The authors first attempted to systematize the formula in 2017 (Shishkina & Lavrova Z. I., 2017). The mathematical and economic formula proposed by the authors should be interpreted as follows: the primary goal in investing in human capital is to improve the company's metrics, through increasing (improving) the human capital of the company's employees. Thus, the indicators of knowledge, skills and abilities of employees should increase, and, for example, the timing of projects (an example of a company's metric) should decrease, while the employer's net profit should increase as a result of investments made in the human capital of the company's employees.

It should also contribute to the creation of technological innovations and new solutions on the part of employees.

Assessment of knowledge is not always carried out, but only if it will be possible to draw up a questionnaire (survey) or check employees before acquiring new knowledge (investing in human capital) and after obtaining it.

Expenses. The general formula looks like in (1). The authors decided to apply the labor rationing approach and divide all the employee's work into labor elements. Thus, the formula for labor expenses (1) was calculated. And, if the duration of an element of labor was easy to calculate using a stopwatch, then the financial cost of performing an element of labor could be calculated as the cost of time per element of labor under a time-based wage system, or as the value of the result of labor produced for a given element of labor.

$$\sum_{i=1}^{m}(T_{e_i} \times M_{e_i} \times K_{e_{i*}}) = Ex \tag{1}$$

where N — number of elements of work, T_{e_i} – i-th element of time expenses, time spent on performing an element of labor; M_{e_i} - i-th element of expected expenses, financial cost of performing an element of labor; $K_{e_{i*}}$ – i-th element of knowledge expenses, the cost of knowledge (a conventional designation of knowledge of skills and abilities that must be used to perform an element of labor), is determined by testing before work, is used only during certification; Ex – Expenses. To notice, ^{i}*refers only to indicators that measure knowledge, that is, $K_{e_{i*}}$, as it can be excluded from the formula if there was no preliminary testing (Shishkina E. V. & Lavrova Z. I., 2015).

Results: After the Expenses formula (1) was derived, the following type of formula for assessing labor results (2) was proposed:

$$\sum_{i=1}^{m}((T_{r_i} + T_{s_i}) \times (M_{r_i} + M_{s_i}) \times K_{r_{i*}}) = Rt \tag{2}$$

where T_{r_i} – i-th element of time result, time spent on achieving the result of labor in the end; T_{s_i} – i-th element of time studying, time spent learning; M_{r_i} – i-th element of financial result, financial costs of labor for all completed elements of labor in the end; M_{s_i} – i-th element of cost of studying, finances spent on employee training; $K_{r_{i*}}$ – i-th element of knowledge result, the knowledge that was used for all the completed elements of labor in the end is determined by testing based on the results of the work, is used only when carrying out certification; Rt – results, actual labor costs.^{i} refers only to indicators that measure knowledge, that is $K_{r_{i*}}$, as it can be excluded from the formula if there was no final testing (Shishkina E. V. & Lavrova Z. I., 2015).

Summarizing formula. Further, a summarizing formula was derived, which connects the expenses estimation formula and the formula for evaluating the result of investment in human capital:

$$k_{j=1}^N = \frac{Rt_j}{2Ex_j} \tag{3}$$

where N – number of projects, Rt_j – j-th element of Results, Ex_j – j-th element of Expenses, k_j – K-coefficient, the coefficient that interprets changes in investment in human capital is a proportion of changes in financial, time and knowledge, skills and abilities, $k \to 0$, but it will always be $k \neq 0$. The formula for the K-coefficient can be derived from formula above (3) in an expanded form:

$$k_j = \frac{\sum_{i=1}^m ((T_{r_i} + T_{s_i}) \times (M_{r_i} + M_{s_i}) \times K_{r_i*})}{2 \sum_{i=1}^m (T_{e_i} \times M_{e_i} \times K_{e_i*})} \tag{4}$$

If $k \geq 1$, then we can conclude that the employer acted rashly and ineffectively, since his investments in human capital did not bring a positive effect. It is important to note that each of the training that an employer decides to produce (as well as the time and cost) must be the same for each individual training. The higher the efficiency of investment in human capital, the lower the value of the coefficient k (0; 1), should be.

Conditions for the functioning of formulas. The above formulas are correct if the following identities are met:

$$\begin{cases} \sum_{i=1}^m (M_{r_i} + M_{s_i}) < \sum_{i=1}^m M_{e_i} \\ \sum_{i=1}^m (T_{r_i} + T_{s_i}) < \sum_{i=1}^m T_{e_i} \\ \sum_{i=1}^m K_{r_i} > \sum_{i=1}^m K_{e_i} \end{cases} \tag{5}$$

During the execution of work, a work employee explores a limited set of knowledge, skills and abilities, which is less than the set of knowledge, skills and abilities at his disposal. Thus, the assessment of knowledge, skills and abilities that could be improved and were not used in the employee's work is impossible. It is important to understand that this mathematical-economic formula assesses only those knowledge, skills and abilities for which the tests were developed, as well as those that the employee directly uses in the performance of his duties.

A good example of a skill that cannot be directly related to the performance of a job would be the skill of speed reading or the skill of typing on a computer "blindly", while these skills were acquired incidentally, during the basic training of the employee. If an employee has not undergone direct training in making managerial decisions, time management, but at the same time these skills have developed sideways in him during the course of other training, they also cannot be evaluated.

When calculating the result of investment in the human capital of employees, such "hidden" or incidentally acquired skills will not be taken into account, but this will not prevent them from indirectly improving the quality of an employee's work by optimizing his work using the same time management or making more effective management decisions. And, despite the fact that these side skills will not be taken into account in the dynamics of knowledge inherent in the human capital of employees, they will have a positive effect on the growth of the efficiency of using the human capital of the company's employees, and the assessment of the effectiveness of investments in human capital is taken into account in changing quantitative and qualitative indicators employee performance.

3.2. Approbation of the Effectiveness of Investments in Human Capital Using Data of LLC "Alternativa"

Thanks to the data provided by LLC "Alternativa", the authors of the article were able to evaluate and check the profitability of the developed formula and propose a possible rationalization (alternative options) of how investments in the human capital of employees could be made more efficiently (Shishkina & Lavrova Z. I., 2017).

LLC "Alternativa" carries out its activities in the field of laying networks and pipes. To do this, she uses various methods, such as punching, as well as performing works in a trenchless and open way. The company is based in St. Petersburg, but also occasionally operates in the Leningrad Region. The head office is located in St. Petersburg. The company has 34 employees as of June 2020.

During the initial measurements of the indicators, it was decided to conduct testing to identify changes in the knowledge that employees demonstrated using the test results before and after the training, as well as after the successful implementation of two projects in which employees had the opportunity to apply the knowledge gained. The test was developed in collaboration with a company that provided two consultants to advise and train in the work process and the training was delivered remotely. This company provided test results in the form of average scores.

The management of the LLC "Alternativa" demanded not to disclose the data of the itemized rationing of labor and labor standards, therefore the company's management approved the decision to combine the elements of rationing into groups for further analysis. The work items were divided into the following groups:

Table 1. The calculated data for the work elements

Work element name	Initial data		Project # 1		Project # 2	
	hours	p/h*, T_e	hours	p/h, T_{r1}	hours	p/h, T_{r2}
Preparatory work	17.6	52.8	13.2	39.6	14.1	42.2
Equipment and materials	11.0	33.0	11.0	33.0	10.6	31.7
Soil (surface) preparation	26.4	105.6	22.0	66.0	21.6	64.7
Geodetic works	52.8	211.2	52.8	211.2	44.0	176.0
Installation of cables / pipes	41.8	167.2	39.6	158.4	40.9	163.7
Installation of the equipment	22.0	66.0	17.6	52.8	17.2	51.5
Connecting cables / pipes	44.0	176.0	44.0	176.0	44.0	176.0
Functional check	22.0	88.0	22.0	88.0	22.0	88.0
Burying pipes	17.6	52.8	19.8	59.4	19.4	58.1
Cleaning the place &equipment	13.2	39.6	8.8	26.4	9.2	27.7
Customer acceptance	10.0	30.0	10.0	30.0	9.0	27.0
Total	278.4	1022.2	260.8	940.8	251.9	906.6

*p/h – person-hour, - unit of accounting for hours worked, corresponds to the hour of work of one person.

The starting point was a real project, in which three permanent employees and one surveyor were involved, whose presence was not required on an ongoing basis, but he was involved for certain categories of tasks during the project. He was involved in the execution of the following elements: from geodetic work, controlling next points, till the point of functional check (included). Thus, during these works, not 3, but 4 people worked. The duration of the shift of workers is 10 hours, and the total duration of the working day of the engineer-surveyor under the contract is no more than 8 hours, but his working day can be flexible.

In terms of wages, a surveyor gets $ 8.5 an hour, while a worker gets $ 6.5 an hour. The company decided to train its employees, for this purpose it hired a consultant who provided training for the surveyor engineer and workers, respectively. The authors consider payment for the services of consultants in the form of investments in the human capital of the company's employees.

Table 2. Data for calculating time and financial indicators

Name	Clarifications	Standarts	Project # 1	Project # 2
Survey engineers (pers.)	-	1	1	1
Working (pers.)	-	3	3	3
p/h, expected (Te)	-	1022.2	-	-
p/h, result (Tr)	-	-	940.8	906.6
Expenses	Equipment rent	$ 55680	$ 52160	$ 50376
	Materials	$ 2435	$ 2435	$ 2435
	Wage			
	Bonus	-	$ 2000	$ 2000
Expected expenses (Me)	-	$ 65133	-	-
Result expenses (Mr)	-	-	$ 63027	$ 61005
Bounty	-	-	$ 590	$ 888
Investments in HR (Ms)	-	-	$ 800	-
Total contract amount	-	$ 67000	$ 68279	$ 67181

The consultation (studying)for workers was carried out using the Skype program, the cost of consultations was $ 800. Since the training took place on the job, there was no time spent on the event ($T_s = 0$). To complete the project, the company needed to rent additional equipment. Its cost was US $ 2000 per day, including delivery of equipment at the beginning of work, as well as return transportation of equipment to the warehouse at the end of work.

The original contract amount was $ 67000. The contract concluded between the company-executor of the work LLC "Alternativa" and the customer of the work implied a bonus for the company-executor in the form of 0.05% of the contract amount for every day, in case of early execution of the contract. Such an item was discussed at the conclusion of the agreement in view of the fact that the customer company was interested in the early completion of the work. According to the contract, the term of work was 28 calendar days (working) days.

Planned project costs (Me) were calculated as the product of planned equipment use costs, material costs and planned labor costs. The actual costs of the project (Mr_1 and Mr_2) were calculated as the product of the actual costs of using the equipment, the costs of materials and the actual costs of wages (Shishkina E. V. & Lavrova Z. I., 2015).

In order to increase the motivation of employees and stimulate them to shorten the project execution time, the company's management introduced a bonus for early project completion. Such a bonus, provided that both projects are completed ahead of schedule, amounted to USD 250 per person for each project. The bonus fund was $ 2,000 for two projects equally.

The data for Project #1 in Table 1 and Table 2 are provided for comparisonof the planned financial indicators for both projects. To calculate the assessment of the effectiveness of investments in the human capital of the company's employees, data on Project #2 were used, since they included the test results after training and made it possible to take into account the indicators Kr and Kein the calculation.

Table 3. Results of the "knowledge level" of employees before and after training

Staff	Test before training	Test after training
Worker 1	7.25	8.50
Worker 2	6.80	8.00
Worker 3	7.50	8.25
Engineer surveyor	7.75	8.75
Average score	7.33	8.38

The assessment of the employees' knowledge was carried out in the form of testing before the start of training and after training. Various tests were used for the workers and the surveyor engineer, testing was carried out by a third party. The results of pre-testing and post-training testing are below in Table 3.

From Table 1 it can be concluded that the awareness of the employees has improved and the training event was successful. Below is the calculation of the coefficient of efficiency of investments in human capital:

$$k_{Project\#1} = \frac{Rt}{2*Ex} = \frac{(940.8+0)\times(63027+800)\times8.38}{2(1022.2\times65133\times7.33)} = \frac{503205941}{976047445} = 0.516 \qquad (5.1)$$

$$k_{Project\#2} = \frac{Rt}{2*Ex} = \frac{(906.6+0)\times61005}{2(1022.2\times65133)} = \frac{56031613}{133157905.2} = 0.421 \qquad (5.2)$$

The data from Table 2 allow us to draw the following conclusion: the number of hours worked by employees during the implementation of Project #1 turned out to be less than the planned number of hours. In the second project, the number of hours worked decreased in comparison with the first project.

The coefficients belong to the intervals:

$$\begin{cases} k_{Project\#1} \in [0 < 0.516 < 1] \\ k_{Project\#2} \in [0 < 0.421 < 1] \\ k_i \to 0 \end{cases} \qquad (6)$$

From formula (6), one can estimate the level of efficiency of investments in the human capital of the company's employees. As can be seen from formula (6), investment in human capital in the second project turned out to be more effective than in the first.

In Figure 1 shows the indicators of the planned and actual wages of employees based on the results of the first and second projects.

If you pay attention to Figure 1, a similar trend can be noted in the form of an increase in the wages of workers and an engineer-surveyor in comparison with the planned level of wages.The trend in which wages for the second project are higher than the planned wage level but lower than the wages in the first project is related to the hourly wage system. That is, the second project required fewer working hours than the first project.

The authors decided to further investigate the possibilities of using the developed formula, but already at the moment the formula has shown its effectiveness and reliability in assessing investments in the human capital of the company's employees.

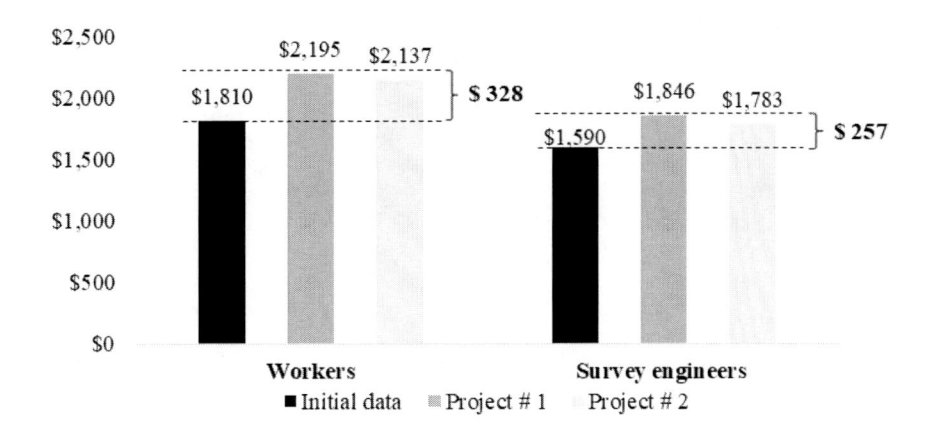

Figure 1. Comparison of total employee salaries.

4. DISCUSSION

Calculations for assessing the effectiveness of investments in human resources were carried out earlier by such authors as Shultz in "Human Capital in the International Encyclopedia of the Social Sciences" (Schultz, 1971), Borshcheva in the article "Investments in personnel training in the structure of human capital: theoretical aspect " (Borshcheva Y. A., 2011), Becker in" Human Capital " (Becker, 1964). The disadvantages of the methodologies proposed by other authors were that there was no uniform unification of the indicators considered, the calculations were mainly based on testing, and the results were empirical. At the moment, a similar development in the form of a mathematical and economic formula has not been developed. The calculations that are proposed by other authors and were studied by Shishkina and Lavrova in articles (Shishkina E. V. & Lavrova Z. I., 2015) (Shishkina E. V. & Lavrova Z. I., 2016) earlier are prerequisites for the creation of this article.

Further research could be conducted on the basis of the digital models in logistics and trade networks (Barykin, Kalinina, et al. 2021; Barykin, Kapustina, Sergeev, et al. 2021; Barykin, Bochkarev, et al. 2021; Barykin, Kapustina, Valebnikova, et al. 2021; Barykin, Smirnova, Sharapaev, et al. 2021).

CONCLUSION

The bonus fund, which was planned by the company for the accelerated execution of contracts, allowed to increase the final salary of employees and justified itself from an economic and motivational point of view.

Figure 2 graphically reflects the relationship between the total amount of contracts and the company's net profit.

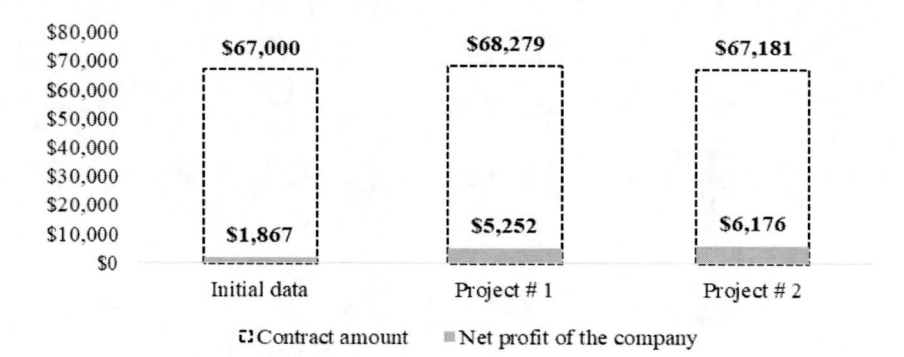

Figure 2. Comparison of net profit and final amounts of contracts.

The economic benefit for the company was expressed in the increase in net profit. According to the plan, the company's net profit was to be $ 1867 for each of the projects. According to the results of the projects, the net profit from the project 1 amounted to $ 5252, which is more than 2 times the planned net profit by $ 3385. When Project #2 was completed, it amounted to $ 6176, which is $ 4309more than planned.

The net profit was to be 2.79% of the contract value in case of a preliminary agreement. Net profit in project # 1 amounted to 7.69% of the contract amount, and in project # 2 it amounted to 9.19% of the full amount of the contract. These results allow us to make an unambiguous conclusion about the effectiveness of investments in the human capital of employees, as this is confirmed by positive changes in the company's financial indicators.

Understanding the nature of the accumulation of knowledge (a part of human capital that is integral to its carrier) allows us to conclude about the long-term positive effect of the measures taken. An employee can use the knowledge gained as a result of cooperation with consultants (training) in the further work process and integrate it into his work as a whole, extending it to other tasks and (Prikhach A. Yu., 2015).

Not the most obvious effect of investing in the human capital of company employees through investment in their training is an increase in loyalty to the company. This phenomenon can be explained by the Hawthorne effect[1] (Adair, 1984). Thus, the positive effect on employee loyalty could be more pronounced not due to the acquisition of new knowledge, but due to increased attention and satisfaction of the needs of employees through the satisfaction of the need for training and advanced training.

Summing up the use of the formula - it has shown its effectiveness in forecasting and working with data comparisons to assess the already made investments in human resources and for a universal assessment of the impact of current activities on the company's human resources.

---

[1]The Hawthorne effect is the effect of increasing labor productivity due to increased attention to employees during the study. Identified by Elton Mayo while conducting productivity research at Western Electric from 1924 to 1932.

ACKNOWLEDGMENTS

The authors of this article express their deep gratitude to the company Alternativa LLC for agreeing to provide data for calculations, the opportunity to test the results of the study and assistance in its organization.

REFERENCES

Adair, J. G. (1984). The Hawthorne effect: A reconsideration of the methodological artifact. *Journal of Applied Psychology*, 69(2), 334–345. https://doi.org/ 10.1037/0021-9010.69.2.334.

Aleksandrov, I., & Fedorova, M. (2020). Development of e-commerce, transport and logistics in rural Russia: Attitudes and obstacles. *E3S Web of Conferences*, 164. https://doi.org/10.1051/e3sconf/202016407008.

Barykin, Sergey Yevgenievich, Andrey Aleksandrovich Bochkarev, Sergey Mikhailovich Sergeev, Tatiana Anatolievna Baranova, Dmitriy Anatolievich Mokhorov, and Aleksandra Maksimovna Kobicheva. 2021. "A Methodology of Bringing Perspective Innovation Products to Market." *Academy of Strategic Management Journal* 20 (2): 19. https://www.abacademies.org/articles/a-methodology-of-bringing-perspective-innovation-products-to-market.pdf.

Barykin, Sergey Yevgenievich, Olga Vladimirovna Kalinina, Irina Vasilievna Kapustina, Victor Andreevich Dubolazov, Cesar Armando Nunez Esquivel, Elmira Alyarovna Nazarova, and Petr Anatolievich Sharapaev. 2021. "The Sharing Economy and Digital Logistics in Retail Chains: Opportunities and Threats." *Academy of Strategic Management Journal* 20 (2): 1–14. https://www.abacademies.org/articles/the-sharing-economy-and-digital-logistics-in-retail-chains-opportunities-and-threats.pdf.

Barykin, Sergey Yevgenievich, Irina Vasilievna Kapustina, Sergey Mikhailovich Sergeev, Olga Vladimirovna Kalinina, Viktoriia Valerievna Vilken, Yuri Yevgenievich Putikhin, and Lydia Vitalievna Volkova. 2021. "Developing the Physical Distribution Digital Twin Model within the Trade Network." *Academy of Strategic Management Journal* 20 (1): 1–24. https://www.abacademies.org/articles/developing-the-physical-distribution-digital-twin-model-within-the-trade-network.pdf.

Barykin, Sergey Yevgenievich, Irina Vasilievna Kapustina, Olga Aleksandrovna Valebnikova, Natalia Viktorovna Valebnikova, Olga Vladimirovna Kalinina, Sergey Mikhailovich Sergeev, Marisa Camastral, Yuri Yevgenievich Putikhin, and Lydia Vitalievna Volkova. 2021. "Digital Technologies for Personnel Management: Implications for Open Innovations." *Academy of Strategic Management Journal* 20 (2): 1–14. https://www.abacademies.org/articles/digital-technologies-for-personnel-management-implications-for-open-innovations.pdf.

Barykin, Sergey Yevgenievich, Elena Aleksandrovna Smirnova, Petr Anatolievich Sharapaev, and Angela Bohuovna Mottaeva. 2021. "Development of the Kazakhstan Digital Retail Chains within the EAEU E-Commerce." *Academy of Strategic Management Journal* 20 (2): 1–18. https://www.abacademies.org/articles/development-of-the-kazakhstan-digital-retail-chains-within-the-eaeu-ecommerce-market.pdf.

Becker, G. S. (1964). *Human Capital: A Theoretical and Empirical Analysis with Special Reference to Education, First Edition.* https://www.nber.org/books-and-chapters/human-capital-theoretical-and-empirical-analysis-special-reference-education-first-edition.

Bondarenko G.I. (2005). *Human capital: the main factors of its reproduction and development. Rostov-on-Don* (Vol. 254). Tera . https://search.rsl.ru/ru/record/01002717371.

Borshcheva Y. A. (2011). Investments in personnel training in the structure of human capital: theoretical aspect. *Bulletin of the Volga Institute of Management*, 3, 132–136. https://elibrary.ru/item.asp?id=28895806.

Brand, A. M., Van Der Merwe, R., & Boshoff, A. B. (1974). The Measurement of Investment in Human Resources. In *Personnel Review* (Vol. 3, Issue 2, pp. 26–35). https://doi.org/10.1108/eb055252.

Csath, M. (2019). The key to increasing competitiveness is investing into human resources. *Annals of Marketing Management and Economics*, 4(2), 31–46. https://doi.org/10.22630/amme.2018.4.2.15.

Dyatlov S.A. (1994). *Theory of human capital* (Vol. 156). Publishing house SPbUEF. https://www.ozon.ru/context/detail/id/5221005/.

GARY S. BECKER. (1976). *The Economic Approach to Human Behavior,* Becker. M.: GU HSE. https://press.uchicago.edu/ucp/books/book/chicago/E/bo5954985.html.

Intangible investment and human resources. (n.d.). Retrieved February 11, 2021, from https://www.researchgate.net/publication/24057935_Intangible_investment_and_human_resources.

Investment in Human Resources--A Dilemma? (n.d.). Retrieved February 11, 2021, from https://www.researchgate.net/publication/234708458_Investment_in_Human_Resources--A_Dilemma.

Kalinina, O., Suschenko, V., Shchegolev, V., & Barykin, S. (2018). Logistic development and use of personnel motivation system based on the chosen strategy of sports organization. *MATEC Web of Conferences*, *193.* https://doi.org/10.1051/matecconf/201819305063.

Kendrick J. (1978). Aggregate capital of the United States and its formation. In *M.: Progress.* https://rusneb.ru/catalog/002072_000044_ARONB-RU_Архангельская+ОНБ_DOLIB_-889753/.

McConnell K. R., B. S. L. (1992). *Principles, Problems, and Policies.* T. 2. M .: Republic.

Milana, M. (2014). Incentives and disincentives to invest in human resources. In *Challenging the "European Area of Lifelong Learning": A Critical Response* (pp. 61–73). Springer Netherlands. https://doi.org/10.1007/978-94-007-7299-1_6.

Novikov, S., Kazakov, O., Kulagina, N., & Ivanov, M. (2019). Organization of data gathering and preparing on the basis of blockchain for the supporting system of making decisions in the sphere of developing human capital of region. *IOP Conference Series: Materials Science and Engineering*, 497(1), 012046. https://doi.org/10.1088/1757-899X/497/1/012046.

Prikhach A. Yu. (2015). Active innovative activity of personnel as a competitive advantage. *Personnel Management*, 1–2, 69–71. https://elibrary.ru/item.asp?id=23438970.

Prikhach A. Yu., V., P. N., & Kazymov F. A. (2015). *Formation and implementation of labor potential in modern economic conditions.* 6, 389–395. https://elibrary.ru/item.asp?id=24901673.

Rachlin, R., & Rachlin, R. (2019). An ROI Approach to Evaluating Investments in Human Resources. In *Return on Investment Manual* (pp. 222–236). Routledge. https://doi.org/10.4324/9781315503813-18.

Relation of investing in human resources and the results. (n.d.). Retrieved February 11, 2021, from https://www.researchgate.net/publication/266387084_Relation_of_investing_in_human_resources_and_the_results.

Ritchie-Calder, Lord. (1970). Investment in Human Resources. In *Aslib Proceedings* (Vol. 22, Issue 8, pp. 399–405). https://doi.org/10.1108/eb050255.

Rudskaia, I., & Rodionov, D. (2018). The concept of total innovation management as a mechanism to enhance the competitiveness of the national innovation system. *ACM International Conference Proceeding Series*, 246–251. https://doi.org/10.1145/3230348.3230349.

Schultz, T. W. (1971). *Investment in Human Capital. The Role of Education and of Research.* The Free Press, A Division of The Macmillan Company, 866 Third Avenue, New York, New York 10022 ($8.75).

Shishkina E. V., & Lavrova Z. I. (2016). Development of the human potential of a company in a crisis. *Global Problems of Modernization of the National Economy: Materials of the V International Scientific and Practical Conference*, 257–262. https://elibrary.ru/item.asp?id=26156079.

Shishkina E. V., & Lavrova Z. I. (2015). Investments in people as an opportunity to realize the company's potential in a crisis. In L. Z. Shishkina E. V. (Ed.), *Problems of the socio-economic development of Russia at the present stage: materials of the VIII Annual All-Russian scientific and practical conference* (pp. 244–250). https://elibrary.ru/item.asp?id=25129680.

Shishkina, E. V., & Lavrova Z. I. (2017). Labor rationing as a tool for assessing the effectiveness of investments in human capital. *Strategies and Tools for Economic Management: Sectoral and Regional Aspects: Materials of the VII International Scientific and Practical Conference.* https://elibrary.ru/item.asp?id=36932334.

Succeed with automation: Invest in human resources. (n.d.). Retrieved February 11, 2021, from https://www.researchgate.net/publication/296945671_Succeed_ with_automation_Invest_in_human_resources.

Tonhäuser, C., & Seeber, S. (2015). *Assessing the Return on Investments in Human Resource Development* (pp. 69–87). https://doi.org/10.1007/978-3-319-08186-1_5.

Torosyan, E., Tcukanova, O., Smesova, K., Feiling, T., & Kalinina, O. (2020). Development of human capital management system in the transportation industry. *E3S Web of Conferences*, 164. https://doi.org/10.1051/e3sconf/202016410012.

Zhilenkova, E., Budanova, M., Bulkhov, N., & Rodionov, D. (2019). Reproduction of intellectual capital in innovative-digital economy environment. *IOP Conference Series: Materials Science and Engineering*, 497(1). https://doi.org/10.1088/1757-899X/497/1/012065.

In: Global Challenges of Digital Transformation of Markets ISBN: 978-1-53619-754-9
Editors: E. de la Poza and S. E. Barykin   © 2021 Nova Science Publishers, Inc.

Chapter 41

Computer Vision, AI and ML in HR and Event Management

Elena Shishkina[1,], Ekaterina Pozdeeva[1], Ismail Aliyev[1], Victoria Vilken[2] and Lyn Yinan[3]*

[1]St. Petersburg State University of Economics, St. Petersburg, Russia
[2]Peter the Great St. Petersburg Polytechnic University, St.Petersburg, Russia
[3]China Pharmaceutical University, Nanjing, China

Abstract

In this article, we look at a non-trivial way to use machine learning, computer vision and artificial intelligence in the field of personnel management. The second aspect of using these technologies is our attempt to apply neural networks for categorization, analytics, and an attempt to classify the unique behavior of people at exhibitions and major events. The main goal of our research is to imply, test and share our experience of using computer vision in HR and event analytics. For HR, we used computer vision to collect, analyze and identify the activities that an employee performs in order to analyze his productivity during the working day and suggest ways to optimize the use of working time. The result of our work was an increase in the efficiency of using working time by an average of 20%. As for event analytics, we will tell you about the case of analyzing people's behavior at exhibitions and conferences without identifying a specific person.

Keywords: labor productivity, HR, AI, ML, computer vision, marketing research

---

* Corresponding Author's Email: dctu@bk.ru.

1. Introduction

Neural networks are universally known, but they are not used in all areas. The area of HR and the area of event management has become such a little affected by artificial intelligence technologies (Miller, 2019). No research has been done to date on computer vision technologies aimed at studying labor productivity (Lawry & Lawry, 2020) due to legal difficulties (Gulliford & Parker Dixon, 2019). Such legal restrictions are due to the fact that the legislation (Rana, 2019) of most countries in the world does not allow the installation of surveillance cameras over the workplaces of employees (Altemeyer, 2019), but install them only in places where it is necessary to control their safety (Ahmed, 2020).

In this way, companies protect the personal data of employees, but this complicates the process of optimizing the work of personnel (*Artificial Intelligence and HR: A New Era*, n.d.).

The authors of the article, in cooperation with LABRA LLC (*LABRA*, n.d.) conducted a study of the company's activities and this article was the result of this work. LABRA's team (*LABRA*, n.d.) has been engaged in HR analytics (A.Bataev, 2019) for the last 5 years and consists not only of HR specialists (Shishkina E. V. & Lavrova Z. I., 2016) (Evseeva et al., 2020), but also analysts, programmers, IT architect and data scientist (Novikov et al., 2019) (*The Challenges of AI and Blockchain on HR Recruiting Practices*, n.d.), a year ago they got an idea on how to automate this process and invited the authors of the article to jointly research this issue.

From March to October 2019, they were engaged in hypothesis testing and MVP development, and the team of authors of the article was involved in the data analysis process.

This MVP contained not only computer vision tools that determined a person and his movements, but also a pre-trained neural network. The MVP demanded video recordings from surveillance cameras from workplaces (mainly from production workplaces). Further, our specialists marked operations, workplaces and work areas on video recordings and noted the time.

After that, the neural network itself selected the criteria by which it identified each of the marked operations and could independently mark the remaining part of the video recordings from the surveillance cameras.

2. Materials and Methods

2.1. Technologies Used

It should be noted that data on technologies, method of work execution and on data provided for the study are the property of LABRA LLC (*LABRA*, n.d.) and one of the authors, Elena Shishkina, as a member of the LABRA (*LABRA*, n.d.) team.

The program is written in the Python programming language using the following libraries: OpenCV computer vision algorithm library, NumPy high-level math functions library, Scikit-learn machine learning libraries, TensorFlow and Pytorch, Postgresql database, JavaScript library, Bootstrap, HTML, CSS, and JS library, Robust email syntax and deliverability validation library for Pythonpython-multipart, Matplotlib Python 2D plotting, Werkzeug is a comprehensive WSGI web application library, openpyxl is a Python library to read / write Excel, pytz the Olson tz database, Python Data Analysis Library Pandas.

Thus, LABRALLC (*LABRA*, n.d.) used computer vision technologies, publicly available libraries, a database provided by LABRA LLC (*LABRA*, n.d.) for analysis.

The above libraries and technologies were used for both analytics options, both for HR and for event analytics.

2.2. Methodologies Used

The principle of the program is to track the movement in the fragments specified by the user, and the time of this movement (Shishkina E. V. & Lavrova Z. I., 2019a). Operations are identified using ultra-precise neural networks. Thus, each normalized operation is matched to a set of monitored video sections (for which movement should or should not occur), unique for each operation (Kendrick J., 1978), which are marked directly on the screen.

As a result, this makes it possible to automate the process of taking photographs of working hours and timing of various work processes (Shishkina E. V. & Lavrova Z. I., 2018b) (Shishkina E. V. & Lavrova Z. I., 2019b). In order for the program to work correctly, the following conditions must be met:

1. The video camera, from which the program will then receive a video recording, must clearly see what the employee is performing, the photograph of whose working time (or timing) is being taken. Thus, it should be located in front of him, on top or on the side so that nothing obstructs his actions (*Management AI Architecture*, n.d.).
2. It is necessary that the correctness of the selection of areas for each operation is checked by a specialist who understands the production process displayed on the video, since he can correctly distinguish the beginning and end of operations.

Video is a set of static images of the same format, displayed at a certain frequency. In the first step, LABRA's (LABRA, n.d.) team open the video pointing to the desired file (Shishkina E.V. & Lavrova Z.I., 2018d). Start streaming the looping broadcast of the first video frame. The user's mouse actions are tracked and when the left button is pressed, drawing a rectangle on the frame begins; the coordinates of the two corner points are recorded. Then, after the user clicks on the "OK" button under the video, the frame is closed, and the program in turn demonstrates the trimmed fragments, and the user indicates whether there should be movement in this rectangle for the current operation by clicking on the corresponding buttons "YES" and "NO."

At the next stage, the program sequentially examines frame by frame, selects from them similar to the specified zones with the same coordinates, cuts and stores. Then each of these fragments is compared with a similar fragment from the previous frame as follows: the distance between the two fragments is calculated and a new frame is obtained. Each point from the frame is a set of three values, ranging from 1 to 255, for red, green, and blue (RGB). The resulting new frame is a set of points, each of the values of which is obtained by taking the geometric mean between the corresponding values for two points. The created function is used for this.

Applies the Gaussian distribution from OpenCV to the new mean frame and thresholding is applied.

Thus, a table of values is obtained, which shows where the movement takes place and where it does not. Now you need to calculate the standard deviation to eliminate the influence of video quality and other errors. If it is larger than the selected one, then it is considered that motion occurs on this frame.

The numbers of frames on which the movement occurs are recorded and the exact time in seconds of the beginning or end of the operation from the beginning of the video is calculated by their numbers.

Then the obtained data is collected and for each second of the video it is determined whether there is motion (or, accordingly, not present) in the desired fragments. In this way, the start time of the operations and the end time can be obtained.

The above principles and methodology are used for both options for creating analytics, both for HR and for event analytics, the difference in approaches lies in the differences in the final requirements for the result and the various tracked indicators and metrics.

2.3. Metrics

The services themselves were implemented as cloud services on the Yandex.Cloud (*Yandex.Cloud Homepage*, n.d.) platform in the form of subscription services with the possibility of customization for the needs of specific customers. Below, in Table 1, the primary analyzed metrics are indicated that relate to HR analytics.

In addition to analyzing labor productivity, LABRA's (*LABRA*, n.d.) team tried to consider the safety of employees in the workplace. Prevention of emergency and dangerous situations for employees at workplaces through monitoring compliance with safety measures.

LABRA's (*LABRA*, n.d.) team tried to deploy the security option in the form of a streaming service that sends push notifications in real time to the production administration if computer vision detects a danger to an employee.

Table 1. Primary metrics for automated HR-analysis

Indicator number	Description	Alpha-version	Beta-version
1	Accuracy of determining the operation.	> 90%	> 96%
2	Support for a large number of users (the solution was developed in the form of a cloud service Yandex.Cloud (Yandex.Cloud Homepage, n.d.), which makes it possible for us to deploy computing power for any number of users.	> 50concurrent users	> 200concurrent users
3	Detection of the resource to improve the efficiency of using working time.	At least 10%	At least 12%
4	Possibility of constant access to analytics from the company's management.	To all required management	To all required management
5	Determination of the availability of personal protective equipment.	> 80% of cases	> 90% of cases
6	Determination of the unwanted presence of an employee in the danger zone	> 80% of cases	> 95% of cases

Table 2. Primary metrics for automated event-analysis

Indicator number	For stands/ exhibits	For conferences /lectures / debates:
1	The number of unique visitors (including staff) in general.	The number of unique visitors (including staff) in general.
2	The number of unique visitors at the showpiece / stand.	Time spent by a unique visitor at the conference / debates.
3	Route of each unique visitor.	The effectiveness / popularity of the conference.
4	Time spent by a unique visitor at the stand / exhibit.	Discussion within the section (people talk to each other).
5	Behavior at the stand / exhibit (dialogues with other visitors, fixation, photos).	Number of questions (and duration of answers to them).
6	The effectiveness of the stand / popularity of the exhibit (in comparison with other stands), depending on the goals (how can the stand be considered that it was not in vain).	The dynamics of finding unique visitors (how many sat in relation to the number of seats, were there standing visitors, how many people left the audience during the lecture / debate).
7	Attendance of the stand / exhibit.	Attendance of the conference.
8	Revealing quality standards (omitted ballots / signed / completed transaction / purchase / etc.).	Behavior in the hall during the conference (being on the phone, looking at the lecturer, taking notes, and so on).

LABRA's (*LABRA*, n.d.) team tested the alpha version of our HR analytics for more than 5 companies, who wished to maintain their anonymity, with a total of more than 2,000 employees, and LABRA's (*LABRA*, n.d.) team got a result that exceeded our expectations: on average, LABRA's (*LABRA*, n.d.) team identified an opportunity to improve the efficiency of working time usemore than 20%. This was possible due to the simplification of the production line, the application of more efficient working methods, which LABRA's (*LABRA*, n.d.) team tracked down from the most efficient employees and proposed to extrapolate to the rest of the employees, the reorganization of workplaces and the improvement of internal logistics.

The idea to expand our platform to event analytics came to us in May 2020 during a pandemic and tightening of work measures in many industries. LABRA's (*LABRA*, n.d.) team believed that quarantine would end sooner or later and people would again start going to face-to-face conferences, exhibitions and technology parks.

Based on our HR developments, LABRA's (*LABRA*, n.d.) team decided to try to create metrics that would allow us to analyze the effectiveness of stands at exhibitions(Ianenko et al., 2019), the involvement of people at conferences and offer our solutions to optimize the use of space.

In this case, LABRA's (*LABRA*, n.d.) team developed the following beta metrics, which are presented in Table 2. The metrics are divided into two groups: those related to exhibitions and booths, and those related to conferences, booths, lectures and public debates.

This version was tested in a private gallery in St. Petersburg (*Master, Gallery's*, n.d.) and allowed us to build a heat map of the movement of unique visitors.

Thus, metrics were developed that would allow us to estimate the occupancy rate - the number of people who came (the number of unique people), to assess the intensity of the discussion (conversations between people), to assess the degree of involvement of people and visitors (how many people and how did they spend time on their phones during the conference), how many visitors who came to the conference got to its various sections and how much time they spent there, how quickly they left the conference or exhibition, where they stayed, what was their path (heat map).

3. RESULTS

3.1. Automation of HR Analysis

A convolutional neural network from the open access (*Pytorch*, n.d.) receives a video that has been pre-cut into frames. The figure below shows a comparison of the arrangement of operations by a human and a neural network during testing the beta version of the program.

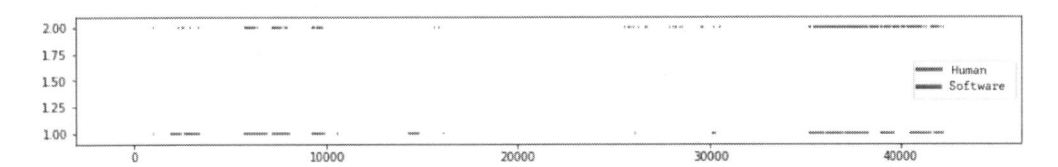

Figure 1. An example of a heat map of one of the gallery rooms with automatically generated layout of stands and visiting areas.

As you can see from this figure, the neural network showed a good result. Seconds from the beginning of the video are located horizontally, and the comparison of human markup and neural network is located vertically, respectively.

At the input, the convolutional neural network receives a frame from the video, at the output, the resulting factor becomes a set of probabilities that the image belongs to different classes of images (*GitHub, Map_clsloc*, n.d.). Then the obtained probabilities become factors for the subsequent binary support vector classification. The classifier determines the presence or absence of an operation on the image.

The classifier is trained with a linear kernel and with unequal weights for the presence or absence of any operation. After processing all frames of one video by the classifier, the obtained probabilities are smoothed using the median filter method with a kernel of size 3.0.

Then, if the probability of finding the operation on the frame is more than 0.5, then it is considered that the operation is present in the frame, otherwise, it is absent. The result of this is getting an area where the operation is considered to have occurred with a probability higher than 90% (Shishkina E. V. & Lavrova Z. I., 2018a).

Then the employee reviews the transactions with the aim of detecting errors by the computer, or bringing the accuracy of determining the transaction and 4%. Please note that the first paragraph of a section or subsection is not indented. The first paragraphs that follows a table, figure, equation etc., does not have an indent, either.

3.2. Automation of Event-Analysis

The developed tool for the analysis of events has shown its effectiveness in measurements at the exhibition held in the Master gallery (*Master, Gallery's*, n.d.). An example of a heat map is shown in Figure 2.

In order to transfer the dimensions of a real room and not to lose a unique person on the cameras, a special tool is used, which is located in each room on the floor before the start of the exhibition in order to set up and calibrate the cameras and compare the coordinates of people with coordinates in space and on the plane of the cameras.

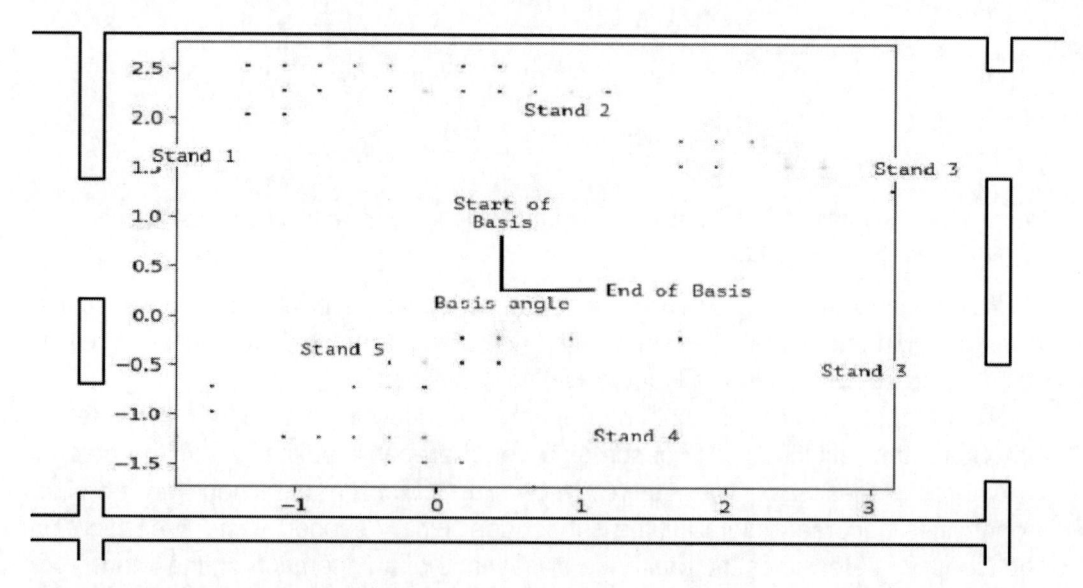

Figure 2. An example of a heat map of one of the gallery rooms with automatically generated layout of stands and visiting areas.

This tool, the basis is shown in Figure 2 as an angle of two black straight lines. It marks the beginning of the basis, the angle of the basis and the end of the basis. It doesn't matter where exactly the base will be located (Aleksandrov et al., 2020), but it must be placed in each room in order to set up the cameras (Krasyuk et al., 2019) (Verevka et al., 2019).

Before the start of the exhibition, the base can be removed. It doesn't matter how many cameras are in the room, it is important that there are no "blind spots" in the room.

3.3. Technology Application

The companies whose data were analyzed confirmed the effectiveness of the results. The indicators are shown below. Since the companies wished to remain anonymous, they will be named Company 1, Company 2, etc. For event-analysis it would be Gallery (*Master, Gallery's*, n.d.).

Company 1 belongs to industrial companies and the authors and LABRA (*LABRA*, n.d.) employees were faced with the task of assessing the labor productivity of working personnel. Company 1 experienced 23% downtime, which shocked management. Thus, thanks to the technology developed by LABRA (*LABRA*, n.d.) and E. Shishkina, new labor standards were adopted, which optimized the work of personnel by more than 16%. The level of accuracy in determining operations was 98%.

Company 2 also belongs to industrial companies, but the main task in this case was not just to increase labor productivity, but to identify dangerous situations at work and avoid them. Thus, downtime of 14.2% was identified for Company 2, new labor standards were adopted, which optimized the work of personnel by more than 7.8%.

The level of accuracy in determining operations was 97.6%. Thanks to the technology, dangerous areas and employees were identified who violate safety rules. This made it possible to take measures to influence the situation in a positive way.

Company 3 had a task similar to Company 2, namely, to track and control the safety of employees, the presence of certain groups of employees in certain areas assigned to them, and also to analyze labor productivity. The level of accuracy in determining operations was 99.5% and showed the highest accuracy relative to other companies. Thanks to the technology, dangerous areas and employees were identified who violate safety rules, so downtime of 15% was identified for Company 3, new labor standards were adopted, which optimized the work of personnel by more than 10%.

Companies 4 and 5 did not agree to disclose the results of the analytics, but allowed mentioning that thanks to the developed technology, it was possible to halve the detected downtime, as well as improve the safety of production and office workers.

In the Gallery (*Master, Gallery's*, n.d.), the results of event analytics showed the most popular paintings, which made it possible to raise their price and sell them at a better price.

4. DISCUSSION

The use of neural networks for the analysis of processes in personnel management, namely the analysis of labor productivity using computer vision technology has not been recorded at the moment and, relying on numerous studies, for example, A. Bataev, Z. Selezneva, A. Glushkova, N. Suslova in the article "Evaluation of development trends in the Russian big data market" (A. Bataev, 2019) and S. Evseeva, O. Evseeva, O. Kalinina in "HR staff leasing: Opportunities in the digital economy environment (case of Russia)"(Evseeva et al., 2020) by other authors, as well as studies of one of the authors of this article, E. Shishkina (Shishkina E. V. & Lavrova Z. I., 2019a) (Shishkina E. V. & Lavrova Z. I., 2018b) (Shishkina E. V. & Lavrova Z. I., 2018d) and co-author Z. Lavrova allows us to conclude that despite the widespread use of artificial intelligence, there are still areas in which it has not been used (Ianenko et al., 2019), despite the fact that the technology of computer vision and training of neural networks is not new. As for the use of this technology in the field of event management, in general, marketing technologies (A.Bataev, 2019) (Verevka et al., 2019) are more aimed at studying the audience by digital metrics (Krasyuk et al., 2019) than physical analysis of people's behavior at exhibitions, conferences, lectures, and so on. Thus, we can conclude that in the field of event management there is also an area for the application of computer vision technologies, and the researchers, the authors of this article and the LABRA (*LABRA*, n.d.) employees will continue their work on optimizing algorithms and improving the operation of software. The topic for furter research could be based on the models of digital logistics and thrade networks

(Barykin, Kalinina, et al. 2021; Barykin, Kapustina, Sergeev, et al. 2021; Barykin, Bochkarev, et al. 2021; Barykin, Kapustina, Valebnikova, et al. 2021).

CONCLUSION

This software can be effectively used in calculating exhibition marketing indicators, analyzing the effectiveness of stand placement and applying various metrics in order to increase traffic, public engagement and increase visitor conversion.

Summing up, we can make an unambiguous conclusion that machine vision and the use of neural networks can significantly improve the quality of HR processes, and also allow you to analyze the area that has not previously used machine vision, namely event analytics.

Further study of the use of neural networks in HR and event analytics can show more accurate results and identify other areas of application of computer vision technologies, process automation, machine learning and related developments.

This article can be called an overview of the current state of technology on the example of LABRA (*LABRA*, n.d.), which offered its vision and a non-trivial solution to optimize the use of working time, and optimize the use of space at exhibitions and conferences.

Creation of labor standards (Shishkina E. V. & Lavrova Z. I., 2020a) using machine vision, including mathematical methods (Shishkina E.V. & Lavrova Z. I., 2020b) and neural networks, and enable people to realize their potential (Shishkina E. V. & Lavrova Z. I., 2018c) in a company much more efficiently.

ACKNOWLEDGMENTS

The authors thank Labra (LABRA, n.d.) LLC for the information provided, as well as its partners, who wished not to be disclosed, but agreed to process the data they provided.

REFERENCES

Bataev, A. Z. S. A. G. S. (2019). Evaluation of development trends in the Russian big data market. *International Business Information Management Association Conference, IBIMA.* https://www.elibrary.ru/item.asp?id=41816328&.

Ahmed, O. (2020). *Artificial Intelligence in Human Resources.* https://doi.org/10.31221/osf.io/cfwvm

Aleksandrov, I., Fedorova, M., & Parshukov, A. (2020). E-commerce in Russian rural areas as a tool for regional development. *E3S Web of Conferences*, 175. https://doi.org/10.1051/e3sconf/202017513046.

Altemeyer, B. (2019). Making the business case for AI in HR: two case studies. *Strategic HR Review*, 18(2), 66–70. https://doi.org/10.1108/shr-12-2018-0101.

Artificial Intelligence and HR: A New Era. (n.d.). Retrieved February 11, 2021, from https://www.researchgate.net/publication/348620107_Artificial_Intelligence_and_HR_A_New_Era.

Barykin, Sergey Yevgenievich, Andrey Aleksandrovich Bochkarev, Sergey Mikhailovich Sergeev, Tatiana Anatolievna Baranova, Dmitriy Anatolievich Mokhorov, and Aleksandra Maksimovna Kobicheva. 2021. "A Methodology of Bringing Perspective Innovation Products to Market." *Academy of Strategic Management Journal* 20 (2): 19. https://www.abacademies.org/articles/a-methodology-of-bringing-perspective-innovation-products-to-market.pdf.

Barykin, Sergey Yevgenievich, Olga Vladimirovna Kalinina, Irina Vasilievna Kapustina, Victor Andreevich Dubolazov, Cesar Armando Nunez Esquivel, Elmira Alyarovna Nazarova, and Petr Anatolievich Sharapaev. 2021. "The Sharing Economy and Digital Logistics in Retail Chains: Opportunities and Threats." *Academy of Strategic Management Journal* 20 (2): 1–14. https://www.abacademies.org/articles/the-sharing-economy-and-digital-logistics-in-retail-chains-opportunities-and-threats.pdf.

Barykin, Sergey Yevgenievich, Irina Vasilievna Kapustina, Sergey Mikhailovich Sergeev, Olga Vladimirovna Kalinina, Viktoriia Valerievna Vilken, Yuri Yevgenievich Putikhin, and Lydia Vitalievna Volkova. 2021. "Developing the Physical Distribution Digital Twin Model within the Trade Network." *Academy of Strategic Management Journal* 20 (1): 1–24. https://www.abacademies.org/articles/developing-the-physical-distribution-digital-twin-model-within-the-trade-network.pdf.

Barykin, Sergey Yevgenievich, Irina Vasilievna Kapustina, Olga Aleksandrovna Valebnikova, Natalia Viktorovna Valebnikova, Olga Vladimirovna Kalinina, Sergey Mikhailovich Sergeev, Marisa Camastral, Yuri Yevgenievich Putikhin, and Lydia Vitalievna Volkova. 2021. "Digital Technologies for Personnel Management: Implications for Open Innovations." *Academy of Strategic Management Journal* 20 (2): 1–14. https://www.abacademies.org/articles/digital-technologies-for-personnel-management-implications-for-open-innovations.pdf.

Evseeva, S., Evseeva, O., & Kalinina, O. (2020). HR staff leasing: Opportunities in the digital economy environment (case of Russia). *E3S Web of Conferences*, 175. https://doi.org/10.1051/e3sconf/202017513041.

GitHub, map_clsloc. (n.d.). Retrieved February 8, 2021, from https://gist.github.com/aaronpolh-mus/964a4411c0906315deb9f4a3723aac57.

Gulliford, F., & Parker Dixon, A. (2019). AI: the HR revolution. *Strategic HR Review*, 18(2), 52–55. https://doi.org/10.1108/shr-12-2018-0104.

Ianenko, M., Ianenko, M., Huhlaev, D., & Martynenko, O. (2019). Digital transformation of trade: Problems and prospects of marketing activities. *IOP Conference Series: Materials Science and Engineering*, 497(1). https://doi.org/10.1088/1757-899X/497/1/012118.

Kendrick J. (1978). Aggregate capital of the United States and its formation. In *M.: Progress.* https://rusneb.ru/catalog/002072_000044_ARONB-RU_Архангельская+ОНБ_DOLIB_-889753/.

Krasyuk, I., Kirillova, T., & Amakhina, S. (2019, October 24). Marketing concepts development in the digital economic environment. *ACM International Conference Proceeding Series.* https://doi.org/10.1145/3372177.3373304.

LABRA. (n.d.). Retrieved February 8, 2021, from https://labrahub.com/.

Lawry, T., & Lawry, T. (2020). When AI Meets HR. In *AI in Health* (pp. 91–104). HIMSS Publishing. https://doi.org/10.4324/9780429321214-10.

Management AI architecture. (n.d.). Retrieved February 11, 2021, from https://www.researchgate.net/publication/324039620_Management_AI_architecture.

Master, gallery's. (n.d.). Retrieved February 8, 2021, from http://masterclassfund.org/gallery-master.

Miller, T. (2019). Explanation in artificial intelligence: Insights from the social sciences. In *Artificial Intelligence* (Vol. 267, pp. 1–38). Elsevier B.V. https://doi.org/10.1016/j.artint.2018.07.007.

Novikov, S., Kazakov, O., Kulagina, N., & Ivanov, M. (2019). Organization of data gathering and preparing on the basis of blockchain for the supporting system of making decisions in the sphere of developing human capital of region. *IOP Conference Series: Materials Science and Engineering*, 497(1), 012046. https://doi.org/10.1088/1757-899X/497/1/012046.

Pytorch. (n.d.). Retrieved February 8, 2021, from https://pytorch.org/docs/master/torchvision/models.html.

Rana, D. T. (2019). The Future of HR in the Presence of AI: A Conceptual Study. *SSRN Electronic Journal.* https://doi.org/10.2139/ssrn.3335670.

Shishkina E. V., & Lavrova Z. I. (2016). Development of the company's human potential in the conditions of the crisis. *Global Problems of Modernization of the National Economy*, 257–262. https://www.elibrary.ru/item.asp?id=26156079.

Shishkina E. V., & Lavrova Z. I. (2018a). Information technology: artificial intelligence and living workforce. *Hypothesis*, 1 (2), 56–59. https://www.elibrary.ru/item.asp?id=39155770.

Shishkina E. V., & Lavrova Z. I. (2018b). Information technology: artificial intelligence VS living workforce. *Digital Economy in the Social and Economic Development of Russia*, 309–313. https://www.elibrary.ru/item.asp?id=35341185.

Shishkina E. V., & Lavrova Z. I. (2018c). Role of human potential in the national economy. *Global Problems of Modernization of the National Economy*, 173–179. https://www.elibrary.ru/item.asp?id=35025604.

Shishkina E. V., & Lavrova Z. I. (2018d). Use of video equipment in labor rating. *Information Technology in Economics, Business and Management*, 22–27. https://www.elibrary.ru/item.asp?id=37635045.

Shishkina E. V., & Lavrova Z. I. (2019a). Digitalization of labor rating as a tool for increasing the efficiency of processes. *Foresight "Russia": The Future of Technology, Economy and Man SPEC-2019*, 542–550. https://www.elibrary.ru/item.asp?id=43050650

Shishkina E. V., & Lavrova Z. I. (2019b). Improving the quality of working life by popularizing the use of video cameras to identify resources for optimizing the work of company employees. *Problems of the Development of the National Economy at the Present Stage*, 406–415. https://www.elibrary.ru/item.asp?id=41707618.

Shishkina E. V., & Lavrova Z. I. (2020a). Labor rating as an investment in human capital. *Social Modernization: Russian Specificity and Some Lessons*. https://www.elibrary.ru/item.asp?id=42427074.

Shishkina E. V., & Lavrova Z. I. (2020b). Use of mathematical methods in solving issues to increase productivity in an organization. *Transformation of the National Social-Economic System of Russia*, 494–500. https://www.elibrary.ru/item.asp?id=42815145.

The challenges of AI and blockchain on HR recruiting practices. (n.d.). Retrieved February 11, 2021, from https://www.researchgate.net/publication/332697930_The_challenges_of_AI_and_blockchain_on_HR_recruiting_practices.

Verevka, T. V., Gutman, S. S., & Shmatko, A. (2019, October 24). Prospects for Innovative Development of World Automotive Market in Digital Economy. *ACM International Conference Proceeding Series*. https://doi.org/10.1145/3372177.3373320.

Yandex.Cloud Homepage. (n.d.). Retrieved February 8, 2021, from https://cloud.yandex.ru/.

ABOUT THE EDITORS

Elena de la Poza, PhD
Professor, Finance
Universitat Politècnica de València, Valencia, Spain

Dr. Elena de la Poza holds a PhD in Finances from Polytechnic University of Valencia (UPV) in 2008. Associate Professor in Finances at the UPV since 2018. She coordinates the PhD Program of Business at the UPV. She has published more than 40 international scientific papers. Her research interests are focused on Sustainability, Finance, Valuation and Human Behavior.

Sergey E. Barykin, PhD
Professor, Economics
Peter the Great St. Petersburg Polytechnic University, St Petersburg, Russia

Dr. Sergey E. Barykin holds a PhD in Economics since 2010. He is a Professor at the Great St. Petersburg Polytechnic University. He has more than 45 research scientific publications. He is member of the editorial board of the journals International Journal of Business and Economics Research and Audit and Financial Analysis, HAC of The Russian Federation. His research interests are connected with the theory of the digital economy, the methodology of managing logistics flows, methods of financial management and models of the theory of logistics, corporate logistics, scientific discourse and innovation management.

INDEX

C

D

E

F

G

H

I

J

K

L

N

O

T

U

V

W

Y